THE MONUMENTS OF SYRIA

A Guide

Ross Burns

I.B. TAURIS

LONDON · NEW YORK

Reprinted twice in 2010 by I.B. Tauris & Co Ltd
6 Salem Road, London W2 4BU
175 Fifth Avenue, New York NY 10010
www.ibtauris.com

In the United States of America and Canada distributed by Palgrave Macmillan,
a division of St. Martin's Press, 175 Fifth Avenue, New York NY 10010

First published in 1992 by I.B. Tauris & Co Ltd
Paperback edition published in 1994 by I.B. Tauris & Co Ltd
Revised edition published in 1999 by I.B. Tauris & Co Ltd
This edition published in 2009 by I.B. Tauris & Co Ltd

ISBN: 978 1 84511 947 8

A full CIP record for this book is available from the British Library
A full CIP record is available from the Library of Congress

Library of Congress Catalog Card Number: available

Printed and bound in India by Replika Press Pvt. Ltd.
from camera-ready copy edited and supplied by the author

Contents

Maps and Plans

(north is at the top of the page)

Plates

(photographs by the author)

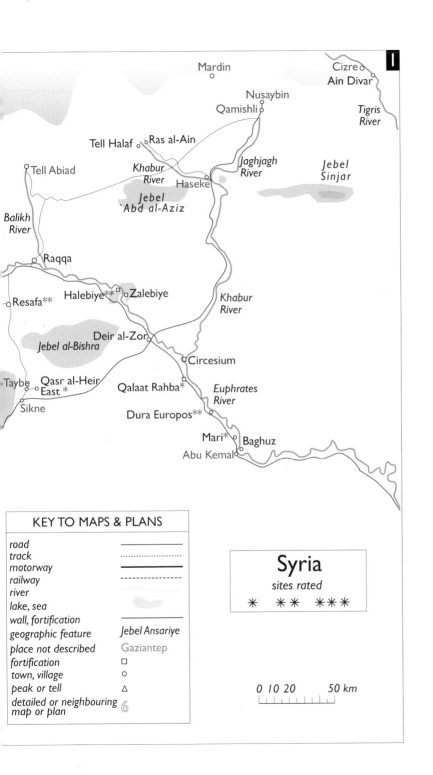

Mardin

Cizre
Ain Divar

Nusaybin
Qamishli

Tigris
River

Tell Halaf   Ras al-Ain

Jebel
Sinjar

Jaghjagh
River

Tell Abiad

Khabur
River

Haseke

Jebel
`Abd al-Aziz

Balikh
River

Raqqa

Halebiye**   Zalebiye

Khabur
River

Resafa**

Deir al-Zor

Jebel al-Bishra

Circesium

Taybe   Qasr al-Heir
East *

Qalaat Rahba*

Euphrates
River

Sikne

Dura Europos**

Mari*   Baghuz

Abu Kemal

KEY TO MAPS & PLANS

road
track
motorway
railway
river
lake, sea
wall, fortification
geographic feature   *Jebel Ansariye*
place not described   Gaziantep
fortification   □
town, village   ○
peak or tell   △
detailed or neighbouring   6
map or plan

Syria
sites rated
*   **   ***

0 10 20   50 km

Abbreviations, Ratings and Symbols

ABBREVIATIONS

Abd	Abbasid (750–968)	Rom	Roman (64 BC– AD 395)
AH	after Hijra (Islamic calendar)	Sem	Semitic
alt	altitude (metres)	Tur	Turkish
anc	ancient	Umd	Umayyad (661–750)
Arb	Arab (includes Ayyubids (1176–1260), Mamluks (1260–1516))		

Ayy	Ayyubid (1176–1260)
b	born (year)
BA	Bronze Age
bib	biblical
Byz	Byzantine (395–636)
C	century (eg 12C = 12th century)
c	circa (about)
Cru	Crusader (1097–1292)
d	died (year)
EBA	Early Bronze Age (c3000–1900 BC)
Fr	French
Grk	Greek
ha	hectare
IrA	Iron Age (early first millennium BC)
Ism	Ismaeli (mid 12C–mid 13C)
Itn	Italian
km	kilometre(s)
Lat	Latin
LBA	Late Bronze Age (c1550–1200 BC)
m	metre(s)
m²	square metre(s)
Mam	Mamluk (1260–1516)
MBA	Middle Bronze Age (c1900–550 BC)
Ott	Ottoman (1516–1919)
Phn	Phoenician (early first millennium BC)
REFS	references (main sources used in compiling gazetteer entries)
r	ruled (date range)

RATINGS
(after a place name)

***	essential
**	well worthwhile
*	worth a detour if time allows
–	limited or specialised interest
T	of interest for historical topography of site

SYMBOLS

*	before a place name indicates a separate gazetteer entry under that title
+	before a number indicates '.. km (or m) further on'
+	after a number means 'more than .. km (or m)'
?	before a name indicates a doubtful identification
??	indicates an unlikely identification

OTHER

- for the purpose of establishing alphabetical order, the definite article 'al-' before an Arabic place name is ignored
- 'St' (saint's name) is also ignored
- key to maps and plans is given on Map 1 (Syria) pages viii–ix
- all dates are AD unless otherwise indicated

Preface to the Third Edition

This book was originally undertaken in the hope that it would help stimulate new interest in the riches of Syria's past and provide a reference work suited to the informed modern traveller. 'In this living museum', as the first edition put it, 'some sort of handbook is needed to guide the visitor through the layers of history, to link the remains to the deeds of men such as Alexander or Saladin and to convey the fact that these are not just pretty stones but remarkable signposts to a complex past ... to make history come alive through the monuments of Syria.'

The exploration of Syria is one of the most satisfying pleasures that remain in the world of travel, a world where many destinations are now overwhelmed by the press of visitors. While conditions for travel in Syria have greatly improved in the past 20 years, it is still a destination that retains a freshness and, above all, a genuine welcome for visitors, especially those who have a lively interest in the country's past. Moreover the country has preserved an openness that has survived all the vicissitudes of the Middle East in recent decades.

'Monuments of Syria' is intended as less and more than a guidebook. Less, in that it does not convey any information on hotels, restaurants or banks though it does as much as possible guide the reader to locations which may not be evident from maps. More, in that while it does not claim the authority of an encyclopaedia, it can be used in the same way – to be dipped into as necessary by those interested in a particular site or area, with an additional perspective provided by the sections on historical and architectural developments.

The main changes to this edition come from a thorough revision based on the torrent of information which has been published in recent years and on the impressive work which has been done by the Syrian authorities to improve sites and extend or upgrade the country's network of museums. It is gratifying that so much has improved that the information in the first two editions is already seriously out of date. While the book will look familiar to readers of the earlier versions, the opportunity has been taken to rework the text, add a handful of sites (usually those easier of access or better presented than in the past) and add Arabic place names for each entry. The maps and plans have been revised or reworked and in lieu of the small itinerary maps, larger regional maps form a mini-atlas section towards the end of the book.

I have attempted no new solution to the problems of transliteration from Arabic. I have instead adopted several arbitrary rules:

- Use the simplest commonly accepted versions even when they are not necessarily the most accurate – hence Latakia, not Ladhiqiye. (The 1965 English edition of the Hachette World Guide *Middle East* was adopted as a benchmark but there are a few variations where later more accurate versions have become accepted usage – eg Arwad, not Ruwad; Muhammad, not Mohamed.)
- Keep to 'al-' as the Arabic definite article (rather than confuse the reader by trying to represent the pronunciation slide in, for example, 'Deir ez-Zor').
- As no single method reconciles the differing requirements of spoken and written Arabic in recording *ta marbuta* endings I have followed the Blue Guide's practice in rendering them variously as -a, -eh, -e. The Blue Guide is also followed with regard to medial vowels and not attempting to represent the `ain except in rare cases of direct transliteration of Arabic names or titles.
- Where monuments have passed into history under a non-Arabic name, leave it that way (Krak des Chevaliers in lieu of the modern Arabic Qalaat al-Husn; Palmyra, not Tadmor).

In setting the Gazetteer and the Index, articles such as the Arabic 'al-' are included but passed over in setting the alphabetical sequence. Arab names are indexed according to the most distinctive part of the string – e g 'al-Zaher Ghazi' is listed as 'Ghazi, al-Zaher'; 'Mohi al-Din Ibn al-Arabi' under 'al-Arabi' and hence in sequence, 'Arabi'. 'St' before a saint's name is also included but ignored for the purposes of alphabetical order. In the Index, all mosques and madrasas are listed under their city or town of location then under 'mosque' or 'madrasa'.

I have not cluttered the gazetteer with notes on how and when access to particular buildings may be secured. The general rule is to look perplexed and someone will offer advice as to who might have the key. Smaller mosques are closed between prayer times. Rather than disturb the prayers, a visit just before the midday or evening prayers is the best option. Keys for churches can usually be hunted down from the priest living nearby or a local shopkeeper. Official monuments are much more predictable. Although their hours tend to be standardised (most monuments and sites maintained by the Antiquities Department are closed on a Tuesday), there are local variations regarding the choice of summer and winter hours, the afternoon break and Friday prayers.

The main works consulted for each site or walking tour are summarised in the REFS section at the end of each gazetteer entry with full details in the Bibliography.

All photos – as well as maps and plans – have been prepared by the author who retains copyright. They may, however, be used freely for educational purposes (journal articles, lectures, academic publications up to a limit of ten photos or line drawings) without specific clearance as long as they are clearly attributed.

As this new edition represents the fruit of over 20 years of research and travel, it would be invidious to attempt a definitive list of those who have assisted my work and so risk serious omissions. I have benefited greatly over the years from the assistance of Syrian officials and from the dedicated work of researchers from many countries. The amount of research in the years since the work was first undertaken has increased exponentially. The task of updating the text was correspondingly even more complicated than undertaking it in the first place. As a result of the work of these researchers new frontiers have been broached in our understanding of the region and in demolishing many of the old myths. I hope that by summarising their work in this format, this process can be further advanced.

For Syria is a great laboratory for understanding the flows of one of the world's most significant and dynamic regions. It preserves a greater cross section of the past than most countries of the region (even Egypt) and it is a tribute to the resilience of Syrian society that it offers a welcome to everyone seeking to find in the complexities of the past a better understanding of the present.

Ross Burns
2009

I

SYRIA – HISTORICAL SKETCH

Prelude

For a piece of land which has been fought over for millennia, Syria hardly gives the impression of a lush prize. In shape, present-day Syria is a distorted quadrilateral, pushed out to the northeast to take in a small portion of the Tigris River. The coastline is short (160 km), sandwiched between Turkey and Lebanon. Much of the land is barren or semi-arid with the central Syrian Desert (a rocky steppe, alt 700–1000 m) opening towards the great historical chasm of the Arabian Desert to the south. Along the edges of the Orontes and Euphrates valleys, there is good pasture but much of the area near the coast that benefits from the winter Mediterranean rains is occupied by steep and rocky mountainsides (Jebel Ansariye), leaving little room for the coastal plain.

Yet Syria lies within the crescent that has seen most of the great breakthroughs in agricultural, economic and social life that propelled the key historical changes of the past six millennia. This Fertile Crescent extends from Iraq's irrigated lands in the east to the Nile Valley to the south, taking in its sweep the edges of the hill country in southeastern Turkey and the mountains that hug the Mediterranean coastline between Antioch and Jerusalem. At its heart lie the pastures, orchards and grainfields of Syria.

If today, exhausted as much as anything by the surfeits of history, this land looks at times bleak and unyielding, it occupies a strategic position of incomparable value. Syria bears the traces of many caravan routes, Roman roads, pilgrimage trails and superhighways that testify to its role as a corridor for east-west trade. Across its plains, the rich valley of the Tigris-Euphrates system was linked to the outer world that began at the Mediterranean. Across these steppes, as stability and secure trade developed, goods from as far away as China and India were exchanged. The Persian conquests of the sixth century BC broke down the east-west barriers further. Alexander crossed Syria in his efforts to develop a new order based on an amalgam of Greek and Oriental.

Through Roman, Byzantine and Arab times, Syria became the focal point in efforts to maintain a universal empire.

Possession of Syria was essential to any power that wished to control the arteries of history. The task was complicated in that Syria has little in the way of natural borders to ensure its security. To the east, the Euphrates is a highway into Mesopotamia that has never bothered potential aggressors. To the southeast, the great Arabian Desert has historically funnelled its excess energies in the direction of Syria, causing population changes that have marked several of its major historical eras. The northern plains have likewise been a magnet for the disaffected, marginalised by successive changes in Turkey. Much of the historical channelling of forces has focussed on the northwest of Syria at the point where the natural corridor between Europe and Asia spills out onto the plains after negotiating the uplands and circuitous coast of Asia Minor. Here the Greeks and Romans placed their major urban centre, Antioch (now in the Hatay province of Turkey), Alexander defeated the massed armies of Darius and the Crusaders first realised what they had taken on in challenging Muslim supremacy.

But beyond the natural chokepoint in the northwest, Syria is an open land without doors. It has learnt to survive on its wits, by trading and statecraft rather than closing itself off as a fortress land. It has been the classic buffer, though not in the sense of having little coherence of its own and thus perpetually at the mercy of others. It has learnt to transmit rather than to block – to absorb the first ethnic waves from the steppes and desert to the south; to pass on the great themes and ideas that have moved between east and west; to provide a footing between the religious currents that have swept the region.

As this study is concerned with the buildings and monuments that remain in recognisable condition, we will pass over Syria's role in prehistory and its central part in the rise of the methods of agriculture, domestication of animals and development of urban life that first brought this area out of the obscurities of pre-urban civilisation.

Early Bronze Age (c3100–2150 BC)

When the earliest written records emerge in the Early Bronze Age (third millennium BC), Syria shared in the development of city states that arose in the Sumerian lands to the east, along the Tigris-Euphrates system in Mesopotamia. Though of different (Semitic) origins to the Sumerians, the population of the Mid Euphrates city, *Mari, based its social structures on analogous systems. Literacy, through the development of a system of cuneiform writing (wedge shaped markings in soft clay), stimulated complex legal and trading practices, the local monarchs' power depending on the effectiveness of their control of irrigation and trade. The end of Mari's early phase coincided with the rise of the first truly imperial power in the region, the Akkadian Empire (2340–2150) under the leadership of Sargon whose conquests, reaching from Mesopotamia both towards the Persian Gulf and the Mediterranean coast, were consolidated by his grandson, Naram-Sin.

To the west, Mari enjoyed close relations with another trading centre of major importance, *Ebla. Ebla had a Semitic population and by 2400 BC had created a complex web of political links across much of northern Syria though it lacked the basic underpinning that irrigation control gave to other city-states. Under the subsequent rule of the Dynasty of Ur, Mari retained a degree of importance under the Shakkanaku dynasty while Ebla became a subsidiary state.

Middle Bronze Age (c2150–1600 BC)

By 2100 BC, the early experiments in urban societies were disturbed by new population movements that brought Amorite people (of Semitic stock) from the Syrian desert into the settled lands of the Fertile Crescent. This period of urban decay and disruption initially brought an end to much of the pattern of regional trade on which Ebla had thrived and the city fell into decline. After the initial disruption of the Amorites' invasion, many towns absorbed the new population and the development of urban civilisation resumed. The Kingdom of Yamkhad (Aleppo) became a major power in this period, absorbing Ebla into its orbit. Mari enjoyed some independence during the 19th–18th century BC as an Amorite city. The Babylonian leader to the south, Hammurabi (another Semitic ruler, c1792–50) ruled with reformist zeal at home (he promulgated a codified system of law in his name) but this did not distract him from developing an appetite for conquests which caused him to raze Mari around 1759 BC thus terminating the precarious balancing act that the ruler of Mari, Zimri-Lim (r 1775–60), had maintained between Babylon and Aleppo.

For much of northern Syria, this new golden age brought a flowering of international trade (19th–18th centuries BC). The Amorite kingdoms of the north managed to resist direct Babylonian rule but traded extensively to the east – Yamkhad, Alalakh (Tell Achana in the Amuq Plain east of Antioch), Zalmaqum (Harran) and *Qatna (the modern Mishrifeh north of Homs).

Late Bronze Age (c1600–1200 BC)

The next major change to the regional power game came from the northwest. The Hittites (Indo-Europeans by origin) had installed themselves in central Anatolia and brought an end to Babylonian power c1595. To the south, Egypt was thrown into chaos for two or more centuries by the secondary effects of this movement. The Hyksos, a people whose roots are still unexplained but who may have been related to the Amorites or the Canaanite inhabitants of the coastal mountains of Syria-Palestine, were pushed south by Indo-European pressure.

A non-Semitic people (with Indo-European connections) called the Hurrians had been moving into Syria in large numbers from the north. A second analogous wave, the Mitanni people, soon arrived to blend with the Hurrians to form a federation of Hurrian principalities, the Kingdom of Mitanni (16th–14th centuries BC), centred on the present Northeast Province around the Khabur River with links to the 'land of Amurru' to the east. Their region (including the vassal kingdoms of Yamkhad and Alalakh) pressed against the area of Hittite dominance in the northwest. They installed themselves firmly enough to form part of the triangle of powers that fought for dominance in Syria in the 15th–14th centuries BC – Egypt, Hittites and Mitanni – until they were made a client state of the Hittites after a series of marriage alliances in the late 14th century.

Egypt had sought tentatively since the Middle Kingdom (20th–18th centuries) to extend its influence in Syria especially to cultivate the coastal cities to gain access to important inland sources of timber for shipbuilding. After the disruption of the Hyksos period, the Pharaohs returned under the more grandiose pretensions of the New Kingdom in the great campaigns of Thutmose III (early 15th century), Amenhotep II (mid 15th century), Thutmose IV (late 15th century), Seti I and Ramses II (early to mid 13th century). By the 14th century, their main foe in Syria was the Hittite Empire which had come to dominate the local city states (Damascus was taken c1360) who did their best, however, to play the powers off against each other. The chaos of the Amarna period in Egypt helped their purpose. In the end, even the vainglorious Ramses II met his match when ambushed by the Hittite chariotry under Hattusilis II at Qadesh (*Tell Nabi Mend) c1286.

At about this time to the south, the tribe of the Israelites was moving into Palestine from the east with consequences still to be resolved 3000 years later.

The Mediterranean coast as a whole enjoyed a more prosperous and untroubled life based on the sea trade routes built up by the Phoenicians – peoples of Semitic origin who had moved into the region at the beginning of the second millennium and had established a culture that blended Mesopotamian,

Anatolian, Aegean and Egyptian influences. In this zone of relative prosperity, the port cities of Ugarit, Gabala (*Jeble) and Arwad were left to get on with the business of making money. Some especially privileged enclaves like Ugarit, which benefited from the copper trade with nearby Cyprus, had succeeded in working with both Egypt and the Hittites against the other or a third party. Their trading contacts brought wider connections including with Mycenae (after 1500) and the Aegean. The tradition was continued in the next millennium by their Canaanite descendants to the south, the Phoenicians, whose 50 plus colonies around the Mediterranean served to spread the first alphabet in the Semitic and Greek worlds.

Iron Age (1200–539 BC)

Syria's ethnic and political chess board, however, was again scattered by the arrival of the Sea Peoples around 1200 BC. Moving in from the west, possibly from the Aegean, the Sea Peoples brought an end to the apogée of Ugarit as well as the Hittite Empire; they were only stopped at the edge of the Nile Valley by the land and sea campaigns of Ramses III (r 1198–66).

In the confusion left by the Sea Peoples' passing, further Semitic population movement arrived from the south in the form of the Aramaeans, a people who concentrated particularly in the north where around 20 so-called 'Neo-Hittite' principalities had arisen – Haleb (*Aleppo), Arpad (30 km north of Aleppo), Tell Barsip, *Tell Halaf, Hattina and Hamath (*Hama). Except for some continuity in dress and language, there was, in fact, no link between the Hittite Empire and the principalities whose original leadership was probably Luwian-speaking (from southern Asia Minor). The arrival of the Aramaeans from the desert further scrambled the mix. The art of northern Syria post-900 reflects this diversity of origins in a clumsy attempt to rival the monumentality of their Assyrian adversaries to the east. In the south, the city-state of Aram-Damascus led a coalition of forces that checked the ambitions of the kingdoms of Israel and Judaea. On the coast, the Phoenician cities survived the dark age that followed the Sea Peoples' invasions and continued to serve as a conduit for products and ideas between Greece, Egypt and the Asian mainland.

The fragmented Aramaean states, however, were unable to maintain their autonomy in the face of new and vigorous forces from the east. The Assyrian Empire (1000–612) under Shalmaneser took permanent control of parts of northern Syria and Phoenicia from 856 and was confronted by a coalition of Aramaean states at the Battle of Qarqar in 853. Under Tiglath-Pilaser (r 744–27 BC), the Assyrians pushed even more firmly into Syria, ending Damascus' independence in 732. But it required further action by Sargon II (r 721–05), after renewed unrest in Syria and Palestine, to confirm the submission of Damascus.

The Assyrians imposed a skeletal administration in their western lands, being largely content to exploit them for opportunistic booty and slave labour. The spoils and tribute from their raids adorned the palaces of Nineveh and Khorsabad which so fascinated 19th century archaeologists. Even centres such as *Arwad and Sidon (southern Lebanon) could not escape the vehemence of the late Assyrians' ambitions though Sidon resisted even when Assurbanipal came down on it 'like a wolf on the fold' in 668. Eventually it fell, not to the Assyrians, but in 587 to Nebuchadnezzar, one of the first of the Chaldean rulers whose short-lived dominance in Syria (605–539) followed their defeat of the Assyrians (they took Nineveh in 612) after a long period of rivalry in their common home territory in northern Mesopotamia. This was the era of the legendary Babylon, the Chaldean capital, with its palaces and hanging gardens.

Persian Period (539–333 BC)

The Achaemenid Persians annexed much of Syria as a consequence of their move westwards and their defeat of the Neo-Babylonians with the capture of Babylon by Cyrus in 539. Syria was made their fifth satrapy or province (Abar Nahara – 'beyond the river') with its capital possibly at Damascus. They recognised the pervasive spread of the Aramaean language and its neo-Phoenician script by adopting it as the lingua franca of their empire, ensuring its survival well into the Roman period. The Persians brought a regular and comparatively benevolent system of administration to their 23 provinces but above all the integration of the Syrian coast into the network of exchanges across the east Mediterranean to Greece heralded the first of the great east-west clashes that have focussed on Syria. In their efforts to find a sphere of influence in the eastern Mediterranean, countered so arduously by the Greeks (eg the Battle of Marathon in 490), they focussed in Syria much of the struggle for supremacy throughout the sixth and fifth centuries BC, bringing a uniquely Persian element to the land, of which only a few traces remain (*Amrit).

Hellenistic Period (333–64 BC)
(Map T1)

This Greek-Persian contest was decided in the great battles (the first at Issus in 333) in which Alexander the Great defeated the forces of Darius III. Issus lies just to the north of the pass in the Amanus Mountains called the Syrian Gates. After Alexander's death at Babylon in 323, it took some time to settle the apportioning of his lands between the generals. Syria was contested, with northern Syria falling to Seleucus I Nikator (who had already been assigned Mesopotamia) after his victory over Antigonus at the Battle of Ipsus (Phrygia) in 301. The south (including Damascus) and the regions of Lebanon and Palestine were seized by Ptolemy I Soter who had already been given command of Egypt. The Seleucid Kingdom began on an ordered and rational basis but never succeeded in welding Syria into a secure base for the Macedonian dynasty. Applying the principles of government and administration found elsewhere in Alexander's domains, new satrapal headquarters were established – Antioch, Seleucia (now Suweida at the mouth of the Orontes), *Apamea and Laodicea

(*Latakia) were the major centres. Subsidiary centres settled included *Cyrrhus, Chalcis ad Belum (*Qinnesrin), Beroea (*Aleppo), Arados (*Arwad), Hierapolis (*Menbij), and *Dura Europos, the latter to defend the connection between the two main Seleucid domains, Syria and Mesopotamia.

While the Greek soldier-settler element was probably no more than 50,000, the Hellenization of the region was firmly set in process. Many of the city states, however, preserved a high degree of independence and, though they shed their local dynasties to become republics loosely affiliated to the Seleucid Kingdom, retained an increasing degree of freedom of manoeuvre as the Seleucid hold on Syria weakened in the second century. The Ptolemies lost control of southern Syria by 198 BC when it fell to the Seleucid king, Antiochus III Megas (the Great) (r 223–187 BC). This marked the beginning of a temporary resurgence of the Seleucid dynasty which resulted in the Romans (recent masters of Greece) checking Antiochus' forces at Magnesia, obliging him under the terms of the Treaty of Apamea (188 BC) to cede all his conquests across the Taurus. A successor, Antiochus IV Epiphanes (r 175–164 BC) was forced to withdraw from Egypt, again following Roman intervention (168 BC). Attempts to force a policy of Hellenization on the Jews (including the profanation of the Jerusalem temple by setting up an altar to Zeus – the 'abomination' referred to in *Daniel* 9,7) – brought a fierce resistance, including the Maccabees' role in fostering the post-166 BC resurgence of a Jewish state in Palestine. By the beginning of the first century BC, Seleucid Syria was fraying badly at the edges with inroads by the Armenians to the north, the Parthians to the east and the Arab Nabataeans to the south.

Roman Syria (64 BC–AD 395)
(Map T2)

The Romans, who since their conquest of Greece had shown interest in the fate of Syria, became increasingly involved. In 64

BC, the Roman legate, Pompey, formally abolished the Seleucid Kingdom and created the Roman province of Syria with its principal city (metropolis) at Antioch. For a time, Syria became part of the setting for the great leadership struggle that brought an end to the Roman Republic. The main centres played with relish the game of switching allegiance between Augustus and Mark Antony as fortunes changed. The Augustan peace and the era of consolidation and prosperity that followed advantaged Syria which became one of the principal provinces of the Empire, remaining under the Emperor's jurisdiction, locally represented by a legate of consular rank. Antioch particularly flourished to become the third imperial city after Rome and Alexandria but other centres such as Damascus, Beroea and the trading hub of Palmyra, also benefited greatly. Under Augustus, four legions came to be stationed in Syria, the level of threat being considerably less, for example, than Germany which garrisoned eight.

Roman administration in Syria gradually took more direct control with previously semi-independent city-states such as Arados, Emesa (*Homs) and members of the loose confederation called the Decapolis (eg Damascus, Deraa and Canatha (*Qanawat)) quietly brought under direct rule by the early first century AD. The process was more slow-moving in Palestine where the collaborative Hasmonaeans had been permitted by the Senate to carve out their own kingdom under Roman protection, partly at the expense of the Nabataeans in southern Syria. (The Nabataeans were also dislodged from Damascus and retreated to semi-independent status in the fastness of Petra (in southern Jordan), fitfully retaining control as far north as Bosra.) The Hasmonaeans were succeeded by the sometimes more rowdy line of Herod the Great (r 39–4 BC) but the Romans took the opportunity of the death of Herod's heirs, Agrippa II in 92/3, to integrate Palestine into the province of Syria.

Economically, Syria flourished and became not only an entrepôt zone of

Roman Provincial Divisions

The following summarises the administrative divisions under which the broader region of Syria was ruled in Roman and Byzantine times. The original province of Syria did not include a number of principalities or city-states which the Romans allowed to continue within its provincial bounds, including the cities of the Decapolis – Canatha (*Qanawat), Deraa, Dion and Damascus within present-day Syria – and Emesa. These were gradually absorbed under direct rule from Augustus' principate until Trajan's incorporation of the Nabataean Kingdom in 106.

DATE	EMPEROR	PROVINCES	CAPITALS
64 BC	[Republic]	Syria	Antioch
AD 69	Vespasian	Syria	Antioch
		Judaea	Caesaria
106	Trajan	Syria	Antioch
		Judaea[1]	Aeolia Capitolina
		Arabia	Bostra
194	Septimius Severus	Coele Syria	Laodicea
		Syria Phoenice[2]	Tyre
		Arabia	Bostra
		Syria Palaestina	Aeolia Capitolina
		Mesopotamia	Nisibis
295	Diocletian	Arabia	Petra
		Augusta Libanensis	Bostra
		Syria Palaestina	Caesarea (after 365)
		Phoenice	Tyre
		Coele Syria	Antioch
		Augusta Euphratensis	Cyrrhus
		Osrhoene	Edessa
		Mesopotamia	Nisibis
c395	Arcadius	Syria Prima	Antioch
		Syria Secunda[3]	Apamea
		Phoenice Maritima	Tyre
		Phoenice Libanensis[4]	Damascus or Emesa?
		Palaestina (three provinces)	
		Arabia	Bostra
		Euphratensis	Cyrrhus
		Osrhoene	Edessa

In many cases, provinces cover only limited parts of present-day Syria.

NOTES: (1) Renamed Syria Palaestina in 135 when Jerusalem (Aeolia Capitolina) became the capital; (2) Included the main towns of southern Syria – Damascus, Emesa, Palmyra; (3) Justinian (mid sixth century) created a third Syrian province (Theodorias in honour of his wife) out of the coastal area around Laodicea; (4) Chief towns were Damascus, Emesa, Heliopolis (Baalbek) and Palmyra.

central importance in the east-west trade in luxuries (from China, India and Trans-Oxiana) but a major agricultural producer whose grain and wine supplied a good share of the Roman market. To service this commerce, trade routes were systematised through the building of roads, including the north-south Via Maris and Via Nova Traiana and the east-west route through Palmyra that saved considerable time and effort over the northern route following the Euphrates. Settlement and agricultural activities were pushed out into new areas such as the rocky hill country between Antioch and Beroea (*Dead Cities/Limestone Massif), the marginal zone south of Beroea or the region south of Damascus known as Auranitis (box on Hauran under *Suweida page 289). The cities were upgraded to reflect this prosperity and the energy of the urban upper classes who underpinned it (largely Greek-speaking, though of varied origins). Thus Damascus, already replanned by the prosaic Greek military, was given a more monumental appearance through the provision of a widened and colonnaded axial thoroughfare (immortalised in the New Testament as Straight Street) and a vastly enhanced sacred precinct for the Temple of Jupiter-Hadad (*Damascus – Umayyad Mosque).

Other cities such as Apamea, Palmyra, Laodicea-ad-Mare (Latakia), Canatha (*Qanawat) and Bostra (*Bosra) were given similar treatment. The latter two were replanned after Trajan's more aggressive policy of direct control resulted in the annexation of the Hauran in 106 and the creation of the province of Arabia (in the area south of Damascus and east of Palestine). Rome regarded Syria as a prized province and the position of legate was a valued appointment. Visits by several Emperors brought particular privileges to cities such as Bostra (capital of the new province of Arabia), Damascus (raised to metropolis by Hadrian, 117) and Palmyra (renamed Palmyra Hadriana in 129).

The second century AD was an era of unparalleled stability with Syria particularly favoured by contrast with the troubles that still beset the Romans in the province of Judaea to the south where, after the first Jewish-Roman war of 66–70, a second revolt under Bar Cochba in 132 brought an even more vehement Roman campaign to efface the insurrection and scatter the Jewish population. Syria's eastern borders took on an increasingly strategic significance to the Romans in the face of the perceived threat from the Parthians whose presence across the Euphrates had resulted in successive Roman attempts to dominate the Parthian heartland since the late first century BC. As the Parthians hit back into Roman territory, the campaigns in the east became more vigorous and draining, requiring imperial command from the early second century. The military presence in the region grew and with it the influence of Syrians in Rome itself became more direct not the least through links formed by Roman commanders on station in Syria, such as the future emperor, Septimius Severus. His marriage in 187 to Julia Domna, the daughter of the High Priest of Emesa (Homs), brought a line of 'Syrian' emperors which reached its nadir in 218–22 in the alarming eccentricities of Elagabalus.

By the late second century, the Parthian wars were a dominant pre-occupation with Parthia the only organised power anywhere along Rome's frontiers able to conduct a centralised campaign against the Empire's might. The challenge began to affect the prosperity even of such a flourishing centre as Palmyra which had successfully lived off its ability to act as a go-between in trade across hostile frontiers. The permanent military presence was pushed out as far as the Khabur River by the mid second century. Palmyra came under direct Roman rule (colonia from 212) and the sleepy local garrison at remote *Dura Europos on the Mid Euphrates was reinforced with imperial forces.

The sporadic confrontation with Parthia became more persistent by the end of the second century and turned into a more aggressive and focussed Sasanian threat following the takeover of Persia after 224 by Ardashir and particularly under his successor, Shapur I. Successive emperors

Roman Syria – Routes and *Limes*

Roman control of Syria was based on a highly developed system of roads and frontier forts which reflected both defensive and commercial needs. After the mid second century, the main axes were thoroughly replanned. North-south communication along the traditional Via Maris following the coasts of Syria and Phoenicia was supplemented by the new north-south routes – the Strata Diocletiana which ran from Sura on the Euphrates to Damascus via Resafa, Palmyra and Dumeir and the Via Nova Traiana which continued the axis southwards via Bosra to Aila (modern Aqaba, Jordan's port). East-west routes either crossed the desert on partly-improved carriageways (provisioned with milestones and watering points) or skirted it along the fertile lands to the north (eg the route via Cyrrhus and Zeugma and on to present northeast Syria; or further south via Chalcis ad Belum (Qinnesrin)). Within the bounds (*limes*) of the closely administered province, roads were now constructed to a high standard of durability (*Roman Road, Bab al-Hawa) better able to negotiate difficult and circuitous terrain (*Roman Road, Wadi Barada). Most roads, however, were of loosely compacted stones with a surface of gravel, on an average 6 m wide and slightly sloping from the centre. In steppe areas, a border of stones sufficed to mark a carriageway cleared of protrusions.

While the initial deployment of four Roman legions reflected as much internal security as frontier defence, by the end of the second century AD, the military deployments and creation of a fixed line of forts reflected the shift of priority to the east. The system of forts was generally aligned along the eastern frontier zone with a particular concentration in the northeast to meet the Parthian (later Sasanian) threat. The thick clustering of forts and sub-forts in the Euphrates/ Tigris zone was intensified by the fourth to sixth centuries though most of the remains of this activity are identifiable only by aerial photography. By the Byzantine period, the major building effort shifted further to the west and sites such as Resafa or Halebiye were re-constructed under Justinian's great defensive works program.

Roman forces in Syria rose to a total of six or seven legions (30–40,000 troops?) by the end of the second century supplemented by provincial auxiliaries, many of them locally recruited. The legions and their probable bases were as follows: VI Ferrata, Latakia; X Fretensis, Cyrrhus; XII Fulminata, Raphaneae; III Gallica, Zeugma.

over four centuries were to pit themselves against the Sasanian determination directly to challenge Rome's presence. By the mid third century, the situation on the eastern frontiers of Syria was parlous, the low points being the fall of Dura Europos in 256 and the capture in 260 of the Emperor Valerian in person by Sasanian forces at Edessa (southeastern Turkey), in spite of the presence of a Roman force of 70,000.

The humiliation of Valerian's capture, his torture and subsequent death were telling blows to Roman pride but symbolic of the general loss of authority at many points on the imperial *limes* by the mid third century. The Sasanians had already challenged Rome as far west as Antioch and the Romans were happy to exploit any assistance they could get to hold the situation.

They thus eagerly backed the ambitions of a Palmyrene oligarch, Odenathus, who campaigned on Rome's behalf deep into Sasanian territory (Ctesiphon 262) but who was unfortunately murdered in 266. His wife, Zenobia, carried on but had a rather different view of the relative power of Rome and Palmyra. She sent forces to Egypt and tried to engineer the takeover of Antioch in 271. The Emperor Aurelian clearly felt the challenge to central authority had gone too far and took to the field to check Zenobia. She fled Antioch, her forces failing to put up any challenge to Aurelian's outside Emesa in 272. Back in Palmyra, she again decided confrontation was best avoided and slipped out of the besieged city towards the Euphrates. Captured by the Romans in her attempt to cross the river, she was led off to Rome to grace Aurelian's triumph; Palmyra, after a second revolt against its occupying forces, was razed.

Syria's agricultural base was not fundamentally undermined by the repercussions of these events to the east and the building programs of the third century in much of Syria reflected the continued prosperity of the region, now divided further with the creation of the new province of Coele Syria after 194.

Christianity

By the time the Emperor Constantine gave official recognition to Christianity after 313, increasingly encouraging it as the state religion, Syria (and particularly Antioch) was already an area of intense Christian activity going back as far as the missions of St Paul in the mid first century. Christianity, with its blending of Jewish and Greek influences, was at first one more element, albeit a powerful one, in the Syrian melting pot. Before Christianity became part of public life in the fourth century, churches (as in the house-church unearthed at Dura Europos) were merely adapted dwelling places. After the official recognition of Christianity, they took on the form and scale of Roman public buildings. The pilgrimage phenomenon sponsored by Constantine's mother, St Helen, with her visit to the holy sites of Jerusalem in 324 later proliferated in Syria, complemented by the arrival of the monastic tradition (from Egypt) and the veneration of places associated with ascetic and saintly figures. By the sixth century, Syria was dotted with countless village or monastic churches as well as major pilgrimage centres such as those honouring the ascetic, St Simeon Stylites, or St Sergius in northern Syria.

But the diverse ingredients in the Syrian church were never totally at rest with each other. The philosophical debate over subjects as arcane as the division between Christ's physical and divine natures became overriding pre-occupations that divided eastern and western strands within the Church (Monophysites-Oriental versus Orthodox-Western), often seemingly

becoming codeword debates with deep political and social undercurrents.

Byzantine Era (395–636)

The adoption of Byzantium (renamed Constantinople) as the second capital of the Empire under Constantine foreshadowed the final transfer of the Roman capital to the East in 395, the start of the Byzantine era. Under Theodosius II (r 408–50), a '100 year peace' with the Sasanians brought some respite from the debilitating eastern wars but they became a major distraction again by the mid sixth century, absorbing much of the resources of Justinian's reign (r 527–65).

In spite of the troubles on the frontiers and the deep divisions that rent the Church (the Arian heresy in the fourth century; Nestorianism in the fifth century; and the dogged controversy over Monophysitism that continued from the fifth to the seventh century), it was a time of continued prosperity in the more settled parts of Syria. The limestone country west of Aleppo continued to prosper, based on its olive oil exports; the Hauran was intensely exploited; the cities remained thriving. Church and monastic projects abounded and Syrian builders developed a repertoire of styles (see pages 222–4 below) that adapted metropolitan and neo-classical models and blended them with elements from the east, often achieving a rather bizarre local mix whose remains are richly evident. In fact, no area of the Mediterranean world contains such a wealth of evidence of this period as can be found in the many churches, village and monastic remains of Syria.

For all its efforts to marry the eastern and western elements in Syrian society, continuing the process which had begun even before Alexander, Byzantine rule by the sixth century had begun to run out of solutions. The controversy over Monophysitism had become a corrosive element provoking intense local resentment against the imposition of orthodoxy from Constantinople. The Sasanian Persians made increasing inroads into Syria, their destructive raids punctuated by a devastating series of earthquakes. In spite of the efforts of Justinian and later emperors to stabilise the eastern frontiers, by the early seventh century, Syria was virtually incapable of putting up serious resistance to the prolonged occupation by Chosroes II who brought his presence in Antioch to a climax with the slaughter of 90,000 of its inhabitants. The Byzantines had tried diplomacy under Maurice (r 582–602) but were subsequently divided by their leadership struggles. By the time they rallied themselves to recover Syria (626), the country was so perpetually wearied by war, famines, earthquakes and plagues that it seemed virtually indifferent to its fate. After centuries of warfare, the Roman and Persian worlds had fought each other to a standstill.

Arab Conquest (632–61)

Into this near-vacuum came the armies of early Islam. After the death of the Prophet Muhammad in 632, his successor in the leadership of the faithful (the Caliphate), Abu Bakr, encouraged his forces to take further steps beyond the tentative moves begun by Muhammad himself to find new outlets to the north for the military, religious and commercial energies of the new Arab leadership. Few Syrian centres put up much resistance. Damascus surrendered twice, the second time in 636 after the crucial defeat of the Byzantine forces at Yarmuk. The small element of new population that the desert Arabs initially introduced gradually blended with the existing Semitic-based people, the distinctions further blurred by the unhurried process of conversions to the new faith of Islam. In contrast to the often heavy-handed imposition of Byzantine orthodoxy, Islam's introduction depended more on tax incentives than coercion and thus aroused little active resentment from the local (and for many centuries, still basically Christian) population.

For almost two decades, the new leadership remained based in Medina and southern Iraq. After Abu Bakr, the Caliphate passed to Umar (caliph 634–44), Othman (caliph 644–56) and then Ali (caliph 656–61), the four comprising the group of Rashidun or 'right-guided' caliphs. Ali's leadership, however, was challenged by Muawiya Ibn Abi Sufyan, the leader of the Umayyad faction who believed Ali had not sufficiently dissociated himself from the murderers of Othman. Ali was murdered by a disaffected former supporter. Of Ali's two sons, Hassan and Hussein, Hassan did not press his claim to the succession. Muawiya had already taken the Caliphate and promptly decided to move the capital to Damascus (where he had built up his power base as Governor).

Umayyads (661–750)

The Umayyad Caliphate brought in what is perhaps one of the most fertile and inventive periods of Syrian history. The perpetual search for an east-west balance was given a new and vigorous interpretation in an eclectic blending of Byzantine, Persian, Mesopotamian and local elements. This interaction resulting from the collapse of the antique world and the rise of Islam is still not fully explored or explained but the snapshot we are provided in the remains of the period attest to the complexity of forces at play in Umayyad Syria. The establishment of the supremacy of Arabic and the centrality of Islam within the Empire was done with a skilful hand. It was a period of great intellectual curiosity which flourished in an atmosphere of laissez-faire under Muawiya's judicious and moderate political leadership. The warrior-aristocracy of the Umayyads readily absorbed ideas from Syria's rich mixture of cultures and aspired to be the successors of the Romans and Byzantium. Damascus became a major centre (the Umayyads' realms eventually stretched from the Indus to Spain), a focus of political, religious and artistic creativity that gave the city a dynamism it had rarely enjoyed.

Gradually, however, the Umayyads' focus turned away from the larger Mediterranean world. Not only did they find few interlocutors interested in dealing with the new power (western Europe had not even begun to emerge from barbarian night; Byzantium was still struggling to hold itself together in its remaining lands) but it had to meet to the east a new trend towards a much harder-edged form of Islamisation. The germ was sown as early as Muawiya's reign (661–80). His assumption of power had exacerbated the split between the Umayyad clan and the followers of Ali, led by Ali's remaining son, Hussein, on the death of Hassan in 669. Muawiya was succeeded by his son, Yazid (r 680–3). Pro-Yazid forces drew the small band of Hussein and his followers into battle at Kerbala (southern Iraq) on 10 Muharram 61 AH (680), slaughtering Hussein and all but a few of his companions. Among those taken into captivity in Damascus was Zainab, sister of Hussein. The tragedy of Kerbala was to rankle for centuries. Eventually it would perpetuate the division between orthodox followers of the Umayyad Caliphate (later to be called Sunnis) and the unrequited supporters of the house of Ali (Shiites); it gradually deflected the focus of the Umayyad world towards the challenges to its cosmopolitanism that were germinating to the east.

At first, however, the opposition to their Caliphate having been driven underground, the Umayyads embarked on the most confident period of their administration. This was marked by major building projects at home and expansion abroad, especially under Abd al-Malik (r 685–705) and al-Walid (r 705–15). The latter was responsible for the immense project of the new congregational mosque in Damascus (*Damascus – Umayyad Mosque) which 1200 years later still bears striking witness to the richness and variety of the Umayyads' inspiration.

After the defeat of the Umayyad attempts to dislodge the Byzantines from Asia Minor, the Empire turned increasingly away from efforts to seek a place in the hostile or indifferent Mediterranean world to address the challenges from the east. Hisham (r 724–43) was the last of the great Umayyad rulers. After him the dynasty declined, exhausted by Shiite disaffection and the military incursions from Central Asia, Byzantium,and in North Africa. The line petered out in a succession of debauched or incompetent caliphs, palace

tensions and rebellions in the provinces of Persia and Iraq. A pretender, Abu al-Abbas, emerged in Iraq and marched on Damascus in 750. The Umayyads were eliminated, one grandson of Hisham fleeing to Spain where the Umayyad line survived for a further 500 years.

The new dynasty, the Abbasids, represented the eastern (Persian) tradition and a more theocratic version of the Caliphate, consciously spurning the attempts of the early Umayyads to marry eastern and western influences. The Abbasids transferred the Caliphate to Iraq (Kufa, until the founding of Baghdad in 762) and Syria became merely a neglected backwater, punished for its adherence to the corrupt and lax line of the Umayyads.

Abbasids (750–968)

The Abbasids never matched the vigour or the territorial spread of Umayyad power. The promise held out in the plan of Caliph Mansur for a new capital on the Tigris banks at Baghdad (built on a bold circular plan) was never carried through by his successors. Only Harun al-Rashid (Abbasid Caliph 786–809) had the flair to give the Caliphate wider status. He attracted an embassy from Charlemagne, the latter gaining from his gesture the right to protect Christian pilgrims to Jerusalem.

But the Abbasids failed to give sustained momentum to the development of a unified Islamic polity. Within two centuries, the heartland was increasingly invaded by Turkish nomads who displaced the Arab-Persian political elites. Regimes based on alien leadership now became the rule that marked virtually every era until modern times. The Turkish and other successive infiltrations prevented efforts to restore a Mid East-wide empire (a situation which was only securely reversed with the rise of the mamluk system in the 12th and 13th centuries). The process began in the mid ninth century with the Abbasid domains fragmenting through independent dynasties assuming power in provinces such as Egypt (Tulunids after 868; Fatimids after 905) and Persia (Sasanids after 874).

The caliphs themselves became hostage in Baghdad to foreign 'protectors' such as the Seljuk Turks from 1037.

Syria, once again, was contested from many directions. In this period of unparalleled confusion, the struggle for political dominance was matched by a resurgence of the Shiite-Sunni tensions as various factions fought to impose their views on an increasingly Islamicised population. Heterodox sects of all persuasions sprang up in this no-man's-land of empires with Shiism (and its Ismaeli variant) the dominant trend even in the cities (especially Aleppo). Rebellions and disaffection abounded and many sects simply retreated to the mountainous and desert areas, there preserving a separate identity which is evident today in the country's ethnic and religious complexity. (It was at this time that the Maronite sect took refuge in the mountains of Lebanon, illustrating that diversity and fragmentation were not the sole prerogative of Muslims.)

Syria's political history during this period can only be traced at the local level, separate lines of political succession being established in northern and southern Syria, depending on their degree of exposure to events in Egypt, Iraq (especially Mosul, the seat of Seljuk power), Byzantium and Turkey. Aleppo was controlled by the Hamdanid dynasty (944–1003) whose impetuous adventurism only served to make Aleppo a virtual protectorate of the Byzantines and later of the Fatimids. The Bedouin Mirdasid family then nominally ruled the city (1023–79) in a balancing act that recognised Fatimid suzerainty without provoking Byzantine intervention. The Seljuk Turks who had extorted from the putative Abbasid caliph a mandate to govern northern Syria effectively took over under Alp Arslan as sultan (1070–2). The Byzantines had been seeking to profit from this instability by intermittently seizing parts of northern Syria under Emperors Nicephorus II Phocas (r 963–9) and John I Tzimisces (r 969–76) but their campaign had petered out with the signing of a treaty in 997 accepting Fatimid supremacy in Syria.

Damascus, like Aleppo, experienced in the ninth to 11th centuries a time of anarchy, with a period of rule in the ninth century by the Cairo-based Ikhshidid dynasty. After 961, the Fatimids, a Shiite dynasty, supplanted them in Cairo. Though the Ikhshidids paid nominal allegiance to the Abbasid caliphs in Baghdad, the Fatimids set up a rival Caliphate. The significance of this Baghdad/Cairo polarisation was to make Syria a battleground for inter-Muslim tensions, a situation which prevailed until a viable centre of power was effective in uniting the Middle East.

The continued rise of the Seljuks (nominally subservient to the Baghdad Caliphate) now brought the struggle for Syria to a new phase. The supremacy of the Seljuk Turks was sealed at the Battle of Manzikert (in eastern Turkey) in 1071 which saw their victory over the Byzantine forces of Romanus IV Diogenes who was taken prisoner. They went on to take most of Syria, including Damascus in 1075, and by 1078 were in Jerusalem. By the late 11th century, under Alp Arslan and Malik Shah I (sultan 1072–92), the Seljuks were sufficiently strong in Syria to block the Fatimid dynasty's efforts to maintain control of southern Syria, though Damascus oscillated between the two centres for some time. The Seljuk supremacy began to ring alarm bells in Europe, particularly given the apparent weakness of the Byzantines, and was in large part the stimulus that led to the 12th–13th century crusading movement which called for the recovery of the Holy Places by Christian arms.

Crusades (1098–1291)
(Map T3)

After centuries of comparative isolation, the Crusades brought to Syria another of the great clashes of worlds which have marked its history. After Pope Urban II (1088–99) made his stirring appeal to arms at the Council of Clermont-Ferrand in 1095, the Christian army that poured into Syria in 1097 found that the Seljuk leadership had disintegrated and that the land lacked any unified command for resistance. Not that the Christian armies were much more united, rent by serious problems of leadership and disputes over tactics. During the nine month siege which resulted in the brutal taking of Antioch (when little respect was paid to the city's still-considerable Greek Orthodox population), the armies divided. Baldwin of Boulogne headed east to set up a separate principality at Edessa (southeastern Turkey). Bohemond was made Prince of Antioch while Raymond, Count of Toulouse set out for Jerusalem with what remained of the largely rabble army. Their taking en route of *Maarat al-Numan produced another gross massacre but still there was no concerted Muslim resistance.

From Maarat, the Crusaders marched south along the Orontes Valley and then turned towards the coast again through the Homs Gap, taking on the way the Kurdish fort which was to become the site of the great castle now known as the Krak des Chevaliers. Tripoli (northern Lebanon) was the next major objective but the city put up a fierce resistance and had to be by-passed while the army went on to take Jerusalem in 1099. It took some time for the various Crusader princes to consolidate their hold on the Syrian coastal areas. Tripoli was finally taken in 1109 but smaller centres such as *Latakia and *Tartus as well as the mountainous region around *Masyaf fell earlier. But the Crusader domains were never a compact and tightly defended entity. The division of control between various families – Raymond, Count of Toulouse, now installed in Tripoli; Bohemond and later Tancred in Antioch; Baldwin in Edessa – their mutual rivalries and separate designs on the Jerusalem Kingdom and their lack of sizeable or professional standing armies meant that many compromises had to be made with the Syrian environment. The divisions between the Muslim cities and leaderships, the fact that the Muslim/Christian gulf was often less important than the temptation to make alliances of convenience in pursuit of local power struggles, the ambiguous position of local Christian communities – these factors and more blurred the great faultline that theoretically ran between the Muslim and Christian worlds.

Yet the confrontation ran on for almost two centuries. To the Muslims, the Crusaders' religious pretext for intervention was never credible, Christian subjects of the Islamic states rarely suffering any distinct disadvantages and Christian pilgrims having long been accepted in the Holy Land. The Crusaders' presence was thus seen as a straight invasion in which religion was a veil cast over territorial motives.

The Franks, as they were known to the Muslims, stayed on in their main bastions, controlled some areas of countryside and precarious communication routes between, brought in fresh recruits through renewed crusading campaigns in Europe, married, died and constructed castles and churches. Though they held on to the slender coastal strip, their hold inland (even when consolidated after 1150 by the transfer of key fortresses to the Hospitaller and Templar orders) was at best precarious given the lack of manpower and popular support in the countryside. They rarely managed to threaten the main Muslim population centres. They got little help from – and did little to advance the position of – local Christians (usually Greek Orthodox and thus aloof from the aspirations of the Westerners). As the Muslim forces rallied to the new centres of Sunni power in Damascus and Aleppo, the process of slow attrition of the Crusaders' positions set in.

Islamic Resurgence

Aleppo was the first centre for Muslim consolidation under the Zengid regents (atabeqs), Zengi (r 1128–46) and his second son, Nur al-Din (r 1146–74), nominally subservient to the Seljuk sultan of Mosul and through him to the caliph in Baghdad. They continued the Seljuk policy of restoring Sunni orthodoxy, rolling back the gains made by Shiism under Fatimid encouragement and through the Persian-inspired Ismaelis. Sunni Islam became a more distinct rallying point against the alien threat, its concepts of inner character and righteous living being embodied in the Sharia (Islamic law code) and systematised through the work of the urban religious leadership, the *ulama*, and a new network of educational and religious foundations.

The Zengids complemented this consolidation of the spiritual defences of their realms with a consolidation of their physical preparedness. They regained the Crusader outpost at Edessa (1144) and destabilised the Crusader presence in the Orontes Valley. By 1154, they had brought Damascus under their control, uniting for the first time the resistance to the Crusades in Syria into a single front and thus refining the concept of jihad.

The consolidation of orthodoxy and the encirclement of the Crusader forces took most of the century to complete before Muslim forces in Egypt and Syria were linked under one command (thus denying the Crusaders the capacity to play off Cairo against Damascus). Nur al-Din completed the process, making serious inroads into the Crusader presence in the Syrian coastal mountains, but it was taken further by Saladin, the nephew of his commanders, Ayyub. Saladin (a Kurd by origin) wrested the succession from Nur al-Din's infant son in 1176, having earlier (1171) ended the Fatimid era in Cairo by nominally restoring the authority of the Abbasid Caliphate. Damascus, for long the frontline centre of resistance to the Crusader presence in Jerusalem, became his preferred forward base and there he initiated the line of Ayyubids (1176–1260 – after his family name) which later took the form of separate dynasties in Damascus and Cairo. From there he completed the unification of Syria, taking full control of Aleppo in 1183 and thus securing strategic depth for a vigorous campaign against the Crusader forces. By 1187 he had lured King Guy of Jerusalem into the disastrous battle at Hattin in Galilee which saw the mass destruction of the Christian army and brought the fall of Jerusalem to the Muslim forces.

Crusader Syria withstood the loss of Jerusalem. The concept of a jihad to unite Muslim ranks rarely had much currency outside the areas directly affected by the Crusaders' depredations. Even Saladin's

brilliant campaign in 1188 (see box page 16) did not touch off a consolidated effort to dislodge them from the great fortresses at the Krak or Marqab or from the cities of Tartus, Latakia or Antioch. After Saladin died in 1193, the inspiration had gone. Disputes resulted in the fragmentation of his realm between rival sons and it took nine years before the Ayyubid lands came together again under his brother, al-Adil (sultan in Damascus 1196–1218; in Cairo 1200–18). One of his successors in Cairo, al-Kamil I Nasr al-Din (1218–38), even handed back Jerusalem to the Crusaders by treaty with Frederick II in 1229, a move that provoked outrage and rebellion in Damascus. (It was recovered by the Muslims after falling to a Turkish marauding army in 1244.) The Ayyubids' line petered out by 1260, crippled by squabbles between Saladin's many descendants, though there were occasional signs of local vigour, for example the rule of his third son, al-Zaher Ghazi as Governor at Aleppo (1196–1215).

Mamluks (1260–1516)

By the mid 13th century, the focus of the Muslim/Crusader struggle had moved to Egypt which became the target of the later Crusades. From Cairo came the second great Muslim revival with the rise to open political power of the Mamluks (professional guards usually of Central Asian or Turkish background) in a palace coup of 1250. The first of the Mongol invasions of Syria, under Hulaga, inspired the Mamluks to rally the flagging forces of Islam (Battle of Ain Jalud – 'Goliath's Fountain' – on 3 September 1260) and to take over Damascus from the last Ayyubid, al-Malik al-Nasr II. The ruthless leadership of the Mamluk sultan, al-Zaher Baybars (r 1260–77), gave renewed momentum to the anti-Crusader cause and the debilitated Christian presence was rapidly dislodged from Antioch (1268) and from the bastions at the Krak and nearby *Safita (1271). The concurrent campaign against heterodox Shiites brought the Ismaeli castles of the coastal mountains under Sunni rule (*Masyaf). The process continued under Sultan Qalawun (r 1280–90) who routed the remaining Crusader

Saladin's Campaign of 1188

After Hattin and the taking of Jerusalem, Saladin spent the next campaign season in a series of whirlwind strikes against Crusader positions in Syria. His main concern was to block the incursion of a German Crusader army then en route through Asia Minor and to complement his diplomatic contacts with the Byzantines aimed at discouraging them from giving the Germans access through Byzantine territory. His tactical objectives were not to drive the Crusader presence in Syria into the sea but to reduce the extent of territory they could make available to a German force. Thus he decided against any frontal assaults on the main Crusader strongholds where resistance developed but rather to roll up their weakly manned positions inland and bottle up the Christian forces in major centres – Tortosa, the Krak, Marqab and Antioch.

His tactics were a brilliant success. The taking of over 50 Crusader positions (for the moment, reducing the Kingdom of Jerusalem to a small enclave around Tyre) fatally weakened the Crusader presence, denying them the capacity to interdict the major inland north-south routes. The weak Crusader response to his campaign justified his assumptions about the capacity of an alien force to maintain its presence on hostile territory. The last gesture of Saladin, the occupation of the castle of Baghras, virtually under the nose of Bohemond, Prince of Antioch, showed the ultimate powerlessness of the Frankish forces. What is perhaps most remarkable, however, was that it took almost another century for the Muslim successors of Saladin to capitalise on this realisation and nudge the remaining Crusader forces out of the East.

LIST OF MAIN ENGAGEMENTS

1187

4 July	Battle of Hattin
2 October	Jerusalem falls

1188

30 May	arrives at Krak – decides not to attack
3–8 July	sacking of Tortosa, passes Marqab, burning of Baniyas
16 July	takes Jeble
23 July	siege of Latakia succeeds
29 July	Château de Saône (Qalaat Saladin) falls after three days
1 August	Balatonos (Qalaat al-Mehelbeh) falls
5 August	Bakas falls
12 August	Shugur falls
20 August	arrives at Qalaat Burzey
23 August	Burzey falls
28 Sept	Baghras besieged

forces with their successive retreats from Marqab (1285), Latakia (1287), Tripoli (1289) and Tartus (1291).

The Mamluks, though aliens, rapidly built themselves networks of alliances with the principal families and religious establishments (*ulama*) of the main Syrian cities. Under their guidance and with the aid of the endowments often funded by their governors, the early Mamluk period was another golden age

for Damascus. Though not the centre of the Mamluk realms (that remained Cairo), it was made the second capital by the early 14th century, greatly favoured by the early sultans as demonstrated in the 171 building projects undertaken during the period. Its governors were highly connected and often very effective (most notably Tengiz, Governor of Damascus 1312–40). Elaborate chains of command were set up to ensure that they did not arrogate independent authority. By

1312, the Mamluks had largely achieved all they had set out to gain and a period of sustained prosperity set in for most of the century. After 1380, however, a series of disastrous civil wars weakened the leadership and renewed threats of bedouin and Tartar assaults. After the last, and most disastrous, Mongol invasion of 1400–1 under Timur (Tamerlaine), the Mamluk sultans never quite recovered their stride.

In 1390, the succession of Bahri Mamluks (1260–1382 – mainly Turks or Mongols) had been replaced by a largely Circassian line of Burji Mamluks (1382–1516). A period of consolidation began in 1422 and the long rule (1468–95) of Sultan Qait Bey brought renewed stability to Syria. But the most notable reminders of the late Mamluk period are the numerous mausoleums. (Elisséeff notes that the Mamluks 'who lived uncertain of what the next day would bring, tried at least to secure themselves a sepulchre'.) In the end, Mamluk rule collapsed as much from its unpopularity (due to the extortionate demands placed on its Syrian subjects) as from the swift inroads of a new Turkish incursion, this time in the form of the Ottoman military.

Ottomans (1516–1918)

The Ottoman Turks had already taken much of Asia Minor (including Constantinople from the Byzantines in 1453) before they moved in on Syria. Many of the upper class rallied spontaneously to them in 1516, the Mamluk garrison quietly slipping out of Damascus to allow the new Sultan to make his entrance. Shortly after, under the long reign of Suleiman (known to Europe as Suleiman the Magnificent – r 1520–66), the administration of Syria was systematised, its population counted and its revenues stabilised. The early Ottoman period (especially the 16th–17th centuries) brought a new impetus to the development of the three Syrian provinces (*vilayat*) – Aleppo, Damascus and Raqqa. The role played by the Syrian provinces in the administration and provisioning of the annual pilgrimage (Hajj) to Mecca did much to advance the economy and

external trade grew. Under the provisions of the Ottoman 'capitulation' treaties with European powers, Aleppo became the base for a substantial foreign trading presence, a role that Damascus shared only to a limited extent.

Ottoman rule was a reasonably loose arrangement, considerable power being devolved to the local governors (*wali*, holding the rank of Pasha), as long as the central coffers were supplied with tax revenue, the Hajj provisioned and the security interests of the empire respected. The sultan's role as caliph was broadly accepted by Sunnis and helped confer legitimacy on Ottoman rule. There was little attempt to impose a Turkish cultural identity and what borrowing there was of ideas and projects from the capital often became modified in local detail. The millet system which ruled minority communities through their religious leaders tended to reinforce the existing forces which had set up distinctive minority quarters in the cities and enclaves in the more remote parts of the countryside. The minorities largely thrived under Turkish rule, the Christians in particular playing an intermediary role in the rise of external commerce under the watchful eye of the Western powers. By the 18th century, however, Turkish rule was stagnating and the economic fortunes of Syria began to diminish with more intense competition from trade routes via the north or via the sea routes to Asia.

The 19th century was again a troubled period for Syria. The 1831 expedition of Ibrahim Pasha, the son of Muhammad Ali who had set up his own power base in Egypt in defiance of Ottoman authority, pushed the Ottoman forces back across the Taurus. Egyptian rule brought in a more tolerant dispensation that saw the first European residents of Damascus and encouraged the Christian communities to play a more assertive role in public life. Ibrahim Pasha was forced out in 1840 and Ottoman rule uneasily restored. In 1860, partly as a result of the Druze-Christian troubles in Lebanon, a terrible massacre broke out in Damascus after a Muslim attack on the Christian quarter.

The Ottomans restored calm but the situation provoked the landing of French forces on the Lebanese coast. By now, Syria was considerably more open to foreign influence. European educational institutions began to operate in the second half of the 19th century but much of the initiative had already been lost to the more outward-looking cities of the coast, notably Beirut.

Damascus was thus slow to adopt the Arab nationalist sentiments that were encouraged in the case of Cairo, for example, by the development of the Arabic-language press. (There was no Arabic newspaper in Damascus until 1897.) Some reformist Ottoman governors such as Midhat Pasha (1878–80) were well in advance of most of their subjects and introduced on their own initiative civic improvements that enhanced the amenities and sanitation of the main cities. The first paved road for wheeled traffic since Roman times was opened between Beirut and Damascus in 1863. A railway from Beirut to Damascus and the Hauran was opened in 1894 and a supplementary line from Rayyak (in the Beqaa Valley in Lebanon) north to Homs and Aleppo was later completed. In 1908, the German-built Hijaz Railway connected Damascus with Medina.

Syria anticipated a new deal for the Arab subjects of the Empire with the overthrow of the Ottoman Sultan Abd al-Hamid II in 1909 by the Young Turks. Disappointment at the continuation of Turkish rule and the imposition of policies of 'Turkification' gave new stimulus to Arab nationalism. In 1914, Damascus was made the general headquarters of German and Turkish forces in Syria, Lebanon and Palestine. Damascus became a base for rising Arab feeling against

Turkish domination, focussing particularly on the aspirations of Amir Feisal, son of Hussein, the Sharif of Mecca, to liberate the Muslim holy places. World War I was a time of extreme privation in Syria and Lebanon with Turkish indifference and maladministration aggravating the effects of food shortages, leading to starvation and serious epidemics.

French Mandate (1922–45)

Allied and Arab nationalist forces entered Damascus on 1 October 1918, the city having been abandoned the day before by its Turkish garrison. Elections to a National Syrian Government the next year and the appointment of Feisal as King cut across British and French ambitions and were overturned by the establishment under the provisions of the Versailles Treaty of a French Mandate in Syria (along with a corresponding French Mandate in an enlarged Lebanon and British Mandates in Palestine and Trans-Jordan). The mandate was imposed by force of arms in 1920 and was accepted at best grudgingly thereafter.

France faced a hostile population and wearying resistance. In 1925, a serious revolt broke out in the Hauran and spread to Damascus where the French resorted to mass bombardment of the city. Having tried to break Syria up into more malleable portions (separate 'states' were declared in the Hauran, the Alawi area and northern Syria), the French succumbed to rising nationalist agitation with limited constitutional independence in 1943, the Vichy French by then having been dislodged in favour of the Free French. The Mandate formally ended in April 1945 with Syria's admission to the United Nations.

2

DEVELOPMENT OF ARCHITECTURAL FORMS IN SYRIA

Bronze and Iron Ages

Although Syria is of critical importance in the scientific study of the remains of the Bronze and Iron Ages and provides an extraordinary range of sites that have been researched over the last century, the scope of this book is restricted to remains that are recognisable as buildings or as monuments to the past. Only a limited number of remains of these early periods are covered in this volume namely those of major historical importance (*Ebla, *Tell Halaf) or where the physical remains uncovered by researchers provides unusually rich evidence of the architectural practices of the period (especially *Ugarit, *Mari, *Ain Dara).

The early sequence of buildings does not represent in itself a continuous tradition, the pattern was continually disrupted by the waves of invasions and cross-currents of influences that washed over Syria. While the remains of temples at sites such as Ugarit do show the beginnings of an architectural style that will emerge later as a steady trend (box on Syro-Phoenician Temples below), most of the architectural development is only broadly related to common themes such as the evolution of the internal courtyard as the basis of palace design. If the results are thus ad hoc and cumulative, the effects are nevertheless striking when seen on the scale achieved in the Palace of Zimri-Lim at Mari with its 275 rooms or in the main palace of Ugarit with 90 or more rooms on the lower (stone-built) floor plus upper storeys. Major settlements were generally fortress-cities, walled for defence against newly-developed weapons such as cavalry (based on the horse-drawn light chariot) and archers. A citadel was located on the highest ground, defended by two or three outer walls of beaten earth or stone, surrounded by a moat, intended to resist siege devices such as moveable towers and battering rams. Within the walls, houses were usually of mud brick, some with an upper storey.

The development of decorative elements in palace and temple design is likewise only randomly visible in our survey. At Mari, there are fragments of wall-painting

Syro-Phoenician temples

Several temples in Syria which are variously described as Roman, Palmyrene, Phoenician or in the style of Baalbek, actually bear many traces of a common lineage which is largely local in inspiration, but takes on many Roman or classical attributes. What is common to the Allat, Bel and Baal-Shamin temples at *Palmyra, the Phoenician-Persian temple at *Amrit, the Roman temple compound at *Husn Suleiman and even the Temple of Jupiter in Damascus (*Damascus – Umayyad Mosque) is a common Syro-Phoenician ancestry.

The idea of isolating the temple cella from the clutter of its surrounds and locating it in an open compound is an idea that first appeared in Syria (Ugarit temples) and later gave rise to the fully free-standing Greek version. The earliest clear example is the late fifth or fourth century compound at Amrit, a curious site just south of Tartus which betrays an eclectic mixture of influences from local Phoenician to Mesopotamian-Persian. Here can be seen the basic idea of a large open temple compound at the centre of which stands a small naos or cella. The areas for public assembly are kept open and the room reserved for the image and priestly worship of the gods is enclosed in a relatively small space. (The same idea can be seen in reconstructions of Old Testament religious buildings.) In front of the naos are an altar for public sacrificial rites and a small pool for lustrations. The provision at Amrit of a sacred lake around the central island is not found at any other sites.

In later examples, the naos increases in size, even taking on some of the appearance of the classical temple itself (surrounding colonnade etc) but is still small compared to the vast spaces of the walled and/or arcaded enclosure. The altar and lustral pool survive (Palmyra). So too does the corner tower, a format found in the *Palmyra – Bel temple as well as in the curious building at *Dumeir. The most flamboyant achievement is the Temple of Jupiter Heliopolitan at Baalbek (Lebanon) which is outside the scope of this book but which represents an overblown version of forms found in the major classical and Phoenician sites of the region.

and the use of orthostats to line gateways or courtyards is evident by the early Iron Age, developing into the bold use of stone-carved panels or free-standing sculptures at Tell Halaf (*Aleppo – Museum) or *Ain Dara.

Seleucids

Virtually all of Seleucid Syria has been lost to posterity in later re-building[1], though the tendency in the Roman period to respect the Greek town plan (based on the Hippodamian grid – *Damascus – Straight Street) means that the principles used in planning Greek cities endured even if the actual fabric was considerably embellished (usually on a grandiose scale – *Palmyra, *Apamea). *Dura Europos is a good example of a Greek fortress adapted to Persian and Roman needs. In fact, until recently there was no evidence of a major Hellenistic fortress that was not rebuilt by the Romans indicating that at least the Greeks' capacity to pick strategic sites could not be improved on even if some of their cities (eg Beroea – *Aleppo) failed to prosper as major civilian centres in Roman times.

Roman Period

Though remains of the early imperial period are scarce, in architecture the second century AD seems to have seen a drift away from the orientalising trends of the Hellenistic and early Roman periods and a closer observance of imperial norms. The mixture of styles that marked the vast project developed from the late first century BC, the *temenos* of the Palmyra Bel Temple, is a last throw in terms of the heavy use of the orientalising repertoire for major projects. But local preoccupations survived at the level of individual sponsorship, for example in the rectangular tower tomb and in funerary art at Palmyra (see box under *Palmyra – page 229).

Syria is well furnished with 12 examples

1 A French team has excavated the Hellenistic fortress at *Ras al-Basit. An extensive citadel has also been found by an Australian team at *Jebel Khalid.

of Roman theatres (of which at least six are preserved in substantial form), including one of the most intact in the Mediterranean world, at *Bosra. Although its construction in sombre basalt gives a different impression from the dazzling stone of Leptis Magna (Libya) or Aspendos (Turkey), its survival virtually intact (only the *scaenae frons* had to be reconstructed) and the sweep of its nearly intact *cavea* make it a monument of singular significance. Though not the largest in Syria (see box below), other examples only manage to suggest their former proportions, though the small examples at *Jeble and *Shahba are reasonably well preserved.

The theatre boom in Syria does not seem to have begun until the mid second century, reflecting the increasingly prosperous basis of the communities and their acquisition of more distinctly Roman tastes. We have no evidence of theatre construction in the Hellenistic period (though Damascus and Antioch are reported, from written

Roman theatres			
site	diameter	capacity	date
Apamea	139 m		late 2C
Bosra	102 m	6–9000	late 2C?
Cyrrhus	115 m		c150
Jeble	90 m	7000	–
Palmyra	90 m		2C?
Shahba	90 m		mid-3C

evidence, to have had theatres by the early first century AD). The remaining examples follow Roman models though the Syrian builders were more inclined to chose sites on flat ground (eschewing the advantages of building the huge structure into a hillside) and construction is almost always in stone (as opposed to brick used in the Roman world to the west).

City Plans

Other manifestations of the classical period can be found in diverse forms in Syria. The expansion of cities generally

Roman city plans

city	main axis	width	grid elements	date
Aleppo (Beroea)	1.00 km	20–25 m	120 by 46 m	?
Apamea	1.85 km	37.5 m	105 by 53 m	115–180
Bosra	900 m	23 m	V	105+
Cyrrhus	400+ m	7 m*	?	?
Damascus	1.35 km	26 m	100 by 45 m	late 2/3C
Laodicea (Latakia)	1.50 km	5–7 m	112 by 57 m	192–211?
Palmyra	1.20 km	25 m	V	mid 2– 3C

* = between columns only   ? = not known   V = variable

respected the basic Hippodamian grid of Hellenistic times (see box above). To this was added, however, a specifically Syrian embellishment – the principal axis (*decumanus* or *cardo maximus*) was considerably enlarged and lined with colonnades to shelter pedestrians from the sun, frame the commercial booths or shops to the rear and provide a sumptuous setting to major civic buildings. The effect is still observable at *Palmyra and on an even grander scale at *Apamea. Few new cities were founded under the Romans. An exception is Philippopolis (*Shahba), a curious attempt to establish a later Roman 'model town' to commemorate the local ancestry of the reigning emperor, Philip the Arab (r 244–9).

Temples and Civic Works

Roman temples are found in various locations, mostly remote from population centres which might have re-used their stone for subsequent construction. There are several examples of Roman baths (*Barad, *Shahba, *Bosra) but few extant examples of houses. Some prosaic but impressive engineering accomplishments survive (eg sections of stone-clad Roman roads – *Roman Road – Bab al-Hawa; the bridges east of *Cyrrhus; the cistern at *Bosra), attesting to the intensive nature of Rome's development of this prized and largely peaceful province. Perhaps most impressive, though, are the lonely sentinels on the outer frontier – the outposts at Dura Europos and Cyrrhus, both fortress cities of Greek origins. But the centre-piece of Rome's accomplishment in stabilising the area is Palmyra which also bears witness to the intense (and finally tragic) attempt to build from an isolated society a culture blending eastern and western styles bound together by recognition of the commercial advantages of the Pax Romana.

Byzantine Period

The transition to the Byzantine period with its emphasis on architecture in the service of Christianity is the theme of the fourth to fifth centuries in Syria. Leaving aside the notable fortresses of *Resafa, *Qasr Ibn Wardan and *Halebiye, the Byzantine period is largely measured by its extraordinary variety of churches, with which Syria is exceptionally well endowed. (For this reason, and given the profusion of sites in this category, the architectural development of church styles is examined here in some detail.)

Churches

Syria being a crossroads of diverse influences, more than one tradition is reflected in the evolution of architectural styles of early Christian churches. Influences include: the Roman basilica model, adapted to religious use; local domestic architecture; eastern styles (including the surmounting dome); and temple architecture. Also to be factored in are regional variations, often reflecting availability of materials, and (after the fourth century) liturgical and doctrinal fissures within the Christian hierarchy which influenced architectural practice.

The earliest churches of which we have evidence were converted private houses. The example at *Dura Europos is the most remarkably preserved (it was transported in the 1930s to a museum at Yale University) and the earliest (early third century), before the official recognition of the Church under Constantine. From the next century comes the house converted to a church in the village of *Kirkbizeh.

The tradition subsequently became more evidently diverse, the availability of building materials playing a large role in regional variations. In the north, the chalky local limestone was easily worked. Usually the basic plan followed the basilica tradition. In the Hauran, the local basalt was heavy and unyielding. The lack of wood and the need to work basalt into roofing slabs no longer than 2 to 3 m imposed a different range of technical needs including the transverse arch and the centralised dome plan. This gave rise to an inventive local tradition different from that of the north and remote from any major metropolitan

centre such as Antioch.

Evolution of Church Plans

Most of Syria's early churches are dated, making it relatively easy to trace the variations in their design. Some even record the name of the architect. By the end of the fourth century, church design had become highly ambitious, for example the cathedral at *Barad (built by the architect Julianos – 27 m wide by 39 m). The buildings may lack the refinement of design of counterparts in the area of Antioch, more readily influenced by imperial and metropolitan styles, but the construction is solid and precise.

By the second half of the fifth century, Syrian churches were beginning to show signs of the bold experimentation that is evident in other parts of the Mediterranean world. At *Qalb Lozeh, the plan had become so big in scale that new structural devices were needed, especially in order to allow for the opening up of the side aisles. Whereas the outer aisles were previously divided from the central nave by a row of columns, the latter were replaced by broad squat piers which support wide sweeping arches, with added devices such as the dramatic archway enclosing the apse and solid towers flanking the west entrance (an idea which has precedents in Hellenistic buildings).

Syro-Byzantine church plans

By the early fifth century, the elements of the typical northern Syrian church plans from this heyday of Christianity were largely in place. The design, repeated in scores of villages of the 'dead cities' zone, comprised a basilica plan with the nave terminating to the east in a semi-dome over the sanctuary housed in a half-circular apse. On either side of the sanctuary was a small chamber – on the north, the *diaconicon* or sacristy/vestry and a room often used as a martyrium for the veneration of saints' relics. (One of these chambers might support a tower.) The roof above the nave was usually of pitched timber, avoiding the arched stone or domes found in the south. In many churches, the centre of the nave was occupied by a horseshoe-shaped *bema*, a raised platform or tribunal, perhaps intended to serve for the celebration of the Liturgy of the Word.

The entrance to the church was often through a doorway on the south side, especially in early examples. Later there was a tendency to develop the west front with either a wide *narthex* or vestibule or a narrower one enclosed between flanking towers. Social convention prescribed in many areas (but especially in the neighbourhood of Antioch where greater orthodoxy prevailed) the separation of women and men, the former being confined either to the western end of the church or in a separate gallery above the nave.

Shortly after, a project of massive proportions was undertaken a little to the north at *Saint Simeon to commemorate the monk who had spent the later part of his life as a hermit on a small platform atop a pillar. The pilgrimage to commemorate St Simeon had taken off with great vigour even before his death. The imperial authorities probably sought to use it to divert the local population from their heretical attachment to Monophysitism and thus poured funds into the ambitious project – a four-basilica pilgrimage centre, constructed in the last decades of the fifth century. This gigantic construction re-introduced many aspects of classical decoration to the Syrian repertoire, probably via architects and craftsmen imported from Antioch or further afield.

Pilgrimages to the shrines of martyrs inspired many of the churches constructed during the remainder of the Christian period in Syria. The cathedral dedicated to St Sergius at *Resafa represents the 'final stages of majestic authority' of the basilica plan.[2] Dating from the sixth century, it typifies the bold concepts employed post-Qalb Lozeh to divide the centre from the side aisles by means of leaping arches carried on stout piers. The same principle is employed in the Church of Bissos at *Ruweiha (sixth century) though both show the structural weakness of a design which failed to provide sufficient lateral support to hold the towering arches and their surmounting masonry clerestories.

Materials, Decoration

The use of stucco and plaster provided a finish to most churches quite different to that now conveyed by the mellowed and mottled stone. In the south, most were plastered inside and out; internal plastering (and probably the application of frescoes) was employed in the north. Traces of floor mosaics have been found in some churches and transferred to museums for preservation.

Centralised churches

In a different stream is the tradition of centralised churches, usually based on a circular domed structure placed on top of square lower walls. The earliest dated example found in Syria is the cathedral at *Bosra (511–2). The basic method of resolving a round room within a square building by the use of corner exedrae flanked by niches had been used in Roman architecture, particularly in the construction of baths (as at Bosra itself) but its translation into Christian buildings is a southern Syrian initiative. Later examples were found at Jerash (nearby in northern Jordan) and at Constantinople (Church of Sts Sergius and Bacchus (518–27); Baptistery of Hagia Sophia).

The second notable element of the Bosra design is the central circular arcade, technically called a colonnaded quatrefoil. The device also came from classical sources and had already passed into church architecture by the time the Bosra cathedral was built. Such examples are found in the Church of San Lorenzo in Milan, the martyrium at Seleucia ad Pieria (near Antioch) and (later) in the centralised churches at *Resafa and *Apamea.

The Bosra church thus has clear roots in the Hellenized traditions of the Mediterranean world and the local tradition of centralised dome structures. The trend was taken much further in, for example, Hagia Sophia, once the technical problems of expanding the centralised design had been resolved by the later development of pendentives and flying buttresses to spread the excessive weight bearing down on vulnerable points.

Another remarkable non-basilica design is the Church of St George at *Ezraa in southern Syria, probably the oldest continually-used church in Syria whose origins go back to AD 515. It differs from other centralised churches in that its basic shape is octagonal, thus rendering the problem of resolving the transition to the circular dome less formidable. The shape is heavy and solid, the effect inside sombre with little natural light but the impression is remarkable for the sheer survival power of the building.

2 Milburn 1988: 126.

The use of external ornamentation in stone is, in the early period, restrained. In the south, external appearance and proportions are not considered important, basalt being the sole structural and decorative resource. In the north, the limestone is carved and moulded to elaborate shapes from the mid sixth century on, either in the classical repertoire (*St Simeon) or in multitudinous examples of the flamboyant local taste for swooping moulded decoration, linking door and window frames.

Monasteries

On the whole, monasteries were more sober and practical buildings reflecting particularly the monastic boom that developed in the Antiochene hinterland after the middle of the fourth century. (There were 60 in the area by the end of the sixth century.) There was no standard plan but elements that were often included were a chapel, a monastic tower, a dormitory building up to three storeys high and a collective tomb, usually arranged around a courtyard.

The Muslim conquests of the 630s brought an end to new church building in Syria for many centuries though a few of the churches were later adapted as mosques (eg Cathedral of St Helen at Aleppo – * Aleppo – Great Mosque). Many of the older churches, however, remained in use and were constantly adapted and expanded throughout the centuries (eg St Elian's at *Homs; the monastery of *Mar Mousa near Nabk). Most of the larger churches and cathedrals now in use, however, were constructed during the 19th and 20th centuries.

Justinian's Defensive Works

A major and increasing preoccupation of the Byzantine period after the fifth century was the defence of Syria against the Persian threat from the east. After a relative lull in the fifth century, by the time of Justinian (r 527–65), the need to stem incursions against the Empire on several fronts led to a major commitment of resources in Syria where a strategic plan was entrusted

to his general, Belisarius. The results are seen today in the remains of Justinian's fortification or re-fortification program to contain the revived Persian threat – the palace/barracks complex at *Qasr Ibn Wardan, the fortified/pilgrimage centre at *Resafa, and the fortress at *Halebiye, still grimly maintaining its watch over the Mid Euphrates. A number of other centres were up-graded during the same period including Balis (*Meskene), *Qasr al-Heir West, *Palmyra, *Circesium, *Anderin and *Cyrrhus.

Islamic Architecture

Islamic architecture in Syria burst into flower with extraordinary vigour within decades of the establishment of the Umayyad Empire. There is no single monument in Syria which rivals the Umayyad Mosque in its capacity to sum up the energy and cross-currents of an era the way this building does, for all the imperfections visited on it by subsequent sackings, earthquakes, fires and reconstructions. It is virtually the history of Syria in less than a hectare. However much it was a synthesis of existing architectural and decorative influences, its main purpose was to bear witness to the glories of the new faith and to Islamicise the forms of old in a brilliant, new and monumental structure. The fact that many of its parts (the outer structure, the mosaics, the concept of the basilica prayer hall and the transept dome) were taken from an older repertoire is part of the conscious purpose of the building, absorbing the past into a new order.

Umayyads

Apart from the Umayyad Mosque, the architecture of the early Islamic centuries is largely a mystery to which few clues are available. The Abbasids effaced most of the tombs and palaces of their predecessors and sought to leave Syria a wilderness. Fortunately they neglected to obliterate the evidence of the Umayyads' castles or model settlements in remote desert regions as illustrated in the two *Qasr al-Heir (East and West) and in the more fragmentary remains at *Jebel Seis. The most interesting aspect of these secular projects is not their basic plan, which is largely derived from Roman military models but the eclectic, incessant nature of the decoration, the best examples we have of the budding Islamic decorative style. The concern seems to be to cover every part of the surface in a restless repertoire of diamonds, false arches, rosettes, frieze bands and triangles, drawing on every tradition known locally from Roman to Sasanian – an effect most readily seen on the reconstructed façade of Qasr al-Heir West which forms the main entrance to the *Damascus – National Museum.

Abbasids

Since the Abbasids adopted a conscious policy of neglecting Syria, their architecture is absent from the main towns, the most notable exception being *Raqqa which was re-colonised in an effort to revive the Jazira's central role linking the horns of the Fertile Crescent.

Likewise, the centuries of confusion from the ninth to 11th centuries resulted in little which has survived beyond a few remains of Seljuk fortification works that were incorporated in later reconstructions. The first notable example of the emergence of a new Syrian style is the minaret of the *Aleppo – Great Mosque. But it is only towards the end of the Ayyubid period (particularly with the emergence of the madrasa – see box page 27) that we find a substantial range of buildings that remain intact.

Crusades

In the 12th and 13th centuries, Syria's remains bear witness to the intensity of the great struggle between the Crusaders and the Islamic dynasties that established in Syria their forward bases against the Frankish presence.

The Crusaders came with little in the way of an active tradition of fortification in stone but within decades established a formidable range of fortresses based on Byzantine precedents as well as new ideas concurrently tried out in 12th century

France. Syria has preserved virtually intact one of the greatest examples of medieval fortification, the *Krak des Chevaliers, rarely equalled in thoroughness of design and construction. Other examples such as the Château de Saône (*Qalaat Saladin) reveal a more varied ancestry but few match the grim steadfastness of the massive fortifications of *Qalaat Marqab, overlooking the Mediterranean and guarding the access route from the Crusaders' homelands.

Islamic Resurgence

The promotion of Sunni orthodoxy (which began in the late tenth century but was given new impetus by the Crusades) reached a peak of energy under the Zengids and Ayyubids (12th to 13th centuries). The great struggle between Europe and the East also stimulated the development of Arab military architecture, largely a Syrian adaptation of Turkish, Persian and domestic precedents. The walled enclosures of Damascus and Aleppo were rebuilt under the Zengids and Ayyubids, the most spectacular result being the monumental gateway to the Aleppo citadel (built under al-Zaher Ghazi, early 13th century) which remains the supreme example of the Arab style. The fortress at *Bosra was built by surrounding the extant Roman theatre with towers and bastions. Arab military architecture on a smaller scale can be found at *Harim, *Qalaat Rahba, *Qalaat Najm, *Qalaat Jaabr and the citadel at Damascus (*Damascus – Citadel, and North Walls).

The Minaret

The origins of the minaret is a contested issue among experts, accounts giving different weight to the precedents set by Christian church towers, lighthouses or signal towers. One of the first uses of the tower was at the Umayyad Mosque in Damascus. It was several more centuries before the attachment of towers to mosques became the invariable practice.

During the period of Shiite expansion (tenth to 11th centuries), the mosque tower was not favoured but with the resurgence, under Seljuk influence, of Sunni orthodoxy, the minaret returned with renewed vigour. The tower of the Great Mosque in Aleppo (late 12th century) noted earlier is the first example that proudly proclaimed the local mastery of an assured Islamic style. From then on, minarets are found in virtually every conceivable style in Syria, from the varied confections of the Mamluks to the severe simplicity of the Ottoman pencil version, often deployed in multiple formations.

of caravanserais or fortresses, rubble in mortar was the common technique.

Domes were adopted in Syria from a variety of sources, not least the local tradition dating from the Christian/ Byzantine period where Roman and Persian techniques were used. The basic concept of dome-on-cube proliferated in a variety of uses ranging from serial arrays for the prayer rooms of major mosques to solitary and undecorated examples

The Madrasa

The promotion of Sunni orthodoxy (which began in the late tenth century) reached a new peak of energy under the Zengids and Ayyubids (12th to 13th centuries). This era saw the introduction of the madrasa, a school-cum-mosque, established by a civic or political leader for the promotion of Islamic exegesis or jurisprudence. The arrangement was funded by an endowment (waqf), usually the income from an area of land, an orchard, a market (suq) or a bath (hammam). (The corresponding institution for the sufi mystics was the khanqah of which few have survived into modern Syria). 82 were constructed in Damascus and 47 in Aleppo during this period but the earliest example is found in the additions to the Mabrak Mosque in *Bosra (1134–6).

The madrasa in its classic form (derived from tenth century Persia) followed a cruciform plan with four iwans facing an internal courtyard but there was no strict adherence to this model in the many variations developed in Syria. Early examples included rooms for the living quarters of the students and teachers, though in the later Mamluk period, the living quarters were usually in a separate commercial building which generated the income for the religious institution. By then, the madrasa as a propaganda weapon had fallen into disuse. It tended to have a broader civic function, serving as a congregational mosque for the quarter, the earlier fashion for a large central congregational mosque replaced by neighbourhood mosques throughout the cities. The madrasa later included the mausoleum of the benefactor, separated from the street by a large grilled window to attract the blessings of passers-by.

Although madrasas are found in some form throughout much of the Muslim world, their prevalence in Syria was particularly marked. The scale of the madrasa, however, was relatively small and their location discreet, perhaps reflecting the fact that it was often not the wealthiest members of the élite who funded them but the local leadership or their wives or mothers and for pious reasons rather than prestige.

Materials, Decoration

The materials used in construction depended, once again, on the local sources. Brick was common in areas influenced by the Mesopotamian tradition (Raqqa, Qalaat Jaabr) but masonry was more prevalent elsewhere. Pointed arches are found as early as the eighth century and were virtually universal by the tenth century with the use of elaborate joggled voussoirs for decorative effect being highly developed by the Zengid period. For non-prestige jobs, such as the vaults

serving as simple tombs of holy men.

In the Ayyubid period, builders began to use the muqarnas as a device to convert the traditional squinch or pendentive into a more complex and architecturally harmonious means of reconciling the round base of the dome to the square plan of the supporting walls. Muqarnas was also used as a stylized stalactite decoration around portals, first developed in an elaborate way in Syria in the 12th century, probably through Mesopotamian influence transmitted via northern Syria. Likewise the use of striped or *ablaq* stonework (contrasting black and white/cream bands) originally came into fashion in Syria in the 13th century and from there became part of the repertoire of the Mamluk style. Arabic calligraphy, often in highly stylized patterns, was used for decorative effect, usually as bands around or on top of doorways or windows. Decoration in carved stone, encrusted marble or stucco was remarkably restrained, being confined to areas such as windows, doorways, stylized bands of inscription or mihrabs.

On the whole, pre-Mamluk Islamic architecture in Syria avoided the over-striving for effect that is found elsewhere with the use of multiple decoration and contorted shapes. Buildings were usually on a human scale, not seeking to dominate their surroundings as in some of the more prestigious projects in Cairo. Decoration was confined to a few surfaces or areas and ornamentation usually restricted to interlace devices, mosaic or muqarnas effects. Given the sustained influence of the Umayyad Mosque on the Syrian creative repertoire, the survival of the Hellenistic tradition in decoration continued through much of the Islamic period.

Specialised Buildings

Mashhads, essentially a Shiite phenomenon in the form of commemorative foundations dedicated to descendants of the Prophet, are represented in Syria, among traditional buildings, by the 12th–13th century Mashhad al-Hussein and the nearby Mashhad of Sheikh Muhassin (Aleppo).

Other notable building forms of the Islamic middle ages which survive in recognisable form are the hospital-cum-medical school or *maristan* (Maristan Nur al-Din in *Damascus – Khans) and the public bath or hammam. Of the latter, virtually none have kept their original decoration given later reconstructions but good examples which preserve much of their original plans can be found in the Hammam Nur al-Din (*Damascus – Khans) and the Hammam al-Nahasin (*Aleppo – South Quarter).

Mamluk Period

During the later Mamluk period, the indigenous Syrian style became more clearly subordinated to the leadership's Cairo-based tastes. Syrian craftsmen were less free to pick and choose from the traditional range of local styles and were under greater pressure to imitate the more ostentatious repertoire of the Mamluks in a gimmicky and thus provincial way. On the whole, the Mamluks brought little that was new or inventive to the city, preferring towards the end of their rule to plumb for the picturesque. 'Everything was sacrificed to outward appearances and the monument was no more than a support for showy ornamentation.'[3]

Ottoman Period

The Ottomans, their styles based largely on those prevalent in Turkey, introduced for a time a cleansing influence with the preference for simpler, cleaner shapes, particularly in minarets. But most of the examples of Ottoman building in Syria were also provincial in both scale and inspiration. The exceptions, in the area of public buildings, are the projects partly transplanted from the metropolitan context, for example the Tekkiye Mosque (*Damascus – Tekkiye Mosque) by the renowned court architect, Sinan. The *tekkiye*, the successor to the Mamluk *khanqah*, returned to the tradition of a series of cells around a courtyard with a central pavilion for the conduct of lessons.

Khans, Caravanserais

For the Ottomans, the importance of Syria lay in its export opportunities and its entrepôt role in the Levant trade as well as its part in provisioning and protecting the annual Hajj from Asia Minor to Mecca. Thus much of the Ottoman period survives in the suqs (markets) and khans (depots/hostelries) of Damascus and Aleppo and in the sequence of caravanserais (overnight accommodation for travelling caravans) that dot the north-south route. The latter

3 Elisséeff 'Dimashk' in *EI*2.

can still be seen in centres such as *Latakia, *Maarat al-Numan and *Apamea where they have been turned into museums. But many suqs and khans are still part of the commercial infrastructure of the towns and it is often difficult to pick out from the work-a-day world of the modern suqs the functional 'monuments' described in our walking tours. The best examples of the suqs of the Muslim middle ages are in Aleppo whose walled city houses one of the most authentic market areas in the Middle East. The heavily-vaulted thoroughfares still follow the pattern of the Hellenistic grid (with many subsequent amendments and narrowing of the axes). The present structure of the vaulted suq area dates from the 12th to the 16th centuries.

The Ottoman khan is on a considerably more monumental scale than its predecessors of the Mamluk period where the central courtyard was left open to the sky. Generally, in the Ottoman period, the court (where goods were stored and bartered) was originally covered either with one or two domes or a series of domes surrounding a central cupola, as in the impressive Khan Assaad Pasha in Damascus (*Damascus – Khans). The storage rooms around the court were supplemented by further rooms off upper galleries, often used to accommodate travelling merchants. While some of the decorative treatment shows Syrian origins, the basic design of the larger scale halls derived from metropolitan Ottoman precedents. Sadly many of the domed spaces now lie uncovered, the roofing having succumbed to weather and earthquake damage, but some of the scale of these virtual 'temples of commerce' can be seen in the recent restoration of the Khan Assaad Pasha.

Houses

In the field of private housing, the Ottoman period is also more resourceful. For the élite families favoured by the Ottomans, the opportunities of successive periods as *wali* or governor of the main cities inspired the construction of homes on a grand scale. The Azem Palace in Damascus, its counterpart in *Hama (both now museums) or the houses of the Jdeide quarter in Aleppo are good examples of the blending of Syrian and Turkish practices in domestic architecture with the common emphasis on the internal courtyard with its fountain and the adaptation of the *iwan* as an open reception area (usually on the south of the courtyard, with a winter reception room (*qa`a*) on the north). The rest of the ground floor would comprise a study, office and service rooms/kitchen with bedrooms on the upper floor. All domestic architecture followed the Arab pattern of a plain façade to the street with walls high enough to preserve privacy. Wealthier Muslim houses provided a separate area (*selamlek*) for the reception of male visitors, apart from the family quarters (*haremlek*).

Twentieth Century

Our survey closes with the start of the French period. This saw the continuation of the attempts during the late Ottoman era to improve public amenities (electricity and piped drinking water), open the cities to public transport (trains and trams) and to develop new quarters for the operations of government and the needs of the defence forces. By the late 19th century, housing styles more closely followed Turkish taste with houses in the 'Konak style' the norm, marked by the notable new feature of windows on (or even overhanging) the street. The major improvements to infrastructure belie the image of the late Ottoman years as a one of slow decline, a correction recently illustrated in Stefan Weber's masterly survey of late Ottoman architecture in Damascus. Fortunately, much of this development was done on the margins of the older cities, preserving the walled centres (or, rather, often leaving them to decay) while the newer facilities opened out into 'garden suburbs' that still lend grace and a sense of spaciousness to Damascus and Aleppo.

3

GAZETTEER OF SITES

A

Ain Dara (Plate Ia)

عين دارة

VARIANTS: Kinalua (?IrA); PERIOD: IrA
RATING: * MAP: R3

LOCATION: 10 km south of Afrin in the
valley of the Afrin River (classical Oinopa-
ras), a picturesque orchard area near the
Turkish border. You can either: take the
Afrin road from Aleppo (60 km) then
south down the river valley after passing
the town or combine your visit with some
of the sites near *Saint Simeon. From the
south flank of Saint Simeon, take the road
that forks left of the hill and runs through
the ruins of Deir Semaan to Barsuta. At
17 km north, mound is on the left across
fields (track from Ain Dara village).

Ain Dara has remains from many periods
(with a gap during Roman times) but its
main interest lies in the 'Neo-Hittite' period
at the beginning of the first millennium BC
when Ain Dara was one of the fragmented
principalities established following the Sea
Peoples' invasion of the Levant. It seems to
have been incorporated into the Seleucid
domains, lying on the direct route from
Antioch to *Cyrrhus (and on to the
Euphrates crossing at Zeugma) though
the identification with Strabo's Gindaros
(Grainger) now looks doubtful.

The eclectic nature of the Neo-Hittite
period is reflected in the temple which is
the main point of interest on the mound.
The format of the temple comprises main
hall and inner chamber, antechamber and
peripteral corridor. It dates from the
tenth to ninth centuries BC and continues
several traditions from Bronze Age Syria,
Palestine and Turkey though its layout is
simpler than the contemporary temple at
*Tell Halaf.

As you approach from the south entrance
to the temple, the steps are flanked
by two carved lions, a common Hittite
theme continued in the frieze of lions

and sphinxes that runs across the lower
façade and vestibule. Note the three huge
footprints (each 1 m long) carved into the
paving of the entrance as if left by some
giant extra-terrestrial visitor. A fourth is
carved on the threshold of the main hall.
(There are other Iron Age manifestations
of such footprints, perhaps intended to
signal that the building is the home of a
god/goddess of super-human proportions.)
A shallow vestibule leads into an antechamber then a main hall which originally
housed the shrine to the rear, a typical
layout. A distinctive feature, however, is
the continuous corridor which ran around
three sides of the building, decorated with
80 fine relief panels. Abu Assaf surmised
that the temple was devoted to Ishtar, the
Semitic goddess of fertility for whom the
lion is often a symbol. Since 1994, a Syro-
Japanese project is seeking to consolidate
and restore the relief panels of the temple
base.

While it is difficult to distinguish the
various levels of occupation on the rest
of the sizeable mound, the site is littered
with carvings. The city remained occupied
as late as the Umayyad periods and was
walled for defence. (It was still occupied
in the 16th century.) The defences were
rounded off by a citadel or acropolis at the
highest point. There are beautiful views
from here of the Afrin Valley which flows
away to the south to join the Orontes at
the Plain of Amuq northeast of Antioch.

REFS: Abu Assaf 1985; Abu Assaf *Tempel*; Cohen
2006: 171; Grainger 1990: 107–8.

Ain Divar (Arab Bridge)

عين ديوأر

VARIANTS: Sapha (Grk); Jeziret Ibn Umar[1]
(Arb) PERIOD: Arb RATING: T MAP: R5

LOCATION: On the Tigris River, where it
forms the Turkish-Syrian border, 116 km
east northeast of Qamishli via Qahtaniye
(29 km); left after al-Jawdiye (+28 km); al-

---

1 The site name for the Arab ruins on the
Turkish side of the Tigris (see below). Hassan
Ibn Umar was a local leader of the ninth
century – Bell 1911: 296.

Malkiye (+40 km). The bridge lies c3 km southeast of the Turkish town of Cizre, an Umayyad foundation originally bearing the name al-Jezira ('the island'). The strip of Syrian territory which terminates on the Tigris is called the 'duck's beak'.

Some care should be exercised in approaching this site which is in a sensitive border area. The bridge is on the west bank of the Tigris (near the point where Alexander crossed in his march towards the Persian heartland in 331) and is heavily watched by Turkish soldiers on the opposite side. Take a local guide and check with Syrian security authorities (the nearest major police station is at al-Malkiye 16 km before Ain Divar) before approaching. It may be advisable to confine your visit to the magnificent perspective over the deep Tigris Valley with the mountains of southeastern Turkey in the distance.

To reach the bridge you will need (besides a police escort) a guide and either be willing to hire a four-wheel drive vehicle or be ready for a 10 km round trip on foot from the motorable road. A final problem is that the bridge is only accessible when the river is low (late summer).

The original bridge was Roman (second century) but what survives is largely of Seljuk and Arab origin (11th, 12th century), partly reconstructed in recent centuries. It consists of a series of pylons with a single surviving arch in basalt, 20 m wide. One of the piers (on the western end of the south face) carries eight inset sandstone panels representing the signs of the zodiac with explanatory inscriptions in Arabic. Gertrude Bell noted that the lion figures resembled the panels over the gate of the citadel at Cizre, over the border to the north. The Roman fortress of Bezabde, once assumed to lie on the west bank straddling the Syrian-Turkish border, is now reliably located at Eski Hendek c20 kms upstream from Cizre on the west bank of the Tigris.

REFS: Bell *Amurath* 1911: 296–7; Sinclair *Eastern Turkey* III 1989: 351–6.

Aleppo

حلب

VARIANTS: Halap   (Amorite),   Khalap (Hit); Beroea (Grk); Alep (Fr); Haleb (Arb) PERIOD: All   ALT: 390 m   RATING: ***
MAPS: 2–8

LOCATION: 350 km north of Damascus. Aleppo lies alongside the Quweiq River (the classical Chalus) at a point where the plains of northern Syria begin to rise towards the Taurus mountains.

> No Eastern city has impressed me with a greater sense of its mystery. To drift with the crowds in the bazars, those vaulted avenues cool and dim as cathedral naves, is to enter another world.
> (H V Morton *In the Steps of St Paul* 1936: 72)

Aleppo and Damascus vie for the title of 'oldest continuously inhabited city in the world'. Both can claim an impeccably ancient lineage and it would be a brave outsider who would express an opinion on which city is older until we have firm proof. Until recently, neither of these densely occupied sites offered much opportunity to the archaeologist to penetrate the layers of millennia. It is enough to say that Aleppo is one of the oldest continuously inhabited cities on earth and still flourishing.

Moreover it is a city that readily leads you back into the past; a sort of time continuum in which flashes of the past, rather than dissipating with time, accumulate in the present. It is still an animated Arab bazar city where the traditions of the Middle Ages do not seem all that remote. It still (perhaps more than any other city of the Levant) works according to the conventions of commercial life unbroken since Mamluk times. There are glimpses further back into the past, including the Arab resistance to the Crusades and the recently discovered Iron Age Temple of the Weather God. Less evident is the period of Byzantine, Roman or Greek occupation though their stamp is there in the present street layout and the basic shape of the walled city and *Citadel.

Aleppo may not be the international trading hub it was in the 16th to 18th centuries, when it lay on the land trade routes between, on the one hand, Central Asia, Mesopotamia and India and Europe, on the other. The Suez Canal and superhighways have meant it can readily be by-passed. But a more gradual economic boom has encouraged Aleppo in its old habits of turning in on itself, to preserve its traditions and its architecture.

complexity of Aleppo's history. Settled for at least eight millennia, its recorded history first comes to light in the archives of Ebla (2250 BC) and later of Mari and of the Hittites in the early to mid second millennium BC. The Amorite Kingdom of Yamkhad, centred on Halap (Aleppo), controlled many of the cities and towns of northern Syria at the beginning of the millennium but after 1800 BC it was subject to pressures from the east

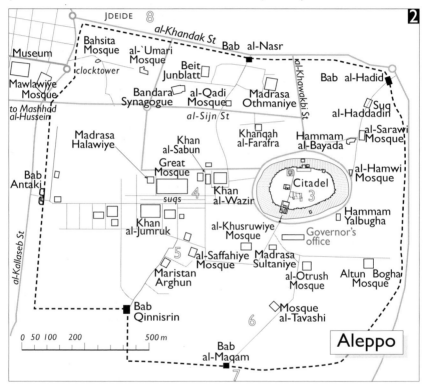

Relatively untouched by the contemporary tourism surge, the rediscovery of Aleppo is arriving in an age when its past can be more sympathetically preserved. Aleppo remains one of the treasures of the Middle East that should be savoured carefully lest its dignity and fragility be lost.

History

No summary could adequately evoke the

from Mitanni and, from 1600 BC, the overall supremacy of the Hittites whose homeland lay in central Anatolia. Unlike Damascus (whose links were largely with Palestine to the south and beyond to Egypt) northern Syria and Aleppo have always been more exposed to events to the north (Turkey) and the east (Mesopotamia). By the 15th century BC, however, the two worlds clashed directly with the short-lived Egyptian bid to extend their direct control to the north. After the catastrophic invasion of the Sea Peoples around 1200 BC which affected the eastern Mediterranean seaboard, a series of small inland **Neo-Hittite** states (*Ain Dara, *Tell Halaf) sprang up, one of which was centred on Aleppo.

The Assyrians were the next foreign power to exert their dominance in the area (eighth to seventh centuries BC), followed by the Neo-Babylonians then the Persians (539–333) whose supremacy lasted until Alexander's great campaign cleared the way for the **Seleucids** to establish their claim on the area. Seleucid control, though often tenuous, brought a new dimension to Aleppo's role. A true urban centre arose on a mound near a bend in the River Quweiq while further to the east, a hill provided a natural site for a citadel. Under the Greeks, this urban centre was given the Macedonian name, Beroea, and was laid out according to a Hippodamian grid pattern (cf *Apamea, *Cyrrhus and *Damascus – Straight Street to Bab Sharqi). As Seleucid control dissolved, the city was probably ruled by a separate dynasty from 96 to 69 BC. The **Romans** took control of Syria in 64 BC bringing to an end a period of internal anarchy which had left northern Syria prey to invasions from several directions, including the Armenian kingdom (in present-day eastern Turkey).

Roman control lasted almost 600 years (including the period of **Byzantine** rule from Constantinople) and brought unparalleled prosperity. The area became closely settled and highly developed agriculturally. A network of roads was established, the Limestone Massif to the west became the centre of a major olive oil export industry and Beroea was one of the bases for the defence of the imperial frontier to the east and northeast. Beroea became an important secondary centre but its role was later limited by the fact that it did not lie on a major transport route, falling between the Antioch/Chalcis (*Qinnesrin) corridor to the south and the trading/military route to Mesopotamia via Cyrrhus and Zeugma to the north.

Aleppo fell to the Arab armies without resistance in 637. It played a secondary role to Damascus (under the Umayyads) and Baghdad (under the Abbasids). It became the centre of autonomous power in the tenth century under the swashbuckling dynasty of the Hamdanids (944–1003), themselves Arab refugees from Iraq, particularly under Saif al-Daula (r 944–67). However, Saif al-Daula's aggressive style taunted the Byzantines into reasserting their power in the area with an invasion of northern Syria in 962 under General (from 963–9, Emperor) Nicephorus II Phocas who methodically sacked Aleppo. After a period of renewed local rule under the Mirdasids (1023–79), Aleppo was conquered by the Seljuk Turks in 1070, the Mirdasids staying on temporarily as vassals. Even the annexation of Aleppo to the Baghdad Caliphate (now under Turkish dominance) in 1086 did little to end the chaos which peaked just as the greatest threat emerged in the form of the Crusades.

Following their capture of Antioch in 1098, the Crusaders took much of the environs of Aleppo, strangling the city by cutting off its access to the coast. The leadership of the Seljuk governor, Ridwan, proved ineffective in staving off the challenge and the Crusaders installed themselves only 10 km away. It was the city's fiercely orthodox religious leader or *qadi*, Ibn Khashab, who rallied the Muslims and invited in Seljuk forces from Mosul (northern Iraq). Their first success was at the battle of Sarmada in 1119. (Because of the Crusaders' extensive losses, the battle was known as Ager Sanguinis ('field of blood') in their chronicles – *Harim.) In 1124/5 during a fierce siege by Christian forces under Jocelyn of Edessa, Bursuqi, Atabeq of Mosul, came to the rescue of the city and took the opportunity to stay on. His successor, Zengi, a Mosul Turk, possessed a sense of mission and dedication which most of his predecessors in recent decades had lacked. He built up Aleppo as a centre of resistance to the Crusades. This period of **Zengid rule** (1128–70) continued under his son, Nur al-Din. Measures were taken to restore the city's crumbling facilities after years of neglect. In order to restore Sunni orthodoxy, the first madrasas and Sufi monasteries (khanqahs) were established as centres of counter-propaganda. The union between Mosul's military strength and Aleppo's commitment to jihad was the basis on which in the coming decades the Muslim front against the Crusades was slowly forged.

Saladin, initially a Zengid protegé, after 1160 gradually extended his base from Egypt to realise his ambition of uniting most of the central Muslim lands (Egypt to Iraq) under his rule in 1176. Direct control of Aleppo, however, was not secured until after the death of the last Zengid, Nur al-Din's son, al-Salih, in 1183. The **Ayyubid period** (1176–1260) saw the rule in Aleppo of one of its most illustrious governors, al-Zaher Ghazi (effectively ruler from 1193 to 1215), a son of Saladin. Ghazi's contribution to the re-fortification of the Citadel is still evident. The work and driving personality of Ghazi made Aleppo one of three premier cities of the Islamic world. Its new international trading role was recognised by a series of treaties with Venice (1207–54) which established in Aleppo a factory (with ancillary church and hammam) providing direct access to the Muslim market, leap-frogging the Crusader ports on the coast.

Northern Syria, including Aleppo, was devastated by the Mongol invasion of 1260 which gave the impetus to the Egypt-based **Mamluks** to seize control of Syria. The Mamluk period lasted from 1260 to 1516. Given Aleppo's exposure to the northern threats, it was many decades (marked by earthquakes, plagues and further Mongol raids) before confidence in the city was restored, one modern historian noting that the early Mamluks 'virtually abandoned Aleppo to its fate'.[2] The first Mamluk construction projects did not begin until 1313. The collapse of the Armenian Kingdom to the north resulted from a sustained (1335–75) campaign in which Aleppo served as the Mamluks' base. Subsequent economic recovery in the 15th century owed much to the diversion through Aleppo of the silk

2 Lapidus 1988: 15.

caravans that since the Mongol invasions had preferred the more northerly route via factories on the Black Sea or in Cilicia. Thus began the era of the great khans or warehouses. The spices and fabrics, the gems and precious metals of the camel traffic from the East were traded and re-loaded for the mule trip across the mountains to the Mediterranean while European manufactures (including woollen cloth) were exchanged in the opposite direction.

In 1516, Turkish **Ottoman** forces chased the Mamluks out of Syria. Aleppo became the seat of a Turkish governor (*wali*). Though it was often subject to the anarchy that beset other Ottoman centres in times of weak government, its commercial role thrived. During the first Ottoman century, the earlier Venetian presence was complemented by French (1562), English (1583) and Dutch (1613) factories and consulates established under 'capitulation' treaties with the Ottomans. Aleppo became the principal entrepôt of the Levant, now unified under one power; a role which brought the construction of the great suqs which still grace the city. Aleppo met increasing competition from the sea route to India and China but the resulting decline did not become marked until during and after the 18th century with further competition from routes to the east through the Red Sea, the Persian Gulf and across Russia. Even then the city reserved enough of a local entrepot role to remain a centre of prosperity. The Christian and to a lesser extent Jewish, communities thrived given their protected status under the capitulations, as well as through their favoured positions as middlemen and the protective role of the consuls.

The mixed population of the city reflected its importance as a trading centre and remained more varied than the more enclosed and orthodox Damascus. Though figures are largely guesstimates, the population of Aleppo which had been around 120,000 at the beginning of the 18th century, declined to less than 100,000 at the century's end – still marginally above Damascus' 90,000 – and probably a doubling of the figure two centuries earlier. It was not until the second half of the 19th century that the population again rose steadily, reaching 150,000 after World War I with the influx of Armenian refugees from Turkey.

The late Ottoman period, an era of tentative reform and westernisation, saw construction of new quarters such as al-Aziziye and the linking of Aleppo to Damascus by rail as part of the Hijaz project (1906) and to Istanbul (1912). Ottoman rule lasted until Allied forces occupied Syria at the end of World War I. The political separation of Turkey and Syria has brought a severing of much of Aleppo's natural economic hinterland to the north.

Organisation of Visit

Aleppo is described here in ten itineraries. Even these surveys only touch the surface of this city still steeped in time. At least three days are needed for an adequate visit to the town and more time should be allowed for touring in the area (*Saint Simeon, *Limestone Massif, *Cyrrhus etc). For those with the time to spare, there are many more monuments than could be included in these itineraries and readers will find the survey of the city prepared by Abdallah Hadjar an, excellent companion. It includes detailed cadastre-based maps.

In addition, some time should be spent savouring the atmosphere of the suqs and of the 20th century city developed under and since the French Mandate, notably the Aziziye quarter (not described here) and the public gardens (1948–50) that border the Quweiq. Aleppo is best visited on foot. Few parts of the old city are accessible by vehicle though major distances can be covered by taxi. It is best to avoid high summer or mid winter.

REFS: Marcus 1989; Hadjar 2000; Saouaf 1975; Sauvaget *Inventaire* 1931; Sauvaget *Alep* 1941.

Aleppo – Citadel (Front cover, Plate 2a)

PERIOD: Arb RATING: ** MAP: 3

LOCATION: Aleppo – old city (east of the main suq area).

It needs an effort of the imagination to appreciate fully how the structure impressed itself on the citizens of 13th century Aleppo: An enormous expanse of bare stone, rearing to its full height of 50 metres, shimmering white in the harsh sun. At mid point on its gleaming flanks stood out in stylized black the legend of the fortress' foundation. [Sauvaget *Alep* 1941: 146]

History

The small hill on which the Citadel is located is a natural feature utilised as far back as the Amorite federation under Yamkhad before the Hittite conquest in the 16th century BC. The first citadel may have been constructed by the Seleucids (333–64 BC), separate from the ancient town to the west. It is not clear whether the Romans continued to use the site as the military headquarters of their city, called by its Greek name Beroea. In the fourth century of our era, the Roman Emperor, Julian ('the Apostate') (r 361–3), who had abjured the link between Christianity and the empire established by Constantine, pointedly visited the hill to offer sacrifice to Zeus. The citadel of Beroea is mentioned in the Byzantine accounts of the sixth century Persian wars as still serving as a fortress and there may be Byzantine remains beneath the structure of the medieval palace.

After the Arab conquest, Aleppo as a whole fell into decline. The role of the Citadel is again obscure. In the tenth century, for example, it appears not to have housed the residence of Saif al-Daula whose Hamdanid dynasty gave Aleppo one of its most flourishing periods of activity. Its strategic importance in the struggle against Byzantium resumed in the Crusader period when it became the impregnable base for Muslim power in northern Syria. Towards the end of the 12th century, after Saladin's successes against the Crusaders and with the Ayyubids in firm control of Syria, the Citadel was made the focal point of the new city established by al-Malik al-Zaher Ghazi, a son of Saladin who initiated the line of upper walls seen today, though much was destroyed in the subsequent Mongol invasions. After the first Mongol wave in 1260, the Citadel was restored in 1292, only to be razed again by Timur in 1400.

German program which has unearthed important remains of the Bronze and Iron Ages. Major work on the restoration of the enclosure and the Ayyubid palace is being undertaken by the Aga Khan Trust.

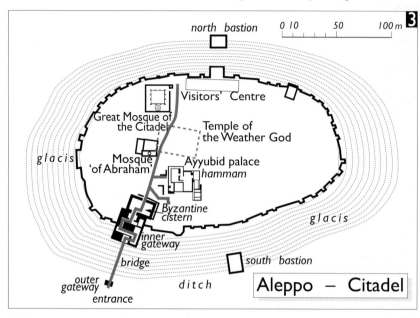

Aleppo – Citadel

The remains that you now see date from various attempts (mainly Mamluk) to reconstruct or strengthen the fortress' role following these episodes of devastation. The most significant work was probably that undertaken by Ghazi who dug the encircling ditch, paved the glacis with stone and built the great gateway. As the Mamluks' control tightened after 1400, the citadel again assumed a more civilian character though the Ayyubid towers were rebuilt, apparently on a smaller scale. (A few remains of the Ayyubid citadel survive under the base of the present walls.) The town had expanded to embrace the fortress on all sides, thus making its role as a bastion against marauders somewhat redundant. The palace of the Ayyubids, sacked and destroyed by the Mongols, was replaced by the Mamluk staterooms intended to provide a fitting setting for visits by the sultan. The Citadel has recently been excavated as part of a Syrian-

Visit

The most striking view of the Citadel is the approach to the sole entrance bridge and monumental gateway. This masterpiece of Arab military architecture combines the practical with the flamboyant. The bold sweep of the rising bridge, the depth of the ditch (22 m) and the steepness of the surrounding glacis (48°) culminate in the entrance façade rising several storeys and incorporating a deep arch and a complex range of defensive devices. The effect is emphasised by the window surrounds of contrasting stone in black and white.

The huge ditch, the stone-faced glacis that encircle the lower two thirds of the 55 m high mound and the upper ramparts were built by Ghazi in the closing years of the 12th century. Note (left) how the lower reaches of the glacis were strengthened against the weight of the upper slope by sections of re-used Roman or Byzantine columns to anchor the stone.

The entry bridge is preceded by a rectangular tower, 20 m high, originally constructed c1211 and refurbished in the 16th century, hence the inscription from the reign of the penultimate Mamluk sultan, Qansawh al-Ghawri, recording the work undertaken by the local governor, Abrak al-Ashrafi al-Saifi (1507). Among the earlier elements included in the renewed tower is the outer door dated by inscription to 1211.

Now cross the bridge which is supported on eight arches with internal channels to carry water to the citadel. Before you enter the great gateway built out from the line of walls note the defensive arrangements. Any attack, having penetrated the outer tower and straddled the gap normally spanned by a draw-bridge (exposed all the while to fire from the walls) would lose momentum as it met the blank face of the fortress. The entry door is set on the right, blunting the attack and exposing assaulting troops to the full range of defensive devices above. In addition to slits and parapets, the face of the gateway is furnished half way up with machicolations and strengthened underneath with re-used ancient columns to guard against undermining. Note also 50 m on the right an island bastion, once connected to the fortress by a draw-bridge. This was added in the 14th century to provide flanking cover to the main entrance and (like the corresponding tower on the north side) served to strengthen weak points in the defence of the walls.

Originally, the two towers comprising the gatehouse ended at the level of the machicolations. Major work on the entrance was carried out after the 1260 Mongol attack. The Mamluk sultan, al-Ashraf Khalil (r 1290–3), had his subsequent contribution grandiloquently commemorated in a long inscription on the band that runs across the gatehouse and between the towers. This records his victories not only in expelling the Franks and the Mongols but also over the Armenian Kingdom of Cilicia to the

north. The upper façade and deep arch joining the two towers were added during the conversion of the building to more ceremonial purposes by the Mamluk governor, Saif al-Din Jakam in 1415. Further work was carried out in the 15th–16th century.

Above the first doorway, note the intertwined dragons. This brings you to the first of five bends including two more gateways before emerging at the upper defences. As you follow the twists and turns of the passageway, look out for two further carved devices near the next two gateways: the first, above the lintel, two lions facing each other; the second, two lions represented frontally flanking the opening. All three carvings were believed to have some mystical role in guarding the entry. The third (cross-vaulted) gateway also provides side-chambers for the guard.

After following the bends of the entrance complex, you emerge into the daylight at the start of an ascending path. On the right are several doors, the last one leading to a series of dungeons and a cistern, possibly of Byzantine origin. These may have been the dungeons used to imprison Crusader leaders captured in battle including Jocelyn, Count of Edessa, and Reynald de Châtillon.

The path now leads you to the top of the mound. Many of the buildings on the summit have recently been excavated or partly reconstructed. The main thoroughfare was probably originally an axial covered passage in the style of other Islamic fortifications.

The **palace** built by the Ayyubid ruler al-Aziz in 1230 lies on the right. What remains (much was destroyed by the Mongols) is grouped around a series of small courtyards. The entrance (ascend stairs to right to upper level) is decorated with a superb example of *muqarnas* vaulting with a frame in striped stone (basalt and limestone). The first courtyard is built around four *iwans*, a pattern increasingly common in Arab architecture. Behind it, part of the complex, is the hammam or baths (1367, plate 2a), recently extensively restored. Return now to the main thoroughfare.

Ten metres on the left is the **Mosque of Abraham** (Makam Ibrahim al-Asfal) attributed to Nur al-Din by an inscription dated 1167. The reference is to the tradition that a stone on which Abraham used to sit was preserved on this site, earlier commemorated by a church (of which two columns were preserved in the north wall). The church is also supposed to have contained (yet another) burial place of the head of St John the Baptist moved here in 435 from Baalbek.

Opposite, on the right, are the newly-excavated remains of a **Temple of the Weather God**, originally dating from 1700 BC and reconstructed around 1000 BC. The excavations have given us a spectacular glimpse of the richness of Hittite temple culture of the Bronze and Iron Ages with a series of basalt panels, stretching over 10 m, depicting gods and mythical figures. (The site was not open to the public at the time of writing.)

Near the end of the way, on the left, lies the **Great Mosque of the Citadel**. It is rather small in size but a gem of a building in its austerity and simplicity. Originally possibly a Mirdasid mosque (built on the site of a Christian church), it was rebuilt in 1214 by Ghazi. Almost square in external plan, the doorway leads into a stark internal courtyard, beautifully proportioned. The prayer room is equally sparse with a central cupola and *mihrab*. The elegant minaret to the north, square in plan, is contemporary with the mosque.

From the terrace and parapets above the mosque there are superb 360⁰ views of the city. On the right of the mosque is a barracks building built in 1834 by Ibrahim Pasha who controlled Syria on behalf of Muhammad Ali of Cairo, now restored as a museum and Visitors' Centre. On the lower slopes of the glacis can be seen the shell of the northern tower, a counterpart to that on the south face.

On your way back, ascend to the terrace at

the rear of the gateway building from where you enter the large throne room built in 1415 by the Mamluk governor, Saif al-Din Jakam, after the last and most devastating Mongol invasion of 1400. It is approached through a courtyard decorated in black and white stone paving. The throne room reflects the increasingly civilian emphasis of the complex given the encroachment of the town around the walls of the Citadel. The roof of the hall was rebuilt with nine domes by Qansuh al-Gawri (late 15th century, early 16th century) but when the hall was reconstructed in the 1970s (partly using materials from the al-Aidi house in Damascus), the domes were replaced with a flat roof. Nevertheless the room is grand in its dimensions – 27 m by 24 m. While the decoration and upper spaces may have changed, the hall remains a rare example of a Mamluk reception hall, there being no counterpart in Damascus or Cairo.

From here, stairs descend through the tower to the entrance.

REFS: Allen 2003: chapter 5; Hadjar 2000; Herzfeld 1955 I: 77–139; 1956: 309–12; Saouaf *Alep* 1975; Sauvaget *Alep* 1941; Tabbaa 1997: 111.

Aleppo – Great Mosque and Environs (Plate 1b)

VARIANTS: Umayyad Mosque; Jamia Zakariye³ (Arb)
PERIOD: Byz/Arb RATING: * MAP: 4

LOCATION: Aleppo – old city, north of the main suq area. Begin at the new square immediately north of the Great Mosque. The tour takes in the areas along the pedestrian zone to the west.

The popular attribution of the Great Mosque to the Umayyads applies only to its basic plan and not to any of the present fabric. It was founded c715 by the Umayyad Caliph Walid I (r 705–15) and probably completed by his brother and successor, Suleiman (r 715–17). It thus followed by ten years the building by Walid of the great mosque within the compound of the Cathedral of St John in Damascus and <u>may well have been</u>, on Suleiman's part, a

3 After Zachariah, father of St John the Baptist.

deliberate attempt to echo his brother's achievement in Damascus. In the case of Aleppo, the new mosque was also built in the enclosure of a cathedral, namely the garden or cemetery of the Cathedral of St Helen. (This, in turn, had previously been the site of the *agora* of the Hellenistic-Roman city.) Of this original mosque, nothing survives, given the amount of subsequent destruction and rebuilding. In 1169 it was burnt down and Nur al-Din (r 1146–74) rebuilt it entirely with the exception of the tower. Later alterations have in turn replaced most of Nur al-Din's work.

The 45 m minaret (plate 1b) in its own right is worth particular note. It was erected under the first Seljuk sultan,

treatment of this top level is almost identical to the tower of the mosque at *Maarat al-Numan.) The stone for the tower may partly have been obtained from the remains of the nearby cathedral.

You enter the mosque proper from the northwest door. The effect of the white stone flagging and the arcading is pleasing, particularly in strong light. The elements in common with the plan of the Damascus mosque are the broad arcaded courtyard where the majority of worshippers are accommodated and the division of the prayer hall into three aisles running lengthwise with a small dome placed over the middle aisle. The Mamluks, however, substituted a more ambitious system of cross-vaulted arcades for the original

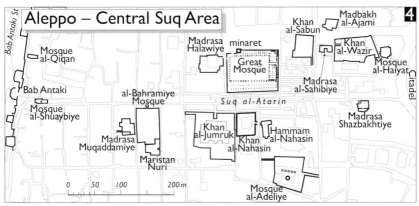

Tutush, between 1090 and 1092 and is one of the first notable examples of a growing sense of assured style in Syrian Islamic architecture, heralding the developments of the Ayyubid and Mamluk periods. It has been described as 'the principal monument of mediaeval Syria'[4] and is the work of a local architect, Hassan Ibn Mukri al-Sarmani. The façades are divided into four principal registers, each treated differently but with a strong sense of unity and balance. Note particularly the Kufic (early stylized Arabic script) inscriptions which run around the bands between the registers. Above a final band of *muqarnas* niches, the gallery for the muezzin is covered by a wooden verandah. (The

4 Herzfeld *Damascus – II* 1943: 35.

colonnades of the courtyard and prayer hall. The beautifully carved wooden *minbar* (pulpit) is 15th century. The room to the left of the *mihrab* is said to contain remains of Zachariah, the father of John the Baptist.

In the street running alongside the west door of the mosque, the **Madrasa Halawiye** marks the site of the sixth century Cathedral of St Helen, mother of the Emperor Constantine. It comprises a courtyard with students' cells on two sides and, opposite the entrance, a columned prayer hall with dome. This hall incorporates all that remains of Aleppo's original cathedral, a quatrefoil plan like that at *Bosra. Only the four L–shaped piers and one of the quatrefoil semi-circular rows of six columns that formed the western end of the church remain intact. The sixth century Byzantine origins of the columns (of which the first third lie buried under the risen ground level) are obvious in the superb, richly decorated capitals. The *mihrab* (kept locked in the north *iwan* off the courtyard) is particularly noteworthy, dating from 1245, a century after Nur al-Din's reconstruction of the building. The remains of the Cathedral of St Helen were used for Christian worship long after the construction of the mosque in the cathedral's garden. It was only in 1124 that it was among four churches seized by the *qadi* of Aleppo and reconstructed as a madrasa in retaliation for the atrocities against Muslims committed by the Crusaders.

One hundred metres east of the square in front of the Umayyad or Great Mosque lies a smaller square on the east side of which is the entrance to the **Khan al-Wazir** a 1682 caravanserai, one of the finest in Aleppo though the courtyard has been reconstructed on the north side following street widening in the 1950s. The monumental doorway is framed in alternating courses of black and white stone. The courtyard is extensive with arcaded galleries on the upper floor. Before you return through the entrance passageway, look up to the two windows set in indented and richly ornamented frames closely resembling the decoration of the inner face above the doorway of the earlier Khan al-Jumruk (below).

[If you have time, an interesting mosque west of the citadel moat which does not fit easily into other itineraries, could be included now. The **Mosque al-Haiyat** ('Snakes' Mosque') or the Madrasa Nasiriye is found immediately behind the east wall of the Khan al-Wazir (currently closed). The mosque apparently stands on a site of great antiquity and it includes a number of basalt columns clearly of antique origin which enclose a peaceful courtyard. Before it was turned into a mosque (1327, initially serving as the Madrasa Nasiriye) it had functioned as a synagogue bearing the name Mithqal. (A Hebrew inscription on a basalt panel along the east wall records the reconstruction of the

synagogue in 1241.) Burnt during Tamerlane's assault on the city, the references to snakes apparently derives from the stylized reptiles dividing the vault of the entrance.]

Nearby, in the Suq al-Zarb, northern section of the main suq, the **Madrasa Shazbakhtiye** (or Mosque of Sheikh Marouf), founded in 1193 by a eunuch employed by Nur al-Din. A *muqarnas* doorway leads to a courtyard with vaulted *iwan* to the north. Tomb of the founder in the northeast corner. Fine *mihrab* in the prayer hall.

West of the Khan al-Wazir is the **Madrasa al-Sahibiye** (or Fustuq Mosque, 1349) with a beautiful stalactited portal. On the north side of the same square is the **Matbakh al-Ajami** a Zengid (12th century) palace which formerly housed a small museum of folklore (now in *Aleppo – Jdeide Quarter). The façade was reconstructed when the street was widened in 1950. The rebuilt entrance incorporates a doorway rescued from another palace, of the Ottoman, Othman Pasha. The doorway may be Ottoman or Mamluk but consciously imitates the Ayyubid love for fantastic interlaced decoration. The *muqarnas* of the north *iwan* is particularly notable.

From the west side of the square, take the lane that leads south into the suq. After 40 m, on your right, look back to take in the entrance to the famed **Khan al-Sabun** whose gateway façade is rightly considered one of the greatest examples of Mamluk architecture in Aleppo (constructed in the late 15th, early 16th century by the Mamluk governor, Adzemir). The facade is decorated in a rich variety of carved detailing. Note the surrounds of the window above the main entrance, particularly the intertwined colonnettes. The courtyard, cluttered by a central warehouse, includes much beautiful arcading and a fine arch (now blocked) on the north. (Most of the north side was truncated in the 1950 street widening.)

REFS: Hadjar 2000; Bloom *Minaret* 1989: 163–4; Butler *EC* 1929: 170–1; Ecochard *Note*; Elisséeff *BEO* 1949–51; Herzfeld 1955 I: 143–171 (Great

Mosque), 205–21 (Halawiye); Herzfeld *Damascus* I 1942: 34–5, Herzfeld *Damascus* III 1946: 118; Lassus *Sanctuaires chrétiens* 1947: 153; Sauvaget *Alep* 1941: 59–60.

Aleppo – Suqs and Khans

PERIOD: Arb/Ott   RATING: ** MAP: 4

LOCATION: The main suq area of the old city.

This tour will lead you through the main area of **covered suqs** behind the Great Mosque, visiting some of the old khans and continuing to the old city gates, Bab Qinnesrin and Bab Antaki (Qinnesrin and Antioch Gates).

Largely unchanged since the 16th century (some go back as far as the 13th), the suqs preserve superbly the atmosphere of the Arab-Turkish mercantile tradition. In summer, the vaulted roofs provide cool refuge; in winter, protection from the rain and cold. While many of the products on sale have been updated, there are still areas where the rope-maker, tent outfitter and sweetmeat sellers ply their trade much as they have done for centuries. Treasures it doesn't flaunt to any great extent. The rug section is poorly provided though the gold suq (Suq al-Siyagh) flourishes. On the whole this is a practical, living bazar, not an upmarket collection of boutiques. Most of all, it is worth simply absorbing the passing parade of faces, a mixture of Arab, Kurdish, Armenian and Turkish with a variety of dress that ranges over several centuries. Even the prosaic is of interest. In the Suq al-Manadil, the public latrines date from the 12th century, restored in 1357, and are a notable and rare example of medieval sanitation.

From the square in front of the Great Mosque head along the lane running east of the mosque into the main suq area of the old city. This lane immediately cuts across the main passageway of the suq, the Suq al-Atarin. The **suqs of Aleppo** (see map 4) form a labyrinth totalling 7 km in length and are unsurpassed in the Middle East for sheer interest and atmosphere. This tour concentrates on the area to the south and

west of the Great Mosque, the *medina* or central market area largely rebuilt during the period of economic expansion in the early Ottoman period. The Suq al-Atarin follows the route of the Roman *decumanus* or principal axial thoroughfare, gradually hemmed in over the centuries by commercial buildings and booths.

From the main suq continue west (right), taking the first major side street (left) which eventually leads to the Bab Qinnesrin. In the 19th century, the Venetian Consulate was located in a small caravanserai (**Khan al-Nahasin**), first on the right along this street. In the same 16th century building, the Belgian consulate was established from the 1930s until the death in the mid 1980s of Adolphe Poche. (The house, spread between the south side of the courtyard and the north side of the neighbouring Khan al-Burghul, contains many treasures and is under the supervision of the Belgian Consulate in the Khan al-Khattin, immediately south of the Khan al-Wazir.)

Almost opposite the entrance to this khan is the **Hammam al-Nahasin** or Hammam al-Sitt, 12th or 13th century in origin and still functioning as a public bath. A modern reconstruction has obscured its original treatment.

Return to the main passage of the suq. On the left (150 m) look out for a high dome over the thoroughfare that marks the superbly decorated entrance to the **Khan al-Jumruk**. This is one of the most famous and certainly the largest of the Aleppo khans. The whole complex (including the two rows of suqs at the front) comprised 344 shops spread over 6,400 m². It accommodated after it was completed in 1574 the banking houses and consulates of the French, English and Dutch merchants stationed in Aleppo. The building is still in use for commercial purposes. Go through to the courtyard and turn back to admire the exceptional carved windows with slender columns above the entrance passage (later emulated in the Khan al-Wazir, above). In the centre of the courtyard stands a small mosque obscured by modern buildings.

Keep going to the west along the main thoroughfare (Suq al-Atarin). On the left, you will reach after 150 m the al-Bahramiye Mosque, a large mosque built in the Turkish style in 1583 by Bahram Pasha, governor of Aleppo. The tall minaret fell during an earthquake and was reconstructed in 1698. The *mihrab* of the prayer hall rivals that of the Firdows Mosque (*Aleppo – South Quarter) in its bold arabesque decoration. Behind this mosque (70 m on right down the cross street to the east) was the Maristan Nuri founded by Nur al-Din c1147 of which only the doorway (protected by an iron grille) and a small section of the street wall survive in a precarious state.

Off the second lane to the left is the entrance (50 m on the left) to the **Madrasa Muqaddamiye,** the oldest madrasa in Aleppo. Formerly a church, it was converted into a theological school endowed by Izz al-Din Abd al-Malik al-Muqaddam (inscription dated 1169) following its seizure in 1124 by the *qadi* of Aleppo (Ibn Khashab) as a reprisal for the Crusaders' ruthless siege of the city.[5] The building has a fine portal with complex vaulting and two arabesque medallions. Inside, only the prayer hall dates from the madrasa and no traces of the church survive.

On the intersection, 20 m before Bab Antaki (centre of a forked intersection), is the small **Mosque al-Shuabiye** (or al-Tuteh, 'Mosque of the Mulberry Tree') a Zengid project, recently extensively restored. The west façade of this most curious building was once assumed to have incorporated elements of the Roman triumphal arch which marked the beginning of the main east-west *decumanus* but recent studies establish that the 'classical' entablature was a medieval element. This fine work blending Kufic inscription and interlaced decoration dates from the 1150 mosque constructed by Nur al-Din. The narrow mosque was preceded by a porch (left on façade) originally open on three sides. The portal (now hidden behind

---

5 The *qadi* seized other church property including the Cathedral of St Helen – see *Aleppo – Great Mosque.

infill masonry and a wooden door) is an elaborate work in the mid 11th century 'decorated style' using two layers of joggled voussoirs. What remains of the fountain (also dated 1150) on the right of the façade lies behind a modern stone panel. An earlier mosque on this spot, reputedly the first mosque built by the Muslims in the city, commemorated the taking of Aleppo by Umar Ibn al-Khatib.

North of Bab Antaki, the ground rises over Tell Aqaba, the mound of the ancient village which was incorporated in Hellenistic Beroea. If you follow the street that runs just inside the walls, 50 m on the right is the small Mosque al-Qiqan ('Mosque of the Crows'). Two ancient columns in basalt mark the entrance. A Hittite relief block (14th century BC) was re-employed in the wall of what is probably an early Mamluk construction. From the top of the rise, a good view of the northwestern quarter of the city. Return to Bab Antaki.

Bab Antaki or Antioch Gate consists of two great hexagonal bastions with a jagged entrance path and is a reconstruction by the Ayyubid governor, al-Nasr Yusuf II (r 1242–60) grandson of Ghazi, on an 11th century base. It was further reconstructed in the 15th century. Through the earlier gateway on this spot the Arab armies entered Aleppo in 637.

The line of city walls north of Bab Antaki have recently been cleared of obstructions. Particularly notable is the huge (15 by 12.5 m) tower, a Mamluk reconstruction on an Ayyubid base. Note the two lions (mid way up the outer face), usually an insignia of Baybars but in this case probably older, marking the city's 11th century Hamdanid rulers.

REFS: Allen 1986: 1–16; Hadjar 2006; Herzfeld 1955: 222–7; Saouaf *Alep* 1975; Sauvaget *Alep* 1931.

Aleppo – South of the Suqs

PERIOD: Arb/Ott RATING: * MAP: 5

LOCATION: This itinerary continues from the central suq area covered in the last walk and heads south to the Bab Qinnes-rin. A relatively short excursion, it takes in a traditional residential quarter that is also sprinkled with mosques and institutions of the Ayyubid and Mamluk eras.

From the Hammam al-Nahasin (see page 43), continue south 70 m. On the left a gradual rising passage leads to the Mosque al-Adeliye built in 1557 by Muhammad Pasha Dukakin, governor of Aleppo, as part of the mid 16th century expansion into an area previously occupied by a Mamluk exercise field. It is the second oldest Turkish-style mosque in the city, resembling in design its forerunner, the al-Khusruwiye Mosque (*Aleppo – South

Quarter). A wide portico with five domes precedes the prayer hall (large central dome, the fine *mihrab* and superb faience panels produced locally).

Take the next street left and 100 m on the right you will find the Mosque al-Saffahiye. Built in 1425, the mosque is entered through a tall portal decorated in black and white bands. The minaret above is octagonal in shape with beautiful, richly carved decoration.

Go back to the intersection of the first street. Continue on to the south, crossing an intersection and after c80 m (following a slight dog-leg to the right) you reach on

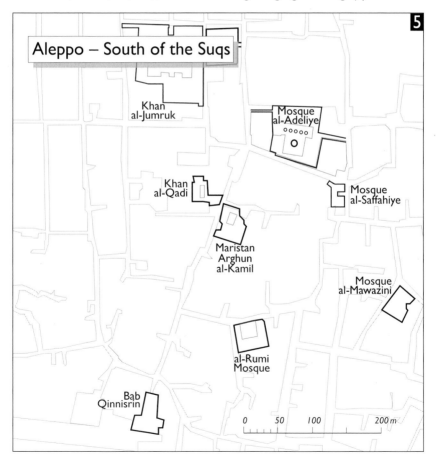

Aleppo – South of the Suqs

5

Khan al-Jumruk

Mosque al-Adeliye

Khan al-Qadi

Mosque al-Saffahiye

Maristan Arghun al-Kamil

Mosque al-Mawazini

al-Rumi Mosque

Bab Qinnisrin

0   50   100   200 m

the right the Khan al-Qadi. This is a rare example of a reasonably intact khan of the Mamluk era. It was built in 1450 by the *qadi* (chief judge) of Aleppo and distinctly follows the plain Ayyubid style. A passage deflects to the right and leads to a courtyard with arcaded galleries above.

Virtually opposite is the Maristan Arghun al-Kamili converted from a house to an asylum in 1354 by the Mamluk governor, Arghun al-Kamili. The entry is through a tall, honeycombed portal (probably surviving from the Ayyubid house on this site) leading through a vestibule to the central courtyard. Diagonally across is a tall vaulted passage leading to a confined octagonal courtyard designed to house the dangerously insane. A central fountain is surrounded by twelve cells, still used to house chained inmates at the beginning of the last century. Two other small courtyards lie north and south, each provided with a central water basin. The southern courtyard has room for *iwans* north and south of the central open space. Sauvaget considered this the best preserved Muslim hospital in Syria or Egypt.

A diversion to the east takes you to two Mamluk mosques, each with an interesting minaret. Turn left 100 m past the *maristan* and after c 70 m you see on your right the Mosque al-Rumi (sometimes called the Mankalibugha Mosque). The minaret is remarkably tall and is a rare example of a cylindrical form. The mosque was built by Mankalibugha al-Shamsi, governor of Aleppo and later commander of the Mamluk armed forces (d 1380). The mosque was built in the 1370s to commemorate Mankalibugha's part in defeating the forces of Armenia, Cyprus and Rhodes at Ayas (Cilicia) in 1367.

From the al-Rumi Mosque head east (as you leave the mosque door, right). At the next intersection, right, then left and second left again which brings you along the western wall of the Mosque al-Mawazini (also known as the Taghribirdi Mosque). This is a mosque of considerable interest as it was built on the site which may also once have served as a church. The present mosque was constructed in 1366 by Prince Saif al-Din Taghribirdi al-Zahiri. Herzfeld noted the massive columns of the prayer hall and concluded that this may have been one of the four sites appropriated from the Christian community after the 1124 Crusader attack on Aleppo. The five columns (more or less in line but slightly off the vertical) may have formed a part of a basilical church's internal colonnade. Interestingly, the prayer hall (25 by 10 m) deviates from the normal orientation to the south by 25°. Other classical stones lie left of the entrance to the courtyard.

Return now to the street leading to Bab Qinnesrin. This is the most intact of the gates of Aleppo. The tenth century gate was re-constructed in 1256 and restored in 1501 by the Mamluk, Qansawh al-Ghawri. West of Bab Qinnesrin, the walls of the city have been cleared of accretions to display two massive towers, probably Mamluk. At this point the walls follow the traditional alignment before they turn north and run to Bab Antaki on the western edge of the old city (see *Aleppo – Suqs and Khans) though the line is often obscured by ramshackle shops. (The area to the east of Bab Qinnesrin is described in *Aleppo – South Quarter.)

REFS: Hadjar 2000; Herzfeld 1955; Saouaf *Alep* 1975; Sauvaget *Inventaire* 1931; Sauvaget *Alep* 1941; Tabba *Architectural Patronage* 1982: 266.

Aleppo – South of the Citadel

PERIOD: Arb/Ott RATING: * MAP: 6

LOCATION: Those parts of the old city lying to the south of the Citadel and along the road leading to Bab al-Maqam.

This tour begins in front of the entrance to the Citadel and takes you south along the road leading to Bab al-Maqam. It can be combined with the next itinerary which continues through the gate and into the burial area to the south but this would make a long program involving at least 3 kms on foot. This section of the old city appears to have been consciously developed as a prestige zone leading up to the Citadel, particularly under the Ayyubids and Mamluks but continued under the Ottomans.

Across the road and a little to the left as you look from the entrance to the Citadel lies the **Madrasa Sultaniye** completed in 1223/4 by Governor (Sultan) al-Aziz, to serve as the mausoleum of his father, Sultan al-Zaher Ghazi (d 1216) who had initiated the project. The *mihrab* of the prayer room is particularly commended. To the left lies a modest room which contained the cenotaphs of Sultan al-Zaher Ghazi and his family. The east and the portico, covered by five domes, is wider than the prayer hall. The minaret is distinctly Turkish in style.

The khan immediately north is the **Khan al-Shuna**, built as a *qaisariye* in 1546 to generate income for the Khusruwiye Mosque and currently housing a handicraft suq.

The **Governorate**, 300 m east, is housed in a 1930s building conceived in a 'neo-Saracanic' style. Beyond it to the east is the

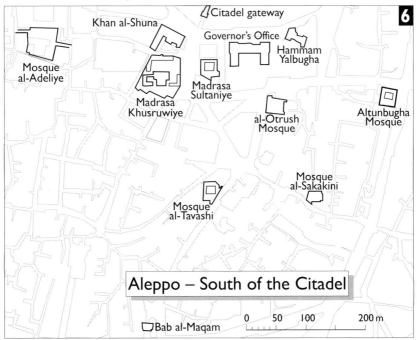

Aleppo – South of the Citadel

0   50   100   200 m

west wings of the building replace sections which were ruined before the mosque was restored in the 1940s.

To the west, 40 m right is the entrance to the **Madrasa Khusruwiye** initiated in 1537 by Khusruv Pasha, governor of Aleppo. Perhaps constructed under the supervision of the famous Turkish architect, Sinan, then at the beginning of his remarkable career (*Damascus – Tekkiye), this is the first of the Ottoman-style monuments in Aleppo. Note that

Hammam Yalbugha, the grandest baths in Syria which have been reconstructed and revived for their original purpose by the tourism authorities, having been rescued from service as a felt factory. The hammam was built in the mid-14th century and restored by the Mamluk, Saif al-Din Yalbugha al-Nasiri (1387–9). The recent restoration has been done in a sober style and the domed warm and hot rooms achieve a striking impact.

Immediately south of the Governor's

Office stands the **al-Otrush Mosque** a funerary mosque commissioned to serve as his mausoleum by Amir Aq-Bogha al-Otrushi in 1403 (and completed by his successor, Amir Damir Dash). The tall *muqarnas* entrance portal and main façade (west side of intersection) are offset by a striking series of recessed window frames, one of the finest façades of any Mamluk building in Aleppo. Under the minaret, left of the portal, the inscription reads: 'This is the work of God's slave, the famed Aq-Bogha al-Zaheri. God grant him mercy'. From the courtyard inside, a corridor right of the entrance gives access to the burial chamber, a small square room covered with a dome resting on four honey-combed corners. The prayer hall is divided into five broken-vaulted segments supported by a row of four columns.

From the intersection of the al-Otrush Mosque, continue to the east. On the right (200 m) is the **Altunbugha Mosque** the work of governor Altun Bugha al-Nasiri (built 1318). Impressive in its plain severity; a small courtyard with deep, cross-vaulted arcades.

Return to the square behind the Governorate and resume walking south. After 100 m a street heads due east (left), and brings you after 120 m to the **Mosque al-Sakakini**, a 1371 foundation of a Mamluk governor of Aleppo, Asheq Timur. The fountain, left of the façade, is boarded up. Returning to the square, take the road that heads southeast towards Bab al-Maqam. Just after a small traffic circle (100 m) is the **Mosque al-Tavashi** whose impressive façade is punctuated with recessed window frames decorated with colonnettes. The window immediately left of the entrance is framed on the left by a colonnette topped with a windswept Corinthian capital, obviously in imitation of the Byzantine capitals on the portal of *Saint Simeon. The mosque was built in the 14th century by the Mamluk, Safiye al-Din Jawar Tavashi, but renovated in 1537.

REFS: Hadjar 2000; Herzfeld 1955; Saouaf *Alep* 1975; Sauvaget *Inventaire* 1931; Sauvaget *Alep* 1941; Tabbaa 1997: 168–98.

Aleppo – Bab al-Maqam and South

PERIOD: All RATING: ** MAP: 7

LOCATION: From the south gate of the city, this itinerary leads you through the burial area and shrines to the south of the old city.

This itinerary begins at **Bab al-Maqam** ('Shrine Gate') 300 m south of the end point of our last itinerary and takes you through the main Ayyubid funerary complexes outside the walls including a shrine associated with legends of Abraham. The gate was a project of al-Zaher Ghazi, rebuilt under Barsbay (r 1422–38) and later (1493) Qait Bey. The gate, while deeply recessed between bastions, in the Arab fashion, is more ceremonial than defensive with three openings, the wider central one for wheeled vehicles. From the small tree-shaded square south of the gate, take the street branching slightly to the right (southwest), Deir al-Khatun St. Forty metres on the left lies the **Mausoleum of Kheir Bey** commissioned in 1514 by Kheir Bey al-Ashrafi. A Mamluk official, he went over to the Ottomans after 1516 and was transferred to Cairo as governor thus missing the opportunity to be buried in the mausoleum he had planned. The façade is particularly fine with two recessed panels.

Continue 300 m south and you will reach a major intersection. To the south, two roads branch off at a 'V'. Take the left fork. Fifty metres to the left is the **Madrasa Zahiriye**, another superbly restrained Ayyubid project with an attractive courtyard and deep fountain, originally intended as the funerary college of the great builder, Sultan al-Zaher Ghazi, and constructed in 1217. Ghazi, however, is buried elsewhere (see Madrasa Sultaniye above). Now a Koranic school; no photos permitted.

Return a little way along the street which brought you from Bab al-Maqam and head southwest, taking the right fork between high-walled cemeteries. A small street on the left after 200 m leads to the **Madrasa**

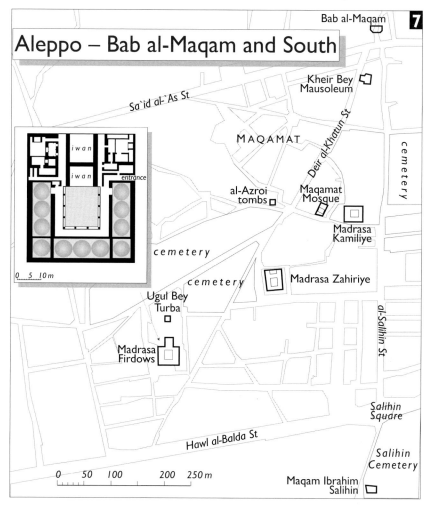

Aleppo – Bab al-Maqam and South

Bab al-Maqam **7**

Kheir Bey
Mausoleum

Sa`id al-`As St

MAQAMAT

Deir al-Khatun St

al-Azroi
tombs

Maqamat
Mosque

Madrasa
Kamiliye

cemetery

Madrasa Zahiriye

cemetery

cemetery

Ugul Bey
Turba

Madrasa
Firdows

al-Salihin St

Salihin
Square

Hawl al-Balda St

Salihin
Cemetery

0　　50　　100　　　200　　250 m

Maqam Ibrahim
Salihin

0　5　10 m

iwan

iwan

entrance

Firdows or School of Paradise, truly the most beautiful of the mosques of Aleppo. The religious school was built by Daifa Khatun, the widow of Sultan al-Zaher Ghazi[6] in 1234–7. She was regent at the time for her grandson, al-Nasr Yusuf II (r 1242–60) and had taken a particular interest in encouraging Sufi mysticism. This certainly comes through in the superb architecture, a masterpiece of simplicity and balance. A

long inscription band, carried on the rear walls of the *riwaq*s, underlines the Sufi affiliations of the community. An *iwan* at one end looks out on an octagonal pool in a courtyard framed by arcading of simple broken arches supported on fine ancient or imitation columns. The capitals are particularly well proportioned, based on a honeycomb pattern. The prayer hall is covered by three honeycombed domes supported on twelve-sided bases. The central *mihrab* is a restrained but assured masterpiece, decorated in simple

6 Daifa Khatun had two connections to Saladin being the wife of his son and the daughter of his brother, al-Adel.

interlaced straps of arabesque. Unusually, a separate *iwan* lies on the northern side of the madrasa.

Thread through the lanes to the major street to the south, Hawl al-Balda St, and proceed east to al-Salihin Square. The road south from here leads (100 m on the left) to one of the Aleppo shrines commemorating the legend of Abraham and his transit from Ur to Hebron. The **Maqam Ibrahim Salihin** (like the two mosques on the Citadel with Abrahamic associations) was apparently a Zengid-Ayyubid project though the site was first honoured by the Seljuk sultan, Malik Shah, in 1086. The 1106 inscription over the entrance to the prayer hall claims that the rock honoured in the room dates from Abraham's visit. The minaret above the portal may be part of the work attributed to al-Ghazi. The surrounding graveyard contains 12th century tombs.

REFS: Hadjar 2006; Herzfeld 1955; Saouaf *Alep* 1975; Sauvaget *Inventaire* 1931; Sauvaget *Alep* 1941; Tabbaa 1997: 168–98.

Aleppo – Museum, Bab al-Faraj Quarter

PERIOD: All RATING: **   MAP: 2

LOCATION: Central Aleppo, corner of al-Maari and Baron Sts. West of old city and opposite tourist information office.

The Aleppo Museum contains an important collection of items from many periods with a strong emphasis on Iron Age and classical finds. The museum building is a hollow square with two storeys arranged around a central courtyard. To the right of the entrance to the main building is the administration annexe with a mosaic collection yet to be installed on the ground floor.

The main entrance is framed by elements from the gateway to the temple excavated at *Tell Halaf by a German expedition in the 1920s. Huge and rather ungainly animals support three *caryatid* figures in a style found in a range of statuary from this early first millennium BC site. Around the entrance forecourt are other items

of stone sculpture found in the Aleppo region.

After the ticket office, you enter a large foyer in which are often displayed neolithic exhibits or (upstairs) recent finds from foreign expeditions in northern Syria. It is recommended you visit the Museum in an anti-clockwise direction, beginning on the right of the ground floor.

The first large hall begins with finds from the Jezira area of northeastern Syria. These include (right of entry) many of the discoveries made by Mallowan at *Tell Brak** in the 1930s among which are examples of the votive offerings found in the Eye Temple (case 2 facing entry). Note especially the altar (case 1) decorated with friezes comprising bands of coloured stone bordered by gold strips. The next section is devoted to finds from *Mari**, the Early Bronze Age site excavated by Parrot under the auspices of the Louvre from 1933 to 1974. Among the major objects displayed are a superb vase decorated with intertwined snakes (case 1) and the distinctive statues in case 2, including that of King Lamgi-Mari. Beyond are larger statues from Mari including: a black diorite figure of Ishtup-Ilum found in the main throne room of the palace of Mari (facing, in front of case 5); limestone statue of the god Shammas (headless, left); the figure of a spring goddess holding a flowing vase (considered one of the most notable pieces of scupture found in Syria, 18th century BC); and a superb statue of a man wearing the leaved skirt or *kaunakes* (between cases 4 and 5). A small selection of some of the 20,000 or more early second millennium cuneiform tablets found at Mari is also displayed.

The next section contains objects from *Hama** including finds from the excavations (1931–8) of the Danish archaeologist Ingholt on the town's citadel mound. Note the large basalt lion (first millennium BC) along the left wall. *Ugarit** (Ras Shamra) is the theme of the last section of this hall, displaying many items from this major site of the Late Bronze Age. Note (case 1) a collection of bronze figurines, some displaying Egyptian influence; (case 2) gold platelets and bronze bracelets; dark stone stele of the god El on his throne approached by the King of Ugarit (case 5).

You now enter the hall which runs along the rear of the building. This is divided into three sections, each devoted to a different Iron Age site. The first covers *Tell Halaf (Guzana, statues from which you saw at the entrance to the building). Here are displayed several of the huge standing or seated black figures (in some cases, copies) produced by this Aramaean culture of the early first millennium BC. This style of art strives for monumentality along Assyrian lines but the rendition is clumsy and eclectic; Frankfort has observed that 'there is no pronounced style, either as an imitation of better work or as a result of a vivid original conception of the nature of statuary'.[7] More aesthetically pleasing are several carved stone slabs which once protected the brick walls of the Tell Halaf temple, depicting battle and mythological scenes. Most notable, against the east wall, is a low relief panel depicting Gilgamesh between two bull-men carrying a winged sun disk above his head, from the ninth century BC palace. On leaving this section, the last figure on the left is of a scorpion-man from Tell Halaf's 'Scorpion Gate' (ninth century BC).

The middle section of the rear hall is devoted to two sites of the northern Jezira, Tell Hajjib and Arslan Tash. The latter is another Aramaean city (ancient name Hadatu) of the early first millennium BC, excavated by a French expedition from 1928 which also dug the companion site, Tell Hajjib, 20 km to the east. The style is also heavily influenced by contemporary Assyria. Note in the wall cases the ivory engraved panels found at Arslan Tash (Hadatu), tribute from King Hazael of Damascus (ninth century BC). Items in case 1 were probably made in the Phoenician (coastal) cities, thus showing Egyptian influence. The Assyrians later installed the panels in their provincial palace at Arslan Tash where they were found by Thureau-Dangin and Dunand in the 1930s. The hall ends with the two

7 Frankfort 1970: 291.

huge basalt lions that once guarded the city gates of Arslan Tash (right one heavily restored).

The third section displays finds from another Aramaean site, Tell Ahmar (or Tell Barsip), excavated by the French in the 1920s. The site is located on the Euphrates, 20 km downstream from Jerablus (on the Turkish-Syrian border). The palace was built in the Assyrian style in the reign of Salmanasar III (858–24 BC) when Tell Ahmar was the seat of an Assyrian governor. The palace was used as late as the reign of Ashurbanipal (668–29 BC). Wall paintings taken from the palace of the governor have been restored and displayed in this gallery. On the north wall, two huge panels in basalt commemorating victories by the Assyrian king Esarhaddon (r 680–69).

Turn the corner and enter the large gallery that runs along the north side of the building. This houses finds from several sites including Tell Mardikh (*Ebla) and *Ain Dara (section of a notable basalt frieze – right). Note especially two limestone basins arranged along opposite walls of the central section of the hall. From the last great flowering of Ebla (18th century BC) one (south wall) bears a fascinating carved relief scene possibly recording a treaty ceremony.

The first of the major halls upstairs contains an impressive collection of classical and Byzantine finds including pottery, statuary (from *Palmyra and *Menbij), coins, bronze objects, glass and mosaics. The rear hall is devoted to the Arab period including a full model of the city of Aleppo, panels illustrating the restoration work done at *Meskene and *Qalaat Jaabr and a wide range of ceramics. (The last gallery displays modern art.)

Behind the Museum lies the Tekkiye Mawlawiye, an important link with the Dervish tradition in Aleppo. Though the gateway and façade are relatively modern the mosque (built probably in the early Ottoman period) commemorates Jalal al-Din al-Rumi, the founder of the Dervish order who died and was buried in Konya (Turkey) in 1273. Rumi had spent some time in Aleppo and Damascus before returning to Konya in his final years. The Dervish order was prohibited in Turkey in 1925 and the last adherents took refuge in this complex. Entrance from the north with minaret to the side; large courtyard with rooms for the dervishes and their teachers to the west; kitchen to the south. A further courtyard to the south provided open space (dating back to 1250) for the whirling ceremonial dances.

If you leave the *tekkiye* by the north door and turn right (east) you quickly reach the busy square in the centre of which stands the **clocktower** endowed on the city in 1899 through the initiative of Raef Pasha with local financial support. A little to the east along the south side of the old street leading into the Bahsita Quarter you can see above the shopfronts a small section of the city gate, **Bab al-Faraj**. Most of the gate was removed in a 1904 street widening. Continuing on to the east, the lane passes (right) the **Bahsita Mosque** (1350) with a fine minaret and, where the lane peters out after 250 m, the **al-Umari Mosque** (1328). They comprise the few elements that survived the redevelopment of this quarter to make way for the long-delayed construction of commercial and government offices as well as a five-star hotel.

REFS: Khayyata *Aleppo Museum Guide* 1977; Saouaf *Alep* 1975.

Aleppo – Jdeide Quarter, North Walls

PERIOD: Arb/Ott   RATING: *   MAPS 2, 8

LOCATION: The traditionally Christian area immediately north of the old walled city of Aleppo.

This itinerary covers the Jdeide Quarter, which, though outside the medieval walls, is one of the most charming areas of the city, with stone-flagged streets and vaulted laneways winding between houses which preserve the best traditions of domestic architecture. The quarter developed during the late Mamluk period (hence its description, 'new quarter'), probably largely in response to the arrival of Maronite and Armenian Christians attracted by employment as middlemen in the Venetian trade. The area has greatly changed its role in recent years as many family homes or charitable institutions have been converted to 'boutique' hotels and restaurants preserving much of the charm of the quarter.

The houses described all bear common features of Arab domestic architecture of recent centuries. The house is oriented around a courtyard at the centre of which stands a pool or fountain. Shade and contrast is provided by planted trees and vines. At one end is an *iwan* or large vaulted room open to the courtyard with a tall arch framing the opening. The open space is often surrounded by benches for guests. Reception and service rooms (usually including a large reception room for winter) are distributed around the courtyard while upstairs off a gallery lie the private rooms and sleeping quarters for the family. Some buildings are now charitable or commercial institutions so gaining entry can be a bit of a lottery.

Begin at the clock tower at Bab al-Faraj Square (*Museum, Bab al-Faraj Quarter). Head 300 m north to the point where Quwatli St continues east as al-Khandak St. Cross the intersection and continue north (left of the police station) up Tilel St, the animated pedestrian mall lined with haberdashery and perfume shops. The first sizeable cross street on the right leads to the Maronite church. Stop in the square in front of the church before entering this maze of alleys.

The Maronite Church is relatively new (1873–1923) as is the Greek Catholic Church (1849, right from the square). Some older churches of considerable interest, however, will be found nearby. From the Greek Catholic church follow the dog leg turn for 100 m until you reach a T junction. Again turn right and 10 m on the right is the **Greek Orthodox Church** built in 1861 in a consciously Syrian style of decoration – ebony *iconostasis*, interesting icons; grave of a Russian consul in the courtyard. To reach the **Gregorian Armenian Church of the Forty Martyrs** (15th century – icons and paintings in the Armenian tradition) turn right from the Greek Orthodox Church and follow the bend in the street for +20 m. If you return to the T intersection, the **Syrian Catholic Church** is a few metres left on the left side of the street but is normally now closed due to the drift of the community to other parts of Aleppo.

from Mamluk to Rococo, blending them in an exuberant synthesis. The reception room opposite the *iwan* has a superb ceiling in gilded and painted wood.

Turn left into Kayyali St and after 40 m you will reach on the left the second of our houses, **Beit Ghazale**. This large house of the 17th century has been acquired for use as a Museum of Folklore. (Fine polychrome wood inlay in the reception room (domed), *iwan* and waiting rooms; beautiful interwoven designs in the

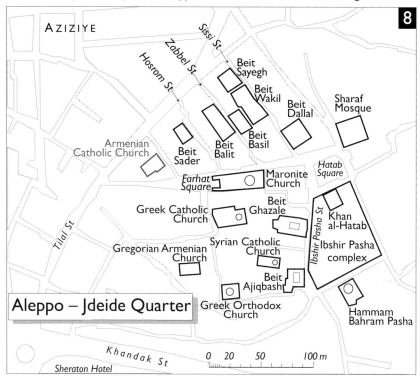

Continue east and at the intersection of the next cross street on the left, you will find one of the most impressive traditional houses in Syria, restored in the 1980s and now used as a Museum of Popular Traditions. This is the **Beit Ajiqbash** (plate 2b), built in 1757 by the wealthy Christian trading family of that name. It has a harmonious courtyard, extravagantly decorated in a style that borrows elements

wide frames around the windows of the courtyard; to the west, a bath area.)

Forty metres on is Hatab (or Jdeide) Square which lies at the back (east) of the narrow rectangular block that began with the Maronite Church. On the northeast corner of the square lies the **Sharaf Mosque**, with a fine Mamluk minaret. The Mamluk inscription dates the mosque to

1491 but Hadjar believes the mosque may be earlier in origin, the name referring to al-Hajj Sharaf (d 1393) who was buried on the site.

To the south of the square lies a whole block endowed in the 1650s by the governor of Aleppo, Ibshir Mustafa Pasha. A variety of commercial operations, including khans and a coffee house, funded the mosque and fountain within the complex. Much of the block has been radically altered but the **Khan al-Hatab** provides an authentic frontage to Jdeide Square. To the rear of the block, across the street to the south, is the currently disused **Hammam Bahram Pasha** (16th century) with a notable doorway and banded façade.

From the street that borders the northern side of the Maronite Church, three narrow and picturesque streets run off to the right.

The first is Sissi St, On the right (20 m) is **Beit al-Dallal** a 17th century house also occupied by an Armenian school. (Large courtyard with fine marble pavement; gazebo in iron; off the *iwan* (to the east) a dining room with polychrome painted ceiling; grand reception room (south) with vault in painted wood; above this a terrace for the women). **Beit Wakil** (20 m on left) is now a boutique hotel with marvellously decorated walls including stylized gargoyles in the north (now covered) courtyard. The two rooms that flank the *iwan* are beautifully decorated in wood. But the true glory of Beit Wakil was once the wood-panelled reception room that was sold before the World War I to the Museum of Eastern Art in Berlin which it still graces.

In the next street (al-Rahab Buhayrah or Zabbel) you will find mid-way along on the right **Beit Basil** once a Roman Catholic orphanage now housing a school for business studies. (Early 18th century; fine relief decoration in painted stucco around the *iwan* which has been converted into a chapel.) The houses on the left side of the street have been radically re-organised and re-named. The first is now a restaurant

(Sidraat). Further along lies the Armenian orphanage, **Beit Balit** (also known as the Beit Saghil) – 18th century; painted wood ceiling of room off the *iwan*; courtyard walls elegantly decorated. The orphanage is not usually accessible but part of the complex to the north has been turned into another boutique hotel, Tourath, where you can inspect a complex cave system that once stored ice and provisions during the heat of summer.

REFS: Hadjar 2006.

Aleppo – North Walls, Bab al-Hadid

PERIOD: Arb RATING: – MAP: 2

LOCATION: The northern city walls of the old city and the quarter inside the northwestern gate, Bab al-Hadid.

This itinerary also starts 300 m north of the clocktower at the intersection where al-Khandak St continues the alignment of Quwatli St following the old ditch (Arb: *al-khandak*) that ran outside the city walls. A walk of 650 m brings you to the **Bab al-Nasr** (Gate of Victory). The gate which is buried amid shops 10 m along a narrow lane on the right (south) side of the road is largely Ayyubid in origin. It was reconstructed by al-Zaher Ghazi – an inscription to that effect on the gate. The wall between the two bastions has been dismantled to give direct access through the gateway whose original design required two right-angle turns through the left bastion.

Take the first street right after the Bab al-Nasr. After 120 m, turn left then 40 m on the right is the entrance to the **Beit Junblatt** a 17th century house built by a governor of Aleppo. The *selamlik* of this large complex is currently under restoration by the Kuwait-Syria-Arab Fund and will serve as a cultural centre and library. Two *iwans* face each other across the large courtyard, that on the south being exceptionally high and grand. Both carry faience tiles and marble decorations.

The area south and west of Beit Junblatt (Bahsita) was the traditional Jewish quarter of Aleppo. The **Bandara Synagogue** lies in the street that runs behind the Syrian Insurance Company office on Abd al-Munem St. The building, deserted since the 1950s, has recently been partly restored (access arrangements are posted on a notice next to the door). The building is of exceptional interest. It dates in part from the 12th century but a synagogue probably stood on this site from the fifth century.

To reach the **Madrasa Othmaniye** return to Bab al-Nasr and keep going on the street that skirts south of the gate. This soon takes a right turn. The madrasa is on the left. The large building (1730–8), endowed by Othman Pasha al-Duraki, is distinguished by the highest minaret of the traditional mosques of Aleppo, in the round Turkish style. A large courtyard has the prayer hall on the south preceded by a three-domed portico and flanked by two *iwans*; 42 student rooms surround the other sides of the court.

[For those with sufficient time, two monuments south of the Othmaniye can be reached by a short diversion. On leaving the Madrasa Othmaniye navigate your way to the lane that runs along the south wall of the madrasa. Turn right (west) and walk until you reach a street. Turn left and head for the intersection of al-Mutanabbi St (often confusingly called al-Sijn at this end). On the corner to your left stands the mosque known as the '**al-Qadi Mosque**' but also as 'al-Mahmandar', honouring its founder the 14th century Hassan Ibn Balaban or 'Ibn al-Mahandar', chef to the then sultan. The minaret with its wave-patterned ribbing, according to Hadjar, is in the Mongolian style.]

To continue to the next site is a little tricky. Cross al-Mutanabbi St and head left almost half-way along the remainder of the street to the east. In between modern shops is a passage that leads to a rear lane. This brings you to the northwest corner of the **Khanqah al-Farafra**, a rare example of a Muslim (Sufi) monastery. The rather severe but pleasing building was constructed in 1237 in the name of the Ayyubid Governor, al-Nasr Yusuf II,

son of Sultan al-Aziz (Ayyubid governor of Aleppo 1216–36) but probably actually endowed by his mother, Daifa Khatun (see Madrasa Firdows above). Note the honeycombed entrance, the large *iwan* in the courtyard and the marble *mihrab*. Cells surround the courtyard. Next door (to the east) is the headquarters of the Office for the Protection of Old Aleppo.

To reach our next destination, the **Bab al-Hadid**, return to Bab al-Nasr and continue east along al-Khandak St. After 600 m, the road joins a roundabout in front of the gate. The present remains are largely Mamluk but the gate was first constructed under Ghazi. It originally had a counterpart bastion to the north, a typical Arab configuration with two towers protecting a lateral entry through one of the bastions (*Aleppo – Citadel). The Arabic inscriptions refer to the role of Sultan Qansawh al-Ghawri (r 1500–16), effectively the last Mamluk ruler, in its reconstruction. Two-storeyed bastion with machicolation and firing slits; passage takes a right angled bend.

If you are returning to the Citadel area, continue along the street bending south into the Bayada Quarter. After 75 m you come to a striking tunnel-like structure that continues the ironmongers' quarter through which you have just passed, hence 'Iron Gate'. This 'tunnel' is actually a late Mamluk suq built to accommodate the city's 'heavy industry' at the time. (Today, Hadjar informs us, the suq is known as **Qubu al-Najjarin** or 'carpenters' basement'.)

Following the bend south (Bayada St) you pass on the left the **al-Sarawi Mosque** just before an intersection with a right T. This mosque was built by Hajj al-Din Muhammad al-Sarawi in 1402. The façade is noteworthy for its two stalactite-decorated entrances. On the southwest side of the T junction lies the **Hammam al-Bayada** (1450), one of the oldest surviving baths in Aleppo. At the end of the street, where it joins the road encircling the Citadel, on the right is the **al-Hamwi Mosque**. The name commemorates not the original benefactor (1560) but Hussein al-Hamwi who restored the mosque in 1768.

REFS: Gaube & Wirth 1984; Hadjar 2000; Saouaf *Alep* 1975; Sauvaget *Inventaire* 1931; Sauvaget *Alep* 1941.

Aleppo – Mashhad al-Hussein

PERIOD: Arb   RATING: –   MAP: –

LOCATION: Western outskirts of Aleppo, on the slopes of Jebel Jaushan. Take the Damascus route from downtown. Just after you pass the old stadium (on the right) you cross under the railway viaduct. The street immediately after on the left leads you south. (Vehicles cannot turn left at this point and have to detour via the next passage to the north.) 600 m on the right is the Mashhad al-Hussein, a short walk up the rise.

Aleppo was once a city rich in Shiite associations, at least until the 12th century. The rise of the great Sunni orthodox dynasties (partly inspired by the need to rally the faithful to the Muslim cause against the Crusades) brought an end to a mainstream Shiite tradition in northern Syria. These two institutions, however, both linked to the martyrdom of Hussein at the hands of Umayyad forces, indicate how Shia associations managed to survive in a remarkable way.

The **Mashhad al-Hussein** (Memorial to the Martyrdom of Hussein) has been described as 'the most important medieval Shia structure in all of Syria'.[8] It was originally built over the period 1183 to 1260 in honour of Hussein, son of Ali, as a conscious challenge to resurgent Sunni orthodoxy. The building was half destroyed in an explosion in 1920, having served as a munitions store for the Turkish forces. Shiite community contributions brought about its reconstruction in the 1970s using the photographs and plans of the German researcher, Herzfeld, and what remained of the original fabric. The mosque is also called the Masjid al-Mukhtar, commemmorating the spot (*al-mukhtar*) where a drop of blood from Hussein's head is said to have fallen (for background, see *Damascus – Umayyad

8 Tabbaa 1997: 110.

Mosque). The *mashhad*, one of the most important Shia shrines in Syria, is now the centre for a considerable pilgrimage traffic from Iran and recent alterations to handle the crowds have robbed the building of much of its poetry. The central courtyard, for example, is now enclosed by a soulless roof that denies the building the play of light and shade.

After passing through the outer courtyard, the reconstructed honey-combed entrance doorway, whose vault is described by Allen as 'by far the most elaborate in Ayyubid architecture' (note the delicate carved frieze), leads you into a large inner court now covered by that graceless modern roof. The court is surrounded by: to the west (straight ahead) a large *iwan*; to the south (left as you enter) a prayer hall with three domes; and to the north a portico (behind which lie service rooms and latrines). The stone said to bear the mark of the drop of Hussein's blood is in the grilled enclosure on the left side of the *iwan*. The mihrab of the prayer hall is monumental in size (1.4 m by 3.9 m), a superb example in geometric marquetry flanked by imitations of ancient columns.

Three hundred metres further south along the same road turn right. Straight ahead is another Shiite shrine, the **Mashhad of Sheikh Muhassin** (also known as al-Dikka – 'the platform'). Nothing remains of the original shrine built at the peak of Shiite influence in the mid tenth century by the Hamdanid ruler, Saif al-Daula, on a site linked to earlier Shi'ite tradition. The present fabric dates from the 12th and early 13th centuries[9] when the building was reconstructed by Nur al-Din and the Ayyubids. The entrance gateway (almost a half-dome decorated with honeycomb vaulting) is the oldest *muqarnas* stone portal in Aleppo (1189). It is preceded by a pavement in contrasting basalt and limestone. The large courtyard is flanked

9 Especially under Saladin's son, al-Zaher Ghazi. Sauvaget 'Deux Sanctuaires' notes (1928: 326–7) that there are many details in common between the two Shiite shrines, suggesting perhaps that the same team worked on the reconstruction of the second and the construction of the first.

on the south (left) side by the prayer hall topped by three domes. Immediately to the left of the gateway is a mausoleum containing a fine cenotaph in carved wood (13th century, now covered and locked). The room is covered by twin domes with a central arch terminating in vase-capitals (whose shape is Mesopotamian in inspiration). The columns supporting the arch and those framing the *mihrab* appear to be of ancient origin. The memorable view over Aleppo celebrated in engravings in recent centuries is now obscured by trees but can still be appreciated from a little higher up the hill.

REFS: Eliséeff *BEO* 1949–51; Hadjar 2000; Herzfeld 1955: 193–200; Sauvaget *Alep* 1941: 124–5; Sauvaget 'Deux Sanctuaires' 1928; Tabbaa 1997: 109–21.

Amrit (Plate 3a)

عمريت

VARIANTS: Marathias, Marathos (Grk); Marathus (Lat)
PERIOD: Phn/Grk RATING: * MAPS: 9, R2

LOCATION: 8 km south of *Tartus. Take old coast road towards Tripoli. 2.7 km south of the roundabout on the southern outskirts of Tartus, fork right along a narrow road that branches at an angle towards the coast. (The turn-off is just before the two radio transmission masts and the citrus research station.) After +2.5 km, cross the small stream, the Nahr Amrit (classical Marathias), and after 80 m take the track left 300 m to temple remains. The stadium is at the end of this track.

Amrit was a Phoenician religious centre heavily influenced in its architectural style by the Achaemenid Persians (who controlled as far west as the Syrian coast and went on to threaten classical Athens). It is the only extant site in Syria whose remains, though fragmentary, convey this mixture of civilisations, reflecting the ability of the Phoenicians to absorb and syncretize outside influences. It was also the mainland port for the Phoenician settlement on *Arwad, the island 2.5 km to the west. After the decline of *Ugarit, Arwad had become the principal

Phoenician commercial power on the Syrian coast, rivalling Sidon in the south of present-day Lebanon.

Amrit is an important site having 'escaped the Romanisation that all but eclipsed Phoenician remains elsewhere'.[10] It uniquely preserves pre-classical forms of Semitic religious architecture without the classical veneer other sites later acquired.

History

The earliest constructions on the tell date to the end of the third millennium BC. The site was probably founded by people from Arwad and the town virtually functioned as a mainland suburb and religious centre. Many of the buildings date from the period of Persian dominance after Cyrus' conquest of Babylon in 539 BC. The most significant monument, the temple compound dedicated to the gods Melqart and Eshmun, was built at the end

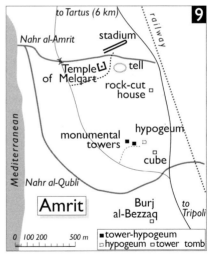

of the sixth century BC with elements freely borrowed from Mesopotamian and Egyptian architecture. It was still functioning as a temple when Alexander the Great paused here in 330 BC, though Dunand believes that the temple may have been desecrated and its statuary thrown into the sacred lake earlier (mid fourth

10 Ball 2000: 366.

century) during the general breakdown of Persian control in the area. Alexander waited at Marathos, as it was then known, while his army diverted to Damascus. By the Roman period, Amrit had been abandoned, the port of Antaradus (*Tartus) to the north offering better access to larger ships.

Visit

The site is large, extending over an area 3 km long by 2 km wide. The most striking remains are those of the Phoenician temple of the Achaemenid Persian period (late sixth to mid fourth century BC). The **temple** dedicated to the god Melqart (assimilated in the Greek period to Heracles) with a secondary association to the Egyptian god of healing, Echmoun, was excavated and partly restored under a Franco-Syrian program from 1954 to 1959 (plate 3a). The temple was built around an artificial lake (c48 m by 39 m) with a small sanctuary (*naos*) on a platform of living rock at the centre, topped by an Egyptian-style cornice, terminating in a frieze of stepped triangular merlons. A spring (whose healing properties gave rise to the cult) was channeled towards the sacred precinct from the foot of the tell to the east. The rectangular pool was surrounded on three sides by a colonnaded arcade whose facade (formed from plain rectangular pillars in the Egyptian style) was originally topped by a continuous row of merlons (in the Mesopotamian tradition). Two towers flanked the northern ends of the east and west colonnades, again reflecting a Mesopotamian inspiration. On the open platform between the towers was a high altar facing south towards the opening in the *naos*.

A **stadium** (230 m by 30 m) lies on the other side of the Nahr Amrit to the north. Constructed in the third century BC, it is one of the few reminders we have of the early Hellenisation process in Syria. The seating was partly cut from the living rock and includes a widened turning circle at the eastern end. Four hundred metres southeast of the tell lies a house whose 30 m façade and interior walls are cut from the rock.

The remaining monuments are in a zone still under military control, south along the sealed road. After 1 km a track (left) leads to the remains of a necropolis with two **monumental towers**, also fourth century BC but in use up to the end of the first century BC. The southern tower is 4 m high, cylindrical with four unfinished lion sculptures around the square base (a Persian motif). The decoration echoes that of the temple compound. Two burial chambers lie in a *hypogeum*. The second tower, also cylindrical, is 7 m high and ends in a five-sided pyramid with a burial chamber below.

A **funerary monument**, with some traces of Egyptian influence, is to be found +1 km south in an enclosed military zone. Burj al-Bezzaq ('snail tower') is a cube formed of massive blocks formerly surmounted by a cornice and ending in a pyramid. Inside were two superimposed funerary chambers. The remains of a fallen obelisk lie still further to the south.

REFS: Dunand & Saliby 1985; Rey-Coquais *Arados* 1974: 212–3; Saliby *CFAS* 1989: 118–20.

Anderin

الاندرين

VARIANTS: Androna (Lat) PERIOD: Byz RATING: T MAP: R4

LOCATION: From *Qasr Ibn Wardan (62 km north-northeast of Hama), the road continues in the same direction +25 km to Anderin, on the western edge of the northern Syrian steppe.

An extensive site scattered over nearly 3 km², this was once a Byzantine settlement comparable to the nearby complex at *Qasr Ibn Wardan. The countryside from here north to Aleppo was probably rich grazing land in late antiquity, rainfall sources supplemented by extensive irrigation works. The region came to play a role in the Emperor Justinian's (r 527–65) plans to block access to Antioch from the east. The need was not, however, for one of the massive fortifications Justinian used to counter the Persian threat but smaller complexes which combined a base for locally-raised militia units intended to counter any nomad threat with intensive agricultural exploitation. The site is currently being researched by German and British teams in collaboration with the Syrian antiquities authorities. The results have given considerable new insight into the area in late antiquity. Anderin provided an extraordinary level of luxury and comfort for its yeoman forces presumably raised from the wealthy landed class. The complex remained in use in Umayyad times. (A lavish Umayyad bath was built to replace a Byzantine predecessor.)

For the most part, the town was constructed in mud brick with the lower parts of the more significant buildings in stone, largely the local volcanic basalt. The central elements were a square barracks building and a cathedral dating from the last years of Justinian. The ruins (which include ten other churches) reveal little of the plan of the city but there were probably two main cross streets on north-south, east-west axes, intersecting slightly to the east of the cathedral.

The dating of the **walls** may reflect an earlier defensive role. The question is still problematic but the site may have been used as a defensive position at least from the early sixth century. The town wall still visible in Butler's day was 1.5 m thick with rectangular towers. The original walls and towers were possibly mined for the construction of the churches and replaced with a second, inner ring.

The most interesting result of the recent German research is the clearing of much of the structure of the **barracks** or *kastron* which was based on a square plan, each side c80 m. The complex dates from 558, virtually contemporary with Qasr Ibn Wardan. Significant elements of the structure illustrate the high degree of comfort provided to the yeoman contingent. The work was funded by a local benefactor, Thomas. An inner courtyard was surrounded by a colonnade at the centre of which was a chapel. Hexagonal towers stood at each outer corner and the gates and halls within the complex's walls were often stylishly decorated. (A section

of painted wall has survived.) Courses of basalt alternated with brickwork in a style closely related to Qasr Ibn Wardan. There were gates on the west and south sides, both provided with ramps for equestrian access to the upper levels.

The **Byzantine baths**, contemporary with the barracks (opposite western side), were funded by the same benefactor. They too were richly decorated (wall mosaics and painting, marble cladding) and larger than the baths at *Serjilla. To the west, a later baths project constructed by the Umayyads has recently been excavated by the Syrian authorities, correcting an earlier assumption that this was a Byzantine *praetorium*.

Only a few segments of the **cathedral** survive. The building was a reasonably typical product of the sixth century Syrian style, triple-naved with an apse ending in a semi-circle slightly projecting beyond the rear baseline. The overall dimensions were 43 m by 25 m. The half-dome of the apse was built of brick. Three vaulting arches separated the naves in the style of the Church of Bissos at *Ruweiha.

At **Stabl Antar**, 8 km southwest, a Byzantine farmstead follows the pattern of smaller fortified posts in the area.

REFS: Butler *PE* II B 2 1908: 47–63; Butler *EC* 1929: 80–2, 158–60, 169; Mango *DOP* 2002: 307–15; Mango *DOP* 2004: 293–7; Mouterde & Poidebard 1945: 174; Strube *Arch Anzeiger* 2003: 25–115; Strube *25 Years* 2005: 105–9. Stabl Antar: Decker 2006.

Apamea (Plates 3b, 3c, 4a)

أفاميا

VARIANTS: Niya[11] (pre-Grk); Pharnake, Pella,[12] Apameia (Grk); Afamia, Fémie, Fémia (Cru); Qalaat Mudiq (Arb); Apamée (Fr)

11   The name used in the Egyptian account of the expedition of Amenhotep II to Syria in 1447.
12   A Macedonian occupation (named in memory of the birthplace of Alexander's father) pre-dated Seleucus' re-naming of the settlement c300 BC.

PERIOD: Hel/Rom/Byz/Arb RATING: ***
MAPS: 10, R2

LOCATION: 55 km north of *Hama. Northwest exit from Hama by road to Mhardeh (23 km), then +6 km to *Shaizar, +20 km to Suqeilibiye, +5 km to Qalaat Mudiq village. For ruins, sharp turn right north of village takes you behind citadel mound; follow road to ticket office. Also accessible (22 km) from Khan Sheikhun north of Hama on the highway to Aleppo.

From Apamea, overlooking the Orontes Valley before the green starts to fade towards the desert to the east, you look out on a stunning sight, over rich farmlands reclaimed from swamp towards the hazy outline of the Jebel Ansariye to the west. Palmyra may offer sheer dramatic contrast between the starkness of the setting and the beauty of the ruins, but Apamea compensates through the juxtaposition, no less dramatic, of stone against lush pastures and distant mountains.

Apamea has been excavated since 1930 by Belgian teams,[13] but a good deal of reconstruction work was done in the 1990s by the Syrian Department of Antiquities, particularly in order to restore the columns of the *cardo maximus* (plate 4a). The results are now evident and the sight of the long stretch of columns, bearing in some cases curious twisted fluting, provides a new perspective on the huge scale on which Roman Apamea was conceived.

History

The mound of *Qalaat Mudiq ('fortress of the defile') lies west of the classical walled city and is still occupied by some of the town's inhabitants. The mound, an artificial accumulation on a natural rocky outcrop, has indications of settlement going back at least to the Bronze Age. The site was chosen as the location for one of the four cities founded by Seleucus I Nicator at the end of the fourth century

BC.[14] Originally named Pharnake, the name was changed to Apameia to honour Seleucus' Persian wife, Apama. The old citadel was probably incorporated when the new city's enclosure walls were extended to the west. It became one of the main centres of Seleucid Syria and a forward military base. Its rich pastures made it a natural breeding centre for the horses of the Seleucid cavalry and it lay astride the kingdom's main north-south communications, slightly to the rear of the buffer zone with the Ptolemaic lands to the south. By the second century BC, however, it had fallen well behind Antioch in economic and political importance. In 64 BC, Apamea was taken by the Romans under Pompey and its citadel was razed. Under Roman rule, it was again favoured as a military base. The theatre, baths, temples and villas, constructed during the town's period of peak prosperity, the boom years of the second century AD,[15] were perhaps initiated when Trajan ordered the rebuilding of the city after a severe earthquake in 115. The colonnaded main street was completed in its present form under Marcus Aurelius (161–80) and served both as an axis and a market, lined with stalls and shaded arcades.[16] In the third century, the city was made the winter base for the élite II Parthica legion. In addition to its economic and military importance, Apamea became the centre of an influential school of neo-Platonic philosophy which flourished particularly under Iamblichus (early 4th century).

Apamea remained a centre of considerable importance into the Byzantine period. It was made the capital of Syria Secunda province in the early 5th century and was the seat of a bishop. The Persians sacked and burnt the city in 573 during the troubled century which also saw a succession of major earthquakes. The Persians again held it from 612 to 628

14 The other three were Laodiceia (*Latakia), Antioch and Seleuceia (the port for Antioch).
15 One estimate gives the population of the town including extra-mural suburbs as half a million.
16 J-C Balty describes the *cardo* as 'one of the most esteemed avenues in world architectural history' – 'Apamée' 1977: 128.

13 The Belgian researches are one of the most prolonged programs of archaeological work carried out in Syria, apart from *Ugarit.

and the Byzantine 'liberation' came only a decade before it fell to the Arabs, changing hands without resistance.

The town came under Crusader control (attached to the Principality of Antioch) in 1106 when it was taken by Tancred. In July 1149 it fell to Nur al-Din. In 1157, an earthquake caused major damage. The castle was re-fortified by the Ayyubids and some remains of this phase are found on the citadel mound. The 16th century mosque and caravanserai indicate the role the town later played as a staging post on the pilgrimage route from Istanbul to Mecca.

Visit

The site falls naturally into several groups of ruins:

• The main columned street or *cardo maximus* which runs precisely north-south, bisected by a modern road. The cardo was crossed in ancient times by several east-west axes (less distinguishable) or *decumani*.
• Roman residences and extensive Byzantine **ecclesiastical remains** about 400 m to the east of the *cardo*
• the **theatre**, between the *cardo* and the modern village
• the **walls** surrounding the classical site
• the Ayyubid **citadel** (on the site of its Seleucid predecessor) on the tell above Qalaat Mudiq.
• the Turkish caravanserai which now serves as a **museum**, located east of the approach road entering the village from the south.

Leave a couple of hours for a leisurely walk along the length of the *cardo maximus* which served as the spine of the typically Hippodamian grid pattern, later adopted by the Romans as the standard layout for their military and other colonies. The grid was based on elements 106 m by 53 m. Though the *cardo* follows the line of the Hellenistic axis, its present form dates from Roman rebuilding after the disastrous earthquake of 115. The thoroughfare is oriented precisely north-south and

stretches 1.85 km, considerably longer than *Palmyra (1.2 km) or Damascus (1.35 km). It was lined with buildings of civic and religious significance. The street, 37.5 m wide with a carriageway of 20.8 m, was accessible to wheeled transport (you can still see the ruts at some points). Some of the columns along the colonnade carried brackets, a Syrian practice intended to support statues of civic or imperial dignitaries.

Our tour of Apamea will begin at the intersection marked by the café and main ticket office located where the modern road bisects the *cardo*. (Visitors may also enter from the north where a second ticket office is located.) Begin with the northern sector, reserving for later the quarters south and east from here. The northern *cardo* falls into three segments each of 250–500 m, defined by honorific columns that mark important cross-streets. It should be kept in mind, however, that work on the *cardo* after AD 115 proceeded from north to south and you will thus be seeing the thoroughfare in reverse chronological order.

On leaving the ticket office, head north. 100 m right, the remains of a *nymphaeum* or public water fountain, are seen just behind the main colonnade. Its deeply curved *exedra*, 10 m wide, was decorated with statues arranged in niches. In a survey (1978–84) of around 50 marble fragments, these sculptural works (probably late second century) were found to have been imported and closely followed Hellenistic models. The structure behind served as a latrine.

On the mound 100 m to the left is the site of the **Temple of Zeus Belos**, dismantled in 384–5 by order of Bishop Marcellus. A further 200 m to the north, you will see a monumental columned entrance pavilion, the eastern entrance to the *agora* or forum, behind the main colonnade. The *agora* was a long narrow open space, 45 m wide including the porticos on each side and possibly 200 m long (the full extent remains unexcavated). It was under construction around AD 130 but, like parts of the *cardo* at this point,

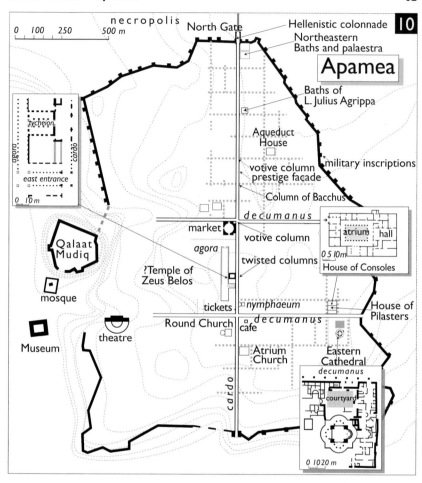

necropolis   North Gate   Hellenistic colonnade   **10**
0   100   250   500 m   Northeastern
                                                    Baths and palaestra

Apamea

Baths of
L. Julius Agrippa

tycheion
agora   cardo   Aqueduct
east entrance   House
0   10 m

Qalaat
Mudiq

mosque

Museum

theatre

votive column   military inscriptions
prestige façade
Column of Bacchus

decumanus

market   votive column   atrium   hall
agora   0 5 10m
            twisted columns   House of Consoles
?Temple of
Zeus Belos

tickets   nymphaeum   House of
Round Church   cafe   Pilasters
            decumanus
            Atrium   Eastern
            Church   Cathedral
                      decumanus
                      courtyard

0 10 20 m

the full plan may not have been realised for some decades.

Returning to the *cardo*, notice on the right the section marked by columns with twisted fluting, an effect emphasised by rotating the grooves in alternate directions (plate 3b). This device was a specialty of Apamea for which there are few parallels. The columns and the elaborate entablature with carved trails of acanthus show a baroque taste which foreshadows late Roman style. They probably date from c AD 166. The choice of these columns at this point, according to the Belgian archaeologist, J-C Balty, was perhaps influenced by the siting on the left of the imposing façade, tentatively identified as a Temple of the Tyche ('**tycheion**') honouring the city's protecting goddess. To the north, the agora is approached by a second entrance at its northern end marked by columns standing on beautifully carved bases (also c AD 130).

After 100 m you enter the lower segment of the **northern cardo**. (Note the base of the honorific column marking the intersection.) This second 400 m section contains two points of interest. In a hollow on the right after 130 m, a pillar that once supported an arch over a cross street (*decumanus*) depicts the legend of Bacchus: Lycurgus entrammelled by Bacchus in the trails of a vine; Pan with a flock of goats. Further up on the right, a prestige façade (purpose unknown) juts out from the line of the cardo. At the end of this section, the next major cross street is marked by a reconstructed votive column raised on a triangular base.

Along the final 700 m section of the northern *cardo* (plate 4a), about 150 m on the right past the column, remains of **baths** can be seen. Built in the last year of Trajan's reign (AD 117), they are lavish in scale with two large halls for the cold and warm baths. It is worth noting the richer, more classically portentious lines of the columns in this northern sector, reflecting the imperial inspiration for this early phase of the project as opposed to the more razzle-dazzle style adopted further south. This reflects Trajan's role in giving impetus to this first phase of the *cardo*. The columns with their beautiful classical entablature above also date from AD 117. Note too the sections of the shop façades that once lined the length of the colonnaded porticos.

The area of the second century AD triumphal arch and the outer North Gate has been excavated by the Belgian mission, unearthing evidence of a Hellenistic (c 100 BC) phase. From the outer gate, one of the city's three necropoleis extended to the northwest. The town was surrounded by 6.5 km of **walls**. The walls on the north and west sides are particularly well preserved. (A good view can be had from the road that encircles much of the site). Note the effect here of Justinian's rebuilding of the walls (the base is Hellenistic) and the addition of square bastions.

To visit the remains south of the principal *decumanus* return to the starting point at the tarmac road; 50 m on the right (west) are foundations of a **round church** dating from the reign of Justinian (527–65). The church comprised a circular chamber, 25 m in diameter, extended out to the east to end in a semi-circular apse. Even the

foundations suggest in their confident shapes and the four-square precision of the masonry the imperial will that drove so many projects of this era.

A slightly smaller building, the **atrium church,** lies 50 m south but on the east side of the *cardo*. This was an enlargement, from Justinian's time, of a fifth century building. (The latter in turn replaced a fourth century synagogue of which the mosaic floor (391), based on purely geometrical motives, survived and is now in the Musées royaux d'Art et d' Histoire, Brussels.) The style of Justinian's church reflects metropolitan rather than local architectural trends, probably resulting from imperial patronage of Sts Cosmas and Damien whose relics were venerated here. Under Justinian, the original chapel was enlarged – two side aisles and a courtyard were added. The remains of the saints were originally contained in two large stone reliquaries found (empty) in the northeast chapel in 1934.

At the east end of the *decumanus*, 400 m east of the starting point on the *cardo*, there is a group of buildings, the most important of which, the eastern cathedral, is said to be 'one of the most significant architectural complexes of the Christian East'.[17] To reach this area, take the modern road east. The original *decumanus* ran 20 m to the right, its line marked by a row of excavated columns. The first site you will notice (right, 50 m) are the remains of a large complex of 80 rooms built around a peristyle court (southwest corner). There were in addition two subsidiary courts as well as three reception or dining rooms (hence the description, *triclinos*), each ending in an apse. The complex (mid fourth century and later) was richly decorated with marble cladding and fine mosaics. (Several are now displayed in the National Museum in Damascus and in the Musées royaux, Brussels, including a superb hunting scene mosaic.) J-C Balty speculates that the house may have been upgraded to serve as the official residence of the governor of Syria Secunda after the province was created at the beginning of the fifth century. The shop complex along

17 Balty, J-C *Guide* 1981: 115.

the *decumanus* at this point apparently remained in use until the 12th century.

The **eastern cathedral** occupies the next two segments of the city grid to the east. It was approached by steps from the *decumanus* which provided a monumental entrance to the building. This gave access to the *narthex* (the exposed pavement can be seen) and then a large court, originally surrounded by a peristyle. This grand entry court dates from 533. The earliest Christian construction was the centralised church built on the site of an earlier pagan building on the south side of the court. The plan was based on a *tetraconque,* a square defined by massive pillars expanded on each side by a semi-circular row of six columns, further carried out to the east by a chapel with semi-circular apse. The same plan was employed at other centralised churches in the region (box page 24), including *Bosra (511) and *Resafa (520+) ,though the present example is earlier, probably fifth century.

A second construction phase, however, was necessitated by the earthquakes of 526 and 528. In 533, a monumental entrance was added north of the *tetraconque*. Advantage was taken of the rebuilding to adapt what had basically evolved as a pilgrimage church housing the famed relics of the True Cross to serve a new purpose as the seat of an archbishop. To the southeast, the complex of rooms was built to house the ceremonies connected with baptism. Most interesting in liturgical terms, however, was the alteration of the open tetraconque shape of the church through the replacement of the east colonnade with a wall, in front of which was built a *synthronon* to frame the archbishop's ceremonial seat. All this, as well as the mosaics[18] and richly decorated capitals of the nave were inspired by Bishop Paul who played a strong role

18 The most significant of the fourth century mosaics that predate the Christian cathedral and were found under its structure have been removed, some to the local museum (see below), some to Brussels or Damascus. They indicate the strength of the late Roman neo-Platonist school in Apamea with their concentration on subjects from the Greek myths.

in maintaining orthodoxy against the Monophysite 'heresy' at the Council of Constantinople in 536.

On the northern side of the *decumanus*, opposite the eastern cathedral, you will find remains of three **Roman houses** excavated since 1973. The most interesting is the so-called House of Consoles (plate 3c) whose façade has been reconstructed (northern end of the grid segment). The house is arranged around a large peristyle of six by nine columns. A gallery ran along three sides, the fourth (to the east) opening on to a hall through three doors. In the style later common in the east, the hall was provided with a central fountain, marble paving and wall decorations, high ceiling and benches around the walls. To the south is the House of Pilasters. The rooms are grouped around a peristyled courtyard with the main reception rooms off the courtyard to the north, though the plan is less symmetrical and more obscured by later rebuilding. (The third house is less fully excavated, its plan partly concealed by the modern road.)

To reach the **theatre**, head back to the orientation point on the *cardo* and keep going along the modern road west. It is located behind a row of houses in a natural hollow left of the road immediately before it reaches the citadel. The ancient remains (tentatively dated to the late second century AD) are rather hard to appreciate from close quarters. Most of the masonry seems to have been carried away to support building activity in the town over the centuries. Some idea of the theatre's scale (it was perhaps the largest in the Roman world – 139 m in diameter with a façade of 145 m) can be gauged by looking back from the walls of the citadel.

The Ottoman caravanserai lies on the southern end of the modern village just below the escarpment. The 16th century building has been converted into a **Museum** of mosaics, inscriptions, sarcophagi, funerary stelae and statuary collected from the region of Apamea. The caravanserai itself is an impressive building, 80 m square with a vast internal courtyard entered by a single gateway from the north. It is perhaps the most imposing of the surviving caravan stops built in Syria by the Ottomans to service the pilgrimage route from Istanbul to Mecca.

The courtyard has an impressive range of military stelae underlining Apamea's role as a legionary headquarters comprising a strategic reserve for the eastern frontier. The stones, mostly commemorating members of the II Parthica legion (first half of third century AD), were recovered by dismantling one of the towers of the eastern wall where the inscribed stones had been reused in the late Roman rebuilding of the defences. Enter the museum by the door to the left of the entrance passageway and proceed clockwise. As there is no catalogue, the following notes, in part based on Janine Balty's survey, give a brief account of the more easily identifiable finds displayed.

The large mosaic set into the floor of the northeastern wing as you enter depicts **Socrates and the Sages** – 2.62 m by 1.3 m, third quarter of fourth century – from the building which preceded the eastern cathedral, dated 362–3. Socrates surrounded by six bearded sages, each wearing the plain *pallium* of a philosopher, seated at a curved table. The faces are superb examples of late Roman mosaic work and reveal the presence in Apamea of a strong centre of neo-Platonic philosophy, attracted by the teachings of Iamblichus. Janine Balty notes the resemblance between this scene and the depiction of Christ at table surrounded by his disciples. Perhaps, she observes, this is Christ 'repaganised', part of a process of rediscovering the Hellenism of the past given new impulse at this time by the decrees of Julian the Apostate (361–3).

A number of funerary stelae are displayed on the exterior wall to the left. They are set out in chronological order from Hellenistic times to the third century AD.

In the middle of this (northern) outer wall is a sarcophagus decorated with cupids found in the northern necropolis – second century AD. The Latin inscription is to a 44 year old ex-legionnaire of 22 years'

service, dedicated by his wife. In the middle of the wall opposite, another sarcophagus from the same tomb, this time dedicated by a centurion in the II Parthica Legion in honour of his wife of 28 years.

Turn the corner but stay with the left (outer) wall. The fourth object on the left after the turn is a plaque found at pavement level on the *cardo* recording the dedication of a statue installed on the column bracket above, in honour of a Lucius Julius Agrippa. Other inscriptions were carved onto the consoles of the columns as can be seen further on to the left.

Further again along the left wall, opposite the second mosaic set into the floor, is a statue of a woman (head missing) found near the *nymphaeum* and which probably was part of the decoration of the monument. The mosaic just mentioned is a long scene depicting the **Judgment of the Nereides** – 7.69 m by 1.56 m, third quarter of third century – from the *triclinos*. A work of exceptional interest, this frieze of 13 figures depicts a contest between the Nereides and Thetis on the one hand and Cassiopeia on the other to determine who was the most beautiful. The winner, Cassiopeia, is the nude figure second from the right. The judge of the contest, Poseidon, is fourth from the right. Next is an Amazon mosaic from the *triclinos*, Apamea, fifth century.

The southwest corner and west wing of the building now display finds of the Christian era.

• Huarte, Church of St Michael (AD 487), hunting scene, animals capture
• ossuary (AD 483)
• same church, animal scene
• West hall
• Huarte, Church of St Michael (AD 487), mosaic from the portico including figure of Adam
• animal mosaic from Huarte baptistery (AD 384).

The provenance of many of these mosaics is **Huarte**, 11 km to the northwest, in the Jebel Zawiye (tarmac road from northwest corner of ruins). The monastery of Huarte (fourth or fifth century) comprised two parallel churches – that to the north is dedicated to St Michael the Archangel; the larger southern one was built in 487 by Bishop Photios. They are largely confined to foundations and lower walls. The existence of two churches is perhaps explained by the need to keep some distance between the official cult (which discouraged giving too much attention to angels) and the popular traditions of the parishioners. A mithraeum, apparently frequented by soldiers from Apamea, was recently found under the western end of the Photios church. The 7.2 m by 4.8 m chamber and vestibule contained mural paintings representing typical mithraitic scenes including a figure of Helios (now in the *Hama museum).

See separate entry on the Ayyubid citadel, *Qalaat Mudiq.

REFS: Apamea: Balty, Janine (ed.) 1984: 103–34; Balty, Janine 1977; Balty, J-C Guide 1981; Balty, J-C 'Groupe episcopal' 1972; Balty, J.& J-C ANRW 1979; van Berchem & Fatio 1914: 189; Sauvaget 'Caravanserails syriens' 1937: 110; Viviers 2007. Huarte: Canivet, M-T & P 1979; Canivet, P 'Huarte' CFAS 1989: 215–9; Gawlikowski 'Un nouveau mithraeum' CRAI 2000.

Arwad

ارواد

VARIANTS: Arvad (Phn/bib); Arados (Grk); Aradus (Lat); Ruwad
PERIOD: Phn/../Arb   RATING: T   MAP: R2

LOCATION: 3 km offshore (southwest) from *Tartus. Take ferry service from jetty along the Tartus esplanade (opposite the old fortress walls, south end).

History

At the beginning of his study of Arwad's role in the classical world, J-P Rey-Coquais notes that on first sight descending the hills towards the coast the tiny island appears lost in a vast sea. Tiny though it is, Arwad has had an extraordinary history. Any place that has its origins written up in Genesis (X, 18) must be destined for a role of some significance. As the sole habitable island off the Syrian coast and

the only sizeable natural port between Tripoli and the mouth of the Orontes its inhabitants were able at times to dominate large areas of the fertile coastal region. The island's natural role as a fortress (the name derives from the Phoenician word for 'refuge') was made possible by a fresh water spring which rose from the seabed between Arwad and the coast, providing a capacity to resist sieges beyond the limited resources from rainwater.

Originally settled as an urban centre by the Canaanites, Arwad was a prosperous trading centre (mentioned in the Amarna archives) by the late second millennium. It was taken by the Pharaoh Tuthmosis III during his fifth campaign in Syria. Under the Phoenicians, it became the base for a series of settlements of the coast as far as *Jeble (25 km south of *Latakia) and inland almost to Homs and to the cult centre at Baetocecea (*Husn Suleiman). Like Tyre (southern Lebanon), its seafaring skills gave it an important role in eastern Mediterranean trade in the first half of the first millennium BC. It used its status in the mainland federation to secure access to timber for shipbuilding.

Arwad was later taken by the Assyrians and the Achaemenid Persians. (Arvadites fought in Xerxes' fleet in 480 BC at the Battle of Salamis – Herodotus VII, 98.) In 333 BC, Arwad's King Gerostratos quickly put his domains at the disposal of Alexander. His voluntary association with Greek rule enabled Arwad to retain a measure of independence under the Seleucids, especially when the Seleucid monarchs needed to engage its support against the Ptolemies to the south. (Like other Phoenician centres, its local monarchy had quietly been dropped by the mid third century BC.) In the mid second century BC, however, Arwad fell out of favour after siding with the Egyptians, though it later recovered its limited autonomy until the Roman conquest in 64 BC. (It was subsequently punished for siding with Pompey in the civil war of 46 BC and was caught off-side again in 41 when the islanders burned alive an envoy of Mark Antony who had come to demand the return of a brother of Cleopatra.) Its freedom of manoeuvre was further eroded under Roman rule. It lost control of the federated mainland centres and its role diminished with the rise of a new mainland town, Tartus. The island became, in Rey-Coquais' words, a sort of 'museum town'. St Paul is said to have stopped there on his journey to Rome. It was a Byzantine naval base but fell to the Arabs late (640), holding out after mainland Syria. The Templars were given custody of the island during the Crusader presence. From Arwad, the Crusaders made their last stand, hanging on until 1302, many years after the fall of the great mainland bastions – the *Krak (1271), *Qalaat Marqab (1285), Tripoli (1289) – and a decade after the loss of Acre and their last bases on the mainland, Athlit and *Tartus (1291). In 1302, however, the last Crusader troops were slaughtered, the surviving Templar knights taken into captivity in Cairo and the Frankish fortress largely demolished.

Visit

Arwad has become something of a local tourist attraction, especially in summer with many visitors to its fish restaurants.

Oval in shape and aligned approximately northwest-southeast, the island is small (less than 800 m long; 300 m wide) and can be visited in a couple of hours. The port lies in the northwest quarter, its position facing the coast providing relatively safe anchorage from winter storms. The anchorage is divided by a low promontory which was artificially built up to serve as a jetty in ancient times. On the western and southwestern sides, the island was once protected by a long wall of the Phoenician or later periods. Remnants of the huge retaining blocks can be seen.

There are two small castles. The one in the middle of the island was originally the 13th century fort held by the Templars and is open as a national monument. The other, an Ayyubid fort ('al-Burj') protecting the port, is usually locked.

REFS: Grainger 1990: 92–5 *et passim;* Rey-Coquais *Arados* 1974.

Atil

عطيل

VARIANTS: Athela   (Lat)   PERIOD: Rom
RATING: * MAP: R1

LOCATION: 12 km south of *Shahba (6 kms north of *Suweida) on the Damascus/Suweida road.

Two apparently identical small temples were constructed here in Roman times. Sources give no explanation as to why the same plan, design and ornamentation were used in each building, one on the north edge of town, the second about 250 m to the southwest. The southern one is better preserved in that its façade is fully exposed. The plan is two Corinthian columns *in antae* (each carrying a bracket) on a high portico supporting a semi-circular arch interrupting the entablature. The northern temple was until recently encumbered by a modern dwelling and the façade has been partly reassembled. It preserves, however, the internal lateral arch which supported the roof. The quality of the rich decoration is quite fine and recalls the temple at *Mushennef.

Like many other settlements in the Hauran (ancient Auranitis – see box 'Hauran' page 300), Atil's building program seems to date from the second century AD when the area's prosperity derived from the grain trade. On the southern temple, an inscription records its construction in the 14th year of the reign of Antoninus Pius (AD 151). The other temple was built in 211–2, the high-water mark of the imperial classical style in the Hauran, probably dedicated to the Nabataean deity, Theandrites.

REFS: Abu Assaf 1998: 47; Butler *AE* II 1903: 343–6; Butler *PE* II A 5 1915: 355–6; Dussaud 1927: 349.,

B

Baghuz (Abu Kemal)

الباغوز

VARIANTS: Nagiateh, Corsoteh (anc); Irzi
(Arb) PERIOD: Rom RATING: – MAP: R5

LOCATION: 130 km southeast of *Deir
al-Zor on the left bank of the Euphrates.
Take the Euphrates crossing 4 km before
Abu Kemal. The five towers are strung out
over 4 km on the edge of the bluff bordering the river flats. Follow tracks along the
escarpment as far as the point where the
river makes a wide sweep south before
the border with Iraq. As this is a sensitive
border area, check conditions.

Those with a passion for funerary towers
in the style of Palmyra can satisfy their
spirit of adventure by visiting the small
group on the left bank of the Euphrates at
Baghuz, opposite the Syrian-Iraqi border
town of Abu Kemal.

The funerary towers date from before
the high Palmyrene period when this was
the necropolis area for a Parthian frontier
settlement (possibly established in the
second century BC).[1] Two towers are in
reasonable condition with recognisable
architectural detail on their façades
(two pilasters enclosing semi-columns;
staircases rising to upper storeys) though
the protective plaster facing has largely
disappeared. The largest ('Abu Jelal', the
central of the group of five) is 5.7 m² in
plan. The tomb's northern façade is the
best preserved with a stepped base,
corner pilasters and two engaged columns
supporting a bulky entablature. There is
some resemblance to the later Palmyra
towers which used a system of niches or
loculi to hold the remains of the dead in
the tower superstructure but the Baghuz
towers also used basement chambers for
burial. The main purpose of the tower
above was probably to provide a roof

terrace for funerary rituals. Certainly
the style, methods of construction and
architectural treatment are cruder than at
Palmyra. The tombs, however, provide a
rare glimpse of the Parthian architectural
style: 'the Doric order under the Parthian
mask' (Toll).

Baghuz was the site of the even more
ancient Nagiateh with pottery remains
going back to the fifth millennium BC
and an extensive necropolis of the early
second millennium BC. The ruins of
Corsoteh, mentioned by Xenophon (c
400 BC), were located here.

REFS: Bell *Amurath* 1911: 83–4; Clauss 'Les tours
funéraires du Djebel Baghouz' *Syria* 2002: 155–94;
Toll 1946: 146–50, pl LXV 1–4; Will 1949: 258–
312.

Bakas (Shugur Qadim)

الشغو قديم

VARIANTS: Bakas-Shugur[2]; Bakas Shoqr
PERIOD: Cru RATING: T MAP: R2

LOCATION: Reaching the village of
Shugur Qadim is easy enough. Take the
Latakia road from Jisr al-Shugur (starting point, main square). At 6.6 km, turn
right, following the sealed road +4.5 km
to village. Now the hard bit. Though the
remains of the castle are almost at arm's
length across a ravine from the village
mosque, you will need to choose one of
two routes to try on foot – either a brief
but hair-raising scramble across the rock-
face of the ravine; or a longer circuit, looping through the ravine below the village
(20 minute hike). A good view of the site
(but no access to the castle) can be obtained 1 km before the village by walking
down the ridge to the right.

The most breath-taking castle site in Syria.
The minimal remains of this Crusader
fortress perch precariously on a high
promontory hundreds of metres above a
sharp bend in the river, the Nahr al-Abiad
(a tributary of the Orontes). The nearby
village of Shugur Qadim is a stop on the

---

1 The Parthian town was probably on the
river flats and has long since been swept away
by the seasonal floods.

2 In recent centuries, the two castles were
given different names – Bakas (the Crusader
name for the whole complex) was applied to
the south and Shugur to the northern part.

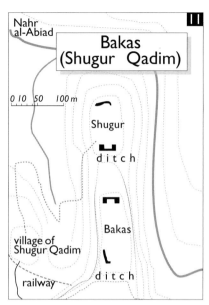

Bakas
(Shugur Qadim)

0 10 50 100 m

Shugur

d i t c h

Bakas

village of
Shugur Qadim

d i t c h
railway

Nahr
al-Abiad

Aleppo-Latakia railway and the ridge that runs down to the castle is pierced by a railway tunnel. While the remains are hard to relate to the original construction, it is worth the effort of the final walk to enjoy the splendour of the scene and the views of the mountainous country to the north, with the river rushing away at a dizzying distance below to the east.

The northern end of the site had been fortified by the Byzantines. It was rebuilt and extended along the southern reaches of the promontory by the Crusaders but the date of their occupation is not known.[3] Due to the narrowness of the site, the Crusaders divided the fortifications between two separate compounds. The lower northern keep, Shugur (over 200 m long but only 30 m wide), was separated from the southern fortification, Bakas, by an open space protected by two small ditches. To separate the southern compound from the adjoining heights, a deep trench was cut in the rock.

The twin castles fell to Saladin in his famous campaign of 1188 when he rolled back the greater part of the Crusader presence on the eastern side of the coastal mountains (see box on Saladin's Campaign of 1188 – page 16). The attack began immediately after the fall of the Château de Saône (*Qalaat Saladin) on 30 July. The southern compound fell to Saladin on 5 August, the Crusaders taking refuge in the lower redoubt to the north. The garrison surrendered on 12 August having failed in their attempts to attract help from Bohemond III, Prince of Antioch, in whose realms the castle lay. The Mongols took the fortress, probably in 1260, but Baybars seized it from them in the next decade. An earthquake caused serious damage in 1404, beginning the process of decay which has reduced the ruins to a few fragments of walls and cisterns.

REFS: Deschamps *Châteaux III* 1973: 349–50; Dussaud *Topographie* 1927: 155–62; Huygens 1972: 279–80; Runciman II 1965: 470; van Berchem & Fatio 1914: 251–59.

Bamuqqa

باموقا

VARIANTS: Bamuka PERIOD: Rom/Byz ALT: 590 m RATING: – MAPS: R3, R3a

LOCATION: 55 km west of Aleppo. From the Bab al-Hawa turnoff (starting point of Itin 9b) follow the road to *Harim for c10.5 km until you reach the village of Bashmishli (at the point where the road turns left to Barisha). Keep going to the western edge of Bashmishli and just before the edge of town turn right onto a small tarmac road 500 m .

Once you reach it, it is hard to resist the charm of this setting, one of the most perfect picnic spots in all of Syria. The remains are scattered about the oak grove on a ridge that looks down over the Plain of Amuq, east of Antioch. As a place of refuge from the heat on a warm day and to savour the beauty of the Limestone Massif environment, Bamuqqa is well worth the short hike.

Moreover, the site includes a remarkable Roman ruin, a sizeable **villa** with which

---

3 There is no mention of the castle in Crusader records. Our information comes from Arab written sources, especially the accounts of Saladin's campaign of 1188.

are associated (140 m to the south) a large cistern and an underground tomb with a pillared façade. There are remains (north) of 16 more modest farmhouses of a later period and, in the same area, a small church (sixth century).

Tchalenko dates the original farmhouse as early as the first century AD and speculates that the easy communications from this area to Antioch and the favourable soil made it one of the first areas settled by the moneyed class which Roman occupation brought into existence. He describes this farmhouse as 'one of the most interesting monuments of the region'. It comprises two rooms, one above the other and connected by an external staircase. The local (Alawi) villagers use them these days to hold fuel lamps as the grove and farmhouse harbour the tomb of a local saint, Sheikh Khalil Sadeq.[4] The use of the grove for religious purposes has probably discouraged the dismantling of the remains for building materials.

The dating of the villa (and the tomb, probably commemorating the first proprietor) is disputed. Butler believed it dated from the second or third century. Tchalenko prefers the first century because of the earlier style of the decoration: 'Since its characteristics recall no other Syrian building influenced by Roman styles, we have to resort to a local Antiochene tradition of which this is perhaps the sole extant example.' He also compares the tomb to the one in *Beshindlaye but notes the richer decoration of the latter. Tchalenko surmised that the villa was the occasional residence of a landlord who lived most of the year in Antioch, leaving the running of the olive farm to a local overseer and visiting for the harvest season, one of the first signs of the systematic agricultural exploitation of the mountainous area. (Beshindlaye was probably settled about the same time.) Most other Roman sites in the area date from the second century.

4 Pena et al Inventaire 1990: 53 notes that the stele marking the saint's tomb was erected in 1196, some time after Nur al-Din had taken *Harem and the area of Jebel Barisha from the Crusaders.

No other houses seem to have been built in Bamuqqa until the fourth century. The 16 independent farm houses (north of the Roman villa – see above) established by the fifth century reflect the explosion of small-holder operations in the Byzantine period. After the curiously late construction of the main **church** (apparently not built until the decades immediately before the Muslim conquest – extreme north of the site), the town was abandoned in the seventh century but reoccupied in the 12th century.

REFS: Butler AE II 1903: 63, 79; Pena (et al) Cenobites 1983 : 62; Pena Inventaire 1987: 52–6; Tchalenko Villages I 1953: 300–18; II 1953: pl XCII–XCIX, CXIV, CXXXV.

Banastur

See **Burjke, Fafertin, Surkunya & Banastur**

Baqirha

VARIANTS: Burj Baqirha, Bakirha (Arb)
PERIOD: Rom/Byz RATING: * MAP: R3, R3a

LOCATION: From the turn-off just before Bab el Hawa (starting point) turn left; go via Sarmada, take right road and ascend steep hill (Harim road); at 9.4 km, a sign in English points right to Baqirha; follow the road (past Babuta on right) for +1 km to Roman temple of Zeus Bombos on the right; churches and town are lower down the slope.

An exceptionally interesting site on the edge of the hills looking over the Plain of Amuq (east of Antioch) and the Amanus Mountains to the north. In the distance are further 'dead cities' up to the Turkish frontier.

The **Roman temple** whose surprisingly intact remains stand on the southern edge of the site consists of a *cella* preceded by a four-columned portico of which one shaky column (with a superb Corinthian capital) was until recently still standing. The surrounding compound wall has been removed except for the monumental gateway dated by inscription to AD 161. The temple is dedicated to Zeus Bombos (Zeus of the Altar) but was probably established on the site of an earlier Semitic cult centre. Butler notes: 'The site may easily have been one of the 'high places' of the early inhabitants which the Roman conquerors chose further to sanctify by the building of a shrine which should give a Greco-Roman character to this ancient Oriental place of worship and clothe the old tradition with the dignity of classic architecture'.

There were other temples to Zeus in the area, notably the one whose remains can still be traced on the top of nearby Jebel Sheikh Barakat (*Qatura).[5] The Baqirha temple, however, is the best preserved and is a remarkable sight in this sweeping landscape. Butler described 'the treatment of the whole edifice and its decorative effect (as) the most chaste and dignified in all Syria' – ie lacking the later 'coarse over-elaboration' found at Baalbek. The fact that most of the fabric of the temple *cella* remains makes it a prime candidate for reconstruction one day.

Tchalenko's researches in the area emphasise the importance of the olive oil processing industry in the establishment and subsequent prosperity of the town. He notes that the first presses were probably set up in the second century AD under the auspices of the temple but later greatly expanded in private hands. The industry flourished given the area's easy access to Antioch and the sea. It laid the basis for the later expansion of the settlement during the Byzantine period, hence the remarkable extent of the ruins in the lower town.

A kilometre down the hill from the temple, the jumbled ruins of this extensive Byzantine town contain much of interest but at first sight the confusion seems total. There are two important churches, however, the first of which can be identified relatively easily. This the **eastern church** standing on the eastern

5 At Baqirha, Zeus Bombos (Grk: 'altar'), is equivalent to the Aramaic version, Zeus Madbachos, on Jebel Sheikh Barakat.

edge of the town, the western façade and *narthex* of which have survived almost intact although the rest of the building is in ruins. The church is dated, by inscription, to 546 and is a columned basilica of six bays. Even for the Jebel Barisha region, where heavy use of decoration prevailed, the degree of moulded decorative courses is extraordinary, the effect being somewhat like drooping spaghetti. The interior decoration is also free-wheeling, with considerable departure from classical models in the column bases, capitals and mouldings of the chancel arch. The western portal is a copy of the famous doorways of the architect Kyros.

The second **(western) church** was probably part of a monastic institution. Little survives except the eastern wall. The central nave included a *bema*. In date it is earlier – 501 according to the inscription on the northern gate, though parts of the compound are perhaps earlier (first half of the fifth century). The compound includes a baptistery, almost a cube in shape and richly decorated with grooved mouldings. Note especially the classic shape of the east door to the courtyard, originally preceded by a portico.

A good tarmac road allows access to the sites to the northwest – Burj al-Deruni, Dar Qita and Babisqa.

REFS: Butler AE II 1903: 66–9, 190–3, 209–12; Butler EC 1929: 133–4, 139, 145, 148, 153, 157; Butler PE II B 4 1909: 195–201; Callot & Marcillet-Jaubert 1989: 184–5; Lassus Sanctuaires chrétiens 1947: 35, 45, 59, 222, 292; Mattern 1944: 70–3; Pena Inventaire 1987: 72–5; Tchalenko Villages I 1953: 51 n3, 106–7, 110–1; Tchalenko & Baccache 1979–80: pl 323–334.

Bara

بارة

VARIANTS: Kapropera (Grk); Kfer al-Bara, al-Kfer (Arb) PERIOD: Byz ALT: 670 m RATING: ** MAP: R3

LOCATION: From Aleppo, follow the main Damascus highway for 67 km, taking the Latakia road (right) at Saraqeb junction. Pass the al-Riha turnoff and continue on c+5 km to Urum al-Joz (25 km from Saraqeb). From here take the road south (left) for +14 km to Bara. The site can also be reached (from Damascus) by turning off the Aleppo road at *Maarat al-Numan and taking the road west to Kfer Nabil then north (+5 km) to Bara.

In terms of size and variety of remains, this is one of the most impressive of the 'dead cities' and one which those unfamiliar with the area might choose as a good starting point. The site is huge, extending over an area of 2 km by 3 km and although some motor access roads to the parts of major interest have recently been laid, you need to be prepared for a fair bit of rock fence climbing and walking across often muddy fields.

History

The importance of the settlement resulted from its location between the two major sections of Jebel Zawiye, the trough in which it is located forming a north-south corridor essential for internal access. Though it expanded rapidly during its boom period in the fifth and sixth centuries, settlement at Bara only began in the fourth century. The site was blessed with a plentiful supply of underground water and the first settlers gathered around a church on the eastern edge of the Wadi al-Goz (west of the modern village, running parallel with the main road). At about the same period, a second development, originally isolated in its own compound (temenos), began at the great basilica today called al-Husn (north of the main agglomeration).

The settlement rapidly enriched itself through its olive oil and wine industry. By the fifth century, according to Tchalenko, Bara became the processing point for other surrounding villages. An area to the north, called al-Muallaq, developed around huge monastic properties. A series of private farms also sprang up in the sectors known as al-Deir, Deir Sobat, Braij and Deir Debbane. It eventually included five churches which can still be recognised (and another three referred to in sources). The style of buildings was lavish, indicating the high level of

prosperity, and the processing facilities, particularly olive oil presses, were built to industrial standard. The people who could finance these buildings could also afford to bury themselves in style and there are two pyramidal-roofed tomb buildings from the sixth century built on a monumental scale.

Settlement here does not seem to have been disrupted by the Muslim conquest, perhaps because the scale of the centre was much greater than the average. Its location on a natural transport route and relatively near the edge of the limestone region gave it a more diversified role. Its economy thus survived the collapse of the export trade following the disruption of trade routes to the west.

When the Crusaders reached Bara after their capture of Antioch in 1098, they found a Bishop still in residence (affiliated to Constantinople). Raymond de Saint Gilles, Count of Toulouse (later Count of Tripoli), took control of the town on 25 September 1098, and later installed a Latin Bishop. (The latter distinguished himself by urging on those responsible for the horrendous massacre at nearby *Maarat al-Numan in January 1099 when 20,000 Muslims – men, women and children – were slaughtered by the Crusading forces.) The area remained under Crusader control until 1148. They fortified their presence with the building of Qalaat Abu Safian but thereafter Bara reverted to the Muslims.

Visit

Given the difficulty of finding your way between the olive groves, the rock-piled fences and broken terrain, many visitors will be tempted simply to take the site as it comes, which is not a bad first approach. However, for a visit aimed at taking in as many of the main buildings as possible in a period of three or four hours, the following sequence may be useful.

The ruins run roughly north-south, to the right of the Urum al-Joz–Kfer Nabil main road as you head south. A good place to start a tour would be the monastery of

Deir Sobat which lies on the southern edge of the ruins. You reach it by a laneway which heads west out of the southern part of the village of al-Kfer al-Bara and crosses the deep *wadi*. The monastery is on the slopes as you ascend the *wadi* and is reasonably well preserved, part of its upper walls recently reconstructed.

The central building is dated to the sixth century. It comprises a large central chamber off which corridors and rooms are arranged. The room on the east side was probably an oratory for the celebration of Mass. Two other monasteries were located in the south – Deir Debbane and al-Deir – but are in a poorer state of preservation.

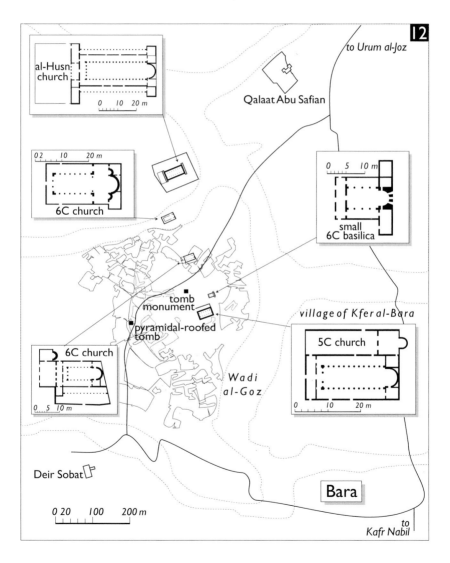

al-Husn church

0   10   20 m

12

to Urum al-Joz

Qalaat Abu Safian

0 2   10   20 m

6C church

0   5   10 m

small
6C basilica

tomb
monument

pyramidal-roofed
tomb

village of Kfer al-Bara

6C church

0   5   10 m

5C church

Wadi
al-Goz

0   10   20 m

Deir Sobat

Bara

0 20   100   200 m

to
Kafr Nabil

Working your way north, you should now head for the first of the **pyramidal-roofed tombs**, visible about 200 m away. (A tarmac road now leads past it; turn off before you descend the *wadi* again.) This is the larger of the two examples and has a roof based on a considerably elongated pyramid. A beautiful band of carved acanthus leaf decoration surrounds the top of the cubed base and is repeated over the lintel of the door. It is interrupted by the interweaving of the Christian 'chi-ro' symbol. The corners were terminated in pilasters of Corinthian design. Altogether, the effect on a building of relatively exuberant shape is to add an element of restraint and classical balance. Inside, the burial chamber contains five sarcophagi with further decoration. The substantially smaller second tomb is in excellent condition.

The five **churches** of Bara stretch along the central line of ruins from a point roughly 100 m east of the large tomb monument. The group ends 500 m to the north in the church known as al-Husn. You may wish to explore this central area of churches and substantial villas by planning your own fence-hopping.

Beginning from the south, the first church in the sequence is a large (25 m by 17 m) example from the fifth century. Immediately to the northeast is a smaller (sixth century) church, perhaps part of a monastery. Eighty metres north of the large tomb monument is the third church and, 200 m north-northwest, the fourth. Mattern notes that the latter, a sixth century construction, barely distinguishable in its ruined state, has each of its three aisles terminate in a semi-circular apse. Continue another 50 m north and you should end up at the al-Husn compound which provided a convenient point for the Arabs to fortify in the late Crusader period. The church of al-Husn is notable for its size (c50 m by 35 m within a compound of 100 m by 60 m), its side porticos and the use of a gallery above the side aisles but very little of this can be appreciated given the lack of walls.

About 400 m to the northeast, you will find the remains of another Crusader-period fort **Qalaat Abu Safian**. It comprises a donjon, protected by walls of 4–5 m and a surrounding wall with bastions in two corners.

REFS: Butler AE II 1903: 97; Butler EC 1929: 66–7; de Vogüé I 1865–77: 93, 105–6; Tchalenko II 1953: pl XII, LXXXI, CXXXVII–IX, CCXII; Mattern 1944: 35–4.

Barad

بر اد

VARIANTS: Kaprobarada (Grk), Barade (Lat) PERIOD: Rom/Byz ALT: 490 m RATING: – MAP: R3

LOCATION: From Deir Semaan, 14 km north along Afrin road. On north edge of al-Barsuta (Crusader Basuet), turn right along a road that ascends the plateau and continues southeast for +10 km. It is also possible to reach Barad via the Azaz road north of Aleppo via Nabbul to the east.

An extensive site (in area, the largest in the Jebel Semaan zone) located on a plateau with a rich variety of remains including a classical tomb, a public bath house and three churches (one a major basilica). From the second century, Barad was a small provincial city with its own industries, rather than a rural settlement. It was probably the headquarters of an administrative district controlling the northern part of the limestone country. The oil industry was considerably expanded in the fourth century when the principal cathedral replaced the pagan temple. The surrounding terrain offered a variety of crops in addition to olives including grains and grapes.

The only notable surviving building in classical style is the **monumental tomb**, probably dating from the second or the first half of the third century AD and located on the northern edge of the town. The style is rather heavy (not unlike the monumental arch in *Latakia though on a smaller scale) with four typically Syrian-Roman arches holding up a medium-pitched pyramidal roof. This structure rests on a podium base under which is the burial chamber, originally housing five sarcophagi, four within burial niches, one free-standing. Within the open structure itself, two further sarcophagi were placed on the podium. It is, says Butler, 'the earliest, and quite the most sumptuous, of this particular type of tomb structure which continued to be built through the fourth century in northern Syria.'[6] The idea of the four-faced arch is essentially classical but much of the detail is oriental in inspiration, particularly the horseshoe shape of the arches and the moulding of the cornice. At the top of the arches originally stood a series of four busts.

in southern Syria) but Tchalenko believes they were built in the second century as part of the landowner's mansion that preceded the later village.

The great **cathedral** of Barad (or Church of Julianos, centre of the town) is one of the largest church buildings in Syria, apart from the pilgrimage centre of Saint Simeon. Sadly, it is almost a complete ruin and there is little to appreciate beyond a few piers and part of the east wall. The plan is typical of the period (399–402) in northern Syria, the rear wall, for

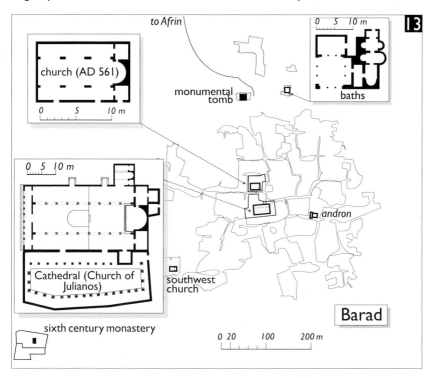

The ruins of the **baths** complex (northern edge of the settlement, 100 m northwest of the mausoleum) provide one of the few examples from the Roman period in Syria. In style the low-vaulted rooms are quite different from the fifth century baths at *Serjilla. Butler dates the building to the third century (cf baths at *Bosra

6 Butler *PE* II B 6 1920: 299

example, being flat and the curved apse accommodated by complicated masonry to square the circle. The arcades of the nave are supported on eight columns and two piers. A *bema* stood in the central nave. There are still some classical touches such as the rectangular west central doorway with dignified jambs and lintel. But above it, the Syrian influence is strong in the more flamboyant use of arches (seen in Butler or Tchalenko's reconstructions). The west entrance was preceded by a colonnaded portico. To the south stood an oblong atrium.

Slightly to the northeast lies the **northern church** dated by inscription to 561. Better preserved than the cathedral, the naves are divided by three sweeping arches carried on two free-standing piers, an arrangement more common at this time in the southern parts of the limestone country (*Qalb Lozeh, *Ruweiha) and in southern Syria. The sixth century taste for swooping moulded decoration is indulged in the external treatment of the upper windows.

The *andron* or meeting place lies 100 m to the east of the cathedral. Not unlike a large house in appearance, with double portico along the front, the fact that the lower storey was undivided favours the interpretation that it had some civic purpose. The second storey was supported on three wide (5 m) arches spanning the ground floor. The building is dated to 496. To the east lie the remains of an inn (207–8) and an oil press.

The **southwest church** (sixth century) lies in that quarter of the main quadrilateral of ruins. The nave is undivided and the sanctuary square in plan. Along the southern wall runs a colonnade. The windows are framed by looping incised decorations, a rather overdone effect in this case.

1200 m to the southwest of the main agglomeration lie the ruins of a sixth century **monastery** (also known as Qasr al-Barad) on the crest of a knoll. Access is difficult as there is no road. Best path is to follow the footpath from the southwest church. The single-naved chapel is reasonably intact and remains can be seen from the high tower (22 m south of the western end of the chapel) and other buildings including the hostelry (17 m east of the chapel).

REFS: Butler *EC* 1929: 109–10, 142; Butler *PE* II B 6 1920: 299–315; Mattern 1944: 140; Tchalenko

Villages II 1953: pl XV, XIX, CXXXIII, CCVII; Tchalenko & Baccache 1979–80: pl 5–32.

Basofan

باصوفان

VARIANTS: Basufan PERIOD: Byz RATING: – MAP: R3, R3a

LOCATION: Take the road which heads north from Saint Simeon. Continue for 5 km as the road bends south then heads northeast. Ruins of the church on eastern side of village, south of the road. (NOTE: +1.5 km east are the remains of Kfer Lab.)

The remains are not particularly striking at first sight as the ruins are disguised among modern houses. The Church of St Phocas (dated 491–2)[7] is one of the largest churches in the Jebel Semaan area (it measures 15.4 m by 24 m) and was apparently destroyed by fire. The columned basilica is closely related in style to the martyrium of *Saint Simeon, particularly in the way in which the curve of the rear wall of the apse is retained on the exterior instead of being filled in by a straight wall between the line of the two side chambers as in earlier examples. Tchalenko speculates that it could have been built by the same craftsmen as Saint Simeon. Butler also draws attention to the two columns with Corinthian (wind blown) capitals and spiral fluting that once supported the chancel arch. (The column capitals are no longer in situ.) The decorative treatment of the south wall is particularly interesting. (The wall is partly enclosed in a farmstead and a medieval tower; the rest is covered by vegetation.) The use of moulded bands to divide the wall and surround the windows with festoons, was a style Beyer believed stemmed from the nearby church of St Simeon.

Butler comments[8] that 'it is a pity this

7 The inscription recording the date is in Syriac, the language much more commonly found in the Jebel Semaan area than in the south of the limestone country more directly influenced from Greek-oriented Antioch or Apamea.
8 *EC* 1929: 67.

church is so ruinous for in it we have a summing up of the architecture of the fifth century and a carrying to their ultimate forms of expression of a number of motives that have been developing for a century'.[9]

REFS: Beyer 1925: 58; Biscop and Sodini p 282; Butler EC 1929: 67–70, 127; Butler PE II B 6 1920: 284–7; Krautheimer 1981: 160; Tchalenko Villages II 1953: pl LXXIV.

Batuta and Sinhar

باطوطة و سنهار

VARIANTS: Simkhar PERIOD: Byz RATING: – MAP: 3a

LOCATION: Batuta is 4 kms northeast of Dar Tazeh, approachable by a sealed road but the route may be confusing given the proliferation of settlements. Can also be reached by branching south off the road to *Basofan c2.5 km after St Simeon's. After +1 km along the Burjke road, branch again south and follow track for +2.3 kms to Batuta. Sinhar is +2.3 km along the continuation.

In **Batuta** a single-nave chapel with rectangular plan and distyle porch intact, described by Butler, is now ruined. A separate church, of early date, retains its apse and south arcade. Each column capital is a different type. Villa dated AD 363. Hadjar notes that many homes are in polygonal stone and date to the Roman period.

The main destination of this diversion, though, is **Sinhar**. 'There is not a more interesting or beautiful ruin than this in the Jebel Semaan'. Butler's description is borne out by the superb remains of decorated facades in the rich local tradition. Fourth century church whose dimensions are 11m by 20 m. As Hadjar notes, a huge project for this isolated area. A single-nave chapel was added in the sixth century onto the southeastern façade; its western face carries beautiful decoration in the form of stylized garlands.

REFS: **Batuta**: Hadjar 2000: 116; Butler PE II B 6 9 EC 1929: 67.

1920: 330–2; Villages II 1953: pl CXXVIII; **Sinhar**: Butler PE II B 6 1920: 334–5; Hadjar 2000: 116.

Behyo

بهيو

PERIOD: Byz ALT: 720 m RATING: – MAPS: R3, R3a

LOCATION: See *Beshindlaye. Before Beshindlaye, stop at 28 km and climb up the steep hill to the left – 10 minute scramble. (The ruins are not visible from this point on the road.)

At first sight, this village lying on the crest of the Jebel al-Ala and looking down over the Plain of Self to the east presents an indecipherable jumble of huge rocks, impossibly tumbled in disorder. On closer inspection, you should be able to distinguish two sizeable churches. Why such a large community would have gathered in this isolated spot, surrounded by no apparent plots of arable land, is still difficult to fathom. The researches of Tchalenko have devoted considerable attention to this site. It was apparently a late starter, being developed for olive growing only after other, more easily exploited, sites had been settled. (The more arable areas such as *Bamuqqa had been farmed as early as the first century AD.)

Behyo did not attract settlement until the boom in olive oil prices in the fifth century justified the development of its relatively marginal potential. By this period, the olive oil industry was no longer dominated by the large landlords but had been transformed by the activities of small-holders. According to Tchalenko 'it is probably this village ... which represents most faithfully the changes in the ancient habitat of the region which evolved from the great aristocratic holdings into an agglomeration of small agricultural establishments.'

The ruins include a variety of house types of the fifth and sixth centuries – villas, farmhouses, workers' cottages. Remains of many olive presses are found around the edges of the ruins. The two churches lie to the east of the settlement. The church on the northeast corner of the ruins dates from the first part of the sixth century but is badly ruined. It employed the same type of sweeping lateral arches as at *Qalb Lozeh a little to the north but on a smaller scale. The second, older, church lies immediately to the southwest, its eastern wall still relatively intact. It dates from the middle of the fifth century and Tchalenko noted in it a horseshoe-shaped *bema*. The church takes the form of a basilica with five columns on each side of the central nave. The façades are sober and the scale of the blocks convey an impression of massiveness.

REFS: Butler AE II 1903: 204; Butler EC 1929: 141, 204; de Vogüé II 1865–77: pl 113, 137–8; Tchalenko *Villages* I 1953: 346–72, II 1953: pl CIX–CXXIII, CXXXV, CXCIX–CC; Tchalenko & Baccache 1979–80: pl 399–417.

Beshindlaye

بشندلاية

PERIOD: Rom/Byz RATING: – MAPS: R3, R3a

LOCATION: Take the *Harim road for 14.9 km and then turn left. At 22.5 km, turn right up a steep hill and continue through *Qalb Lozeh past *Behyo. At the 30.3 km point, take the road on the right and follow it through Kfer Kila until 32.2 km from starting point.

In this Roman tomb of the second century AD was buried Tiberius Claudius Sosandros and his wife. The following touching inscription was supplied by his son: 'Tiberius Claudius Philocles to Tiberius Claudius Sosandros, his father, and to Claudia Kiparous, his mother; witness to his piety and remembrance; in the year 182, 27 Dystros [27 April AD 134]. Sosandros, my father.'

The name has no historical associations but indicates descent from a slave freed in the reign of Emperor Tiberius Claudius. 'Sosandros' is of Greek origin and it is possible that the family is that of a soldier who was settled in the area on release from military service.

The facade is improbably elaborate, with festooned garlands barely suspended above the muddy courtyard that was the entrance to the underground tomb. If you can manage to make your way through the animals, in the dim light you can discern the three burial niches but no decoration.

Perched above the descent to the *hypogeum* is a curious monolith column, square in shape. The Marquis de Vogüé, who visited in the mid 19th century, describes on it a set of portrait figures but the carvings and inscriptions illustrated in his engraving cannot be distinguished these days.

Around the village, remains of olive presses and a sizeable villa (presumably Byzantine) but no church.

REFS: Butler AE II 1903: 60; de Vogüé II 1865–77: 92.

Bosra (Plates 4b- 5 c)

بصرى

VARIANTS: Busrana (BrA); Bostra (Lat, Cru); Busra Eski Sham (Arb) PERIOD: Nab/Rom/Byz/ Arb ALT: 800 m; RATING: *** MAPS: 14, 15, R1

LOCATION: 140 km south of Damascus. The faster route is to take the highway to the Deraa/Bosra exit (102 km) and from there turn east on a secondary road (+40 km) to Bosra. A slower trip that enables you to take in other areas of Jebel al-Arab and the Hauran is to take the road to *Suweida (106 km from Damascus). Continue directly south from Suweida for +22 km and turn right (west) +10 km to Bosra.

After Palmyra, Bosra is the most important site of the Roman-Nabataean period in Syria. Its main point of interest was for long the magnificent and exceptionally intact Roman theatre (second century AD) but recent clearing of modern dwellings from the ancient city makes a detailed visit worthwhile. Bosra has recently been intensively researched under a program coordinated by the Syrian antiquities authorities and involving French, German, Italian, Lebanese and Polish teams.

No visit to Bosra should be crowded into less than half a day, preferably a full day allowing for the trip to and from Damascus. The sombre and unyielding basalt of this volcanic region may dull for many the impact of the Roman remains (so often associated with bleached stone and marble) but if you visit on a sunny day, especially in winter, the effect can be memorable.

Any visit to Bosra begins with the theatre which, since its restoration (post-1946), has been one of the major monuments maintained and supervised by the Antiquities Department. The theatre owes its exceptional state of preservation (from both the ravages of earthquakes and the building programs of later centuries) to its conversion into an Ayyubid fort guarding the southern approaches to Damascus.

As you enter the theatre from the main square of the town, there is little to indicate its Roman origins. The horseshoe internal shape is jacketed by stout Arab walls with heavy bastions and an imposing gateway. Only when you enter do you realise that the fortifications conceal the underpinnings of a Roman theatre – arches, ribs of tiered seating and curving corridors.

If you follow the itinerary marked by arrows, you ascend the outer rim of this maze and come out on the upper parapets of the theatre (plate 4b). Here a most extraordinary site greets you – a classical theatre more spectacularly and authentically preserved than virtually any other around the Mediterranean, described as 'the most perfect of all Roman and Italian theatres' (Rey-Coquais). The

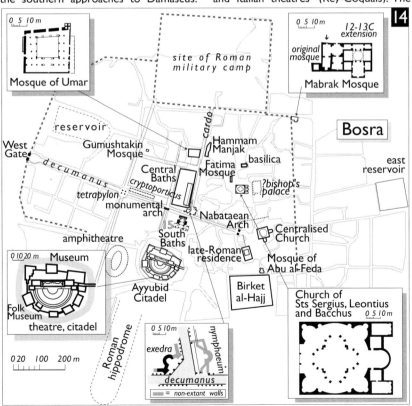

seating is almost entirely intact, in places up to the last row before the crowning colonnade. The huge façade behind the stage and the wings on either side are preserved with much beautiful detail (some unique in style).

History

It is perhaps best to pause here and consider how this splendid monument to the persistence of Roman civilisation originated. While the *Hauran (the classical Auranitis – see box page 289) today is an area which is beginning to find a new prosperity, it had until recently been a comparatively backward region, beset, even during the French period, by banditry and disaffection. Its agriculture had thus been neglected and the stone-littered terrain, the windswept flatness of the volcanic plain and the treeless slopes of the Jebel al-Arab left a harsh impression.

In Roman times, however, the Hauran was probably one of the granaries of the Empire – like Egypt but on a smaller scale. Its sudden rise to prosperity as the Pax Romana took hold in the first century AD is reflected in the ambitious scale of the civic replanning later in the century. Bosra, however, had already played a role in earlier periods. An Early Bronze Age settlement, it is mentioned in Egyptian 18th dynasty records as Busrana. It is not to be confused with the Bozrah mentioned in the Bible as one of the towns in Edomite territory (now southern Jordan). It became part of the Seleucid domains after Alexander's conquests and was seized by Judas Maccabeus in 163 BC (I Macc V, 26, 28). When the Nabataean Kingdom rose to local prominence in the first century BC, Bosra came within the northern reaches of their control though it was later the object of Herodian ambitions from Palestine. From AD 70 to 106, in the final stages of the Nabataean Kingdom (reign of Rabbel II), Bosra was made the capital.

In AD 106 the Romans extended direct rule and established Provincia Arabia, a new province with its headquarters at Bosra. Direct Roman control and the implantation of 5000 legionaries must have fundamentally altered the Nabataean town. It became heavily influenced in its cultural and civic life by Roman models, even more profoundly than the other major Nabataean centre, Petra. Once the more easily travelled route bordering the desert became a safer option, Bosra was made the hub of an important trade network linking Egypt – Red Sea – Syria and the Mediterranean – Mesopotamian regions. The axis of this network was the Via Nova Traiana, Trajan's great trunk road built (probably immediately after 106) to connect Damascus, through Bosra and Philadelphia (Amman), to the Gulf of Aqaba. The road was protected from the nomadic Arabs to the east by a series of forts of which some remains can be seen in northern Jordan. (The routes closer to the coast had to negotiate difficult ravines and mountainous country.)

The city's existing plan was ambitiously expanded. The Nabataean town on the eastern edge of the present ruins, probably centred on a sanctuary dedicated to Dushares, was greatly extended by the establishment to the west of a vast new grid which housed the installations and amenities of the Roman administration, the new grid continuing at an angle to the orientation of the eastern quarter. Trajan (r AD 98–117), the creator of the new province, particularly favoured the town, renaming it Nova Trajana Bostra. It was visited by Hadrian in 129 during his tour of the eastern provinces. Under Alexander Severus (r 222–35), it was made a Roman *colonia*. It retained strong imperial patronage through the reign of Philip the Arab (r 244–9) who was born in the neighbourhood (*Shahba) and who declared Bosra a *metropolis*.

Bosra retained its importance into the Christian era, becoming the seat of an influential bishopric (hence the innovative and sizeable cathedral described below – one of the largest in the east). It was, however, a strongly Monophysite centre and thus often at odds with Constantinople. (Monophysitism was adopted by the Christian Arab tribe, the Ghassanids, whose influence was predominant in the region.) The Prophet Muhammad probably visited the city during a trading journey before his religious mission began with the Hijra and there are legends of his consulting here a revered Christian monk, Bahira (see basilica, below). Bosra lay on the prime access route into Syria from the Arabian Desert and was the first Byzantine city to fall to the Arabs in 634 in the opening phase of Islamic expansion.

After a devastating earthquake in 749, Bosra fell on more uncertain times and its fortunes fluctuated for many centuries. The area diminished in agricultural significance as it became prey to political uncertainty. Lying close to Palestine, it was drawn into the long struggle between Crusaders and Arabs, being attacked at least twice (1147 and 1151) by Frankish armies unsuccessfully challenging Nur al-Din's control of the Hauran. It was too exposed on the southern approaches to Damascus to recover its prosperity during the decades of rivalry between Cairo and Damascus. The Ayyubid effort to fortify the theatre from 1202 to 1251 (improving on earlier Fatimid and Seljuk work) reflected rivalry between the Ayyubids as well as the continuing fear of a renewed Crusader (and later Mongol) invasion (plate 5a). The fortress was considerably restored by Baybars in 1261 after the first Mongol invasion.

Given this perpetual insecurity, the caravan and pilgrimage routes to Mecca gradually moved back to the west where greater security prevailed, out of Bosra's orbit. The area became neglected agriculturally and by the 19th century it was only lightly inhabited, thus making it attractive for new settlement when many thousands of Druze fled Lebanon during the Druze-Christian tensions of 1840–60. Yet the area has retained the more traditional elements of its population, including a sizeable Greek Orthodox community which has one of its principal bishoprics at nearby *Suweida.

Visit

Having fixed Bosra's position in history, continue to visit the rest of the theatre.

It is easy enough to distinguish the original fabric from the reconstructed elements added during the restoration. (Note particularly that the middle columns of the stage scaenae frons are reconstructed or copies of the rather battered originals.) At the beginning of the 20th century, much of the interior of the theatre had been filled with Mamluk structures as well as sand deposited by the wind over the centuries, a further stroke of good fortune which accounts for the theatre's preservation. After Syria's independence, a program of clearance work and research was undertaken lasting from 1946 to 1970.

Having removed the debris and some minor Arab additions, the main restoration work was devoted to the stage area and the upper rows of seats. The full extent of the theatre's seating was thus revealed with room for 6000 spectators distributed over 37 tiers (14 + 18 + 5), plus room for a further 2–3000 standing. The width of the semi-circular theatre is 102 m. This is one of a handful of classical theatres which did not take advantage of a natural slope to support its massive proportions (cf *Jeble and *Palmyra). The acoustics are excellent.

The auditorium was originally covered with retractable cloth shading (velum), the stage being protected by a more permanent wooden roof. Only the lower level of the decoration of the scaenae frons remains, the fine Corinthian columns (probably Severan) giving some indication of the richness of the treatment, once ornate with coloured marbles, statues, windows and sculptured friezes like the façade of a fantastic palace. The three entrances respected the conventions of the Roman theatre. The theatre's construction must post-date the expansion of Bosra following AD 106, probably spread over much of the second century.

On either side of the stage, the versurae, providing access between the stage building and the auditorium, are well preserved and retain part of their beautifully symmetrical colonnades. Behind these and the huge scaenae frons lies a series of Ayyubid-period additions which formed the citadel's headquarters.

In plan, the **Ayyubid fortifications** fit like a jacket around the half-circle of the Roman building, with major towers at the northeast and northwest corners, a central bastion along the diameter (north) and five subsidiary towers around the arc of the semi-circle. The first use of the theatre as a fortification dates back to the Umayyad and Fatimid eras and the first three towers (east and west of the stage and on the southeast rim of the theatre) were constructed under the Seljuk governors, Gumushtakin (1089) and Altuntash (mid 12th century). However, the major work, including the encircling ditch, dates from the Ayyubid response to the Crusader threat after 1200, particularly under al-Adil (sultan in Damascus 1196–1218) and his son, al-Salih Imad al-Din, who alternated as governor of Bosra and sultan of Damascus between 1218 and 1238. The later work relies less on smaller recycled stones and more on massive blocks up to 4.5 m long, particularly in the central tower of the north face.

The Ayyubid upper ramparts now house, on the upper terrace, a collection of sculptures from the Roman period as well as Roman and Arabic inscriptions. Al-Salih established a palace complex and mosque within the Roman auditorium, remains of which were removed during the reconstruction program. One surviving remnant is the water basin of the palace hammam which has been transferred to the ethnographic (folklore) collection in the southwestern tower.

This **Folklore Museum** can be found as you proceed anti-clockwise around the ramparts to the south. From here you can continue back to the entrance via the Ayyubid parapets, with good views over the modern town and of the area once covered by the hippodrome (right of Cham Hotel – see below).

Starting again from the main entrance to the citadel-theatre, strike out to explore the old town to the north, distributed on either side of the main east-west axis. From the entrance, turn left and walk down

the alleyway that runs from the northeast corner of the theatre. After 75 m, to the left, are the remains of the Roman **South Baths**. The baths were constructed in several phases. The alignment of the first bath construction (dating to around the time of the incorporation of Bosra into the Roman Empire as the capital of the province of Arabia) is at an angle to the *decumanus* as it follows the orientation of earlier buildings on the site. The full monumental development of the baths was not realised until the third century.

In its final form (4th–8th century), the complex formed a T-shape with an entrance from the north through an eight-columned portico which led immediately into a great domed vestibule, octagonal in shape. The dome, built of volcanic scoria set in hard mortar, has largely collapsed. Four major chambers served as warm (*tepidarium*) or hot (*caldarium*) rooms. To the east, remains of a late Roman courtyard or *palaestra* were partly covered by a Byzantine church.

Running west-east along the northern face of the baths is the once-colonnaded axis of the town, now partly cleared of dwellings. The axis was probably re-aligned in the second century to provide the spine of the enlarged provincial capital but the monumentalisation of the street as now seen probably dates from the early third century. The carriageway was almost 8 m wide, bordered by a raised colonnaded

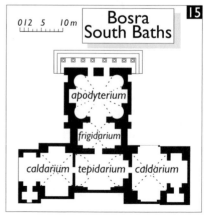

0 1 2   5   10 m

Bosra South Baths   15

apodyterium

frigidarium

caldarium   *tepidarium*   *caldarium*

pavement (5.5 m wide) on each side. Here and there, some of the columns of the colonnade (with Ionic capitals) can be seen. To the left you can see 600 m as far as the western gate of the Roman walled town. To the right, the perspective along the axis ends after 250 m in a gateway of the Nabataean period which led into the temple compound of the pre-Roman period.

On the northeast corner of the South Baths, the colonnaded north-south street (*cardo*), discussed later, heads in a northerly direction. Left of the cardo lie the remains of a series of shops and behind them the Central Baths complex, also examined later. Take as your orientation point this intersection where the *cardo* joins the main east-west street. Here four soaring columns (on the left), 13 m tall on octagonal bases, mark a monumental **exedra** (once assumed to be a *nymphaeum*). The Corinthian capitals of the columns are superbly executed. The half-domed *exedra* was framed by walls provided with niches, probably constructed in the second century AD as a shrine to the imperial cult. The diagonal alignment of the columns cuts the corner between two main streets thus providing a small public space at the intersection. On the opposite (right) side of the north-south *cardo* stood a structure once identified as a *kalybe* but which appears to have been a **nymphaeum**, probably dating from the late second century. Two tall handsome columns towering 14 m above the street level and a piece of the magnificent entablature connecting the southern column with its *anta* (plate 5b) survive. The *nymphaeum*, too, was aligned to frame the triangular space but at a less oblique angle.

Continuing down the main axis to the west, you will see the substantial remains of a gateway or **monumental arch**, dating from the mid third century, which framed a contemporary street running north from the theatre, colonnaded with limestone columns. The arch follows the traditional pattern with a high (13 m) central opening flanked by two smaller arches. Transverse arches allowed continuous pedestrian

traffic along the east-west street's southern footpath. The original upper structure has probably been re-arranged in a later reconstruction though only the northern façade has survived.

At a point beginning 50 m beyond the monumental arch, an underground storage area was built under the raised portico on the right, marked by a series of slit openings in the stepped footpath. This **cryptoporticus**, as it is called, can be entered through a courtyard to the north. The recently cleared gallery consists of a corridor 5 m wide, 4.5 m high and 108 m in length, serving as cool storage for the shops on the northern side of the *decumanus*. The 34 openings noted from outside were intended to admit light and air. It was probably constructed late in the second century AD or early in the following century. To the east, remains of a *macellum* (provisions market, second-third century) have been identified, its entrance marked by four columns of larger dimensions.

As you proceed west, the next major cross-street was once marked by a **tetrapylon** (late third century or early fourth century) standing in a circular open space. It is another 200 m to the **West Gate** (Bab al-Hawa or Gate of the Wind). The original paving of this sector continues to the oval forum (cf the Damascus Gate at *Palmyra) just inside the gate. The latter shows an unusually sober style for the Syrian environment, perhaps reflecting origins in the mid third century given the resemblance to Philip the Arab's city at *Shahba. The single opening is spanned by two super-imposed barrel vaults, the upper reaching 10.5 m above the ground. The lower vault frames the actual opening and was surmounted by false façades, thus avoiding a huge superstructure imposing a crushing load on the arch. The vaults are supported on towers flanked by pairs of pilasters with unadorned bases and capitals. On each side, the pilasters frame a vaulted niche topped by a small pediment. The simplicity of treatment is striking. Stretching left and right of the gateway, you can still see some of the line of Roman **walls** (third century), much cannibalised to serve later building programs.

Head back now to the orientation point midway along the main east-west axis marked by the *nymphaeum-exedra* complex. The development of the principal colonnaded north-south street (*cardo*), heading north from here, probably dates from the late second century and was planned to provide a fitting axis between the Roman military camp and the centre of the civilian city. Recent examination of the newly cleared area west of this *cardo* has revealed extensive remains of a huge baths complex, now called the **Central Baths**, earlier fancifully called the Khan al-Dibs ('molasses caravanserai').

The Central Baths conveys the impression of an extensive complex, conceived along the lines of other grand imperial examples but recent research has revealed a more improvisatory series of development stages. Its beginnings were reasonably modest, confined to a group of rooms directly west off the elongated courtyard or *palaestra* entered via two doorways off the *cardo*. The probable date of this initial project (which preceded the transformation of the *cardo* into a colonnaded axis) was mid second century AD. Later, a duplicate set of warm and cold rooms were provided and the whole complex made more monumental in style, probably in the late third century. Two more *palaestrae* were added to the north and south. In a final stage, a set of latrines (probably also accessible from the street as well as from the northern *palaestra*) were added to the northeast. Accommodating up to 130 at a time, they are the largest set of Roman latrines discovered in the Middle East.

The scale of these baths and the fact that they appear to have been built in parallel with the stages of the baths to the south, underlines the importance of Bosra in Roman times and of its resident military population who would have provided much of the baths' clientele.

If you continue along the *cardo* heading north, you will come to an intersection with a second east-west street. On the left across the intersection, a fine façade groups five almost-intact doorways. Most are entrances to second to third century shops but the larger one probably once gave access to a house or warehouse.

Continue to the north and a little way on the left is the **Mosque of Umar**, once considered to be one of the oldest surviving mosques. Though attributed to the great Caliph Umar (caliph 634–44), responsible for the conquest of Syria in 636, the first mosque on this spot was the work of a later caliph, Yazid II (r 720–4) according to a foundation stone later re-used in the north wall. This first mosque was rebuilt or heavily reconstructed by the Seljuk ruler of Damascus, Abu Mansar Gumushtakin, in 1112–3. In 1221–2 under the Ayyubid al-Salih Ismael the courtyard was enlarged to the north and a new northern *riwaq* added. Carefully restored between 1938 and 1965, it one of the few surviving mosques from the earliest days of Islam which may to some extent preserve its original plan.

You enter the mosque from the east through a colonnaded portico, added in the 12th century using elements borrowed from the ancient *cardo*. Inside, the mosque comprises a courtyard surrounded on two sides (east and west) by double arcades and on the south by the prayer hall, also double arcaded but of wider dimensions. Note the surviving scraps of a decorative panel in sculptured plaster which surrounded the *mihrab*, an important clue to the Seljuk decorative scheme. The square-plan minaret on the northeastern corner was reconstructed during the 13th century improvements. The pyramidal roof over the courtyard and the flat cement ceilings of the arcades are new.

Immediately to the east acoss the *cardo* lies the partially restored **Hammam Manjak**, a Mamluk baths complex in Damascene style built in 1372 by the governor of Damascus, Manjak al-Yusufi, and the last major Islamic addition to the city before its steady decline set in. Described in a recent survey as 'a masterpiece of medieval architectural engineering' (Meinecke) it dates from the heyday of the the city's role in servicing the Hajj traffic to Mecca. After two entrance rooms, a corridor leads to the (originally domed) reception room. A maze-like corridor led the visitor through the 11 chambers of the baths proper, today housing a small museum of Islamic Bosra.

Return to the group of shop façades south of the mosque and take the street 200 m to the west bordering the northern edge of the Central Baths. This brings you to the **Gumushtakin Mosque** (named after its re-founder, Gumushtakin, who was also responsible for the rebuilding of the Mosque of Umar and the central part of the Mabrak Mosque). A small (7 m by 7 m) building with a bulky minaret separated on the west by a 1.5 m gap from the mosque itself, it probably largely dates from the 1134 reconstruction of an earlier mosque. The mosque (also given the name al-Khidr) follows closely the architectural traditions of the Hauran (transverse arches carry the flat basalt roof). Note the Roman ornamental grilles used as windows on the north and west façades. The minaret may be a later addition (13th century) having taken its cue from the design of the Umar Mosque's minaret. To the west, the **mausoleum** (attributed to St Elias but also linked in local tradition to St George) probably marks the site of a former church built into the remains of a Roman courtyard house.

Re-trace your route to the southeastern corner of the Mosque of Umar and from there head east 120 m, crossing the line of the central *cardo*. On the right just beyond the vaulted section of the street is the **Fatima Mosque**, a reference to the daughter of the Prophet. The northern half of the prayer hall was constructed in the Ayyubid period. The three southern arches are 19th century while the 19 m minaret dates from 1306, again following the Mosque of Umar.

Immediately northeast lies the **basilica**, originally an administrative building probably constructed in the third century AD, later converted to serve as a Christian church. It is a large rectangular building with a semi-circular apse on the eastern end. The church came to be associated with the monk Bahira, the Nestorian holy man who, according to tradition, was consulted by the Prophet Muhammad during his visit to Bosra. Certain elements of the Koran which borrow from Mosaic law and Christianity (at least the Nestorian version) are attributed to his influence but the legend seems somewhat tenuous.

If you divert 250 m to the northeastern corner of the city from the basilica (across a Muslim cemetery), you will find near the road that leads to Jemrin, another important early mosque, the **Mabrak Mosque**, restored by the Syrian Antiquities Department and the German Archaeological Institute between 1986 and 1989. According to legend, the first copy of the Koran brought to Syria rested here, carried on a camel. An important centre of learning grew on this spot. Some idea of the original simplicity and beauty of the early Islamic architectural style survives despite numerous changes. The building falls into three segments. The earliest is to the west and used the Roman city wall as its western limit. In front of its *mihrab* (note the shell niche re-employed from antiquity) is a stone said to bear the marks where the camel carrying the Koran rested (hence the Arabic title, 'mosque of kneeling'). The small oratory east of the first mosque also uses recycled classical elements – colonettes flanking another shell-niche *mihrab*. The northern and central courtyards were added a little later. The larger eastern part of the building was constructed on a more monumental scale, dated by inscription to 1136. This new wing was cruciform in plan, probably the first manifestation of the new fashion for madrasas of this style during the Sunni revival in medieval Syria. The stucco decoration around the *mihrab* is one of the best illustrations of Islamic use of sculptured plaster. The dome over the central courtyard of the madrasa is fairly rare in Syria. Meinecke believed that the use of a tall dome shape in the reconstruction reflected local tradition dating back to Byzantine times. The minaret was probably added around 1221.

Returning to the basilica and continuing a little further to the south you reach the so-called **Cathedral**, a pilgrimage church dedicated **to Sts Sergius, Leontius and Bacchus** (511–2), a building of considerable importance in the annals of early Christian architecture. The plan is somewhat complex, being basically a circle within a square with the transition from the inner to the outer shapes carried by corner *exedrae* flanked by niches. The plan is extended to the east to take in a choir with four side rooms or chapels. The central chamber was 36 m in diameter (as large in scale as the first version of Hagia Sophia in Constantinople). At its centre stood a sanctuary enclosed by four L–shaped pillars joined by semi-circular colonnades. This complex variation of circular and square shapes is a pioneering masterpiece of early Christian architecture, though rather more heavy and ungainly in its final results than the smaller and slightly later version at *Resafa. (For an examination of the Bosra cathedral, see the box on Centralised Churches, page 24.)

Unfortunately the remains are badly ruined, some of the worst damage having been done in the last century. Virtually all the walls, apart from the apses, were reduced to ground level by mining for building material. No evidence remains of the roofing of the original church, the assumption being that it consisted perhaps of a wooden lantern with a conical top. The lantern, 24 m in diameter, sat upon a circular clerestory which housed at least 50 windows, bringing a high level of natural light into the church, illuminating internal walls which were once probably plastered and painted, perhaps even clad with marble. An alternative reconstruction prefers a square central tower with polygonal apses on each side. The external walls are virtually undecorated, in contrast to the contemporary carved stonework of churches in northern Syria.

The church is dated by its dedication in 512–3 by Julianos, Archbishop of Bosra, in honour of three of the most celebrated martyrs of early Syrian Christianity, Sergius, Leontius and Bacchus. (Sergius is the saint associated with the great fortress city of *Resafa in northern Syria.) Julianos, known for his courage and forthrightness, was dismissed from his post shortly after the Cathedral's construction, having refused to accept the authority of Severus, Patriarch of Antioch, whom he regarded as an adherant of the Monophysite heresy.) Behind the church, and originally linked to it, fragmentary remains of the bishop's palace of the Byzantine period have been found.

Work your way from the cathedral (head south through the alleyways) to the eastern end of the east-west *decumanus*. At its extremity lies the **Nabataean arch** (plate 5c). The drabness of the basalt stone does not diminish this remarkable blending of a basically Roman shape with Nabataean-orientalising decoration. While conforming to the Roman canon of civic architecture, the arch shows many Nabataean touches: the plain undecorated capitals which look like Corinthian blanks left uncarved; the high vaulting central arch which nearly swallows the whole structure; the fascination with semi-circular arched niches; and the (conjectured) addition of triangular indentations to the top of the structure (cf the crow-feet merlons on the parapet of the *cella* of the Bel Temple at *Palmyra). These features would date the construction to the second half of the first century AD, perhaps at the point when the last Nabataean king had moved his capital from Petra to Bosra. The effect is not inelegant, the division of the façade into two main orders being well proportioned. Above a recently excavated lower structure (marked by a simple rounded niche), the middle panel balances a niche between columns framed by pilasters; the upper level comprises a rounded niche between two rectangular niches, divided by simpler pilasters. There were no parallel pedestrian thoroughfares through the flanking pylons which instead have transverse passages probably aligned to a pedestrian thoroughfare on a north-south street.

The gateway led to a colonnaded *temenos* of a Nabataean temple, possibly dedicated to Dushara. Only fragments of the enclosure remain. (See part of the colonnade just inside, orientated at an angle to the gate.) This arrangement of the city's principal axis leading to the main shrine is also found at the western end of Petra ('Qasr al-Bint' compound). Only a few possible remains of the temple have been found on the site of the later **Centralised Church** 100 m to the east. Recent excavations have revealed that this second 'circle in a square' church, even larger than the 'cathedral' described earlier, was built after the fourth century re-using columns of the Roman (Antonine) temple for the central circular colonnade.

Immediately south of the Nabataean gateway lie the remains of a substantial **residence** which Butler ascribed to the Roman governor of the province of Arabia, but which has also been interpreted as the seat of the Christian bishop (fifth to sixth century). The complex was 33 m by 50 m in extent and arranged around a central court. Two-storeyed colonnades preceded the rooms on the northern and southern sides of the court. On the south, the central chamber or dining room (*triclinos*) was an elaborate hall with semi-circular apses at each end and a central space of grand proportions. The external facade on the east incorporates the wall of an earlier building, perhaps part of the Nabataean temple complex with alternating square and curved niches.

Further south again, it is hard to miss the sizeable **cistern** (Birket al-Hajj), over 120 m by 150 m in extent. A Nabataean/Roman construction restored in Ayyubid times, it was originally 8 m deep, the walls strengthened with pilasters. It is one of the largest town water storage facilities found in the Roman east. The supply of piped water to the town was an important preoccupation and much evidence remains throughout the site of the brick and lead conduit system. (There is a further cistern 300 m from the eastern limits.)

The **Dabbagha Madrasa** is situated on the northeastern corner of the Birket al-Hajj. Literally the 'Dyers' School' (a dyeing industry drew its water from the *birket* until the early 20th century), it dates from the Ayyubid period (1225 according to

an inscription on the south façade) and was restored 1982–5. The madrasa was built under the Ayyubid ruler of Bosra, al-Salih Ismael, in 1225–6 though the real initiative was probably due to his officer, Shams al-Din Sunqur ('al-Hakim'). It followed a four-*iwan* layout with the south *iwan* extended to form an enlarged prayer hall. The courtyard was initially uncovered. Later, several changes were made. A tomb for Sunqur was built in the southeast corner in 1232–3 and next to it a minaret was added, either just before or in the decades after the changeover from Ayyubids to Mamluks (1260). At some stage the courtyard was roofed to provide a long continuous prayer hall.

[Sites of lesser interest on the outskirts of the Roman perimeter include:

• South-southwest of the theatre (200 m), the location of the Roman **hippodrome** can be clearly seen from the theatre's parapets (see above page 96). The hippodrome, with its curved end to the south, covered an area 440 m by 130 m and seated 30,000, one of the largest in the Roman east. (Date uncertain, possibly mid-third century.)
• To the north (west of the citadel), recent excavations have exposed remains of an **amphitheatre**. Relatively rare in the Roman east, amphitheatres housed gladiatorial or wild animal contests.
• The base for the Roman legion was located on the northern outskirts of the town at the end of the *cardo* that passes the Mosque of Umar. No remains survive.]

REFS: Butler EC 1929: 124–7; Butler PE II A 4 1909: 215–95; Creswell Early Muslim I 1979; Crowfoot Churches at Bosra 1937; Crowfoot Early Churches 1941; Dentzer, Blanc & Fournet 2002; Dentzer Guide 2007; de Vogüé I 1865: 63–7; Finsen 1972; Meinecke (et al) 1990; Meinecke & Aalund 2005: 87–96; Mukdad 2001; Mougdad 1974; Ory 1999: 371–8; Piraud-Fournet 2003; Sartre Bostra 1985.

Braij

البريج

VARIANTS: Breij, Breig   PERIOD: Byz
ALT: 455 m   RATING: –   MAP: R3, R3a

LOCATION: From the Bab al-Hawa turn-off, follow the road to *Harim. 4 km after the village of Sarmada, the monastery can be seen c450 m across the field to the right.

The remains of the Monastery of St Daniel at the western edge of the Jebel Barisha massif are in a surprisingly good state of preservation. The main building is inserted into the cliff face, the first storey being cut out of the rock and the stone used to build the upper two storeys. The complex of three buildings includes some oil presses, cisterns and a conventual tomb.

Tchalenko describes this as 'the most interesting monastic grouping in the area'. It was built relatively late in the monastic 'boom'. The building dates from the late sixth century, though sources differ as to whether it was built in one or two phases. Located on the edge of the Dana Plain – an area notoriously infested with Monophysites, heretical in the eyes of the central Byzantine Church authorities – it was probably a Monophysite institution.

REFS: Mattern 1944: 88–90; Pena (et al) Cenobites 1983: 203–12, 261–3; Pena Inventaire 1987: 84; Tchalenko Villages I 1953: 124–5, 158–9, 173.

Burj Haidar

برج هيدر

VARIANTS: Kaprokera (anc), Burj Heidar
PERIOD: Byz RATING: * MAP: R3, R3a

LOCATION: Take the road leading north from the eastern slopes of the ridge of St Simeon. The road bends but eventually heads northeast. Burj Haidar is reached after c6 km. (Burj Haidar is also c4 km west of *Kharrab Shams.) To the north and northeast respectively lie Kfer Nabo (2 km), Kalota (4 km).

Burj Haidar's origins go back beyond the adoption of Christianity as the official religion of the Roman Empire (AD 324). A survey mark of 298 indicates that the settlement was registered at that time under the ancient name above. Later, it apparently became a fervent Christian community judging by the unusual number of churches (six) for such a small settlement. The agriculture of the area was based on an extensive basin of arable land below the village.

The columned arcades of a mid fourth century three-aisled church (centre of the village, north of the road) survive somewhat incongruously. The two rows of Doric columns are left standing while most of the walls of the church have disappeared. The building was of medium dimensions and typical in style of the period. The exception was the prothesis, the chamber to the right of the apse, which was enlarged during the fifth century, apparently to provide a martyrium. The early date is evident in the virtual absence of decoration. Traces of a bema were found in the central nave. Other remains include a tower (90 m northeast) and an andron or meeting room and a monastery (sixth century, both on the western edge of town – take lane heading northeast from bend in the road).

A more extraordinary survival is the small chapel, on the eastern edge of town, north of the modern road. The chapel itself is described by Butler as 'one of the most attractive in the Jebel Semaan'. Added to it at a rakish angle is a plain elongated building which was presumably the clerical residence. The chapel is richly decorated on the outside with fluid mouldings. Inside the main decoration is around the extant chancel arch. Note the two bosses sticking out from the arch whose purpose is unexplained. In Butler's day, evidence could be seen of the plastered and painted ceiling of the sanctuary.

One hundred metres southeast lie remains of the **east church** (sixth century) difficult to distinguish south of the road as it bends southeast. Butler noted that the chancel arch showed early signs of the horseshoe shape development seen in other late Christian experimentation (*Ruweiha – Church of Bissos) but which is developed much further in subsequent Christian and Islamic architecture.

REFS: Butler AE II 1903: 32, 150; Butler EC 1929: 32; Butler PE II B 6 1920: 288–93; Tchalenko Villages I 1953: 170, II 1953: pl CXXIX; Tchalenko & Baccache 1979–80: Album pl 33–46, Planches pl 23–8.

Burjke, Fafertin, Surkunya and Banastur

VARIANTS: Fafirtin, Fafartin   PERIOD: Byz
RATING: – MAP: R3, R3a

LOCATION: Burjke is 4.5 km east of Saint Simeon in a direct line. From Saint Simeon, take the right fork below the east flank. Follow this road as it winds for c4 km before turning right along a tarmac road for +2 km. For Fafertin, continue 1.5 km to the east along the same road. Surkunya lies over the rise 800 m south-southwest of Fafertin. It can be reached by a vehicle track (1.2 km) forking south-east just before Burjke. Banastur is 2.5 km along the same track to the southeast.

A sixth century church with a meandering band along the side façade and central doorway lies just to the left of the road as you arrive in **Burjke**. Like the chapel at nearby *Surkunya, the chancel is rectangular and had a flat roof of stone. There is also a tower of the sixth century, 11 m (originally five storeys) high, probably once part of a monastery. In Islamic times, however, it was fortified at the base for defensive reasons.

Fafertin is a Kurdish village largely devoid of charm, built on a shelf underneath a crest and overlooking a valley which descends to the east. The chief point of interest is the oldest dated basilica church in Syria, though a house has recently intruded on the edge of the site. The remains consist of the stubs of the columned aisle, terminating in the intact semi-dome of the apse. The building is dated by inscription to 372, making it also one of the oldest churches surviving anywhere. Nothing remains of the *bema* once located in the centre of the main nave.

The deserted ruins of **Surkunya** lies 800 m south-southwest of Fafertin (see road access directions above). In the centre lie the remains of a small single-naved church of the fourth century. South-southeast (200 m south of the track) is another single-naved church whose rectangular apse still preserves its sloping stone roof. The chancel is formed by a single but elegant arch. The external window frames carry the drooping decoration typical of the period. Underground burial chambers and remains of villas lie scattered about.

Banastur, Butler notes, 'is one of the smaller and less important places on the eastern slopes of the Jebal Siman'. For the most part, large private residences, plain in decoration. Butler speculates on whether the tower might not be a particular form of 'dwelling house' not a monastic retreat. Hadjar describes a convent with a 'recluse's tower'; residence for monks alongside.

REFS: **Burjke:** Hadjar 2000: 113; Butler *AE* IV B 1909: 138; Butler *PE* II B 6 1920: 329; Tchalenko *Villages* III 1958: 117; Pena *Reclus* 1980: 272–3 **Fafertin:** Butler *EC* 1929: 33–4; Butler *PE* II B 6 1920: 327–9; Tchalenko *Villages* II 1953: pl CXXVIII; Tchalenko & Baccache 1979–80: pl 80–96. **Surkunya:** Butler *PE* II B 6 1920: 326; Hadjar 2000: 114; Tchalenko II 1953: pl. CXXVIII; **Banastur:** Butler *PE* II B 6 1920: 325; Hadjar 2000: 111.

Burqush

برقش

VARIANTS: PERIOD: Rom/Byz   ALT: 1580 m
RATING: * MAP: R1

LOCATION: 33 km west of Damascus. Take the Beirut highway. At 17 km from Umayyad Square, right exit then cross over highway to south. +4 km, left at T- junction then immediately right. +4.5 km, right turn just past Kfer Kuk. +6.5 km, military checkpoint. Leave vehicle here. 30 minute walk along along dirt road to south-southwest. For Rahleh, continue along tarmac road from checkpoint for +6 km.

From this ridge on the lower slopes of Mount Hermon, breathtaking views out to the east provide a setting for the remains of a Byzantine **basilica** of the sixth century. It is difficult to imagine how blocks of such dimensions were transported to this site but part of the narrow ridge was cut away to form an artificial platform which was extended to the southwest by a huge vaulted sub-structure. On this terrace measuring some 46 m by 34 m a three-aisled basilica was constructed on an impressive scale with pillars rounded at each end by half-columns. The basic plan has much in common with other transverse-arched churches of the sixth century. The remains of the capitals which topped these half-columns are scattered about in the general confusion of blocks that litter the site. Most of the supporting wall of the sub-structure has collapsed but enough can be seen of the northeastern wall to reconstruct how the lower space comprised a huge chamber some 6 m wide over which the upper platform was carried on a series of arches supported on consoles. Stairs in the southwest corner led down from the basilica.

The site had earlier been used for religious buildings in the pre-Hellenistic and Roman periods. To the northeast (90 m) lie the remains of a *cella* of a Roman **temple** (Krencker suspects it may have been a mithraeum) in a severely plain style, oriented broadly northeast-southwest with the opening on the lower face. A semi-circular apse was contained within the walls, forming an internal *cella*.

Lower down are the remains of a monastery of which only the foundations survive as well as traces of other religious buildings.

There are a number of other remains of Roman temples in the neighbourhood of Mount Hermon (eg the ruins at Rahleh 6 km northwest – *distyle in antis* preceding a domed *exedra* – dated by inscription to AD 296–7) but access is currently difficult given military deployments in the area.

REFS: Brands 2007 (website at www.orientarch. uni-halle.de); Krencker & Zschietzschmann 1938: 235–48; Mouterde 1951–2.

C

Circesium (al-Buseira)

البصيرة

VARIANTS: al-Buseira or Basira (Arb); Phalga, Phaliga Rummunidu, Nabagath (anc); Carcis (Grk); Qarqisiye PERIOD: Rom   RATING: T MAP: R5

LOCATION: At the confluence of the Euphrates and Khabur Rivers. From Deir al-Zor, cross to the left bank of the Euphrates and take the road to Haseke and Qamishli for c7 km. Follow signs to the right for al-Buseira or Basira +30 km southeast.

Circesium, a Greek foundation (of Seleucus II Callinicus r 245–26 BC), once played a role in the defence of the Roman domains in Syria against the Persian and Sasanian threat from the east. In the second century AD, its importance was secondary or complementary to *Dura Europos, the Seleucid foundation on the right bank of the Euphrates, with Circesium offering first haven in Roman territory for caravans proceeding down the Khabur River (the classical Chaboras) from the east. It was essentially a Roman military outpost consolidated under Trajan's policy of pushing out the frontier to the Khabur. It fell temporarily to Shapur in his push into Syria in AD 256 which also saw the fall of Dura. It was later re-fortified by Diocletian who may have revived the Seleucid place name, designating it Circesium. It housed in the fourth century Legio III Parthica until it was transferred to Beroea (Aleppo). The defence post was revived under the Byzantine Emperor Justinian (sixth century) as part of his major defensive network in northern and northeastern Syria. It was still in Byzantine hands when it fell to the Arabs in 637.

Virtually nothing remains of the ancient fortifications. There is an incongruous stub of massive Byzantine wall in the centre of the old town, probably part of the central *castellum* whose remains were distinctly evident to travellers of a century ago. The northern city walls can be traced in the raised terrain north of the old town. The erratic course of the river (which is now considerably to the west) erased the original walls along the Euphrates.

REFS: Bell *Amurath* 1911: 74–5; Chapot 294–6; Dussaud 1927: 466, 486–8; Geyer (*et al*) 2004: 93, 130; Musil *Middle Euphrates* 1927: 334–7; Poidebard 1934: 89, 134, 145; Ulbert 1989: 293–5; Wiesehöffer in *Encyclopedia Iranica* 'Circesium'.

Cyrrhus (al-Nabi Huri – Plate 6a)

النبي هوري

VARIANTS: al-Nabi Huri (Arb); Khoros; Kyrrhos, Hagiopolis (Grk); Coricié (Cru); Qurus. PERIOD: Hel/Rom/Byz   RATING: * MAP: 16, R3

LOCATION: 76 km north of Aleppo, almost on the Turkish border. Take the main north road out of Aleppo. At 45 km, right turn to Azaz. +4 km small round-about at the entry to Azaz. Follow the signs +24 km to Cyrrhus (Nabi Huri). Alternatively, at the 45 km point, continue +5 km along the Afrin road to the turn-off to Bulbul. Follow that road for +16 km, then turn right +16 km for Cyrrhus.

The first road is more interesting, if only for the experience of crossing two steep hump-backed Roman bridges that still carry traffic. This experience is not for the faint-hearted given the sharpness of the hump and the narrowness of the roadway (remarkably slippery in wet weather). The Romans didn't seem to have four-wheeled vehicles in mind when they designed these things, though to be fair the bridges probably originally had parapets.

History

Like many cities that became major bases in the Hellenistic-Roman period, Cyrrhus was founded by Seleucus I Nicator after 300 BC (and named after Cyrrhus in Macedonia) as part of a program of military colonies to secure his share of Alexander's inheritance. There is no documentary reference to Cyrrhus until 220 BC but it was probably the headquarters of one of the four original satrapies created by

Seleucus before 294 BC on the site of a pre-301 settlement. It seems, however, to have lacked the economic and security attributes needed to remain the centre of a satrapy under the Seleucids, lying as it did so close to the rival Commagene and Armenian Kingdoms to the north. By the late second century BC, it had foundered and in the early first century BC, was annexed to the Armenian Kingdom. It was absorbed into the Roman province of Syria following Pompey's conquest (64 BC) and lost all administrative and political identity. The area was badly affected by invasions from the east and subject to brigandage. By the first century AD its fortunes recovered and it was visited by Germanicus (adopted son of Tiberius) in AD 19. It became both an administrative centre and the headquarters of a legion (the X Fretensis until its transfer in AD 66 to Jerusalem). In the second century, it served as a base for the campaigns in Armenia.

Its role depended on imperial interest in sustaining its military and commercial advantages rather than on the agricultural resources of the surrounding countryside. It lay on the reasonably secure route from Antioch to the bridge crossing of the Euphrates at Zeugma (now flooded by a dam north of modern Birecik in Turkey). Its role in supporting the bridgehead to the east, however, was usurped in the third century by Hierapolis (*Menbij) which had the added attraction of being a major cult centre.

Cyrrhus was occupied at least once during the Persian invasions of the mid third century AD. It recovered to become a centre of some importance (under the name of Hagiopolis) in the early Christian era, Sts Cosmas and Damian being venerated here. Theodoret, Bishop of Cyrrhus from around 423 to 450, was a prominent early father of the church. Justinian re-fortified and garrisoned it in the mid sixth century as part of his program of frontier works commissioned during the renewed confrontation with the Persians. It fell in 637 to the conquering Arab armies. It was taken for a time by Crusaders (early 11th century) and made dependent on Edessa

under the name Coricié. Nur al-Din took it back in 1150 but it subsequently lost its strategic significance and the site is now lightly inhabited though the area is being developed for olive farming.

Visit

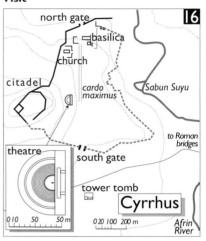

En route, the tell of **Azaz** marks the location of the Crusader fortified position, Hazart, that was taken from a Turcoman amir at the beginning of the First Crusade (1097). Though precariously held, it served to protect the route Antioch-Edessa via the Afrin Valley and as a point to harass Aleppo until taken by Nur al-Din in 1150.

The two second century AD **Roman bridges** on the road to Cyrrhus are worthy of particular note. Though much modified in Byzantine and Arab times, the construction is basically late Roman, a singular tribute to the empire's engineering skills. Coming from the southeast (Aleppo), the first bridge (plate 6a) crosses the upper reaches of the Afrin River and employs three arches. The second, 1 km later and less than 1 km from the edge of Cyrrhus, crosses the stream of the Sabun Suyu River with six arches. The carriageways are 5 m wide and the slope of the rise does not exceed 15 percent.

Cyrrhus has less to show above the ground

than other major Hellenistic-Roman cities in Syria but it is situated in a wild and romantic setting and has sufficient of interest to justify a visit for which you will need a good six or more hours, including the trip to and from Aleppo. Spread out between the citadel hill and the Sabun Suyu River to the east, the site bears traces of a planned settlement of the period. These include a grid pattern centred on a colonnaded main street (*cardo maximus*) and major amenities including a theatre. The *cardo* runs north-south, 7 m wide and was once paved with basalt. At the southern end of the *cardo*, a monumental gate formed one of the principal entrances to the city (recently partly reconstructed). Lower down the valley, near the northern gate, are sketchy remains of a church surrounded by a large enclosure wall and a basilica. Sections of the northern *cardo* were also exposed in this area.

Cyrrhus was investigated by the French in several campaigns in the 1950–60s. Further work has been done to reconstruct parts of the town which have succumbed to earthquakes or were mined for building materials. The reconstruction effort concentrated particularly on the **theatre** which probably dates from the mid second century. At 115 m in diameter, it is, after Apamea (139 m), one of the largest examples in Syria. Its original dimensions are larger than the contemporary theatre at *Bosra (102 m). The stage wall seems to have fallen pell mell into the *cavea* during an earthquake. Only the first 14 rows of seating embedded in the earth have been preserved, the free-standing upper structure that once provided 11 more rows has collapsed and the stones have been re-used elsewhere.

The **citadel** (above and west of the theatre) gives sweeping views of the countryside and the outlines of its heavy fortifications (including an inner keep) can still be traced. An inscription on the entrance gate (northeast corner) confirms that at least the acropolis walls are the work of Justinian. The **walls** of the lower town are extensive, the lines being determined by the contours of two ridges radiating from the low hill on which the citadel was built. It is unclear whether the outer line of walls belongs to Justinian's sixth century re-fortification program (which may have been confined to the citadel), though the line seems to follow the Hellenistic foundations.

To the southwest (visible 600 m left of the access road) is a curious hexagonal **Roman tower tomb**, a good example of the eclectic tastes of the period (probably second or third century AD). The upper storey is formed by a six-sided pyramidal roof topped by a knosp of carved acanthus leaves. Inside, the upper storey is surrounded by arches separated by marble monolith pillars ending in Corinthian capitals. It has been made even more eclectic, however, by the conversion of the lower floor in the 14th century into the burial place of a legendary Muslim saint, al-Nabi Huri (inscription of AH 703, AD 1303), and the addition of a pilgrimage mosque. Behind the tower is the first of two necropoleis associated with Cyrrhus, the other lying to the northwest.

REFS: Dussaud 1927: 470–1; Frézouls 'Cyrrhus' *ANRW* 1979; Frézouls *Mission archéologique* 1989: 175–80; Tchalenko *Villages* II 1953: pl LXXXVI/10.

D

Damascus – Introduction

دمشق

VARIANTS: Dimashqa, Dimaski (BrA); Arsinoia, Demetrias (Grk – Ptolemaic); Damascus (Lat); al-Shams, Dimashq (Arb) PERIOD: All ALT: 691 m RATING: *** MAPS: 17–27

LOCATION: Capital of Syria, occupying the ancient site in the oasis fed by the Barada River flowing from the Anti-Lebanon Range.

If Paradise be on earth, it is, without a doubt, Damascus;

but if it be in Heaven, Damascus is its counterpart on earth.

(12th century Spanish Muslim traveller, Ibn Jubair – adapted from Ziadeh 1964: 24)

She measures time not by days and months and years, but by the empires she has seen rise and crumble to ruin. She is a type of immortality. ... Damascus has seen all that ever occured on earth and still she lives. She has looked upon the dry bones of a thousand empires, and will see the tombs of a thousand more before she dies.

(Mark Twain *Innocents Abroad*)

Preamble

Damascus is described in ten walking itineraries (the order described depending on their distance from the heart of the city, the Umayyad Mosque). The exploration of Damascus in this detail amply repays the effort for it is one of the rare historical centres which has managed to preserve much of its atmosphere in the face of mounting population pressures.

Nestled at the foot of the Anti-Lebanon Range where the waters of the Barada (the Abana or Chrysorrhoas of antiquity) rush out of the mountain gorge to water an oasis 30 km or more in extent, it is easy to appreciate how this city has come to play such a continuous role in history. This is perhaps best appreciated by beginning your visit with a taxi trip up to the lookout points along the slopes of Mount Kassyun which dominates the city and oasis. The mountain itself has attracted several legends including the belief that here Abraham had the unity of God revealed to him. A mosque at Berze, at the foot of the eastern slopes, commemorates the reputed birthplace of Abraham. Other legends which have passed into Muslim tradition include the belief that Jesus and his mother found refuge there (Koran XXIII, 50). It is from this point, too, that legend has the Prophet Muhammad looking down upon Damascus for the first time and proclaiming that if man could have only one paradise, he would have to forego the earthly paradise of Damascus in favour of the other.

Looking south and east from the lookout, you see how the desert which has swept relentlessly from southern Arabia and the Indian Ocean abruptly confronts this fragile band of cultivation as the Barada fans out into the semi-wilderness. This accounts for Damascus' abiding importance; like a port on the edge of this harsh sea of infertility, it is the natural first landing for the desert traveller.

From Kassyun, you can also gain a good appreciation of the Anti-Lebanon Range which stretches to the west and north. At the southern extremity lies the peak (often snow-covered – alt: 2814 m) of Mount Hermon (Jebel al-Sheikh).

History

No large scale systematic excavations have been possible in a city so continuously and densely inhabited as Damascus. Much of the evidence for the earlier phases of its history is thus fragmentary, resulting from either literary sources or fortuitous archaeological digs. The settlement of the oasis, however, clearly goes back to the earliest phase of post-nomadic economic development – the fourth millennium or before – making Damascus one of the oldest continuously inhabited urban centres in the world.

The first historical records of 'Dimashqa' (Damascus) are in the *Mari tablets (c2500 BC) and a little later as 'Dimaski' in the Ebla archives. **Amorite** settlement began around the beginning of the second millennium BC. Later in the millennium it came into the Egyptian sphere of influence and is mentioned in the Amarna archives (18th dynasty, 14th century BC). After the great disturbance of the Sea Peoples' invasion c1200 BC, it recovered under the **Aramaeans**. They established here their principality of Aram-Damascus which took a leading role in checking the expansion of the biblical kingdoms of Israel and Judaea. The city fell to the **Assyrians** in 732 BC. In 572, the neo-Babylonian (or **Chaldean**) King, Nebuchadnezzar, conquered Syria and Palestine but the Chaldean dynasty itself was overwhelmed shortly after in 539 when the Persian King, Cyrus, took the whole region in the course of his sweep towards the Aegean. Damascus was the seat of a Persian governor or satrap.

Alexander's great campaign brought Damascus under Greek control in 332 following the battle of Issus. Though Alexander's own path took him directly along the Phoenician coast, a small contingent under his general, Parmenion, secured Damascus. The subsequent rule by **Greeks** brought town-planning to Damascus (*Damascus – Straight Street) but wrangling for control between Seleucids and Ptolemies weakened Greek authority and the lack of effective administration by the first century BC introduced a phase

The Gates of Damascus

The walls of the old city of Damascus are described in three itineraries (*Damascus – Citadel and North Walls; *Damascus – Southwest Quarter; *Damascus – Straight Street). The following provides a consolidated listing of the city gates which interrupt the 6 km of wall (excluding the gates to the Citadel itself which were reserved for the army or ruling class). Cross-references are given to the gates' locations on the separate itineraries. A walk around the full circumference of the walled city would be feasible in a rather long morning or afternoon but would not allow time for the exploration of buildings en route. The nine gates (eight are extant) are listed clockwise, starting at the Citadel, at the northwest corner of the city walls.

ARAB NAME	TRANSLATION	ROMAN NAME (i)	ITINERARY
Bab al-Faraj	Deliverance	(no gate)	Cit
Bab al-Faradis	Orchards	Mercury	Cit
Bab al-Salaam	Peace	Moon	Cit
Bab Tuma	St Thomas	Venus	Cit
Bab Sharqi	Eastern	Sun	St
Bab Kaysan	(proper name)	Saturn	St
Bab Saghir	Small	Mars	SW
Bab al-Jabiye	Water Trough	Jupiter	SW
Bab al-Nasr	Victory	(not known)	-

Cit = *Damascus – Citadel; St = *Damascus – Straight Street; SW = *Damascus – Southwest Quarter (i) As cited in Arab chronicles.

What is remarkable in following the walled enclosure is the extent to which the city plan over the centuries continued to observe its basically Roman outline. The walls retain the locations of the Roman gateways (though Nur al-Din moved the northern alignment up to the banks of the Barada) though they do not always follow the Roman alignment between the gates. Where the alignments correspond, however, many of the original Roman blocks can be found at the base of the walls, in spite of much mining and plundering in the last 2000 years.

of uncertainty (including a period of Nabataean domination) that was ended by the Roman conquest in 64 BC.

Roman rule lasted (in one form or another) 700 years. Though Damascus was not a major centre for Roman administration (Antioch was the third city of the Empire for the Romans and the base for the administration of Syria), Damascus flourished under Roman rule. From 37 BC to AD 54, it remained nominally a city-state (though with a heavy Nabataean presence at times) and kept its major trading role given the growing importance of the eastern route via *Palmyra. The cult centre, originally a ninth century BC Aramaean temple dedicated to the god Hadad, was appropriated by the Romans through the syncretisation of Hadad with Jupiter. From the first century AD, the temple compound was rebuilt to a grandiose imperial plan (*Damascus – Umayyad Mosque). The town plan was improved further, an aqueduct system brought the waters of the Barada to homes and baths and the city's walls were provided with seven or eight gates (see box on page 95).

Damascus, which housed an important Jewish colony, was associated with the earliest phase of the spread of **Christianity** and the mission of St Paul (*Damascus – Straight Street). Hadrian gave it the rank of *metropolis* (117), later raised to *colonia* under Alexander Severus (222). After the adoption of Christianity as the imperial religion in the fourth century AD, the Temple of Jupiter-Hadad was adapted to house the Cathedral of St John. In 635–6 the city surrendered twice to a Muslim army, the first time to Khalid Ibn al-Walid after a six month siege. It was made the capital of the **Umayyad Empire** under the fifth caliph, al-Muawiya, in 661, thus ending a thousand years of western supremacy.

The Umayyad Empire survived only 90 years but it provided Damascus with the most lasting and impressive monument to its fame, the great Mosque of the Umayyads, built by the Caliph al-Walid after 706 on the site of the Cathedral of St

John. Little else remains of the Umayyad period in Damascus (the great palace complex, for example, to the southeast of the Great Mosque, has been obliterated).

Under subsequent **Muslim dynasties**, Damascus stood at the intersection of competing spheres of influence and was eclipsed by other centres associated with the regimes that sprang up in Baghdad, Mosul, Aleppo and Cairo. The Abbasids, successors to the Umayyads, based their rule on Baghdad and deliberately defaced or dismantled much of the Umayyad city on the grounds of the alleged apostasy of the earlier caliphs. The fall in population and status continued under the turbulent days (tenth–12th centuries) of the competing Tulunid, Ikshidid, Fatimid, Hamdanid and Seljuk dynasties which struggled for control of Syria from their power bases in Cairo and Aleppo/Mosul. There are virtually no remains in Damascus of these centuries of disruption which gave the main impetus to the process by which the open grid plan of the Greco-Roman city was broken up into self-contained quarters, each walled for protection of communities segregated along confessional lines. (The Muslims congregated around the Great Mosque and the Citadel to the west; the Christians to the northeast; the Jews to the southeast.) The street plan was further modified by the narrowing of thoroughfares and the creation of meandering laneways.

The Muslim resistance to the **Crusades** began the reversal of this decline. It brought a rallying to Damascus as a bastion of the Muslim cause and thus of Sunni orthodoxy. The refugee influx (particularly after the barbaric slaughter associated with the Crusaders' taking of Jerusalem in 1099) began the process by which the city's population spread beyond the walled city into the Salihiye quarter along the lower slopes of Kassyun and later towards the Midan to the south. To this era belongs the reconstruction of the defences of the city including the major gateways, the Citadel and its surrounding walls.

Damascus was twice attacked by Crusader forces (1129, 1140) before the first serious effort to take it was mounted in 1148. At the opening of the Second Crusade, King Louis of France and Conrad, King of the Germans, impetuously decided to divert their forces to Damascus. The Crusaders abandoned their siege after a sustained two-day battle on the outskirts of the city, having been alerted to the expected arrival of further Muslim forces from

weakened the dynasty's cohesion and insecurity prevailed in the face of the first of several Mongol invasions (in 1260 under Hulaga – later invasions which did much to raze the fabric of the city came in 1299–1300 under Ilkhan Ghazan and in 1400–1 under Timur).

Gradually, however, the **Mamluk**

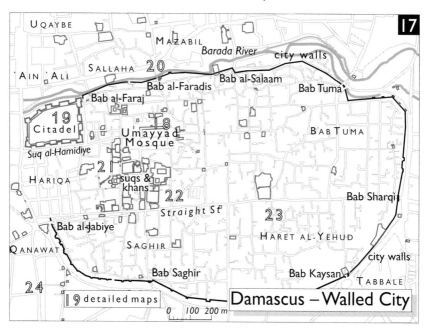

Aleppo. Under the **Zengid**s, Nur al-Din took the city more by charm than by arms in 1154. During his reign and that of his successor (and founder of the **Ayyubid** dynasty), Saladin (1176–93), Damascus again became a political centre of note and its economy recovered much of its vigour. Contemporary European travellers noted that the city was considerably larger than either Paris or Florence. It attracted leading theological and philosophical figures, as well as poets, from the more troubled environments of Baghdad and Palestine. This was the great age of the madrasas, their number more than quadrupling in the 13th century in order to reinforce Sunni orthodoxy (see box on page 27). The later Ayyubids' family quarrels, however,

dynasties based in Cairo restored prosperity to the city after 1260 and put a final end to the Crusader presence in Syria. The early phase of Bahri Mamluk rule was a third golden age for Damascus, particularly during the reign of Baybars (1260–77) who spent much of his time in the city, and under the governorship of Tengiz (1312–40). Some of the most resplendent monuments of Islamic Damascus date from these decades when the city was the second capital of the Mamluk Empire. It began to expand further beyond the confines of the walled city of Roman times and a new era of endowments resulted in the construction or restoration of 43 institutions between 1260 and 1311. However, internal Mamluk feuding became an increasingly debilitating distraction and in 1400 a campaign against Cairo by the Damascus governor, Tanabak, left the city undefended against the worst of the Mongol invasions, that of Timur. Mamluk rule was restored after the unprecedented devastation and depopulation but the city did not recover the sustained confidence it had gained under the early Mamluks. Instead a phoney 'boom economy' developed in supplying the Mamluk ruling class and soldiery (the rest of the population being left to struggle under the increasing burden of taxes and extortion).

In 1516, the **Ottoman** Turks conquered Syria and incorporated it into their empire. At first relatively enlightened and progressive, Ottoman control varied in its effects with the capacities of its governors. The Azem family, originally prosperous landholders from *Maarat al-Numan in northern Syria, monopolised the post of Governor of Damascus for the greater part of the 18th century. A governor such as Assaad Pasha al-Azem did much to improve the amenities of the city as had earlier governors, notably Darwish Pasha and Murad Pasha. Much of the importance of the city for the Ottomans lay in its position as the last of the major population centres where the Hajj from Turkey could assemble before it set out on its arduous three week crossing of the desert to Mecca. Ensuring the security of the Hajj and provisioning it with mounts, camping material and food was an essential element in the Ottoman claim to the caliphate and the growth of the Midan Quarter to the south of Damascus grew in step with the increasing emphasis on the pilgrimage.

The 19th century was a more troubled period with local resentment against the Ottomans rising and the city readily supporting the cause of Muhammad Ali (who had led a revolt against Istanbul from Cairo). Ibrahim Pasha was his lieutenant in Damascus and he concentrated on administrative and military reforms. Direct Ottoman rule was restored in 1840 but in the face of the rise of Arab nationalism in the late 19th century, continued Turkish rule had little to offer to advance

modernisation in economic terms and Damascus was rapidly overtaken by Beirut as the economic and intellectual centre of the region. In 1860, serious rioting touched off by Druze-Christian tensions in Lebanon led to a massacre of Damascus Christians. In spite of some 19th century civic improvements which tended to move the city's centre of gravity towards the newly-built Merdje Square, by the time of the French Mandate, old Damascus was a rather dispirited version of its former self. Some expansion of the city was undertaken under the French Mandate, especially in the quarters southwest of Salihiye where a garden suburb based on the Abu Roumaneh axis was developed by French planners.

Figures recording the population of Damascus across these millennia are virtually non-existent. The city perhaps reached its peak of prosperity under the Romans but declined thereafter for many centuries. Its population was still only 52,000 at the end of the 16th century and that figure was achieved after a reasonably long period of regeneration. It grew to 90,000 by the end of the 18th century, expanding only slowly for the first half of the 19th century. Clearly, historic population growth rates are outstripped by last century's explosion of the city's size from around 150,000 (1900) through 300,000 (1946) to over 3.5 million today.

The evidence of the history of the city can still be traced in its topography: hence the residual broad divisions into quarters. These were either traditionally associated with significant minority populations (Christians in the eastern quarter (Bab Tuma); Jews south of the central part of Straight Street; Shiites to the northeast of the Umayyad Mosque (Amara Quarter)) or identified with religious, charitable and trading institutions in the orthodox Sunni heartland between Suq al-Hamidiye and Straight Street (western part of the city). Over the centuries, the city's commercial heart had been steadily moving westward since Greek-Roman times when civic life was centred on the *agora* that once lay east of the Temple of Jupiter. After shifting to the middle of Straight Street by the

Arab middle ages, the commmercial heart moved to the quarter southwest of the Umayyad Mosque, the area that housed the first Mamluk and Ottoman khans. The westward trend was locked in with the construction of the Suq al-Hamidiye in the late 19th century thus completing the 180 degree rotation of the axis which had once linked the *agora* to the temple.

In recent centuries, Damascus' conquerors tended to expand further west beyond the walls to gain space for their new institutions, for their bureaucratic and military presence, or for recreation – the Turks along the present Sharia Quwatli; the French, as noted above, to fill in the space between the Turkish city and Mount Kassyun. The city acquired room to move without the need to cannibalise its past. Damascus has thus guarded its traditions perhaps more than any other of the great cities of the Middle East outside Cairo, unconsciously preserving in the process much which in other centres has been imprudently abandoned, especially last century.

REFS: Burns *Damascus* 2005; Elisséef *Dimashq* in *EI*2; Rihawi *Damascus* 1977; Sack *Damaskus* 1989; Sauvaget *Esquisse* 1934.

Damascus – Umayyad Mosque
(Plates 6b, 7a)

VARIANTS: Jamia al-Umawi (Arb)
PERIOD: Rom/Byz/Arb/Ott   RATING: ***
MAP: 18

LOCATION: Damascus old city – eastern end of the Suq al-Hamidiye.

In Damascus, there is a mosque that has no equal in the world. (al-Adrissi, 1154)

This itinerary is principally devoted to the Great Mosque of the Umayyads but includes as options one or two sites to the east of the mosque which are not easily reached from other routes. It can be combined with *Damascus – Suqs.

The Umayyad Mosque sums up in one site much of the complexity and continuity of Syrian history. The effect is almost overwhelming on first sight; scarcely less so on repeated visits. Along with the Dome of the Rock in Jerusalem (691), it is one of the great monuments to the creative energy of early Islam.

History

This site has been marked by sacred enclosures as far back as the early first millennium BC. The worship on this spot of the Semitic god, Hadad, later assimilated to the Greek Zeus or the Roman Jupiter, was promoted under imperial patronage. The temple was developed on lavish lines in the first century AD. Restored and redecorated under Septimius Severus (r 193–211), it formed part of his program of public works to underline his authority following the civil war of 193. In accordance with Syro-Phoenician tradition, the temple compound consisted of a large open enclosure with a central chamber and sacrificial altar. The compound extended over an area even larger than the present mosque, the inner enclosure (*temenos*) being surrounded by an outer *peribolos* of which a few traces can still be observed in the surrounding streets of the old city.

After the adoption of Christianity as the imperial cult, the temple was used to house a church ostensibly dedicated to John the Baptist. This is often attributed to the Emperor Theodosius (r 379–95) who is said to have ordered the tearing down of the inner shrine of the pagan temple in 379. With the taking of Damascus by the Arabs in 636, the Christians were allowed to continue to use their churches and Muslims were settled in new areas of the city. At least for the first 70 years, the Church of St John remained as the principal Christian place of worship though it seems likely that the extensive compound was for a time shared with Muslim worshippers whose prayers were oriented towards the south wall which faced Mecca.

The embellishment of the huge sacred area for the glory of Islam, however, proved a tempting objective for the great Umayyad builder, Caliph al-Walid (r 705–15). As the Muslim population of Damascus grew he recognised the need for a congregational assembly area capable of accommodating the entire community. The obvious place was the Greco-Roman temple compound, now housing the Christian church. After unsuccessful negotiations with the Christian community for the ceding of the church, he converted the inner compound into the magnificent mosque that you see today.[1] The work was commissioned in 708 and construction finished in 714–5, the year of al-Walid's death. It soaked up seven years of the state's revenue.[2] The caliph used local Syrian (and imported) craftsmen to execute much of the glorious mosaic work which survives only in part. The prayer hall was based on the mosque built by the Prophet in Medina. The southern half of the temple courtyard was covered by a massive roof supported on an elongated basilica plan (three aisles separated by two rows of internal columns). In order to re-orient such a wide building to the south, a central transverse aisle terminated in the *mihrab* and was topped by a magnificent dome.

The rest of the mosque consists of a huge courtyard (now paved in white marble) surrounded by a colonnade that borrows elements from several periods from Roman to Arab. This pastiche of elements comes together with striking effect.

The mosque has survived the intervening 1200 years with surprising integrity in spite of successive invasions, Mongol sackings and the ravages of earthquakes and fire. Perhaps most devastating was the fire of 1893 which destroyed much of the inner fabric of the prayer hall, leaving the outer walls, transept and courtyard intact. The Ottomans replaced the interior columns, the central dome and most of the roof in a rather severe

1 Several accounts (eg Ibn Asakir – Elisséeff trans. 1959: 36–8) relate that the Christians were compensated with permanent rights to four church sites elsewhere in the old city including the site of the present Greek Orthodox Patriarchate. For the architectural and symbolic background see Grabar's article in *Synthronon* (1968).

2 Muqadassi quoted in Creswell *Early Muslim* I 1969: 151.

and simplified style but the original plan has been retained.

Visit

There is no better way to prepare for the experience of visiting the mosque than to approach it along the 500 m length of the Suq al-Hamidiye (late Ottoman). Though the hubub of the suq may grate at times and its wares seem tawdry, it is the life blood of Damascus and its street life still represents what has drawn people here for thousands of years. As the long stretch of suq comes to an end, you see dramatically rising from the chaos the bizarre remnants of a grand and classical order: fragments of the geometry of the tall *propylaeum* or triumphal arch that proclaimed the western outer entrance to the Temple of Jupiter. The *propylaeum* took the common Syrian form of a huge semi-circular arch framed by a triangular entablature, the whole supported on six soaring columns (almost 12 m high), topped with superb Corinthian capitals. After this a few arches of a Byzantine arcade (built as part of a shopping complex of 330–40 that linked the outer and inner enclosures) bring you past the Koran sellers (Suq al-Miskiye) to the newly opened square that reveals the full extent of the western wall of the mosque.

Pause here and get your historical bearings. You are now between the outer and inner enclosures of the ancient temple. The outer complex was built in the first to third centuries of our era, at a time when the stability and prosperity introduced by Roman rule had taken hold. The outer perimeter of the compound (*peribolos*) was a vast rectangle measuring 305 m on the eastern and western edges and 385 m on the northern and southern sides. A monumental gateway stood on each side of the outer enclosure, each preceded by a tall *propylaeum* (the remains of the western one have just been noted). In ancient times, a portico ran around the inner side of the outer wall giving protection to an extensive bazar.

The inner Roman compound or *temenos* originally also had entrances on all four

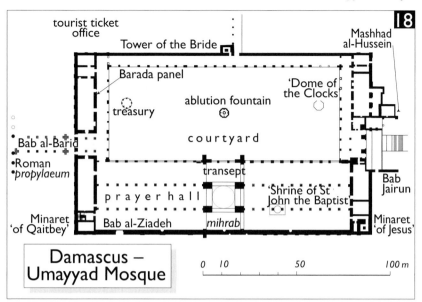

tourist ticket office

Tower of the Bride

Mashhad al-Hussein

18

Barada panel

treasury

ablution fountain

'Dome of the Clocks

Bab al-Barid

courtyard

•Roman
•*propylaeum*

transept

Bab Jairun

prayer hall

'Shrine of St John the Baptist'

Minaret 'of Qaitbey'

Bab al-Ziadeh

mihrab

Minaret 'of Jesus'

Damascus – Umayyad Mosque

0   10   50   100 m

sides (cf *Husn Suleiman), though the principal religious axis was through the eastern entrance. The inner enclosure whose west wall you see in front of you measures nearly 100 m by 150 m and is the cumulative result of all the construction phases since Roman times. The large lower blocks show the Roman mastery of size and precision. (Note the use of 18 shallow pilasters on the western wall to relieve the massive effect of so much masonry.) The upper reaches of the wall show later patching and reconstruction. The beautiful tower above the southwestern corner (described later) is the work of the late Mamluk period, constructed on the base of one of the lower Roman-Byzantine towers which were set at each corner of the compound.

The tourist entrance to the mosque is on the northern side. The ticket office (female visitors are required to don cloaks; men must cover their legs) is on the northwest corner of the compound. Continue on to an open area preceding the door in the centre of the north wall. (This recently paved area includes the tomb of Saladin (*Damascus – Suq al-Hamidiye) and some stray remains of the classical columns

found re-used in this area.) Taking the mosque's north door (Bab al-Amara or Bab al-Kallaseh, to the left of the Tower of the Bride), you enter the courtyard (*sahn*).

In the great **courtyard**, the full splendour of the mosque's design has lost little of its impact over 13 centuries (plate 6b). This huge space (approximately 50 m by 122 m) is flagged in stark white marble (a late 19th century project succeeding the 11th century stone or baked tiles that had replaced the original mosaic paving), thus reflecting the intensity of the sun with brilliant effect. Except on the southern side where the prayer hall is located, the courtyard is arcaded – or rather double arcaded – with an upper row of smaller arches resting on the lower. On the lower course, 47 supports comprise a mixture of columns and piers.[3] Note the use of slightly horseshoe-shaped arches, a design that was found in some late Byzantine churches (Church of Bissos at *Ruweiha)

3   Creswell *Early Muslim* 1 1969: 170–3 notes that the original pattern was: pier-column-column; pier-column-column etc but that the columns on the north side were progressively replaced over the centuries with stouter piers.

but, while it was transmitted to Muslim architecture in Umayyad Spain, where it became even more popular than in its Syrian homeland.

On the western side of the courtyard, note the small domed octagonal building raised on a cluster of eight truncated columns with Corinthian capitals, all obviously recycled from antiquity. This was the mosque's **treasury** (Kubbet al-Khazneh or Beit al-Mal), raised above the ground for security reasons. The beautiful mosaic decoration probably dates from the 13th or 14th century restorations of the original early Abbasid building.[4] Little else disturbs the dramatic simplicity of the paved court except for the late Ottoman central ablution fountain and on the eastern side another domed pavilion employing eight Byzantine columns with diverse capitals. (Until 1958, it was used to store the mosque's clock collection, hence its popular title, the Dome of the Clocks.)

The decorative scheme for the walls of the arcaded areas and the prayer hall façade is now only a faded version of its original splendour. To imagine the richness of the original, you have to picture virtually every surface of the courtyard covered in patterned marble and glistening **mosaics** of unparalleled splendour. What you see is partly the result of an unsatisfactory reconstruction of the mosaic work in the 1960s but enough remains of the original mosaics to convey the extraordinary richness of treatment. There can have been few buildings anywhere in the world which employed mosaic decoration on this scale.[5] The unbroken pattern weaved across walls, arcades, arches and under porticos without once resorting to the human figure for dramatic relief

4 Dussaud attributes the treasury, on the basis of an Arab historian's account, to the work of the Abbasid governor of Damascus, Fadil Ibn Salih in 788 – Dussaud 1927: 23.

5 A singular exception is the great Cathedral of Monreale built in 1172–6 by the Norman king of Sicily, William II, near Palermo which clearly borrowed from the same decorative tradition as the Umayyad Mosque through the Arab craftsmen employed on the project.

or emphasis: an extraordinary tribute to the vitality of the Umayyad synthesis. The mosaics still lead the eye through groves, orchards, fields, cities, rivercourses, pavilions and palaces, creating a universe of fantasy threaded by lush vegetation and stylized trails of acanthus leaves in a treatment that hovers between classical and oriental. For generations of desert dwellers or travellers, these mosaics fixed in two dimensions the Koranic vision of paradise:

> *Such is the Paradise promised to the righteous; streams run through it; its fruits never fail; it never lacks shade.*
> (Koran, Sura 13 'Thunder', 35)

Much of the mosaic work has been lost in fires and reconstruction efforts over the centuries but a good appreciation of its original condition can be gained from the sections under the western portico (especially the 1964 restoration of the Barada panel on the western wall) and in the darker, unreconstructed sections of the façade of the transept mid-way along the wall of the prayer hall. Restoration work carried out after 1963 has been criticised for its unsympathetic adaptation of the original styles and techniques and the use of garish and stereotyped designs.

[For those interested in a more detailed examination of the mosaics, the main surviving panels are:

- vestibule leading to the western portico – cleaned and restored 1929 with later work pre-1963, otherwise unchanged
- outer façade of the western portico – partly restored pre-1963
- inner façade of the western portico – restored pre-1963
- soffits of the western portico – uncovered 1929, restored pre-1965
- inner wall of the western portico, facing the court – the **'Barada panel'** (34.5 m by 7.3 m) – Umayyad work with some patching under Baybars (late 13th century) – uncovered 1929, restored post 1963
- walls of the 'Treasury' – ?Abbasid period
- façade of the northern portico (right) – three fragments, restored c1954
- façade of the transept of the prayer hall

(plate 7a) – except for two (darker) sections, the façade was much restored in the 1960s
- within the prayer hall – inner face of the transept – largely restored in the Seljuk period (late 11th century)
- upper façade (left) of the east portico – fragments only, some restored under Nur al-Din (mid 12th century).]

On all surfaces, the mosaic extended down to a level 6.5 m above the ground. Below this, the Umayyads had decorated the arcades and other façades with **marble panelling**. Most of the geometrically-patterned cladding you see now is post-1893 but fragments of the original treatment can be detected in the eastern vestibule, around the southern lateral door (Bab Jairun – discussed later). This would have been interrupted by small pilasters and marble grill panels based on elaborate geometrical patterns (among the first examples of such geometrical designs later a hallmark of Arab decoration).

As you walk around taking in the details of this great monument, note particularly the three **minarets** that crown the walls of the mosque compound. The southern minarets were erected on the truncated bases of earlier Roman-Byzantine corner towers. The lack of towers on the northern corners has been seen as resulting from the extensive restructuring in the Arab middle ages of the whole northern wall including the addition of a single central minaret. The southern towers were probably the earliest versions of the minaret in Syria and proclaimed the presence of the Islamic community in a city which was still largely Christian.

The existing minarets are as follows:

- Immediately to the right of the western entrance (southwest corner), the **Western Tower** (Madhanat al-Gharbiye) built by the Mamluk sultan, Qait Bey, in 1488 in the Egyptian style.
- On the southeastern corner, the tallest of the minarets, the **Tower of Jesus** (Madhanat Issa). According to Islamic popular tradition, Jesus will descend from heaven via this tower

in order to combat the Antichrist before the Last Judgment. The minaret was built in 1247 on the site of an Umayyad structure but the upper part is Ottoman.
- On the middle of the northern wall, the **Tower of the Bride** (Madhanat al-Arus). The lower part dates from the ninth century but the upper structure is from the late 12th century when the northern wall was extensively reconstructed.

At the western and eastern ends of the courtyard is a series of narrow halls, dating from the Roman construction. On the western side lies the former tourist entrance and ablutions hall. On the east, the larger room to the north of the eastern entrance leads into an inner chamber which has become a major Shiite place of pilgrimage (**Mashhad al-Hussein**) associated closely with the powerful tradition of the martyrdom of Hussein at Kerbala (modern Iraq) at the hands of the Umayyads. Legend has it that the head of Hussein was brought here from Kerbala and placed by the caliph in a niche, with the aim of ridiculing Hussein and the supporters of Ali.[6] In some accounts, the Umayyads later sent the head to Medina for burial but there are also legends (unsupported by any physical evidence of a grave or shrine) that the head was buried in the mosque precinct.

Before entering the prayer hall of the mosque, pause again in front of its **façade** to take in the overall shape of the great chamber. Note how the long (137 m) façade is broken by a central transept, the face of which carries some of the most spectacular of the mosaic work already described. The transept façade, clearly based on Byzantine precedents, consists of three lower arches topped by three

6　Hussein's sister Zeinab and his son, Ali, were also brought back to Damascus to participate in this humiliation. Zeinab's burial mosque on the southern outskirts of Damascus (a largely modern re-housing) is another major centre of Shiite pilgrimage. Hussein's daughter, Ruqaye, is also commemorated in a new Shiite mosque in the Amara Quarter.

smaller ones framed within a sweeping arch. This lower area is bordered by two stout pilasters to provide stability. Above, a triangular entablature surmounts an extensive panel of mosaic work.

Immediately inside the western entry used by the faithful, the **Bab al-Barid** (Postal Gate), is the magnificent vestibule which retains many elements of the earliest phase of the mosque's construction. The doors of the Bab al-Barid decorated with bronze panels are dated by inscription to 1416. The vestibule's patterned roof in painted wood (restored) dates from the 15th century and is supported on arcading (possibly Byzantine). Note particularly on the upper parts of the walls and above the western doorway remains of the earliest phase of mosaic work (the overall design was discussed earlier).

You should now enter the **prayer hall** by the western door. (The doors separating the prayer hall from the courtyard were not, incidentally, part of the Umayyad building which had no fixed panels enclosing the arches.) Though elements of the prayer hall may have Roman or Byzantine precedents, the overall plan is a departure from the earlier tradition of the triple-aisled basilica. Its length and relatively narrow proportions are broken by the central transept, the purpose of which is to steer the worshipper towards the middle of the south wall rather than the east or west ends which are blank. At this focal point, the *mihrab* oriented towards Mecca was placed, one of the first recorded uses of this device. The transept (rare in buildings before that date and usually confined to a *narthex* at the western end of Byzantine religious buildings) was further emphasised by the use of a dome to crown its centre. The design was thus an Umayyad adaptation of various elements found in the wider Mediterranean and eastern traditions.[7]

---

7 Grabar *Grande Mosquée* 1968: 38 notes the influence of the first mosque, at Medina, with a Byzantine basilica plan for the prayer room substituted for the hypostyle hall. He believes the transept or axial nave was intended to emphasise the area reserved for the Caliph.

The modern (post-1893) building broadly follows this plan but the dome has been reconstructed in a Turkish style adapted from European models. (Its predecessor was itself an 11th century replacement in stone of the Umayyad original in wood.) The columns are new but neo-classical in their inspiration and the arcading of the aisles is a simplified version of the Umayyad original. A few remnants of the inner structure of the pre-1893 building remain, notably the beautiful wood panelling of the transept ceiling on the courtyard side and the fragments of mosaic work (probably 11th century) on the northern wall. Note too the six eighth century windows at both ends of the transept enclosed by marble grills. They are the earliest Islamic examples of geometric interlace-patterned marble.

The site of the legendary burial of the head of St John the Baptist[8] is commemorated by the extravagant marble monument to the east of the transept. The monument is late Ottoman, having been constructed in place of a mausoleum destroyed in the fire of 1893.

Those interested in further exploring the history of the mosque may wish to make a tour of the **outer walls**. Exit by the northern entrance and turn left, following an anti-clockwise direction to the long southern wall of the prayer hall.[9] Note that all the mosque windows are placed high (8 m at least above the ground). This reflected the fact that the Roman inner *temenos* wall was kept intact and the mosque's windows placed above it. On the left of the transept façade (partly covered

---

8 There is no evidence at all that the head of St John was bought to Damascus though many legends have sprung up on the subject. An Arab historian, Ibn al-Asakir, recounts many versions of the discovery of the head by the Caliph al-Walid who ordered that the spot be commemorated by the placing of a distinctive column above it. The head was left in place and the spot commemorated by the Muslims on account of St John the Baptist's role as a precursor of Christ, one of the Prophets recognised by Islam.

9 The door immediately after the corner is Bab Ziadeh.

at the moment by an electricity sub-station building) is the original southern entrance to the Jupiter Temple inner compound, a triple doorway whose upper moulded lintel can still be seen. When the mosque was constructed, the Roman doorway was blocked as part of the new arrangement orienting the prayer hall towards Mecca (south). Before that time, Creswell believes, Christians and Muslims used this same doorway to gain access to their separate mosque and church within the temple compound. The inscription in Greek over the central doorway reads:

Thy Kingdom, O Christ, is an everlasting Kingdom, and Thy dominion endureth throughout all generations.[10]

South of the point you have reached is the probable site of the Umayyad palace, al-Khadra, erected shortly after the Arab conquest in the mid seventh century.

A left turn at the next corner brings you to the eastern **façade** of the inner compound and the great gateway now known as **Bab Jairun** or Bab al-Nawfarah (Fountain Gate). In Roman times the monumental main entrance, a triple doorway, was preceded by an imposing *propylaeum* 33 m wide jutting out 15 m from the eastern wall. With its 15 steps, this massive gateway must have been a powerful climax to the colonnaded axis that led up to the temple from the *agora* to the east. To trace the axis, go down the stairs past the coffee shop (right), and follow the street (Badreddin al-Hassan St) that heads directly east for 120 m. You will come to another triple gateway that led into the outer compound. Two monoliths form the sides of the central passage but the rise in the level of the ground in the past 1800 years has left the side doorways almost buried beneath the surface.

From the gateway, Qaimariye St leads down the broad colonnaded axis which once led 250 m east to the *agora* of Hellenistic-Roman   times.[11] No trace

remains of this open gathering space in the maze of houses. This avenue between temple and *agora* provided a second west-east axis to complement the commercially-oriented thoroughfare perpetuated to the south in Straight Street.

Continue down the road east of the gateway. There is an interesting mosque worth the short diversion from Bab Jairun along Qaimariye St which, after a short dog-leg to the right, continues the axis eastwards (see map 20). After 150 m on the right is the entrance to the **Mosque al-Qaimariye** built in 1743 by Fathi Effendi, an Ottoman treasury official. 'A plan of obviously Ottoman origin (a portico of three domes giving access to a prayer hall covered by a large dome) but with a decor so profoundly influenced by Syro-Mamluk traditions (stone in alternating white, black and ochre tones) that the imported character of the architecture is somewhat overshadowed by the local exuberance of the patterns of colour' (Raymond). The effect of the quiet courtyard, the vegetation and the mellowed stone is striking. One street to the north is the Madrasa al-Qaimariye (possibly Mamluk).

To return to the north wall of the Umayyad Mosque, you need to enter the alleyway second right west of the Roman gateway and skirt the northeastern corner of the Mosque. Turn left immediately before the Epigraphy Museum (Madrasa Jaqmaqiye – *Damascus – Suqs) (map 20). Here (as in the western entrance), part of the Byzantine arcade joining the outer and inner walls remains but (as noted earlier) most of the Roman wall on the north side has been replaced over the centuries. You are now back at the northern doorway of the mosque.

REFS: Bahnassi *Great Umayyad* 1989; Burns *Damascus* 2005; Creswell *Early Muslim* I 1979; de Lorey; Dussaud *Temple*; Ettinghausen & Grabar 1987: 37–45; Freyburger 'Jupiter-Heiligtums' *DaM* 1989; Grabar *Grande Mosquée* 1968; Raymond 1985: 101; Sack *Damaskus – Beitrag*; Sack *Damaskus*

---

10 The translation of the inscription adapted from Psalm CXLV, 13 (Septuagint) comes from Creswell *Early Muslim* I 1969: 164.

11 The quarter is now called Zukak al-Saha. Elisséeff disputes Sauvaget's earlier thesis that

the *agora* was established in Hellenistic times, preferring to attribute it to the monumental building projects of the Romans. See his article in Hourani *Islamic City* 1970: 170.

1989; Sauvaget *Monuments* 1932: 12–38; Wulzinger & Watzinger *Damaskus – islamische* 1924.

Damascus – Citadel and North Walls

PERIOD: Rom/Arb   RATING: * MAP: 19, 20

LOCATION: The itinerary begins with the western face of the Citadel then follows a clockwise direction along the branch of the Barada that flows besides the northern walls, ending at Bab Tuma. [NOTE: This is a somewhat long walk (3+ km) and, especially in hot weather, is better done in the morning.]

To orient yourself, you may wish to begin by visiting the Museum of Damascus which is located in the Beit Khalid al-Azem, 200 m north of the Citadel. (Take al-Thawra St, turn right just as the overpass ends. Museum is immediately behind the high-rise building.) The palace (donated to the state by a former Prime Minister) follows the Turkish pattern of two distinct zones, *haremlek* (for the family – north) and *selamlek* (for reception of visitors – south). The *haremlek* court is used for the museum and includes several salons ranged around the open space. That on the north of the western side contains an interesting fountain in the form of a double meander course, used for competitions between floating objects – a sort of early pin-ball machine. The room to the east contains several models of the old city which will usefully give visitors a perspective on its layout.

Return now to the Citadel along al-Thawra St. On the left is the Suq al-Khail (horse suq – replanned during the late Ottoman period) and the vegetable and saddlery markets.

Citadel – History

The Damascus Citadel may surprise those who expect to see a formidable Arab military fortification on a par, for example, with Aleppo. Given its setting on flat ground, hemmed in by cluttered urban surrounds, the fortifications never presented the same forbidding front. Now

that the Citadel's courtyard, however, has been opened to visitors, it is possible to appreciate that the size of the Citadel is vast. Most of the construction is from the Seljuk, Ayyubid and Mamluk periods. Heavy use since then (in the Turkish, French and independence periods) has not been kind to the fabric. Work to restore some of the inner apartments is continuing but already a visit is a must, particularly for the chance to appreciate the beauty of the eastern gateway linking the Citadel to the city.

Suppositions about the existence of Roman remains within the Citadel structure have recently been disproved. While it is not inconceivable that the site was used before the medieval fortifications were undertaken (material going back to the third millennium BC has been uncovered in the post-2002 excavations), there is incomplete evidence so far of any Roman structures in situ.

The remains recognisable today largely date from the 11th century and later. Extensive remains of a Seljuk fortified enclosure lie within the later Ayyubid fortifications. When the new fortifications were renewed on a more massive scale by Sultan al-Adil in 1207, Damascus had become the key centre of resistance to the Crusader presence, a role built up particularly under the leadership of Saladin (r 1176–93). The city had experienced Crusader attacks three times in the 12th century. Al-Adil (a brother of Saladin who replaced the latter's son, al-Afdal, in Damascus in 1196 and ruled until 1218) spent 12 years on the refortification project. It included, besides the enlargement of the Seljuk fortifications to a rectangle 220 m by 150 m, a new palace complex in the northeastern sector. The Ayyubid enclosure, however, was badly damaged in the first of the great Mongol invasions in 1260. The 16 towers and walls with three levels of firing slits were partly dismantled. Baybars, the Mamluk sultan (r 1260–77) rebuilt most of them. Just as well, otherwise later Mongols – particularly Timur during the fierce siege of 1400 – would have had nothing to knock down; which they did with ruthless efficiency. The Turks over 500 years made less than a 100 percent effort to repair the damage though they continued to use the Citadel as a military base.

to the Suq al-Hamidiye. The southern wall unfortunately cannot be seen as the Suq al-Hamidiye presses up against the enclosure comprising three towers (two well-preserved) with fine machicolations.

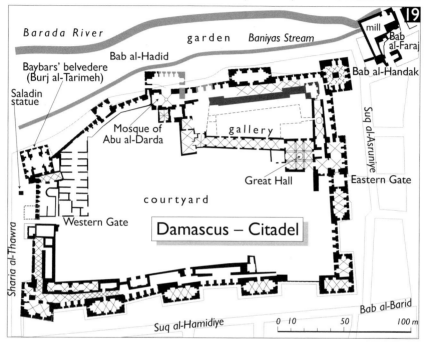

Citadel – Visit

At the time of writing, the Citadel is still undergoing extensive reconstruction including continuing excavations. Visitors can sometimes cross the courtyard between the western and eastern gates and certainly make an external circuit of the massive fortifications and towers. The Citadel is roughly a rectangle in shape but with the northwestern corner cut off. It is protected by 12 surviving towers, the southwestern one having been heavily reconstructed in the 1980s. The work shows the features typical of the Ayyubid masons – large rusticated blocks, massive regular towers, vaulted interiors and use of machicolation and arrow slits.

For an external circuit, begin at the southwestern corner north of the entrance

Within the southern circuit, a series of two-storeyed 12th century halls flanked a later Mamluk gallery between the Ayyubid and Seljuk enclosures.

The central entrance on the western side once lay between two substantial towers, now largely gone. A little to the north you can see the opening by which the Baniyas stream of the Barada was channeled under the Citadel replenishing its cisterns before flowing under the rest of the old city. This also provided a means of filling the ditch surrounding the Citadel with water in the event of attack.

The tower on the northwestern corner where the Akrabani stream cuts off a corner of the quadrilateral was embellished with a high platform from which Baybars could review his troops, hence its title,

Belvedere Tower.

Continue your tour along the northern side where the river divides the walls from the suqs to the north. The partly ruined double towers in the centre of the north wall protected the Gate of Iron (**Bab al-Hadid**) whose twisting passages required any attacker to negotiate five closely-defended bends. The key element in the northeastern defences was the corner tower dated by inscription to 1209, the most massive (21 m by 23 m) in the complex.

A small park has recently been created north of the Citadel, occupying the space between the Akrabani and main channel of the Barada. This recreates the centuries-old use of this area for relaxation and coffee-drinking, its pleasant and cooling environment having been noted by early European travellers to Damascus.

Continue around to the eastern flank of the Citadel where the main access gate to the civilian city was protected between two salients. Its position on a less exposed side allowed for a more aesthetic treatment of the doorway placed obliquely in the space between the towers. The entry vestibule (1213), hemmed in by the two huge central towers of the eastern wall, is a beautiful example of honeycombed vaulting (*muqarnas*). This northern Syrian device, until then rarely used in Damascus, was employed here with striking effect.

You may be able to complete your circuit of the Citadel by continuing through the eastern gateway into the outer chamber of the Ayyubid ceremonial complex. At the moment, the passage takes you only through a corner of the magnificent columned hall with a central pool. This hall, its central dome supported on four massive columns, almost certainly salvaged from the remains of the Temple of Jupiter, was the centre-piece of al-Adel's staterooms. To the west, still under reconstruction, an impressive cross-vaulted gallery led from the main (northern) gate of the Citadel, providing an equally daunting approach for any visitor.

Walls – History

Though there are some traces of Roman work on the lower courses, the city walls as you see them today are largely post-11th century. They reflect the greater need for security in the face of Crusader incursions and Mongol attacks (1260–1400). The gates, however, largely coincide with Roman gateways. There were nine gateways in the Arab period of which seven (and traces of an eighth) remain (see box under *Damascus – Introduction on page 95).

The city's defensive plan was probably largely the achievement of Nur al-Din in the mid 12th century. Much of the work of that period, however, had to be extensively reconstructed under the Ayyubids during the next century, particularly under Sultan al-Salih Ismael (sultan twice, 1237–45). Generally, the phases of construction can be recognised by the quality of the masonry. The Roman blocks are large and precise. The work of the mid 12th to mid 13th centuries follows regular courses 50–60 cm high. Mamluk courses are smaller (20–30 cm) while later Turkish work is largely irregular in pattern. Much of the fabric of the walls has been lost to domestic building in recent centuries, though the practice has now ended given the exodus of population from the narrow confines of the old city (largely impossible for car access) and legislation controlling the modernisation of the streetscape.

Walls – Visit

Return now to the northeastern tower of the Citadel. It will be some distance before the line of walls becomes evident as you head east, taking the street which leads from the northeastern corner of the Citadel. Almost immediately, you turn left, through the double gateway, the **Bab al-Faraj** (Gate of Deliverance). The inner doorway dates from the earliest phase of Ayyubid reconstruction (1239–41). The 1154/5 outer door, around a double bend, was reconstructed in the 15th century. There was no Roman gate on this site where the first opening in the wall dates from the time of Nur al-Din.

Continue east, by going straight ahead, not through the outer gate, skirting the Shiite quarter of the old city (Amara) which lies behind the 1154–74 walls of this sector. Along a picturesque, often-vaulted alleyway (Bain al-Surain St), you reach after 250 m a modern Shiite mosque in the Iranian style (Sitt Ruqaye). Turn left to the second of the gateways, the **Bab al-Faradis** (Gate of the Orchards) named after the extra-mural district to the north. The Roman gate stood a little to the south of this site but the present structure dates from the Ayyubid efforts to rebuild the city's fortifications (1132–42). Originally a double gateway, only the outer door is intact. The inner door was reconstructed in the 15th century but only an archway survives.

[Those interested in exploring some of the mosques to the north of the walls should at

The long inscription on the lintel records the extravagant attributes of the Ayyubid ruler, al-Salih Ismael (sultan twice, 1237–45).

From the Bab al-Salaam, the road continues to the east for another 300 m at last rejoining both the line of walls and the rivercourse (which has only been glimpsed to the north since leaving the Citadel). The wall is well exposed on the right and the different types of masonry can be distinguished.

At the end of this stretch, the road brings you to the square that opens around the fourth of the gateways, **Bab Tuma** (St Thomas' Gate). Bab Tuma has become synonymous with the Christian quarter of Damascus. The gate itself is now stranded in a busy square and traffic circle. It consists of a 1227 Ayyubid reconstruction

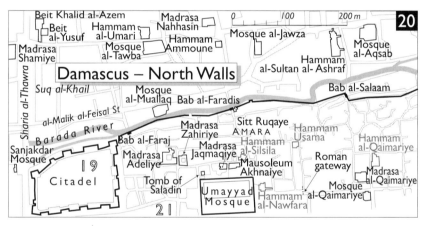

this point follow the itinerary described at the end of this entry.]

A 200 m walk to the east along the lane north of the Ruqaye Mosque (passing after 50 m the house on the left that once was the winter residence of the Algerian patriot, Abd al-Kader al-Jazairi – *Damascus – Salihiye Quarter) brings you to the most impressive of the Arab gateways, the **Bab al-Salaam** (Gate of Peace). Stones from the Roman gate were re-built in the present form by the Ayyubids in 1243 following a 1171/2 reconstruction.

of the Roman gate with the machicolation added during the restoration of 1333/4 by Tengiz, the Mamluk Governor of Damascus. The Roman gate marked the northern end of the eastern *cardo*.

The eastern and southern limits of the old city are described elsewhere (*Damascus – Straight Street; *Damascus – Southwest Quarter) but you may wish to round off this tour with the **Tower of al-Salih Ayyub** (sultan of Damascus 1239, 1245–9) whose remains (base and first storey only) stand at the northeastern corner of the walls (100 m to the east). The tower dates from the final (1248–49) Ayyubid re-fortification of the city. The relatively open area to the east (agricultural land until recently almost touched the old city here) marks the point where the Arab armies camped before taking Damascus in 635–6. Across the road immediately east (behind a modern mosque) is the **Tomb of Sheikh Arslan** (original parts are 13th–14th century), a local saint and poet (d 1146) whose reputation for piety and asceticism earned him the title of 'protector of Damascus'.

[The tour finishes here. Those who are returning on foot to the starting point at the Suq al-Hamidiye may want to make their own itinerary through the winding streets of the old city.]

Mosques North of the Walls

As noted above, a short excursion from Bab al-Faradis takes in several mosques in the busy commercial quarter north of the walls. Head directly north along the suq until it meets the tree-lined al-Malik al-Feisal Street. 200 metres on the left is the Mosque al-Muallaq. The façade is the most noteworthy part of the building – particularly beautiful honeycombed doorway on the right.

Return to the point where you emerged from the suq leading north from the Bab al-Faradis. Cross al-Feisal St and continue towards the north ascending the lane which branches to the left. After 200 m, this leads you to the street which has come from the Suq al-Saruja At this intersection, you find the **al-Tawba Mosque** (Jami`a al-Tawba) built as the city's third congregational mosque in 1231–4 on the site of a caravanserai which had become a house of ill repute, hence the Arabic title 'Mosque of Repentance'.

Take the continuation of Saruja St in the easterly direction. You are now in the area that lay at the southern limit of the Hellenistic hippodrome) now largely covered by a major Muslim burial ground, the Dahdah Cemetery. At 150 m along the street on the left you will find after

a few metres the **Madrasa Nahhasin** (1457/8) (School of the Copperworkers) with a fine stalactited entrance portal. The Dahdah Cemetery itself is worth inspection, its origins going back beyond the Islamic conquest when the disused ancient hippodrome served as the main burial ground for the city.

Return to al-Malik al-Feisal St and walk eastwards for 100 m. You come to a Y-intersection which encloses a small minareted mosque, the **Mosque al-Jawza** of 1676 (note Roman monolith column in the courtyard). Return to the main road and continue east (right) for 200 m. Look carefully for the narrow façade of an old bath house, the **Hammam al-Sultan.** The coat of arms of the Mamluk Sultan Qait Bey (r 1468–96) decorates the honeycombed doorway, but inside the changing room of the baths is now in ruins and what remains serves as a furniture factory. The rest of the baths (probably early 14th century) are reached by the entrance in the side street to the left that leads to Bab al-Salaam.

Sixty metres on the right is the **Mosque al-Aqsab** (also called the Mosque al-Zainabiye) founded in 1301 and reconstructed in 1408 after the last Mongol invasion by one Nasr al-Din Muhammad, son of Manjak. The square minaret is the most notable feature. Beautifully constructed in contrasting stone, it is divided into several layers by cornices. The windows of the top layer comprise twin enclosures within a single frame, a design not unlike Gothic windows though the decorative treatment is purely Arab. Two Roman columns are re-used in the courtyard (left arcade). The mihrab is decorated with marble mosaics encrusted with turquoise faience, a masterpiece of Mamluk decorative treatment. This was once the site of a Byzantine church.

REF: Burns *Damascus* 2005; Ecochard and le Coeur 1942; Herzfeld *Damascus Studies* IV 1948; Cathcart King 'Defences of the Citadel of Damascus' 1951; Omran & Dabboura *The Citadel of Damascus* Damascus 1997; Rihawi *Damascus* 1977; Sauvaget *Monuments*; 1932 Sauvaget 'Citadelle' in *Syria* 1930; WW *Damaskus – islamische* 1924.

Damascus – Suq al-Hamidiye Area

PERIOD Arb/Ott RATING: * MAP: 21

LOCATION: The old city immediately north and south of the Suq al-Hamidiye. Begin at the open area in front of the western entrance to the suq. This itinerary covers the busiest section of the old suqs of Damascus. The route involves around 1.5 km of walking with some poking into obscure corners and alleyways. You may wish to combine this itinerary with *Damascus – Umayyad Mosque.

The **Suq al-Hamidiye** is the grandest of Damascus' bazar streets, a radical departure from the city's traditional commercial architecture. It is built along an axis of the Roman city that probably matched on the western side the eastern monumental approach to the great Temple of Jupiter-Hadad. This 500 m thoroughfare had been lost over the centuries and the area had been used for a mixture of suqs and houses, interspersed with gardens. It was not until the reign of the Ottoman Sultan Abd al-Hamid II (r 1876–1909) that the eastern sector, Suq al-Jadid (built in 1780–1 along the line of the southen ditch of the Citadel), was widened and extended eastwards to the mosque. The governor, Rashid Nasha Pasha, sought to rival the great shopping precincts in the European style, increasingly popular in Istanbul. The gallery was lined with two-storeyed shops. It was built using such new materials as plate glass for the shopfronts and steel girders to support the second storey. In 1886 the thoroughfare was given an arched roof, originally in wood but, after 1912, metal as a fire precaution. (The iron roof was later peppered with the evidence of the French bombardments or aerial machine-gunning of the suq area.) The suq quickly became popular for its elegant and quiet environment. Workshops, offices or storerooms were relegated to the floor above. It was named in honour of the reigning sultan.

The western end of the suq also marks the site of the former Bab al-Nasr (Gate of Victory – see box page 95), an Ayyubid gateway which was pulled down in 1863 during the widening of Sinaniye St. The association is commemorated in the broad street that leads directly west towards the Hijaz Station, Sharia Nasr.

Head down the suq, counting the cross streets on the right as you go. After 250 m, just as the roof gives way to clear sky, turn right. After about 75 m on the left, you will notice a white-painted honeycombed arch over a gateway. This is the entrance to one of the most remarkable Islamic institutions in Damascus, the **Maristan Nur al-Din** (Hospital of Nur al-Din).[12]

The building is now a fascinating museum of Arab medical and scientific history. The institution was originally founded as a hospital and medical teaching centre by Nur al-Din in 1154, immediately after adding Damascus to his domains. The *maristan* functioned as a healing centre until the construction of the National Hospital in the 19th century. The building as you see it now owes much to the restorations of 1283 and of the 18th century.

The honeycomb-domed doorway is a notable piece of architecture. Its shallow dimensions are unusual in Syrian architecture. While it provides an indication of early Mesopotamian influence, the ideas were later adapted to the Syrian idiom. (For instance, the moulding of the *muqarnas* shapes, here worked in plaster on a wooden framework, quickly gave way to the skilful use of stone for the same purpose.) The lintel of the outer doorway is recycled from antiquity (possibly it once topped a window of the outer enclosure of the Temple of Jupiter). Note the disused fountain to the right with a striking *muqarnas* canopy culminating in a shell half-dome. The doors are encrusted with geometric decoration executed in copper nails with carved wooden panels on the inside. The *muqarnas* dome inside the vestibule is also a Mesopotamian feature introduced to Syria by the Seljuk Turks. The plaster-on-wood dome is supported on two semi-domes with the shell above

---

12 There were two others in Damascus – Maristan Dakaki; Maristan al-Qaimariye (Salihiye Quarter, constructed c1256).

in cement, a Mesopotamian idea that was quickly superceded.

The courtyard of the *maristan* (15 m by 20 m) provides a beautiful retreat with *iwans* on each side. The principal *iwan* (opposite the entrance) served for consultations and lessons in medicine. Though smaller, the south *iwan* which houses the *mihrab*

towards the Umayyad Mosque for another 200 m. As you reach the remains of the Roman *propylaeum*, take the cross street on the left and follow it for about 100 m. This will bring you to a point where two grand entrances face each other.

That on the right is the **Madrasa Zahiriye** or Mausoleum of Baybars which contains

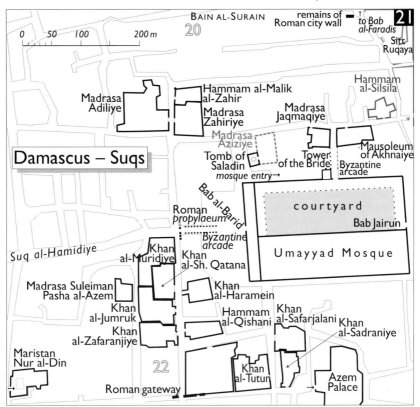

is more richly decorated. The *mihrab* includes a semi-circular slab in white marble beautifully decorated with vines and grapes. More marble is used to provide an upper frieze, also richly decorated with cornucopias and vegetal themes, and below it, four other slabs, two of which seem to have originally come from Byzantine offering tables.

Return now to the main suq and continue

the tomb of the Mamluk sultan who did more than any Muslim leader to secure the Crusaders' final departure from the east (plate 8b). On the death of Baybars in Damascus in 1277, his son acquired the building, then a private house, the Beit Akiki, in which Saladin's father, Ayyub, had lived and where Saladin had spent part of his youth. It was converted into a funerary college or madrasa by adding the gateway and domed burial chamber (recently restored). The entrance is a singular masterpiece, executed in contrasting black and yellow stone, with marble inserts which carry three bands of finely executed inscriptions. (The top two relate to the endowments that funded the madrasa, the lowest one to the date of construction.) The *muqarnas* work which forms the half-dome over the entrance is particularly impressive, falling in a cascade of shells and arches to make the transition between semi-circle and rectangle. Note too the superb geometric medallions on the entrance façade and the south wall.

The madrasa served until recently as an academy of art. It is now under restoration but it is usually possible to inspect the inner courtyard and the mausoleum of Baybars and his son, Muhammad Said – a domed chamber with four shallow *iwans*. The chamber, the work of the famous architect, Ibrahim Ibn Ganaim, contains an impressive range of decorative work: the polychrome patterned marble on the walls is striking in its boldness; several friezes of carved marble, stone marquetry, gilded plaster or wood; an extraordinary *mihrab* in patterned marble with a mosaic half-dome framed by colonnettes. Perhaps most unexpected is the surmounting wide band of mosaic work executed in a style which imitates that of the Umayyad Mosque 500 years beforehand, though in a somewhat coarser treatment.

The baths to the left of the madrasa, Hammam al-Malik al-Zaher, have recently been restored and again function for their original purpose. They may in part date from the original Beit Akiki (tenth–12th century). The dressing room is new in its treatment but the warm and hot rooms behind survive from earlier centuries.

The entrance already noted on the western side of the street leads to the **Madrasa Adiliye** which once housed the Arab Academy and the manuscript collection of the National Library. The name refers to the burial in this building of Sultan al-Adil Saif al-Din (d 1218), the brother of Saladin and the man who contributed most to the re-fortification of Damascus. The construction of the madrasa began

earlier (1172–3), however, and was left unfinished until al-Kamil completed it in 1222–3 to serve as the burial place of his father. In style it is purely northern Syrian, with many features in common with the Madrasa Nuriye (*Damascus – Khans). The entrance is a fine example of simplified *muqarnas* with a hanging keystone and bold decorative treatment, almost a rival to the doorway to the Mausoleum of Baybars opposite. After a narrow vestibule, you reach the courtyard, once surrounded by the rooms of students and teachers with an open *iwan* to the right (the reading room of the library). In the near left corner is the burial chamber of al-Adil whose large dome rests on unusual sloping honeycomb supports.

The next group of buildings lies on the north side of the Umayyad Mosque. Retrace your steps as far as the southern wall of Baybars' mausoleum, then follow the broad street to the left for about 100 m. Here, after passing the ticket office for the Umayyad Mosque, you will find amid a small oasis of trees and foliage on the left, the enclosure which houses the Tomb of Saladin.

Most of the original Madrasa Aziziye which housed **Saladin's tomb** has disappeared, leaving an isolated arch and the burial chamber completed in 1196 after the death of Salah al-Din Yusuf Ibn Ayyub (Saladin) in 1193. Certainly it is one of the most understated tombs of any great historical figure, befitting the unassuming pretensions of this outstanding Muslim leader who died without personal wealth though his writ ran from northern Iraq to Libya. The modesty of the site perhaps contributed to its neglect over the centuries. En route to the Holy Land in 1898, the German Kaiser Wilhelm II passed through Damascus and funded the restoration of the chamber as a tribute to Sultan Abd al-Hamid II. (A new cenotaph had already been provided by Abd al-Hamid in 1878.) The silver lamp over the new tomb bears the monograms of the kaiser and of the sultan.

The kaiser also bestowed an honorific wreath on Saladin's tomb. Though still safely preserved in a glass case when observed by the redoubtable Gertrude Bell in 1911 it was misappropriated by T E Lawrence in 1918 and 'given' by him to the Imperial War Museum in London.[13] The French General Gouraud, following the Allied victory at the Battle of Maysaloun in 1918, is said to have made his way to Saladin's tomb and proclaimed: 'Saladin, we're back!'. The sultan's cenotaph is in white marble but the remains of the original in humbler wood (with intricate floral design described by Sauvaget as among the great achievements of 12th century decorative art) is preserved behind glass to the right. The inscription in green lettering reads: *Oh Allah, be satisfied with this soul and open to him the gates of Paradise, the last conquest for which he hoped.*[14] The faience panels are 17th century.

If you return to the street which brought you from Baybars' Mausoleum and continue along it a little way to the right, you will reach the building which serves as the Museum of Epigraphy. The Museum is housed in the **Madrasa Jaqmaqiye** built in 1418–20 by the Mamluk governor of Damascus, Jaqmaq al-Argunsawi (who later went on to become sultan in Cairo, 1438–52). The façade is a beautiful example of polychrome work of the period. Inside, the marble and pearl shell mosaics are striking but the wood and marble sculpture are mediocre. The museum has a collection of Arabic inscriptions including some early examples in Kufic lettering.

Adjacent to the east (a side street separates them) is the **Mausoleum of Akhnaiye** dedicated in 1413.

REFS: Burns *Damascus* 2005; Flood *Muqarnas* 1997; Kayem; nd Meinecke *Mamlukische Architectur* I 1992; Sack 1985; Sauvaget *Monuments* 1932; Sauvaget &

13 The Museum's acquisition certificate carries a note from Lawrence: 'removed by me as Saladin no longer required it' – Malcolm Brown *Lawrence of Arabia, the Life, the Legend* London 2005: 135.
14 Adapted from translation in Herzfeld *Damascus* III 1946: 47. For Baha al-Din's account of Saladin's death, see Gabrieli 1984: 246–52

Ecochard 1938–50; Scharabi 1983; S Weber 2006: 209–23; WW *Damaskus – islamische* 1924.

Damascus – Khans, Azem Palace (Plate 7b)

PERIOD: Arb/Ott RATING: * MAP: 22

LOCATION: The area south of the east end of the Suq al-Hamidiye and the Umayyad Mosque, extending to Straight Street.

The itinerary begins at the square in front of the western entrance to the Umayyad Mosque, at the eastern end of the Suq al-Hamidiye. In addition to the most outstanding of the Ottoman residences of Damascus (Azem Palace) it covers the main concentration of traditional khans – the warehouses for the receiving, storing and sending of trade goods and the provision of accommodation to traders. The Damascus khan follows the broader Mamluk and Ottoman traditions. Earlier types (eg Khan Jaqmaq) were arranged around an open rectangular court; later examples (eg Khan Suleiman Pasha) usually centred on a central area covered by soaring domes, often now in ruins or only partially restored, and were thus covered halls in the Persian tradition rather than courtyards.

The 18 surviving principal khans were mostly constructed in the Ottoman period and are concentrated in the area to be described. This development represented a westward movement of the main bazar area of the city which had previously centred on Straight Street southeast of the Umayyad Mosque but many examples have been obliterated by subsequent development. (Many commercial structures were lost when the entire Hariqa quarter, immediately south of the Suq al-Hamidiye, was destroyed by a French bombardment during the revolt of 1925. The area was later reconstructed along geometric lines.) Not all the khans mentioned here are worth detailed examination, many barely surviving in dilapidated conditions.

Start to head west along the Suq al-Hamidiye but turn left immediately at

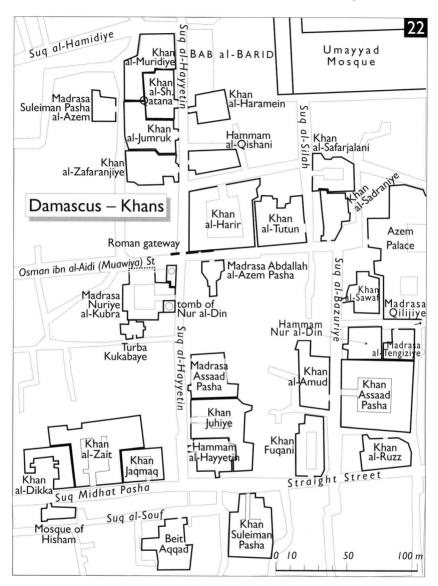

Suq al-Hamidiye

Khan al-Muridiye

Suq al-Hayyetin

BAB al-BARID

Umayyad Mosque

22

Khan al-Sh. Qatana

Madrasa Suleiman Pasha al-Azem

Khan al-Haramein

Khan al-Jumruk

Hammam al-Qishani

Suq al-Silah

Khan al-Safarjalani

Khan al-Zafaranjiye

Damascus – Khans

Khan al-Harir

Khan al-Tutun

Khan al-Sadraniye

Azem Palace

Roman gateway

Osman ibn al-Aidi (Muawiya) St

Madrasa Abdallah al-Azem Pasha

Suq al-Bazuriye

Khan al-Sawaf

Madrasa Qilijiye

Madrasa Nuriye al-Kubra

tomb of Nur al-Din

Hammam Nur al-Din

Madrasa al-Tengiziye

Turba Kukabaye

Suq al-Hayyetin

Madrasa Assaad Pasha

Khan al-Amud

Khan Assaad Pasha

Khan Juhiye

Khan al-Zait

Khan Jaqmaq

Hammam al-Hayyetin

Khan Fuqani

Khan al-Ruzz

Khan al-Dikka

Suq Midhat Pasha

Straight Street

Suq al-Souf

Mosque of Hisham

Beit Aqqad

Khan Suleiman Pasha

0 10   50   100 m

the Roman gateway whose remains poke above the intersection. Take the street (Suq al-Hayyetin – Tailors' Suq) which heads south (eventually towards Straight Street). fifty metres on your left is the first of the khans, **Khan al-Haramain**

or Khan al-Juwar. The original building dates from 1630 but was substantially reconstructed in 1900 when the area was reorganised. Immediately opposite, a 10 m corridor leads off the Suq al-Hayyetin to the small **Khan al-Sheikh Qatana**

(18th or 19th century) whose dome and pendentives have been restored. Twenty metres further down the same street on the right is the striped stone gateway to the **Khan al-Jumruk** (Customs Khan) an L–shaped gallery constructed in 1608/9 under Murad Pasha). Now covered with six large domes resting on pendentives, the original nine-domed structure was considerable altered in two major rebuildings. Its name dervies from the fact that for part of the 19th century it served as the customs house.

Past the Khan al-Jumruk, 15 m on the left, is a smaller suq which was once the changing room of a 16th century public bath, the **Hammam al-Qishani** (Tiled Bath) – domed with modern painted decoration in the pendentives; tiled panel above inside doorway. Opposite the Khan al-Jumruk down a stone passage (right) is the 19th century **Khan al-Zafaranjiye** – arcaded courtyard, note the re-used classical columns. About 30 m further south, take the first street on the left. A little way on the right lies the **Khan al-Harir** (Silk Suq) built by the Ottoman governor of Damascus in 1573/4, Darwish Pasha – rectangular court; upper gallery once covered by domes.

Return to the street heading south. At the next corner, look back and you will notice a Roman gateway, once part of the outer limits of the Temple of Jupiter. Turn left (east) down a narrow street that is often clogged with motor vehicles. Twenty metres on the right is a former madrasa (1779), the **Madrasa Abdallah al-Azem Pasha** built by the man who later became the last of the illustrious Azem governors; now an antiquarian shop with a superb courtyard – uncovered; double arcading (third storey in timber relatively modern); good view of Umayyad Mosque from terrace.

Continue to the east. After 80 m, the street reaches another crowded crossroad. Take a left turn into the Suq al-Silah (or Assagha – once the weapons market) which leads back towards the southern wall of the Umayyad Mosque to visit two further khans of lesser interest.

The first, 15 m on the left is the **Khan al-Tutun** (18th century – of the three original domes, central one is closed, outer two open). Fifty metres down the Suq al-Silah, on the right, is the entrance to the **Khan al-Safarjalani**, dated 1757/8 – 10 m corridor leads to a rectangular (5 m by 16 m) courtyard covered with three part-domes.

Return now to the southern end of the Suq al-Silah and turn left. The main thoroughfare follows a turn immediately to the right (south) but ignore that for the moment. On the left is the **Khan al-Sadraniye** also built in 1757/8 in two segments, the first a 15 m domed corridor and behind it a small courtyard covered with twin part-domes. Now pass into the small square that terminates Othman Aidi St and in which on the right stands the antique shop named after its original founder, George Dabdoub. This unprepossessing forecourt brings you to one of the major points of interest in the old city.

This is the **Azem Palace** (Beit al-Azem – Plates 7c, 8a) built in 1749–50 by the Ottoman governor of Damascus, Assaad Pasha al-Azem.[15] (Officially, the building is now the Museum of Popular Arts and Tradition.) The Azem Palace displays all the notable features of Arab domestic architecture in a restful and harmonious setting. The building was erected on the ruins of the Palace of the Mamluk governor, Tengiz, remains of which have been found in the present structure. (The Mamluk fountain is now in the National Museum.) The 18th century construction

15 There were five Azem governors of Damascus at nine different periods between 1725 and 1809 – (1) Ismael Pasha (gov 1725–30); (2) his brother, Suleiman Pasha (gov 1734–38, 1741–43; (3) Assaad Pasha (gov 1743–57 – son of (1), builder of the Azem Palace); (4) Muhammad Pasha (gov intermittently 1771–83 – nephew of (3)); and (5) Abdallah Pasha (gov 1795–9, 1805–7 – son of (4)). For a complete genealogy, see Barbir 1988; Schatkowski Schilcher 1985. The period of the Azem governors is examined in Rafeq, Abdul-Karim *The Province of Damascus 1723–1783* Beirut 1966.

was twice partly rebuilt after renovations in the 1830s and a fire in 1925. After 1930, the building served to house the French Institute but reverted to the Azem family on independence. The palace was purchased by the Syrian Government in 1951 and opened as a museum three years later.

Follow the red arrows which lead you first to the northwest corner, leading off a western extension of the main *selamlek* (public entertainment area). This corner comprises mostly service rooms not now open to the public including the kitchen and a vaulted storeroom. Continue clockwise around the principal court (plate 7b) whose rooms are used to display the museum's collection of household and decorative items as well as furniture of the 18th and 19th centuries. The marked tour takes you successively to a school room and a series of rooms behind a long columned portico along the north wall – a drawing room, a *diwan* and a library with stucco and painted wood decoration (note especially the latter with geometric carved decoration on the ceiling). Next is a room set up as a 'marriage chamber' with marble inlay, stucco and painted wood decoration.

At the narrow (eastern) end of the court, three more rooms, the first of which has a fine ceiling with relief geometric decoration (1750). Along the south wall, as you continue clockwise, an *iwan* faces on to the court, flanked by two rooms decorated in painted wood. Continuing clockwise, you will find across the wide passage that once led to a smaller court to the left a small entrance leading to the palace baths. After the large domed room for changing and relaxing, a succession of warm and hot rooms led to the central steam room (domed roof). Behind this is a cleansing room with two massage chambers to the left.

Next in sequence is the main reception hall (*qa'a*) of the palace, with a fountain in the centre of its marble floor and raised wings on each of the three enclosed sides. Note particularly the south wing – painted ceilings; three superb stalactited niches;

Delft porcelain panels in the waterfall of the central niche.

The last section of the palace visited is the *haremlek* or private quarters (access by following the arrows through the 'Jebel al-Arab' room off the reception hall). The central courtyard of the *haremlek* is unusually large with a water pond and a cooling canopy of citrus trees. This area was much affected by the 1925 fire but parts have since been restored.

As you leave the Azem Palace, take the broad street on the left that leads south towards Straight Street. Thirty metres on the left along this spices and confectionary suq (Suq al-Bazuriye) a small sign indicates the entrance to the badly deteriorated Khan al-Sawwaf (Ottoman). Along the next street on the left are two interesting façades. The first, on the right is the **Dar al-Hadith** built by the Mamluk governor, **Tengiz** (1338–9) with a fine *muqarnas*-topped portal. A little further on the left lies a badly deteriorated madrasa built a century earlier – **Madrasa Qilijiye** (1247–54). The entrance is hidden behind later rebuilt but this Ayyubid building is the first façade in Damascus completed entirely in *ablaq* (contrasting) stone. (Nur al-Din's funerary madrasa, to be visited in a minute, was built a decade later.)

Return to the Suq al-Bazuriye. Twenty metres further on, still on the left, signs indicate the **Hammam Nur al-Din** or Hammam al-Bazuriye which still functions as a public bath. The hammam, one of the oldest in Damascus, was founded between 1154 and 1172 by Nur al-Din in order to provide income to his funerary madrasa which you will visit in a moment. Though much restored over eight centuries (it was a soap factory early last century), it is still a good example of a classic Arab public bath. The domed chamber immediately inside the entrance is unusually grand and dates from the Ottoman period. To the left lie successively an octagonal chamber and a warm room.

The building 40 m to the left along the spice suq towards Straight Street has recently undergone extensive reconstruction, the

Khan Assaad Pasha (plate 8a). This, conspicuously the boldest and most striking of the Damascus khans, is another project (1752) of the remarkable mid 18th century Ottoman governor of Damascus who built the Azem Palace. The caravanserai was conceived on a grand scale with an uncovered central space flanked by eight domes, the whole covering 2500 m². The monumental effect is increased by the use of severely contrasting stonework in basalt and limestone. A central fountain lies under the circular aperture in the roof. Though restoration is complete, no plans for the future use of the khan have been announced.

Opposite lies the entrance to the **Khan al-Amud** a badly dilapidated 17th century building formed around two courtyards (the first iron-roofed), still a warehouse.

Before continuing 60 m on to Straight Street, you may want to divert 20 m before the intersection down a small lane to the left. 20 m on the right is the **Khan al-Ruzz** – 18th century; square courtyard of 9 m by 9 m once covered by twin domes.

Straight Street – known in Arabic as the Suq al-Tawil (Long Street) – is the Via Recta of the Roman city, the main transverse thoroughfare whose fame has been amplified by the account in Acts of St Paul's eventful sojourn in Damascus. (Full details in *Damascus – Straight Street).

There is a further khan of limited interest in this area. To the right (12 m) behind a grille doorway as you turn right along Suq al-Tawil is the **Khan Fuqani**, another 18th century construction, sometimes known as the Khan al-Sanaubar and now in a bad state, used as a coffee-roasting plant – rectangular courtyard, once covered by triple domes.

Continue right (west) along Straight Street along the section known as the **Suq Midhat Pasha** (cloth, cotton articles, bedding, household items, oils, soap). This was one of the first (1878) Ottoman attempts to open the city up to wheeled traffic and the first to use a corrugated

iron roof system. About 50 m on the left is the striped entrance doorway to the **Khan Suleiman Pasha** built in 1732 by the Ottoman governor, Suleiman Pasha al-Azem (governor 1734–43). A 15 m gallery leads to an ambitious central courtyard once covered by twin domes with a broad upper gallery.

About 20 m further along Straight Street (continuing west) is the entrance on the right to the street (Suq al-Hayyetin) which you followed at the beginning of this itinerary and which leads eventually back to the Suq al-Hamidiye. If you wish to inspect three further khans in the next block to the right along Straight Street, ignore this turn for the moment. The first khan (20 m, right) is the **Khan Jaqmaq.** Founded by the Mamluk amir, Saif al-Din Jaqmaq al-Argunsawi, (governor of Damascus, 1418–20) it is one of the earliest surviving khans, extensively rebuilt in 1601. Forty metres further on the right is the **Khan al-Zait** – late 16th century; once the depot for the olive oil trade. One of the most pleasant of the khans, it has a partly tree shaded open courtyard enclosed by vaulted arcades with an upper gallery in semi-circular arches. Twenty metres further along Straight Street on the right are the fragmentary remains of the **Khan al-Dikka** (date uncertain), another early example much altered. Remains of Roman columns, probably transported from the Roman Via Recta, were used to support the courtyard arcades.

Returning to the Suq al-Hayyetin, follow this north for 20 m. On the right are the remains of the Hammam al-Hayyetin, possibly part of the endowment of the first of the Azem Pashas, Ismael (d 1723/4), now a market – painted dome. A further 20 on (right) is the **Khan Juhiye**, or Khan al-Hayyetin, built in the mid 16th century by the Ottoman governor, Ahmad Samsi Pasha. Further on, 25 m still on the right, is the entrance to the **Madrasa Assaad Pasha al-Azem** (1748, now known as the Masjid al-Hayyetin), originally endowed by the builder of the Azem Palace.

A further 60 m along the street, just after the thoroughfare narrows, look out for a long stone wall and the unheralded entrance on the left to a madrasa. The **Madrasa Nuriye al-Kubra** houses the tomb of one of the great Muslim rulers, Nur al-Din, whose achievements united Syria behind the anti-Crusader cause. The original building (1167–72) survives only in part, notably along the street frontage. The tomb itself is to the left of the entrance. (If unattended, the white cenotaph can be seen through the grille behind the drinking fountain.) This was the first madrasa-mausoleum complex in Islam, an architectural combination that was to have a great impact in Syria and Egypt. The tomb chamber is covered by a *muqarnas* or honeycomb dome, a magnificent example of this Mesopotamian device. This last example of this form in Damascus post-dates the entrance to the Maristan Nur al-Din (*Damascus – Suq al-Hamidiye) and this time the structure is built in plastered brick. (A view of the external 'sugarloaf' structure can be seen from the north wall along al-Aidi St.) The *mihrab* of the tomb chamber is framed with two porphyry columns with acanthus capitals, probably Byzantine. The northern *iwan* of the original four-*iwan* plan of the madrasa was severely truncated by the widening of al-Aidi St in the 1950s and the courtyard as seen today is prosaic.

To reach the last monument on our tour, double back a few metres towards Straight Street, taking the first street on the right. On the right (80 m) lies the **Turba Kukabaye**, the mausoleum built for Sotaita (d 1330–1), wife of Tengiz, the noted Mamluk governor of Damascus. The honeycombed entrance at the centre of a simple and symmetrical façade leads to a twin-domed interior decorated with sculptured plaster.

If you return along the street you have just entered and turn left, continuing past Nur al-Din's madrasa, you can follow the Suq al-Hayyetin back to the area of the Suq al-Hamidiye where the itinerary began.

REFS: Burns *Damascus* 2005; Omiry, Ibrahim & Jabbour, Khousama Khan *Asa'ad Bacha* Damascus nd; Sack 1985; Sauvaget *Monuments* 1932; Scharabi; Wulzinger and Watzinger *Damaskus –*

islamische 1924; Tabaa 1982 120–32, 189–90; S Weber 2006.

Damascus – Straight Street

VARIANTS: Via Recta (Lat); Suq al-Tawil (Arb)
PERIOD: Rom/Arb RATING: * MAP:23

LOCATION: A walk along the main thoroughfare of old Damascus from west to east. Begin 250 m (fourth intersection) south of the western entrance to the Suq al-Hamidiye. This is a somewhat long walk (3+ km) through difficult traffic conditions. There is a lot to be said for doing it on a Friday when commercial traffic is light, preferably avoiding the heat of the day.

Since Hellenistic and Roman times, this has been the major west-east thoroughfare of Damascus. When it was taken by the Greeks after Alexander's conquests, the already ancient city (centred on a hillock just north of the central section of the street) was re-oriented on a grid pattern. The **Hippodamian grid** (based on the ideas of the fifth century BC Greek, Hippodamus of Miletus) reflected the sense of order the Greeks sought to bring to many centres throughout the east (including *Apamea, *Latakia, *Aleppo and *Cyrrhus). Little of the orthogonal plan survives to the earth-bound eye though topographical surveys indicate the extent to which the seemingly random web of streets and alleyways of old Damascus still conforms at many points to the ancient plan. The segments of the grid (*insulae*) were based on rectangles each 45 m (east-west) by 100 m (north-south). The footprint of the Greek city as expanded by the Nabataeans (to the east) and the Romans (west), largely corresponded to the old city within the current walls though the edges probably conformed more strictly to a rectangle (some 1330 m by 850 m) than the present more rounded shape. (See also box 'Gates of Damascus' page 95.)

The Romans who were considerably more ambitious in their civic embellishments and concerned to display in public works the sense of a new imperial order, added many improvements. In the first century AD, they expanded enormously the enclosure of the Temple of Jupiter (*Damascus – Umayyad Mosque), established a military compound possibly on the site of the present Citadel (*Damascus – Citadel and Northern Walls) and widened Straight Street (Via Recta) to serve as a broad axis with much the same purpose as the colonnaded streets that can be seen in the remains of *Palmyra or Apamea. It became a principal thoroughfare (*decumanus maximus*) lined with solidly built stalls, the whole overshadowed by

Alas, the dignified ambience of the Roman thoroughfare has gone. The broad Roman street (at 26 m it was four times the width of the present roadway) has over the centuries (especially since Abbasid times, eighth century) gradually been encroached upon by the building line on each side. Commercial establishments and workshops now crowd the thoroughfare allowing only one lane of vehicles with barely room for pedestrians at the sides. The columns are gone, as have the stone-

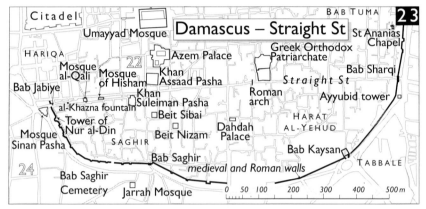

the forest of columns that lent dignity at the same time as supporting a canopy. But even the Greeks and Romans had to bend to the logic of the existing street pattern at some points. Straight Street followed the path of an existing thoroughfare that dodged the low hills and settlements in its passage, hence the slight deviations which aroused Mark Twain's sense of irony: 'The street called Straight is straighter than a corkscrew, but not as straight as a rainbow'.[16]

framed shops and the shading.[17] You are now left to brave alone the elements, the noise and impatient traffic. Nevertheless, the experience of Straight Street is an indispensable part of a visit to Damascus, and the intense commercial life continues the role the street has played for over 2000 years.

You may notice that Straight Street for its first 400 m runs parallel with two (later one) narrow suqs to the south. In Roman times, the *decumanus* embraced this whole width. As the buildings encroached on the pedestrian and wheeled thoroughfares the street, at this western end, was divided into several narrow thoroughfares by the encroachment of stalls.

The market area immediately south of the beginning of Straight Street is described in

16 Twain does exaggerate a bit. Along its 1.35 km length, Straight Street makes two slight changes of alignment, both originally marked by an arch placed at the intersections. Twain went on to observe in *Innocents Abroad* (1869) that 'St Luke (assumed author of Acts) is careful not to commit himself; he does not say it is the street which *is* straight, but the 'street which is *called* Straight'. It is a fine piece of irony; it is the only facetious remark in the Bible, I believe.' (Quoted in Yapp *The Travellers' Dictionary of Quotations* London 1988.)

17 Not to mention the civic facilities including a theatre and an odeon that once stood to the south of the first stretch of Straight Street, Suq Midhat Pasha.

*Damascus – Southwest Quarter. For our present purposes, locate the Arab gateway (Bab al-Jabiye) that lies 20 m south of the start of the street, immediately behind the Mosque of Sinan Pasha (green ceramic-tiled minaret). Continue along this clothing market for 100 m until you spot, on the left, the **Fountain** (*Sabil*) **al-Khazna** (1404/5) erected by Amir Saif al-Din Jarkas, a grand chamberlain of Damascus under the Mamluks. The mouldings inside the arch are said by Sauvaget to derive from a Crusader monument.

A minaret, attached to the **Mosque al-Qali** (1431), is found 70 m to the left along the Suq al-Qutn (cotton suq). Described by the Syrian writer, Talass, as 'one of the most beautiful minarets in the Islamic world' for the rich harmony of its decorations, it is the last of the square-plan minarets in the Mamluk tradition in Damascus. Note the blue faience decorations left incomplete on the south panel. Another 100 m on the right is the fine octagonal minaret of the **Mosque of Hisham**, built four years earlier (1426–7) by a chancellor of Damascus under the Mamluks and decorated with fine *muqarnas* work. The theatre that Herod the Great had built in Damascus (first century BC), mentioned in literary sources, was located south of the Via Recta a little east of this point. Further along on the right is the Danish Institute, housed in the Bait al-Aqqad, a Mamluk-Ottoman house built into remains of the Roman theatre's stage.

Take any passage to the left that brings you back into Straight Street. This section, the Suq Midhat Pasha, is described under *Damascus Khans. Pass along it quickly until you reach the south entrance to the spices suq (Suq al-Bazuriye) on the left (leading to the Azem Palace and the Umayyad Mosque) and the wide street leading to the Bab al-Saghir on the right. You are now at the beginning of the long (1 km) stretch that takes you through the edges of the Jewish and Christian quarters, past many shops established for the tourist trade offering brass and wood mosaic wares. 100 m left, amid the densely settled laneways, you can just

distinguish the mound (Tell al-Samaka) which marks the original settlement of the pre-Hellenistic period including the era's royal palace.

As you proceed east, shortly after you pass the ruined remains of the Hammam Kharab (early 18th century), you reach (450 m) the next landmark. The small **Roman Arch** (Bab al-Kanise, partly reconstructed in newly cut stone) stands in a minute oasis of park. The triple arch stood on the *decumanus* at the intersection of a major cross street (*cardo maximus*) but such has been the rate of accumulation of debris over two millennia that by last century, the arch had been buried and forgotten below the surface of the modern street. It was excavated and re-erected at surface level during the French Mandate. The original arch was probably constructed in the late second century AD and may have been part of a *tetrakionion*, a common device for marking important intersections.

The intersection where the arch stands is a useful orientation point for those who wish to explore more of the neighbouring back streets of the old city. Facing east, the traditionally **Christian quarter** of Damascus begins to the left (northeast segment) with the area known as al-Qaimarie (and beyond that Bab Tuma – *Damascus – Citadel and North Walls). The concentration of Christians in the eastern part of the city reflects the decision of Khalid Ibn al-Walid, the Muslim conqueror of Damascus in 636, to confirm their continued access to their churches in that area. The Patriarchate of the Greek Orthodox lies immediately to the left beyond the arch. A Christian church was located on this site as far back as the Byzantine period. The immediate quarter is named al-Mariamiye after the church dedicated to the Virgin Mary (al-Mariam). The buildings and patriarchal church are largely modern but the church has a fine marbled *iconostasis* of the 18th century.

The area to the right was traditionally inhabited by the Jewish community (Haret al-Yehud). One of the most remarkable buildings in this area is the Dahdah Palace, originally Beit Murad Farhi after the financier who funded much of the activities of the Azem rulers at the end of the 8th and early 19th centuries. To reach it, take the laneway on the right immediately before the arch. Continue 150 m, then turn right, looking for the small sign pointing to the Dahdah Palace. The house (still in private hands and usually closed) is an excellent example of Syrian domestic architecture of the late 18th century with its large summer *iwan* at the western end decorated in superb style. The reception room on the north side is unusually large for a private house.

Continue your walk eastwards. The remaining stretch of Straight Street (550 m) brings you to the east gate of the city, **Bab Sharqi** (the Gate of the Sun to the Romans). This is the oldest extant monument in Damascus and the only one of the Roman gates of the city to preserve its original form. The gate comprises a triple passageway, the central one for wheeled traffic, the outer two corresponding with the arcaded passages along the colonnaded street reserved for pedestrians. Note the beginnings of the colonnades that once carried the arcading. From Arab times until last century, the central and south passageways had been blocked by masonry but the gate was cleared and restored in the 1960s. The treatment of the façades is rather plain but well balanced. The gate, formerly attributed to the period of Septimius Severus or Caracalla (late second, early third century) is more recently assigned, in its original version, to the reign of Augustus (d AD 14) and partly rebuilt in the late second century. It is through this gateway that the Arab commander Khalid Ibn al-Walid entered Damascus in 635. The mosque perched on the northern side dates from Nur al-Din's rebuilding of the city's defences. (To the south of the gate lie two other Christian patriarchates, that of the Armenian Orthodox and of the Greek Catholics.)

While you are in the vicinity, there are two other monuments worth visiting at the eastern end of the city both of which are associated with St Paul and the story of his visit to Damascus (Acts 9). In brief, Saul (as he was before his conversion to Christianity), a Jew from Cilicia, was brought up as a Pharisee and thus a confirmed opponent of the followers of Christ. He was instructed to go to Damascus to arrest followers of Jesus. As he approached the city, 'a light from heaven shone all around him'.[18] He fell to the ground, and heard a voice saying 'Saul, Saul why are you persecuting me?' Saul was blinded and led into Damascus by his companions. At the same time, a Christian called Ananias was directed by a vision to go to a house in Straight Street, where he met Saul, sheltered him in his house and initiated him into Christianity. Saul began preaching in the synagogues proclaiming 'Jesus the Son of God', thus arousing the resentment of the Jews. Eventually made aware of a plot to kill him, Saul evaded capture by having himself lowered over the walls of Damascus in a basket.

The first site associated with these events is the **Chapel of St Ananias** which can be reached by going down the lane immediately inside the arch on the north. The chapel is at the end of the lane (150 m) and is reached by descending the stairway in the corner of the small court. The chapel reputedly includes a part of the house of Ananias where Saul took shelter.

The second site is more clearly apocryphal, namely the spot where Saul was lowered over the walls in a basket. To reach it you leave the old city via Bab Sharqi and take the broad and busy street curving to the right. En route there are two remarkable features revealed by recent roadworks in the area. The first is a huge tower that originally stood outside the line of the southeastern walls but which is now buried under the present road level. It can be reached by descending the pedestrian underpass just south of Bab Sharqi. The tower dates from the Ayyubid period, reflecting the work done to refortify

18 The exact spot is only conjectural but the Greek Orthodox recently erected a chapel 15 km southwest of Damascus at Kawkab to commemorate the incident.

Damascus. It originally stood out from the walls and was intended to protect a weak point in the circuit. Return to ground level and keep to the curve of the road as it hugs the walls. After 400 m you approach a roundabout from which the road to the airport originates. The course of the southern walls has now been exposed as part of recent road improvements. Note the Roman blocks at the base of this stretch of wall, the upper courses dating from Nur al-Din's time and later. In part, the Arab re-fortification followed the Roman lines but added seven towers.

Just before this major interchange, set into the walls is a 20th century **St Paul's Chapel** at **Bab Kaysan** built and maintained by the Greek Catholics. Except for a few stones incorporated in later walls, nothing remains of the original Roman gateway which marked the southern point of the *cardo* that ended at Bab Tuma, running through the eastern quarter of the city. Whatever was left of the Roman gate was rebuilt when the aperture was blocked in 1154 under Nur al-Din. It is the Mamluk gate built in 1364 whose traces are incorporated in the chapel. At the top of the stairs leading from the street entrance is an arch reconstructed on the remains of the Mamluk gateway.

There is no historical evidence that this is the spot where St Paul was lowered and the tradition ascribing it to this section of the wall seems recent in origin, perhaps not much older than the chapel. The incident, of course, could have happened at any point on the 6 km or more of Roman wall. As Saul may well have lodged in the eastern quarter and took off in the direction of Jerusalem, this is a tempting interpretation but would it really be logical to plan an escape at a gate which would have been one of the most heavily watched points on the Roman circuit?

The rest of the south walls beyond the recently landscaped area deflect from the Roman alignment and are covered in the next entry, *Damascus – Southwest Quarter*.

REFS: Bredel & Lange *A House in Damascus*

Copenhagen 2003; Burns *Damascus* 2005; Kader *Propylon und Bogentur* 1996; Meinecke 1992; Freyburger 'Jupiter-Heiligtums' *DaM* 2 1985; Rihawi *Damascus* 1977; Sack 1985; Sauvaget *Monuments* 1932; Sauvaget *Plan* 1949; Sauvaget *Esquisse* 1937; Talass 1943; S. Weber 2006; WW *Damaskus – antike* 1921; WW *Damaskus – islamische* 1924.

Damascus – Southwest Quarter

PERIOD: Arb/Ott RATING: * MAPS: 23, 24

LOCATION: The area extending south from the western entrance to the Suq al-Hamidiye as far as the cemetery of Bab al-Saghir. This itinerary involves a walk of c3 km. It is preferable to avoid undertaking it during the heat of the day or when commercial activity is at its peak.

The tour begins at the western entrance to the Suq al-Hamidiye (map 24). As you face the entrance to the suq, take the road that leads south (right), officially named Zaghlul St but later becoming Midan St as it eventually leads to the pilgrim quarter known as the Midan (*Damascus – Midan). Walk along this busy street for about 75 m. The first **mosque** on the right commemorates the Ottoman governor of Damascus from 1571–4, **Darwish Pasha**, who built it in 1572–5 and whose tomb lies in the small octagonal domed building (1579) to the south, joined to the mosque by an arch. The entrance, consciously Syrian in style with the octagonal minaret above the portal, leads you into a small courtyard. Note the decorative faience panels of the portico of the prayer room on the left, following a Turkish domed plan.

The quarter which lies behind (west) is known as **Qanawat** (canal or aqueduct). This is a reference to the ancient water intake which entered Damascus above ground at this point. Remains of the Roman aqueduct can still be seen in the Qanawat Quarter whose houses are largely the product of the 19th century. Take the side street that runs between the Mosque of Darwish Pasha and the tomb. After about 100 m take the winding lane to the left which eventually brings you to a short flight of steps which rise onto a street. In fact, you have just emerged under one of the arches of the Roman aqueduct whose course can be traced in the embankment supporting a row of white-painted houses. This was part of the aqueduct system which brought water to the city from the Barada River. Return now to Midan St by continuing southeast. Double back north a few metres along Midan St to reach the next mosque on the itinerary.

A rather striking façade frames the entrance on the left (a little raised above a row of shops) of the **Madrasa Sibaiye**, a funerary college commemorating Sibai, governor of Damascus (constructed 1509–15). Given Sibai's proclivity to strip other mosques for interesting features, the mosque carries the popular name Jamia al-Jawami or 'mosque of mosques'. Built at the very end of the Mamluk period, the architecture shows a rather debased and heavy version of the style, the minaret in particular being lumpy and earth-bound. The façade follows the Mamluk preference for alternating bands of black and white stone with *muqarnas* treatment of the doorway. Inside, the elements of the prayer hall taken from earlier buildings include Kufic inscriptions on marble offering tables (11th century) and marble marquetry.

Continue another 35 m south, crossing to the eastern side of Midan St. Just past the entrance to Straight Street, another small street runs parallel eastwards. On the corner is the **Mosque of Sinan Pasha** (Jamia al-Sinaniye). Sinan was Governor of Damascus when the mosque was completed in 1591 under an endowment which also included a hammam, school and market. The

minaret is distinguished by its colouring of green-enamelled brick. The courtyard is small but charming, an oasis from the chaos outside. Though none of its parts are particularly striking, the overall effect is a pleasing blend of Ottoman and Syrian. Note the faience panels of the portico, of local manufacture but in the tradition of Iznik. The prayer hall is exceptionally beautiful, a miniature Turkish domed chamber with galleries.

Some remains of the Roman/Arab western wall of the old city lie behind the buildings that now line Midan St. Immediately behind the Sinaniye Mosque (first right past the mosque's side entrance) can be seen what remains of the **Bab al-Jabiye** (named after the first Arab settlement in the Hauran, later abandoned). To find it, you will have to hunt among the crowds and stalls of the second hand clothes market known picturesquely as the Suq al-Kumeile, 'lice market'. As with other gateways (*Damascus – Citadel and North Walls), its reconstruction, partly using Roman blocks, dates from the era

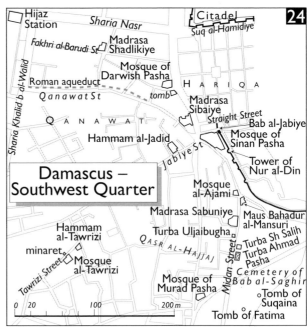

of Nur al-Din (1164) with further work completed in 1227. The Roman gate on this site marked the western end of the Via Recta the main colonnaded axis of the city (*decumanus maximus*) which ran 1.3 km to Bab Sharqi (*Damascus – Straight Street).

Forty metres south of the Sinaniye Mosque, look for a narrow-arched entrance in zebra-stripes leading to a hotel (Funduq Islakh). In the courtyard are the remains of the **Tower of Nur al-Din**, a round structure built in surprisingly small blocks with a bold inscribed band, as part of his improvements to the defences of the city in 1173.

Midan St continues south via a suq covered by a curved roof of corrugated iron (Suq Sinaniye). A little further, on the right, lies the **al-Ajami Mosque** (or Turba Afriduniye) intended both as a tomb (*turba*) and Koranic school (madrasa). Built after 1348, the building commemorates the Persian merchant Afridun al-Ajami. The plan is a rare example (for Damascus) of the cruciform mosque. The façade is in the familiar Mamluk striped masonry with door and window surrounds in *muqarnas*. Frankish capitals are employed in the *mihrab* of the prayer hall.

Al-Badawi St diverts left around the southern limits of the old city. At the fork, the intersection encloses another Mamluk monument, the **Mausoleum of Amir Saif al-Din Bahadur al-Mansuri**, a military leader in whose honour the domed tomb was built in 1329.

On the land behind this mausoleum lies the extensive **Cemetery of Bab al-Saghir**. This is the most notable of the cemeteries around the old city and contains several tombs of interest. Before visiting them, however, you may wish to note two other funerary buildings along Midan St.

On the right side of the street as you continue south is the **Madrasa Sabuniye**, a Koranic school founded as a funerary endowment in 1459–64 by a rich merchant, Shihab al-Din Ahmad Ibn al-Sabuni. Highly-patterned façade with black

and white banding; medallion panels over each set of windows; tall deeply stalactited doorway; minaret; dome decorated inside with painted floral designs.

After 20 m, still on the right side of Midan St, you come to the **Turba Uljaibugha al-Adil (Turba 'al-Jianiye')**. Façade with black stone banding and decorations; entrance with stalactited treatment and arms of the founder. The name refers to the 14th century governor who authorised the construction, Uljaibugha al-Adil.

Returning to the left side of Midan St, a series of mausolea backs on to the cemetery a little beyond the point you have reached. The first is the 14th century **Turba Sheikh Salih** (façade only remains). The second tomb is that of **Ahmad Pasha** with twin domes (1535), a rather messy façade dated 1535 but still in the Mamluk idiom. The last, the Turba Mankabaiye, is an unremarkable building.

From the next intersection, 50 m west along a small side street, is the grand **Mosque and Mausoleum of Murad Pasha**, built in 1575–6 by the Ottoman governor who sought to leave his mark on this area outside the walls as a new Ottoman precinct. The mosque catered for the Naqshbandi order of Dervishes, one of many Sufi institutions encouraged in this area frequented by Ottoman troops. The style manages to retain some of the late Mamluk traditions.

To enter the cemetery, retrace your steps to Midan St and continue along al-Jarrah St that continues northeast and cuts across the cemetery. Enter by the gate 80 m on the right. Two tombs are worthy of particular note, both reached by continuing south through the cemetery towards the central cluster of tomb chambers. As the Cemetery of Bab al-Saghir has been in use since the time of the first caliphs, it has, not unnaturally, attracted a store of legends relating to its early tombs. The first **tomb** to note is that **of Suqaina**, a daughter of Hussein and great-granddaughter of the Prophet. The attribution of this twin-domed building, however, appears doubtful. Suqaina died in Medina (after many marriages) and the coffin and inscription are dated a good deal after her lifetime. Nevertheless, the coffin, decorated with Kufic lettering (which it is difficult to appreciate displayed behind glass in the confined space) is noteworthy and has been dated to the first half of the 12th century.

The second tomb, single-domed, to the south, has become a centre for Shiite pilgrimage as it is held in popular legend to be the burial place of **Fatima**, daughter of the Prophet and wife of the Shiites' revered Ali. Sauvaget preferred to see it as the tomb of another Fatima, the daughter of one Ahmad al-Sibti who was perhaps a descendant of Ali. In any event, the tomb attracts considerable crowds of pious visitors, particularly from Iran.

South of Fatima's tomb (150 m) lies the reputed site of the burial of the founder of the Umayyad dynasty, Muawiya Ibn Abi Sufyan (caliph 661–81). The site is now marked by a simple white domed cube, recently clad in stone and encased in an iron grille. Virtually all trace of the Umayyads was fiercely effaced by their Abbasid successors but it is not impossible that sufficient memories remained of the spot where the founder of the Umayyid dynasty was interred to locate his cenotaph with reasonable accuracy in later centuries.

[At this point, the energetic visitor may want to continue 700 m south to pick up the starting point (Bab Musalla Square) for *Damascus – Midan but this would add considerably to the distance covered and time required.]

We return by tracking further to the east to take in part of the south walls of the city (map 23). At the northeastern corner of the cemetery, just before it meets Badawi St, the mosque on the right is the **Jarrah Mosque**, one of the earliest congregational mosques outside the walled city – courtyard plan, square minaret. It was built by the Ayyubid sultan, al-Ashraf Musa in 1233, rebuilt in 1250 and much altered since given its exposed situation outside the walls. Continue on to Badawi St, the thoroughfare that you earlier saw forking

away from Midan St at the Mausoleum of Bahadur al-Mansuri. Walk 60 m east along Badawi St then 50 m left along a side street to the remains of another Roman gateway, heavily reconstructed in Ayyubid times. This is the **Bab al-Saghir** (Little Gate). The Arab army of Yazid Ibn Abi Sufyan camped outside this gate during the first siege of Damascus by the Muslim armies. It was reconstructed as part of Nur al-Din's defences of the city in 1156 but on the foundations of the Roman Gate of Mars. The scale is small (hence the Arabic nickname) and the Arab work sits rather awkwardly on the large Roman blocks. The minaret on top adds a final bizarre touch.

Continue north through the gate and along the street (Amin or Hassan Kharrat St) that leads 300 m to Straight Street and was widened as part of Jamal Pasha's improvements after 1915. In the quarter to the right are two old houses of considerable interest. Both are now owned by the Syrian Government and access is usually possible. For the first, turn right at 130 m, left at second cross street and 10 m on the left is the **Beit Nizam**. Originally two separate houses, it was built between 1780 and 1840, originally for the family of Ali Agha. For the second, go back one street towards Hassan Kharrat St and turn right, left, then right. Immediately on the left is the **Beit Sibai** (1769–74).

Resume your walk northwards along Amin St to the intersection that leads to the spices suq (Suq al-Bazuriye) and the Azem Palace (*Damascus – Khans). You can return to the starting point by turning left along Straight Street. This 300 m stretch of corrugated iron-covered suq, also known as the Suq Midhat Pasha after the governor of Damascus who had it constructed in 1878, is described in *Damascus – Khans and *Damascus – Straight Street.

REFS: de Lorey & Wiet 1921; Keenan 2000; Meinecke 1992; Moaz & Ory 1977; Rihawi *Damascus* 1977; Sauvaget *Monuments* 1932; S. Weber 2006; WW *Damaskus – islamische*. 1924.

Damascus – National Museum
(Plate 9a)

PERIOD: All RATING: ** MAP: –

LOCATION: Al-Quwatli St, east of the former Damascus Fairgrounds and west of the *Tekkiye Mosque.

The National Museum of Damascus is one of the world's great collections of archaeological treasures and it would be impossible to do it justice in a few pages. This survey is intended only to introduce the scope of the collection and its broad layout. A thorough visit is best facilitated with a copy of the Museum's *Concise Guide*. or Abed Issa's *Illustrated Guide*.

The museum was founded in 1919 and was originally set up, along with the Arab Academy, in the Madrasa al-Adeliye (*Damascus – Suqs). In 1936, the east wing of the present complex was built. From 1939 to 1952, the building's entrance was embellished by the reconstruction of the gateway from *Qasr al-Heir West, an Umayyad desert palace of the eighth century. The three-storeyed west wing of the Museum was added in 1953 and expanded from 1956 to 1961.

The archaeological and historical collections of the museum are arranged in four departments: pre-historic; ancient Syrian; classical; and Arab-Islamic antiquities. (There is a fifth department, not covered here, for modern art.) The layout of the building, however, does not follow chronological sequence.

You may wish to start by taking in the formidable array of largely classical-period sculpture in the gardens of the museum, left of the entrance avenue. Continuing down the avenue from the ticket office, you enter the building through the monumental **gateway of Qasr al-Heir West**, a superb example of the eclectic Umayyad style. It borrows elements from Persian, Byzantine and local Syrian sources but provides its own synthesis. The gateway comprises two semi-cylindrical towers enclosing a rectangular portal, the latter surmounted by a large blank Syrian arch, familiar in the local repertoire for several centuries. The tympanum above is embellished with niches, false windows and colonnettes.

The gateway has been described as 'as extravagantly sham as anything built by Ludwig II of Bavaria', pointing out that the various visual images of the façade are thematically unrelated (Hillenbrand 1982). The concern with restless decoration applied on every surface, apparent in Arab art of later periods, is already evident. The stucco surfaces are divided into panels of distinct elements, each treated according to a geometric or floral theme. Yet the effect is not frenetic and chaotic. The whole develops a strange harmony in spite of the two-dimensional nature of the decorative skin. This is perhaps due to the strong basic shapes adopted for the architectural elements – semi-cylinder, triangular crenellations, Syrian arch, rectangular doorway and copious niches and colonnettes.

Once inside, the vestibule offers other elements from the Umayyad palace (with more in the large hall upstairs including two striking painted panels). From the vestibule, the building offers you two choices. To the right is the west wing with its collections of pre-classical and Islamic art. To the left are the classical and Byzantine collections in the original part of the building. It is suggested you begin to the left though this means that you will have to double back chronologically when you come later to the pre-classical rooms.

The elements of the east wing will be taken in the following order:

• entrance hall
• corridor at left
• galleries of Jebel al-Arab and the Hauran (left of corridor)
• continuation of main corridor
• galleries of Palmyra and Dura Europos (off the corridor, to the right)
• Dura Europos synagogue (through vestibule at the end of the corridor, then across a small courtyard)

- Tomb of Yarhai from Palmyra (downstairs off the same vestibule)
- Hall of Byzantine Art (behind Palmyra and Dura Europos galleries).

The Museum was about to undertake a major refurbishment at the time this book was being revised and some items may not be in the locations described.

Begin with the **entrance hall** immediately to the left of the vestibule, containing classical statues. To the left off the main corridor is the **second corridor** in the museum handbook. Two large **galleries** extend off it to the left, largely covering the **Hauran** in the classical period. Finds displayed include a mosaic found at Shahba ('Glorification of the Earth'), a mosaic pavement depicting the Orontes as a god (from Latakia), basalt statues, several bronze helmets from the Hauran and a magnificent marble sarcophagus with a complex battle scene found at Rastan on the Orontes and dated to AD 3.

Return now to the first corridor and enter the Palmyra wing that leads on directly from the entrance. This is devoted to sculpture and jewellery of the classical period found at Latakia, Apamea and Palmyra. Especially notable is the bust of a woman which stands out from its circular frame and the statuette of Aspasia from Hama.

The first room off to the right is the **Hall of Palmyra** which contains many items of sculpture, notably busts or groupings taken from tombs. Note on the south wall (right) the superb mosaic of a nude Cassiope revealing her beauty to the Nereides (from a house of the third century AD, Palmyra). Second to the right is the **Hall of Dura Europos** in which are displayed jewellery, ceramics, bronzes and frescoes from this Hellenistic-Parthian-Roman site on the Euphrates. Note especially the remarkable set of horse armour (central case on the right) and the significant wall paintings from the Temple of the Palmyrene Gods.

The most celebrated find from Dura Europos, however, is the reconstructed **synagogue** found during the excavations under Cumont in 1931–2 and transported to the museum later in the decade. The circumstances of its discovery are related in *Dura Europos. The synagogue can be visited across the small vestibule and courtyard that lie at the far end of the wing. (The synagogue is usually kept closed to prevent light fading the wall paintings.) This is a remarkable building not only for the fact that a synagogue of the mid second century has survived at all, but also that its walls are covered in representations of the human form in scenes from scripture depicted in a unique mixture of Parthian and local painting styles. The shape of the building is itself of interest, prefiguring many aspects of later church and mosque design.

Off the same vestibule, reached by a descending staircase is the *hypogeum* (underground tomb) **of Yarhai**, reconstructed from the Valley of the Tombs in Palmyra. You enter through stone doors carved to imitate wood. The main vault (truncated in the reconstruction) ends in the customary *triclinium* with officials of the temple preparing the funeral ceremony. The two side walls are covered with portrait relief slabs enclosing *loculi*. In the alcove to the right is a carved banquet scene topped by two niches. The tomb was dedicated in AD 108 and used during the following two centuries by members of the family.

The **Hall of Byzantine Art** is divided into several sections representing jewels and coins, Syriac finds and other works including pottery. Note especially the treasury from Resafa (case 1 on left in first room), a remarkable find of 1982 comprising five 12th century gold-on-silver items probably buried to escape the Mongols' attention. The third room includes several cases showing textile finds from Palmyra, evidence of the city's role in trade with China via the Silk Route.

To reach the west wing of the Museum return to the main entrance vestibule and continue though to the other side. A courtyard in the Arab style includes a wall fountain with *muqarnas* hood, rescued from a section of Tengiz's palace exposed by excavations in the courtyard of the present Azem Palace in the 1930s. You then enter the first of the rooms devoted to **Ras Shamra** (*Ugarit). Exhibits display the high standard of craftsmanship in various materials and a sample of the important archives in syllabic cuneiform, a system of writing which foreshadowed a true alphabet. A second room devoted to Ugarit is found through the doorway.

Follow now the long gallery which continues on from the second Ugaritic room and keeps to the western wall of the building. This covers a variety of Bronze and Iron Age sites of the inland and coastal regions of Syria. Immediately on the left, note the basalt panel, a griffin figure found re-used in the north wall of the Umayyad Mosque. This stone is the only remains of the Aramaean temple to Haddad to have survived. Double back now along the next series of rooms beginning with the **Hall of Ebla**. The next section covers **Mari** on the Mid Euphrates, another Bronze Age site of major importance. Case 39 (along the wall to the right) contains an unmatched selection of votive gypsum figures. Note especially the beautifully worked lapis lazuli figure of Imdugud in the form of an eagle with a lion's head in gold (case 39, from the 'Treasure of Ur' found in the temple of the late Early Dynastic palace, third quarter of third millennium BC).

Continuing through another Mari gallery (most remarkable are the ivory inlaid friezes in case 40 and the figures of the singer, Ur-Nanshe, and of King Ikun Shamagan) you reach a vestibule off the first courtyard displaying finds from *Raqqa including remnants of the Abbasid palace. Centred at the eastern end is the ceramic figure of the Raqqa Horseman from the Ayyubid period. From here, again change direction along the gallery along the right (east) side of the building, the area devoted to Islamic collections of the museum including coins, jewellery and arms. This brings you to a hall displaying finds in wood, some of exceptional interest. Note particularly the sections of the 13th century sarcophagus that

once graced the Mosque of Khalid Ibn al-Walid in *Homs. A little back to the left, a section of screen of great historic interest (1103), once enclosing the tomb of Duqaq. This fragment of Burid Damascus is a rare reminder of the art of the period that was marked by the opening of the Crusades.

Beyond lies the reconstructed 'Damascene Hall' based on a room taken from a palace of the 18th century in the old city of Damascus. The room was reconstructed in 1958–62 following a gift of the marble and timber panelling by Jamil Mardam Bey, a former prime minister. The hall does not follow the dimensions of the original and has been considerably extended and supplemented with reconstructed panels. Among the original sections are the central element of the ceiling (raised section); the marble basin; the two niches surrounding the fountain; and the chimney. Return now to the main entrance along the remaining part of the Islamic wing.

REFS: Arush (et al) Concise Guide 1982; Arush Antiquités arabes 1976; Hillenbrand 'Dolce Vita' 1982; Issa Guide 2007.

Damascus – Tekkiye Mosque

VARIANTS: Tekke Mosque
PERIOD: Ottoman RATING: ** MAP: 25

LOCATION: The most notable buildings of the Turkish period in the area between al-Quwatli Street (east of the National Museum) and the entrance to the Suq al-Hamidiye are covered in this itinerary with a diversion to the Suq Saruja area to the north.

If you are approaching the Tekkiye from the northern side of the Barada, passing the huge new Four Seasons hotel complex, you may notice the two Ayyubid tombs, both commemorating generals of Saladin, which are now almost swallowed by the western end of the complex. Farrukshah (northernmost of the tombs) was a nephew of Saladin. His tomb lost all its internal decoration when it was turned into a mosque in the 1920s. Bahramshah was Farrukshah's son (d 1229–30, probably assassinated).

Across the river is the Tekkiye Mosque, the most gracious and perhaps the most under-rated monument in Damascus. Damascus' first major work in the authorised Ottoman style, it nevertheless borrowed many elements from the local Syrian repertoire. It was the work of the foremost architect of the Ottoman period, Sinan. The complex was intended to service the great annual pilgrimage to Mecca whose custody was one of the most important duties of the governor of the *vilayat* (province) of Damascus and the income from which was one of the city's major sources of prosperity. The complex was built on the site of the Qasr al-Ablaq, a Mamluk palace built by Baybars. Earlier, the area from here west to the former fairgrounds had served as a parade or exercise ground (Midan al-Akhdar) for Ayyubid and Mamluk troops and a convenient assembly point for pilgrims as the Hajj set out each year.

Though modest in scale by comparison with many of Sinan's other projects (for others in Syria see *Aleppo – South Quarter; *Damascus – Salihiye Quarter), it was begun in 1554 to honour the great Sultan Suleiman I (Suleiman the Magnificent r 1520–66). The work of Sinan is prominently represented in Istanbul, particularly in his superlative Suleimaniye Mosque, and in other parts of Turkey and in the Balkans. The assurance and sensitivity of his style can be seen on a small scale in this Damascus project but the effect is nevertheless as striking as in his more monumental achievements. While the project was planned by Sinan's Istanbul studio, it was probably supervised by a local subordinate employing Syrian craftsmen.

The complex consists of three parts:
• the mosque itself
• the arcaded buildings which enclose the courtyard on the north, east and west sides, forming a khan to house the pilgrims with, on the northern side, the former kitchens and refectory
• the compound to the east, now used as a handicrafts suq, the Madrasa

Selemiye, actually built as a Koranic school (or hostelry) a decade after the Tekkiye and not the work of Sinan.

Relying to a great extent on Ottoman Turkish designs (the domed prayer hall), Sinan's local craftsmen interposed local Syrian elements including the function and shape of the courtyard and its central

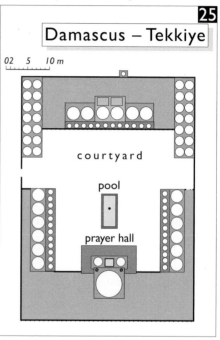

Damascus – Tekkiye

02 5   10 m

courtyard

pool

prayer hall

tank, the use of *muqarnas* work over the entrance to the prayer hall and the alternation of light and dark courses in stone. (In fact some of it is coloured plaster skilfully applied). The overall effect is calm and magical with the trees providing a cool oasis on a hot day though the vision until recently was marred by the incongruous paraphenalia of the military museum. (The complex was under reconstruction in 2008.)

In 1554 the design contract was given to Sinan by Sultan Suleiman. The construction took five years. The use of the slim Turkish minarets gives the complex much of its careful sense of proportion. Note that each cell of the accommodation blocks was covered by a dome and provided with a chimney.

The **Madrasa Selemiye** was added under Suleiman's successor, Sultan Selim II (Sultan 1566–74). Its style, though more distinctly Syrian, blends well with Sinan's work. The prayer room of the school (off the small courtyard to the south of the main suq) is still used for that purpose.

Note too the recently restored **Turkish Law Institute** (Dar al-Muallim) on the northeastern corner of the block. Built in 1910–11 to serve as a teachers' college, it became the Law Institute in 1918 and is now the headquarters of the Tourism Ministry.

Among other buildings of the Turkish period in the neighbourhood (continue east to Port Said St then up the hill past main Post Office), the Damascus terminus of the **Hijaz Railway** (1913) is worth noting. The building, though small in scale, is notable for its blending of Turkish and Syrian elements. Note especially the intricate ceiling, in Damascene style, in the ticket hall. The station has only recently been taken out of service and with the removal of all the platforms in preparation for a major complex behind.

A short continuation to the east (towards the entrance to the Suq al-Hamidiye) will take you past some other notable buildings which line the street (Sharia al-Nasr) which was widened and straightened under the late Ottoman governor, Jamal Pasha, during the First World War. This area housed the central administrative headquarters of the late Turkish and French administrations. On the left is the headquarters built for the Societé des Eaux Fijeh (1924) that took over the concession to supply Damascus with drinking water from the Anti-Lebanon. (The provision of fresh drinking water through a separate system was the work of the late Ottoman governor, Hussein Nizam Pasha.) Further down on the left is the **Mosque of Tengiz**, Mamluk governor of Damascus (r 1312–40). The mosque suffered from its use as a military

school under Ibrahim Pasha (r 1832–40). It was restored as a mosque after a fire in 1945 and given a new street façade. The only elements surviving from the original mosque façade are the gateways at either end. Besides the wonderful minaret (best seen from the rear lane), the mosque is rich more in its historical associations, having been built in 1317–8 on the site of the former church of St Nicholas. To the right on Nasr St is the domed tomb built for Tengiz. Opposite was once the military headquarters of Ibrahim Pasha and further on, just before the Suq al-Hamidiye, is the impressive main courts complex, a French Mandate project on the site of the late Ottoman military headquarters.

Continue east and turn left at the busy intersection at the western end of the Suq al-Hamidiye, along al-Thawra St. Continue north for 70 m (the Citadel is on the opposite side) until you reach the **Mosque of Sanjakdar** – originally built by the Mamluk governor, Argunshah al-Nasiri (1347–9) but altered in the late 19th century when the street to the north was opened to provide room for a tramway. Though the façade now looks rather cramped, the portal is the highpoint of the building, dramatically rising to a superb *muqarnas* canopy and below it a panel of interlaced circles in coloured stone.

Suq Saruja

Keep walking north from the Sanjakdar Mosque for 200 m. Recent urban redevelopment work in Damascus has left isolated a rather charming quarter, the Suq al-Suruja, a little way north of here, beyond the Barada. The most interesting group of buildings is at the eastern end of Suq Saruja where it meets al-Thawra St.

The Saruja Quarter was originally developed in the Ayyubid period and contained sites built or endowed by relatives of Saladin in the late 12th century with subsequent development in the Mamluk period. The most important building lies behind high white stone walls, recently refurbished and now surrounded with gardens to the south and west – the **Madrasa Shamiye**, often known simply as Sitt al-Sham ('the Lady of Damascus'). The lady in question is the sister of Saladin, Sitt al-Sham Zumurrud Khatun, one of a series of formidable Kurdish women of the period. The madrasa was formerly her house and she buried in the complex a brother (Turun Shah, brother of Saladin and Lord of Yemen d 1180), a husband (Nasir al-Din Muhammad d 1186) and a son Hosam al-Din Muhammad d 1191). She survived until 1220 and was also probably buried in the complex though her grave is not marked. To the west are two other tombs of the period, dubbed the lesser Sitt al-Sham. First (on the southwest corner of the madrasa) is the **mausoleum of** a young martyr of the struggle against the Crusades, **Zain al-Din** son of Ala al-Din (d 1172) and the second (a little to the west) is **Turba Najmiye** (second half of the 12th century), again containing the burials of relatives of Saladin including Shahanshah (brother of Sitt al-Sham and Saladin) and Malik al-Mansur, a son who died early.

To finish the circuit, take the quiet leaf-shaded lane, Suq Saruja, to the west, all that remains of a quarter saved from the runaway development of new traffic systems in the 1980s. The most prominent landmark is the garishly striped **Mosque al-Ward** (Mosque of Barsbay) with its square minaret (recently restored) topped by a prominent balcony. The mosque was built in 1427 by the Mamluk chamberlain, Barsbay al-Nasiri, and served as his funerary mosque on his death in 1448–9. Following the lane to the end takes you to the busy square in front of the Central Bank and the Cham Palace Hotel, Yusuf al-Azmeh Square.

REFS: Goodwin *PEFQ* 1978–79: 127–9; Goodwin 1987: 256; Meinecke 1992; Moaz 1994: 1–3; Sack *Damaskus* 1989; Sauvaget *Monuments* 1932: 78–81; S Weber 2000: 494–5.

Damascus – Salihiye

PERIOD: Arb/Ott RATING: * MAP: 26

LOCATION: The Salihiye Quarter lies 2 km north of the walled city on the lower slopes of Mount Kassyun. The following itinerary begins at the busy traffic intersection, Jisr al-Abiad ('White Bridge' denoting an original crossing of the Tora arm of the Barada).

History

The more gently sloping ground on the lower reaches of Mount Kassyun has long been used to take spill-over population from the walled city of Damascus, to house the tombs of pious benefactors, or to accommodate the wealthier class seeking a more salubrious climate. It has also provided a refuge for new immigrant groups, particularly non-Arabs (Kurds, Circassians and Cretan Muslims) or refugees from persecution elsewhere (Palestinians fleeing the Crusaders). The settlement in the Salihiye area has thus been unplanned compared to the relatively ordered beginnings of the old city which from the Greco-Roman period was provided with a grid plan and a systematic water reticulation system. The historic importance of the quarter is indicated by the 70 monuments officially recognised, a significant proportion of the 250 or so for Damascus as a whole.

The area to be visited in this itinerary is a 1.4 km segment of the extensive arc of settlement spread across the lower slopes of the mountain, reaching areas where the ground is precipitous and wheeled traffic impossible. This segment (also known as al-Chaharkasiye) lies between al-Muhajjirin (the quarter established between 1895–1911 to settle Muslim refugees from Crete; on the left as you face the mountain) and al-Akrad (Kurdish quarter, established 19th century; on the right). Lying at the end of the main access route from the old city, Salihiye represents the first part of the Kassyun slopes to receive permanent settlement in Arab times and it continued to attract major building projects. The first impetus to the development of civic services, however (including the channelling of the Tora and Yazid arms of the Barada River), came in 1159 under the patronage of Nur al-Din. He settled Hanbali refugees from Crusader-occupied Jerusalem, under the leadership of Sheikh Abu Umar Muhammad al-Maqdisi, in the

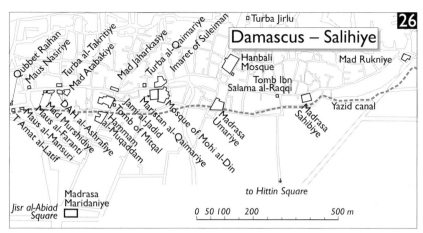

Damascus – Salihiye **26**

Turba Jirlu

Hanbali Mosque　　　　Mad Rukniye

Tomb Ibn Salama al-Raqqi

Yazid canal

to Hittin Square

Jisr al-Abiad Square　　Madrasa Maridaniye

0 50 100 200 500 m

Salihiye Quarter to prevent rivalries in the old city where adherents of the Shafei school were dominant. 'Hanbali' derives from Abu Salih al-Hanbali, the early Islamic scholar whose followers constructed the Hanbali Mosque described later.

Salihiye became a centre for Hanbali influence in Damascus, especially after the arrival in the 13th century of a large number of Hanbali refugees from Harran in Mesopotamia, fleeing the Mongols. 'Salihiye' is also popularly taken as a reference to the number of devout (*salihoun*, 'saints') buried there.

In the Ayyubid period, the Hanbalis consolidated themselves around the Hanbali Mosque, founded in 1202 as the first Friday mosque outside the old walled city. Further development was sponsored by endowments from leading figures of the ruling class, usually for the establishment of funerary mosques or madrasas (Maridaniye 1213–27; Rukniye 1227; Sahibiye 1231; Murshidiye 1252). The area also served as a place of burial, including for the notable mystic Mohi al-Din Ibn al-Arabi (d 1240) whose tomb (Mosque of Mohi al-Din) still attracts crowds of pilgrims to the quarter.

The Salihiye Quarter, essentially without defensive walls or strongpoints for refuge, was sorely affected by the three great Mongol invasions (1260, 1300, 1400) of

the Mamluk period as well as by internal strife. Its development thus slowed, at least until private endowments from prominent trading families gave new impetus to the quarter in the late 14th century. In the early Ottoman period, the quarter benefited from the works to enlarge the tomb of al-Arabi, as well as charitable projects such as the Imaret of Sultan Suleiman of 1552 (see below). After the 16th century, however, it largely stagnated, a process hastened by the earthquake of 1759.

Visit

The following itinerary surveys the major historic monuments of the Salihiye Quarter but it should be noted that many are open only rarely or are used for other purposes (e.g. schools). The majority of mosques (apart from the Hanbali and Mohi al-Din Mosques) are closed except, in some cases, at prayer times. However, given that the façades are usually the aspect which retains most of the original character of a building, even a short visit conveys a good deal of the atmosphere of this richly historic quarter.

The tour begins with the building which stands on the north side of the intersection at Jisr al-Abiad, the **Madrasa Maridaniye**. Unfortunately much of the simplicity of the original Ayyubid building erected after 1213 but endowed in 1227 has been lost with later additions. The title refers to the benefactor, a princess of the house of the lords of Mardin, southeastern Turkey – Ikhshawra Khatun, the wife of the Ayyubid ruler, al-Muazzam Issa, and probably a niece of Nur al-Din. She died in Mecca and was thus not interred in the building she had endowed. The best view of the complex is from across the busy street to the south but the entry is on the north side – note the fine lintel in carved wood, the carved wooden panels in the prayer hall and three early coloured glass windows. The funerary chamber is to the left. The minaret (right of entrance) was probably built around 1413 by the Mamluk Amsanak Ibn Uzdamur who is buried in the mosque.

There are two streets which branch from the north side of the Jisr al-Abiad square near the Madrasa Maridaniye. Take the left street (al-Afif St) and ascend for c120 m. After skirting the French Embassy on the left, the road veers left across a triangular intersection but continue to ascend 20 m to the next cross street to the left. Immediately on the left are two buildings of interest. The first is the **Mausoleum of Amir Kajkun al-Mansuri** (1322) (Turba al-Kajkariye). Small building – dome with two side arches; long carved inscription on the façade, now used as a centre for a government welfare agency. Almost immediately next left is the **Turba Amat al-Latif**, tomb of a wife of an amir of Homs (d 1255–6) and descendant of a prominent Hanbali sheikh – uninscribed *tabula ansata* on door lintel. Next on the right, a domed mausoleum, **Qubbet Raihan** (1243) built by a tutor to one of the Ayyubid princes.

Return to Afif St and head uphill (north), taking the first street on the right. You will now find the majority of buildings described in the rest of the itinerary along this main thoroughfare (Madares Assaad al-Din) which cuts across the quarter for 1.4 km from west to east.

Second building on the left is the **Mausoleum of Nasiriye** al-Balabaniye, usually given the name Nabi Yunis, an attractive dome resting on *muqarnas* squinches; probably late 13th century.

On the right you now approach a group of four buildings, the first of which is the **Mausoleum al-Faranti** (Turba al-Farnatiye), the tomb of Ali al-Faranti (d 1224), a Hanbali sheikh and ascetic – with a small dome; restored since 1981.

Immediately after, on the right, **Madrasa Murshidiye** (1252), a strangely contorted building plan due to the need to have the tomb and prayer hall oriented true south. Funerary college commemorating Khadija Khatun, daughter of the Ayyubid leader, Malik al-Muazzam Issa (whose wife was commemorated in the Madrasa Maridaniye above). The simple square minaret is the only example surviving from the 13th century in Damascus. Immediately after is the doorway to the **Dar al-Hadith al-Ashrafiye** (1237), a Koranic school reflecting the return to basic Sunni traditions under the Ayyubid ruler, al-Ashraf Musa. The courtyard behind the prayer hall is abandoned but the tomb chamber survives on the east.

Also on the right, across an intervening laneway, is the **Madrasa Atabakiye**, a building with a notable honeycombed entrance. Erected in memory of Tarkan Khatun, daughter of a ruler of Mosul and grand-niece of Nur al-Din who married Malik al-Ashraf Musa (d 1242). A square minaret is apparently a later addition.

Returning to the left, immediately opposite the Dar al-Hadith al-Ashrafiye, is the **Turba al-Takritiye** (or Madrasa Tabutluk), the mausoleum of Taqi al-Din al-Takriti (d 1299), a senior official under Qalawun. The building comprises a beautiful *muqarnas*-treated entrance doorway, a domed funerary chamber on the right and a small prayer room to the left. Most of the building follows Syrian tradition of the time (it was the work of the famed architect, Ibrahim Ibn Ganaim) but the decoration of the prayer room shows Andalusian influence.

You now enter Salihiye's Friday market. 100m on the right is a street which descends to the Jisr al-Abiad square. On the left (northwest segment) of this intersection is the **Madrasa Jaharkasiye** founded by the Ayyubid Amir, Fakhr al-Din Jaharkas ('the Circassian'), commander of Saladin's mamluks (d 1211), and enlarged by the former mamluk Khutluba (d 1237) for his own burial. Two linked funerary chambers with segmented melon domes and a separate prayer hall to the west (under restoration in 2008).

25 m down the street on the right, a gateway leads into the compound which houses the **Jami al-Jadid** (the New Mosque) and the **Turba Khatuniye**. This is the mausoleum of Ismat al-Din Khatun who was the wife of Nur al-Din and of his successor, Saladin (d 1185/6). The site was incorporated into the mosque in the 14th century. The burial chamber (behind the main courtyard) is richly decorated in sculptured plaster. In the separate prayer room, note the Crusader capitals.

On the opposite side of this street, you will notice the remains of another **tomb** now in crumbling disrepair, that **of Amir Sabiq al-Din Mitqal**, a *jamdar* (knight) of Saladin who died in 1224. Though the dome has collapsed, the tomb is intact and the inscription commemorates his service including at Saladin's great victory over the Crusaders at the Battle of Hattin (1187) and at the subsequent capture of St John of Acre and of Ascalon.

Continue to descend. The building on the next corner (lower right) is the **Hammam al-Muqaddam** (late 14th century?), still in use as a bath house. The original layout is preserved but covered, in a 1980s renovation, with a violent concatenation of new bathroom tiles in showroom-style profusion.

Return now to the main street and continue your walk across the slope to the east. At 70 m on the left, you will notice the red-domed **Turba al-Qaimariye**. The Saif al-Din Qaimari (amir of the Kurdish regiment, the 'Qaimariye' – d 1256) in 1248 endowed the nearby Maristan al-Qaimariye. His son who died in 1260 at an early age, is also buried in the building. The **Maristan al-Qaimariye**, is 10 m further on, on the right side of the street. The building's sobriety and

balance illustrate the development of the earlier design of the Maristan Nur al-Din (*Damascus – Suqs). Note particularly the honeycombed entrance doorway with supporting colonnettes and the sculptured plaster decoration of the main *iwan* (south) which also contains two large medallions and an elegant inscription. There is a good view of Damascus from the window of the *iwan*. The *maristan* was originally supplied with water from the Yazid stream of the Barada.

Next, almost immediately on the left, is a small building of singular interest, the **Imaret of Sultan Suleiman**. This was the work of the famous Ottoman architect, Sinan, who was also responsible for one other building in Damascus, the superb Tekkiye Mosque (*Damascus – Tekkiye). The architect of some of the most famous mosques of Istanbul, Sinan's building was commissioned (possibly to replace a building burnt in a fire) by the great Sultan Suleiman (1520–66) for the distribution of food to pilgrims visiting the tomb of al-Arabi opposite. It was completed in 1552, two years before the Tekkiye. It comprises two domes over a central chamber surrounded by service rooms. It is still in use as a charitable food distribution centre. The recently reconstructed interior clearly demonstrates Sinan's masterful control of shapes and volumes even in the most mundane of constructions.

Immediately on the right stands one of the most interesting mosques in Damascus, the **Mosque and Mausoleum of Sheikh Mohi al-Din** or Jamia al-Selimi, one of the first projects of Damascus' new Ottoman rulers when they took power in 1516 and part of their program to encourage Sufism. The mosque honours the burial chamber of the celebrated Sufi mystic, Mohi al-Din Ibn al-Arabi (b 1165 in Andalusia, d 1240). The four-aisled mosque above was built in 1518 by Sultan Selim I and widened and restored in 1947/8. The style is an amalgam of late Mamluk (the minaret) and early Ottoman influences and was hurriedly constructed during the passage of Selim through Damascus.

Sufism

The relationship between Sunni Islam and Sufism has been amibguous since the movement originated in the 12th century in parallel with the efforts of the Zengids and Ayyubids to restore orthodox Islam in the face of prevailing Shiite beliefs. Sufis attempt to create, through a life of self denial and piety, an individual link to the Creator through *gnosis* or knowledge as opposed to the more communal basis of Sunni mainstream Islam. It has often been rejected by the orthodox as verging on polytheism though a synthesis of Sunnism and Sufism was achieved by the notable *alim* (theologian), al-Ghazzali, in the early 12th century. Ibn Arabi was the great Sufi mystic of his age. Born in Andalusia in 1165, he moved gradually east, settling in Damascus which provided a freer atmosphere for his teaching than Cairo or the Muslim west. He died in 1240 in Damascus. His writings drew together the mystical speculations of a wide range of Sufi and other religious sources.

Al-Arabi is buried behind a silver grille in the domed chamber which pre-dates the mosque and is reached by descending the staircase to the left of the entrance courtyard. Described as the 'greatest speculative genius of Islamic mysticism',[19] his shrine is still a centre for the Sufis (see box above) as well as attracting a constant stream of women. The limestone cenotaph was constructed for the Algerian patriot, Abd al-Kader al-Jazairi, who resisted the French conquest of Algeria from 1830 to 1847. After his eventual surrender, he went into exile in Damascus. (The body was transferred to Algiers following Algerian independence.) Other tombs include those of two sons of al-Arabi; of a devoted follower and fellow mystic, Sheikh Muhammad Kharbutli; and of a son-in-law of an Egyptian khedive, Mahmud Pasha Sirri al-Khunaji.

Continue now past the street vegetable market (Suq al-Jumaa), keeping left at

the V–intersection (25 m). After +75 m, take the small street ascending the slope to the left; +30 m on the right you will come to another major mosque, the **Hanbali Mosque** (or Jami`a Mozafari). This was built between 1202 and 1213 for the Hanbalis of Damascus under Sheikh Maqdisi's patronage (see next building), and completed by Mozafar al-Din Gokburi, a prince of Irbil.[20]

The street façade is exceptionally dull but the interior, including the extensive courtyard, is worth close inspection. The courtyard uses six classical or Crusader columns with capitals and the tall minaret is particularly striking in its four-square simplicity, particularly after its recent restoration. The prayer room (basilica plan, timber roof) suffers from a 1970s treatment but note the *minbar* of 1207/8 said by Sauvaget to be of a 'fine style' and the beautifully carved window over the first door into the courtyard.

To the north (120 m) is the **Turba Jirlu**, an Ayyubid tomb taken over by the Mamluks, who provided a beautiful portal frame (1319–20).

Return to the main street but cross it to continue descending the hill. On the left (50 m) lie the ruins of the **Madrasa Umariye**, the oldest building in the Salihiye area whose origins go back to the exodus of Muslims from Jerusalem after its capture by the Crusaders in 1099. On this site, refugees from the terrible massacre that the Crusaders carried out in Jerusalem built an Islamic school named in honour of a descendant of a leader of the original refugees, Sheikh Abu Umar Muhammad al-Maqdisi (d 1210/11). The school once comprised two courtyards, the one on the west dates from the 13th century reconstruction (student cells; prayer room; *mihrab* with Crusader capitals); the eastern one from the first years of the 13th century (lined with student cells and an *iwan*). Though decayed almost beyond recognition by the 1980s

---

19 Hitti 1951: 652. Hitti claims that much of the schematisation of hell in Dante's poetry can be traced to al-Arabi's writing.

20 He was married to Rabia Khatun, sister of Saladin, and was one of the foremost proponents of the restoration of Sunni orthodoxy to Syria.

the complex is being restored, largely with new materials.

Return now to the main transverse street. Continue eastwards 120 m. On the right is the **Tomb of Ibn Salama Al-Raqqi** (1213 – identity unknown).

Another 50 m on the right, the **Madrasa Sahibiye** built between 1233 and 1245 by Rabia Khatun, a sister of Saladin and wife of the benefactor of the Hanbali Mosque, Prince Gokburi. It was established under a *waqf* for the benefit of the Hanbalite sect. Sauvaget notes that this alone of the madrasas of Damascus preserves its original plan unchanged. The style of the façade is northern Syrian: fine honeycombed portal; restrained geometric decoration around the door and windows. The courtyard includes two *iwan*s. Herzfeld notes that 'the building uses no cupolas, but only barrel vaults, cloisters and cross vaults. It is built in the very best Ayyubid style, with conscious simplicity, displaying perfect mastery over stone'.

To reach the final building on our itinerary, continue 200m along the lane until it widens and joins a descending road amid modern apartment buildings on the edge of the al-Akrad Quarter. Turn right and 25 m on the left is the **Madrasa Rukniye**, the funerary college of Amir Rukn al-Din Mankuris, a governor of Egypt under his half-brother, the Ayyubid Sultan al-Adil (one of Saladin's sons). Recently reconstructed and given a new minaret, the madrasa includes a mosque and the mausoleum of its founder. The façade (now disfigured by an ugly shade structure) is most impressive for its geometric decoration and Kufic lettering (lintels of the doorway and windows). The long inscription on the tomb (dated 1224) praises the many qualities of the founder and lists the endowments whose income funded the madrasa.

REFS: Sauvaget & Ecochard 1938–50; Herzfeld *Damascus* – III 1946: 1–71; Meinecke 1983: 189–241; Sauvaget *Monuments* 1932; WW *Damaskus* – *islamische* 1924.

Damascus – Midan Quarter

VARIANTS: Meidan
PERIOD: Arb RATING: – MAP: 27

LOCATION: Southwest of old city of Damascus. Begin at Bab Musalla Square, 700 m southwest of old city. (Can also be reached as a continuation of the itinerary *Damascus – Southwest Quarter).

This itinerary takes you through the extension of the old city of Damascus that developed in late Ayyubid and Mamluk times and continued under Turkish rule to cater for the growth in the pilgrimage traffic to Mecca. The name (from *midan* – Arb: 'field') resulted from the use of the area as an exercise field (Midan al-Khasa). (A second *midan* was established by Nur al-Din in the area west of the city later occupied by the *Damascus – Tekkiye.) These open areas attracted pilgrim caravans from the north keen to rest and provision themselves before the difficult desert journey to Mecca. The association with the Hajj and the road to Mecca also ensured it became a favoured burial zone. The main street leading from the old city became lined with shops, houses, mosques, other pious institutions and schools.

The pilgrimage was a 'gigantic enterprise'[21, particularly important to the economy of Damascus, especially under the Ottomans whose claim to most of the Muslim world meant that a great deal of the Empire's credibility and its claim to the Caliphate depended on escorting the pilgrimage safely to Mecca and back each year.[21] Up to 30,000 pilgrims would converge on the assembly point in the Midan Quarter to join the consolidated caravan for the six week journey across the desert to Mecca. After 1708, the governor of Damascus was himself commander of the caravan and accompanied it to the Hijaz where his authority prevailed even over the local guardians of the Holy Places.

Today, Midan St is a rather straggling thoroughfare which pays little respect to the old buildings that appear between the modern apartment blocks and shops.

21 Barbir 1980: 177.

Originally considerably broader than the present thoroughfare, the roadway became confined as its commercial role, including the provision of the city with grain and meat, grew more important. It is also now heartlessly chopped in two by the city ring road system. Nevertheless, there are many buildings of interest and it gives a chance to savour an old quarter of Damascus which is not strangled by intense traffic. This is a long itinerary on foot, particularly if combined with *Damascus – Southwest Quarter, and the final mosque is only practicable by taxi.

Upper Midan

We begin at the busy traffic circle, Bab Musalla Place, which lies c400 m south of the Bab al-Saghir cemetery (*Damascus – Southwest Quarter).

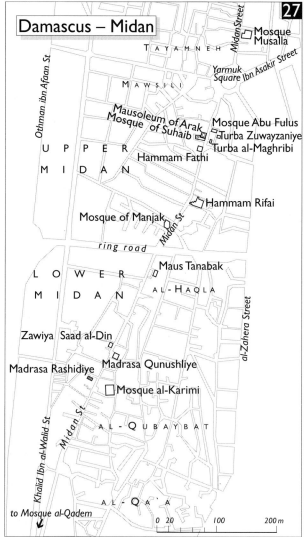

The first mosque, after which the modern square takes its name, lies north of the intersection (100 m on the right). The **Mosque Musalla al-Idain** was built in 1209 during the reign of al-Adil Saif al-Din (Saphadin) on a site formerly used for open-air prayer on feast-days. Inside, the prayer hall is surprisingly large and elongated with a sloping wooden roof structure. This was the second congregational mosque permitted outside the walls of the old city.

Cross now to the south side of the traffic circle, selecting the street diagonally opposite the one you have exited. 150 m on the left set back from the street is the **Mosque Abu Fulus** of which little but the façade survives from the original construction of the first part of the 13th century. In the prayer hall, a *mihrab* said to be Fatimid. In the street behind, a typically

Ayyubid tomb, **Turba Zuwayzaniye**, is witness to the use of this area for burials well before its more intensive development in Mamluk and Ottoman times.

On the right, opposite the Abu Fulus Mosque is the **Mausoleum of Arak** (1349), named after a former governor of Safad (d 1349) – two-coloured façade with turquoise faience inlay above the honeycombed doorway. Double mausoleum with a fine cenotaph in carved wood under the north dome. Adjoining immediately to the left is the **Mosque of Suhaib** al-Rumi whose origins go back to Ayyubid times (1227). On the opposite side of Midan St, the **Turba al-Maghribi** (c1329, founder unknown) now offset by a small paved square.

On the right (150 m) is the **Hammam Fathi** built in 1743 by Fathi al-Daftari, a senior official under Suleiman Pasha al-Azem; recently restored façade. 100 m further, on the left, is the substantially more intact **Hammam Rifai**, a 14th or 15th century building of 'an extraordinarily picturesque and unusual design' (Sauvaget), still a good example of a functioning Damascene hammam. The street façade is narrow and leads into a dressing room probably re-built after the 1925 bombardment by the French.

Seventy metres on lies the **Mosque of Manjak,** a 14th century building commissioned by Amir Ibrahim, son of the Mamluk governor, Saif al-Din Manjak (1368). It was built in the grand Mamluk style as a congregational mosque but only the lower courses of the street façade have escaped a fanciful modern reconstruction. The original minaret (now enveloped within a revamped courtyard) was used to hang the lamps marking Ramadan.

Lower Midan

Beyond the huge elevated structure of the Damascus ring-road lies the lower Midan.   As you resume your course along Midan St, opposite the modern police station, take the lane left that leads to the **Mausoleum of Tanabak** al-Hasani (or Mosque of Yashbak) the 1394

mausoleum of the governor of Damascus (1392–1400). Two domed halls – prayer hall (south); mausoleum (north); fine façade with *muqarnas* gateway, spectacular polychrome decoration and coats of arms, recently restored. The domes rest on *muqarnas* pendentives.

To the south, 300 m on your right, is the **Zawiya Saad al-Din** al-Jabawi (or Mastabat Saad al-Din) planned as a tomb (1438) but converted in the early 16th century into a meeting room for a Sufi mystic group, followers of the 14th century spiritual leader, Saad al-Din al-Jabawi. In 1516, under their then leader, Hussein al-Jabawi, the 'Saadiye' or 'Jabawiye' took part in the handover of the city to the Ottomans. The group lasted to the end of the Turkish period. Turkish style with twin domes (opened out into a continuous space in 1570); under the south dome, stucco medallion and fine faience panels. Cross Midan St. Tucked away behind a small park, is the **Madrasa Qunushliye** a small mausoleum (1320–1). The curious coat of arms within the door frame gives no clue as to the person honoured.[22]

Further along Midan Street, after 100 m take a small street to the right. 20 m on the left, behind modern shop façades, is the **Madrasa Rashidiye**, with twin domed chambers, probably 14th century. The entrance doorway has the arms of the founder set in interlaced decoration, topped by a stalactited frame. The identitiy of the person interred, however, is not certain though if may be the Mamluk relief governor of Damascus, Mankalibugha al-Shamsi (1363–6). Behind the façades on the eastern side of Midan St, **Mosque al-Karimi**, an early 14th century congregational mosque with a plain rectangular minaret and large arcaded courtyard with patterned stone paving.

Our final monument lies 2 km south, 900 m beyond the new Damascus railway terminal. The **Mosque al-Qadam** (16th century) comprises an irregularly shaped

22 The date was established by Meinecke by comparison of the round window of the portal with the same detail on the façade of Turba Jirlu (*Salihiye).

court (*iwan* on south) at the centre of which stands an octagonal prayer hall covered by a dome. In the centre of the prayer room, the tomb of Ahmet Pasha (1636) is topped by a large stone turban. This mosque was associated with legends going back to the 14th century that the Prophet Moses was buried nearby. It was later used by the governors of Damascus as they waited for the pilgrims to assemble in what has been described as 'one of the greatest of mediaeval pageants'.[23]

REFS: Atassi *Midan Sultani* 1994; Ecochard & le Cœur 1942; Rihawi *Damascus*; Marino 1997; Meinecke 1992 ; Roujon-Vilan 1997; Sauvaget *Monuments* 1932; Sadan 1981; VVW *Damaskus – islamische* 1924. ' Sa'diyya' *EI2*.

Dana (South)/Qasr al-Banat

دانا

PERIOD: Byz RATING: * MAP: R3

LOCATION: Take main road from *Maarat al-Numan to Aleppo. 5 km north of Maarat, turn left (west) and take the side road which heads into the Jebel Riha. +3 km to Dana (South).

The village was called **Dana (South)** by Butler to distinguish it from the other Dana, on the plain below Jebel Sheikh Barakat, south of Saint Simeon (*Roman Road – Bab al-Hawa).

The style of the remains at Dana (South) are strongly reminiscent of *Bara. There are three buildings of note:

· a **pyramidal-roofed tomb**
· a third century or fourth century **tomb monument to Olympiane** comprising four columns with a low pyramidal canopy
· and a 'monastery' or 'convent' (**Qasr al-Banat**), 500 m north of the village.

The **pyramidal-roofed tomb** (recently reconstructed) is a remarkable building especially on account of its state of preservation. The roof is steeply pitched. It is preceded by a small portico supported on four elegant Ionic columns,

23 Barbir 1980: 152.

a graceful touch a little out of character with the towering roof. This building is dated by inscription to 324 (the year of Constantine's adoption of Christianity as the official religion of the Roman Empire). It is thus considerably earlier (and totally pagan in inspiration) compared with the sixth century re-creations of this basically Hellenistic concept at *Bara.

The **tomb monument to Olympiane** nearby comprises four smooth shafts with Ionic capitals supporting a stone canopy and was dated by Butler to the third or fourth centuries on the basis of a comparison with architectural details found in southern Syria.

The remains of **Qasr al-Banat** (500 m north) are also surprisingly intact. The building is compact but three storeyed, the lower two levels on the south faced with a double portico in square, simplified columns. The style is unreservedly plain and severe. The plan resembles somewhat the monastery known as Deir Sobat at Bara but given the small scale of the rooms, the lack of courtyards and the small size of the chamber that might be seen as a chapel, Butler prefers to classify it as an inn, perhaps with a small room set aside for prayer, rather than the monastery or convent of tradition. Scattered remains including a sixth century church.

REFS: Butler *AE* II 1903: 73; Butler *PE* II B 3 1909: 138–42; de Vogüé I 1865: 106; Tchalenko *Villages* I 1953: 178–9.

Dayhis

ديهيس

VARIANTS: Daes, Dehes, Dahe
PERIOD: Rom/Byz ALT: 606 m RATING: –
MAPS: R3, R3a

LOCATION: From the Bab al-Hawa turn-off, follow the road to Harim for 10.2 km. Turn left to Barisha. After +2 km (or 1 km before Barisha), take the sealed road to the right. Follow this for c+1 km looking out for the ruins on the left. (Road continues on, after 2.5 km, to Khirbet Hassan.)

The ruins of Dayhis extend over a considerable area. Situated on the crest of the Jebel Barisha, and not far from *Bamuqqa (2 km north), Tchalenko compares its economic base to its northern neighbour. Intensive agricultural exploitation dates from the first century AD, like Bamuqqa, taking advantage of an arable zone of 2000 ha. Its main period of prosperity, too, was in the fourth to sixth centuries. The village was inhabited long after the Muslim conquest, probably until the tenth century. In the late tenth century, the area of Jebel Barisha became the frontier between Byzantine Antioch and the Muslim Amirate of Aleppo and there are signs of military occupation.

The extensive remains include a badly ruined **basilica** (northeast quarter) with baptistery (late fifth or early sixth century) and a columned basilica with *bema* and rectangular sanctuary, adjoining to the southeast. Another church (**west church** – sixth century) lies to the west, another columned basilica with rectangular sanctuary. Butler also describes reliefs in a rock-cut tomb from the Roman period but all are badly weathered. There is a variety of villas scattered between the religious buildings as well as some monumental tombs and a cistern covered with a low-arched vault.

The **monastery** lies 700 m southwest of the main ruins. (Take the second tarred road on the left to reach it.) Its remains include a tower, church (another columned basilica with rectangular sanctuary) and an inn for pilgrims (*pandocheion*).

REFS: Bavant (*et al*) CFAS 1989: 189–94; Butler AE II 1903: 46, 72, 205–8, 274–6; Butler EC 1929: 134–5, 153, 209, 215, 237, 250; Pena (*et al*) *Reclus* 1980: 196–9; Pena *Inventaire* 1987: 93–6; Sodini 1980; Tchalenko *Villages* II 1953: 191, pl CXXXVI; Tchalenko & Baccache 1979–80: pl 335–360.

'Dead Cities' (Limestone Massif) – general note

PERIOD: Byz RATING: ** MAP: R3

LOCATION: The so-called 'Dead Cities' are found in the elevated limestone country (the Limestone Massif) between the Orontes and Afrin Rivers to the west and the Aleppo-Hama highway to the east.

Approximately 20–40 km in width, the zone spreads over a much greater length, covering most of the 140 km between Cyrrhus in the north and Apamea in the south.

The Limestone Massif is a great archaeological puzzle. How is it that this extensive area, once a heartland of Greek-Roman influence in Syria, was apparently so abruptly abandoned that much of the visible remains of its culture survive to this day?

The region lies at 400 m to 500 m in elevation, with some crests up to 800 m. The Limestone Massif can be divided into three groups of hills (see map R03) running from north to south:

• Jebel Semaan with Jebel Halaqa as a subsidiary (Itin 9a)
• Jebel al-Ala with Jebel Barisha running parallel to the east (Itin 9b). The two are separated by the Plain of Self.
• Jebel Riha (or Jebel Zawiye) (Itin 9c).

The Massif can present an inhospitable face to the visitor. The limestone hills are usually denuded of vegetation and even of soil. There are small patches of arable land in the valleys and closer to the plains but few permanent streams. Agriculture today has begun to revive as population pressures have brought new migrations into the upper reaches of the hills but the appearance is still often forbidding and windswept.

Because agricultural life was largely abandoned since the tenth century, the area provides a rich source of insight into Roman and Byzantine rural life, comparatively undisturbed by subsequent settlement and rebuilding. Moreover, the fact that the peak of agricultural exploitation (fifth to sixth century) came at a time when life in most parts of the later Roman or Byzantine Empire was severely disrupted adds to the inherent interest of the area.

The main phases in the occupation can be summarised as follows:

- First century to AD 250[24] – first settlement
- AD 340–550 – intensive exploitation (with a significant increase in the quality of life in the fifth century)
- mid sixth century – saturation point
- seventh century – life undisturbed by Arab conquest
- eighth century – decline coinciding with Abbasid takeover
- tenth century – region deserted, becomes a frontier zone between Byzantines and Arabs.

The prolific range of remains is partly a result of the materials used. The scarcity of wood meant that most permanent buildings were of stone. Architectural styles, perhaps partly because of the limited choice of materials, evolved conservatively. Especially in domestic architecture, there was little outside influence and while the results are stolid and somewhat repetitive, they pass on to us an incomparable picture of a culture that might have departed only a few decades and not 13 centuries ago.

Only a selection of the seemingly limitless number of sites are described – 36 out of over 100 sizeable sites and a theoretical total of 780 settlements. In the past, historians have sought a single coherent explanation why the sites were abandoned during the eighth to tenth centuries. The single-purpose explanations (Muslim invasion, Byzantine persecution of Monophysites, nomad incursion destroying the forests and leading to erosion of the arable land etc), however, are almost all fanciful.

Tchalenko's masterly study completed in the 1950s under the auspices of the French Institute for Near Eastern Studies (now IFPO) in Beirut gives the best (and simplest) explanation though not without

24 Some (eg Tate 1983) believe settlement began as early as Hellenistic times though the first villages date from the first century AD. Around AD 250, much of the Roman Orient was devastated by the plague named after St Cyprien. This probably brought an abrupt slowing of development before it resumed with new vigour in the Byzantine period.

subsequent challenge. Though the ground was marginal compared with the rich Plain of Amuq below, the fortunes of this area marched with the rise and decline of nearby Antioch, one of the imperial mega-cities. Population pressures made exploitation of these uplands economic, supplying olive oil to the Mediterranean world through Antioch. Once that trade was disrupted by the Arab-Byzantine confrontation, the peasants were forced back to self-sufficiency and moved to the outer edges of the zone where they had access to grain-growing terrain. There was some resettlement after the Muslim recapture of the area in 1164 but this was reversed under the Ottomans until it resumed last century.

Though the area was heavily Hellenized, the architectural methods used were essentially rustic – reflecting, perhaps, the discrepancy in backgrounds between the wealthy Antiochene (Hellenized) upper classes who were the landlords and the impoverished peasants of local (Syriac-speaking) stock. Masonry walls are built without cement; stone is used for almost all purposes; stairs, porticos, balconies, benches and cupboards. Vaulting is replaced by stone slabs supported on arches. The only exceptions are the roof tiles and the wooden framework which supported them. There has been much debate as to how the local architectural and decorative styles evolved and whether they were essentially native to the area. Certainly they are distinct from the practices followed in other areas of Syria at this time. The style of houses (which showed little change over the five centuries or more of settlement) and public buildings reflected both local circumstances (village rather than urban settlement, lack of wood, ready availability of stone) and a mix of metropolitan and eastern traditions. In the more ambitious public buildings of later centuries (particularly the great basilica complex at *Saint Simeon) imported craftsmen and architects were no doubt employed, though probably operating within the Antiochene tradition rather than influences further afield. This issue is examined in greater detail under Churches in section 2 (page 23).

Further studies since Tchalenko have followed up his work with an emphasis on finding ways of preserving this remarkable zone from urban and village encroachment. Among ideas being considered is a series of archaeological parks covering the most significant clusters among the hundreds of sites.

REFS: Mattern 1932; Pena (et al) Stylites 1975; Pena (et al) Reclus 1980; Pena (et al) Cenobites 1983; Pena (et al) 1987; Pena (et al) 1990; Sodini 1980; Tate 1992; Tchalenko Villages 1953–8.

Deir Mar Mousa

دير مار موسى

VARIANTS: Mar Mousa al-Habashi PERIOD: Byz/Arb ALT: 1500 m; RATING : ** MAP: R1

LOCATION: 10 km east of Nabk, Qalamoun (81 km north of Damascus on the Homs highway). A new road provides easy access from the Qaryatein road which runs below the Atiye escarpment. Take the road heading east out of Nabk and descend the escarpment. At c 15 km turn left. Follow side road for 3 km; park and walk last 500 m.

After a long period of neglect, the monastery of Mar Mousa has been restored through the initiative of an Italian priest (Paolo dell'Oglio) and the Syrian Catholic communities of Nabk and Damascus.

There is textual evidence that the monastery was founded in the sixth century and was rebuilt in the late 11th and again in the 16th century. The church, though small, is divided into three aisles and contains some extraordinary frescoes dating from the period 1088 to 1192 – 'the only full program of mediaeval church decoration to have survived in greater Syria'[25] according to the recent study by Erica Dodd.

The frescoes provide important evidence of the survival of a Syrian school of painting into the middle ages and its likely influence on Crusader art through the presence of Syrian-rite churches in Jerusalem. The magnificent Last Judgment on the western

25   Dodd 1992: 61.

wall is particularly striking. According to Dodd 'these figures … are painted in a style so different from mediaeval painting in either Byzantium or the West that the unaccustomed eye feels strange in their presence. [They] … belong to a current flowing through Syria from much earlier sources.' She concludes: 'The physical grandeur of the saints in Mar Mousa, the simple, bold colours, colourful display of pattern and elegant sensitivity of line, belong to a tradition altogether different from Byzantine 12th century painting in the rest of the Mediterranean and quite different from western painting' and points to the absorption of influences from Muslim Syria and Iraq which, via Jerusalem, were carried to western Europe by the Crusaders. The recent tracing of this tradition through the reconstruction of the churches at Mar Mousa, *Qara and the Chapel of the Prophet Elijah (*Seidnaya) has been a remarkable contribution to our appreciation of art history in the region.

The monastery is today associated with Mar Mousa (St Moses the Ethiopian – feast day 28 August) was a fourth century Egyptian ascete revered in the Syrian rites. The monastery, however, was probably first named to honour the Prophet Moses. The association was changed in the 15th century when the monastery received an influx of Ethiopian monks from northern Lebanon. The monastery was abandoned by the 19th century but is now functioning again with a resident community. From the terrace, there is a superb view eastwards into the desert below the escarpment.

REFS: Dodd 'Monastery of Mar Musa' Arte mediaevale 1992; Dodd Frescoes of Mar Mousa 2001; Sauvaget 'Les Caravanserails syriens' Ars Islamica 1937: 117.

Deir Semaan

دير سمعان

VARIANTS: Telanissos (Grk); Tell Neshe (Syriac); Deir Sema'an (Arb) PERIOD: Byz ALT: 495 m RATING : * MAPS: 28, R3, R3a

LOCATION: At the foot of the hill on which the Church of *Saint Simeon is located.

History

Originally, the Greek settlement (Telanissos or 'mountain of women') was founded to exploit the two neighbouring fertile plains on the route from *Apamea to *Cyrrhus. This agricultural community (probably located at the northern end of the later settlement) was transformed in the beginning of the fifth century AD by the establishment of a monastery. In 412, an ascetic who was later to become famous as St Simeon Stylites, joined the monastery. In search of a more arduous life-style, he later abandoned the community and took up residence on the hill above, confining himself to a small platform perched on a tall pillar. His presence attracted a stream of pilgrims from 425. After his death in 459, a major centre of pilgrimage under imperial patronage came into being in the lower village with hostelries, a church and three major monasteries. The village was joined to the huge new basilica on the hill by a triumphal way.

Construction seems to have taken place in several phases. In 470–80, three hostelries were constructed. The northern church was built in 491–2, along with the southwestern monastery. The period of peak activity was the sixth century when the large pandocheion (hostelry) was built. The centre continued to be mentioned as a pilgrimage destination until as late as 12th century.

Visit

The ruins cover an extensive area, almost two third of a square kilometre and roughly rectangular in shape. The best place to gain an appreciation of their layout is from the hill of St Simeon's Church. The following groups of ruins can be recognised, scattered between the fields:

- **monumental arch** marking the beginning of the via sacra ascending to the Cathedral of St Simeon
- the **small pandocheion** and **bazars** (where the via sacra begins)
- the **north church** (100 m to the right)
- the **northwest monastery** (450 m west of the north church)
- the **southwest monastery** (400 m from the bazars)
- the **large pandocheion** with tomb chapel to the rear (150 m to the south, nestling into the base of the hill).

In between are remains of many poorly constructed dwellings and of a few more substantial private houses or smaller inns.

The **monumental arch**, reconstructed from the tumbled stones, marks the beginning of the ascent along the sacred way.

The **north church** preserves much of its west façade. The plan is typical (late sixth century), with the addition of a tower above the prothesis (chamber right of the apse) and small portals each supported on two columns over the south and west entrances. The decoration is restrained.

The central grouping lies 160 m to the south, west of the Afrin road. Close to the road lies a building called by Butler a basilica (perhaps an **andron** or law court). The interior was supported by a high transverse arch. Though somewhat classical in style and civic in purpose, it probably dates from the fifth century. To the west of this building is a complex described as a **pandocheion**, dated by inscription to AD 479 – ie not long after St Simeon's death (459) had begun to attract the major pilgrimage traffic to the town. Just to the south is a long row of eleven **bazar** stalls built along the main east-west axis of the settlement.

About 120 m to the west of the bazar stalls, Butler's **house no 1** (probably early fifth century) can be identified. Originally three storeyed, each level bearing a colonnaded porch, it must have been a substantial building for a private residence.

The **southwest monastery** consists of three colonnaded buildings (at least two of them, north and west sides, probably serving as pilgrim accommodation) grouped to form a courtyard. From the southeast corner protrudes a sizeable

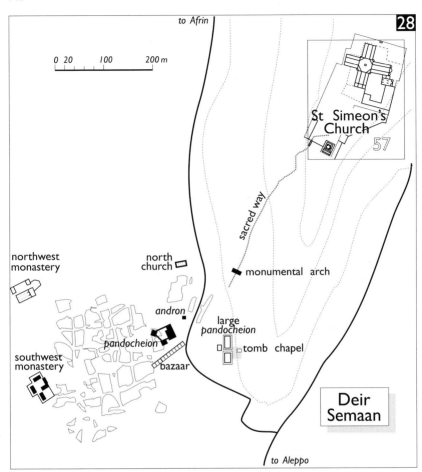

chapel, remarkably well preserved. The building to the east (joined to the chancel end of the chapel) and that to the south (both tri-roomed structures) provided further accommodation, the former probably for the monks themselves. Butler dates the complex to the sixth century.

The **northwest monastery** is described by Butler as 'an exceptionally fine group of buildings in a remarkable state of preservation'. It consists of an irregular collection of hostel buildings grouped around a mid fifth century church (south side) of some size (18 m by 22 m). East of the church was a burial ground, a rock-

hewn colonnaded court preceded by an entrance narthex.

The **large pandocheion** lies on the lower slopes of St Simeon's mount on the eastern edge of town and comprised the major accommodation complex for pilgrims. The remaining ruins make a remarkable sight with many stretches of arcading and parts of the huge structure still intact. It comprises two separate buildings set 70 m end to end, surrounded by wide porticos in two storeys. Both are typical shapes for this type of accommodation for pilgrims but considerably larger than usual. The south building is the better preserved, with large stretches of its porticos intact. A stone bridge at the rear leads from this building to a terrace carefully cut from the rock. At the back of this terrace stands a tomb chapel, half hewn out of the rock. Into the chapel wall (and along the rock side of the terrace) is set a series of *arcosolia* or burial niches. This burial facility gives some substance to the view that the complex (in spite of its modern description) was intended to house a monastery with pilgrim accommodation, rather than solely as an inn for passing pilgrims.

REFS: Butler *EC* 1929: 105–9; Butler *PE* II B 6 1920: 266–80; Mattern 1944: 135–8; Hadjar *Saint Simeon* nd: 47–57; Tchalenko *Villages* I 1953: 205–22; II 1953: pl CXXXII.

Deir Soleib

دير صليب

PERIOD: Byz   RATING: –   MAP: R2

LOCATION: c4 km south of the Hama-Masyaf road. From Hama continue west 30 km (or from Masyaf, 10 km east on Hama road). Sign points c+5 km south to Deir Soleib. Church 1 km on left before village. A second church can be reached on foot, 30 minutes walk southeast of the village.

The first church (Mattern's **west church**) is an interesting basilica which gives a different perspective on Syrian church building from that provided in the contemporary *Dead Cities to the north. The dating of the church is not entirely clear. It is probably, judging by its style, from the sixth or second half of the fifth century.

The semi-dome of the apse and the lower walls are largely intact. The entrance porch or *narthex* is large and has a baptistery off the south end. The surrounding compound is large (65 m by 45 m) with an atrium (30 m by 26 m) in front of the *narthex* and to the south a mausoleum (now blocked) which contains three monolith sarcophagi in niches.

Internally, the church is basilica plan but

almost square in shape. The semi-circular apse protrudes beyond the rear wall of the building, whereas buildings before the sixth century usually enclosed the curved shape behind a straight external wall at the back, thus requiring a good deal of fill-in masonry. The windows are much larger and based on bolder shapes than in earlier examples in northern Syria and the columns are thin enough to bring the naves together rather than form a barrier between them. There is virtually no decoration except the capitals and the occasional carved crosses. The two side rooms, the *prothesis* and the *diaconicon* were not placed in the normal positions at the end of the side aisles but are positioned outside the northeastern and southeastern corners of the church.

A second church (**eastern church**) is found 2 km southeast of the nearby village. It comprises a basilica with three naves, the arcades carried on pillars. The semi-circular apse (with three windows) is enclosed in a five-sided chevet. An inscription above the central portal dates it to 604–5, only three decades before the Arab conquest of Syria. The ruins are in a considerably more depleted condition.

REFS: Mattern, Mouterde & Beaulieu 1939: 6–18.

Deir al-Zor

دير الزور

VARIANTS: Auzara (Lat), al-Rumman (Arb?)
PERIOD: –   ALT: 195 m   RATING: –   MAP: R5

LOCATION: Right bank of the Mid Euphrates. 440 km from Damascus. The Museum is located on al-Imam St, 800 m on the left after the Post Office as you head towards the Aleppo road.

Deir al-Zor is now a good base for the Jezira region particularly with the opening of its new museum which provides an excellent briefing on the rich history of the Mid Euphrates-Khabur region.

Deir al-Zor, in Arabic 'the monastery in the grove', was probably coined to preserve the association with the town's classical name Auzara. The town has always been an important crossroads where the routes from northern Mesopotamia via Palmyra to Damascus and from Aleppo to southern Mesopotamia converged. After the classical period, its importance as an urban centre diminished (possibly in favour of nearby *Qalaat Rahba/Mayadin) until it became the headquarters of a Turkish *sanjak* in 1858, later raised to a full governorate (*muhafazat*). A small Christian community partly include descendants of Armenian refugees who, rounded up during the First World War in response to the Russian invasion of Turkey, were driven as far as Deir al-Zor where a small fraction escaped their intended fate – death from exhaustion and privation.

The town itself reveals little of this grim past. What you now see mostly dates from its renaissance during the French Mandate, hence the lovely suspended pedestrian footbridge (completed 1931, 450 m long) which crosses the river to the old port area. Nowadays, Deir al-Zor is experiencing a new boom with the exploitation of the oil and gas resources of the area. The new **Museum** transferred to its present building in 1996. Finds from many famous sites along the Euphrates and Khabur Rivers have been installed here including a reconstructed doorway from the Assyrian palace at Shadikanni (Tell Ajaja) and another from the Early Bronze Age town at Tell Bderi.

REFS: Bonatz (*et al*) *Rivers and Steppes* 1998.

Deraa

در عا

VARIANTS: Adraa (Lat) PERIOD: Rom/Arb RATING: – MAP: R1

Southern Hauran, just north of the Syrian-Jordanian border. Highway from Damascus to Amman, take Deraa turn-off. Ancient remains and Great Mosque on south side of Yarmuk River, east of the old main road to Jordan.

A restoration program for the Great Mosque is underway. Constructed in dark basalt and long assumed to be one of the oldest mosques in Islam, it has not made a favourable impact on visitors. (Creswell, not one to hold back an opinion, pronounced it gave a 'hideous impression'.) It is, however, a building of considerable interest. Like many congregational mosques it imitates the layout of the Great Mosque in Damascus but is largely Ayyubid in its present form including its curious sloping minaret.

Other aspects of Deraa's past are currently being uncovered. An extensive archaeological zone south of the Great Mosque includes a Roman theatre, temple and a section of an east-west colonnaded street. A new museum, not open at the time of writing, is under construction on the road leading into the town from the northeast, before the railway station (itself of historic interest as it was one of the main stations on the Hijaz Railway and the junction with the line coming up the Yarmuk from Haifa).

REFS: Korn II 2004: 172–3; Meinecke *AAAS* 1997: 101–2.

Dumeir (Plate 9b)

الضمير

VARIANTS: Thelsae (Lat), al-Dmeir (Arb) PERIOD: Rom RATING: ** MAP: R1

LOCATION: 40 km northeast of Damascus. Take *Palmyra road (leave Damascus-Homs highway 24 km north of Damascus). Continue +16 km. Do not take the diversion which skirts Dumeir but go straight into town. Before you reach the centre, look out on the right (300 m) for the outline of the temple (second street on right after crossing the *wadi*).

The **temple** as seen today, restored after much research and reconstruction work, represents one of the fruits of the intensive phase of construction activity in third century Syria. It was dedicated to Zeus Hypsistos in 245 during the reign of the Emperor Philip the Arab (emperor 244–9) who was born in the Hauran region of Syria (*Shahba). (Butler believed the portraits carved in relief in the south tympanum are of the Emperor and his wife,

Otacilia.) However there was an earlier reference to the building in a document relating to a law suit in 216. There may thus have been some changes of plan during the long construction period. An earlier altar dedicated to the Semitic deity, Baal-Shamin, in AD 94 (now in the Institut du Monde Arabe in Paris) indicates that a Nabataean religious building previously stood on the site.

The genesis and original purpose of the building, however, are not clear. The shape is highly unusual. Construction may have commenced as a public fountain or as a staging post at the intersection of two important caravan routes (hence the quadrilateral plan).[26] Perhaps it was even an elaborate triumphal arch or an entrance gateway to a now-buried (or never realised) sacred compound. The argument for seeing it as a temple, at least in its final form, is underlined by the use of corner towers and staircases giving access to the roof for ritual purposes in the Syro-Phoenician tradition. It was fortified in the Arab period; the arch on the rear wall remains completely filled in with stones and defensive devices.

Four kilometres to the east of Dumeir, on the road to Palmyra (to the right of a road leading (south) to a Syrian air force base – access thus difficult), are the remains of a complex once identified as a second century Roman military camp. The remains can be seen from the road. Each side is pierced by a central door guarded by twin semi-circular towers; round towers on each corner. Recent research has indicated that the complex is more likely to have been a **Ghassanid** or Umayyad **palace**.

REFS: Amy 1950; Brümmer 1985; Butler AE II 1903: 400–2; Dussaud 1927: 263, 300; Klinkott 1989; Nasrallah 1952–58; Lenoir Syria 1999; Poidebard 1934: 43.

---

26 Dumeir was the crossroads for the Emesa (*Homs)–*Palmyra and the Strata Diocletiana (*Resafa–Damascus) routes.

Dura Europos (Tell Salihiye)

تا الصلحئة

VARIANTS: Dura (pre-Grk); Dura Nicanoris (Grk); Tell al-Salihiye (Arb) PERIOD: Hel/Rom RATING: ** MAPS: 29, R5

LOCATION: From Deir al-Zor, follow the main Abu Kemal highway for 93 km southeast along the right bank of the Euphrates. Sign points left to Dura and ruins can be seen across the plain.

When the first wall paintings at Dura were uncovered by accident by a British expeditionary force in April 1920, few could have expected that the incident was about to provide a new perspective on early Christian and Judaic art. Dura's remains would not only illustrate the part it played in blending cultural, political and military influences from east and west but would shed an unexpected new light on early representational art of the Christian and Jewish traditions. This 'Pompei of the Syrian Desert' (Rostovtzeff) is thus of major historical and artistic interest even though most of its more important treasures have moved elsewhere (Damascus; the Louvre; Yale University). Nevertheless, a visit is well worthwhile if you gain some impression beforehand of its historical importance and acquaint yourself with some of its major finds, notably the Dura synagogue which has been installed in the National Museum in Damascus.

History

Dura Europos was established at the beginning of the Hellenistic period when the empire of Alexander was divided among his heirs and northern Syria-Mesopotamia was apportioned to Seleucus I. The first fortress (south of the wadi on the eastern edge of the ruins) was founded in 303 BC by Seleucus' general, Nicanor, to guard the river route to Lower Mesopotamia. According to the most recent research, the grid-planned city to the west was not established until the mid second century BC. The fortress ('dura' means 'fortress' in Old Semitic) was the focal point of a network of military colonies implanted to secure Seleucid control of the Mid Euphrates. The troops were given land in the area up to 80 km north along the Khabur River. It also provided a strongpoint on the route between the two major military centres, Apamea and Seleucia-on-the-Tigris (southern Iraq). The name chosen, Europos, referred to the birthplace of Seleucus I Nicator in Macedonia. The ambitious plan to establish a city on the plateau to the west was left incomplete in view of the political uncertainties that dogged the Seleucid Kingdom.

Seleucid dominance faltered and Dura was continually threatened from the east with the rise of the **Parthians** who pushed their frontier to the Euphrates in 141 BC. The settlement came under Parthian control from 113 BC but the townspeople managed to preserve their Greek institutions and retained considerable freedom as a regional headquarters for the section of the river between the Khabur and modern Abu Kemal (Iraq border). In exchange the city's military role was abandoned. Its population, originally based on the Greek settler element, were increasingly outnumbered by people of Semitic stock and by the first century BC, the city was predominantly eastern in character. However, the Greek town layout was preserved as the town expanded to fill the space embraced by the surviving walls.

When the Romans took Syria in the first century BC, Dura remained a Parthian city, the Romans establishing themselves at *Circesium to the northeast at the confluence of the Euphrates and Khabur Rivers. A 'live and let live' policy along the Euphrates was recognised by a treaty with the Parthians signed under Augustus in 20 BC.

Trajan, however, broke the entente and occupied Dura in AD 115 as part of his ill-advised attempt to push the frontier across the Euphrates into Mesopotamia. He briefly took over the Parthian domains

as far south as modern Basra (southern Iraq) but the conquered population in the north quickly revolted and the campaign turned into a shambles.[27] Exhausted and demoralised, he stumbled back towards Europe but died en route at Selente in southern Turkey. Trajan had left his nephew and adopted heir, Hadrian, as governor of Syria. On succeeding his uncle, Hadrian reverted to a softer frontier policy and gave Dura back to the Parthians.

In 161, an earthquake severely damaged the city and three years later Rome took direct control under Lucius Verus (co-emperor with Marcus Aurelius), stationing its own troops there and for the first time incorporating Dura into the province of Syria. It was declared a Roman colony in 211.

The period of full Roman control saw a remarkable flourishing of religious architecture in pagan, Jewish and Christian styles, with some notable similarities between the three. The town still recognised its Greek cultural origins and the language of civic life, as in most of Syria, was Greek. Greek influences served as the common thread that joined the syncretist elements in all three religious traditions in a remarkable way, with some addition of Parthian artistic styles.

Dura was a polyglot town by nature of its origins, its location on the frontier between east and west and its trading function. Though the great bulk of east-west trade by-passed Dura, heading directly across the desert to Palmyra from a river crossing further south around Abu Kemal, Dura's merchants played a role in local facilitation and had their own direct interests in trade and shipping as far as the mouth of the Tigris-Euphrates system. The days of unbridled mercantilism, however, ended when the more aggressive

27 Perowne (*Hadrian* 1960: 43) depicts the tragedy of Trajan's blunder in the following terms: 'The scene might have come from a Greek play. Amid the ruins of Babylon, already a by-word for beauty made desolate, the Roman conqueror confronts failure where his Greek model had encountered death.'

Sasanians replaced the Parthians in the east in 224. The Sasanians regarded themselves as the heirs to the Achaemenid realms and sought to press the terms of the 20 BC treaty between Rome and Parthia. Rome built up its Dura garrison (using as its initial core a Palmyrene cohort) and began a substantial building program in the northern quarter to provide home comforts in the form of a theatre, baths and barracks. The local commander was given the title of Dux Ripae. The Romans spent the last few years leading up to 256 in a hurried effort to build up the long and vulnerable walls of the city and strengthened its Palmyrene garrison with detachments from the Syrian legions.

Having made several thrusts against Dura in the preceding decades (and indeed as far as Antioch in 238) a major assault in 256 under Shapur I resulted in the fall of Dura and ended the brief and uncertain Pax Romana on the Mid Euphrates. Shapur decided to destroy the town and banish its people rather than make it a Sasanian fortress. Except for a brief occupation by the Palmyrene Arabs (whose power was at its zenith in 260–73) the Mid Euphrates was left for centuries without a substantial strongpoint to stabilise the shifting frontier between east and west. Justinian preferred to locate his defences of the Byzantine Empire further to the north (*Halebiye) and when the real threat to the area developed the next century, Arab forces arrived from Iraq without real hindrance.

Excavations

Dura was extensively excavated from 1922 to 1923 by a French team and from 1928 to 1937 by a Franco-American expedition whose work is surveyed in a book published in 1979 by one of the American directors, Hopkins. The excavations were on an enormous scale by today's standards: annual seasons of six months with 300 workers, exposing over a quarter of the surface area of the city. Hopkins evokes the importance of the finds unearthed, particularly the second to fourth century religious buildings. Most remarkable was the synagogue, one of the few examples from the period identified

anywhere. The synagogue owes its survival to the fact that the defenders of the city against the Sasanian threat in 256 piled sand against the inner face of the walls to prevent mining. The sand covered part of the inhabited quarters of the city against the west wall, including the area of the synagogue and the Christian chapel.

Even more notable was the fact that the synagogue bore frescoes which carried human representations, largely in the Parthian manner – clearly a break with traditional rules on representational art. Hopkins' excitement on discovering the find is conveyed in the following passage describing the removal of the synagogue's overburden: 'I clearly remember when the foot of dirt still covering the back wall was undercut and fell away, exposing the most amazing succession of paintings! Whole scenes, figures and objects burst into view, brilliant in colour, magnificent in the sunshine.'

The paintings from the Dura synagogue were transferred to the National Museum in Damascus after the 1932–3 excavations and carefully reconstructed in a courtyard off the wing devoted to Roman and Palmyrene remains (*Damascus – Museum). The synagogue comprises a columned forecourt beyond which is a hall of assembly. It is dated to the second year of the reign of Philip the Arab (r 244–9). At this time, the Roman suppression of the two major Jewish revolts had left few physical remains of Jewish culture in Palestine and the Dura find is an important indication of its survival in an eastern idiom.

The building as reconstructed represents the synagogue refurbished in a more opulent style after its modest origins as a house-synagogue in the late second century. Hopkins sees the building as inspired by a resurgence of Judaism in the Mesopotamian region as a result of the liberal policy towards non-Iranian religions adopted by Shapur I. A shift towards Sasanian-Parthian styles influenced Mesopotamian Jews to abandon the traditional injunctions against pictorial representation. The Dura synagogue has

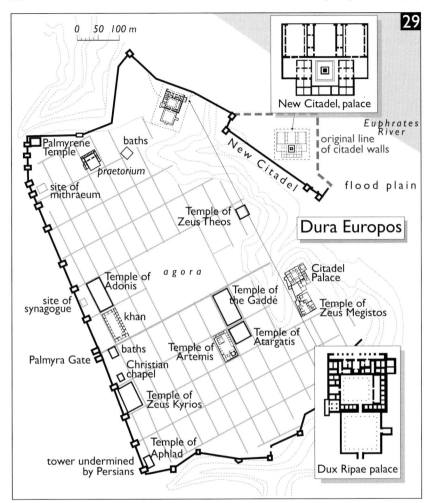

0 50 100 m

29

New Citadel, palace

Euphrates River

original line of citadel walls

flood plain

Palmyrene Temple

baths

praetorium

site of mithraeum

Temple of Zeus Theos

Dura Europos

New Citadel

Temple of Adonis

agora

Citadel Palace

site of synagogue

Temple of the Gaddé

Temple of Zeus Megistos

khan

Temple of Atargatis

Palmyra Gate

baths

Christian chapel

Temple of Artemis

Temple of Zeus Kyrios

Temple of Aphlad

tower undermined by Persians

Dux Ripae palace

had a major impact on the appreciation of the development of religious iconography in the first centuries of our era, before the Roman Empire went over to Christianity after 312. Dura's significance was reinforced by the discovery of a house converted into a Christian chapel – the earliest recognisable Christian cult centre in Syria, also richly decorated with wall paintings.[28]

28   The Christian chapel paintings are held in the Yale University Art Gallery but have suffered serious deterioration. Efforts are

On the whole, though of immense historical interest, the local style is rather heavy and crude, lacking the technical skill and feeling for psychological insight found in Palmyra where a more successful synthesis of oriental and Roman art was developed.

A re-examination of the Dura site is currently underway through the work of a joint Franco-Syrian mission. One of its currently underway to conserve them for display in a refurbished gallery in 2010.

first fruits was to challenge the assumption of the earlier teams that Dura had been created in its present walled boundaries from the beginning of the Greek period. One of the new mission's more urgent tasks is to arrest the damage done to the site since the exposure of many of its buildings to the elements since the 1920s. This painstaking further research should also correct many of the gaps left by the 1930s excavations which were not fully recorded.

Visit

If you start out from *Deir al-Zor, it would be worthwhile to visit the town's museum which contains some of the finds unearthed at Dura, as well as from other sites along the Mid Euphrates including *Mari and *Halebiye.

Though little remains of Dura Europos above the ground, a visit to the site takes a good two to three hours if you wish to gain an impression of its layout and the scale of the walls and the Citadel. The walled area covers 80 ha and is based on a very approximate rectangle, the shape being distorted by the need to accommodate natural features. On all but the west side the site is bordered by natural *wadis* or the river itself.

The **walls** on their present alignment were probably initiated by the Seleucids as late as the second half of the second century BC, the original fortress having been confined to the area of the 'first citadel' (see below). To some extent, the river on the east and the *wadis* to the north and south provided a degree of natural protection to the site. The perimeter was fortified by a system of stone towers (of which 26 remain) joined by curtain walls 3 m thick. The walls, begun in dressed stone but topped with mud brick in a frantic effort to fend off the Parthian threat, still stand, in places, to a height of 9 m. Their survival is largely the result of the later Roman efforts to strengthen the walls to meet the threat of a Sasanian invasion in the 250s by throwing huge quantities of sand against both faces. The long western side open to the desert was the most

vulnerable and it was here that the Sasanian forces concentrated their effort in 256. The Sasanians mined under the Roman defences. A mine under tower 19 (second to the left of the main gateway) was met by Roman counter-mining, the two sides meeting in hand-to-hand combat. The mines collapsed, burying the troops. Their remains were found still carrying their last pay, the date of the latest coin giving the year of the city's fall.

As you approach by the side road from the west, you see on the left the remains of a Roman **triumphal gate** built in honour of the III Cyrenaica legion during Trajan's brief imposition of Roman direct rule (115–7). You enter the city by the 'Great Gate' or **Palmyra Gate** on the west side. The remains of the Hellenistic gate are reasonably substantial (20 m²). It comprised two stout bastions each with two guard rooms, the upper rooms linked by a passageway over the inner archway. The passage was defended by three successive doors.

From here, the main street, twice as wide as the other principal streets, crossed the city towards the river. This was the axis of the Greek late second century 'new town' leading towards the *wadi* that descended to the port area (long since swept away) and to the original citadel. The city was laid out according to the strict grid plan invariably employed in the Macedonian cities founded in the east though the *insulae* or blocks employed were rather smaller (30 m by 60 m) than other examples while retaining the 1:2 ratio.

Immediately inside the Palmyra Gate, the original layout of several religious buildings can be discerned. 100 m north, on the left against the wall, (in the middle of the second *insula*) is the site of the **synagogue** (see above). On the right, after one of three Roman bath sites, the Christian **chapel** (AD 232) and the **Temple to Zeus Kyrios** (before AD 28) were located against the wall at 50 m intervals.

Heading east (to the river), half way along the *decumanus*, you will find on the left the site of the **agora**. The original *agora* was probably planned to cover eight *insulae*, four bordering the main axis and the adjoining four to the north. In the Greek period, only the northern four were developed with a central open space surrounded by an inverted U-shaped cluster of shops. In the Parthian period, all eight *insulae* were gradually over-built with further shops and houses, forming what the excavators called a 'crowded bazar quarter'.

[We might digress here to mention several religious buildings dotted around the area south of the *agora*. All follow a similar plan in the Parthian tradition with a *cella* standing within a *temenos* and ancillary structures within the enclosure wall.

- Separated by one block to the south is the **Temple of Artemis**.[29] The layout is that of the 40–33 BC Parthian rebuilding of the Greek original. This served as the centre of the city's principal official cult throughout the Greek, Parthian and Roman periods. The cult of Artemis was merged with that of her Persian equivalent (Nanaia) and the temple was built along Parthian lines (with some Greek elements), originally a simple layout of entrance, altar and *cella* divided into three.
- On the next block directly east of the Artemis-Nanaia temple, a **temple** was built in AD 31–2 to a similar plan in honour of the 'Syrian Goddess', **Atargatis**. (On the cult, *Menbij.)
- On the block between the Atargatis temple and the *agora*, a third **temple** (pre-AD 159) served two Palmyrene gods of the Baal family, the **Gaddé**.

Another cluster of pagan religious buildings lay on the edge of the eastern ravine.

- **Temple to Zeus Theos** (AD 114) northeast of the *agora* and opposite the south end of the 'new citadel'
- The **Temple of Zeus Megistos** (AD 169) adjoining the 'first citadel' on the south (described below). This temple originated in 95–70 BC in the hybrid Parthian-Greek style.]

---

29 A statue of Aphrodite recovered from this temple can be seen in the Louvre, Paris.

The eastern end of the *decumanus* leads to the '**first citadel**' complex established by the Greeks. Described over the decades as a *strategion* (residence for the *strategos* or chief magistrate) or as an inner redoubt, it lies across a *wadi* that cuts into the southeastern sector of the city. This early acropolis built on a natural prow-shaped site was later superseded in its military role by the 'New Citadel' across the ravine to the north. It may have remained in use as the residence of the civil governor of the city. Efforts are underway to attempt to stabilise the northern end of the 'palace' which has been threatened by collapse since its excavation.

Most of these remains, frankly, will cause little excitement, except to the specialist, consisting largely of foundations or a few courses of masonry. The main point of interest in this eastern sector is the spectacular sight of the '**New Citadel**' spread along the city's river frontage. Though the eastern part of the Citadel has been swept into the river over the years, what remains of its western face consists of stonework which is robust and massive in scale, reflecting the Citadel's purpose as the main defence against a concerted attack. Almost 300 m long, it includes three towers over 20 m high, originally topped with crenellated terraces. There are three gates, two with semi-circular arches, leading to an internal palace.

The earlier theory that this second (hence 'new') citadel was largely the work of the period of Parthian dominance in the first century AD, has been disproved by recent research which attributes the whole building to the Seleucids (second century BC). The conscious use of 'orientalising' features is particularly clear in the triple *iwans* (see insert on map 29). Similar buildings are to be found at the Parthian capital, Hatra, and at Ctesiphon (both in Iraq). Unfortunately, the plan has had to be reconstructed from only partial evidence as the southwestern corner of the palace is virtually all that remains behind the walls.

Further to the north, on the western side of the deep ravine that divides the New

Citadel from the city, you should be able to identify the later palace erected for the Roman garrison commander, sometimes called the **Palace of the Dux Ripae** (Commander of the River Bank). This was part of the post-227 military quarter mentioned earlier, and marks the phase of full militarisation of the city in the struggle against the Sasanians. The palace was built around two internal courtyards with an arcaded front to the east looking out over the sweep of the river.

The rest of the **Roman military camp** occupied the area between this point and the western walls. This is a rare example of an encampment inserted into an existing town plan, most being located outside the established perimeter. It was a virtually self-contained military colony with its own *praetorium*, exercise square, baths and temples. Of the latter, two should be mentioned, both in the northwest corner.

- In the northwestern angle of the walls, the Temple of Baal or **Temple of the Palmyrene Gods** (mid first century AD)
- A little further around to the south, a **mithraeum** (209–11), a centre devoted to the Persian cult whose practice spread throughout the Roman Empire and was particularly favoured in the legions. The single chamber was originally covered with wall paintings including scenes from the life of Mithras (now at Yale).

You may want to complete your tour by taking in some parts of the extensive **walls**. Most interesting is the southwestern sector which extends south of the main gate. Note the arched gateway, probably a temporary entrance used during the construction of the Greek fortress as it was later blocked up in Roman times. It is possible to walk along parts of the upper walls. Tower 14 on the southwestern corner is a precarious witness to the effectiveness of the Parthians' siege techniques. The tower perches at an angle due to one of the Persian mines whose work was exacerbated by the removal of the walls' internal ramparts in the 1930s. The huge amount of overburden used to strengthen the walls largely survives on the outer face.

REFS: Downey 1986; Edwell 2008: 93–148; Leriche & al-Mahmoud *Doura-Europos Etudes* Beirut 1988; Leriche & Gelin *Doura-Europos Etudes IV* Beirut 1997; Rostovtzeff *Caravan Cities* 1932; Rostovtzeff *Dura Europos and its Art* 1938.

E

Ebla (Tell Mardikh – Plate 10a)

VARIANTS: Tell Mardikh (Arb)
PERIOD: EBA/MBA RATING: * MAP: 30, R2

LOCATION: Leave Aleppo on the Damascus road. At 51 km (6 km south of Saraqeb interchange where the Latakia road diverges), turn east (left) at the signpost marked Tell Mardikh/Ebla. +3 km on a good sealed road to the tell, just past the village of Tell Mardikh.

One of the most important Bronze Age sites discovered since the Second World War, Ebla is described by its excavator as 'the first true capital of ancient Syria'. Though the remains require some interpretation to the lay visitor (now assisted by a series of explanatory panels) an hour's walk around the site gives a good impression of the scale of the ancient city and its main defensive works. The importance of Ebla, however, is even more remarkable for the scholarship emerging from the painstaking research since 1964 of Dr Matthiae and his team coordinated by La Sapienza University, Rome. In the last few years, the Italian program is placing more emphasis on the conservation and presentation of the city as well as on diversifying the sectors investigated.

History

The history of Ebla and its place in the Bronze Age civilisations of the area is a fascinating piece of historical reconstruction once marked by controversy. The discovery in 1975 of a major archive of clay tablets at Ebla has thrown much light on the period and the inter-relationships between the kingdoms and city-states of the area but the work of translating and publishing the tablets is a painstaking process.

It is clear that Ebla was an important power in northern Syria in the late third and early second millennia, particularly as a trading hub. The discovery of Ebla thus fills an important gap in our understanding of the third millennium BC, revealing a Syrian counterpart to the major centres of Sumer and Akkad in southern Iraq with links which spread into Mesopotamia, southern Syria and as far as Anatolia (central Turkey). Ebla was probably founded by people of Western Semitic descent. Their archives were written in a language dubbed Eblaite. The inhabitants of Ebla had succeeded in adapting Akkadian cuneiform as a means of recording their own Semitic language.

The sweeping plains of northern Syria at this time encompassed an advanced network of urban societies whose sophisticated political and economic systems were based on the area's considerable agricultural and trading potential. The tell was first occupied before 3000 BC. Ebla reached the peak of its prosperity in the period 2400–2250 BC, lying at the centre of an important trading network stretching from the Mediterranean to Mesopotamia. Its political domain was probably less extensive but covered most of the western part of northern Syria. It also tussled after 2300 with Akkad for control of the Mid Euphrates including *Mari. The kings of Ebla (we know of six in this early phase) seem to have been appointed by the trading élite and the type of monarchy was different from the more absolute rulers of contemporary Mesopotamia.

The days of glory of the early Eblaite dynasty peaked around 2300–2250 BC when the rising power of Akkad (either under Sargon or Naram-Sin) took the city. However, Ebla's fortunes revived around 2200 BC and it re-established its mastery of northern Syria. From this phase of Amorite occupation date the massive mud-brick ramparts and the Temples of Ishtar and Rashaf. Ebla's economic and political dominance ended around 1800 BC and it was incorporated into the Kingdom of Yamkhad (Aleppo). After a new flowering under the hegemony of Yamkhad in the 18th–17th centuries (palace E), a final blow was delivered by the Hittite king who sacked the city in c1595 BC.

The last historical mention of Ebla is from c1450 BC when the Egyptian pharaoh, Thutmose III recorded on a monument at Karnak that the Egyptian army marched through Ebla on its way to the Euphrates. There are some remains of a fortress from the ninth to eighth centuries BC and limited remains from the Persian and

visitor to make the best use of time.

The outer **walls** were up to 30 m thick (and stood up to 22 m high), coated with plaster and with a course of stone to stabilise the lower slope. The enclosure was pierced by four gateways flanked by wide mud-brick bastions and separate forts. The surviving circuit of earthen ramparts date from the MBA, probably replacing a mud-brick EBA enclosure. As suggested in the red itinerary on the panels, it is worth taking the time to inspect the southwestern side of the outer defences where the monumental proportions of the Middle Bronze Age gate's ashlar panelling have been exposed.

Map of Ebla showing: to Saraqeb, resthouse, Aleppo Gate, walls, road, Ebla, scale 0 100 200 m, ceremonial palace, Temple of Shamesh, tickets, Ishtar Temple, 'Lion Terrace', MBA palace, Citadel, Royal Palace G, Crown Prince Palace, archives, princely burials, Southwest Gate, Southeast Gate, = excavated area

The **Citadel** (located on the central mound) includes two extensive exposed areas on the north and west sides of the acropolis. The most interesting are the sections of **Royal Palace G** on the west side of the acropolis, giving some idea of the city's splendour during its EBA IV apogée. The lower parts of the EBA palace were saved when the upper sections collapsed on top providing a base for the post-2000 BC rebuild. Note the huge (35 by 60 m) audience courtyard with a dais for the king in the northern portico (left of the section seen in plate 10a). In the northeast corner, a ramped passage winding around the four sides of a square core provided private access from the royal quarters on the Citadel.

Byzantine periods but otherwise the city was largely abandoned.

Visit

Begin your visit at the orientation point reached by the access road from Aleppo. The outer ring of the mound and its sizeable central citadel immediately convey an impression of the scale of Ebla (60 ha). (Its population has been estimated at 30,000 at its maximum.) Though the Bronze Age remains are of enormous dimensions the new descriptive panels give three itineraries which will guide the

An **archives** room, originally part of the EBA palace, was found south of the east portico of the courtyard. The archives from this room and other findspots totalled some 18,000 tablets covering the period leading up to the first destruction in 2300. The languages included a local language dubbed 'Eblaite', a Semitic language. The tablets were hardened by the fire that engulfed the first palace thus ensuring their preservation. They possibly did not comprise the main palace archives of the time but included many administrative, accounting, religious and diplomatic records giving us countless insights into the functioning of a major kingdom of the Early Bronze Age. The most recognisable remains of the royal apartments on the Citadel include the **private Temple to Ishtar**, an elongated arrangement of portico, pre-*cella* and *cella* typical of northern Syria.

North of the acropolis are remains of an early second millenium palace and (to the northeast) a temple to the sun god, Shamash. Recent work has also exposed more of the complex of the **Ishtar Temple** (c1950 BC), below the Citadel mound on the northwest, including the huge stone **terrace** (c 1650 BC). This massive structure, a platform 42 m by 53 m with internal courtyard but no entrance, was undertaken as part of the Ishtar complex but not completed. The terrace presumably housed the lions sacred to the goddess. This formed part of a spectacular complex which foreshadowed the popularity of the cult of Atargatis (Dea Syria) in the Roman era 2000 years later, celebrated most notoriously at Hierapolis northeast of Aleppo (*Menbij). This structure faced at an angle, across an open square, the *cella* (20 m by 12 m) of the earlier temple, which followed a typical Syrian plan with an entrance vestibule on the square.

South lies the Palace of the Crown Prince, traditionally responsible for the cult of the royal ancestors. Further south, underground chambers formed out of natural caves were used for **princely burials** during the period 1825–1650 BC. The location of the burials is explained by Matthiae in terms of an official ancestor cult – possibly a hallmark of Amorite societies and an evolution from the earlier concept of the monarchy at Ebla. Finds from this area include grave goods now displayed in the Museum at **Idlib**, the provincial headquarters town located a little north of the Latakia road, as well as

in the *Aleppo and *Damascus museums.

The Idlib Museum's Ebla hall is on the first floor and contains a rich collection of material including a reconstruction of the tablet room from Royal Palace G, a stele of a seated dignatory from temple P2 (1800–1700 BC) and a headless bust of an Ebla king of the same provenance (east wall). Alabaster finds from the royal necropolis are found to the left.

REFS: Matthiae in *Cluzan* 1993: 102–23, 162–70; Matthiae 1997; Matthiae 2002–3; Pinnock 2001: 1–44.

Ezraa

ازرع

VARIANTS: Andrea Zorava (Grk); Zor`ah, Zorah, Zurca (Arb) PERIOD: Byz RATING: **
MAP: R1

LOCATION: 80 km south of Damascus on the western edge of the volcanic wilderness, the Ledja (ancient Trachonitis). Take the highway from Damascus south towards Deraa and Amman and turn off left to Ezraa, heading east (look for a huge grain silos complex); then north through the town for 2.6 km. Stop on the northern outskirts and inquire; someone will bring the key for the Church of St George (Mar Georgis).

What was once an abode of demons has become a house of God; where once sacrifices were made to idols, there are now choirs of angels; where God was provoked to wrath, now He is propitiated.
(Inscription dated 515 over the middle portal of the west entrance.)

In its historical and religious associations this is perhaps one of the most remarkable buildings in Syria. The Greek Orthodox Church of St George is (after *St Sergius' at Maaloula) the oldest church still in use in Syria, perhaps the oldest in continuous use. Its architecture has been largely unaffected by its changing fortunes. The signs of previous fortification of the building attest to the difficulties of maintaining the community in the face of 14 centuries of often tumultuous change.

The church (which stands on the site of an ancient temple) is dated to 515 from the long inscription on the lintel over the main door (quoted above). Architecturally, the sixth century **Church of St George** is notable as one of the earliest examples of an octagon-within-a-square plan, surmounted by a cupola (see Centralised Churches box on page 24). (The external shape is a rectangle, the line of the basic square being extended to the east to accommodate a chancel with apse. This extension is enclosed in three sides of a hexagon protruding from the east wall.) The 10 m dome, a relatively modern re-construction covered externally by a metal shell, follows the pointed ellipse shape still seen in mud houses in northern Syria. (The original shape of the dome can only be conjectured but may have been a masonry structure.) The sombre stone arcaded interior was probably once covered with painted plaster but the effect is still impressive.

The internal octagon is formed by cutting off the corners of the square, filling the angles with semi-circular chapels. Within this octagonal enclosure, a second octagon (9 m wide) is formed by eight angle piers carrying soaring arches of impressive simplicity. The masonry rises above these arches, rapidly transforming itself from an octagonal to a circular cross-section until it culminates in the tall dome atop a drum pierced with eight windows. The circumambulatory aisle (and the east apse) were covered by flat stone roofing. The main entrance (west) comprises three doorways.

On the left (200 m) as you return to the centre of town, a second sixth century church of equal architectural interest is found though recent work needed to restore the badly deteriorated structure has given it a more bland and austere appearance. The Greek Catholic **Church of St Elias** is dated by an inscription over the main south doorway to 542. The basic shape is a rare example for Syria of a cruciform plan oriented east-west with an apse protruding to the east. The modern dome over the crossing replaces the original wooden dome.

In the same area are remains of buildings (probably domestic) going back to the Roman period.

REFS: Butler *AE* II 1903: 411; Butler *EC* 1929: 122–5; de Vogüé I 1865–77: 61–2; Dussaud 1927: 374–5; Krautheimer 1981: 136, 147, 253; Lassus *Sanctuaires chrétiens* 1947: 139–42, 148; Lassus 'Deux églises' 1931: 1348..

F

Fafertin

See **Burjke, Fafertin, Surkunya and Banastur**

G

no entries

H

Halebiye (Plate 10b)

حلبية

VARIANTS: Birtha (Grk/Lat); Zenobia(Lat)
PERIOD: Rom/Byz RATING: ** MAP: 31, R5

LOCATION: On the right bank of the Mid Euphrates, 100 km south of Raqqa or 66 km north of Deir al-Zor. From Deir al-Zor, take the Aleppo highway north as far as Tibne (46 km). +12 km north of Tibne, turn right at sign-posted intersection and follow sealed road northeast +8 km.

Halebiye was one of the most formidable Byzantine fortifications in Syria, the culmination of the Byzantine Emperor, Justinian's ambitious policy of securing the frontier on the Euphrates. Time has disturbed the fortifications only cursorily and what is left makes a singular impression. The site is particularly splendid at sunset when the shadows fall across the stark hills and the sun gives the stone a warm luminescence.

Halebiye — North Gate, praetorium, palaestra, West Basilica, agora, Citadel, East Basilica, cardo, baths, Euphrates River, South Gate. 0 100 200 m. 0 5 10 m. **31**

History

Though what you now see is basically Byzantine, Halebiye was first fortified during the apogée of Palmyrene control in the mid third century. The site was chosen as the river at this point is confined between substantial hills (known locally as al-khanuqa, 'the strangler'), allowing river traffic to be more readily controlled. When the Romans responded to Zenobia's rebellion by occupying the Palmyrene domains in 273, they took Halebiye (which had been named after the Palmyrene Queen). Diocletian may have rebuilt the fortifications as part of his defences of the limes from Palmyra north and a further rebuilding was undertaken in the reign of Anastasius (491–518).

The remains now seen at the site, however, date from the reign of Justinian (r 527–65), evidence of his pursuit of a forward defence policy on all the Empire's frontiers, including through the recovery of North Africa and Italy. In Syria, he put considerable store by securing against the Persian threat a region which had become an important centre of Christianity. His general Belisarius carried out several important campaigns in Syria during the early years of his reign and the series of fixed fortifications was intended to secure the gains the army had made. Halebiye (probably re-fortified after 650) along with the earlier fortification of the pilgrimage city of *Resafa were the most conspicuous results of this policy.

Such a bold project seems to show the hand of a master builder in its design. Procopius cites two architects as responsible, one being the nephew of Isidorus of Miletus, the architect who rebuilt the dome of Hagia Sophia in 532–7 after the original had collapsed.

In fact, Justinian's grand strategy was eventually a failure. The fixed defences, undermanned, could do little but survey the contraband traffic. Certainly the effort involved in their construction and mistakes in eastern policy by subsequent emperors (Maurice, r 582–602, excepted) helped to drain resources and encourage local disaffection in the crucial decades before the Arab conquest swept past these purely symbolic monuments to Byzantine glory.

The Arabs used the great fortification from time to time but, on the whole, the sealing of the Euphrates frontier was no longer the preoccupation it had been to Rome and Byzantium; indeed quite the opposite, given the Arab interest in opening up contact between Syria and Mesopotamia. The great fortress was thus largely left to decay (though reoccupied for a time, possibly under the Ayyubids). The lack of significant population in the area meant that the stone was not carried away for other buildings, the main deterioration resulting from earthquake damage.

The scale of the fortifications is remarkable, especially given the remoteness of the site from population centres. The blocks were of huge dimensions and little effort was spared to tame the irregularities of the terrain. The stretch of wall along the river, partly designed to contain the river's floods, has been badly eroded over the centuries. On the other two sides, the walls converge from two points along the river towards the Citadel on the heights. The resulting triangular shape has survived well due to the quality of the stone and the care taken to secure firm footings.

Visit

The fortifications originally contained a small **garrison city** with the usual range of amenities within the 12 ha walled area. In times of peace, access was relatively open with three gates along the 385 m river frontage and one large one on each of the north and south sides where the main route met the city. These walls measured 350 m and 550 m respectively. Inside the city the main north-south street was met at a central point by an east-west axis, probably colonnaded. Except for the two churches, the remains within the walls are largely foundation courses and are hard to distinguish. The baths lay a little to the northeast of the crossing point while the forum was to the north of the barely perceptible east-west axis. Of the two churches, one lies to the north of the east-west axis, and dates from Justinian's

time; the other, the smaller one to the southeast, is earlier.

It is the **walls** themselves, built of flinty grey gypsum, which provide the main interest (plate 10b). You may wish to trace them by beginning with the gate on the north side of the site. Heading towards the apex on the hill, you pass four massive square bastions – more or less identical in design – which date from Justinian's time. They were an attempt to outdo the scale of earlier Roman examples. From their two storeyed strongholds, archers could fire arrows at those trying to assault the walls. The towers are inter-connected by a series of internal corridors running on the city side of the walls and by staircases giving access from the bastions. You will soon come to a point in the wall where the bastion shape is extended to contain a three storeyed building, the *praetorium* for the housing of the troops also dating from Justinian's reign. Much of the groin vaulting in gypsum and brick that supported this massive construction remains.

Continuing up the slope from the inside of the fortress, a steep climb will bring you to the **Citadel**. Much of this has been modified by the Muslims who made use of the fortress for a time because of the mastery it gave of movement on the Mid Euphrates. The keep commands all approaches to the fortress including from the desert via the Wadi Bishri to the rear.

You can descend by the longer south **wall** to the river. Here the construction may have been undertaken somewhat earlier. The bastion towers (ten excluding the south gate itself) use the same design as the northern examples.

To the north of the city, about 1 km up river, lie remains of more than 13 **funerary towers** and rock-cut tombs of the late Roman period.

REFS: Lauffray *Halabiyya* 1983, 1991; Procopius *Buildings* II, viii.

Hama

حماة

VARIANTS: Hamath (BrA, IrA); Epiphanea
(Grk, Lat); Emath (Byz) PERIOD: var/Arb
RATING: * MAP: 32, R2

LOCATION: 47 km north of *Homs (226
km from Damascus).

Hama is certainly one of the oldest
continually inhabited cities of Syria. It
enjoyed a reputation as one of the more
charming of the Syrian towns, making the
most of its picturesque setting with the
Orontes (Arb: al-'Assi)[1] serving as the
city's lungs and cooling device. All of that
changed radically after the events of 1982
which destroyed or damaged large parts
of the city. Yet the tensions brought out
in these events had long existed under
Hama's tranquil surface. The 1932 *Guide
Bleu* observed that while Hama was 'the
most picturesque and the least touched by
the West' of the towns of northern Syria, it
was a 'very enclosed town, unforthcoming
to strangers, whose inhabitants border on
the fanatic'.

The town has undergone a process of
reconstruction with a large part of the
old city replaced by new development.
A visit could be combined with a meal
by the river banks watching some of the
enormous wooden water wheels (*norias*)
creak with the flow of the Orontes. Even
on the hottest day, the slow grinding of
the *norias*, the splash of the water and
the drifts of spray suggest some of the
refreshing environment that this town
traditionally drew from its river location.

History

Constant settlement has effaced much of
the remains of previous occupation and

---

1 It is ironic that the Arabic name for the
river ('the rebel') may also be a pun on the
first name given by the Greeks, Axios, after a
river in Macedonia. The Greeks later prefered
the name Orontes which has taken hold in the
classical and later English, traditions. (Frézouls
'La Toponomie de l'Orient Syrien' in *La
Toponomie antique* Strasbourg 1977: 239.)

virtually nothing survives of Hama during
the Bronze and Iron Ages, or during the
Seleucid, Roman, Byzantine and early
Islamic empires. The citadel hill which you
will find to the northwest of the centre of
the city (today a park crowns the summit)
was researched in the 1930s by a Danish
expedition. Traces have been found of
all periods as far back as the neolithic,
including the 11th century BC when Hama
was the centre of the small Syro-Hittite
or Aramaean Kingdom of Hamath. Some
of the evidence is now on display in the
museum.

For a while, Hamath was obliged to pay
tribute to the Israelite Kingdom under
Solomon but recovered full independence
in the ninth century and joined the
federation under Damascus. The city was
destroyed by the Assyrians in 720 BC
and, like the rest of Syria, came under
Assyrian and Persian rule. The Seleucids
established a presence and renamed the
city Epiphanea after one of their foremost
rulers, Antiochus IV Epiphanes (r 175–64
BC). It remained a centre of Roman and
Byzantine administration, falling to the
Arabs by capitulation in 636–7. The city,
lying on the interface between northern
and southern Syria, was often contested
by rival dynasties in Damascus and
Aleppo, especially in the troubled 11th
and 12th centuries. The Ayyubid period
was particularly prosperous and saw the
construction of the first of the existing
norias, supplemented in the Mamluk and
Ottoman periods. A period of decline
began in the late 16th century and from
the 18th century, Hama was under the
control of Damascus in an effort to widen
the taxation net required to fund the
pilgrimage – hence the strong link between
the two towns through the Azem family.

Visit

You will find a good selection of the town's
17 *norias* in the centre of town, around the
park in front of the governor's office. A
walk around the banks of the river to the
west will take you past a number of others.
The great wheels, up to 20 m in diameter,
were designed to raise water from the
Orontes. The river's flow is channelled

into a sluice which drives the vanes. Each spoke has a wooden box device that scoops up water, discharging into towers at the top of its rotation. The water then flows through stone aqueducts into the town or surrounding agricultural areas. Traditionally each consumer was allocated a portion of the flow for a given period of time. Hama and its region specialised in these devices (first developed as far back as the Byzantine period) as the high river banks required a mechanical method of raising the water to the level of the fields.

northern end of the Citadel from where you can continue downstream to a further group of *norias*. The largest is located 250 m west of the Citadel and is known popularly as al-Muhammadiye. It dates back to the 14th century (inscription on the aqueduct) and has been restored since 1977. About 1 km in the other direction from the central park (to the east) is another cluster of *norias* which you can take in at your leisure from a group of outdoor restaurants.

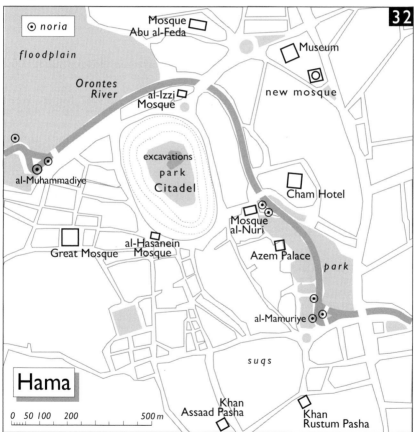

The largest example of this central group (west bank of the Orontes) is known as al-Mamuriye and dates from 1453.

The itinerary will later take you to the

A little north of the central concentration of *norias* on the left bank of the river) is the Beit Azem (**Azem Palace** 1740), the mansion of a former *wali* (governor) of Hama, Assaad Pasha al-Azem (1705–57

– *wali* of Sidon, of Hama pre-1742 and of Damascus 1743–57).[2] Damage caused by the 1982 events required extensive reconstruction of the upper levels on the river side (the room with the cupola was particularly badly hit) but the singular charm of what must be one of the loveliest Ottoman residential buildings in Syria remains, especially the *haremlek* (area right of the entrance). An annexe to the north houses the palace baths and beyond that the public reception area (*selamlek*) with an almost Italian upper *loggia*.

The main collection of antiquities, once housed in the Beit Azem, is now accommodated in the new Museum in the zone rebuilt since 1982 (see below). Beit Azem remains open and serves as the regional Folklore Museum. 100 m north of the Beit Azem, the **Mosque al-Nuri** stands on a square where a small bridge crosses the Orontes. Nur al-Din paid particular attention to Hama, recognising that the city played an essential role in cementing his control of both Aleppo and Damascus. The mosque was completed in 1163 by Nur al-Din following the severe earthquake of 1157. The admirable minaret, strikingly banded with inter-laced black basalt and yellow limestone, follows a local style (an earlier example will be seen in the city's Great Mosque, below). The inscription on the north wall is remarkable for its length (7.2 m). Note the number of large Roman blocks used in the lower courses of the external walls. Off the courtyard, the prayer hall to the east was added under Abu al-Feda (1320–31, see next para). The carved wooden *minbar* (1164), the only surviving example from the time of Nur al-Din, is now in the Museum. The Beit Keilani (another 18th century palace) once stood on the opposite bank.

The **Citadel** has no surviving remains but provides sweeping views of the town and a shady park area (with the crater of the Danish excavations to the north). Northeast of the Citadel a road runs

towards a modern bridge. On the north of this intersection is the **al-Izzi Mosque**, a small Mamluk building of 1323. Continue along the side road to the small bridge left of the modern one and ascend the road as it curves left. This leads to the **Mosque and Mausoleum of Abu al-Feda**, the noted Arab historian and poet (d 1331) who was appointed amir of Hama under the Mamluks (1320–31) though descended from the prominent Ayyubid family of Malik al-Muzaffar Umar, a nephew of Saladin. The building is sometimes given the popular name, al-Hayyat (Serpents') Mosque on account of the interlaced stonework around the windows of the courtyard.

The **al-Hasanein Mosque** stands at the opposite (southwest) corner of the Citadel. An earlier mosque on this spot fell in the great earthquake of 1157. Nur al-Din had it rebuilt, though as the central dome of the prayer hall is ribbed (unusual before 1180) it is possibly a later rebuilding. West of here (100 m) is the **Great Mosque of Hama**. An almost total ruin after 1982, it has been superbly reconstructed by the Antiquities Department in its earlier form. An Umayyad foundation, it was built inside the southeastern corner of the outer compound of a Roman temple (AD third century) and replaced a Christian church. The original basilica plan is reflected (with modifications) in the three aisles of the prayer hall topped by five domes. The east wall (next to the main entrance) uses re-employed Roman material and the west wall of the prayer hall survives from the church (probably sixth century – note the Greek inscription on the inside face). The courtyard is surrounded by vaulted porticos and contains an elevated treasury (cf Kubbet al-Khazneh in *Damascus – Umayyad Mosque), almost certainly Umayyad. To the west is the tomb of the local Ayyubid, Sultan Muzaffar (1280), another descendant of Malik al-Muzaffar Umar. There are two minarets – one, east of the prayer room in the banded local style, has an inscription of 1153; the other, near the north doorway, is Mamluk.

The new **Museum** was developed with assistance from the Danish Government

2 In Damascus he built the even more splendid Azem Palace – see *Damascus – Khans. For a list of the Azem Governors, see footnote under *Damascus – Khans.

and the Carlsberg Foundation and rehoused in a splendid purpose-built building on Muzaffar St, arranged around a central courtyard. It comprises four main sections: neolithic to Bronze Age; Iron Age; classical and Byzantine; and Islamic. With the space now available for the permanent collection and the full labelling of displays, the Museum is one of the most significant in Syria.

You enter from the north side of the hollow square. After the ticket office, a slight deflection to the left takes you through the hall documenting Hama's development from the neolithic into a major Bronze Age centre, particularly in the Late Bronze Age (1550–1200 BC) when it provided the interface between the pharaohs and the Hittite kings. Note #147 (case at end of first corridor), limestone bust from Hama's tell c2800 BC with painted red lips, grooves for eyes, conical cap which almost seems to be conveying realistic expression. You turn the corner of the U-shaped corridor and the following cases contain EBA material including (#176) female figure from Qarqar in terracotta, 2000–1600 BC. In the third case, MBA pottery, notably #204 an incense burner (Hama 2000–1600 BC). As you leave, on the right, a diorama of a burial found 5 km west of Selemiye (2000–1800 BC), reconstructing a typical rock-cut tomb.

The second hall is on the other side of the courtyard and concentrates on Iron Age material from Hama tell. This was the most significant period of Hama's history when the Kingdom of Hamath was a major player in the complex politics of the region. Most notable is the gigantic basalt lion figure found in the courtyard of the Aramaean palace (ninth century BC), a particularly fine example of the monumental art of the period occupying the central position in the hall. The figure had to be 're-assembled from pieces, the result of the sacking of the palace by the Assyrians in 720 BC. Other sculptural pieces line the walls and four re-used stelae stand across the room in front of the lion. On the right of the room as you enter, standing out from the south wall,

is a superb eighth century figurine found near the road to Masyaf and displayed in a window case. The seated figure is in bronze coated with gold leaf and with lapis lazuli inserts for the eyes. The tiara and horned crown are symbols of a deity.

At the end of the hall stands a large model of the palace of the Aramaean kings of Hama which notes the positions of the lion figures guarding the entrance. On the eastern wall (#308), stands a tenth century stele found in the royal quarters at Hama showing an offering scene, above it an eagle with a double lion head. Immediately right of the exit, a stele of King Urhilina of Hama (ninth century BC, basalt) with an inscription in the Indo-European language, Luwian, found at Apamea.

The next major hall devoted to the classical period (right as you leave the Iron Age hall) is equally spectacular. Most noteworthy is the mosaic (#400, right on entry) transferred from a house excavated in the village of Mariamin (northwest of Homs – map R2). The work is from the last quarter of the fourth century AD and measures 5.37 m by 4.25 m. It depicts a group of female musicians and has been described by Janine Balty[3] as 'one of the most significant finds of recent years, as much for the quality of its execution as for the originality of its subject'. It is a rare example of a work devoted to a domestic rather than an allegorical or mythic theme and was probably the centrepiece of a dining room or *triclinium*. Six women perform on various instruments while two infants (dressed as Eros) work the bellows. The woman second from the left plays the organ while others play the flute, lyre (or zither), castanets and six metal bowls placed on the central table. The ensemble is conducted, it would appear, by the woman on the far left holding the cymbals. The mosaic sheds a unique light on musical instruments used at the time. The organ, in particular, is the clearest evidence we have of how this instrument was employed in antiquity.

The hall houses a number of other important finds including a collection

3 Balty, J *Mosaiques* 1977: 94.

of capitals along the east wall, a column (#416) from *Apamea with a representation of Leda and the swan (far end of hall) and three central glass cases, two with fine examples of Roman glass and the third displaying Roman pottery and figurines. Along the west wall (left of entry door) is a large stele (#571) erected in AD 76 by Vespasian. Also notable are the panels temporarily positioned against the north wall discovered by Gawlikowski in a mithraeum under the Photios church at Huarte. The panels are important evidence of the cult from a typical cave site obviously frequented by soldiers of the Roman units stationed at nearby Apamea. The panel 'Helios in front of Mithras' gives many clues to the way this mystery cult was celebrated.

To the left of the exit door, a noteworthy mosaic floor panel of Adam enthroned (#421) identified both in Aramaic and Greek. Also at the Byzantine end of the hall (#1088), a basalt panel representing a stylite saint atop his column. The stylite movement attracted considerable support in northern Syria in Byzantine times (*Saint Simeon).

The final hall shows finds from the Islamic period including excellent examples of Syrian glazed ware. Note particularly #629, a Syrian blue and white dish c 1400 from Hama; #633 blue glaze bowl from Hama tell; #644 Raqqa ware bowl 12th–13th century; #648 lustre bowl with blue and turquoise under a transparent glaze (13th–4th century); #658, black blue painted plate under transparent glaze (Resafa ware, 12th–13th century) found under Hama cathedral. Not to be missed is the *minbar* commissioned by Nur al-Din and which until recently stood in his mosque in the city. This is the only example from Nur al-Din's time which survives.[4] The original basultrade panels are affixed to the wall. The Arabic inscription below the dome quotes Sura 25 of the Koran: ' .. blessed is He who has placed constellations in Heaven and who has set among them a great lamp and a

moon to give light. And He it is who made night succeed day.'

In the commercial centre of the town, south of the river, two **Ottoman khans** can be seen. The 1556 Khan Rustum Pasha: large courtyard; vaulted arcades on four sides; central mosque. The huge façade of the Khan Assaad Pasha (1738), 250 m to the west, now houses a technical school.

REFS: Creswell 1959; Creswell *EMA* 1969 I/1 1979: 17–22; Riis 1965; Herzfeld II 1943: 40–7; Meinecke 1992; Mortensen (*et al*) 2000; Nour 1982: 316–325; Sourdel 'Hamat' *EI2*; al-Tabba 1982; van Berchem & Fatio 1914: 173–77.

Haran al-Awamid

حر اناالعو اميد

PERIOD: Rom RATING: – MAP: R1

LOCATION: Town on the eastern edge of the Ghouta. It can be reached directly from Damascus (exit via the glass factory road) or from the airport road (at c 19 km take exit for +12 km Hejaneh then +10 km north to Haran al-Awamid).

Haran al-Awamid ('Village of Columns') is a largely mud-brick Ghouta town with two items of interest – a mosque which is clearly a pastiche of many centuries and an incongruous group of three tall basalt Roman-Nabataean columns nowadays stranded in a domestic courtyard. Butler says that the column remains are 'structurally and artistically closely allied to the buildings of [the Hauran]'. The three columns belonged to the portico of a temple which stood on a high podium. The basalt capitals are in the Ionic order, similar to the style found in the colonnades of Philippopolis (*Shahba – mid third century). No clue has been found as to the temple's dedication but Thomas Weber speculates it may have been a centre for the worship of the gods who assured the fertility of the Ghouta oasis.

The mosque uses Roman columns and is based on a basilica plan though it is not clear if this was a second Roman temple

---

4 The other splendid example, in the al-Aqsa Mosque in Jerusalem, was destroyed by fire in 1969.

or the columns have been re-used from elsewhere. In the enclosure wall, a number of re-used Roman basalt reliefs including matched eagles supporting a garland. The eagles signal a possible cult centre dedicated to Baal-Shamin or Zeus.

REFS: Butler *AE* II 1903: 398–9; Dussaud 1927: 303; T Weber 'Haran al-Awamid' 1997; T Weber 2005: 26–9.

Harbaqa Dam (Plate 11a)

سدا الحربقا

VARIANTS: Kharbaqah (Arb) PERIOD: Arb RATING: * MAP: R4

LOCATION: From Damascus, take the Palmyra road (turnoff 24 km north on Damascus-Homs highway). At the point (+130 km) where it joins the road coming from Homs, take the Homs road for +10 km, heading northwest. At this point, take left V fork along a faint track curving around a low line of hills. Follow track for c+1.5 km down the *wadi* to the north, skirting the swampy remains of the now-silted lake.

Until recently it was assumed that this project dated from the Roman period (first century AD), improved and adapted during Byzantine and Arab times. It is now seen as more likely that it is a later creation. There is no evidence of a major Roman or Byzantine settlement to justify such a huge project. Genequand argues that it is likely to be the work of the Umayyads in conjunction with the agricultural scheme associated with *Qasr al-Heir West. The survival of the dam wall, the largest such structure built in the Middle East before modern times, is remarkable evidence of the solidity of traditional construction techniques. The wall constructed of a solid stone skin with rubble fill is virtually intact – 20 m high, 18 m thick at the base, 345 m long. Yet the project took no account of the likely build-up of alluvial deposits. This incongruency, as Genequand observes, between magnificence and usefulness quickly limited the dam's life.

It is difficult to discern the traces of the canal system which took the water away

towards the north but evidence is said to lie near the course of the river downstream where the flow was channelled to irrigate the area around Qasr al-Heir West.

REFS: Calvet & Geyer 1992: 79–92; Genequand 2004, 2006; Kennedy & Riley 1990: 79–80; Schlumberger 1986.

Harim

حارم

VARIANTS: Castrum Harench, Harrem (Cru) PERIOD: Arb RATING: – MAPS: 33, R3, R3a

LOCATION: Just before Bab el-Hawa (40 km west of Aleppo) turn left at the main intersection then immediately right through the village of Sarmada and follow the main road for 20 km until it brings you to Harim.

Harim is today a small provincial town, Sunni in population, overlooking the rich Plain of Amuq to the east of Antioch. The houses are a little more colourful than most villages in northern Syria, the locals having a preference for the application of blue paint to bare concrete. The town dates back at least to late Byzantine times but its main asset is a 12th century Ayyubid fortress that dominates the centre of the town from a partly artificial mound.

Its strategic importance resulted from its control of the main route between Aleppo and Antioch (it protected the important Orontes crossing at Iron Bridge, Jisr al-Hadid, 16 km west of Harim) as well as the route which branched off to the south to Jisr al-Shugur and the mid Orontes Valley. Today the road from Antioch to Aleppo runs 4 km to the north on a more direct route across the Amuq Plain but Harim marks the southern limit of the corridor between these two major centres. Harim was occupied by the Byzantines in 959 during Emperor Nicephorus II Phocas' campaign to regain control of the hinterland of Antioch. The Byzantine castle which Nicephorus established fell in 1084 to the Arab, Suleiman Ibn Qutlumish who seized Antioch in the same year. Shortly afterwards, in 1086, the Seljuk Turks took control.

When the Crusaders arrived in the area it took them a nine month siege to capture Antioch in 1098. Harim threatened the rear of their besieging forces and was taken first in November 1097. It was retaken by the Muslim coalition in February 1098 but was abandoned to the Christians before the fall of Antioch (June 1098). It was subsequently held by the Crusaders for over half a century to secure the outer defences of Antioch. In 1119, Crusader forces under Roger, Prince of Antioch, suffered a serious defeat at the nearby battlefield later termed Ager Sanguinis[5] at the hands of the Muslim forces of Aleppo.

Nur al-Din took Harim twice, first in 1149. It was recaptured by the Crusaders in February 1158 after a two month siege mounted by a coalition headed by Baldwin III, King of Jerusalem which included the then Prince of Antioch, the odious Reynald de Châtillon. (Deschamps points out that this was the last major assault mounted by Crusader forces to the east of the Orontes.) In 1164 Harim fell again to Nur al-Din during the first concerted Arab attempt to dislodge the Crusaders from their inland positions. Nur al-Din broke off the siege when threatened by a coalition of Crusader forces (Prince Bohemond III of Antioch, Count Raymond III of Tripoli, Hugh of Lusignan and the Byzantine, Constantine Coloman). He drew the Christian forces into battle on 10 August on the Plain of Artah. The Christians suffered a disastrous defeat and the four leaders were taken into captivity in Aleppo.[6]

Harim remained in Muslim hands right up to the fall of Christian Antioch a century later (1268), a thorn in the side of the Crusader presence in the rich Plain of Amuq below. Just as full Muslim control of the area was restored, however, the Mongol invasions of the late 13th century

resulted in the destruction of much of northern Syria, including the Harim fortress. The fortress was restored and re-used for a time by the Mamluks but before long fell into neglect.

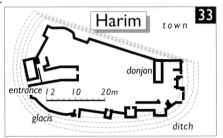

The present remains date from the long period of Muslim confrontation against the Crusaders (1164–1268). The Crusader castle was rebuilt by the Ayyubid governor of Aleppo (and son of Saladin), al-Zaher Ghazi, in the year 1199, according to the Arabic inscription over the entrance gate. The existing mound was pared away to give the truncated cone shape. The sides were covered with a glacis of smooth stone to deny purchase to assailants. (Only a fragment remains, near the main approach from the southwest quarter but the technique is comparable to that of the Aleppo Citadel.) The glacis is broken on the north by the natural rock escarpment which was defence enough. The whole was then surrounded by a moat (again, like Aleppo) of which the outline can be seen in part today.

The state of preservation of the Harim fortress (in part recently restored) and poor sight lines given modern building encroachment diminish its impact as an example, on a relatively small scale, of Arab military architecture before Mamluk and Ottoman times. You approach the castle from the southwest, entering through a gateway defended by two formidable salients, the customary Ayyubid configuration, with a covered corridor originally running though the fortress. The outer shape is semi-circular with the straight wall on the north. On the side opposite the entry, are the remains of the northeastern keep, also the work of

5 'Field of Blood'. The actual location is a little east of Sarmada, not far from the turn-off from the Bab al-Hawa road (see directions above) – map T03.
6 See *Qalat Areimeh for the story of the capture of Raymond III of Tripoli during this battle and its consequences.

Ghazi, placed at this point to strengthen the defences against attack from the hillside opposite.

REFS: van Berchem & Fatio 1914: 229; Deschamps *Châteaux – III* 1973: 341; Korn II 2004: 268–70; Pena (*et al*) *Inventaire du Jebel al-A'la* 1990: 203–12.

Homs

حمص

VARIANTS: Emesa (Lat); Hims (Arb)
PERIOD: var   ALT: 400 m   RATING: *
MAPS: 34, R2

LOCATION: 165 km north of Damascus.

Homs is strategically placed at the intersection of the natural north–south corridor and the access route from the Syrian Desert to the coast through the break in the coastal mountain chains known as the Homs Gap (Buqeia). (The gap lies between the Lebanon range to the south and the Jebel Ansariye range in Syria to the north, map R2.) Homs' location is also determined by the Orontes River which flows through the city. Today it is a key point in the Syrian road and rail networks and the base for several major industries.

Though its location has placed it across many of the major currents of Syrian history, little of that past has survived in what is today a rather drab city.[7] The French historian, Seyrig, wrote in a 1959 study that 'the history of Emesa amounts to no more than a long career of obscurity from the middle of which emerges three centuries of remarkable opulence'. Even that period of prominence in Roman times yields few remains. Beyond some stones in the central mosque, the Roman era in Homs has left no witness to the fact that one of the major imperial dynasties had its origins here.[8] The continuous

7 There has been some improvement, however, since the *Blue Guide (Middle East)* of 1965: 343 languidly recorded: 'Homs offers nothing of very special interest... . You quickly get tired of the depressing streets and the monuments are almost all uninteresting'.
8 Some remnants of the pyramidal tomb of Samsigeramus were still identifiable at the beginning of the 20th century on the western

historic role of the city has meant that its fabric has constantly been redeveloped and renewed, a more effective method of obliterating the past than earthquakes and war.

History

Homs' prosperity, based on the irrigated plain fed by the Homs dam, was probably more enduring than Seyrig argued. The existence of a tell in the centre of Homs attests to the antiquity of the city. It was, however, overshadowed in the pre–Roman period by larger centres in the region, including Qatna (Mishrifeh), Arethusa (al-Rastan) and Qadesh (the classical Laodicea ad Libanum and present *Tell Nabi Mend). After 145 BC, it became the base for the Arab dynasty of the Samsigeramus, one of several pretenders to the crumbling remains of the Greek kingdom. Augustus in 20 BC restored the brother of the Arab ruler, Iamblichus, who had been executed by Antony in 31 BC, and the principality was one of the last to be incorporated into the province of Syria (AD 75 – 85). A recent Syrian researcher points out that Homs did not become a major urban centre until the construction of the nearby dam on the Orontes in the Roman period reduced the risk of flooding along the river's banks.

The territory of Homs (Latin: Emesa) remained hemmed in by its traditional urban rivals. However, to the east, Emesan influence seems to have extended far into the desert. Control of the desert tribes became crucial to the city's fortunes in the first three centuries of Roman rule.[9] Its destiny marched closely with that of Palmyra with which it enjoyed close ties. As long as Palmyra helped to control the security of the central desert and keep the tribes in check, the caravan route based on Homs was viable. Once the desert became unsafe, the caravans by-passed it, preferring the safer reaches of the edge of the city. They had disappeared by the 1950s but items from the nearby necropolis were excavated and are now in the Damascus Museum.
9 The desert Arabs provided the corps of mounted archers (the Hemeseni) much prized by the Roman army.

traditional northern route via the upper Euphrates and Aleppo.

Emesa's first claim to wider fame was its connections with the Severan dynasty, the ruling family of early third century Rome. Julia Domna, a daughter of the high priest of Emesa, married Septimius Severus, the future emperor (r 193–211) around AD 187 following a period in which he was stationed in Syria as a commander of the IV Scythica legion.[10] She was described by Gibbon as deserving 'all that the stars

and Alexander Severus (r 222–35).

The most notorious of the line was Elagabalus, proclaimed as emperor at the age of 14 by the III Gallica legion based at Raphaneae, in the Orontes Valley west of Emesa. His nickname derived from the Baal deity whose emblem, the black stone from the sun temple in Emesa, was transferred to Rome as the basis of a new solar cult. He rapidly declined into insanity, his reign dissolving into four years of chaos and depravity. He was murdered by the

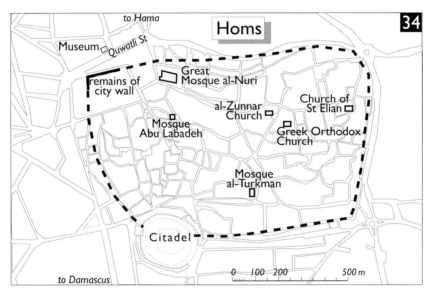

could promise her'. She possessed 'the attractions of beauty, and united to a lively imagination a firmness of mind, and strength of judgement, seldom bestowed on her sex'. Following Septimius' coup of 193, Julia Domna became a central personality in the new dynasty's fortunes. Four of her offspring (or those of her sister, Julia Maesa) and their descendants went on to become emperors – Caracalla (r 211–7); Geta (co-Emperor with Caracalla in 211); Marcus Antoninus (Elagabalus – r 218–22);

praetorian guard; the stone was sent back to Emesa where the sun cult continued at least until the end of the fifth century. (Aurelian took time off from his campaign against Zenobia to visit the Emesa temple and secure the sun god's support for his victory.)[11]

Homs became an important centre after the Arab conquest, rather more fervent

---

10 Recalling stories of a woman in Syria whose horoscope predicted she would be married to a king, Septimius contracted to marry her by correspondence from Lyons following the death of his first wife.

11 For the sun cult see Seyrig *Culte* 1971: 340. Aurelian gave it new impetus in the late third century. Attributing his victory over Zenobia to the god's intervention, he built a new temple to Sol Invictus in Rome and raised the cult to official status. Elagabulus' temple, the Elagaballium, was located in the northeast corner of the Palatine Hill.

and puritanical in its attachment to Islam than the Umayyad court at Damascus. (500 of the Prophet's companions were said to have been settled there.) It later avoided attack by the Crusaders in spite of their strong presence at the nearby *Krak des Chevaliers. Less prosperous than Hama in the Arab and Ottoman eras, it had fallen into a steep decline by the 18th century. By 1914, it had a population of no more than 5000.

Visit

Begin your visit in the centre of town, where the Museum is located on the north side of Quwatli St. The display of finds, particularly from the Roman to the Arab periods, provides an outstanding survey of the area's history, well displayed and labelled, and should not be missed.

The ground floor vestibule divides two wings set at right angles. The three rooms and the corridor to the left houses mosaics, statues and architectural elements from Homs and al-Rastan. Note particularly the mosaic, immediately left as you enter the corridor, showing the Orontes flowing under a stylized bridge, the figures of Orontes himself on the bank and four cupids crossing the stream by boat (one just manages to scramble aboard). In the third room, a huge Baalbek style segment of an entablature includes a water spout formed from a lion's head. To the left, a second century altar to the sun god.

Right of the ground floor vestibule, the corridor contains four enormous sarcophagi from Homs. The hall to the right (east) includes (on entering, left) a third century Palmyrene altar and a selection of other sculptural pieces in the Palmyrene style, most notably of a reclining male figure in Parthian dress (right wall, Palmyra second century).

On the first floor the north hall and corridor (left from the staircase) include pottery from the Neolithic to the first millennium BC as well as gold items, glass and other material from *Qatna, *Qadesh and *Mari. Note the superb 'Susa type' pot (fourth millennium BC) in the angled

case on entering the main hall and the remarkable collection of alabaster vessels from LBA Qatna, presents from the Egyptian court (end of hall). The southern hall and corridor comprise smaller finds from Roman Homs – fine figurines, glass, and (at the end) excellent examples of Islamic pottery including Raqqa and Ayyubid ware.

The **Great Mosque al-Nuri** is 220 m south of the intersection at the western end of Quwatli St. A large rectangular building with an oblong courtyard, oriented east-west, it seems an unlikely candidate for the site of the pagan sun temple (though there are some re-used Roman blocks at the north entry to the mosque, off the suq). Whatever its classical association, it was the site of a Church of St John. The present building dates from the 12th–13th centuries, its name bearing tribute to Nur al-Din. It certainly carries the hallmarks the austere cross-vaulted architecture of the period.

East of here lies the quarter in which the older churches of Homs are located. 400 m east is the **al-Zunnar Church** (Church of the Virgin's Belt). The curious name derives from the discovery under the altar in 1953 of a textile belt said to have belonged to the Virgin. The belt is believed to have been placed in the first church on this spot in the late fourth century. Most of the present church's structure dates from a 1966 restoration but it may rest on Byzantine foundations.

More inherently interesting are ancient frescoes in the south apse of the **Church of St Elian** (continue east for 300 m). The apse stands on the site of a fifth century church dedicated to Elian (Julian), the son of a Roman officer from Emesa martyred in 284–5 for refusing to renounce Christianity. The martyrium (end of the right hand nave) contains the sarcophagus of St Elian and a remarkable series of mural paintings which were uncovered in 1970. They had been covered by a coating of plaster and thus preserved. The church is still a pilgrimage centre due to the miracles associated with St Elian.

A recent study has traced the original layer of paintings (which were retouched in the 19th century) to the second half of the 12th century or first half of the 13th century. The surviving paintings represent:

- Christ in majesty with the Virgin and Mary Magdalene (left) and John the Baptist and one other (St Elian?) (right)
- In the side niches, the four evangelists Luke, John (left); Mark, Matthew (right)
- Medallions of the prophets and apostles.

The saint's sarcophagus is probably a classical import, re-used and embellished with Christian crosses when the remains of St Elian were transferred to the original church in the fifth century. The painted frescoes of the main church (1970s) are devoted to the life of St Elian and were painted by the Romanian artists Gavril and Miha Morasan.

There are a number of interesting mosques though little research available on them. **Mosque Abu Labadeh** (150 m south of the Great Mosque), for example, shows the typical local style of a tall square minaret in basalt, virtually devoid of decoration.

The **walls** of the city and its seven gates were largely demolished in the Ottoman period. Remains of one gate survive in Bab al-Masdud (west). Only a few glimpses of the old walls survive, the most accessible being the short stretch exposed by recent re-development south of Quwatli St.

The remains of the **Citadel** of Homs can be seen on the mound at the southwest corner of the old city. The fortuitous find of an altar to Elagabalus during construction work on the mound in the 1970s appears to confirm that this was the location of the Sun Temple. Recently cleared of its military facilities, it is now being researched by a British-Syrian team. The Arab and earlier remains have been seriously damaged by military use over the past two centuries though 'sufficient

survives ... to show that originally the Ayyubid and Mamluk fortifications ... were comparable to those of Aleppo although they were on a smaller scale' (King).

The **Mosque of Khalid Ibn al-Walid** stands, set back to the right in a park, 500 m north of Quwatli St on the road to Hama. The mosque, completely rebuilt in the late Turkish period (1908–13), is on a site dating back to Ayyubid times and contains (right) the reputed tomb of one of the early followers of Muhammad, Khalid Ibn al-Walid, whose military campaigns in Syria led to the Islamic conquest. He died in 642 his exploits having been eclipsed by his sworn enemy, the Caliph Umar.

REFS: Abdulkarim *AAAS* 2001; Chad 1972; du Mesnil du Buisson 1930: 208–17; Dussaud 1927: 103–5; Elisséeff 'Hims' *EI1*; Gatier 1996; Immerzeel 2005: 149–66; King 2002: 39–58; Moussli 1983; Leroy 1974: 95–113; Sa'ade *St Elian* 1974; Seyrig 1952; Seyrig 1959.

Husn Suleiman (Plate 11b)

حصن سايمار

VARIANTS: Baetocecea (Lat); Baetocécé (Fr)
PERIOD: Rom RATING: ** MAPS: 35, R2

LOCATION: Reaching Husn Suleiman can be confusing. The most straightforward access is from *Safita taking the road which heads north. After c500 m (northern edge of town) take the right fork and continue +20 km, then left +3 km for the village of Husn Suleiman (check by asking as there are numerous road options). Pass through the village and then continue to the top of a narrow valley. It may be more convenient to approach from *Masyaf. Leave Masyaf by the road that goes south, turning right just out of town. Keep heading southwest (road eventually goes to Dreikish). After c20 km, Husn Suleiman lies in a valley to the south-west of a large television relay mast.

Husn Suleiman ('Suleiman's castle') is among the most striking set of ruins in Syria. The remains of the Temple of Zeus Baetocecian are exceptional for the juxtaposition of the gigantic and the picturesque: the cyclopean scale of the component blocks set against the tranquility and beauty of the Jebel Ansariye.

History

A cult centre has existed here for millennia. The first temple was probably constructed under Persian domination when the area known now as the Meshta was settled. The present remains are Greek-Roman but occupy the site of a Semitic-Canaanite cult to the local version

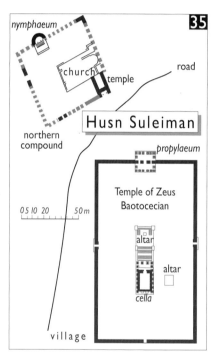

of Baal whose worship was later merged with the Greek equivalent under the title Zeus Baetocecian as lord of the heavens. The cult flourished during Roman times.

The cult was had already been promoted in late Seleucid times when the present compound walls were possibly built and the centre entrusted to a guild of priests. A further program to monumentalise the cult centre began in the second century AD. Much of the surrounding countryside

belonged to the temple which collected the revenue and enjoyed immunity from taxes. Thriving trade activity, including in slaves, supplemented the income stream to fund the upgrade. The Syro-Phoenician cults were still practised into the fourth century after the adoption of Christianity as the official religion of the Empire by Constantine. Thereafter a church was constructed inside the northern enclosure the centre became a Christian pilgrimage destination.

Visit

The enclosure consists of a large open compound (approximately rectangular, 134 m by 85 m) with a *cella* towards the southern end. This is a typical plan for Syro-Phoenician temples (see box on page 20), merging concepts from the Syrian, Roman and Mesopotamian worlds. Some of the cyclopean stones used in the compound wall measure up to 10 m in length and over 2.5 m in height. The taste for huge stones is paralleled in the Jupiter complex at Baalbek as are many of the decorative features found at Husn Suleiman.

There are four gates centrally placed on each of the outer walls. The *propylaeum* that once straddled the north gateway (plate 11b) was the most elaborate, 15 m wide, with porticos of eight columns on each side of the triple doorway. The portico was further adorned with two niches and a Syrian style relieving arch. The columns are now missing but the elaborate decorative treatment can still be seen, reflecting several building phases in which the doorways were inserted into the existing outer walls. An inscription was added around 255 (in the now indecipherable panel right of the west doorway) during the reign of the co-emperors, Valerian and Gallienus, reiterating the privileges originally granted to the sanctuary by the Seleucid kings of Syria and reaffirmed under Augustus. It appears these tax-free privileges had been challenged by Arados which wanted its fiscal cut from the lucrative trade. At both ends of the north wall, the carved figures of lions can be seen (possibly a reference to a symbol seen on coins of Arados).

On the east and west walls, the doorways practically mirror each other with two *aedicule*s (niches) and elaborately-carved lintels supported by winged victory figures. On the eastern version, the portrait head of a man can still be distinguished. On the same (east) doorway, there is a Greek inscription (c AD 224) which records the dedication of the complex by the local people.

All the four gates were adorned with the figures of eagles on the soffits of the lintels, remains of which survive in different stages of preservation (the south gateway example is nearly effaced).

The *cella* took the form of a *pseudoperipteros*, half columns ranged along each side. The entrance (north) is marked by a portico of six free-standing columns preceded by 39 steps divided by a platform. An altar for offerings originally stood on the front of this platform. (A larger altar stood to the east of the *cella*.) From inside the *cella*, a narrow staircase rose within the walls from the right near corner as you enter. It continued to ascend through the rear and eastern walls, eventually coming out on a roof terrace as in many other temples in the Syrian tradition.

It is difficult to describe the purpose of the second compound (across the tarmac road, northwest) though the most recent study of the site (Freyberger) suggests it was established as a market. Dubbed in some sources 'al-Deir' (the monastery, possibly because it was later used as a Christian monastic building), it has a small temple (two columns, Ionic, between *antae*) in near corner. The portico of this temple is quite charming, especially the eagle over the lintel. The rest of the compound, however, is largely bare, except for traces of a Christian basilica north of the temple and the scanty remains of a building on the north side, possibly a *nymphaeum* (water fountain) with an *exedra* preceded by an entrance hall, though there is no trace of a water source.

REFS: *IGLS* VII 1970: 55–74; Amy 'Temples' 1950; Dignas 2003 74–84, 156–67; Freyberger 2004: 13–40; Krencker & Zschietzschmann 1938; Rey-Coquais *Arados* 1974: 213–4.

I

Isriya

اسريـة

VARIANTS: Seriana (Lat); Esriye (Arb)
PERIOD: Rom RATING: * MAP: R4

LOCATION: Northern reaches of the Syrian Desert. Take Selemiye exit from Hama. 33 km, Selemiye – continue to Sabbura (+27 km), Saen (+20 km), Sheikh Hellal (+23 km) then new sealed road 30 km to Isriya.

Nothing shows better to what extent human effort has transformed the Syrian desert than the beautiful Roman temple that is to be found here.

(Blue Guide 1966)

The ancient Seriana was once a crossing point for several Roman routes including from Chalcis (*Qinnesrin) to *Palmyra and from *Resafa to Selemiye, passing through countryside which was considerably more fertile than it is today.

This striking ruin stands alone on the south of the former citadel promontory, its four intact walls of mellowed limestone isolated in a moonscape of flinty stones. It was built in solid limestone blocks, resembling in many ways the techniques used with the same material in Palmyra. The pseudo-peripteral temple is oriented to the east and the walls carry elegant pilasters with capitals in the Corinthian order. There is little trace of either the *pronaos* that preceded the *cella* or the stairs that led up to it. The wide eastern doorway is richly decorated with a typically Syrian semi-circular relieving arch above. A staircase embedded in the masonry to the right of the doorway ascends to what was once a terrace. A *temenos* wall would have surrounded the temple.

The building dates from the early third century, possibly on the site of an earlier cult centre favoured by the local tribes. The style of the doorway bears the same elaborate treatment used in contemporary Baalbek. It was possibly erected by

an imperial offical at this important crossroads of the Roman road system. Alternatively, it was an initiative by local groups concerned to display their 'Romanness'. There is no firm evidence as to the identity of the god to whom the temple was dedicated but the German researcher (Gogräfe) has offered two possibilities, an astral divinity or the local equivalent of the classical Apollo, Nabu, whose statue was found nearby. Latest research indicates that the temple may have had an oracular function with the oracle housed beneath the *cella*. (The building is located above a fissure in the rock base, a *chasm* typical of many ancient religious sites.) In the Byzantine period, the settlement was enclosed by walls which incorporated the temple as a fortified watch-tower. In the Abbasid and Mamluk periods, the remains served as a way-station on the sultan's travels between Damascus and the Jezira.

Khanazir

The track which leads northwest through Sfire and on to Aleppo passes after c 56 km another Roman settlement, Anasarthon (also known as Kunasara or Anasartha, now marked by the village of Khanazir. The flat conical mound on the edge of the village was the site of a citadel which helped guard the channel between the two natural bastions of Jebel Hass to the northwest and Jebel Sbeit to the east. Some ancient stones have been re-employed in the village when it was settled by Circassians at the turn of the 20th century. The fort was probably set up as part of the Roman reorganisation of the area in the third century which also saw the establishment of the Strata Diocletiana running further to the east (*Resafa-Palmyra-Damascus). In the Christian era, the town was sufficiently important to rate six churches, one dedicated in 426 to St Thomas.

There are several other sites to the east of Khanazir but they are largely of specialised interest, including:

• **Zebed** (20 km east of Khanazir, citadel and two large basilicas – one (possibly fourth century) was built largely in

mud brick; the second with some walls
in dark basalt still standing)
• **Muallak** (12 km northeast of Khanazir,
three churches, one dated 606/7).

REFS: Butler *AE* II 1903: 76–7; Gogräfe 1993, 1996;
Mouterde & Poidebard 1939: 59–69; Mouterde &
Poidebard 1945: 89–91; Musil *Palmyrena* 1928: 55.

J

Jebel Khalid

جبل خلد

VARIANTS: Thapsacus?? PERIOD: Hel/Rom
RATING:– MAP: R4

Highway leading northeast from Aleppo
via al-Bab. Continue on bypass south of
Menbij and take road southeast to Tishreen Dam and Abu Qalqal. Jebel Khalid lies
on the Euphrates 3 kms downstream from
the Tishreen Dam (10 km east of Qalqal).
Show identity at dam security perimeter.

Excavated since 1986 by an Australian
team, this fortress site has proved to
be a rare example of a Greek military
settlement not later overbuilt or
disturbed by Roman occupation. It
therefore gives us an important insight
into the type of military colony established
by the Macedonian rulers of Syria in the
third century BC. Probably established
by Seleucus I Nicator, the fortress was
abandoned with the breakup of Seleucid
control in Syria around 70 BC.

While the visible remains consist largely of
lower courses, the rocky outcrop towers
some 100 m above the Euphrates and
gives a spectacular overview of a crossing
point on the river. The fortress (50 ha)
was protected on the landward side by
3.4 km of circuit walls and comprised an
acropolis area (southern spur of the long
ridge), a domestic sector in the north and,
in the saddle between public buildings,
a temple in the Doric order. A palace
arranged around a central colonnaded
court with evidence of both military and
civilian administrative functions was found
inside the acropolis. The most elevated
part of the site, in the northwest sector,
was marked by a substantial U-shaped
tower with commanding coverage of both
river traffic and the land approach from
the southwest.

REFS: Clarke (ed.) 2001; Clarke & Jackson AAAS
2002–3: 189–206; Cohen 2006: 178-80.

Jebel Seis (Plate 12a)

جبل سيس

VARIANTS: Jebel Sis, Says (Arb)
PERIOD:Arb (Umd) RATING:* MAP: R4

LOCATION: A tarmac road now joins
Jebel Seis to the Baghdad road, not long
after it branches from the highway to Palmyra (86 km from Damascus). The Jebel
Seis road turns south at Khirbet Butmiyet, 5 km after the Baghdad turn-off. There
are occasional signs indicating the route
but it is wise to check the odometer. Approximately 60 km south of the Khirbet
Butmiyet turn-off, another tarmac road
branches west. (The road you have turned
off continues south to Khirbet al-Beida
east of Jebel Hauran.) Head for the long
profile of Jebel Seis, 6 km to the west.

This Umayyad complex was built on the
slopes of the outer crater of an extinct
volcano on the eastern edge of a volcanic
wilderness (the Diret al-Tillul). The crater
briefly acquires a patina of vegetation
during the spring and is 500 m broad by
2 km long with steep sides covered in
dark lava and scoria, a scene described
by Sauvaget as 'a truly nightmare vision'.
The inner cone of the volcano rears to
the northwest of the bleak basalt ruins. A
small spring provides a precarious source
of water, which sometimes collects in a
lake to the north. Sauvaget and Brisch,
partly on literary evidence, attribute all
the buildings to the reign of al-Walid I
(r 705–15), the builder of the Umayyad
Mosque in Damascus.

The ruins of the Umayyad settlement fall
into two groups spread over the slopes of
the outer and inner craters – the castle
and ancillary buildings on the southern rim
and a series of ancillary residences below
the inner cone.

The most important building is that wrongly
ascribed by Poidebard in the 1930s to the
Roman period – his 'castle' Built, like
other Umayyad desert lodges, to a square
plan, it admittedly borrowed its outer
shape from Roman military encampments.
The walls (67 by 67 mm; 2 m thick) are

strengthened by eight cylindrical or semi-cylindrical towers. Originally the lower courses of stone were augmented by an upper level of mud brick which has since crumbled. The entrance was through the monumental gateway in the centre of the northern side, the passage cutting through the semi-cylindrical tower. Only this entrance area was finished to its full height in stone. The courtyard (31 m by 31 m) contained a central well and was surrounded by porticos. The arcading showed some decorative elements in common with the recently reconstructed gateway to the Umayyad palace on the Amman Citadel and the main gate shows the early use of the broken arch (plate 12a). The building contained 60 rooms arranged in nine separate compartments (bayts). Other buildings in this lower grouping include the mosque (70 m to the west, divided by a small arcade of two arches, small mihrab) and the baths (150 m to the east of the qasr, originally a large tunnel-vaulted hall (10 m by 4.4 m) with a semi-circular exedra). The only standing remains of the second cluster of domestic ruins is the doorway on the lower slopes to the north.

There is no evidence of Roman remains at Jebel Seis, ruling out Poidebard's identification with Mons Jovis.

REFS: Brisch 1963, 1965; Creswell Early Muslim I 1979: 472–7; Kennedy & Riley 1990: 79–80; Poidebard Trace 1934: 63–4; Sauvaget 'Ruines omeyyades' 1939; Sauvaget 'Châteaux umayyades' 1968.

Jeble

جبلة

VARIANTS: Gabala, Jabala (anc); Gabula (Lat); Zibel, Gebel, Gibel (Cru) PERIOD: Rom RATING:* MAP: R2

LOCATION: Turn-off 25 km south of *Latakia on the highway to *Tartus. Theatre is in the centre of the town, 400 m northeast of the small port.

History

Jeble has served as a small port from the Phoenician period to the present, its fortunes a barometer of prevailing trends. It is mentioned in Assyrian records as part of the Assyrian Empire but received a Greek colony (probably eighth century BC). It formed part of the confederation of Phoenician states controlled by *Arwad in the Persian and Seleucid periods. Nominally under the Seleucids, it was overlooked in favour of Latakia. Pompey's conquest brought Roman control (64 BC). In the early Christian period it served as the seat of a bishop but passed from the Byzantines to the Arabs in 638.

The Crusaders, under Raymond, Count of Toulouse, forced the local Muslim qadi (Fakhr al-Mulk Ibn Ahmar) to pay tribute in 1098, shortly after the fall of Antioch. The qadi spent the next decade trying to find an effective protector among the Muslim leaders of the area (Tripoli and Damascus) but in 1109, Jeble was incorporated by Tancred into the Principality of Antioch and renamed Zibel. The Roman theatre was turned into a Crusader castle.

The town rated its own duke and bishop by the mid 12th century. Saladin re-conquered it during his extraordinary sweep up the coast in 1188, shortly after the Battle of Hattin but his successors abandoned it (as they did many of his re-conquests) and the Crusaders moved back in. The Hospitallers took control but their command was disputed by the Templars. The Mamluk Sultan Qalawun took it by assault in 1285, shortly after his great victory at Marqab which saw the final defeat of the crusading forces on the Syrian littoral. It subsequently passed into less tumultuous obscurity though it became a centre of trade and religious pilgrimage for the Jebel Ansariye.

Visit

While Jeble has played a role in just about every phase of Syrian history, the most substantial reminder of its past is the Roman **theatre** currently under restoration. The scaenae frons lies in ruins but the first 11 rows of seats of this free-standing building have survived, along with the greater part of the next 12 rows and a fragment of the

1a   Ain Dara, Iron Age temple

1b   Aleppo, Great Mosque – courtyard and minaret

2a   Aleppo Citadel, Ayyubid palace baths

2b   Aleppo, Beit Ajiqbash

3a   Amrit, Temple of Melqart

3b   Apamea, twisted fluting of *cardo* columns

3c   Apamea, House of Consoles

4a Apamea, *cardo* – lower north section

4b Bosra, Roman theatre

5a Bosra Citadel, southwest towers

5b Bosra *nymphaeum*

5c Bosra, Nabataean arch

6a   Cyrrhus, Roman bridge (Afrin River)

6b   Damascus, Umayyad Mosque – prayer hall and courtyard

7a   Damascus, Umayyad Mosque – transept façade mosaics

7b   Damascus, Azem Palace – courtyard

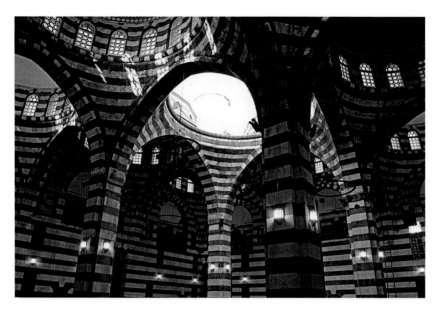

8a   Damascus, Khan Assaad Pasha

8b   Damascus, Madrasa Zahiriye – mausoleum of Baybars

9a   Damascus Museum, Qasr al-Heir West doorway

9b   Dumeir, Roman temple

10a   Ebla, courtyard of Royal Palace G

10b   Halebiye, northern gate and walls

11a   Harbaqa Dam

11b   Husn Suleiman, north gate to the *temenos*

12a Jebel Seis, gateway

12b Khan al-Hallabat, Roman fort

13a   Krak des Chevaliers, from southwest – at dawn

13b   Krak des Chevaliers, *loggia*

14a Krak des Chevaliers, southern inner defences

14b Maalula, from the east

15a   Mushabbak

15b   Palmyra, Bel Temple – eastern columns of *cella*

15c   Palmyra, decorative details of monumental arch

16a   Palmyra, monumental arch and *cardo* – looking west

16b   Palmyra, Valley of the Tombs

17a   Qalaat Marqab, south salient

17b   Qalaat Masyaf, southern outer defences

18a   Qalaat Najm

18b   Qalaat Saladin, from the northwest

19a   Qalaat Shirkuh (Palmyra)

19b   Qalaat Shmemis

20a Qanawat, Seraya – west façade

20b Qasr al-Heir East, eastern castle

21a   Qasr Ibn Wardan, church – basalt lintel

21b   Resafa, Church of St Sergius

22a   Saint Simeon, south façade

22b   Saint Simeon, remains of saint's pillar

23a Serjilla, baths

23b Shahba, Roman theatre

24a   Sheikh Suleiman, Church of the Virgin

24b   Tartus, cathedral (Museum) – façade

third tier, the whole sustained by the solid framework of support piers and arches. In its present state, the theatre gives little indication of its original seating capacity, probably totalling 7000. The free-standing semi-circle of 90 m diameter is oriented to the north. Probably constructed late second or early third century.

The complex north of the theatre houses the tomb of a local Muslim holy man, Ibrahim Ibn Adham (d 778) who renounced life at the princely court of Balkh (Afghanistan) in favour of itinerant asceticism. The mosque has been much restored but stands on the site of a church constructed in the early seventh century.

REFS: Pensabene 1997: 378–84; Rey-Coquais *Arados* 1974: 214–5; Sa`adé 1968.

Jerade

جارادة

VARIANTS: Gerade, Djerade
PERIOD: Byz RATING: * MAP: R3

LOCATION: 2 km southeast of *Ruweiha; or turn off the *Maarat al-Numan-Saraqeb road 4 km north of Maarat.

These picturesque ruins on the outskirts of a modern village are worth a visit of an hour or so. The most interesting is the fifth or sixth century watch-tower, six storeys with latrine arrangements gracing the exterior, one of the best surviving examples in the area. In this case the watch-tower is likely to have had a security function. Pena says that Jerade was once surrounded by walls and speculates that 'the inhabitants must have feared the ravages of the desert' while Tchalenko notes that the villages on the eastern edge of the limestone country were more open to incursions from the east. Notice the lintel which carries the Roman or Byzantine imperial escutcheon. The sole church dates from the fifth century. The central nave is divided from the side aisles by five columns. A *bema* was located in the middle of the nave; base of a tower with an upper loggia at the north end of the narthex.

REFS: Butler AE II 1903: 125, 128–9; Butler EC 1929: 66; Mattern 1944: 16; Pena (et al) Reclus 1980: 273–6; Tchalenko *Villages* I 1953: 30–1; Tchalenko & Baccache 1979–80: 481–96.

Jisr al-Shugur

جسر الشغور

VARIANTS: ?Seleucobelus (Grk); Seleucia ad Belum, Niaccuba (Lat) PERIOD: Rom/ Arb RATING: – MAP: R2, R3

LOCATION: On the eastern edge of the Jebel Ansariye, on the highway between *Latakia (75 km west) and Aleppo (104 km east).

An important bridgehead on the Orontes carrying traffic from the coast to northern Syria, Jisr al-Shugur has been settled since ancient times, hence its inclusion in early itineraries or geographies. The caravanserai in the centre of the old town was originally constructed between 1660 and 1676 and was restored in 1826–7.

Little that is ancient remains in the bustling modern town but incorporated in the bridge that takes current-day eastbound traffic over the Orontes are bits of a much older predecessor, originally built by the Romans. The design forms a broad arrow facing south to withstand the force of the current. This angle and the fact that the bridge was almost horizontal distinguish it from the majority of Roman/Arab bridges. The fabric was much modified in later centuries, its jumbled origins evident in the variety of stones used in the arches and piers.

REFS: van Berchem & Fatio 1914: 260–4; Dussaud 1927: 155–62; Nour 1982: 297–8; Sauvaget 'Caravanserails syriens' 1937: 108.

K

REFS: **Hallabat:**   Bauzou   1989:   329–
30;   Kennedy   1990:   203,   figs   151,   152;
Poidebard   1934:   37,   48,   52,   56,   pl   XL–XLII.
Bkhara: Genequand 2004: 225–42.

Khan al-Hallabat (Plate 12b) and Bkhara

خان الهلبت

VARIANTS: Veriaraca; Avara? PERIOD: Rom, Umm RATING:* MAP: R4

31 km southeast of Palmyra. Take highway in direction of Damascus. At c 25 kms track to west (+10 km). Bkhara lies to the east of the same point on the highway (+ 16 km, initially over tarmac road then follow tracks to north).

A typical Roman desert fort (late third century, probably the classical Veriaraca) can be seen at **Khan al-Hallabat** (Plate 12b). The building, with substantial walls (47 m square) and four round corner towers, has been restored. It provides a typical example of the fortified positions built under Diocletian stretching in a long line diagonally across Syria and linking the settled zones of southern Syria as far as the Mid Euphrates.

Less substantial to visit, but a site of considerable historical importance, is another Tetrarchic fort at **al-Bkhara**. A Roman fort (Avara) was later adapted to serve as an Umayyad palace. Long described as a 'vast field of ruins' whose origins remained obscure, its core is a 35 m by 154 m enclosure with round corner towers and half-moon interval towers (mud brick over stone foundations). Corinthian capitals (now disappeared) indicated an internal colonnaded courtyard. In this palace, the third last Umayyad caliph, Walid II (r. 743–44, the builder of the splendid Khirbet al-Mafjar in Palestine) took refuge but was hunted down by a Yamani hit gang. Around Bkhara are the remains of two Byzantine fortified farmsteads with entrance gateways and watch-towers (Sukuriye 1 km west and Bazuriye 4.5 km southeast). Bazuriye is a cluster of three farms of which substantial remains of one survive and have been recently partly reconstructed.

Kharrab Shams

خرب شمس

VARIANTS: Kharab Shams
PERIOD: Byz RATING: * MAP: R3

LOCATION: Take the road that forks right from the foot of Jebel Semaan (*Saint Simeon) through the Kurdish villages to the northeast, *Basofan, *Burj Haidar (8 km) until the country opens out (+12 km). The ruins, dominated by the tall arcaded church nave, lie across the fields 400 m left. Alternatively, take the Afrin road north out of *Aleppo. At Hayyan (14 km), take the road to the left for +10 km.

The site on the eastern edge of the limestone country around Jebel Semaan has always rated highly among writers on the 'dead cities' area. There are a few remains (including a rock-cut tomb and lintels) which reveal the origins of the settlement before the classical period. It was probably further developed early in the phase of Roman settlement to take advantage of the transport route on which it lies and to exploit the patches of arable land on the neighbouring slopes.

The early remains were cursorily built in polygonal, not dressed, stones. Villas appeared during the Christian period. The dominant ruin, on the southern edge of the settlement, is a **fourth century church** whose side aisles have collapsed, leaving the central arcaded nave of five arches topped by ten windows standing alone, in part perfectly preserved. The resulting effect is enhanced if you visit the scene at sunset when the slanting light plays on the beautifully mottled stone.

According to Butler 'this church is one of the best preserved religious edifices in Northern Syria'. Sources differ as to its date. Butler puts it around 372, on analogy with the church at *Fafertin which is the earliest dated church in northern Syria. The style is in many respects remarkably analagous to the equally well preserved church at *Mushabbak which is usually dated to the late fifth century, about the same time as the construction of the great complex at Saint Simeon. Tchalenko's view is that this fourth century church was rebuilt in the fifth century. The local church architecture is still clearly evolving and the treatment of the arcading and windows is rather heavy. The different phases of construction are illustrated in the north and south clerestories, the first (older) containing five windows, the second ten. The nave contains a *bema*. The wall across the nave added in Arab times accidentally preserved the carved chancel rail behind, the only example to survive in Syria.

Standing by itself further up the hill you will find remains of a small **sixth century church** or chapel with a large enclosure and out-buildings. This was perhaps part of a monastery. Note the variety of capitals, largely based on classical themes but simplified.

REFS: Bell *Desert* 1985: 283; Butler *PE* II B 6 1920: 322–5; Tchalenko *Villages* II 1953: pl CXXIX; Tchalenko & Baccache 1979–80: pl 97–111.

Khirbet Hass

خربت حاس

VARIANTS: Shinsharah PERIOD: Rom, Byz ALT: RATING: – MAP: R3

LOCATION: Take road leaving Maarat al-Numan to the southwest. Take right turn marked 'Madafen Hass al-Asriya' just before Hass (9 km). Follow road for +3 km. The site is now part of a nature reserve.

This ancient village (its origins probably go back to Roman times) became a centre studded with prosperous villas in the Byzantine period when it carried the name Shinsharah. There are many surviving remains of houses, often with superb decoration and with emphasis on the colonnaded courtyard. The church lies on the northeast side of the ruins but only a few walls survive in part. To the south was a monastery, relatively late (sixth century).

REFS: Butler *AE* II 1903: 92–4, 112–3; de Vogüé 1865: pl 82–4; Mattern 1944: 45–50.

Kirkbizeh

قرق بيزة

VARIANTS: Qirqbize, Kirk Birzey (Arb)
PERIOD: Byz ALT: 650m RATING: – MAP: R3

LOCATION: See instructions for *Qalb Lozeh. Stop at 24.5 km, just before you turn left for Qalb Lozeh. The ruins are 200 m to the right.

A settlement of moderate interest with houses dating from the third to the sixth century. The site looks out over the Plain of Self to the south. A patch of arable land nearby allowed for the early exploitation of this area but Tchalenko speculates that the settlers, who joined the community established around the dominant land-holder, needed to supplement olive-growing with exploitation of grain on the plain below.

The buildings include at the top of th rise a house from the third century and adjoining it on the west a fourth century church probably originally a house but large enough to contain a *bema* in the single nave (with its throne still intact at the time of Tchalenko's survey). The church is preceded by a colonnaded portico and a courtyard. There are two other villas which are later in date (fifth to sixth centuries). A little further away are the remains of six modest farmhouses.

Bnabel

Return to the Kirkbizeh intersection (where you turned left to Qalb Lozeh) and continue 3.5 km northwest. An orphaned funerary column (left of the road as you enter the village) is all that is left of a bi-columnar funerary monument, typical in style of the high Roman period. Seek out the prominent remains of a two-storeyed house with a columned portico, one of three houses said to be from the second century AD, described by Butler as 'the earliest residence of the Roman period in North Central Syria'. The village had no building specifically constructed as a church.

REFS: **Kirkbizeh**: Butler *AE* II 1903: 115–9; Tchalenko *Villages* II 1953: pl C–CVII, CXXXV; Tchalenko & Baccache 1979–80: pl 381–399. **Bnabel**: Butler *AE* II 1903: 62, 69–71, 75.

Kokanaya

كوكانايا

VARIANTS: Kaukanaya, Koukanaya
PERIOD: Byz   ALT: 582 m   RATING: –
MAP: R3

LOCATION: Take directions for Harim but before *Qalb Lozeh, at 22.5 km, continue ahead (not up the steep hill to right). +2 km then sharp right, keeping the swampy lake on your right. Continue +4.6 km, through the village, following the steep roadway to reach ruins marked by a distinctive pyramidal-roofed tomb.

A little off the main itinerary, Kokanaya is probably not worth visiting for its own sake unless you have a particular interest in its two principal **tombs**. The moderately extensive ruins lie on the edge of a modern village. Near the road lie two open-sided tombs. One with its pyramidal roof largely standing is inscribed 384 and said by Butler to be an example of his first type of 'canopy tomb'. The second houses an open – and beautifully carved – sarcophagus (to Eusebius, a Christian, dated 369 by inscription).

Further up the hill you will find a two-storey **villa** with attractive columns and fine carving. Pena notes that the purpose of this building is not clear (religious or farmhouse) but Tchalenko says it is a guardhouse. Pena opts for a monks' hermitage (hence the tower). He notes that three **churches** were located in the village, all in poor condition. They are located on the eastern edge (fifth century), to the west (sixth century) and on the southern edge (sixth century).

REFS: Butler *AE* II 1903: 104, 109 (tombs), 146 (church), 173–4 (houses I–III), 213; Butler *EC* 1929: 136; de Vogüé I 1865: 119, 124; Pena (*et al*) *Reclus* 1980: 169–74; Pena (*et al*) 990: 151–5; Tchalenko *Villages* I 1953: 41, 334n, 387.

Krak des Chevaliers (Qalaat al-Husn – Plates 13a–14a)

قاعة الحصن.

VARIANTS: Qalaat al-Husn, Husn al-Akrad (Arb) PERIOD: Cru RATING: *** MAP: 36, R2

LOCATION: Take the highway from *Homs to *Tartus. 41 km west of Homs, a road branches off to the right (north). Several options lead either to the Krak directly or via the village of al-Husn. To gain an appreciation of the castle before visiting, go to the west (seaward) side via the circuit road that skirts the north end.

As the parthenon is to Greek temples and Chartres to Gothic cathedrals, so is the Krak des Chevaliers to mediaeval castles, the supreme example, one of the great buildings of all times.

(T S R Boase 1967: 52)

Many superlatives have been spent on this monument[1] but few do it full justice. The challenge in finding the apt description is that, no matter how many times you visit the great fortress, it never presents the same face. In the winter gales that seek to rend it apart, it is glowering and forbidding; at dawn, it reluctantly shakes off the enveloping mist (plate 13a); on a spring day, its warm hues blend with the wildflowers and the gentle light; in the heat of summer it broods, indifferent to the sun-blasted bare fields.

History

The Krak is certainly the supreme example of Crusader castle building. Though its form evolved over two centuries, it shows the full flowering of the Hospitallers' style which went far beyond the stolid adaptations of Byzantine models that had previously influenced the castles of the first half of the 12th century.

The site lies on a hill called Jebel Kalakh, part of the Mount Lebanon/Jebel Ansariye

1 The origins of the word 'Krak' are intriguing. It could either be a corruption of the Arabic Husn al-Akrad with its reference to Kurds or a medieval French borrowing from the Syriac word for fortress.

range near the famous gap that leads to Homs from the sea via the plain called the Buqeia (*Homs; map R2). This had long been an important defensive site before the Crusaders arrived. There is some evidence that the Egyptians of the 18th Dynasty took an interest in it during their struggle with the Hittites for domination of Syria. Their rivalry worked itself to a climax at the nearby battlefield of Qadesh (*Tell Nabi Mend). Its usefulness was also evident to the Amir of Homs who installed a colony of Kurds and constructed the first fortress in 1031.

The Crusaders reached here first in February 1099 when Raymond de Saint Gilles, Count of Toulouse, resumed his journey south to Jerusalem after the bloody taking of *Maarat al-Numan. The site was reoccupied by the Amir of Homs when the Crusaders passed on. It was not until 1110 that it was retaken by Tancred, Regent of Antioch. The castle was enfeoffed to the Count of Tripoli. But the Crusader presence at this eastern limit of the County of Tripoli was overextended. Without European colonists, the feudal lords lacked the income needed to consolidate the inland castles to form a solid defence against the Muslim towns along the Orontes.

The rationalisation of the Crusaders' resources came in 1144 when Raymond II, Count of Tripoli, transferred the Krak along with his other dependant castles to the Knights Hospitaller. This secular order, originally founded (as its name implies) to shelter pilgrims reaching Jerusalem, was bound by solemn oaths, sanctioned and encouraged by the Church, to protect the Crusader presence in the east. Founded possibly earlier than the 12th century, its presence was extended to other Crusader principalities as the order's influence grew and as the need for an organisation devoted to the common defence of the Crusader states became more evident. Its work was complemented by another secular order, often bitter rivals of the Hospitallers, the Knights Templar.

The Hospitallers' decision massively to

expand the existing fortress after 1170[2] reflected several strategic considerations:

- The Krak, in conjunction with the defences at *Safita and Akkar (northern Lebanon) was vital to Crusader interests along the coast and thus land access between Europe and the Holy Land.
- It prevented encroachment on the rich coastal plain between Tripoli and Tartus. (The Homs Gap is the most easily accessible route from the coast to the interior between Turkey and northern Palestine.)
- It was, moreover, a forward defence position against the threat not only from the Muslim amirs of Homs and Hama but their more distant masters in Damascus and Aleppo (or even Cairo and Mosul).
- The fortress provided a secure base in a region largely populated then (as now) by Christians, albeit of the Orthodox persuasion.
- It guarded the exit from the rich Beqaa Valley in what is now Lebanon.

The Crusader castle survived two major Muslim challenges in the late 12th century. Nur al-Din (then nominally the Fatimid ally as ruler of Aleppo) was beaten beneath the castle in 1163 by a strong coalition of Christian forces from Tripoli and Antioch. In 1188, moving up the coast after his great victory over the Kingdom of Jerusalem at Hattin, Saladin (who had united the Muslim forces of Egypt, Syria and Mesopotamia) by-passed the castle after a one day trial siege but ravaged the rest of the Count of Tripoli's territory.

During the 13th century, the Crusader presence away from the coast thinned further and the garrison at the Krak dwindled as recruitment from Europe fell, especially after the disaster of Louis IX's Crusade in Egypt (1248–9). Nevertheless, the Krak continued to extract tribute from the Amir of Hama until 1267. In that year, however, the Mamluks under Sultan Baybars began a concerted effort to assert Muslim supremacy in Syria.

2 Also the year of a major earthquake in this part of Syria – Runciman II 1965: 389.

Baybars invested the Krak on 21 February 1271 (having already virtually isolated it from 1267). By 31 March he had gained entry at two points in its outer wall (at the southwest tower, no 6, and possibly east of the north barbican gate) thus bottling up the Hospitallers in the inner defences. Faced with the awe-inspiring inner southern battlements, he resorted to a psychological campaign to force the demoralised garrison to surrender which they did on favourable terms on 7 April. They were given safe conduct to Tripoli in return for a promise that they would remove themselves to a Christian country and not stay in Arab lands. The 'key of Christendom' thus passed into the hands of the Crusaders' most ruthless opponent.

The Mamluks themselves used the castle as a base, making considerable improvements to the structure, described later. Gradually, however, as the foreign threat disappeared, it fell into disuse as a military strongpoint. Muslim villagers settled within the walls and remained there until cleared out by the French antiquities administration in 1934. (They were relocated in the present village of al-Husn.) The French arrested the damage (relatively minor) which the centuries of civilian occupation had brought, even declaring the building a 'monument of France'. The castle was ceded to Syria in compensation for the damage inflicted by the French bombardment of Damascus in 1945. Considerable work has been done since 1946 to continue the work of restoring and safeguarding the fabric of the building.

The classic study of the fortress is by Deschamps but a recent German re-study (Biller (et al) 2006) has drawn important new conclusions on the sequence of the building history.

Visit

Even a leisurely visit of three or four hours may result in some confusion over the complex layout of the castle. It is wise to gain a good overall appreciation of how the defences are laid out by driving or walking around to the west side of the building as suggested in the location notes above. Stop a little way along the rise and look back at the magnificent expanse of the castle below you.

The Krak is built on a spur running off the higher mountain range to the south and its defences form an elongated loop. The blunt end is to the south from where it was most vulnerable, hence the greater accumulation of heavy bastions atop an outer ditch dug to isolate the fortress from the connecting spur. There are two distinct lines of fortifications: the outer, a curtain wall protected by round towers; and the inner ring which clings tightly on the south side to the innermost keep, protected by its great sloping base. In the case of the Krak, the keep or donjon is not physically separated within the inner defences but integrated into the south side of the central ring as part of a complex grouping of fortifications. Note especially the western outer ring with its five beautifully balanced and evenly spaced towers along the 150 m stretch of wall that Deschamps has described as 'an architectural perspective based on perfect harmony'. [3]

The two rings of defences were separated by an open space which incorporated many of the refinements in fixed defences that the early 13th century had perfected. A ditch surrounded the inner ring on three sides except on the south where the huge reservoir is located. The talus or glacis behind this fulfilled several purposes: a strengthened footing for the massive weight of wall above, particularly necessary in an earthquake-prone area; solid protection against undermining of the walls; and a smooth surface to discourage scaling. Above, the battlements with loopholes and jutting firing positions as well as the strategically placed bastions delivered fire along the full length of the walls.

This, however, is no theory-driven fortress plan. Partly its shape has been dictated by the site. But it also grew organically from the pre-1170 Crusader castle, the core

3 Deschamps *Châteaux – Crac* 1934: 150.

of the inner fortress. A quantum leap in fortress design separates the fortress in its pre-1170 phase and its subsequent reconstruction and improvement. This leap was driven by a new level of expertise combined with imaginative improvisation. This fresh approach to castle building reflected the lessons of the first Crusades, the secular orders' re-examination of the fortress' role in response to the challenge of Saladin, the adaptation of expert advice from Europe and the need to repair the devastation wrought by the severe earthquakes of 1157 and 1170. However varied the influences that contributed, the resulting complex, even allowing for the reinforcements and additions of the Mamluk period, is a building of extraordinary symmetry without undue concern for a rigid plan: it fully justifies the precepts about 'form following function' without the least self-consciousness.

Nothing identifiable remains of the castle as it stood before the Hospitallers took over in 1144 and certainly nothing of the Kurdish fortress. Much of the first Crusader fort was probably destroyed in the great earthquake of 1170. Under the Hospitallers, the castle was rebuilt in three main phases.

- 1170+ – walls of the inner fortress and chapel. These formed a ring of halls around a central courtyard with external projecting towers and a surrounding ditch on the north,

west and south sides. The standard of masonry is high with large rusticated blocks with flat margins.
- First half of 13th century – talus added to the west and south inner walls;

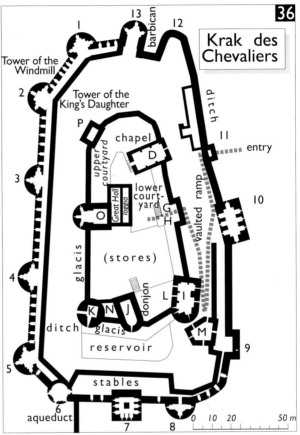

Krak des Chevaliers

greater part of the outer walls. These works too were of a high standard, possibly using Armenian craftsmen, but bossing was not used. Rampart defences on both fortified rings.
- Immediately before 1271– improvements to eastern outer defences.

The main Mamluk additions or improvements include the three outer towers on the south, the outer parts of the two north towers comprising the barbican, and the three square towers and curtain wall on the east which enclose the entrance passage and rising ramp.

Finally, note the aqueduct that once fed the castle's reservoir from the upper hills. Having taken in this view of the castle, return to the entrance on the eastern side.

As you face the entrance, the square tower on the left (no 10) with the sloping base is Mamluk (as is that further to the south (no 9), housing, on the upper storey, the Arab baths). The tower immediately in front (no 11), where the entrance and ticket office are located, is late Crusader but with an Arabic inscription of 1271 commemorating Baybars' restoration of the fortress. It was once probably approached by a drawbridge. The metal-clad door is Arab and brings you into the vaulted base of the tower. From here, the main entry to the upper castle follows a long (130 m) rising passage to the left, vaulted for protection and flagged with low steps to allow horses to negotiate it. (Note too the opening in the vaulting which not only admitted light but allowed missiles or hot oil to be rained upon any attackers who might get this far.) On the way, the ramp passes a gateway connected to tower 10 and then on the left a long chamber built into the outer defences, probably for the housing of guards or horses.

You then reach a point at which the passage turns back on itself in a hairpin bend. We will take that V–turn now as it rises hard right, leaving for later the inspection of the area between the two lines of walls (to which you gain access by going through the short passageway heading off diagonally before the sharp turn). Another steady ascent along a vaulted ramp (another Mamluk addition) leads you to a left turn through a tall vaulted gateway, protected by a series of doors, a large machicolation and a portcullis. This marks the point at which you pass through towers **G** and **H** of the second line of walls and enter the inner fortress. The inner parts of the gate date to the original Hospitaller construction.

Now it gets really confusing since there is little apparent symmetry to this tightly-packed series of buildings and covered chambers. Orient yourself carefully by stepping into the confined court in front of you. Opposite the entrance gateway (on the west) is a curious purely Gothic colonnaded building, a vaulted annexe leading into the great hall behind it. On the right (40 m north) are steps leading to an upper terrace which we shall explore later. Behind these stairs is the castle chapel. To the left of where you entered, a modern cement roof (reached by the stairs which double back above the gateway you have come through) protects an enormous vaulted hall, added to the Hospitaller inner fortress in the second quarter of the 13th century. If you look above this cement terrace, another terrace gives access to the huge southern towers noted in the initial survey.

Taking all these features in turn, begin with the colonnaded arcade or *loggia* (plate 13b) that precedes the great hall, a grouping of which Boase says: 'Apart from the cathedral of Tortosa, nothing of this period that survives in Syria can equal them in faultlessness of charm and elegance'.[4] The *loggia* is a product of the late phase of the Krak, possibly associated with the last major Crusade under Louis (1248–50). The Gothic style was by then established in France under Louis' influence and he may have brought a team to introduce the style to the Frankish east. The stonework is not in good condition (some of it has recently been restored) but it conveys something of the grace and lightness of structure otherwise foreign to the Crusader style. The roof is divided into seven bays of ogival vaulting. Two doorways correspond with the entrances to the great hall beyond and are matched by five windows opening on the courtyard. (The central colonnette and round tympanum above it were characteristic of the new style.) Note the carved Latin inscription on the north lintel of the window furthest to the right: 'Grace, wisdom and beauty you may enjoy but beware pride which alone can tarnish all the rest'.

4 Boase 1967: 56.

This graceful building may be contemporary with the **great hall**, which was an addition to the post-1170 ring of halls. Not quite as uplifting in character as the light-drenched *loggia*, the spacious (27 m by 7.5 m) hall behind it has a certain austere dignity. The two doors leading from the *loggia* end in pointed arches. Above are three windows. The hall's ceiling is divided by elegant cradle vaulting into three segments. The ribs come down to capitals embedded in the walls bearing various patterns of leaves, animals and *caryatids*, all badly damaged. A circular opening in the central vaulting served to ventilate the room. On the north, a double window is externally decorated with trefoiled tympanums.

Behind the great hall, a huge hall stretches for 120 m, taking up one whole side of the inner fortifications and looping around to the north to join the chapel. This hall probably served multiple purposes: kitchens (there is also a well and a bread oven at the south end), storage, accommodation and latrines (the latter can be inspected at the north end of the outer wall, just before the turn). This structure is within the immediately post-1170 Crusader construction forming the basic shape of the central fortress.

The **chapel** dates from the same phase of the Hospitaller fortress (1170+) when Romanesque influence was still evident. The original doorway to the chapel has been largely covered over by a staircase probably built during the final siege. A makeshift new entrance to the chapel was added via the porch to the south. The nave, divided into three bays, ends in an apse roughly oriented towards the east. On the southern side (right as you face the apse) are three roughly-carved niches. These (and the *minbar* or pulpit approached by steps) result from the conversion of the chapel to a mosque following the Mamluk occupation and are intended to orient the faithful towards Mecca during prayers. Otherwise the chapel is bare of decoration except for the barrel vaulting, a plain cornice and the slender support pilasters. There is a small window with a pointed arch driven through the thick masonry of the apse (which gives on to

the outer wall of the inner fortress).

Take the staircase that cuts diagonally across the chapel entrance to ascend to the upper court. Here you will find on the northwestern side a building known as the 'Tower of the King's Daughter' (tower **P**). The lower part is late 12th century but the upper machicolations are probably Mamluk. The upper hall, now a café, contains on the outer wall 12 niches which the recent re-intepretation of the tower assumes were latrines rather than defensive firing slits. (The outer face of this tower which you cannot see from here will be described later.) From the nearby parapets, a view across to *Safita and the coast can be obtained.

Return now to the lower court and concentrate on the two levels at the southern end of the inner fortress. First, inspect the cavernous reaches of the pillared area under the modern cemented roof, probably added in the first half of the 13th century. This space was probably originally intended for a number of purposes – kitchen, refectories, storage of provisions, troop accommodation. A further storage area provided with an oil press is located right at the back but there is no natural light to guide you in the dank interior.

More salubrious is the upper part of the south area. This forms the so-called keep or donjon, a grouping described as 'probably the finest mediaeval line of defence anywhere'[5] consisting of two towers of enormous strength (**I** and **J**) plus a third (on the west – **K**) meant to provide enhanced security and comfort to the senior ranks of the garrison. The central tower (**J** – sometimes called the Tower of Monfret), midway along the south wall, consists of three storeys. In shape rectangular with a round face to the south, it is built of massive masonry to withstand heavy bombardment from the high ground to the south. The upper floor has a large mullioned window and, on the south, a single large loophole. The parapet on the roof has disappeared.

---

5 Cathcart King 1949: 84.

The southeast tower (**I**) is larger in plan and shows the huge scale of the fortress' defences. Its upper chamber is supported on a central pillar 6 m thick. It likewise presents a rounded face to the south. It was joined to the central tower by a heavily fortified and wide structure, the upper defences of which have not survived. On this bridging platform, engines of war could be assembled to confront invaders from the south and the two towers could be linked by protective parapets.

The third tower (**K**), on the southwest corner, is not a part of the heavily fortified donjon, being lighter in construction and different in purpose. (This circular building, however, was also linked to the central tower by a terrace which formed part of the defensive front facing south.) This apartment is interpreted as housing on the upper floor the lord of the castle. This round vaulted room (dated 1260), reached by a spiral staircase, is relatively elegant and light in design, the ribs of the vaults being supported on colonnettes built into the wall. A band of rosettes runs around the walls. Runciman describes this room as 'entirely Western in spirit',[6] a product of the 13th century striving for height and light. The tower's roof (not for the faint-hearted) provides the best vantage point in the castle with stunning views towards Safita and the sea (if haze is not a problem).

We have now finished with the inner fortress. You should retrace your steps along the entrance ramp until you reach the hairpin bend. From here take the doorway noted earlier which leads south to the space between the inner and outer lines of wall. You come out under a large bastion of irregular shape (**M**) and shortly afterwards will see the stagnant waters of the reservoir. Immediately above is the great slope of masonry supporting the three towers (**I, J, K**) of the prestige accommodation wing that you have just inspected. Though you have earlier gained an appreciation of the defences from the upper battlements, it is worth pausing here to admire the great towers surmounting the talus, 'the most striking

and unforgettable aspect of this noble building' (Boase, plate 14a).[7]

From this point, you should also look back to the bastion through which you passed (**M**). Half way up the wall above you note the two (now headless) lions facing each other. Though they have the same stance as the lions of Baybars' insignia, they are Latin in origin, the odd-shaped building having been erected in the second half of the 13th century to protect the bend in the ascending ramp from fire from the south.

Walk across the open space towards the outer southern defences. You will notice in front of you a long (60 m) hall, probably stables to judge by the loops to accommodate rings for the tethering of animals. Above this is a parapet leading to a substantial square tower (tower **7**), the centrepiece of the lower range of southern defences. This was the work of Sultan Qalawun (1285) who rebuilt the Crusader base. The vast interior room comprises a vaulted roof supported on a massive central pillar, a system common to both Muslims and Crusaders. Flanking this at either end of the lower southern defences (and predating it) are round towers (nos **6, 8**), both, according to inscriptions, the work of Baybars' reign. The inner room of the tower on the left (no 8) contains a central octagonal pillar which bears an inscribed frieze in Arabic.

From the west end of the 60 m hall, you can work your way around the reservoir and stroll either along the ditch that runs between the full length of the inner and outer walls or the parapet of the outer wall. On the lower wall are five matching half-round towers (nos **1–5**) that strengthen the curtain wall and whose symmetry was admired in our initial survey.

While you are tracing the lower defences, take account of the western face of the inner fortress – note numerous loopholes between the crenellations. The long talus or glacis (smoothly surfaced sloping front) wraps around from the south continuing along the western front. North of the

6 Runciman III 1965: 383.   7 Boase 1967: 54.

tower which housed the master (**K**), there is only one other break in the sheer wall above the glacis, a semi-circular bastion (**O**) which was linked to a 120 m gallery along the top of the wall. This also linked a series of passageways built into the space between the glacis and the old wall, ending up at a sally-port near the base. This network allowed reinforcements to be rushed to the outer defences.

On the northwestern bend, the Tower of the King's Daughter protudes prominently, its great sheer wall dropping straight to the level of the ditch. This huge mass of stone is relieved by a series of blind arches creating a striking effect. Though architecturally impressive, the origins of this arrangement probably reflect several practical changes of plan after the tower was originally added to the post-1170 fortress to protect a postern gate. The original three tall arches concealed machicolations to rain down projectiles on potential attackers at the base of the wall, a device which Boase has described as 'elaborate and somewhat ineffective'.[8] The machicolation arrangement was later moved higher up the wall, though in the recent re-interpretation by Schmitt the purpose of the slits is not seen as defensive but, as noted earlier, to sluice waste from the latrines.[9]

After the outer wall turns the corner and faces north, the last half-round tower juts out from a more prominent base than the others. This used to house a

windmill and so earned the title Burj al-Tauneh (Tower of the Windmill – no **1**). After a gap in which a modern entrance to the castle has been inserted (originally for the convenience of the Arab villagers) the next two rounded bastions (**12, 13**) formed a barbican which once protected a postern gate.

From this northern curve in the open space between the two walls, you can either return the same way to the bend half way up the ascending entrance passage or continue clockwise and take the stairs and a passage at the left of tower **G**. The second route takes you past the only stretch of the inner fortress that has remained unchanged since the first Hospitaller construction. This leads you back to the top of the vaulted entry passage from where you can descend to the main entrance.

In the town below the castle, a minaret of the early 14th century attached to a mosque rebuilt by Baybars, possibly on the site of a church.

REFS: Biller (*et al*) *Der Crac des Chevaliers* 2006; Boase 1967: 51–6; Cathcart King 1949: 83–92; Deschamps *Châteaux – Crac* 1934; Kennedy 1994: 146–63; Michaudel 2004: 45–77; Rihaoui 1982.

---

8 Boase 1967: 55.
9 See Biller (*et al*) 2006: 136–41.

L

Latakia

 اللزّقيّة

VARIANTS: Ramitha or Mazabda (Phn); Leuke Akte, Laodikeia (Grk); Laodicea, Laodicea ad Mare (Lat); la Liche (Cru); al-Ladhqiye (Arb). PERIOD: Hel/Rom/Arb RATING: – MAP: 37, R2

LOCATION: Major Syrian seaport, 320 km north of Damascus.

Like most other cities of the Levantine coast, Latakia has played its role in entertaining many of Syria's conquerors. Little of that wanton quality remains but there is a residual trace of Mediterranean and Levantine air in the older quarter, conveying a whiff of Alexandria or Beirut when the sea breeze sweeps through in the late afternoon.

History

Even before Alexander or Pompey, the town had known a procession of conquerors. It was a Phoenician village nearly a millennium before Christ but fell to the Assyrians and then the Persians who made it part of their fifth satrapy. In 333 BC Alexander took it, just after the great battle with the Persians at Issus not far to the north (near Alexandretta). It became a major town of the Seleucid Kingdom under Seleucus I Nicator (r 311–281 BC). (Apamea and Antioch were other major Seleucid centres but they were 'new cities' compared with Latakia.)

Named in honour of the mother of Seleucus (later modified by the Romans to Laodicea ad Mare), it played a vital role in Seleucid and Roman times. In addition to serving as a port (more reliable than the fickle conditions at Arwad to the south), it was particularly known for its wine and is mentioned by Strabo[1] as the main supplier to the Alexandrian market. Mark Antony whose eventful relationship

1 *Geography* XVI, 2, 9.

with Cleopatra sent him storming up and down this coast, won the town's temporary support by granting autonomy and some remission of taxes. By the late second century, Septimius Severus declared it capital of Syria (194–202), snubbing the more degenerate Antioch which had supported the aspirations of its governor, Pescennius Niger, his rival for the emperorship. This initiative probably resulted in a major upgrading of the city, including the building of four colonnaded main streets, embellishing the Hellenistic grid plan. The role of capital soon, however, devolved back to Antioch. In the second century, epigraphic evidence indicates that the city became a major port for the Roman army's legionary bases to the east, probably providing a more reliable anchorage for large fleets and the off-loading of equipment than Antioch's port, Seleucia. Zenobia seized it in her ill-advised drive to the sea that so provoked Rome's retaliation in 272.

There were bad earthquakes in 494 and 555, just as Latakia was facing a new Persian threat. Justinian, who fortified many towns in northern Syria against the Persians, rebuilt much of Latakia; he, too, favoured it over Antioch. In 638, Latakia was lost to Byzantium after the Arab armies swept into Syria. The Byzantines mounted a devastating raid in 705 but it was not until 968 that they reasserted their control in the area, fitfully retaining Latakia as their southern-most port until it was retaken by the Turks in 1084.

The Crusades again put it on the fault line between Christian and Muslim. It was taken by a Crusader fleet in the autumn of 1097, even before Antioch fell. It lapsed back to local control and became an irritant in Byzantine-Crusader relations, for a while governed in condominium between Raymond of Toulouse and the emperor. It was retaken by the Crusaders in 1103 and 1108 and incorporated by Tancred into the Principality of Antioch. The city, along with *Jeble, was included in 1126 in the dowry of Alice, daughter of King Baldwin of Jerusalem, who made an unsuccessful bid to assume the regency of Antioch. Later in the century, the town

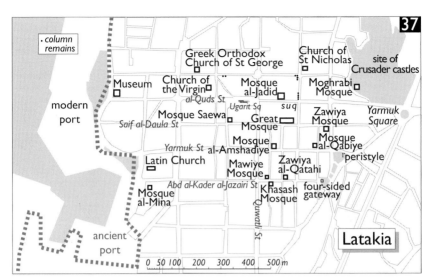

rated a duke who took charge of local affairs.

Saladin took and pillaged it in 1188, his amirs carrying off much of its marble to adorn their houses, according to the Arab chronicler, Imad al-Din. It remained a Muslim enclave on the coast under Aleppo's control until 1260. In that year, in the first of the Mongol invasions, it was returned to the Principality of Antioch whose ruler had shown due deference to the Central Asian invaders. It remained as a truncated Crusader enclave under Bohemond VI even after the fall of Antioch in 1268. But the small Crusader garrison proved incapable of offering effective defence of this last remnant of the principality and it reverted to Arab hands in 1287 during Qalawun's series of victories following the taking of Marqab (1285). In a gratuitous gesture, the neo-Crusaders, the Lusignans of Cyprus under Peter I, returned in 1367 to sack and burn the city. It had housed a Venetian trading colony from 1208 until Sultan Barsbay expelled it in 1436.

By then in a semi-ruined conditioned, Latakia under the Ottomans became merely a dependency of Tripoli (Lebanon) or *Hama. Its fortunes revived somewhat in the 17th century through the silk and tobacco trade and by the 18th century it had again become a major port, comparable to Smyrna or Tripoli. However, it could not sustain this role in the 19th century due to competition from Beirut and Tripoli. By the beginning of the last century it was a fishing village (population 7000) with a silted-up harbour barely able to shelter four to six boats. It resumed a more prominent role under the French when it was the capital of the Alawite state set up during the Mandate period.

Visit

In spite of this complex history, the physical look of the town is less than romantic. The tightly ordered grid plan of the old city indicates a basically Hellenistic pattern refurbished probably in the early third century AD by Septimius Severus when its main streets were lavishly colonnaded. The consistency of its historic role, however, has meant that its ancient remains have largely been obliterated by re-development over the centuries. There are a few columns here and there (often re-erected in ungainly fashion in the middle of some frantic swirling roundabout), the scrubby remains of the acropolis (east of the town), one or two churches with bits of ancient chapels or Crusader rooms and the four-sided Roman monumental gateway (see next para), perhaps commemorating a triumph now forgotten.

In the southern part of the old city, one of the few surviving indications of the town's past glory is the just-mentioned **four-sided gateway (tetraporticus)**, erected at the eastern end of one of the main transverse streets. The French scholar Sauvaget reconstructed the plan of Roman Laodicea in a study completed in the thirties based on a grid (its elements measured 112 m by 57 m) marked by a long (2 km) axis running between the sea on the west and low hills on the east. The gateway was once seen as the eastern entrance to the city. You can still see on the west face the point at which the colonnade of the *decumanus* terminated but there the resemblance to Roman arches marking entry to a city ends as the gateway gave access to a temple compound to the north. Note the remarkable weapons frieze around the attic level of the arch.

The dome within the arch is intact and is set upon an octagon which provides the transition to the rectangular base. As the sides are not quite square, the pendentives which fill the corners are irregular. The stonework and the construction are not particularly fine but the arch is clearly robust having withstood the ravages of 18 centuries, including several major earthquakes, since its construction, probably in the late second century.

Northeast of the arch (125 m), remains of a peripteral temple are found in a small reserve. (There is no evidence that this temple was associated with the tetraporticus.) Other surviving granite columns that once supported the porticos of the main Roman streets still appear haphazardly in the central area with several collected in a small plaza along al-Quds St, once probably the city's *decumanus*.

Latakia has a sizeable Greek Orthodox population. Two of its churches are particularly worth visiting. The **Church of the Virgin** lies in the suq in the

block south of the archbishop's office. The original building may go back as far as Byzantine times, its simple single-nave plan being embellished in the 18th century by an ornate marble *iconostasis*. A smaller chapel with an icon of the Virgin believed to have miraculous properties is on the right. The second church (also undated), the Church of St Nicholas in Maysalun St (one intersection north of al-Quds St), includes a notable collection of icons of the Syrian school of the 17th and 18th centuries and an ebony wood throne dated 1721. Right of the main nave is a chapel to St Moses the Ethiopian.

Several of Latakia's mosques (in the area east and south of al-Quds St – see map 37) are worth inspecting, at least for their façades. They include the early 13th century Masjid al-Kebir (Great Mosque) and the Masjid al-Jadid (New Mosque, 18th century), erected by Suleiman Pasha al-Azem. On the lintel above the entry to the Great Mosque is an inscription (1211) recording al-Zaher Ghazi's construction of a minaret.

The **Museum** (al-Quds St) was originally a tobacco khan (perhaps 16th century). The collection comprises mainly small finds from Ugarit, Ras Ibn Hani, Ras al-Basit and Tell Sukas displayed in three halls.

The rising ground north of Yarmuk Square carries no evidence of the twin Crusader castles. In Jumhuriye Square stands a group of four elegant **monolith columns**, topped with Corinthian capitals. They are said to be part of the Temple of Adonis whose legend, sourced to the mountainous region of northern Lebanon, was prevalent in this area. More likely they are simply part of a colonnaded street rescued and repositioned here for aesthetic reasons. South of the four-sided gateway remains of a sizeable Roman theatre were still visible in the 1920s but are now overbuilt.

REFS: Chéhab 1983: 95; Elisséeff 'al-Ladhikiyya' *EI*1; Kader 1996; Pensabene 1997: 385–98; Rey-Coquais 'Laodicée-sur-Mer' in Dabrowa 1995: 149–63; Sa'adé 1976; Sauvaget *Plan – Laodicée* 1935: 81–114; Wiet 1931: 273–92.

M

Maalula (Plate 14b)

معلولا لا

VARIANTS: Calamona (?anc); Magluda (Byz); Maalloula
PERIOD: Byz/Arb ALT: 1650 m; RATING: * MAP: R2

LOCATION: Take the Damascus-Homs highway north for 50 km. As the road ascends an escarpment, look out for a Turkish caravanserai (Khan al-Arus). Take Maalula exit and follow road +8 km.

Though rich in historical and religious associations, Maalula preserves few remains of its past. Until its recent expansion, it was a village of some charm, its tempered houses piled up on the lower slopes of an escarpment that rises sheer above the village. There is still an uncompromising beauty to the setting with the gorge cutting deep into the escarpment.

Maalula has three claims to fame – its setting; its early Christian associations; and the resistance of the villagers to the replacement of Aramaic by Arabic as the language of communication. There may be some doubt about the extent to which Aramaic, the language spoken by Christ and the popular lingua franca of the area until the Arab conquest in the seventh century, remains in active use. However, even the vestigial survival of Western Aramaic (Syriac) as a spoken tongue is a tribute to the tenacity with which the inhabitants of Maalula have clung to their identity.[1]

There are two monasteries above the village whose loyalty is divided between the Greek Catholic and Orthodox churches. Most interesting historically and architecturally is the Greek Catholic Monastery of St Sergius on the escarpment left of the gorge. Ask for directions to the church of Mar Sarkis and follow the steep road which ascends to the plateau from the left hand side of the village. Icons dating back to the 18th century are worth inspecting but the church which takes the form of a Greek cross approximately 25 by 20 metres is remarkable in itself – perhaps one of the oldest surviving in Syria. Built on the site of a pagan temple (remains of the foundation level lie to the east), it has architectural elements which go back to the Byzantine period (fifth–sixth century). Note particularly the marble offering tables in the central and left apse. The cult of Sergius (and his companion, Bacchus) was particularly widespread in Byzantine times in the Syrian desert and favoured by the Ghassanids (*Resafa).

Descend to the village via the ravine. Just over the escarpment on the right before you descend there are remains of ancient rock-cut tombs. The path descends through a siq (defile) cooled by a bubbling stream and brings you to the second shrine located at the mouth of the gorge, the Greek Orthodox women's monastery dedicated to Mar Taqla (St Thecla). The saint (reputedly a pupil of St Paul and one of the first martyrs of the Church) is believed to have taken refuge in the ravine and, in some accounts, to be buried in a cave above the monastery. There is no indication that any parts of the monastery or chapel date back to the Byzantine period.

There are six other churches (and two mosques) in the village itself. In the Church of St Elias (south of St Thecla), a fourth century mosaic was found but disappeared after its unearthing in 1925.

REFS: Hakim & Jawish 2000; Keriaky 1996; Nasrallah, Elias Ma`loula Damascus 2003; Nasrullah, Joseph 1943–44, 1952–58.

---

1 They are, however, not the only community in Syria to have done so. The Syriac-speaking communities (numerous particularly in the Northeast Province to which they fled last century from Iraq) speak a more diluted form of neo-Aramaic which was preserved during their long exile in Persia and northern Iraq.

Maarat al-Numan

معرة النعمان

VARIANTS: Arra, Megara (Grk); Marra, la Marre (Cru) PERIOD: Arb RATING: * MAP: R2, R3

LOCATION: The Hama-Aleppo highway passes on the eastern outskirts of Maarat 108 km north of Homs, 73 km south of Aleppo.

History

Maarat al-Numan lies in a moderately prosperous agricultural belt on the southern edge of the section of the limestone country of northern Syria, the Jebel Zawiye, which separates the Orontes and the desert. Though known to the Greeks and Romans as Marra, surviving buildings attest only to its history since the coming of Islam. Its modern name refers to al-Numan Ibn Bashir al-Ansari, a companion of the Prophet who was made governor of the region by the Umayyad Caliph Muawiya (r 661–81).

Given its location on the Damascus-Homs-Hama-Aleppo corridor and on the edge of the Limestone Massif, it has been contested several times by forces seeking to control northern Syria. The Byzantines took it in 968 during the attempt by the Emperor Nicephorus Phocas to profit from instability and regain possession of northern Syria. Their destructive occupation was short-lived, however, as the Muslims moved in by 996 and the town returned to Aleppo's orbit. The Crusaders passed this way in 1098 on their initial march south to Jerusalem and halted while they disputed tactics and options. Their three week siege was a particularly frustrating experience, made worse by rivalry between two leaders, Raymond de Saint Gilles, Count of Toulouse, and Bohemond, Prince of Antioch, who had already fallen out over the siege of Antioch. The latter offered to spare the citizens in return for surrender, just at the moment when the impetuous Raymond was successful in breaching the walls. The townspeople were cut down in a famous massacre which saw the slaughter of the town's Muslims including many women and children.

In the subsequent occupation amidst a hostile environment, Christian troops resorted to cannibalism to avoid starvation.

Our people suffered a severe famine. I shudder to speak of it; our people were so frenzied by hunger that they tore flesh from the buttocks of the Saracens who had died there, which they cooked and chewed and devoured with savage mouths, even when it had been roasted insufficiently on the fire. And so the besiegers were more harmed than the besieged.

(Raymond of Fulchre)[2]

From Maarat, the Crusade leadership divided with Raymond leading the march on Jerusalem while Bohemond contented himself with the Principality of Antioch.

Though this point so far to the east into Muslim territory was precariously held, the town did not permanently revert to Muslim control until Zengi reoccupied it in 1135 as part of the first concerted effort to dislodge the Crusaders from inland areas. Under the later Ayyubids, it was dependant on Aleppo and, under the Mamluks, on Hama.

The town has been a notable centre of Muslim pilgrimage and is particularly famed as the birthplace of the blind poet, Abu al-Ala al-Maari (973–1057). A modern tomb marks his burial.

Visit

In the main square in the centre of town, you will find the **Great Mosque**, built on the site of an ancient temple-church and re-using many of its predecessors' remains. The two domed pavilions in the central courtyard rest on ancient columns. Attached to the mosque is a handsome minaret originally erected in the first half of the 12th century but rebuilt after an earthquake in 1170. The

2 Quoted (in translation) in Hallam *Chronicles of the Crusades* 1989: 86–7.

rebuilding is attributed to Kahir al-Sarmani (signature on west face) who sought to rival by imitation the tower of the Great Mosque of Aleppo.[3] The same architect is responsible for the nearby (southwest of Great Mosque) madrasa of the Shafei tradition dated to 1199 – Madrasa Abu al-Fawaris, entry on east side, tre-foiled arch; pyramidal cupola over vestibule; *iwan*; prayer hall to south; tomb of founder in northeast corner.

In the southeastern part of the central area, an early 16th century khan (Khan Murad Pasha – the largest khan in Syria, 7000 m²) has been converted to a **museum** with striking effect. It contains an interesting collection of objects including mosaics and pottery from many periods, a tribute to the work of the late curator, Kamel Chéhadé. The mosaics have been transferred from nearby sites including a fifth century mosaic from as far as Homs. Note especially the mosaic depicting Romulus and Remus, found at al-Firkiye (north of Maarat) and dated to 510. A second mosaic of the same date from al-Firkiye depicts animals in a field bordered by vines. A mosaic from the ruins of a church in Selemiye (second room counting anti-clockwise from entrance) carries representations of animals. In the centre of the courtyard is a *tekkiye* or foundation for the instruction of initiates to the Dervish sect. A doorway to the left once led to the hammam and suq attached to the khan (now managed separately). Opposite the museum is another Ottoman khan, the Khan Assaad Pasha al-Azem (1748 – visit not possible).

On the northwestern edge of town, near the road to al-Riha and the Jebel Riha, you will find the remains of the medieval **citadel**. The scale is surprisingly small. Although subsequent habitation has seriously dismantled the original fortifications, the shape of the enclosure is preserved and the recent removal of housing has exposed more of the fabric. Remains include Ayyubid-style structures, in some cases using Byzantine or earlier decorated stones.

3　The Aleppo tower is also the work of an architect who originated in Sarman near Aleppo, Hassan Ibn Mukri al-Sarmani.

REFS: Herzfeld II 1943: 36–9; Korn I 2004: 263–5; Shéhadé 1997; Elisséeff *Ma`arrat' El*I; Maalouf 1977: 37–40.

Maraclée

خراب مرقئة

VARIANTS: Maraclea, Maraccas (Cru); Marqiye (Arb) PERIOD: Cru RATING: T MAP: R2

LOCATION: Just below the waterline, 16 km north of *Tartus; 11 km south of *Qalaat Marqab. Opposite the village of Kharrab Marqiye.

The small **sea tower-fortress** of Maraclée was built by the local *seigneur*, Barthélemy, in 1277 several years after the fall of the *Krak des Chevaliers and at the end of the Crusader period. The tower-fortress in the sea was built in view of the insecurity of the nearby land castle which had attracted the particular hostility of the Mamluk sultan, Baybars, and which he had had destroyed in 1271 (see below). (Baybars was incensed by Barthélemy's consorting with the Mongol invaders of Syria under Hulaga.) The next sultan, Qalawun, took the nearby castle of Marqab in 1285. Having found the sea tower impregnable, he ordered Bohemond VII whose days were numbered as Lord of Tripoli, to have the tower dismantled, holding him responsible for abetting its construction. (Tripoli itself fell to Qalawun in 1289.) Bohemond apparently obliged, ordering Barthélemy to dismantle it.

Certainly nothing of the building remains above the waterline, though from a boat the foundations can just be discerned below the surface of the sea about 180 m from the shore, at the point where the track to the village of Bezzak leaves the old Tartus-Baniyas road. The remains of the 9 m by 15 m tower come to within a few centimetres of the surface. The stream known as the Nahr Marqiye and the hamlet of Kharrab Marqiye or Merakieh lie near this point.

The **land castle** was established long before the tower and was held by a Frankish family with close links to the lords of Marqab. The site of Maraclée was taken in the earliest phase of the Crusades (1099) and was later important enough to warrant a mention in several Crusader records and to have rated a bishop (shared with Tortosa). It was the subject of a prolonged dispute in the 13th century between the local family, the de Ravendels, and the Hospitallers for its possession. A compromise was reached in 1241. The castle, as noted earlier, was largely destroyed by Baybars in 1271 and no traces remain.

REFS: van Berchem & Fatio 1914: 96; Deschamps *Châteaux* – III 1973: 146, 323–6; Dussaud 1927: 126; Gabrieli 1984: 339–41; Huygens 1972.

Mari (Tell Hariri)

تل حريري

VARIANTS: Tell Hariri (Arb) PERIOD: EBA, MBA RATING: * MAP: 38, 39, R5

LOCATION: 12 km west-northwest of Abu Kemal (Syria-Iraq border). Take the road from Deir al-Zor south towards Abu Kemal. At 24 km south of *Dura Europos, the tell can be seen across the flat land to the left, between the road and the Euphrates River.

History

Mari is a site of central importance, 'a unique example of a bronze age palace' giving 'an exceptionally concentrated picture of the Syro-Mesopotamian world' in the words of its excavator, Jean-Claude Margueron. Discovered in 1935, the excavation of this rare example of a Mesopotamian palace found with its accoutrements and archives relatively intact has been one of the keys to the unravelling of the history of the Syria-Mesopotamia region during the early millennia of recorded history. Its excavation rested for many years in the hands of the French archaeologist, André Parrot, who supervised the excavations from 1933 to 1974; a remarkable record. The research was funded partly by the Louvre where many of the most important pre-war finds can now be seen. Since 1979, excavations have continued under

Margueron with the wider aim of defining Mari's role in the Euphrates Valley and in the context of the Mesopotamian world of the third and second millennia by researching its economic resources and agricultural base.

Mari was the third millennium BC royal city-state par excellence. Margueron has argued that a city as prosperous as Mari could only exist by drawing on a prosperous region. Its key position between the Khabur-Euphrates confluence and the cliffs further south at *Baghuz explain the selection of this site for a new city. It was intended to control access between central and southern Mesopotamia, on the one hand, and, on the other, the drier plains of northwest Syria, the Euphrates-Khabur area and the Anti-Taurus uplands. Caravan routes through Mari also traded metals and metal products both along the east-west and north-south routes.

Mari was first occupied at the beginning of the third millennium (**Mari I** – 2900–2550 BC). Positioned in an area of limited natural agricultural potential, its prosperity relied not only on its trading position but on a sophisticated irrigation scheme. The city was circular in shape (1.9 km in diameter) with an enclosing double rampart and ditch, a notable example of early organised urban planning. Today's mound is only a truncated portion, the southwest sector of the original plan. It lies 2 km from the Euphrates but, in the third millennium, through it flowed an artificial canal meeting the dual needs of water supply and control of navigation on the river. Recent evidence indicates extensive development of other canals, including a 120 km link between the Khabur and Euphrates Rivers. The evidence of the earliest city is still fragmentary and it is still too early to determine the influences (eg Uruk) which played on the first inhabitants.

The next major period of development saw the construction of the first great palace and the Temples of Ishtar, Nini-Zaza and Shamash. Re-populated after a period of abandonment, **Mari II** (c2500–c2200 BC) came under the Akkadian Empire

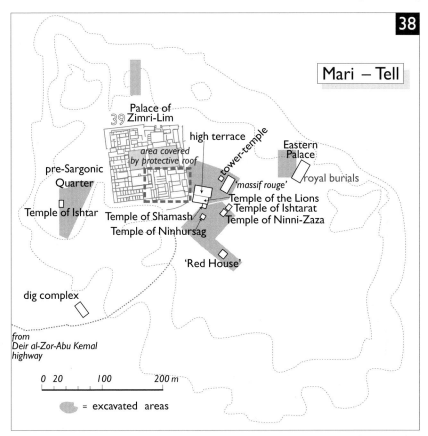

38

Mari – Tell

Palace of Zimri-Lim (39)

high terrace

tower-temple

Eastern Palace

area covered by protective roof

pre-Sargonic Quarter

'massif rouge' royal burials

Temple of Ishtar

Temple of the Lions

Temple of Shamash

Temple of Ishtarat

Temple of Ninni-Zaza

Temple of Ninhursag

'Red House'

dig complex

from Deir al-Zor-Abu Kemal highway

0   20   100   200 m

= excavated areas

(c2300–2150 BC founded by Sargon of Akkad). Mari II may have been destroyed by Naram-Sin of Akkad (r 2254–17 BC). **Mari III** (2200–1760 BC) began with a period during which a succession of local princes (Shakkanakku) perhaps served as governors for a foreign kingdom as early as the period of Akkad, building a new palace on the site of the old. Its population was boosted by the arrival c2000 BC of many Amorites (a Semitic people). Following another period of obscurity, Mari had little chance of holding out against the rising power, Babylon. Occupied for a time by the Amorite leader Shamsi-Adad (1813–1782 BC), it briefly found its independence under Zimri-Lim (1775–60) only to lose it to Hammurabi of Babylon (r c1792–50) in 1760. Mari's walls were razed during Hammurabi's occupation. The temples were sacked and the Palace of Zimri-Lim was stripped of much of its contents, set on fire and its walls systematically dismantled. Babylon was now master of all the trade routes stretching north and west to the Anti-Taurus and the Mediterranean seaboard. The city was no longer a centre of any importance though there are signs of limited re-occupation as late as the Seleucid and Parthian periods.

Visit

While this is the most impressive and best preserved of the MBA palaces unearthed in the region, the largely mud-brick remains, which have been successively peeled off to expose the layers beneath, are difficult to appreciate. The task of orienting yourself is especially challenging if the weather is inordinately hot or muddy as, depending on the season, it often is in this region of Syria. Only a small section of the tell, the sacred enclosure of the pre-Sargonic

East (275 rooms covering 2.5 ha) and was constructed across several centuries though it bears the name of the last ruler, Zimri-Lim. The fact that the building was deliberately destroyed, its mud walls half knocked down to fill in the rooms,

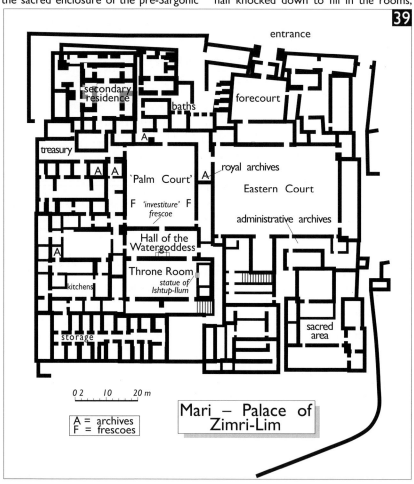

39

entrance

secondary residence

baths

forecourt

treasury

A

'Palm Court'   A

royal archives

Eastern Court

F 'investiture' F
frescoe

administrative archives

Hall of the
Watergoddess

A

Throne Room
statue of
Ishtup-Ilum

kitchens

sacred
area

storage

0 2   10   20 m

A = archives
F = frescoes

Mari – Palace of
Zimri-Lim

palace, is protected by roofing from the eroding effects of rain. Visitors should be conscious that many of the structures unearthed over the years cannot now be readily identified.

The **Palace of Zimri-Lim** (northwest segment of the mound) is one of the most extensive excavated in the Middle

accounts for its preservation.

A rich variety of finds was recovered from the palace including the notable statues of Ishtup-Ilum (governor of Mari) and of a water goddess (now in the *Aleppo Museum). An archive of 15,000 tablets was also found, recording the household accounts of the palace as well as diplomatic and administrative records of the kingdom coverng the period 1810–1760 BC. The walls of the palace survived in places to a height of 5 m and spread across a formidable range of rooms arranged around two courtyards.

The palace bears the name of its last ruler (1775–59) before its destruction though it is probably the work of his predecessors over 250 years. The earlier palace (Mari II) was largely levelled in the building of the new palace. The main gateway was on the northeastern side of the roughly square palace compound which was originally surrounded by a mud-brick rampart. Moving south, a small courtyard gave access via a zig-zag passage to the larger of the two courtyards (east). At its centre was a reservoir inserted into the remains of the earlier palace. A sanctuary, possibly a dynastic shrine to Ishtar, lay on the south side of this courtyard as it had in the Mari II palace. The southeastern corner gave directly on to the area used as a **sacred zone** since the preceding millennium and then to a storage area.

The other (west) courtyard, dubbed the Palm Court, had a more official role, the south façade carrying remains of a frescoe including an investiture scene (now partly preserved in the Louvre). The courtyard gave access (to the south) to a long antechamber (where the water goddess statue, mentioned above, was found) and then to the rectangular throne room of impressive dimensions (25 m by 11 m and at least 12 m high). The throne itself stood against the west wall. To the west of this second courtyard lies a maze of living, administrative and service quarters with the royal apartment probably located above and to the east of the throne room and a secondary residence (for the wives?) in the northwestern quarter. There is evidence in many places of a sophisticated plumbing system. Many of the rooms were decorated with wall paintings (partly preserved now in the *Aleppo and *Damascus Museums as well as in the Louvre).

To the east are remains of a **high terrace** which around 2000 BC replaced an earlier

terrace of red bricks. The great elevated rectangle (42 m by 29 m) with pilastered sides appears to have served as an open space, probably for sacrifices. Probably associated with it was a tower temple to the northeast, an idea in the Syrian rather than Mesopotamian tradition. Around this southeastern corner of the palace were once grouped other **religious buildings**, including the prominent Temple of the Lions (c 2000 BC immediately south of the terrace) and the Temple of Shamash (located southeast of the high terrace).[4] Today these buildings are too eroded to be recognisable. In the Temple of Ninni-Zaza (mid third millennium BC) was discovered a remarkably rich trove of statues including that of the singer Ur-Nanshe, now in the Damascus Museum.

The remains of the **Temple of Ishtar** (third millennium) were found on the western limits of the tell. Its layout comprised an inner sanctum lying within a central hall flanked by rooms reserved for the priests. Other facilities included a well, an oven, a libation basin and a table for offerings. As only the priests could enter the inner sanctum, small votive figures were presented by the priests on behalf of devotees.

REFS: Margueron 2002–3: 47–57; Margueron *Mari, Métropole de l'Euphrate* Paris 2004; Parrot *Mari, capitale fabuleuse* 1974.

Masyaf (Plate 17b)

مصياف

VARIANTS: Marsyas, Marsos (anc); Massiat (Cru); 'Castle of the Assassins' PERIOD: Cru/ Ism RATING: * MAP: R2

LOCATION: Masyaf is 51 km inland from Baniyas along a spectacular mountain road, initially clinging to the southern slopes of the deep ravine of the Baniyas or Jobar River (the ancient Chrysorrhoas) and passing through the village of Qadmus (27 km). More directly accessible from *Hama, 40 km to the east.

4 The lions are found today in the Louvre, testimony to the skill of the Mari bronzesmiths. The idea of guardian lion figures occurs also at *Ebla.

History

Masyaf houses the best preserved, and probably the most famous, of the Ismaeli castles of the mountainous region between the Orontes and the coast. It is superbly located and the sight of the castle outlined against the green of the Jebel Ansariye behind is striking when seen from the road from Hama.

In the 12th century, a network of fortresses established by the Ismaelis (see box next page) protected their presence in the mountains to which they had fled to escape persecution by orthodox Sunni rulers in Aleppo and Damascus. The site had been used in Aramaean, Roman and Byzantine times and the present fortifications include remains going back to the tenth century when the Byzantine and Arab (Hamdanid) forces were active in the area. Written records indicate that it was seized by the Crusaders in 1103, shortly after the establishment of their presence on the coast but it was one of several inland sites that the Crusaders did not have the resources to maintain.

After it was taken in 1140–1 by the Ismaelis, it became a chief centre of their sect, particularly under the leadership of Sinan (see box next page). Sinan's control came under threat from Saladin who, following two assassination attempts by Sinan's followers, sought to assert his mastery over the sect. Saladin aimed to promote Sunni orthodoxy by ridding the country of Shiite influence following the ending of Fatimid rule in Cairo. He laid siege to Masyaf in 1176 but suddenly broke off the campaign. It seems he had been the target of another Ismaeli plot, this time symbolic: the mysterious appearance on his camp bed of a threatening verse, a dagger and a collection of hot cakes. It took another century before the Assassins were subjugated by the Mamluk sultan, Baybars, in 1172 in a new wave of resurgent Sunni orthodoxy.

Some restoration work on the castle was carried out under the Mamluks (the machicolation over the entrance appears to be an example of their work). Parts of the castle were still occupied in the Ottoman period, serving for a while as the palace of the town's governor.

Visit

An hour and a half should be sufficient for an inspection of the castle (and a quick circuit of the central parts of the town where some buildings of the Ottoman and Mandate period retain a certain faded charm).

The castle has been restored by the Aga Khan Trust which has recently undertaken several major restoration projects in Syria. The fortified enclosure sits on a small elongated rocky prominence (running north-south) on the eastern side of the town. Make a circuit of the outer defences on foot, the relatively open area on the east being a particularly good vantage point to gain an appreciation of the fortifications.

The entrance to the castle is on the south. A path ascends through the remains of a barbican gate then takes a hairpin bend rising steeply to the left. Inside the outer door, recycled classical stones embellish the vestibule. (The capitals framing the inner face of the door are sixth century Byzantine.) The overall plan is a central keep (where tenth century remains are most evident) surrounded by an outer wall strengthened by square bastions built onto the rocky 10 m high slopes. The path divides after the vestibule, the right option skirting between the outer and inner enclosures, the left ascending through a corridor to the courtyard on the western side.

The keep lies on the central part of the ridge but the plan is hard to distinguish in the superimposed layout of inner rooms. The whole complex is very much a pastiche, including the re-cycling of ancient elements such as the monolith columns used to anchor the walls to the core of the building. The fact that it is less structured or symmetrical than Islamic or Crusader fortifications of the period is partly explained by its varied origins as well as by the steep nature of the rock

Ismaeli fortifications

The Ismaeli sect originated in Persia. Though first recorded references to the sect date to the late 11th century, the central element in their beliefs is their devotion to the eighth century leader, Ismael (son of the sixth Imam, Jafar al-Sadiq). An element among the Ismaelis later earned the popular appellation 'Assassins' (Hashasheen) on account of their alleged use of hashish in summoning the fierce determination needed to pursue the sect's commitment to murder to advance their ends.

In the late 11th century while the sect was consolidating in Persia, Syria was more than usually fragmented. Nominally under the Fatimids, it was subject to pressures from the Seljuk Turks, Iraq (Mosul) and the Byzantines. The religious scene was in ferment with a proliferation of Shiite sects resentful of the increasingly assertive Sunni mainstream. Persia was still the source of much of this Shiite heterodoxy and the Ismaelis extended their interests into northern Syria.

The Ismaelis were for a time encouraged in Aleppo by the Seljuk ruler Ridwan (son of the great Sultan Tutush). Ridwan exploited a group of Ismaelis to advance his vendetta against his father-in-law, Jenah al-Daula, whose base was at Homs. The group, however, acquired a fierce agenda of their own, taking on the assassination of orthodox figures such as the respected *qadi* of Aleppo, Ibn al-Khashab (1125). Discredited in the main cities during the 1120s for their blatant courting of the Crusaders in their intrigues against the Sunnis, the group of 'Assassins' retreated to bases in the mountainous areas. Their principal headquarters was at Qadmus on the Masyaf-Baniyas road which they took in 1132 from the Banu Munqidh (*Shaizar). (Few vestiges of the Qadmus castle remain though the oval shape of the citadel rises prominently above the modern town.) After 1142, from their widening network of mountain castles (*Qalaat Abu Qobeis, *Qalaat al-Kahf, *Qalaat Maniqa) they extended their influence by playing off Muslims against Crusaders. Masyaf (also acquired in 1140–1 from Shaizar) was relatively exposed compared with other sites hidden deep in the mountains, notably al-Kahf. *Qalaat al-Khawabi was acquired at a later date.

The sect was particularly vigorous during the leadership (1163–93) of Rashid al-Din Sinan. The Crusaders dubbed him the 'Old Man of the Mountain' out of a mixture of fear and respect for his cunning and ruthlessness. Sinan, born in Basra, Iraq, was a charismatic leader who induced his followers to depart further from conventional Islam into mysticism. He had originally been sent from Persia to govern the Syrian province in 1162. The sect by then controlled the central part of the Jebel Ansariye between Tartus and Jeble. The Crusaders held only a narrow strip to provide access along the coast. At their peak, the Ismaelis controlled a total of ten castles, the eastern-most being Masyaf.

The sect's activities continued at a lesser level of intensity after the death of Sinan (1193). Its independence gradually diminished in the 13th century, however, as Sunni control from Damascus and Aleppo was consolidated. Much of their coherence was lost when their headquarters in Alamut fell to the Mongols (1260). In 1270, having forced the Ismaelis to renounce the tribute they had paid to the Hospitallers, Sultan Baybars dismissed their Grand Master and the Ismaelis rose in revolt. By 1273, the Mamluks gained the upper hand and the Ismaelis ceased to retain a political identity, becaming yet another of the minorities (Christian and Shiite) whose adherents sought refuge in the mountains. There they survived till present times though often under pressure from the more numerous Alawi population. Many Ismaelis in the 19th century fled the mountain altogether, settling around the Syrian desert town of Selemiye.

1. Deschamps (*Châteaux – Crac* 1934: 42–3) listed the ten as: *Qalaat al-Kawabi, *Qalaat al-Kahf, Rusafa, Masyaf, Hadid (near Qadmus), Qalaat al-Qrayte (?Qolai'a), Khariba, Qalaat Ollaiqa and *Qalaat Maniqu. He excludes *Qalaat Bani Qahtan and *Qalaat Abu Qobeis which were Ismaeli strongholds for part of their histories. Locations – thematic map T3.

ridge across which the walls and towers, along with their inner chambers, are draped.

REFS: Bianca (ed) 2007; Braune 1993: 297–326; Willey 2005: 220–7.

Meez

ميز

VARIANTS: Ikhkhenis (Grk); Ma`ez, Maaz
PERIOD: Rom/Byz ALT: 382 m RATING: –
MAP: R3, R3a

LOCATION: Jebel Barisha area of the Limestone Massif. Take Harim road from Bab al-Hawa turn-off. After 12 km take the road (left) to Kferdaya (Kfer Darian) – +3 km to Meez.

An extensive site, it probably played a central role in the surrounding region from the second century because of its sizeable fertile area. The town grew up around the *agora* and temple of the second century Roman settlement (west of road). Other Roman remains also include a nearby *andron* (AD 129) and a reservoir. Tchalenko notes that its history seems to be marked by two separate periods of prosperity, one at the beginning, the second at the end of the Roman-Byzantine era.

The most notable ruin of the Christian period is the sizeable church to the southeast which has a richly decorated rear wall including elaborate window placements (first decades of the sixth century). The church compound also includes a baptistery (to the south) and tomb. The second church (mid sixth century, columned basilica – west side of ruins, behind temple) is less lavish and little remains of its structure.

The monastery 1.6 km to the east (local name Deir Aizarara) has an associated monastic tower, Burj al-Assafir, 100 m to the north (probably of the second half of the sixth century).

REFS: Mattern 1944: 95–103; Pena (*et al*) Cenobites 1983: 120–2, 160–6, 219–26, 250–1, 266–9; Pena

Inventaire 1987: 170–1; Tchalenko *Villages* I 1953: 280–4; II 1953: pl LXXXVIII 2, LXXXIX.

Menbij

منبج

VARIANTS: Manbog, Mabog, Bambyce (Br/ IrA); Hierapolis (Grk); Bumbuj (Arb).
PERIOD: Hel/Rom/Arb RATING: – MAP: R4

LOCATION: 88 km northeast of Aleppo.

Menbij. May God protect it. ... its skies are bright, its aspect handsome, its breezes fragrant and perfumed, and while its day gives generous shade, its night is all enchantment.

(Ibn Jubayr)

Nothing [Ibn Jubayr] wrote about Menbij had prepared me for it. If every town on earth were vying for the name 'nowhere', a mere two or three could hope to compete with Menbij.

(Charles Glass *Tribes Without Flags* London 1990)

Menbij has admittedly seen better days. In this alternately dusty or muddy town in the midst of the northern Syrian grain belt little now remains of the famed cult centre whose origins predate Greco-Roman times. Under the ancient name of Hierapolis, the fame of Menbij spread throughout the Roman Empire. Even Gertrude Bell had difficulty relating Menbij to its days of glory. Perhaps just as well. The cult (celebrated, or rather parodied, in the work of the ancient author, Lucian, *De Dea Syria*, 'The Syrian Goddess') centred on the worship of Atargatis (originally a Mesopotamian goddess) and her consort Hadad. The divine pair were appeased by notoriously bloody and sadistic practices, including the sacrifice of children. Its lake (once 100 m wide and surrounded by porticos) where the sacred fish were farmed is now a humble football field west of the town park. A skerrick of wall from the lake's rim survives behind the southern goalposts but nothing of the temple with the bronze altar to Atargatis.

The religious significance of Menbij pre-dated the Seleucids and Romans, a local dynasty having sponsored the cult in Persian times. It was thus a sizeable town when Seleucus I Nicator hellenized it as Hierapolis after 300 BC. Its abundant water supply fed by underground channels (*qanats*) assisted it to become perhaps the chief religious centre of Syria. Its growth was complemented by an important military role as an assembly point for Roman campaigns beyond the Euphrates, a major preoccupation in frontier policy of the second and third centuries. (There is a reminder of this in the number of military stelae in the town park east of the temple site.) The rotation of soldiers through Hierapolis helped spread the fame of its cult throughout the Empire as far as Gaul but it had aroused interest at the highest level even from the time of Nero (mid first century). A sanctuary to Atargatis (second, third century) has been found on the Janiculum Hill in Rome.

Hierapolis remained a centre of importance in Christian times, becoming the seat of a bishop. Justinian fortified it as he did many centres west of the Euphrates. It achieved new fame in the dying days of Byzantine rule when Emperor Heraclius came here in 630 to recover the True Cross, taken by the Persian invaders during their sack of Jerusalem in 614. Heraclius' restoration of Byzantine rule in the area was short-lived and two decades later, northern Syria followed the south in falling easily to the Muslim forces.

Menbij (having returned to its pre-classical name) remained a sizeable centre in the early Islamic period and up until the Zengids (11th and early 12th centuries) when Ibn Jubayr was so impressed by it. The Crusaders from Edessa reached as far as Menbij briefly in 1108, 1110 and again during the period 1119 to 1124. Nur al-Din built a madrasa (1156), of which the tower added by Saladin (1185) was a notable example of the development of the minaret in 12th century Syria.

Some remains of classical Hierapolis survived to be recorded by travellers in the nineteenth century. Nowadays, not only the temple of Atargatis and the

sacred lake but virtually all the other vestiges of Menbij's past have disappeared – the colonnaded east-west axis, Roman baths and theatre, the Byzantine walls and churches, the medieval madrasas. (Sadly even Saladin's minaret was gone when Gertrude Bell passed this way in 1909.) Menbij's decline, however, now seems to have been arrested. The region, settled early last century with Circassian and Armenian refugees, is gaining a new prosperity through irrigation of the rich farmlands of the Sajur River to the north. Menbij's Syriac linguistic root, 'gushing water', is again becoming appropriate.

REFS: Bell *Amurath* 1911: 23; Elisséeff 'Mandbidj' *EI2*; Goossens 1943; Korn II 2004: 275–6; Lightfoot 2003.

Meskene

مسكنة

VARIANTS: Emar (LBA); Barbalissos (Grk); Barbalissus (Lat); Balis (Cru); Eski Meskene, Meskene al-Qadimeh (Arb)[5]   PERIOD: LBA/ Byz/Arab   RATING: *   MAP: R4

LOCATION: From Aleppo, take the road southeast towards *Raqqa (same exit from the city as the airport road). Pass through the modern town of Meskene (90 km from Aleppo). After +2 km, at the point where a sign on the right points to Joumanie, head left at 90⁰ to the road following the unmarked tracks towards the minaret +2 km away.

Meskene marks the site of an important crossing and transit point on the Euphrates where caravan traffic on the Mediterranean-Mesopotamian route transferred from land to river transport. The creation of Lake Assad as a result of the first phase of the Euphrates scheme, however, has totally changed the sleepy remains of the ancient caravan stop. Formerly perched on a small plateau overlooking the river valley, the site has become a lakeside promontory with the waters lapping at the Byzantine fortification walls.

Meskene has been a fortified point since the Middle and Late Bronze Ages. Known

5 'Old Meskene', to distinguish it from the new town created after the filling of the lake.

as Emar, it was mentioned in the Mari, Ebla and Babylonian archives. A palace and three temples from this period were discovered and excavated in great haste in 1973–6 before the greater part of the site was covered by the lake waters. An archive of over 300 tablets in Akkadian and Hittite was found.

Written records corroborate the Hittites' conquest of the site in the Late Bronze Age during their period of dominance in northern Syria. The town was destroyed, however, around 1175 BC at a time when population movements brought great disruption to Syria as to other parts of the eastern Mediterranean.

The site was re-settled in Seleucid times (third to first centuries BC) and was fortified under the Romans. (In the fourth century AD, the Equites Dalmatae Illyriciani was garrisoned there.) The greater part of the remains still visible, however, date from the Byzantine period when the settlement (then known as Barbalissos) was re-fortified by Justinian as part of his major program of fortress cities to hold the line along the Euphrates against the Persians. The remains of this period include the striking 20 m high remains of a *praetorium* (recently stabilised by a team from the University of Tübingen) and the southwest corner of the the walls built in the massive style of Justinian's engineers. In the end, of course, it was a threat from another direction, the Arabs, which overwhelmed the area in the next century and, like most Syrian towns, Barbalissos fell easily to the Muslim armies.

Meskene was again contested during the Crusades. As part of their ill-fated push from Edessa into northern Syria, the Crusaders took the town, then known as Balis, around 1100 but were over-extended and soon lost it. The Mongol invasions of the 13th and 14th centuries finished it off and it fell into disuse as a fortified settlement.

When the valley was threatened in the early 1970s, a rescue campaign was undertaken to move to safety the superb brick minaret of a 13th century mosque

from the ancient Arab village of Siffin near which in 756 was fought the contest between Ali and Muawiya which decided the fate of the Umayyad dynasty (*Qalaat Jaabr). The minaret can now be seen on approaching Meskene, carefully restored in its new location. The simple and striking style shows the continuing influence of the Iranian tradition in northern Syria at the time of the Ayyubids. An internal staircase gives access to the top of the minaret.

REFS: Hillenbrand 'Eastern Islamic' 1985; Margueron 'Emar' in *CFAS* 1989; Sachau 1900: 143.

Mushabbak (Plate 15a)

المشبك

PERIOD: Byz RATING: * MAP: R3

LOCATION: 25 km west of Aleppo. Take the road from Aleppo direct to Dar Tazeh (and Saint Simeon). Turn right from the Damascus road at the Aleppo Scientific College roundabout (starting point). After 400 m, turn left and continue to 25 km point. Take sealed road to left which leads directly to church (+1 km).

The church at Mushabbak, as noted in Butler's survey at the turn of the last century, is 'one of the most perfectly preserved of all the basilica churches of Northern Syria and one that seems typical of the ecclesiastical architecture of the third quarter of the fifth century in this province. The replacing of the fallen stones of the gables, and a restoration of its wooden roofs, are all that would be required to make it a practicable house of worship.'

The three-aisle columned basilica borrows several eclectic architectural ideas. The internal dimensions are almost 18 m by 12 m and the use of nine semi-circular arched windows in a clerestory supported by five 4.5 m columns adds a sense of height which echoes the main church at *Kharrab Shams. The more lavish use of windows is also found on the western façade where six openings above the portal and two on each side were once complemented by a further three in the triangular entablature. The decoration is minimal, restricted largely to the varied carvings of the column capitals. The overall effect shows a considerable evolution from the earlier stodgy church designs based on enlarged house architecture. The striving for greater light and height achieves some success. As usual, two annex rooms lead off the side aisles, but the north one (a martyrium) also has a door leading off the apse.

At the time of construction, nearby *Saint Simeon was being developed as a centre of pilgrimage. Mushabbak was possibly built to serve as a way-station on the pilgrimage route (this would explain the lack of other substantial buildings in the area) thus benefitting from the more advanced architectural concepts tried out in the great basilica by metropolitan builders.

REFS: Beyer 1925: 55–7; Butler *AE* II 1903: 143–7; Butler *EC* 1929: 62–4; Butler *PE* II B 6 1920: 341–2; Mattern 1944: 115–7.

Mushennef

المشنف

VARIANTS: Nela, Nelkomia (Grk?)
PERIOD: Rom RATING: * MAP:

LOCATION: At the roundabout in the centre of *Shahba (87 km south of Damascus on the Suweida road), turn east. Take the road down the hill and through the gap in the Roman wall that still marks the town limits. Follow this road which skirts to the east of the Jebel al-Arab for +25 km, keeping the slopes of the Jebel on your right.

A typically bizarre mixture of ancient and modern in a rather harsh Jebel al-Arab setting with the predominant pallette derived from the black basalt stone of this volcanic region. (Beyond to the east begins the volcanic wilderness known as the Safa.) In the centre of Mushennef is a small Roman temple constructed on the edge of an artificial lake. In spite of the setting and the sombre stone, it manages to suggest a sense of delicacy through its fine architectural decoration

(meanders, rosettes, Corinthian capitals) in the dark unyielding stone. The temple with its portico of two columns *in antis* was oriented eastwards and originally enclosed in a courtyard. The porticoed facade was reconstructed for use as a Druze meeting hall in the 19th century in a hopelessly dyslexic style.

According to an inscription dated AD 171 found near the north gate, the temple of Mushennef was attributed to the Emperor Marcus Aurelius. However, this probably relates to the reconstruction of a building already used for religious purposes. Another inscription, to Herod Agrippa I, indicates the temple was in use in the first half of the first century AD and its origins may go back to the previous century. Freyberger considers the temple's decoration shows the first signs of the unification of decorative style under Roman influence in the first century AD.

REFS: Butler *AE* II 1903: 346–51; Butler *PE* II A 5 1912: 340; Freyberger *Karawanenstationen* 1998: 59–62.

P

Palmyra (Tadmor – Plates 15b-16c)

تدمر

VARIANTS: Palmyre (Fr); Tadmor (Arb)
PERIOD: Rom/Byz/Arb ALT: 600 m
RATING: *** MAPS: 40–3, R4

LOCATION: In the central Syrian Desert, 235 km northeast of Damascus, on a good sealed road. Turn off Aleppo highway 24 km north of Damascus and follow signs for Palmyra.

Palmyra is one of the great sites of the ancient world. The remains of this oasis city, midway between the Mediterranean seaboard and the thin cultivated zone of the Euphrates, seem suspended in time in this harsh desert environment. An elusive and highly romanticised goal of European travellers over the centuries, even today a visit to Palmyra is an experience which alone is enough to make the trip to Syria worthwhile.

History

Palmyra owes its origins to the extensive oasis south of the ruins. The date, olive and pomegranate orchards drew on underground springs emerging from the mountains that enclose Palmyra to the north and west. For this reason, it was settled as long ago as the third millennium BC and is mentioned in archives from *Mari (18th century BC) and as far away as Kultepe (in Cappadocia, Turkey). The Semitic name Tadmor is mentioned in Assyrian archives. Though a Tadmor is listed in the Bible as within Solomon's sphere of influence the reference is based on a confusion of the name with Tamar in the Judaean Desert.[1]

---

1 2 Chronicles 8, 4. The original meaning of the Semitic and modern-day Arab name for the town is probably 'guard-post' – Starcky and Gawlikowski 1985: 33. The Greeks and Romans adopted Palmyra in the belief that Tadmor was a reference to the local date palm (the Semitic root being 'tamar').

The Seleucid settlement has recently been identified as lying south of the main Roman city. The early Romans found Palmyra an elusive prize. In 41 BC, Antony attempted to seize its riches but on arriving in the oasis found it deserted by its inhabitants and thus devoid of booty. It owed nominal allegiance to Rome under Augustus, developing closer links (including Roman city-state political institutions) under Tiberius (r AD 14–37). It was probably integrated into the Province of Syria by the reign of Nero (r 54–68).

Though its rise to prosperity reflected its trading role, Palmyra was not on a long-standing trade route between the coastal-Orontes area and the Mid Euphrates. The natural link arches to the north, following the curve of the Fertile Crescent and skirting the uplands of Turkey. In the first century BC, that route fell prey to the instability that brought the Seleucid kingdom to an end. A coalition of Arab interests was formed between Emesa (*Homs) and Tadmor to secure a new short-cut across the desert. It was an instant success.

Given the conditions of sustained security under the Roman Empire and the impetus to east-west trade resulting from the exotic tastes of the Roman upper classes, Palmyra continued to flourish. Much of the trade between the Mediterranean and the East – India (via the Persian Gulf), Trans-Oxiana and China – flowed through Palmyra. As long as the Arab rulers could control the desert tribes, the commercial viability of the route was assured given the considerable time and effort saved compared with the northern route. But prosperity depended, too, on good relations with the Parthian Kingdom to the east. For the first century and a half of Roman control, Palmyra retained a close understanding with the Parthians (with whom they had many traditional links) while respecting Rome's overall supremacy. It prospered as a sort of neutral zone 'wherein the goods of these two officially hostile powers, Parthia and Rome, might be exchanged'.[2]

---

2 Rostovtzeff quoted in Huxley *From an Antique Land* Boston 1966: 155.

At the height of its prosperity in the second century, Palmyra was perhaps the most active inland entrepôt in the eastern Empire. It was particularly favoured by Hadrian during his tour of the eastern provinces in AD 129, being declared by him a free city (*civitas libera*) and renamed Palmyra Hadriana. Though basically Semitic in population, it increasingly turned to Roman political, social and cultural models while retaining predominantly eastern styles of art and dress. In 194 the city was transferred to the new province of Syria Phoenice. The second century marked

declared a Roman colony (*colonia*). This new period of uncertainty was reflected in the decline of the caravan trade. Palmyra's closer association with imperial strategic interests also reflected the Syrian links of the Severans, Caracalla's mother being a daughter of the High Priest of Emesa. Major building programs initiated in this period include the extension of the colonnaded axis to the Bel Temple.

In the second half of the third century, however, the rulers of Palmyra began to re-assert their independence. Partly

Palmyrene art

Something should be said about the style of art, particularly architecture and relief sculptures, found at Palmyra, if only to head off any assumption that it represents a provincial (and thus debased) version of Roman styles of the first to third centuries AD. True, much of the art (including the overall architectural conventions based on Roman and Hellenistic repertoires) does strive for a metropolitan or standard style. But the differences are significant; and consciously so. The Roman-Hellenistic framework had already been adapted to local usage and tradition through several centuries of blending oriental and Mediterranean styles. This Arab-Parthian synthesis reflected the ripples left by Alexander's great campaign of the fourth century BC as seen in the succession of Nabataean, Bactrian and Greco-Buddhist (Gandara) styles that spread towards the east, including the orientalised Parthian forms found at *Dura-Europos and Hatra (Iraq).

We are thus not simply dealing with a provincial Roman phenomenon but with a Greco-Persian-Parthian synthesis whose roots go back deep into the Hellenized traditions of the east, long before Roman influence became prominent in the first century AD. This semi-'orientalising' or 'other-worldly' element, common to several traditions, is marked by frontal representation; timeless rather than realistic expressions; oriental dress in a heavily stylized treatment; and restless, almost baroque, application of decoration. To some extent, the obsessive formalism of the local style gradually broke down under more direct Roman influence. Realism, introspection and psychological insight in the expressions depicted on late funerary sculptures are thus all the more striking. Ironically, the final victory went to the orientalised-formalised tradition which penetrated even the art of the imperial centre following the move to Constantinople, setting the style for over a millennium of Byzantine art.

the peak of its prosperity as reflected in the nouveau riche lifestyle of its ruling families. Roman culture, however, only superficially cloaked a society still basically tribal and mercantile rather than urban and aristocratic, in spite of all the money sunk into prestige civic projects.

Until the first Roman garrison was installed in the 150s, Roman control was lightly wielded. After the Parthian wars of 162–66, however, the army took a greater role and by 212 under Caracalla the city was

this reflected the breakdown of central control throughout the Empire following successive power struggles in Rome. Palmyra had become a more vital strategic prize as a result of the rise after 224 of the more centralised and aggressive Sasanian dynasty in Persia, founded by Ardashir with its capital at Ctesiphon. At the same time, the Palmyrene economy suffered from the Sasanian seizure of the territory at the mouth of the Tigris-Euphrates from where Palmyra had gained access to traffic on the Indian Ocean thus tapping the cross-desert caravan trade at its eastern source.

With that trade effectively strangled, the mercantilist ethic in Palmyra weakened, making more difficult the city's attempts to act as a go-between linking east and the east at a vital moment when central authority was at crisis point but in pursuing Rome's security interests against the Sasanians, he inevitably became a power in his own right beyond the traditional perimeter of the oasis state.

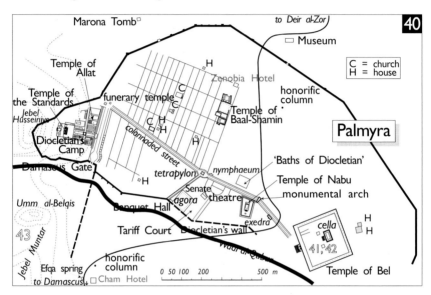

west. The oligarchic rule of the good times gave way to the dynastic ambitions of one family, the Julii Aurelii Septimii. Their leader, Septimius Odainat (Odenathus – r 252–67) rose to prominence as the local strong man by seeking and exploiting Rome's favour. He was apparently put in charge of Rome's legions in the area when appointed consul and governor of Syria Phoenice (256/7) by the Emperor Valerian (r 253–60) at a time of intense Sasanian pressure. (*Dura Europos fell to them in 256.)

Rome was happy to encourage Odenathus, anxious in particular to reverse the disaster brought about by the capture of Valerian by the Persians in 260 and his brutal and humiliating murder. In 266/7, Odenathus campaigned as far as Ctesiphon on Rome's behalf. No doubt his intervention saved Roman fortunes in

Palmyra's ambitions, however, were to assert themselves even more aggressively after the murder of Odenathus in 267/8[3]. During the regency of his wife, Zenobia, on behalf of her son, Vaballath (Vabalathus), Zenobia was determined to realise on her husband's inheritance and to by-pass the constrictions on Palmyra's commercial interests resulting from Sasanian control of the Tigris-Euphrates mouth. Accordingly, she asserted Palmyrene power westwards, taking Bosra and venturing as far as Egypt in 269–70. Asia Minor followed and she began squeezing Antioch from 270. It seems for a time she entertained ambitions of sharing the Roman world with the new emperor, Aurelian (r 270–5) – she (with

3 He and his elder son Herodianus were murdered in Emesa sometime in 267/8. A disaffected soldier did the deed, but on whose behalf, if not his own? Some theories accuse Zenobia herself, others the Emperor Gallienus (r 260–8).

the title of Augusta) would reign in the East, leaving the western Mediterranean provinces to him.

Clearly, for the Romans, things had got out of hand. Aurelian, at first prepared to be flexible, met the new challenge as a cavalry man. He took to the field himself to put down the threat. In 272 he recovered Anatolia and Antioch and defeated a large Palmyrene force outside Emesa. He went on to attack Palmyra. Queen Zenobia attempted to flee eastwards on a dromedary (probably to seek Sasanian support) but was captured by the Romans trying to cross the Euphrates. She was taken back to Aurelian's camp where she formally surrendered Palmyra to the emperor. According to the Augustan History, she was later taken to Rome to grace Aurelian's triumph in 274 in sumptuous bondage.[4] Before that, however, in the spring of 273, the garrison Aurelian had left at Palmyra was overwhelmed in a local revolt and a new and more brutal action against the city was undertaken in 272/3. Aurelian rushed back from the Danube to meet the emergency. This time, he drove home the lesson of Roman power by allowing his troops to massacre indiscriminately and to sack much of the city. Even the Bel Temple was pillaged, its treasure confiscated.

Roman control was now tightened, Palmyra becoming even less a trading centre and more a strategic asset – a nodal point in a network of strategic roads that secured Rome's eastern frontiers. The city was expanded under Diocletian (r 284–305) to encompass an enlarged quarter to house Rome's legion and was walled against the Sasanian threat (given the lesson of Dura's fall in 256).

---

4 The Augustan History (*Life of Thirty Tyrants* XXIX – not necessarily a reliable source) describes the theatrical cortege, complete with elephants and gladiators, culminating in Zenobia, weighed down with gold chains and exotic jewelry. Aurelian's willingness so to humiliate a woman was questioned at the time in the Senate. She was kept in captivity in the neighbourhood of Rome, near Hadrian's villa at Tivoli. The circumstances of her death are not clear.

In the Byzantine period, several churches were constructed in the northern area and the walls further strengthened under Justinian (r 527–65) though much of the city was by then in ruins. In 634 it was taken by Khalid Ibn al-Walid, one of the military leaders under the first caliph, Abu Bakr, but later played only a minor role in the Islamic period though the Umayyads built their desert castles at nearby *Qasr al-Heir East and *Qasr al-Heir West. In 745, a local revolt resulted in the dismantling by Caliph Marwan of the walls rebuilt by Justinian. The area still had some minor defensive role as is illustrated in later centuries by the fortification of the Bel Temple (12th century) and the Arab castle (*Qalaat Shirkuh). By the Ottoman period, the ruins had been surrendered to the desert. The Syrian authorities have carried out numerous projects to excavate and restore important sections of the ruins since the 1970s includings parts of the main colonnaded axis, the tetrapylon, the Temple of Nabu and the theatre.

Visit

The ruins which spread over 19 km² are described in the following order:

- Temple of Bel
- main colonnaded street and associated public buildings
- Diocletian's Camp
- Temple of Baal-Shamin and area north of colonnade
- museum
- Valley of the Tombs
- southwest necropolis
- southeast necropolis.

Though the broad outline of the city suggests some initial grand design, the evidence indicates that it was more the sum of its parts than a strict town plan. Remains of the Hellenistic town have been identified south of the *wadi* that now forms the southern boundary of the main ruins. After the first century AD, some attempt was made to the north to introduce the rigid grandeur of Greco-Roman town planning by imposing a colonnaded axis on this higgledy-piggledy design. However, successive changes of mind about the basic alignment were evident as the axis dodged existing obstacles.

To take in most of these areas, a full day should be allowed. Two days would not be excessive for a more leisurely visit, especially in summer when you need to avoid the heat of the middle of the day (also unsuitable for photography due to the intensity of the light). A day trip out from Damascus allows only a superficial impression of the ruins and no opportunity to experience them either by moonlight or at dawn when they reserve a special magic for visitors.

Bel

Bel is a Semitic god of multiple manifestations. Bel ('lord'(is of Akkadian origins but is found in the Ugaritic pantheon as Baal, eventually equated with the Greek Zeus. He was often accompanied by subsidiary Palmyrene gods representing the sun (Yarhibol) and moon (Aglibol). One of the gods linked to Bel was the Canaanite god, Baal-Shamin, also equated with Zeus and Hadad (*Damascus — Umayyad Mosque). Baal-shamin duplicated to some extent Bel's role as master of the heavens.

Given the mix of populations at Palmyra, numerous other gods were honoured, not least several of Arab origins including Allat (sharing many of the attributes of Atargatis (*Menbij) and Shamash, a sun god probably linked to the cult at Emesa.

The **Temple of Bel** (broadly oriented towards the compass points) stands in its enormous compound at the eastern end of the main colonnaded street. The temple is certainly the most important religious building of the first century AD in the Middle East and is one of the few early imperial projects in the region to survive. The complex was built in several stages:

- Hellenistic temple (probably built on a Bronze Age site) – only fragments survive
- central shrine or *cella* dedicated AD

32 but probably under construction since AD 17 or 19
- AD 80–120 – *temenos* enlarged, surrounded by double colonnaded portico on north, east and south
- late second century – west portico and *propylaeum*.

The undertaking of such a project on a truly imperial scale and to a high standard of craftsmanship reflects both the ubiquity of the Hellenistic tradition which inspired its architecture as well as the prosperity of the late Augustine period and the early years of his successor, Tiberius (r AD 14–37), which provided the wherewithal to construct it.

Before you enter (ticket office on west side), note the massive scale of the second-third century walls, reinforced and converted to defensive purpose during Arab times. In some places, earthquake damage has been reconstructed in a rough and ready manner, Roman details such as niches, pediments and pilasters being reinserted in random order. The general pattern of the Roman walls can still be observed (eg the northwestern corner, opposite the visitors' centre) with pilasters alternating with framed windows topped by triangular pediments. The artificial terrace was built up to the level of the mound on which the original temple had been placed.

To the left of the modern entrance stood the great triple gateway (late second century) – 35 m wide, a broad flight of stairs leading up to a *propylaeum* with a tall central portal. What you see from the outside is basically the fortification inserted into the gate structure by the Burid official, Abdul Hassan Ibn Fairuz (1132–3). The Arab builders constructed in utilitarian style. The *propylaeum* was originally preceded by a portico of eight columns with a huge central doorway. The gateway between the flanking pilasters was filled in, a shallow tower and two sets of machicolation added above the recessed central doorway. Note some sections of the Roman gateway's decorative frieze around the upper machicolation.[5]

5 This gateway is a rare indication of the

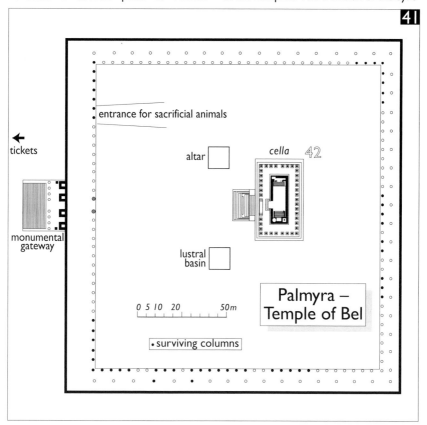

Pass into the compound to get a better impression of the Roman remains. The impressive scale of the gate's triple façade (AD 175) with towering central doorway reflected a second peak of Roman

Though the grandeur reached its climax in this Antonine addition to the first century temple it in no way overshadowed the Augustan *cella* that formed the centrepiece of the complex. The tradition of the Syro-

41

entrance for sacrificial animals

← tickets

monumental gateway

altar

lustral basin

cella 42

Palmyra – Temple of Bel

0 5 10 20   50m

• surviving columns

prestige and prosperity in the late second century. The western colonnaded portico was considerably larger in scale than its counterparts on the north, east and south. The columns are higher (some intact at either end of the portico) and the internal space is uncluttered by the second row of columns that supported the roof on the other three sides.

architectural style used under the early 12th century rulers of Damascus, the Burids and pre-figures many of the elements of later Ayyubid fortifications.

Phoenician temple is traced elsewhere (see box page 20). After Baalbek, the Bel Temple in Palmyra is the supreme realisation of the tradition with its huge compound, surrounding peristyle and relatively small central shrine or *cella*. The *cella* is offset somewhat to the east in the compound whose main axis extends from the great gateway and ascends to the centrepiece by a broad flight of stairs.

Before approaching the *cella*, take in the scale of the compound (205 m by 210 m) and of the colonnades (AD 80–120). The columns, relatively intact on the south, are fine realisations of the Corinthian order. (The purpose of the column brackets will be discussed later.)

As you approach the central shrine, two common features of Syro-Phoenician religious architecture can be traced: the ritual pool for ablutions (right); and the altar for sacrifices (left). A subsidiary feature also worth noting is the passageway that enters the compound north of the *propylaeum*. Animals destined for the sacrificial altar were brought in via a ramp passing under the compound wall through an arch supporting the columned portico above. A little to the right of the passage's end, and in front of the altar, are the remains of a long banqueting hall.

The *cella*, as noted earlier, was dedicated in AD 32 but the site had been used for religious purposes as long ago as 2200 BC. Though it follows the pattern of other Syrian religious centres of the period, the architectural treatment owes much to the Greek tradition as passed on by Rome. The eastern and western traditions vie brilliantly for the last word. In the Semitic tradition, the scale and function of the *cella*, a single chamber enclosed by a colonnaded peristyle, should merely be part of the vast surrounding sacred enclosure. The builders, however, have emphasised its centrality by the bold adaptation of the classical temple concept. The north and south walls of the *cella* are solid, restrained in treatment and furnished with four square or round pilasters in the Ionic order. It is with the peristyle that the oriental opulence begins. The outer columns (eight survive on the east side, plate 15b) were originally capped with metal capitals in the Corinthian order probably bronze plated with gold or silver. But it is the sheer height of the peristyle (18 m) which still impresses, particularly the soaring entrance portal set between engaged columns on the west side. And to top the effect, the peristyle was crowned with stepped merlons, a Mesopotamian device repeated in the four towers that jutted above the roofline of the *cella* itself. This may have been echoed in a frieze of merlons which crowned the whole of

the outer wall of the complex. The neo-Hellenistic bravuro with which the project was realised marked Palmyra's assertion of its new status on the fringes of the Roman world; a brilliant synthesis symbolising the city's role between east and west.

The fact that the *cella* entrance is off-centre and not on a narrower side of the building further emphasises the variation on classical tradition. Opinions vary as to why the main axis of the compound, traditionally oriented north-south, seems to have been switched to the west. The change was evidently made after the construction of the *cella*'s peristyle had commenced. Perhaps it became clear that to the south, the steep walls of a *wadi* prevented the creation of a monumental entrance to the enlarged terrace of the *temenos*. However, the reorientation may also have been required for ritual reasons, to provide two internal chapels within the *cella*.

The reconstruction of the portal was undertaken by the French in 1932. The carved decoration is again typical of the Syrian adaptation of Roman styles. Some may find the effect rather overblown or baroque with no surfaces left unadorned but the style, though exuberant, is controlled and departs judiciously from the classical tradition. The addition of decoration wherever possible is even achieved in the beams that joined the cornice of the peristyle to the top of the *cella* and supported the sloping peristyle roof. Some of the beams that have fallen now lie to the right of the portal and the typically Parthian stylized carving, depicting local gods, is vividly preserved in the crisp limestone.

As you enter the *cella*, you find yourself off-axis within the 10 m by 30 m chamber. Even more confusing is the fact that the chamber has two focal points, namely two shrines for the worship of images of the gods. This lack of a single focus echoes the multiplicity of deities embraced within the Mesopotamian-Semitic concept of Bel. A trinity of gods was worshipped in the compound, Bel himself and the two Palmyrene divinities mentioned earlier,

Yarhibol (a solar god) and Aglibol (a lunar god – see box on Bel, page 210). The setting of the images of the gods in an enclosed *adyton* is a Semitic concept, the Romans preferring to place images of their gods on plinths or pedestals.

The normal place for the statue of the god would be in the north *adyton*. This is where the trinity was worshipped in the Semitic predecessor of the *cella*. The ceiling of the niche is a single stone carved with images of the seven planetary divinities encircled by the zodiac. Superimposed on the carved mouldings of the lintel is an eagle with wings outspread across the soffit, representing Bel controlling the movements of the heavens. He is accompanied by Yarhibol and Aglibol. To the right and left of the *adyton* were two side chambers. Through that on the left, a staircase (one of three) ascends, emerging through a tower at the corner of the *cella* roof which, unlike the surrounding peristyle roof, is flat. This use of the roof as a liturgical platform is a common feature in Syro-Phoenician temples, probably continuing the earlier tradition of conducting sacrifices in 'high places'.

The south *adyton* is somewhat simpler, comprising a smaller niche flanked by two pilasters and a half pilaster on each side. The entablature and the frame of the niche are richly carved. The pillars may once have supported a pediment that would have balanced the rather earth-bound proportions of the current arrangement. Note the gradually sloped stairs leading up to the niche, perhaps intended to facilitate the carrying of the god's image for it is assumed that this niche contained a statue of Bel used in ritual processions.[6] Take particular note of the remarkable monolith ceiling of this south *adyton*. In spite of its soot-stained condition, the superb detail and balance of this design (a central *fleuron* surrounded by a meander band and border rosettes) is one of the great examples of ancient sculptural decoration that influenced the classical revival of the 18th century.[7] To

6 Starcky *Palmyre* 1941: 17.
7 The pattern was carefully reproduced by the English travellers Wood and Dawkins in

the right and left of the south niche are the other two staircases which originally ascended to the roof.

Until the villagers of Tadmor were dislodged from the Bel Temple compound by the French antiquities administration in 1929, the *cella* was used as a mosque, hence the *mihrab* in the south *adyton* and a number of inscriptions going back as far as 728–9.

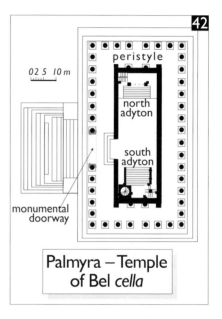

0 2 5 10 m

Palmyra – Temple of Bel *cella*

At the back of the Bel Temple compound, are remains of two patrician **houses** of the third century AD. Both contain rooms grouped around central courtyards. Mosaics of fine quality were found here and have been reassembled in the Palmyra and Damascus museums.

The next stage of our description covers the full length of the **colonnaded street** that serves as the main axis of the Roman city running 1.2 km approximately

their work on Palmyra published following their visit in 1751. Browning 1979: 124–5 notes the important influence which the design had on English decorative arts in the second half of the 18th century.

northwest-southeast in its orientation. For the sake of simplicity, however, the following description will assume a broadly east-west orientation with Qalaat Shirkuh as the western orientation point and the Bel Temple on the east. Note, too, that you will be following the colonnaded axis in reverse chronological order, the western end being the first to be developed.

Start your walk from the point where the tarmac road cuts across the ancient axis. This first section of the street was constructed in the late second or early third century to link the new grand entrance of the Bel Temple to the existing axis. The plan was probably never completed but the first notable embellishment (left) is the **exedra** or semi-circular wall flanked by niches and preceded by a portico with four tall and elegant columns. Such monumental flourishes often served in Roman Syrian cities to display statuary of civic notables.

Sixty metres further on, you come to the first of two bends in the central axis, at which point stands the **monumental arch** (plates 15c, 16a), a structure of considerable architectural interest. It resolves with masterly confidence the problems posed by the street's marked change in direction (30⁰). The solution was a wedge plan, thus angling the façades in two directions while preserving the traditional arch form with a high central opening flanked by two smaller ones. The decoration is rich, in the Syrian style, with resort to the niche to fill the disparate sides of the central opening. The arch was erected under Septimius Severus (Emperor 193–211), more or less the apogée of Palmyra's prosperity when extensive civic improvements were undertaken. It was restored in the 1930s.

Just after the arch, on your left as you continue west, you will find the remains of the **Temple of Nabu**, comprising only the podium of the temple measuring 20 m by 9 m, the bases of the peristyle colonnade and remains of the outer enclosure. The plan is basically eastern in inspiration, comprising a peristyled *cella* opening onto an outdoor altar to the south, with a columned *propylaeum* forming the main entrance from the south. The scale is much smaller than the Bel Temple. Nabu was a Mesopotamian god of wisdom and oracles, equated with the classical Apollo. The compound was thoroughly researched by a Franco-Syrian team in the 1960s and dated to the last quarter of the first century AD. Further work to adapt the northern side of the enclosure to the colonnaded axis' path continued into the third century. The slicing of the north of the enclosure gave it a trapezoidal shape.

Leaving the temple and heading west, you are now well into the main colonnaded street (technically, the *decumanus* given its nominal orientation but also referred to as the *cardo*) at its best-preserved point. The street at this point was the work of the early to mid third century. The central carriageway, 11 m wide, was flanked by porticos 6 m to 10 m broad. In several places behind the colonnaded porticos, the foundations of the market shops can be seen. Note how the columns carry protruding brackets on which statues of civic notables were originally placed. While to the modern observer this may rob the classical columns of their commanding simplicity of form, the Palmyrenes could not conceive of patronage without fanfare; hence the constant reminders of the civic notables to whom everyone was indebted.

In addition to shops, civic amenities were concentrated in this area of the principal axis. An example of the latter is the entry to the '**Baths of Diocletian**' whose location is signalled on the eastern side by four tall monolith columns in Egyptian red granite jutting from the line of arcading. Diocletian's reign (284–305) came after the destruction that followed the defeat of Zenobia. The decision to build up Palmyra as a military centre also brought a new range of civic improvements. The baths were possibly built into the northern section of the palace of Queen Zenobia.

Shortly after on the left, you will notice a semi-circular arch which marks the junction of a cross street which was also colonnaded, at least on one side, and curves around behind the semi-circular profile of the theatre.

Until recently, the remains of the **theatre** gave little hint that it was once in the same league as several other major examples in Syria (*Apamea, *Bosra, *Cyrrhus) in terms of size. Until the 1950s, the theatre was largely buried under the sand. Its lower levels have since been excavated and restored to give a greater idea of its original appearance and the *scaenae frons* or stage façade has been reconstructed. The stage is separated by only a portico from the main street. The Polish archaeologist, Michalowski, dated the theatre to the first half of the second century AD, earlier than the improvements to the colonnaded street. The *scaenae frons,* however, is later (late second or early third century) and lacks the usual facilities for crowd handling and rooms for the actors. This sequence might account for the rather cramped arrangement if compromises had to be made in order to rebuild the stage area in the narrow space left by the later widening or realignment of the main thoroughfare.

The theatre is restored up to its ninth row of seating. (As there is no sign of any substructure for seating beyond the first 12 rows, it has been argued that the upper levels of seating must have been constructed in wood.) The stage is preserved to the first level of entablature over the lowest series of columns, giving some idea of the elaborate stone backdrop. The central doorway is set in a half-oval instead of the usual half-circular *exedra* and there are five doorways leading behind the stage instead of the usual three.

If you walk round to the back of the theatre, you will see on the southwest side of the semi-circle the remains of what was possibly the **Senate**. This was a small building consisting of an entrance hall, a peristyled court and a chamber with an apse at the end around which were arranged rows of seating. The rather truncated form of the building is probably due to the amputation of its north side during the building of the curved street that enclosed the theatre.

Immediately south of the Senate is a large courtyard area known as the **Tariff Court** in which an inscribed stone was found setting out a decree of AD 137 listing the Palmyrene tariff arrangements.[8] It seems reasonable to deduce that it was here that caravans paid the taxes stipulated. The southern entrance to the court (which was not paved) is rather grand in treatment, two of the triple doorways being extant. The outer entrance was once marked by a monumental portico but the arrangement was partly dismantled at the end of the third century during the building of **Diocletian's wall** which cut across the façade at this point.

To the west of this court, you enter the *agora*. This large rectangular enclosure (48 m by 71 m) dates from the first part of the second century AD and has been partly restored since its excavation in 1939–40. The open space was surrounded on four sides by columned porticos. The walls were decorated with windows with richly decorated triangular pediments. The usual brackets for statues of local dignitaries are found on the columns and walls. (There must have been more than 200 in total in this space.) The doorway to the Tariff Court to the east was known as the Senators' Gate and was decorated with statues of the family of Emperor Septimius Severus (r 193–211) who was married to Julia Domna, daughter of a high priest of Emesa. In the southwest corner of the *agora* are the remains of a banquet room or *triclinium* with benches around the walls for reclining guests.

Head back now directly to the main colonnaded street. Almost immediately on your left, you should find the group of four column clusters (tetrapylon) which marks the crossing point of two major streets. Leave this for the moment and note on the right, on the north side of the axis, the remains of a second *nymphaeum*. This takes the form of a columned portico behind which is a curving *exedra* to accommodate a semi-circular water basin. The portico was carried on four tall

8　The 5 m long stone was found in 1881 and is now in the Hermitage Museum, St Petersburg.

columns standing on pedestals.

On the southern side of the *decumanus* at this point note the last eight columns as the street approaches the tetrapylon from the east. The seventh, counting from the tetrapylon, originally carried a statue of Zenobia. On the supporting console is an inscription in her honour dated 271 from which Zenobia's name was effaced in Roman times. The preceding (sixth) column carried a statue of her husband Odenathus. The Romans (perhaps recalling his earlier service to the Empire) left his inscription intact.

At the end of this second section of the main axis, a second, less severe ($10°$) change of direction is marked by the **tetrapylon**[9] which stood in an oval place. Reconstructed by the Polish expert, Ostrasz, and the Syrian Antiquities Department after 1963, this comprises a stepped platform on which are grouped four plinths each of which supports four columns topped by an entablature. Statues originally stood in each of the groupings. The columns were of pink granite from Aswan in Egypt but only one has survived, the modern reconstruction using concrete substitutes.

The remaining 500 m of the colonnaded street to the west is less marked by public buildings and has only been partially excavated. It represents the first stage of the axis, developed in the first half of the second century. The street probably marked the northern limit of the town at this point and the areas beyond were developed later. Browning has noted that the axis may originally have been designed to continue this alignment by driving straight across the city to the entrance to the Temple of Bel.[10] This plan may have been subsequently modified by pressure to preserve the *cella* of the Temple of Nabu and the practical difficulties of cutting into the *cavea* of the theatre, hence the two changes of direction.

9 Technically, the correct description is a *tetrakionion* as it comprises a cluster of four tetrapylons.
10 Browning 1979: 84.

An *exedra* probably marks the site of a second *nymphaeum*, just beyond the tetrapylon on the left. The central *decumanus* has been excavated, exposing remains of a suq built into the axis in Umayyad times. The remaining 500 m brings you to the **funerary temple** (late second century). This is actually more an elaborate temple tomb preceded by an elegant portico with six columns and with a vault below. The portico was standing before the modern reconstruction but the rest has been restored in recent times.

The next part of our description covers the area to the left as you face the funerary temple, commonly called **Diocletian's Camp**. This is reached by the broad transverse street to the left (originally constructed in the second century) some of whose columns can still be traced. After about 300 m, you will come to the remains of another columned avenue leading to the right. This was the principal axis of the Roman camp constructed by Sosianus Hierocles, governor of Syria under Diocletian (r 284–305), the emperor who did much to stabilise Rome's eastern frontier after the Sasanian incursions and Zenobia's revolt. Half way along the 90 m avenue, at the junction of the main cross street, a four-sided gateway was constructed. (Parts of the base and two of the columns which supported the grand entablature remain.)

At the end of the main avenue stood a forecourt followed by the culminating vista of the Temple of the Standards or the legion's *principia*, also the work of Sosianus (293–303). What remains of the temple and its entrance portico is preceded by a huge flight of stairs, intact except that they seem to have collapsed into a melting heap like an ambitious but unstable blancmange. Behind the portico was a hall, only 12 m deep but 60 m wide, at the rear of which was the inner shrine. This shrine for the housing of the Roman legion's standards was a rectangular chamber ending in an apse and flanked on either side by administrative rooms. Above it was an upper chamber and roof reached by a winding staircase. The purpose of the complex seems to combine several ends including the accommodation of the troops and their weapons and the promotion of a military cult. The building's regularity and its imperial scale pay tribute to the confidence of the Empire under Diocletian.

Two other parts of the area called Diocletian's Camp are worth noting. If you return to the main cross street where the four-way arch was situated, continue to the north a little way and you will see on the left the remains of a door frame and several fluted columns. This leads into the **Temple of Allat**, constructed during the second century AD on the site of a first century BC sanctuary before the adaptation of the area as the *principia* for the Roman troops. (*Cella* with a *pronaos* framed by six columns, within a *temenos*). Allat ('goddess') was Arab in origin, equated with Ishtar in Mesopotamia, Atargatis in Syria (see *Menbij) and Athena. A statue of the goddess as Athena copied from a version by the Greek sculptor, Phidias, was found on the site. A giant lion figure of stylized, almost modern, appearance (probably c50 BC) was incorporated into the temple compound wall and is today in the front garden of the Palmyra Museum.

Return to the main transverse street that led off the principal axis and turn south (right). After 60 m you will come to an oval forum (a minor version of the one at Jerash in Jordan) that lay just inside the **Damascus Gate**. The Corinthian colonnading (a segment survives on the south) was carefully coordinated to provide a perspective that framed the gateway.

You have now finished with the areas south of the main axis. For the next stage, areas **north of the axis**, return to the east and head for the group of ruins immediately south and west of the Hotel Zenobia.

Immediately south of the hotel are the remains of the **Temple of Baal-Shamin** (Lord of the Heavens in the Semitic pantheon, responsible for rain and thus fecundity). The complex history of the phases of construction has been

unravelled and the building restored by a Swiss mission in the 1950s. The first work (the northern courtyard) dates as early as AD 17. Further construction was carried out in the early second century funded by a private bequest but improvements were made in the third century under Odenathus. The small *cella* (AD 130, immediately after Hadrian's visit) is a charming building. (The restoration has brought out the almost fanciful or baroque style of the central *exedra* flanked by side chambers – cf the temples at *Slim and *Qanawat.) The *cella* is preceded by a six-columned vestibule, the side walls decorated with pilasters, all in the Corinthian order.

Colonnaded courtyards lay either side of the temple. The court to the north is larger and (as has already been noted) mostly belongs to the earliest phase of construction, except for the west portico which was completed under Odenathus. Whereas the earlier columns were in the classical Corinthian style, the western capitals show an interesting variation. The Corinthian acanthus leaves have been highly stylized and simplified in a distinctly Roman-Egyptian manner. This is one of the few instances of Egyptian influence on the architecture of Roman Syria. The south court is smaller but was also surrounded by a portico. The sole column which remains intact bears an inscription recording the building of the court, commemorated in AD 149.

Though little is left above the ground, other remains in the area north of the main axis include:

- 150 m behind the Baal-Shamin Temple the remains of a Christian basilica, typical in plan of buildings of the sixth century. Six columns separating the central from the northern side aisle remain standing and had been recycled from an earlier period.
- a smaller Christian basilica 100 m to the south of the first
- 150 m to the south of the smaller basilica, the peristyle of two Roman houses can be seen, one virtually intact
- west of the houses, a church complex

immediately north of the *cardo* has been excavated recently by a Polish mission

- sweeping around the edge of this sector are remains of the north wall, possible constructed as part of Diocletian's fortification of the city but reinforced under the Byzantine Emperor Justinian (r 527–65)
- outside the wall (next to the racecourse) stands the fairly intact Marona Tomb, built in 236 as a mausoleum for a patrician merchant.

Museum

The most prolific aspect of the collection displayed in the Palmyra **Museum** (founded 1961 – at entrance to Tadmor town) is the religious and funerary art. The latter, in particular, depicts in all its richness the sculptural tradition through which patrician and wealthy families commemorated their dead. The eastern affinities of the society are clearly shown in their appearance, most notably in their dress; the men in Parthian costume, heavily embroidered and complemented by patterned worked leather; the women in simpler almost Greek robes but veiled and at the same time bedecked with heavy jewellery and head-bands.

Also worthy of note are the mosaics recovered from a private house east of the Bel Temple. Some have been transferred to the Damascus National Museum but among the most notable examples retained in Palmyra is **Achilles at Skyros** – 1.70 m wide, end of third century AD. Achilles' stay on Skyros is a common theme of Roman art, the hero depicted in the company of the king's daughters in a style strictly metropolitan in its inspiration.

Before leaving the museum, you should arrange the services of an accredited guide to gain entrance to the underground tombs described in the following section.

Tombs

The prosperity of Palmyra during the years of its pre-eminence in the caravan trade is reflected in its funerary art. The exploration of the tombs can be divided into three sectors – the so-called Valley of the Tombs (western necropolis) and the southwestern and southeastern cemeteries.

Valley of the Tombs (or Western Necropolis)

The Valley of the Tombs (plate 16b) spreads west from Jebel Husseiniye behind Diocletian's camp extending one kilometre down a barren and forbidding valley. It is an eerie sight at the best of times, even more so under moonlight or at first or last light. Orient yourself by standing on the western slopes of the *jebel*. Around the immediate northern slopes are signs of underground tombs. South of Jebel Husseiniye is a group of tower tombs spread out along the edge of the *wadi*. Head for the eastern-most tower, 120 m west of the Damascus Gate, the **Tower Tomb of Kithoth**, built in AD 40 and standing 10 m high. A relief of a burial feast carved into a niche of the eastern façade is the earliest example found at Palmyra and shows the Parthian rigidity of style later softened by Roman techniques.

You will see 300 m to the south a row of relatively well-preserved tower tombs standing on the slopes of another hill, Umm al-Belqis, to the east of which runs the road to Damascus. Immediately below this row, a track leads right along the Valley of the Tombs. Along the slopes of Umm al-Belqis is the **Tower Tomb of Iamliku** (or Yeliku, AD 83), a handsome and imposing family tomb towards the right of this grouping. The first of the tombs to be built in dressed stone, it was restored in 1973–6 by the Syrian Antiquities Department. The ground floor is impressive with Corinthian pilasters supporting a fine cornice. Three upper storeys survive giving a total capacity of 200 burials. After Elahbel's Tomb (below) this is the most intact among the tower tombs. The tombs to the left in this grouping are of lesser interest.

Head 600 m west along the valley to the

level area in the distance (also reachable by road from just north of the Cham Hotel). Here you will find another group of tombs of which the most notable is the **Tower Tomb of Elahbel** and his three brothers. This is the largest (capacity 300) and most famous of the tower tombs and is distinguishable by its well-preserved lines and the arched niche above the doorway which contains a representation of a sarcophagus. It was built in AD 103 according to the plaque above the door by four members of a family. It incorporates

tower tomb) the upper section collapsed to a conical shape.

A great number of *hypogea* can be found in this area including the site of the **Hypogeum of Yarhai** which has been dismantled and partially reconstructed in the Damascus Museum.

Southwest Necropolis

The southwest necropolis area is reached along the Damascus road, a short distance

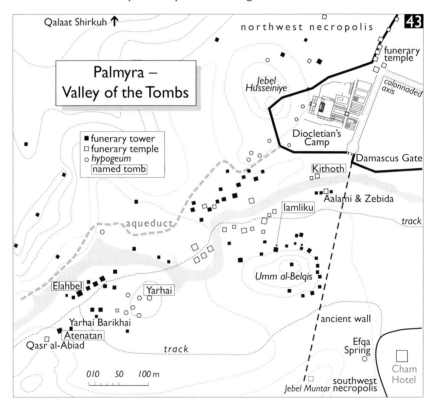

Palmyra –
Valley of the Tombs

■ funerary tower
□ funerary temple
○ *hypogeum*
named tomb

northwest necropolis   **43**

a *hypogeum* underneath (entrance from the north) with four storeys above. The ground floor outdoes even the tomb of Iamliku in its rich use of classical decoration. 100 m southwest is the **Tower Tomb of Atenatan**[11] (9 BC – the earliest dated

11 Not the Atenatan whose tomb is described later in the southwest necropolis.

on the right after the Cham Hotel. The tower tombs in this area are somewhat stubby, the most interesting tombs being the *hypogea* for which a museum guide will be needed. The **Hypogeum of the Three Brothers** (mid second century, restored 1947) offers rich insight into Palmyrene painting styles. (Situated just to

Palmyrene tombs

The Palmyrene upper class seem to have put a great deal of effort into arranging their decent interment. Several broad categories of burials apply:

- Tower tombs were developed earliest, possibly as far back as the Hellenistic period, with the last example dated to AD 128 (though existing tombs were used for later burials up to the third century AD). On each floor of the multi- (up to four) storeyed structure, a central corridor gives onto narrow side passages into which the remains were stacked in layered *loculi*, usually faced with a carved limestone relief or stucco portrait of the deceased.
- Underground chamber (or *hypogeum*). Dated examples AD 81–251. (Comparable styles are found in Phoenicia and Egypt.)
- Combination of *hypogeum* and tower – a transitional phase between tower and underground types. For a while, tower and underground burials were carried out concurrently, bodies sometimes being buried first in underground chambers and later transferred to tower tombs with their economical 'filing cabinet' methods. Later, *hypogea* became the norm and the same efficient methods of stacking remains were extended to the underground chambers.
- House or temple tombs (eg Marona Tomb above) – late fashion (AD 143–251).

Within these categories, many variations in style are found. Our survey is restricted to a few representative examples, particularly given the difficulty of access to the many scores of tombs in the area. Entry to the locked tombs needs to be arranged through the Museum.

the west of the asphalt road, 150 m from the hotel.) You descend a short flight of stairs, noticing the inscription that informs us that three brothers built the tomb as a commercial arrangement. Inside, the main corridor is preceded by two wings. The layout provided 65 side-corridors each of which contained five burial niches or *loculi*.

At the end of the main corridor is a fresco in Syro-Roman style showing the three principal sponsors in circular frames carried by winged victories. Other paintings convey the theme of the spirit overcoming death: Ganymede raised by the eagle of Zeus (ceiling); Achilles gaining immortality in battle (inspired by the valour of Ulysses) having thrown off the garments and the company of women (the aforementioned daughters of the king of Skyros). In the right wing, a dining setting; in the left wing, a funerary monument to Male, one of the brothers (d AD 142/3). Subsequent burials in the tomb span the period up to AD 259.

The **Hypogeum of Atenatan** (AD

98) lies 150 m northwest of the Three Brothers Tomb. The original tomb dates from AD 98 but the main point of interest is the *triclinium* added in 229 by one Maqqai who is depicted on the couch above the sarcophagus at the back. He and the other figures of the group are treated with a subtlety of style associated with the late phase of Palmyrene sculpture.

The **Hypogeum of Hairan** is found a little to the west of Atenatan. Built in 106/7 with a well-preserved frescoe from AD 149–50. The **Hypogeum of Dionysus** lies a little to the south of Atenatan (second half of the second century). It contains a fine frescoe of the god after whom the tomb has been named.

Southeast Necropolis

The southeast necropolis area lies south of the main oasis. Most noteworthy is the **Tomb of Artaban** (second half of the first century AD), discovered in 1957 during construction of an oil pipeline under which you descend to gain entry. The main gallery leads off into four side ones and is covered by a cradle vault. Fifty six niches each contained five *loculi*. Also noteworthy is the **Tomb of Breiki** (early second century AD – 25 m on right), restored by the Antiquities Department following its discovery in 1958. The architectural treatment is on a par with the Yarhai Tomb. The neighbouring tomb (15 m on right) is the **Tomb of Bolha** (inscription of AD 88).

Finally, you should not forget the source of it all, the **Spring of Efqa** which emerged into an extensive cavern under Umm al-Belqis, opposite the entrance to the Cham Hotel, and surfaced just to the left of the hotel entrance. The spring unfortunately dried up in the mid 1990s but it once supplied 60 litres of water per second, at a consistent temperature of 33⁰. Although sulphurous, it was suitable for agriculture and said to be good for a number of complaints.

A little way back towards the ruins, on the rise to the right, are the remains of one of four solitary honorific columns known from Palmyra. Originally they would have been topped by statues of town notables.

For a description of the Arab castle, *Qalaat Shirkuh; for Roman-Umayyad sites southwest of Palmyra, *Khan al-Hallabat and Bkhara.

REFS: al-As`ad & Yon 2001; Bounni and Alas`ad 1982; Bounni *Sanctuaire*; 1989 Browning 1979; Colledge 1976; Gawlikowski 1994; al-Maqdissi 2000; Michalowski *Palmyra* 1970; Millar 1971: 1–17; Richmond 1963: 43–54; Ruprechtsberger 1987; Seyrig *Palmyra* 1950; Starcky *Palmyre* 1941; Starcky *Palmyre* 1952; Starcky & Gawlikowski 1985; Teixidor 1984; Will 1983: 69–83.

Q

Qadesh (Tell Nabi Mend)

تل النبي مند

VARIANTS: Kinza (Hittite),;Qidsha, Kadesh (BrA); Laodiceia (Grk); Laodicea ad Libanum (Lat); Chades (?Cru). PERIOD: LBA/Rom RATING: T MAP: R2

LOCATION: As you approach Homs on the Damascus-Homs highway, watch out for an overhead railway viaduct. Immediately before the viaduct, a secondary road leads off to the left, towards the Anti-Lebanon Range. Follow this for 20 km until you reach al-Qusair. Then northwest +c7 km (towards Lake Homs) until you see a village perched on a mound on the other (west) side of the Orontes River.

The earliest settlement probably goes back to the seventh millennium BC but the site was abandoned and re-inhabited during the Early Bronze Age. After 2000 BC, Qadesh acquired massive fortification walls and was a city of some significance in the Middle Bronze Age, sufficiently prominent for its prince to lead a coalition of Mitannian principalities to war against Egypt only to meet defeat at the hands of Pharaoh Thutmose III c1480 BC at Megiddo in northern Palestine.

Two centuries later, northwest of this unprepossessing site, the 'most famous military engagement in ancient history' before Marathon took place.[1] The battle of Qadesh is a prominent theme of propaganda of the reign of Ramses II in Egypt (c1290–37 BC). A scene of the Pharaoh slaughtering his opponents by the score is repeatedly used in the vainglorious monuments at Thebes (Ramesseum), Abydos and Abu Simbel, in Egypt. His opponents were the Hittites under their leader Muwatallis. The two powers, Egypt of the New Kingdom and the Hittite New Empire, had for some time disputed control of northern Syria.

Ramses II's claim in his monumental propaganda panels to have eliminated the Hittite threat is somewhat overstated. The Hittites threw everything into an attack by chariot forces unsupported by infantry, catching Ramses by surprise and throwing into confusion, though Ramses managed to rally his forces and drive the Hittites back. Both sides subsequently agreed to a balance of power in Syria largely favourable to the Hittites which lasted until the end of the Bronze Age (c1200 BC). The Hittites, from their base in central Anatolia (Turkey), held direct power over Carcemish and Aleppo and had access to the area's important trade (through the port of *Ugarit).

A small tributary stream (the Nahr Mukadiye) comes in from the southwest and joins the Orontes in a marshy area north of the mound, on the edge of present-day Homs Lake. The location of the battle in relation to the present village was the ground to the northwest of the tell. The Pharaoh and the vanguard of the Egyptian army arrived from the south and were attempting to set up camp 600 m northwest of Qadesh when the Hittite chariots attacked, fording the Orontes northeast of the tell and looping around to the south of Qadesh using the mound as a cover. The Egyptians managed to rally their forces with the help of marine auxiliaries which fortuitously arrived from the coast, driving the Hittites back east across the Orontes River.

Qadesh was probably abandoned again after the Assyrian period but was revived by the Seleucids around 300 BC when Seleucus I Nicator established the town of Laodiceia south of the tell. The town bore the same name as the port (*Latakia) on the Syrian coast, both honouring the mother of Seleucus. To distinguish the two in Roman times, the full title of Laodicea ad Libanum was used.[2] This town survived through to Byzantine times.

The significance of the site lies less in

---

[1] Parr 1990/1: 78.

[2] Parr also records an alternative Latin name, Laodicea Scabiosa, a title which he speculates may have referred to the malarial conditions around Homs Lake.

the size of the settlement and its present remains than in its location at an important cross-roads. Not only is it at the point where southern Syria gives way to the flat grain-growing plains of the north, but it also marks the northern exit from the rich Beqaa Valley in Lebanon and lies immediately east of the Homs Gap, the only point between Turkey and Palestine at which the otherwise unbroken coastal chain of mountains allows easy access between the Mediterranean and the interior.[3]

Except for gaining an appreciation of the battle scene (and the views, on a clear winter day, towards snow-clad Mount Lebanon), the site offers little of particular interest to the casual visitor. The 20 ha mound which rises to the unusual height of 30 m above the surrounding ground was excavated between 1975 and 1999 but little sign remains that it was a strategic walled settlement. The rich agricultural and fishing resources of the lake and flood plain, together with its position on significant trade routes, ensured the site's historic importance.

Jusieh

Eight kilometres south of Quseir, a turn-off to the left immediately before the Lebanese frontier brings you to the small village of Juseir al-Amar. To the south (no sealed road access) lie two late Roman-Byzantine fortifications on the lower slopes of the Anti-Lebanon. The first (immediately southwest of the village) is a late Roman fort with a 40 m[2] central citadel. Six kilometres south are traces of a Byzantine defensive complex, Juseir al-Harab. Probably the ancient Maurikopolis, the complex was the last attempt under Emperor Maurice (r 582–602), a few decades before the Muslim conquest, to create a Hellenic 'new city' in Syria. Nothing much remains at either site above the outline of the walls in the soil. The

3 One good way of gaining an appreciation of the Homs gap (Buqeia) is to visit the site on a windy day. The pull of the desert heat often sucks air from the Mediterranean through the mountain gap with incredible vehemence, evident in the slant of the trees. On the significance of the gap – *Krak des Chevaliers.

forts would have guarded access between Emesa and Baalbek.

REFS: Dussaud 1927: 107–8; Mouterde & Poidebard 1945: 31–5; Parr 1983; Parr 1990–91: 78–85; Pena 'Lieux de pelèrinage' 2000: 239–41; Pézard 1931.

Qalaat Abu Qobeis

قلعة لبو قبيس

VARIANTS: Bochebeis, Bokebeis (Cru)
PERIOD: Ism/Cru   ALT: 930 m   RATING: *
MAP: R2

LOCATION: Only 25 km north of *Masyaf but access is by a rather confusing pattern of roads. Best and simplest is to take the road leading from Masyaf to Hama. After 7 km, turn left (north) along the edge of the Jebel Ansariye for +17 km to Tell Salhab from where road west for al-Dalieh. At 6 km (village of Abu Qobeis) continue through the village and take the road left c+2 km southeast around the side of a mountain, past a small Alawi shrine and on to the *qalaat* which looks out over the Orontes Valley.

This small, compact castle affords a superb view over the Orontes Plain towards *Shaizar and *Hama. The castle's upper walls have recently been restored and a road opened to improve access.

The site was utilised by the Byzantines in the 999 campaign of Emperor Basil II to recover Syria. In 1133 it was held by a local Amir, Ibn Amrun. When the Ismaelis moved into this area (see box on 'Ismaeli fortifications' under *Masyaf – page 201) the amir sold them the site, along with Qadmus and *Qalaat al-Kahf.

Bokebeis (to use its Crusader name) may earlier have been occupied for a time by the Crusaders, before the Ismailis were present in strength in the area. There is, however, no evidence of Crusader construction and little reference to the castle in the historical record though it was believed for a time to have paid tribute to *Marqab. (The annual tribute for Abu Qobeis was 800 gold pieces). Under the Ismaelis, the canton of Abu Qobeis may have retained a degree of semi-autonomy from the rest of Ismaeli territory.

In plan, the castle forms two concentric oval-shaped rings. The outer enclosure comprises eight towers. An outer tower protects the main entry to the east lying between half-round bastions. A corridor runs through the centre of the inner enclosure in the style common to most Muslim fortifications. A robust round tower forms the keep at the western end of the inner ring.

More elusive is a Crusader site 4 km to the southwest, **Husn al-Khariba**. Ceded to the Crusader leader, Tancred, in 1105, Khariba was guarded by the Hospitallers from 1163, being handed over to them by the Seigneur of *Maraclée (Guillaume). Like other Frankish posts in the mountains, Khariba would have maintained the watch on Shaizar, north of Hama, from where a fierce Islamic resistance to the Crusades emanated.

REFS: Willey 2005; Vachon in Faucherre (et al) 2004: 230.

Qalaat Areimeh

قاعة الرمية

VARIANTS: Arima (Cru); 'Areima (Arb)
PERIOD: Cru RATING: – MAPS: 44, R2

LOCATION: Take the highway from *Homs to *Tartus. After you have passed through the Homs Gap and descended the low hills, you arrive at the coastal plain, c72 km from Homs. At this point (c19 km from the *Safita turn-off outside Tartus), start looking on the right for a sign which points the way to Deir Mar

Elias. Follow this road as it crosses the old Homs-Tartus road and continue +2 km, stopping when the track to the monastery forks right to ascend a hill. Instead, take the left fork +1 km to the edge of a village called Sefsafe. Road ascends to castle.

Arima was built as a Crusader castle, to help safeguard the routes between Tortosa and Tripoli, to protect the coastal plain leading to the Homs Gap (Buqeia) and to strengthen the outer defences of Tortosa (*Tartus).

Little of the original fabric survives though the scale of the defences can be seen and what remains of the walls shows the quality of the Frankish work. The dates of the original construction are not known but it was in place by 1177 when the Templars were given responsibility for the security of the region around their base at Tortosa.

The castle was there in some form when in 1149 when Bertrand of Toulouse seized it from Raymond III, Count of Tripoli, whom he suspected of having murdered his (Bertrand's) father. Raymond was so determined to retrieve it that he sought an alliance to this end with the Muslim ruler of Damascus, Unur. Unur in turn sought the support of Nur al-Din and the two Muslim leaders dislodged Bertrand and went on to destroy and sack the castle. Bertrand was sent into captivity in Aleppo, together with his sister. (Legend has it that the sister was made a wife of Nur al-Din and bore him a son.) Raymond was captured by Muslim forces in northern Syria in 1164. In 1171, Nur al-Din returned and destroyed what was left of the fortifications as part of the same campaign that saw Safita's original castle razed. The area apparently reverted to

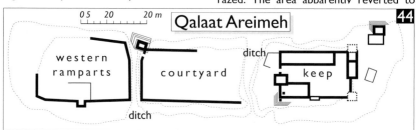

Qalaat Areimeh

0 5   20   20 m

western ramparts   courtyard   ditch   keep

ditch

44

Crusader hands the next year with the restoration of Raymond on his release from captivity in Aleppo, but his debts to the Hospitallers (who seem to have paid the ransom) resulted in the transfer of the castle to the order. The site was briefly retaken for the Muslims by Saladin in his famous campaign of 1188.

Thereafter, the castle apparently remained in Crusader hands until after their general retreat (1291). Much of the present fabric dates from the Arab rebuilding on the Crusader remains but the difference in quality and durability of stonework is readily apparent.

The ruins cover an area of 80 m by 300 m on the crest of a small rise. The land falls away steeply to the east. The site is roughly defined by the confluence of two streams, the Nahr al-Abrash and the Nahr Krach. The parking area (behind the holy man's tomb) lies within the western enclosure. The two distinctly Crusader elements of the complex are:

- the **keep**, which lies on the east side. Rectangular (75 m by 45 m) in plan, it included two towers which can still be noted (the one on the south was probably the donjon) and several (half-buried) vaulted chambers.
- the **western ramparts** (only a little of the south wall remains).

The two are divided by an open courtyard and two ditches, originally surveilled by a tower on the northern face, of which substantial remains can be seen.

Even if you find the remains disappointing, the trip is worth the outlook from the ramparts. Located in beautiful olive-growing country, on a good day the castle enjoys breathtaking views towards the often snow-clad peak of Mount Lebanon well to the south. In theory, you should also be able to pick out from here, preferably with binoculars, the castle at Akkar in northern Lebanon which shared with Arima – and, of course, the great fortress of the Krak – the responsibility for preventing incursions from Muslim-held Homs and Damascus through the

Homs Gap. To the northeast, the donjon at Safita can be detected.

REFS: Deschamps *Châteaux* – III 1973: 313–6; Runciman II 1965 : 387, 395.

Qalaat Bani Qahtan

قاعة بئن قحطان

VARIANTS: Castellum Vetulae, Château de la Vieille (Cru); Bikisrael, Qalaat Beni Israel (Arb)
PERIOD: Cru RATING: – MAP: R2

LOCATION: 24 km inland from Jeble. Coming from the north, turn off the old *Latakia-Baniyas road 25 km south of Latakia where a signpost indicates (on the left) Ain al-Sharqiye, just south of the turn-off (on the right) for *Jeble. Follow the Ain al-Sharqiye road for 10 km, turn left 3 km before the village and head north through Zama (+1 km), al-Thawra (+4 km) then ask for final directions for the last 8 km to Qalaat Bani Qahtan.

Though the trip is worthwhile for the beauty of the mountain countryside, the remains are minimal. A double enclosure (215 m by 51 m) with a trapezoidal donjon, it lies, like Saladin's Castle, on a ridge between two rivers. There are few references to the castle in the historical records, most from the 12th century. It lay on a traditional route between the port of Jeble and the Orontes towns of *Hama, *Apamea and *Shaizar. It is first mentioned as taken by Tancred, Prince of Galilee, in 1111 as part of an attempt to counter the Arab presence at Shaizar.

The subsequent history of the castle is by no means clear. It was seized briefly by a Turcoman adventurer in the 1160s. Recovered by the Crusaders, it seems to have passed to the Ismaeli sect (see box on 'Ismaeli Fortifications' page 201). However, in 1188, during the course of his sweep up the coastal range, Saladin accepted the castle's submission from the Ismaelis. For a while it was linked to the port of Jeble (also temporarily in Muslim hands) to give the interior towns direct access to the sea, the local chieftains having found it expedient to make their peace with the Ayyubids.

If the medieval names listed above are accurate, however, the site reappears in Christian hands as the castle ceded in 1211 by Rupin, Prince of Antioch, to the Hospitallers who had by then assumed responsibility for some of the strategic strong-points in the region, including Marqab and the Krak. This was possibly only a notional transfer of ownership involving occasional payments of tribute from the Ismaelis for the reality was that by the 13th century, the Muslim hold on the area was increasingly unassailable.

Even more difficult to unravel is the other historic name for the site listed above, Qalaat Beni Israel. This implies that there was a Jewish settlement there at some time though Dussaud speculates this might have been as far back as Pompey's time (first century BC) when there was some evidence of local dynasts espousing Judaism (cf Lysias – *Qalaat Burzey).

REFS: Deschamps III 1973: 337–8; Dussaud 1927: 140–1; Runciman II 1965: 118, 120.

Qalaat Burzey

قلعة برزة

VARIANTS: Lysias Bourzo (Grk); Borzé, Bourzey, Borzeih (Cru); Rochefort (?Cru); Qalaat Marza or Barzuya (Arb) PERIOD: Cru ALT: 480 m RATING: ** MAPS: 45, R2

LOCATION: Locating Burzey can be challenging. Although it commands a sweeping view of the Orontes Plain from the inland side of the *Jebel Ansariye, it does not stand out from its surrounds. There are two options from Latakia: Take the Hafeh road (for exit from Latakia, see *Qalaat Saladin) and continue on to Slenfe (40 km). Go past the village and continue straight up the hill (TV transmitter on right). The road curves left along the ridge of Nabi Yunes (alt 1583 m). Keep to the sealed road which will descend after c+5 km to the Orontes Valley floor. At this point, a T-junction, turn left along the edge of the mountain for c+2.5 km. After passing a lake, you should be able to pick out the castle on a spur coming off the lower line of hills.

Be warned: a stiff 45 minute climb over steep and heavily boulder-strewn ground. Keep ruins to your left for easier climb. There is also a donkey track which brings you to the castle from a village half-way down the mountain road described above. The village is called Qalaat Marza and someone there should be able to guide you to the track.

If I had to pick a spot to build a Frankish castle, this would be it. In a wildly romantic location on a rocky crag on the steep side of the Jebel Ansariye, the castle is described by Deschamps as resembling 'the prow of a fantastic ship launched for an assault on the clouds'. The experience is only improved by the relief of arriving after a vigorous and precipitous scramble up the rocky slope. Once you reach it, the scattered remains spread over 3 ha of grassy meadows affording breathtaking 360^0 views of the mountains and the Orontes Plain 500 m below, with only the tinkling of goat bells to disturb the peace.

History

What remains of the castle is minimal. Clearly it was once a sizeable complex; surprisingly so given its remoteness from the main Crusader centres on the coast. It served as the forward defence post, confronting Arab held positions on the eastern side of the valley – Qalaat Mudiq (*Apamea) is 34 km to the southeast – and marking the easternmost line of control held by the Crusaders on a consistent basis along the Orontes Valley.

References to the site as Lysias are found in Strabo's *Geography*. It presumably played a role for the Seleucids in protecting their communications between Laodicea (Latakia) and their military base at *Apamea. Pompey, at the beginning of his campaign (65–4 BC) which resulted in the Roman occupation of Syria, had to dislodge a Jewish partisan (Silas) from the site. The Byzantines fortified it and as late as 975 it was retaken by the Emperor John I Tzimisces from the Hamdanids of Aleppo. It was probably taken by the Crusaders in 1103; five years after they had seized Antioch and shortly before the taking of Latakia by Tancred.

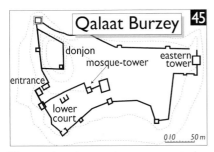

Qalaat Burzey **45**

donjon
mosque-tower   eastern
                    tower
entrance
lower
court
0 10   50 m

The castle whose ruins you see today dates from the 12th century and (like *Qalaat Saladin) marks the first phase of Crusader building in the area. On 23 August 1188 it was taken by Saladin during the whirlwind campaign in which he swept up the coast, besieging Tartus, and took the forts at *Safita, *Jeble, Latakia, Saône, Mehelbeh and Shugur-Bakas (July-Sept 1188). (See box page 16.) Though Burzey had the reputation of being impregnable as no engines of war could be brought near its walls, Saladin struck from the west ridge. His engines having failed to get close enough to make any impression on the walls, Saladin resorted to successive charges by three waves of troops against the western wall, thus wearing down the thin ranks of the defenders and apparently making good use of intelligence from the commander's wife transmitted via her sister, Sybilla, third wife of Bohemond III, Prince of Antioch. (Sibylla was an agent in the pay of Saladin.) The garrison surrendered under the pressure of Saladin's human wave tactics.

While Saladin's rather hit and run strategy did not permanently dislodge the Crusaders from their main defences on the coast, it certainly hemmed in their territory for the second century of their presence and inland sites such as Qalaat Burzey played no continuing role in the Frankish defences.

Visit

If you arrive by the ascent from the valley, you will reach the fortified area on its eastern side. Your scramble should bring you out at the watch-tower which marks the eastern extension of the outer

enclosure. (This is probably a Muslim reconstruction of an earlier tower.) From here, work your way round to the south (left) which should bring you into the area of the lower fortifications.

The fortifications follow a rather random plan resulting from the irregular shape and levels of the crest. The land falls away steeply on most sides but its slope is relatively gradual on the south and west where the main defences are concentrated. The outer walls on the vulnerable sector of the south face were ranged on two levels with a gateway on the westernmost corner giving entry to the inner enclosure. The lower wall consists of four towers with a long curtain wall.

The main donjon was located on the western side and is recognisable today: a rectangular base pushed out to the northwest, with square towers on the corners. To the west of the keep, the castle was most exposed to relatively level ground and was thus protected by five towers and a curtain wall partly faced with a talus. The main entry to the castle was through the central tower on the west side.

Eight kilometres north of Burzey, also on the eastern edge of the Jebel Ansariye, was the site of the Crusader fortress of **Sarmaniye** which was taken by Saladin at the same time as Burzey.

REFS: Boase 1967: 78–80; Deschamps *Châteaux* – III 1973: 345–8; Dussaud 1927: 151–3; Mesqui in Faucherre (*et al*) 2004: 95–136; Runciman II 1965: 470; Sa`adé 1956.

Qalaat Jaabr

قلعة جعبر

VARIANTS: Dausara (Lat); Qalaat Jaabar, Jafar
PERIOD: Arb RATING: * MAP R4

LOCATION: Northeastern shore of Lake Assad. From the new town of al-Thawra (incorporating al-Tabqa) built to service the Euphrates Dam, cross the dam wall to the north bank. At 3 km from dam wall, turn left. +7 km to castle via road curving back towards the lake and the promontory on which the castle is located.

Like other Arab fortresses of the period, Qalaat Jaabr uses a central core of high ground, tightly circumscribed by defensive walls and a ditch (*Aleppo – Citadel is the classic example). Today, though there has been considerable restoration work by the Antiquities Department, much of the fabric of the upper fortress is simply rubble. However, the entrance gateway and ramp and much of the largely brick walls are worth inspection. Moreover the building is dramatically sited. It once overlooked an important crossing point on the Euphrates; it has, if anything, gained in visual impact with the encroachment of the waters of Lake Assad to the base of the castle. The rise on which the castle stood is now an island joined to the shore by a causeway. You look out from the battlements over the intensely blue waters of the lake hemmed between bare promontories.

History

The first fortress on this site may date to the period of Justinian's defences against the Sasanians. The present structure dates from the Zengid, Ayyubid and Mamluk periods. Remains of previous fortifications have not been identified though it was known to be held by the Arab tribe, the Banu Numeir, until taken by the Seljuk sultan, Malik Shah, in 1087. During the First Crusade, probably in 1104, it was incorporated into the territory of the Count of Edessa, the Crusader principality in southeastern Turkey. Edessa (today Urfa), however, fell to Zengi, the atabeq of Aleppo, in 1144 and the subsidiary fortress at Qalaat Jaabr reverted to the Arabs by 1149. However, in an earlier (1146) attempt to dislodge the Crusaders, Zengi was killed before its walls after a quarrel with a Frankish eunuch.

The remains which are seen today date from the rule of Zengi's son, Nur al-Din who, as his father's successor in Aleppo, fulfilled his vision of bringing Syria (less the coastal strip held by the Crusaders) under

united Muslim rule by 1154. His rebuilding of the castle began in 1168. It remained in Ayyubid hands under Saladin and his successors (1176–1260) but it fell victim to the repeated Mongol waves whose incursions, particularly in northern Syria, caused so much devastation between 1260 and 1400. There was, however, some reconstruction in 1335–6 during the rule of the Mamluk governor of Damascus, Tengiz.

Visit

The castle fabric is entirely brick in the upper levels, reflecting the Mesopotamian tradition whose influence was strong in Syria at the time of the Zengids. The main parts of interest are the **entrance gateway** and the corridor which takes you within the battlements to the upper level of the fortified **walls**. You can then make a circuit in a clockwise direction. Much of this upper brickwork has been restored post-1972. On the broad summit (oval in shape, 130 m by 250 m) little remains above the ground except for a fine brick cylindrical **minaret** (the rest of the mosque has disappeared) which recalls others of the 12th century in northern Syria (*Raqqa, *Meskene) probably erected by Nur al-Din. Note the effect of wind erosion on the square brick base. The outlines of a palace with baths may be discerned near the lake side of the summit.

On the right bank of the river at this point lay the Plain of Siffin, where the famous confrontation took place between Muawiya and Caliph Ali, son-in-law of the Prophet, in 657. The forces confronted each other for some months before the issue (the Umayyads' demand that Ali punish the murderers of Othman) was put to arbitration which broadly went against Ali and led to the final undermining of his leadership.

The legendary forefather of the Ottoman sultans, Suleiman Shah, reputedly drowned in the Euphrates near this spot in the 13th century. His tomb was traditionally guarded by a contingent of Turkish troops (a clause allowing for this arrangement was negotiated at the Versailles Conference following the end of Ottoman rule). The practice continued after Syrian independence but as the lake filled, the tomb (and its small garrison) were moved upstream (*Qalaat Najm).

REFS: Bell *Amurath* 1911: 49–51; Hillenbrand 'Eastern Islamic' 1985; Runciman II 1965: 112, 239.

Qalaat al-Kahf

قلعة الكهف

VARIANTS: Khaf PERIOD: Ism RATING: T MAP: R2

LOCATION: Finding Qalaat al-Kahf can be a major exercise and the Ismaelis did well in searching out a location deeply hidden in the folds of the Jebel Ansariye. It can be approached from several directions: from *Masyaf, Baniyas (both via Qadmus) or *Tartus. One proven route is to take one of the Sheikh Badr roads from the coast (turn off either from Tartus or c10 km north). From Sheik Badr, ask for directions north to Ain Breisin (4 km) then al-Nmreije (+7 km). This will take you along narrow tarmac roads, up and down several ravines. Al-Nmreije lies c2 km east of the castle. A new road was recently built to the castle from the village.

History

While Masyaf, which also served as Ismaeli headquarters, may be in a better state of preservation, al-Kahf enjoys an equally rich history for the short period of its prominence.

The castle was originally established by a local lord who in 1132–3 sold the fortress of Qadmus to the Ismaelis from where they began to establish themselves in the area. (See box 'Ismaeli Fortifications', page 209). His son later sold al-Kahf to the sect, part of their program of rapid acquisition of eight castles in the area from 1132 to 1140.

From 1164 to the early 1190s, the Ismaeli leader, Rashid al-Din (known to the Crusaders as the 'Old Man of the Mountain'), operated from this remote mountain fastness. The castle is mentioned in the historical records of the 12th century Crusaders in connection with exchanges between the sect and the Knights Templar with whom they shared an unspoken entente. In 1197, Henry of Champagne, Regent of Jerusalem, sought an alliance with Sinan's successor to counter Muslim pressure on the fragmented Crusader state. He was invited to al-Kahf where, to demonstrate the fanatical devotion of his followers, the Ismaeli leader asked two of them to hurl themselves from the castle parapets; they did so without hesitation.

This ambiguous relationship with the Crusaders continued the next century particularly under St Louis, the French king who led the disastrous Crusade against Egypt in 1248–9. The Ismaeli leader set up an assassination attempt on St Louis but his agents were detected and sent back to al-Kahf with gifts to illustrate Louis' magnanimity. Later Louis sent an envoy, Yves le Breton, to al-Kahf bearing presents, as a result of which an alliance was concluded. Yves was the first Western visitor to the Ismaelis to take an interest in their doctrines.

Not surprisingly, al-Kahf was the last of the Ismaeli strongpoints to fall to centralised Muslim control. It was not until 1273 (two years after his successful siege of the Krak) that Baybars captured the castle in the last phase of his elimination of the Ismaeli presence. The castle remained a military post into Ottoman times, serving as a usefully remote place of detention. In 1816, the British resident of Lebanon, Lady Hester Stanhope, took up the cause of a French captain who had been taken captive and held in the castle. He was rescued at her behest by the Ottoman Governor of Tripoli who also carried out her wish that the castle be razed.

Visit

Of all the mountain castle sites, this is probably the one most marked by a raw and untamed beauty, the environs unsoftened by the cultivation of crops and orchards. The mountain country is either forested or too steep for cultivation in this place where three rivers meet. The castle sits on a ridge, nestled between wild gorges, its fragmentary walls clinging to the rocky flanks. From its elongated heights (running east-west), precipitous cliffs provide their own natural protection. What remains of the castle buildings is debris spread along the 300 m by 50 m site. Most remarkable is the entrance passageway (approached by taking the path which skirts the north side of the ridge) carved into the solid rock with an Arabic inscription to the left. (The artificial 'cave' gives rise to the Arab name for the castle, Castle of the Cave). Legend has it that Sinan was buried near the craggy fortress, the reputed site lying near the northeastern face by which you approach the castle.

REFS: Burman 1987: 139; Runciman III 1965: 89; Willey 2005: 233–7.

Qalaat al-Khawabi

قلعة الخوابي

VARIANTS: Coïble (Cru) PERIOD: Ism
RATING: T MAP: R2

LOCATION: About 20 km (45 minutes' drive) from the coast, Qalaat al-Khawabi is reached by turning off the *Tartus-Baniyas highway 10 km north of Tartus. The turn-off is marked (in Arabic only) Sheikh Badr but is readily recognisable as the road that branches at the northern edge of the cement works. Follow this road inland for c+10 km, passing Dweirtah to reach al-Soda. From here the road heading east for Oaro (+3 km) and Albatteye (+8 km). This road winds on +2 km, around a series of ravines, until it comes within sight of the qalaat perched on a narrow summit amidst a modern village.

History

The castle (in Arabic, Castle of the Ewes) is a purely Ismaeli structure, though well enough known by the Crusaders to have been given a Frankish name, Coïble. The ruins are dilapidated, not helped by being continuously occupied and thus constantly mined (particularly during the 19th century) for building materials. It is the surrounding scenery (as usual, castle builders in the Jebel Ansariye knew how

to pick their site) that impresses most. Located in a ravine, it is perched on a narrow summit surrounded by four hills that tower some 400 m or more above. At its base runs the Nahr Hussein. Olive groves in profusion soften the countryside and provide an idyllic setting. There is even a certain charm in the way the modern village houses improvise around the remains of the medieval fortress.

The history of the Ismaeli presence in the mountains is sketched in the entry for *Masyaf. The historical references to Coïble are scanty but it appears to have been acquired from the local lord in the 1140s. It was certainly well established as an Ismaeli centre early in the active career of Rashid al-Din Sinan who rebuilt it after 1160. In 1213, Bohemond IV of Tripoli (later of Antioch) laid siege to Coïble following the murder by Assassins of his son Raymond in the Cathedral of Tortosa. The siege was a determined one and the Ismaelis, then in alliance with the successors of Saladin, called on the aid of forces from Aleppo and Damascus. Eventually the Crusader siege had to be called off in the face of this coalition. The castle does not seem to have been used by later Arab rulers for defensive purposes once the Ismaeli presence in the mountains had largely been uprooted by the end of the 12th century.

Visit

It takes only half an hour or so to inspect the ruins. The plan is broadly two concentric enclosures, elongated in an east-west direction. A short walk over the Nahr Hussein and up the stone path along the south side of the crag brings you to the gateway which still controls access to the village. The single village street takes you from one end of the narrow castle to the other with diversions down alleyways to gain some impression of the remains of the defensive walls. However, only fragments of the castle buildings survive amid the houses and it is difficult to relate anything to a coherent plan. The quality of the stonework, as is often the case in Ismaeli constructions, is not particularly fine.

REFS: Burman 1987: 105–6, 119–20; Dussaud 1927: 139–40; Runciman II 1965: 138; Willey 2005: 238–9.

Qalaat Maniqa

VARIANTS: Malaicas, Castellum Malavans (Cru); Qalaat Ksabiye, Hisn al-Mainakah (Arb) PERIOD: Cru/Ism   ALT: 656 m RATING: * MAP: R2

LOCATION: 22 km southeast of *Jeble in the Jebel Ansariye. From Baniyas (mid-way between Tartus and Latakia) take the old road north to Latakia for c12 km. Follow the road leading right +10 km to Duweir Baabda then the road heading southeast (not the direct road east to Adele) to the village of Wadi al-Qalaat (+6 km). The castle can be seen looming above the small settlement, a steep 15 minute walk.

This castle, originally Ismaeli, is set amid some of the most beautiful tobacco-growing terraced country in the Jebel Ansariye. The drive from the coast is equally scenic, particularly the last few kilometres, ducking at one point along a convenient ledge behind a waterfall.

The history of the castle is very sketchy. It was originally constructed by local Arabs in the early 11th century but soon was taken over by the Byzantines. The Franks had control at some stage in the 12th century (perhaps as early as 1118) but sometime after 1160[4] it was refortified by the Ismaelis when Rashid al-Din Sinan ('the Old Man of the Mountain') became active in the area (see box on 'Ismaeli fortifications' under *Masyaf, page 201). Somehow, it passed back into the hands of the Crusaders, perhaps as part of their entente with the Ismaelis against their common enemies, the Sunni Muslim forces of Damascus and their allies. By 1186, it had been entrusted to the Hospitallers by Bohemond III, Prince of Antioch.[5] The Hospitallers maintained largely amicable

relations with the Ismaelis and the castle may have stayed effectively under the control of the sect for it was in Ismaeli hands again in 1270–3 when it was taken by the Mamluk sultan, Baybars, during his suppression of the Ismaeli presence in the Ansariye Mountains.

The castle, elongated in plan, is located on a ridge running northeast to southwest between two streams feeding into the valley of the Nahr Hussein. As you ascend, chose the path on the left that will take you to the west face, entering the fortifications through a break in the northwestern wall.

The site is naturally defended by the steep slopes on all but the northeastern side. Here, a lower ridge joins it to the mountain and the defenders cut a ditch in the rock to provide a steep face to discourage assault. This was topped by a formidable wall of solid basalt construction. The defensive positions, notably the keep, were concentrated here, affording commanding views over the spectacular terraces and the mountain ravines to the north.

While the defences to the north are relatively intact the rest of the walls skirting the central court are in a poor state of preservation. (Conservation work recently underway.) Three underground chambers remain including two apparently used for the stabling of horses, judging by the loops provided to attach rings to the stonework. Much of the stone is roughly dressed and has not survived well above the base level. There is, however, some finer work around the windows that survive. Part of a tower is preserved on a lower level in the southeastern corner (overlooking the village).

REFS: Burman 1987: 105; Deschamps *Châteaux – III* 1973: 335–6; Willey 2005: 231–2.

---

4 Perhaps as late as 1180, giving the Ismaeli period of control a span of only six years – Deschamps *Châteaux – III* 1973: 335.
5 At the same time, Marqab was handed to the Hospitallers.

Qalaat Marqab (Plate 17a)

قلعة المرقب

VARIANTS: Margat (Cru) PERIOD: Cru/Arb
ALT: 360m RATING: *** MAP: 46, R2

LOCATION: From Baniyas, follow ascending road for c6 kms reaching the inland
side of the castle, then skirting it to the
south and park on the west (seaward)
side. It is worth pausing on the way up at
the point where you make the right turn,
to gain an appreciation of the southern
defences of the fortress, discussed in detail below.

'The triumph of the gigantic'. The
description of Eydoux, a French writer
on the Crusader fortifications, just
about sums up the first impression of
this formidable castle: predominantly
black, the colour of the extinct volcanic
peak on which it sits, scowling over the
Mediterranean far below. Located at the
point where the coastal plain narrows to
a precarious passage between the sea and
the mountains, Marqab is in many ways the
most baleful of the Crusader fortresses;
certainly the most sombre. From it,
though, access along the sole land route
to the Holy Land could be controlled.

History

The site is the natural location for a
fortified post but it does not seem to
have been used for this purpose until
the Muslims built there in 1062. Baniyas,
at the foot of the mountain, has a much
longer history, dating its foundation to
the Phoenicians, and may have played
the defensive role later assumed by the
massive castle. Baniyas is referred to in
Strabo's *Geography* (c58 BC to cAD 24)
as Balanea. It was used by the Greeks,
Romans and Byzantines and became the
seat of a bishop. The Crusaders installed
themselves first in Baniyas which they
knew as Valénie (Valenia). They reached
the town in November 1098, shortly after
the fall of Antioch, and slaughtered its
inhabitants.

The Crusader presence quickly faded and

it was the Byzantines who took the site of
Marqab from the Arabs in an expedition
of 1104. The date of the return of the
Crusaders is unclear but at some stage
between 1108 and 1140 the site of Marqab
passed to the Principality of Antioch. It
was maintained on behalf of the prince by
a prominent family (Mansoer or Mansour)
in recognition of its strategic potential
particularly in response to the Assassin
threat after 1140.

Later, it was sold by the family to the
Knights Hospitaller (1186). Marqab
avoided the fate of other castles still
held in private hands which lacked the
resources to withstand Saladin's 1188 raid.
Following his victory over the Crusaders
at Hattin (Palestine), Saladin marched past
the fortress of Marqab in his sweep up
the coast in 1188 but, consistent with his
strategy of probing only weak points, did
not attack it.

The Hospitallers converted the fortress
into one of the Crusader strongpoints,
their main effort probably concentrated
on the years 1186 to 1203. They employed
new concepts in military fortification still
only tentatively being exploited in Europe
and exceeded them in scale and boldness,
anticipating many of the achievements
of the military engineers of Philippe II
Auguste in 13th century France. In doing
so, they eschewed the adaptation of
Byzantine concepts which had marked
Crusader defensive works of the first half
of the 12th century. Marqab is thus much
less of a pastiche of different styles than
the more complex fortress, the *Krak
des Chevaliers (also entrusted to the
Hospitallers). T. E. Lawrence saw in it 'all
the best of the Latin fortifications of the
Middle Ages in the East ... informed with
the spirit of the architects of Central and
Southern France'.

Properly manned, there seemed every
reason why the castle should prove
impregnable. It withstood attacks from
the Amir of Aleppo (Malik al-Daher)
in 1204 and by the Turkoman amir, Saif
al-Din Balban, in 1280. The fatal flaw in
the Hospitallers' strategy, however, was
their dwindling manpower resources as

the 13th century brought increasingly fewer volunteers from Europe. By 1271 its status had already been eroded when, following the fall of the Krak to Baybars, the Mamluks of Cairo enforced an agreement for sharing the revenues of Marqab's dependant lands between the Hospitallers and the Sultan. It was besieged, bombarded and undermined by Baybars' successor, Qalawun, beginning on 17 April 1285. One mine brought down the great south tower and with it the castle's reputation for impregnability, convincing the defenders that resistance was useless. The fortress surrendered on 25 May without the need for a final assault, the knights being allowed to retreat to Tartus and Tripoli. Within the next six years, the remainder of the Crusader presence on the coast unravelled, deprived of the strategic strongpoints which had ensured their defences. With the fall of Tripoli in 1289 and Tartus in 1291, the ethos which had sustained such gigantic ambitions ended.

Qalawun retained the fortress and he and his successors strengthened some of its defences, including the south tower. It remained in military hands until Ottoman times but it ended up as a repository for discredited former governors.

Visit

On the ascent by the approach road, take time to gain a good appreciation of the fortress (Arabic name, 'castle of the watch-tower'). The site itself is a natural defensive position, taking advantage of a ridge-like feature which falls away to the north. The plan is basically a huge triangle, the sharp end pointing south where the line of the narrow ridge which joins it to the Jebel Ansariye is interrupted by an artificial ditch. The natural weakness of this southern aspect is the reason for the concentration of the complex defences on this rounded salient (medieval name 'the spur'). Here most of the castle's defensive weight is deployed (plate 17a).

The great donjon served as the central anchor point and the refuge of last resort in the event of the overrunning of the castle. At this point, the second enclosure wall was enormously thickened by the accumulation of functional and defensive constructions making a formidable arrow-head and giving the fortress much of its impression of strength and bulk.

The **south tower** of the outer enclosure wall echoes the great donjon tower above. Note the band of white marble running around the upper part of the outer wall (this can only be observed from the approach road). This typically Mamluk stylistic flourish (stark white on black) carries an Arabic inscription dating from Qalawun's reconstruction of the collapsed south defences. Above it can be found contemporary machicolations or protuding slots for the pouring of boiling oil on potential invaders.

Having reached the main entrance, you will need about two hours to explore the castle adequately. You enter through the **west (tower) gate**. The Arab bridge leading up to it is covered with gradually rising stairs leading via a 90⁰ turn over the ditch and into the entrance gateway (13th century – note the stone brattices and the portcullis) looking out over the Mediterranean. The 12th century outer wall of blocks of dark volcanic basalt joined by white mortar is interrupted to the left by round bastions every 20 m or 30m and the line of the ditch that rings it can still be identified.

After passing through the recessed double-arched gateway, you find yourself in a vaulted entrance vestibule which leads via a right-hand turn into the inner defences. Immediately inside the outer wall is a second defensive wall, somewhat badly preserved in most places. If you continue 30 m between the lines of the two walls, you will reach a **barbican** entrance **gate** (1270).

[Before entering the barbican and the inner defences, those who have time may wish to continue to explore the line of the outer wall. (Note the protected gallery and circuit walk built into the structure.) A newly marked path running for over a kilometre via the southern spur discussed above takes you on a full circuit and provides often spectacular views to the east and north.

The south salient or 'sharp end' of the fortress comprises the main defensive features. The rest of the triangular site to the north and east would have been occupied by more flimsy civilian housing and was certainly heavily built upon in Ottoman times. Although the northern inner enclosure wall has been dismantled, you can still gain some impression of the original extent of the fortified area and the outer walls. Return to the barbican gate.]

From the cross-vaulted entrance chamber, stairs and an archway on the right lead via a subsequent left turn and ascending vaulted stairway into the main **courtyard** of the keep. From the courtyard, the principal parts of the castle to be visited are located around this point, from which you should orient yourself. To the west (right) are the poor remains of the knights' great hall with a segment of Gothic vaulting in one corner.

At the south end of the courtyard, the castle **chapel** can be readily identified. Aligned east-west, its main entrance is on the west (sea) side with a side door to the north. It dates from the initial phase of Hospitaller control (end of 12th century) and is a gem of austere Crusader architecture, inspired by the transition to the Gothic style in France. The beautiful doorways on the northern and western sides are similar in their rich mouldings and elegant colonnettes (only those on the north survive). The interior is divided into two bays by cross-groined vaulting. The central arch dividing the vaulting meets the wall and terminates with two columns encased in pilasters with simplified Corinthian capitals. The absence of internal columns adds a feeling of space in what is a relatively small structure, typical of the striving for openness and light in the Gothic period.

South of the main steps to the chapel, you will find the remains of a two-storeyed building. It was built over a cistern used to store water to provision the garrison and civilians. The southern end of the building is missing. It was linked to the complex of buildings around the **donjon**, the great central tower with walls of massive thickness (5 m in places) probably constructed between 1186 and 1203. Over 20 m in diameter, constructed of dark granite, the donjon's three storeys were pierced with loopholes surveying the perimeter of the southern defences. Another two-storeyed building joins the donjon to the chapel and was probably used as **barracks**.

More than any other site in Syria, the grim but impressive symmetry of this late 12th century construction underlines the determined resourcefulness of the Crusaders' search for security. Ironically, it was not the crumbling of the defences under fire but their undermining by the simple expedient of tunnelling from below which brought the Crusader presence to an end.

Returning to the main courtyard, another series of great chambers northeast of the chapel continues the

46

Qalaat Marqab

outer enclosure
Turkish serail
Arab cemetery
entrance →
west gate
ditch
barbican
great hall
courtyard
ditch
east tower
chapel
donjon
south tower
0 10 20 50 m

line of the fortress defences. They were probably used as **magazines** for storage (though some describe the 46 m long outer room (12th century) which gives on to the second enclosure wall on the east as the great hall). This latter room also leads to the sizeable **east tower** of the castle (built at the same time as the donjon) which gave flanking protection to the southeastern corner and guarded the small postern gate leading to the circuit walk above the first enclosure wall.

Between the main castle and the sea, an isolated watch-tower still stands above the highway as it passes around the lowest ridge extending from the castle. Called **Burj al-Sabi** ('Tower of the Youth'), it protected the access to the castle's port and the coastal route. It comprises a stout tower in basalt, 15 m square, topped with machicolations supported on consoles. Within were two storeys of accommodation and a basement. It was probably built at the same time as the castle itself, namely the end of the 12th or beginning of the 13th century.

Baniyas

Of the town of Baniyas (the Crusaders' Valénie)[6], little of historical interest remains. It is now a small fishing port, commercial centre and base for nearby industries. As late as the mid 19th century, substantial remains of the medieval Valénie were described by European travellers but all have disappeared in the further development of the town.

REFS: Boase 1967: 56–60; Deschamps *Châteaux –* III 1973: 259–85; Eydoux 1982.

Qalaat al-Mehelbeh

قلعة امهلّبة

VARIANTS: Platanus (Lat), Balatonos (Cru)
PERIOD: Cru   ALT: 774 m   RATING: –
MAPS: 47, R2

LOCATION: Leave Latakia by the old Tartus road. After c17 km, after the village of Snobar, turn left along the road to

6 Possibly also the site of the ancient Leucade.

Jobet Borghal. Follow this for +22 km into the hills to the village of Mehelbeh (3 km past Beit Salame). Walk (c15 minutes) up to the ruins.

Qalaat al-Mehelbeh is situated in wild and beautiful mountain scenery, in one of the innermost recesses of the Jebel Ansariye. From here there are commanding views over the plain towards Latakia and over the northern reaches of the range, as far as Mount Casius. The scene is unspoilt and rarely visited. Even though the ruins are at best vestigial, the one hour trip from the coast (perhaps en route to other sites such as Qalaat Saladin or Burzey) is well worthwhile.

History

As with many Crusader sites, the choice of this high ground for a fortification pre-dates the Frankish presence. The local mountain clan, the Bani al-Ahmar, built a fortified post here at the beginning of the 11th century to guard the point at which the route over the range from the Orontes Valley divided into branches leading either to Jeble or Latakia, the two nearby ports on the Mediterranean. The Byzantine governor of Antioch took the post from the clan in 1031 and completed the original fortress. At some stage during the next 80 years, it again seems to have lapsed into the hands of clansmen (the Bani Sulaia), Byzantine control in the area having weakened in the wake of the Muslim resurgency.

After the Crusader presence was progressively established in the area beginning with the capture of Antioch in 1098, Mehelbeh fell into the Crusaders' sphere of interest. The then Prince of Antioch, Roger, took it from the clans in 1118 and made it a dependency of Robert, Lord of Saône, whose castle lay 12 km to the north (*Qalaat Saladin). It remained a Crusader possession for 70 years, affiliated to Antioch via Saône and part of the system of inland castles (Burzey, Saône, Qahtan, Boqabeis) which guarded the passes leading to the Orontes, from where the threat to the coastal Crusader presence emanated.

In the end, though, the Crusaders lacked the manpower to maintain a presence in strength away from the coast. Balatonos, like many of the lightly guarded inland posts, surrendered to Saladin during his sweep through the mountains in 1188, three days after Saône. Under the Ayyubids it was incorporated after 1194 into the possessions of the Governor of Aleppo, al-Zaher Ghazi (see *Harim).

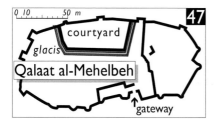

Local tribal chiefs regained control in the mid 13th century probably as a result of the disruption resulting from the first Mongol invasion (1260) but in 1269 it was again brought under centralised control by Baybars as part of his campaign leading to the capture of the Krak (1271). Some work was done on it during the Mamluk period but its importance dwindled as the threat from the alien presence on the coast disappeared and the fabric of the fortifications gradually decayed.

Visit

The castle lies on a rocky prominence at the top of a low mountain. Slightly elongated east-west, its maximum length is 170 m. An enclosure wall runs (much has crumbled away except at the base) around the crest. The wall was broken by square, round or polygonal bastions. Below the walls, the natural escarpment falls away except on the west side where a ditch was used to supplement the natural defences of the site.

The castle was undergoing extensive restoration when last visited (2007). The main gate, on the south, is marked by the remains of a flanking tower, polygonal in shape. This brings you into the main courtyard where care needs to be taken

to avoid cistern openings. What might have been the barracks area lies to the right of the gateway. On the north of the enclosure, note the fine piece of Frankish stonework in the form of a glacis, the remains of an inner defensive wall protecting the redoubt. The rest of the stonework is a mixture, the finer more regular work (especially the great bossage blocks) being Crusader period, the rest later. By curving around to the right, you can gain the upper level which includes another, smaller courtyard, but much of the fabric is in ruins.

On descending, it may be possible to make your way around via the north, circumnavigating the walls via a small local (Alawi) shrine of curious but charming origins set, as usual, in an oak grove. Built upon a spring, the shrine has re-used some of the stones from the castle including a whole arch and part of a scupture of a lion, undoubtedly the work of Baybars' reign of which the Venetian-type lion was a symbol. The shrine is a mausoleum of a local holy man, Sheikh Yunis. An inscription on the water trough is dated to 1285 during the reign of Sultan Qalawun (r 1280–90).

REFS: Deschamps III 1973: 339–40; van Berchem & Fatio 1914: 283–88.

Qalaat Mudiq (Apamea)

قلعة المضيق

VARIANTS: Apamée PERIOD: Arb RATING: – MAP: 10, R2

LOCATION: Western edge of the ancient site of *Apamea, Orontes Valley.

Qalaat Mudiq, the **citadel** of Apamea, dates back to well before Seleucid times and played a particularly important role as an Arab point of defence against the Crusades. The Orontes Valley for long served as the interface between the Frankish and Arab worlds, with most sites on the east side of the valley (notably *Shaizar and *Maarat al-Numan) confronting the Crusader castles on the west (*Qalaat Burzey, *Qalaat Mehelbeh, *Qalaat Abu Qobeis and *Masyaf). The

remains of the medieval citadel show
no trace of the Crusader occupation
(1106–49). The indications of the later
Arab fortress are largely swallowed by
the modern upper village but a tower
pokes up above domestic walls. The main
gateway to the citadel was on the east
side, a typically narrow passage confined
between towers (cf *Harim). The rest
of the outer walls comprise variegated
stonework (some re-used from earlier
periods) including Mamluk (13th century).
There is a beautiful view over the Orontes
valley with the Jebel Ansariye to the west
and Jebel Zawiye to the northeast. An
Ottoman mosque (second half of 16th
century) lies on a southern spur of the
citadel mound.

REFS: Dangles in Faucherre (et al) 2005: 189–204.

Qalaat Najm (Plate 18a)

قلعة نجم

VARIANTS: ?Caeciliana (Lat); Qalaat Nadjim
(Arb) PERIOD: Arb RATING: * MAP: R4

LOCATION: Take the highway to the
Jezira, northeast out of Aleppo (*Raqqa
road, then left turn at airport interchange). After *Menbij (71 km), continue +19
km (7 km before new bridge crossing of
the Euphrates) then turn southeast (right)
for +12 km. The castle is located on the
right bank of the Euphrates.

Caeciliana, an important Euphrates port
and crossing point in this area, was also
the bridgehead for *Menbij, the assembly-
point for Roman forces preparing for
campaigns against the Parthian/Sasanian
threat in the region of Mesopotamia.

Today, while the precise location of
Caeciliana is not clear, the chief point
of interest in the area is the remarkable
Arab castle of the 13th century carefully
restored by the Antiquities Department
using mostly original methods and
materials. Though the wear and tear on
the castle over the years has been great,
enough remains, with the reconstructed
elements, to give you a better idea of
Arab fortification techniques than at any
site outside the *Aleppo Citadel.

The existing remains largely date from the
13th century rebuilding of the fortress
erected earlier by Nur al-Din (r 1146–74)
who in turn had reconstructed an earlier
fortress. The plan largely reflects the
concepts of Arab military architecture
realised from 1208 to 1215 by al-Zaher
Ghazi. This Ayyubid ruler of Aleppo, whose
great achievement was the rebuilding of
the Aleppo Citadel, was a son of Saladin.
By the next century, however, Qalaat
Najm was already in decline, a victim, like
other sites, of the neglect and disruption
which attended the Mongol invasions of
the late 13th and 14th centuries.

The castle takes full advantage of an
existing highpoint in the terrain. The
rocky crag is in itself a natural defence,
towering steeply above the river plain.
On the river side, a cladding of dressed
stone provides an effective glacis and two
towers further discourage scaling of the
heights and defend the entrance gateway.
Above the entrance, an Arabic inscription
pays tribute to the work of Ghazi.

A great vaulted central passage leads
up from the gateway with chambers
on either side. The castle spreads over
a series of these underground rooms
and passageways (some reputedly
giving secret access to the river) and
two upper floors. Some pattern to the
chambers and battlements on top of the
mound is gradually emerging from the
reconstruction. Remains include a small
palace with a central courtyard with iwans
and a mosque.

To visit the modern monument
commemorating the re-entombment
of the Suleiman Shah, forefather of the
Otoman sultans, who perished in the
Euphrates downstream at a site now
covered by Lake Assad (*Qalaat Jaabr),
return to main Jezira road but turn right
(instead of left for Menbij) and continue 12
km to Euphrates bridge at Qara Qozaq.
Tomb is on east bank of the river (north
of road), guarded by a small contingent of
Turkish troops.

REFS: Dussaud 1927: 449; Korn II 2004: 277–8;
Eiden AAAS 1999.

Qalaat Ollaiqa

قلعة العليقة

VARIANTS: Argyrokastron (Grk) PERIOD:
Arb, Cru ALT: 352 m RATING: – MAP: R2

LOCATION: 13 km directly east of Baniyas. Take Latakia road north. Sign c8 km
points to the castle. Follow winding roads
for c20 km via Annazel.

This site was probably first fortified by
the Byzantines in the 11th century. It
was acquired for the Crusaders by the
Mansour family in 1118 but later on-sold
to the Ismaelis after 1160.

The fortress was built on a narrow
triangular plateau atop a conical
prominence in the mountains to the north
of the Baniyas River. The plan follows the
Ismaeli preference for concentric (in this
case, roughly triangular) enclosures with
a keep on the northeast side of the inner
fortifications. The entrance is on the same
side via a rising ramp that negotiates four
gates including a sharp turn left. The few
recognisable remains inside the outer
enclosure include a rather elegant cross-
vaulted chamber leading to the gate of the
inner fort. The latter is a superb example
of precise (probably Ayyubid) masonry.

REFS: Deschamps III 1973: 333; Vachon in
Faucherre (et al) 2004; Willey 2005: 230–1.

Qalaat Rahba

قلعة الرحبة

VARIANTS: Qalaat al-Rahba (Arb) PERIOD:
Arb ALT: 244 m RATING: * MAP: R5

LOCATION: Take the Abu Kemal road
south of Deir al-Zor. After 45 km, the
town of Mayadin lies to the left, on the
river. Castle +1 km south on the right of
the road, accessible by a dirt track.

This small, almost fairy-tale, castle presents
an unreal impression when seen from afar.
Constructed eight centuries ago, the fabric
of the five-sided donjon has been literally
crumbling to pieces ever since. As the

stone disintegrates, the dust accumulates
around the walls above the ditch.

The first fort was constructed on this spot
by Malik Ibn Tauk during the caliphate of
al-Mamun (813–33) but was destroyed
by an earthquake in 1157. A new castle
was built by al-Mujahid Assad al-Din
Shirkuh II, an amir of Homs (r 1186–1240)
and uncle of Saladin, as part of the the
latter's grand design for the unification of
Syria under a single Muslim ruler (a goal
largely realised in 1154). This was part
of a program of castle-building, all in the
style common to Islamic fortifications, in
areas of central Syria controlled by Homs
(*Qalaat Shmemis, *Qalaat Shirkuh).
In 1264, the Mamluk ruler, Baybars,
appointed an Egyptian as governor. As the
successive Mongol invasions ravaged Syria
(1260–1400) the fort's usefulness lapsed
in the face of the damage inflicted by the
invaders.

Although contemporary with many of the
major Crusader castles of Syria, the style
of fortification was altogether different.
Instead of a massive keep area surrounded
by complex rings of curtain wall, bastions,
and ditches, Qalaat Rahba concentrates
on a central mound, ringed by a high but
simple set of walls (a pentagon roughly
270 m by 95 m) rising from a huge ditch.
Enough remains of the inner fabric to
give you an impression of the scale of the
defences. The central enclosure echoes
the five-sided shape of the outer wall on a
smaller scale (c60 m by 30 m). This donjon
had its largest side to the west and was
on three levels, the lowest comprising
a large cistern. Six construction phases
ending probably in the 14th century have
been identified with a tendency to replace
mud brick with conglomerate stone in
later phases. Some of the brickwork in
geometric designs is characteristic of an
early phase of Arab architecture heavily
influenced by Mesopotomia and Persia.

REFS: Bianquis CFAS 1989: 220–6; Bylinski in
Faucherre (et al) 2004: 159–62; Elisséeff & Paillet
1986; Musil Middle Euphrates 1927: 7–8; Toueir,
Bianquis & Rousset CFAS 1996: 220–6.

Qalaat Saladin (Plate 18b)

قلعة صلاح الدين

VARIANTS: Sigon (Grk); Château de Saône,
Saona, Sehunna (Cru); Qalaat Sahyun, Qalaat
Salah al-Din[7] (Arb – mod) PERIOD: Byz/Cru/
Arb ALT: 400 m RATING: *** MAPS: 48, R2

LOCATION: In the mountains 24 km
east of *Latakia. From Latakia (Jumhuriye
Square, starting point) take southern exit
for *Tartus. Take turnoff marked Hafeh
(+15 km). Above Hafeh (+2 km), a sign
points right to the castle. +1.5 km, then
turn left along the spectacular and circuitous road (+2.4 km) that leads across the
ravine forming the northern perimeter of
the fortress. It is worth pausing before descending the ravine in order to gain a full
appreciation of the layout of the site and
to admire the dramatic setting.

*... the most sensational thing in castle-
building I have seen.*

[T E Lawrence – letter to his
mother, September 1909[8]]

While its defences are less intact than
the unstudied symmetry of the *Krak
des Chevaliers and it is less sombre and
brooding in its aspect than *Marqab,
this is an example of Crusader castle-
building at its most romantic. Much of this
is due to the site, a ridge between two
spectacular ravines leading down from the
commanding reaches of the Jebel Ansariye.
(Nabi Yunes, the highest peak in the range
– alt 1583 m – is immediately behind.)
The fall of the land takes the eye down
to the coastal plain and beyond it the
Mediterranean sparkling in the distance.
The castle represents the flamboyance of
the Crusader enterprise – perhaps folly
is a better word – in a raw and beautiful
location, softened today by the peaceful
setting.

History

Long before the Crusaders, the site was
chosen for its defensive properties. From

7 This is the official title bestowed on the
castle in 1957 to commemorate Saladin's
capture of the fortress in 1188.
8 Quoted in Boase 1967: 49.

this secluded spot could be surveyed
the access routes between the Orontes
Plain and the coast via the Bdama Pass to
the north that today carries traffic from
Latakia to Aleppo. While not directly on
this route, the presence of a formidable
strongpoint in the area was a severe
impediment to anyone trying to challenge
control of movement. Moreover, its
commanding location protected the sweep
of the broad plain behind Latakia, the
reason which probably led to the earliest
fortification by the Phoenicians (early first
millennium BC) who were holding it when
Alexander reached Syria (331 BC).

When the Byzantines moved back into Syria
in the second half of the tenth century, the
Emperor John I Tzimisces seized this site
from the Hamdanid dynasty of Aleppo and
began the first substantial defensive works
after 975. It is not known precisely when
the Crusaders took it over, probably in
the first two decades of the 12th century.
Certainly by 1119, a castle on this spot,
a feudal endowment from Roger, Prince
of Antioch, is recorded in the possession
of a local seigneur, Robert of Saône.
The family's extensive domains (which
stretched from Balatonos in the south
(*Qalaat Mehelbeh) to Sardone (east of
the Orontes)) perhaps explain how they
found the resources to undertake the
greatest Crusader building enterprise
of the 12th century. As Deschamps has
observed, other Crusader leaders had
built economically; at Saône, everything
was 'big, solid and magnificent'.

Saône (as it was known to the Crusaders)
was unlike the other major Crusade
strongholds in two other respects. It was
never entrusted to one of the major orders,
the Knights Templar or the Hospitallers;
and its construction dates entirely from
the early phase of the Crusader presence
in the east, namely the years between
1100 and 1188. In the latter year, it fell
to Saladin, the first major casualty of the
Crusader's fundamental problem, the lack
of sufficient manpower to protect their
far-flung positions.

Confident after his major victory over the
Crusaders at Hattin in Palestine in 1187

which resulted in the Arab recovery of Jerusalem, Saladin took his army on an expedition to the north to probe Crusader defences and block the prospective access route for a fourth Crusade bent on re-liberating Jerusalem. He contented himself with softer targets, especially the smaller, more lightly-defended castles. He took all but the inner redoubt of Tartus but moved on when resistance stiffened. Safita fell to him but he marched straight past the great fortress of Marqab. On 23 July 1188, Latakia surrendered.

Saladin moved on the next day to Saône, arriving on the 26th and beginning his siege on 27 July. Saladin's forces pounded the castle from the plateau to the east while his son, al-Zaher Ghazi, moving in from Aleppo, took up position across the north ravine. The Crusaders resisted fiercely but two days later the walls were breached by bombardment from the mangonels of Ghazi, the weak point proving to be the elongated and relatively thin walls of the lower court. Muslim soldiers stormed the breach,[9] gained the western enclosure and from there swarmed over the narrow and incomplete ditch into the upper fortress. The garrison, overwhelmed by the swiftness of events, surrendered after barely a fight. The vast area of the fortress had proved too much for them to defend. Moreover the easy victory by Saladin at Latakia gave little point to their further resistance to an Arab leader who had established his prowess by his triumph the previous year against the united forces of the Jerusalem Kingdom and who enjoyed a reputation for magnanimity.

Unlike the other major fortresses seized by the Arab leader (*Tartus, *Safita, *Latakia), Saône did not lapse back into Crusader hands. It was lost to the cause, along with other smaller strongpoints along the mountain (*Qalaat Burzey and *Qalaat al-Mehelbeh are nearby examples). It was controlled from 1188 to 1272 by a local family, that of Amir Nasr

al-Din Manguwiris, but was ceded by the family to Sultan Baybars as a contribution to his campaign against the Crusader presence; a campaign which also asserted central authority in the mountain region. It was occupied from 1280 by the rebel ex-Governor of Damascus, Sonqor al-Ashqar, but was regained for the Mamluk Sultan Qalawun in 1287 after another siege. In the course of these occupations it acquired a range of Ayyubid and Mamluk additions, including a mosque built by Sultan Qalawun. Though the lower enclosure housed for a time a small town, it was gradually deserted in favour of more convenient locations once the security of the area was assured. Commenting on its neglect as late as 1967, Boase observed: 'It still today keeps something of this remoteness, its solitude rarely disturbed, its secrets not wholly explored'.

Visit

As it is not easy to gain a full perspective of the site, it is suggested that you pause on the other side of the ravine as you approach (plate 18b) and take note of its complex layout. The narrow ridge between two ravines runs approximately east-west and was once joined on the inland (eastern) side to the mountain spine. Probably in Byzantine times, however, this link was broken by a formidable 156 m long ditch cut from the living rock, 28 m deep and 14 m to 20 m wide.

Along the elongated triangular site which follows the remainder of the ridge down to the west the Crusader castle was built on several levels stretching 740 m and covering a total of 5 ha. To the east (left, but not visible from this vantage point) is the main keep, deploying the castle's most formidable defences against a potential enemy utilising the high ground. Next, moving westwards, is a courtyard that precedes the core of the Byzantine fortress, preserved by the Crusaders. West of the knoll on which the earlier fortress stands, a ditch separated the upper and lower courts. The elongated circuit wall descended the hill, encompassing further strongpoints or gateways in the lower court, including a small chapel at

9 The point at which the breach was made can be traced today in a section (partly repaired) of the north wall of the lower court, a little to the west of the point at which the walls narrow.

the narrowest point. These somewhat
thin outer defences petered out with a
Byzantine round tower at the sharp end
where the two ravines meet.

What you see is 'the finest and best-
preserved of the feudal castles built in the
East before the profound modification
of military architecture at the end of the
12th century'.[10] After the great victories
of Saladin in the 1180s and the loss of
Jerusalem, the defence of the Crusader
realms was undertaken with a new
sense of purpose. The Templars and the
Hospitallers were given a key role in the
professional management of the main
defensive positions and a new approach
was taken to military architecture. The

wish to take a closer look at the walls
on the south and east sides where they
are best preserved. The fortifications
here formed the line of defence against
the relatively open and thus vulnerable
southeastern approach. This outer line of
walls, combining round towers to the east
and the stouter square bastions on the
south, show the transition from Byzantine
to Crusader work. The three relatively
slender round towers (east) are Byzantine
in origin, adapted and strengthened in the
Crusader rebuilding of the 11th century.
In the massive square towers (south),
the stone is laid in large blocks finished
with neat bossage in a typically precise
Crusader style.

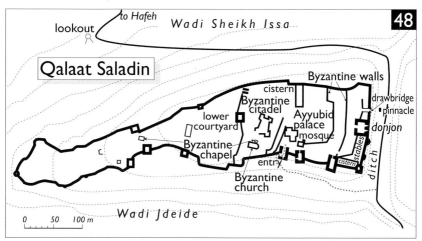

result was the formidable work realised
at Marqab and the vast improvements
made at the Krak. But this came too late
for Saône already irretrievably lost. Its
construction had been part of the more
spontaneous phase of Crusader enterprise
when urgency required an improvisatory
approach adapting local and Byzantine
techniques.

The road continues down, across the
stream and up the other side of the ravine.
After crossing the ridge via the ditch (to
be inspected on foot in a moment), you
park on the right hand side. You may

If you walk back to the east face, a close
examination of the ditch will convey a
striking impression of how much labour
went into carving it out by hand with
relatively basic tools. It is not entirely
clear whether this work was substantially
or entirely completed by the Byzantines
before the Crusaders arrived. Most likely,
it was a Byzantine achievement which the
Crusaders deepened and widened. Note
especially the 28 m tall needle of rock
which was left at the northern end of the
ditch to support the drawbridge leading to
the postern gate (a secondary entrance to
the castle). The postern gate is flanked by
two shallow rounded towers.

10 Fedden *Crusader Castles* 1950: 49.

To gain entry to the castle, return to the main entrance on the south side. A path leads to the third of the square bastions. The entrance door is located on the left flank where it gained most protection from bombardment. The slot above either housed a portcullis or served to rain down burning oil. You enter a spacious vestibule from which a second door opens to the north leading into the castle compound. (Notice the huge monolith stone which forms the lintel of the second door – 3.25 m in length, topped by a shallow relieving arch.)

The tour described will take you in an anti-clockwise direction around the fortifications. The first tower on the right after the entry is marked by two doors on the north face, one leading up to a hall, the other to an underground storage area. Fifty metres east, you come to a second square bastion. It is similar in style to the other Crusader bastions on the south side but includes a sally port to facilitate covert exit. Note that there is no direct access from the towers to the battlements between, indicating the Byzantine origins of the defensive concept.

As you work around from the tower just described, there are two other buildings worth noting. The first is the **cistern** at the southeast corner, one of several for the storage of water. Between the cistern and the donjon is a building in the form of an extensive pillared hall which housed the castle **stables**. From this point, you reach the narrow courtyard flanking the main donjon (or keep) situated in the middle of the east side, above the huge ditch.

The eastern donjon is built on a massive scale with walls over 5 m thick on a base 24 m^2; as formidable as the great donjons at *Marqab or *Safita. Designed for a last-ditch defence of the castle, it presents a largely blank front even to the inner courtyard. The keep comprises two storeys topped by a terrace. The entry is a plain doorway on the west with a straight lintel above, a feature introduced into Crusader architecture from Byzantine examples. The first storey is 11 m high but presents a gloomy appearance due to the

restricted light from the slit loopholes or *archères*. The groined vaulting is supported on a single central pillar. A staircase built into the north wall gives access to the upper storey which duplicates in plan the hall below except for the addition of three windows. A further staircase leads to a panoramic view from the roof parapets.

As you move northwards around the defences, you will reach the postern gate where the **drawbridge** led into the castle. The doorway was protected by two round towers already noted. To the right is a domed room of Byzantine origins.

At this point you can see on the rise to the west, beyond the courtyard and behind the minaret, the remains of the **Byzantine citadel** including the bulky rectangular tower, the core around which the Crusader castle was built. The Byzantine design relied essentially on a series of three or possibly four concentric defensive walls as opposed to the massive concentration of Crusader defences on the most vulnerable outer point to the east where the Byzantine walls were superceded by the Crusader keep. To the northeast, however, part of the Byzantine wall survives though the two huge cradle-vaulted cisterns towards the middle of the north front are Crusader. The largest **cistern** (northeast of the Byzantine tower) is 32 m long and 10 m deep. Across the ridge to the west, the Byzantine defenses followed the line of the wall between the upper and lower fortresses which you can reach by continuing to skirt anti-clockwise around the central rise.

You will reach a point where the upper terrace looks directly down to the lower courtyard. Below it you can detect the outline of the ditch which complemented the inner dividing wall between upper and lower courtyards. Saladin's forces gained entry to the inner castle across this ditch, after storming the lower walls. The forces concentrated in the upper keep then surrendered. The tower to the right was rebuilt in Ayyubid times to replace the structure partly destroyed in the Muslim assault.

If you feel like bashing your way through the heavy (and prickly) undergrowth, you can descend to the lower courtyard. After 150 m, at the point where the thin-walled defences (Byzantine in origin) narrow, there is a small but charming **chapel** (also **Byzantine**), much overgrown with vegetation. There is also a cluster of square towers to protect the twists and turns of the walls at this point and to guard the postern gates giving direct access to the lower town from both north and south. This was the point (north side) at which Ghazi's forces pounded the outer enclosure and first gained entry.

Returning to the upper enclosure, continue in an anti-clockwise path to take in the rest of the inner Byzantine fortress. As you head back towards the entrance gateway, you will pass on the left the remains of the principal **church** of the castle, once assumed to be Crusader but now seen as Byzantine after a 2002 French study.

Before exiting, you will find the main additions of the Muslim period immediately to the left. These include a **mosque** (with minaret) probably dating from the time of the Sultan Qalawun (r 1280–90) and an Ayyubid palace complete with **baths**, partially restored. The baths include an attractive courtyard with four *iwans*. The palace entrance is marked by a superb gateway in stalactited carving (probably late 12th, early 13th century).

REFS: Boase 1967: 49–51; Deschamps *Châteaux – III* 1973: 217–47; Dangles (*et al*) 2004; Sa'ade *Histoire* 1968: 980–1015; Smail 1985: 236–43.

Qalaat Shirkuh (Palmyra, Plate 19a)

قلعة شركوه / إبن معن

VARIANTS: Qalaat Ibn Maan, 'Arab Castle'
PERIOD: Ayy RATING: * MAP: R4

LOCATION: 2 km north of the main ruins of Palmyra. It can be approached by vehicle (road from the northwest outskirts of Tadmor); but that is spoiling the fun. The climb up the pebble-strewn slope (150 m above the valley) takes about 40 minutes.

The castle itself has recently been reconstructed and a visit is an essential adjunct to any exploration of Palmyra. The splendour of the scene either at sunset or at dawn as the sun rises over the ruins and the mountains behind is a memorable souvenir of Palmyra.

The castle has for long been attributed to the Lebanese Maanite amir, Fakhr al-Din (1590–1635), who tested the limits of Ottoman flexibility in the early 17th century by expanding his area of direct control well beyond Mount Lebanon as far east as the Syrian Desert, hoping to present the Ottomans with a fait accompli that they would be too weak-willed to reverse. His calculations were wrong. He was pursued and arrested by the Ottomans in 1635 and kept in captivity in Constantinople until executed later in the year.

Recent Polish research has confirmed, however, that Fakhr al-Din simply briefly (1630–2) occupied an earlier Ayyubid castle (c 1230, post-dating the fortification of the Bel Temple at *Palmyra) built by the Homs amir, al-Mujahid Assad al-Din Shirkuh II (r 1186–1240) who was also responsible for Qalaat al-Shmemis (*Selemiye and Qalaat al-Shmemis) and *Qalaat Rahba.

Relatively small in size, the fortifications are based on an original triangular fortress of seven towers (1230), extended later in the 13th century with curtain walls to the east and west, the whole ringed by a deep ditch. The effect is spectacular. You enter from the south via a metal bridge that brings you to a landing between two towers. Like many Muslim castles, the internal arrangement of chambers and defences is compact, with a steep passage taking you up to the internal court. This is surrounded by battlements with a substantial thickening of the defences on the south side. There are memorable views for 360° around but perhaps the most striking is the view to the north along the spine of the Jebel al-Tadmoria as the rising sun begins to colour its rugged slopes.

REFS: Bounni & Alas'ad 1982: 92; Bylinski 1993: 144–53; Bylinski 1999: 151–208.

Qalaat Yahmur

قلعة يحمور

VARIANTS: Jammura (anc)   PERIOD: Cru
RATING: – MAPS: 49, R2

LOCATION: 12 km southeast of Tartus. From *Tartus, take the road to Safita. At c10 km (village of Ghattazziye, before Khirbet Almazeh) take road to right. At first intersection, fork right. +2 km to Yahmur village.

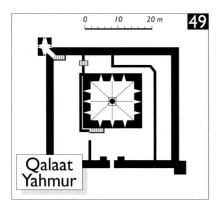

This site provides a wonderful, and relatively intact, picture of a fortified outpost of the Crusader period. There are remains in the environs from periods earlier than the Crusades, including some Roman tombs. There is no evidence, however, that the site of the present small keep was fortified before the Crusades.

Some doubt has recently been cast on whether this is the Castrum Rubrum of the medieval chronicles transferred in 1177 to the Hospitallers who had been entrusted with the defence of the hinterland of Tartus. (The traditional identification was based on the assumption that the Crusaders confused Yahmar with 'ahmar' (red) in Arabic.) Castrum Rubrum is probably to be sought elsewhere in the neighbourhood but this fort, clearly identified as Yahmur, temporarily fell

to the Muslims in 1188 during Saladin's campaign in the area. The Crusaders recovered it and it remained in their hands for another century. It fell in 1289, two years before Tartus, to the forces of the Mamluk sultan, Qalawun.

The keep, essentially a robust watch-tower with a surrounding wall, was probably a fortified farmstead under a seigneur. Along with numerous other smaller towers in the Homs Gap area (a nearby example is Miyar, 2 km southeast), such posts complemented the larger fortifications, *Safita and Arima (*Qalaat Areimeh). The points were often in line of sight, enabling contact by signal fires.

The construction is basic but solid, consistent with Frankish work of the late 12th century. It consists of a stubby square tower with a lower room surrounded by an outer wall obscured by modern housing. Inside the wall, galleries provided accommodation and storage to the east and west. The western gallery roof served as a platform leading to the donjon. The donjon's lower chamber reveals the solid construction with the arched vaults coming down to a central pillar (cf the donjon at *Qalaat Saladin). This gave sturdy support to the upper storey which can be reached by a staircase built into the north wall. The terrace gives a commanding view of the countryside. Note the two watch-towers at the southeastern and northwestern corners of the outer enclosure, the latter still reasonably intact. The site has been under reconstruction since 2005.

REFS: Biller & Burger DM 2004: 233–52; Dangles (et al) 2004; Deschamps Châteaux – III 1973: 317–9.

Qalb Lozeh

قلب لوزة

VARIANTS: Qalbloze PERIOD: Byz ALT: 683 m RATING: ** MAPS: 50, R3, R3a

LOCATION: Follow directions for Harim. After 17.4 km, take the left turn (instead of continuing on to Harim). Qalb Lozeh is on the top of the ridge, after +5 km.

The church at Qalb Lozeh (in Arabic, 'the heart of the almond'), is one of the most celebrated ecclesiastical monuments in Syria. Though there are earlier churches which survive in reasonable condition, this is the first example which realises on a monumental scale the Syrian model of the broad-aisled basilica church. It anticipates (possibly only by a decade or two) the bold experiment at *Saint Simeon and its decoration is of the same order of sophistication. It represents, in short, the full development of a Syrian style as an offshoot from Byzantine models and anticipates many of the features which were to find their way eventually to Europe in the Romanesque period (eg the dramatic entrance arch and flanking towers).

Qalb Lozeh is one of a group of Druze villages which have survived in the Jebel Ala since the tenth century, considerably isolated from the other communities in the area of Jebel al-Arab (Jebel Hauran) south of Damascus and the Golan region near Mount Hermon.

Visit

The church is the only ancient remains surviving in this mountain hamlet and it is not difficult to find it as the road winds its way between the dwellings. You will come upon the church from the north side. If you walk around to the right, you will see the entrance just noted with the three-storeyed towers to each side. These towers once framed a huge semi-circular arch topped by a terrace but only the footings on the left of the arch survive. Behind is the entrance doorway where the arch theme is continued, relieving the weight of masonry above the door. Reconstructions of the main arch show how this bold effect virtually brings to a climax several centuries of Syrian fascination with this device, seen also in the local adaptation of Roman styles in such centres as Palmyra or even the monumental arched entrance *(propylaeum)* to the Temple of Jupiter in Damascus.
To complete a circuit of the exterior, continue anti-clockwise to the south side, marked by three decorated entrance

doorways and the then newly-developed volute band flowing around the windows. Continue on to the east end (behind the altar) and you will come to the semi-circular *chevet* which takes the apse out beyond the rectangular lines of the building. This too is a new development, most Syrian churches having embedded the semi-circular apse inside the outer rectangular shape of the building, using complex and massive stonework to accommodate the incompatible shapes. The *chevet* is finished off by a device soon to be further developed at Saint Simeon, the use of two tiers of colonnettes (the second level has gone) topped by a cornice to embellish the curved wall.

Completing the circuit, you will come again to the north side from which you can now enter the building. The first thing that will strike you as you enter is the dramatic shape of the three sweeping arches which divide the central from the side aisles and once carried the clerestory and roof. This practice of substituting piers for columns, thus integrating the side aisles more fully with the nave, became a feature of later Syrian church building (Church of St Sergius at *Resafa (480–500) or the Bissos church at *Ruweiha (sixth century) are good examples). To support the huge weight of masonry at the critical points, relatively slim piers are used but in later examples the piers become considerably more massive.

Thankfully, much of this structure survives in a remarkable state of preservation at Qalb Lozeh and even some of the stone roofing slabs of the side aisles are still intact. By providing the side aisles with a flat roof, the builders of Qalb Lozeh allowed considerably more light to enter the church through the clerestory windows. Note the elegant treatment of these windows, separated by small brackets and colonnettes which once supported the wooden structure of the roof over the main aisle. The semi-circular apse preserves intact its vaulted semi-dome and the choir in front (raised above the level of the nave) is flanked by two side rooms (the *prothesis* on the left accessible to the faithful; the *diaconicon* on the right reserved for clergy). The outline of a *bema* can be seen in the paving.

The standard of decoration framing the apse's semi-dome is particularly worth noting, rising on each side from beautifully treated pilasters and capitals of almost classical simplicity. Mattern rightly observes that the architects of Qalb Lozeh show an ability to use classical Greek norms 'with unexpected effect ... to give them a new application, even a new life'. Certainly the overall effect is more harmonious than the over-achievement which later churches strive for, often mixing styles and shapes with ungainly effect.

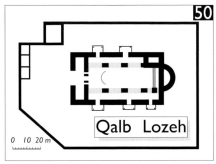

Qalb Lozeh

0 10 20 m

The dating of the church has been much debated. Butler had dated it to around 480. The later expert on the villages of the limestone country, Tchalenko, argues that by comparison with the nearby dated church at Bettir (2 km north), Qalb Lozeh must have been built before 469. Most likely, he feels, the church was built during the lifetime of St Simeon (d 459) or immediately after. Many aspects of the Qalb Lozeh basilica were repeated, often in a more refined way, at the great quadruple basilica erected on the site of Simeon's column, probably after 475.

Except for a few olive trees, the ancient village consisted of little but the church, there being no sizeable patches of arable land on the limestone ridge. The fact that the church was surrounded by a walled compound supports the likelihood that it was intended not to serve a village but to provide a stop for pilgrims, perhaps those bound for the already flourishing

pilgrimage centre at Deir Semaan, at the foot of Simeon's pillar. Whatever, the explanation, clearly a number of seminal influences came together on this site with an unusually productive blending of metropolitan and local Syrian influences most likely inspired by the pilgrimage role. Krautheimer may be right in criticising the unnecessarily monumental treatment of a relatively small-scale building and ascribes this and the emphasis on classical decoration to the Emperor Zeno's attempts to revive the classical heritage.

REFS: Butler *AE* II 1903: 221–5; Butler *EC* 1929: 71–3; de Vogüé I 1865–77: 135–8 pl 122–9); Krautheimer 1981: 160–4; Loosley 2003: 256–62; Mattern 1944: 107–14; Tchalenko *Basilique* 1974; Tchalenko *Travaux* 1973; Tchalenko *Villages* I 1953: 343–4; II XXII, CVIII, CXXXVI; Tchalenko & Baccache 1979–80: pl 418–25.

Qanawat (Plate 20a)

قناوأت

VARIANTS: Kanatha, Kenath, Nobah (Bib)[11]; Canata, Canatha (Grk); Kanawat PERIOD: Rom/Byz RATING: ** MAPS: 51, 52, R1

LOCATION: 90 km southeast of Damascus. Leave Damascus by the *Suweida road. Pass through Shahba (87 km) and at +10 km (*Slim on right) turn left for +4 km then left again and ascend +2 km to Qanawat.

History

Qanawat ('canal' in Arabic[12]) is a site of considerable interest. Though its origins may go back earlier, first historical mention of the town dates to the reign of Herod the Great (first century BC) when Nabataean Arab forces inflicted a humiliating defeat on the Jewish ruler's army. (The campaign was the result of pressure on Herod from Antony who wished to restore the area to Cleopatra's realms.) It remained

11 Numbers 32, 42 relates its conquest by Nobah who renamed the settlement of Kanatha or Kenath after himself. It is later mentioned in Judges 8, 10–12.
12 Perhaps a play on words, referring both to the remains of a Roman water reticulation system and to the pre-Roman Kanatha.

an issue of contention between the Nabataeans and the Hasmonaeans to the south. From Pompey's time until Trajan (r AD 98–117), it was listed as one of the cities of the Decapolis, a loose federation allowed by the Romans to retain some degree of civic autonomy.[13] The first prestige projects were erected in the late first century BC or early first century

(late second century) and transferred to the province of Arabia at the end of the second century. Christianity flourished (as elsewhere in the Hauran) in the fourth and fifth centuries and it became the seat of a bishop. The town fell to the Arabs in 637, after Damascus' capture and then declined. It was virtually deserted by the mid 19th century.

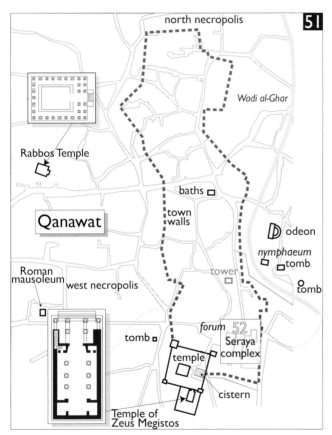

51 The main ruins (popularly called the **Seraya** or palace) are set in a beautiful grove of oak trees. Originally the complex comprised two Roman basilica-shaped buildings – a temple facing north and alongside it on the east a separate basilica. Both buildings were oriented north-south and reflected the dual religious-commercial importance of the town en route to the important pagan cult centre at *Sia in the late first century BC. The complex was upgraded in late second century when an imposing entrance portal was inserted into the existing wall leading to the eastern basilica, perhaps under Septimius Severus who raised the town to the status of *colonia*. An atrium separated the two enclosed spaces. The complex has recently been researched by French and German scholars.[14]

AD. Incorporated into the province of Syria (first century AD), it was titled Septimia Canatha by Septimius Severus

Visit

The first building you enter is the original

13 Most of the Decapolis towns were in northern Jordan. The only towns in present-day Syria listed in the Decapolis were Damascus, Deraa and Dion, the latter possibly located west of Deraa in the vicinity of Sheikh Sa`ad.

14 Amer (*et al*)1982; some findings revised by Breitner – see Kreikenbom (*et al*) 2005.

first century BC Roman temple. Adapted to Christian purposes in the late fourth century, the purpose of the complex was radically altered and this western basilica and probably served as a gathering point and commercial area. To the south behind the magnificently decorated and imposing doorway was the second temple – a hall flanked on each side by seven Doric columns and, at the south end, an apse and two side chambers (remains now hidden by the modern store-rooms). When this temple too was converted to a church, rather awkward in shape being much wider than long, the north wall was rebuilt with the ornamented frame inserted using recycled material. (Note how in the Christianising process a pagan bust that once decorated the central lintel of the grand entrance has been chiselled out, only a small boss carved with a cross remaining.) The church's altar was placed on the east at the centre of a *synthronon*. Behind the altar and the east wall a tomb was added. The long narrow room to the north (east of the atrium) seems to have been a baptistery. Between the two lies a curious room surrounded by a corridor which appears to pre-date the Christian restructuring of the compound. Recent research has speculated that the Qanawat complex became a centre of pilgrimage in the early Christian period, perhaps associated with the legend of the Old Testament prophet, Job. (In the 19th century, the triple *adyton* of the temple was still a site of local pilgrimage honouring Job.)

52

Roman temple

portico

entrance

→ monastery

atrium

?baptistery

monumental doorway

martyrium of Christian church

Qanawat – Seraya

synthronon

tombs

second church

non-extant structure

de Vogüé's reconstruction of Roman eastern basilica

0 1   5   10 m

was switched to an east-west orientation. The south wall whose three semi-circular niches had served as the *adyton* or focal point of the Roman cult centre was screened off and used as a martyrium or side chapel. The Christian building thus rotated the basilica plan 90°, with three naves separated by two rows of columns oriented east-west and a semi-circular apse around the altar set against the east wall. The lower part of the western façade (plate 20a) seen today is entirely re-used classical material, largely of the first century AD, probably part of the fourth–fifth century restructuring when the west wall was pushed out to give the church greater length. To the north lie remains of the temple's portico (also added under Septimius Severus), with its Corinthian columns on square bases.

Go through to the atrium. This was built in conjunction with the eastern temple

Besides the charm of the location amid its grove of trees, the decoration is of a high standard, the Christian buildings having simply re-used much of the classical stonework.

The ruins to the northeast of the Seraya belong to the Christian period (episcopal palace or monastery?). The remains of the tower on the far corner of the complex represent a late addition, presumably at the time when towers were common in monastic establishments of northern Syria.

If you take the first turn left from the square, you will come after 100m to the remains of a **temple to Zeus Megistos**. The temple stood on the upper terrace overlooking the square with the Seraya structures forming the eastern edge flanking the gateway of the ancient route to Sia. The upper (Zeus) temple comprised a *cella* with a four-columned portico, not unlike the temple at *Mushennef. The dimensions, however, are larger (15 m by 30 m in plan) and the interior was supported by six internal columns with a rectangular sanctuary at the south end. The first version of the temple was built in the second half of the first century BC, contemporary with the west temple of the Seraya complex, and was rebuilt in the third century AD.

The main civic part of Qanawat stretched north from the Seraya square. Recent excavations 300 m to the north have unearthed indications of a central forum with a baths complex on its southern side. Along the west side of the gorge of the Wadi al-Ghar a park bordering the stream contains along the opposite bank the remains of an odeon or small theatre (46 m diameter) with nine rows of seats built into the rise. A little further upstream (south) is a curious building which was probably a *nymphaeum* (water fountain) built over a natural fountain. The *nymphaeum* and odeon are now thought to date from the first century BC. Further upstream, the remains of a tower are incorporated into a modern house. On the top of the rise to the left, another tomb, in the form of a round tower.

On a knoll to the northwest of the town (200 m on the right as you take the

northern route back to the main road) is a **peripteral temple** once assumed as honouring the sun god, Helios – a sort of minor version of the Palmyra and Baalbek temples. An inscription discovered in 2002 indicates that the temple was in fact dedicated to a local god, Rabbos. Built on a high platform surrounded by a colonnade on all sides, it commands an impressive view across the Hauran Plain to Mount Hermon. The late second/early third century temple incorporates remains of a first century structure, probably rebuilt after a catastrophic event. Little of the building is extant though the surviving columns indicate that the decoration was rich, in the Baalbek-Palmyra tradition.

Other remains of the Roman period lie scattered around the perimeter of the town. If you descend the road that climbs from the west to the Seraya square you will see on the right after 200 m the fairly substantial remains of a Roman mausoleum, vaulted with multiple burial compartments.

REFS: Amer (*et al*) 1982: 1–15; Breitner in Kreikenbom (*et al*) 2005; Butler *AE* II 1903: 351–61; 402–8; 418–9; Butler *PE* II A 5 1912: 346–51; Donceel 1983; 129–39; Freyberger 1993 : 63–79; Freyberger 2000: 143–6; Sartre 1981: 343–57.

Qara

قارة

VARIANTS: Ocurura (Lat), Cehere
PERIOD: Byz/Umd Rating: – MAP: R1

LOCATION: 97 kms north-northwest of Damascus on the Homs road. Exit 15 kms north of Nabk.

During the doctrinal differences which divided the church in the fifth and six centuries, Qara was a bishopric which resisted the Monophysite trend that swept over much of Syria. Most remarkable of the Christian remains are the beautiful frescoes (12th century) found in the Greek Orthodox Church of Sts Sergius and Bacchus (last street on the right before the main square). The great Basilica of St Nicholas was converted to a mosque in 1266 by Baybars after he had discovered that the Christians of Qara had sold hundreds of Muslim prisoners to the Crusaders as slaves. The mosque lies on the southern side of the ridge that runs through the old town and preserves its Byzantine façade largely intact.

Two kilometres west of the town are the striking remains of a sixth century monastery to the Persian martyr, Mar Yakub, built around the remains of a Byzantine refuge tower. The church's frescoes date from the 11th century with a second layer (the cycle of the life of Christ) applied in the late 12th00/early 13th century. Rescued in 1970 by the antiquities authority (at a time when the church had been abandoned) they have now been restored and returned to the reconstructed tenth–eleventh century church. (On the recent rediscovery of a Syrian tradition in medieval wall painting – *Deir Mar Mousa and *Seidnaya (Chapel of the Prophet Elijah)).

At the eastern edge (southwest of the first major intersection as you reach the village) is an Ayyubid **khan**, ascribed by Sauvaget to the late 12th century or early 13th century. It has a high *iwan* used as a prayer room and the building's decoration incorporates a number of recycled classical elements.

REFS: Nasrullah 1943–44; *idem* 1952–58; Pena *Lieux* 2000: 255–56; Pouzet 1991; Sauvaget 1939: 53–4 ; Schmidt & Westphalen 2005.

Qasr al-Heir East (Plate 20b)

قصر الحير الشرقي

VARIANTS: Qasr al-Heir[15] al-Sharqi (Arb); al-Urd (Arb) PERIOD: Byz/Umd RATING: *
MAP: R4

LOCATION: From Palmyra, take the road towards Deir al-Zor as far as Sikne (68 km). Turn north +24 km to al-Taybe then take the track heading southeast for c +15 km. Can also now be approached directly

15 The Arabic 'heir' or 'hayr' translates as 'walled castle', an archaic word referring to the walls of the gardens.

from the south along a new sealed road from the Palmyra-Deir al-Zor highway.

The purpose of the two desert castle complexes at Qasr al-Heir (in Arabic, 'walled castle') East and West has stimulated much debate in recent decades. In *City in the Desert*,[16] recording the results of an American expedition of 1964–72, Oleg Grabar notes that the monumental façades of these two palaces are not commensurate with the more mundane internal structures and the utilitarian nature of most of the items found. There is, he concludes, 'something grandiloquent, *nouveau riche*, and provocatively expensive about the site'. Nevertheless, it is a bizarre ruin of great interest and although one should not expect another Palmyra or even a Resafa, the diversion is well worthwhile.

History

Studies last century tended to emphasise the possible classical origins of the complex, citing the Roman *castrum* plan and the presence of architectural elements such as capitals. Grabar *et al* believe, however, that the Byzantine and Roman stonework had been transported from neighbouring sites (some around Palmyra) or was provided by Christian craftsmen using Byzantine techniques. When work commenced on the Umayyad complex (728/9 under Caliph Hisham), the area may already have been in use for oasis gardens. The water supply was based on a watercourse leading from a dam at al-Qawm, 30 km to the northwest. The gardens, 850 ha in extent, were surrounded by 22 km of largely mudbrick walls (the remains of which can still be traced in places).

Like the companion castle, Qasr al-Heir West (200 km west), the scale of the *qasr* owes a good deal to the edifice complex that marked the second half of the Umayyad dynasty, particularly under Caliph Hisham. Other castles of the Syrian-Jordanian desert have attracted speculation as to their purpose. Traditional explanations have covered a range of possibilities from

16 Harvard University Press (2 vols) 1978.

pleasure (hunting lodge with oasis gardens) through practical (intensive agricultural development; caravanserai or khan) to military (control of fractious tribes).

The American expedition identified a combination of several practical explanations, speculating that the site was probably originally built as a grandiose agricultural settlement intended to help control warring desert tribes. It later acquired a more distinctly economic purpose with the addition of the east building or caravanserai to encourage commercial traffic. The original motivation for the settlement (probably around 700) was the need to pacify the area after a series of murderous tribal wars. As the Umayyads consolidated their rule in the region, they concentrated on developing the 'Fertile Crescent' link between Mesopotamia and Syria, particularly through ambitious schemes on the Mid Euphrates and the new province of the Jezira (northeast Syria). This new order required a more effective means of controlling the caravan traffic across the desert, along the short-cut route from Damascus to Mesopotamia and Persia.

Shortly after the end of Hisham's caliphate, the Umayyads were overturned and replaced by the Abbasid dynasty ruling from Baghdad. Syria was purposefully neglected, increasingly a backwater and a hotbed of discontent and factionalism. The qasr, however, was not abandoned, with signs that the Abbasids saw economic advantage in bringing the scheme to fruition, albeit on a reduced scale. There was further minor building work up to the tenth century but the area by then had largely been abandoned to the nomads. Renewed occupation seems to have taken place in the 12th century when a small settlement was built between the two enclosures. This settlement survived until the 13th century after which (presumably due to the effects of the Mongol invasions) the site was again abandoned for permanent settlement.

Visit

If you approach the ruins from the south,

look out for the remains of the outer walls which are as far as 5 km distant from the qasr. The outer garden area measured 3 km by 6 km. Closer in lay the palace garden and the civilian town. An inner enclosure wall surrounds the two castle buildings about 200 m out. The central complex consists of two separate castles, 40 m apart and carefully built from fine-grained limestone. The two gateways guarded by semi-cylindrical towers on each side face each other with the minaret between.

The gate of the smaller **eastern castle** (plate 20b) is reasonably well preserved and is the most interesting architectural feature of the complex. The decoration is clumsy but shows a conscious juxtaposition of styles (Mesopotamian, Byzantine and local), a practice much encouraged under the Umayyads (cf the gateway of Qasr al-Heir West in the *Damascus National Museum). The two half-circle towers found on each wall are on the entrance side moved in to flank the gateway. This is decorated with a simple framework of a semi-circular arch above, the architectural device beloved of Syrian builders since Roman times. (Palmyrene inspiration is evident in the two semi-circular niches flanking the arch.) The upper frieze is in brick (a Mesopotamian touch probably added after 760, the first known use of brick patterning in Syria). A jutting machicolation (one of the earliest uses in Arab architecture though it had precedents in the Roman period) protects the gateway.

The purpose of this eastern castle (c70 m²) has been variously interpreted and was seen by Grabar as a caravanserai. While the larger enclosure with its congregational mosque, large *bayts* and an inscribed reference to a 'medina', was seen as an urban settlement, Genequand argues that the description of a 'medina' must refer to the complex as a whole. The smaller enclosure, in his view, formed the palace component. It largely retains its outer walls, 2 m thick and once 12 m high, topped by a circuit walk and fortified with 12 semi-cylindrical towers. Inside its single entrance, however, its remains are in ruins, the courtyard deeply covered in rubble. The structure once consisted of a series of 12 m deep chambers, vaulted in brick in order to support a second storey, probably roofed in timber. The central courtyard was based on an irregular square with sides varying from 28 m to 36 m, once surrounded by a colonnade. The use of brick to finish off the upper level of the walls and for vaulting may indicate that this building was completed under the Abbasids for whom brick was a more natural material.

The **larger castle** (167 m^2) on the west had six times as much space for habitations and common facilities but its walls (with 28 rounded towers) and five gateways are less well preserved. The east entrance gateway opposite the minaret consists of a rectangular aperture topped by a blind arch. The tympanum inside the arch was originally filled with a marble decorated panel. Above this is another early use of box machicolation, the doorway being flanked by semi-circular towers recently reconstructed. Inside, the original plan comprised a central square with streets leading to it from each of the four cardinal gateways. The square was surrounded by a portico and provided with a covered cistern for the storage of water. The buildings comprised 12 segments, each roughly a square – six were living quarters of approximately the same plan; three were ancillary service areas; one was an official building; one housed olive presses; and the last was a mosque (southeastern corner). They formed a small urban centre with limited commercial facilities.

The **minaret**, once assumed to be contemporary with the rest of the complex, was judged one of the oldest in Islam. The American research (confirmed by the Swiss-Lichtenstein survey) has established, however, that it could not have been older than the 13th century. Built of re-used stones of various origins (with a doorway 3 m above the ground on the south side) it formed part of a congregational mosque constructed in the first half of 13th century in mud brick on a stone foundation, the outline of which has recently been exposed. This was constructed by the Ayyubids as part

of their new settlement. The courtyard of the mosque included six tombs one of which had an underground chamber and monumental structure on top. The Ayyubid resettlement (known from Arab chronicles as al-'Urd) reflected the revival of transit routes across the central desert, but was later abandoned again in the face of the Mongol invasions (late 13th century).

Remains of reasonably spacious baths were discovered 60 m to the north of the area between the two enclosures. The baths are Umayyad, built at the same time as the palaces.

REFS: Creswell *Early Muslim* I 1979: 522–44; Ettinghausen & Grabar 1987; Grabar (*et al*) 1978; Genequand *Antiquity* 2005: 350–61; Hillenbrand 'Dolce Vita' 1982.

Qasr al-Heir West (Plate 9a)

قسر الحير الغربي

VARIANTS: Heliarama (Lat); Qasr al-Heir al-Gharbi (Arb) PERIOD: Byz/Umd RATING: – MAP: R4

LOCATION: Damascus/*Palmyra road. At c153 km from Damascus, the road from Homs joins from the left. Follow this road back towards Homs, passing after c+10 km the turn-off for *Harbaqa Dam. Continue +20 km north – castle is +2 km to the east across the desert. See remarks below about the monumental gateway re-erected at the National Museum in Damascus (*Damascus – Museum) before visiting the Qasr.

History

The existence of a settlement in this bleak spot has always depended on the supply of water to its gardens from the nearby dam at Harbaqa. Water was brought by canal and pipe from the dam (17 km south). The Palmyrenes may have established the first settlement here in the first century AD but it was abandoned after their revolt in 273 and no remains have been identified. The Byzantines (under Justinian) and their local Arab allies, the Ghassanid tribe, re-occupied the site in 559 and established a monastery, the tower of which still survive.

(The eastern desert was a favourite area of monastic concentration).

The Umayyad caliphs, who sought to retain their roots in the desert, established here a retreat from the environment and pressures of Damascus. But this 'hunting lodge' reflected the Umayyads' judicious combination of leisure with practicality. It was built on the Byzantine site by the last great Umayyad caliph, Hisham (r 724–43). Construction began in 727–8, about the same time as the more ambitious project at *Qasr al-Heir East 200 km across the desert, beyond Palmyra. As well as pleasure, the complex served the practical purposes of facilitating contact with the tribes, as a post-house for communications and as a means of consolidating defensive arrangements in the desert. The more spartan Ayyubids and, many centuries later, the Mamluks, used the site for military purposes but after the 14th century Mongol invasions, it was again deserted.

Visit

Today, the remains are a disappointment, though it is a worthwhile short diversion (30 minutes in each direction) for travellers visiting Palmyra who may also wish to see the more interesting phenomenon of the surviving Umayyad dam at *Harbaqa. Most of the surviving remains of the curious Umayyad castle were (probably wisely from the point of view of conservation in this harsh environment) taken away to be reassembled to form the striking main entrance to the Museum in Damascus.

A visit to the Museum should therefore precede any call at the ruins of the qasr. The huge monumental gateway constructed largely in stucco and fired brick of a fine consistency is a remarkable testimony to the cultural diversity of Syria at the time of the Umayyads. The patterns of the two large semi-circular towers and the joining gateway are largely geometric, in accordance with Islamic norms but the style juxtoposes elements of Persian, Byzantine and local traditions.

What remains on the ground gives an indication of the size of the Umayyad **lodge** (measuring c70 m^2) which partly incorporated the remains of the Byzantine monastery. The most prominent feature of the latter is the northwestern tower which rises three storeys above the ground. The rest of the compound was originally two-storeyed, made of brick on a lower 2 m course of limestone and with a colonnaded internal court. Except for the Byzantine tower, the corners ended in round towers. In the middle of each face, semi-circular towers provided protection for the walls, except on the east side where the central gateway (now in Damascus) was flanked by twin towers.

To the north, remains of a **hammam** were excavated by Schlumberger. The small reservoir for collection of the waters channelled from the Harbaqa Dam are found to the west. From here the gardens of the lodge (1050 m by 440 m in extent) were irrigated.

REFS: Arush 1976: 155–61; Creswell *Early Islamic* I 1979: 506–18; Genequand 2006; Hillenbrand 'Dolce Vita' 1982; Sauvaget *Châteaux Umayyades* 1967; Schlumberger 1982.

Qasr Ibn Wardan (Plate 21a)

قصر إبن وأردان

PERIOD: Byz　RATING: *　MAP: R4

LOCATION: In the north steppe 62 km northeast of *Hama. From central Hama (starting point) take Hamra road (40 km northeast). Continue to Qasr Ibn Wardan (+10 km).

History

The Byzantine Emperor Justinian (r 527–65) did much to set his stamp on northern Syria. During his long reign, he sought to restore to the Eastern Empire much of the territory lost since the high point of Rome in the second century. Syria was the strategic depth for the defence of the empire's heartland against Persia to the east. Justinian's military commander, Belisarius, conducted several campaigns in the area and in order to secure the fruits of his achievements, a series of impressive fortifications was constructed, largely along the north reaches of the Euphrates (*Halabiye, *Resafa, *Meskene).

Completed in the last full year of Justinian's reign (564), Qasr Ibn Wardan perhaps owes more to local initiative though it used an imported stylistic vocabulary. It lacks the sheer size and stolidity of the more distinctly fortress-like outposts elsewhere. The overall design is more graceful and flamboyant, partly reflecting in concept and choice of materials the high art of the capital at the time.

The complex of palace-church-military barracks on the edge of the great Syrian Desert was intended to control the nomadic Arab population of the desert zone rather than to meet the more strategic threat from Persia. This allowed for greater freedom of expression, elegance of style and lightness of touch. The results are still obvious in this extraordinary complex with its broad-banded brick and stonework silhouetted against the featureless landscape. The old *Blue Guide* does not exaggerate when it calls these ruins 'among the most impressive, and perhaps even the most outstanding, in the whole of northern Syria'.

Visit

The largest part of the complex is the **palace** (east side) (dated by inscription AD 564). This was possibly built to house the military commander of the region. The south side, through which you enter, is the best preserved façade. The complex of rooms on this side reached two storeys and much of the fabric damaged largely by the work of nature over the years has been restored by the Antiquities Department. After noting the carved basalt lintel and the boldly contrasting bands of stone and brickwork of the façade, you enter through a broad vaulted vestibule. On both left and right are apsidal rooms with annexes to each side, probably ceremonial chambers. Stairs from the right chamber lead to an upper (dormitory) area. On the west side of the courtyard is a large cross-vaulted chamber said to be a school.

The courtyard is extensive and contains a variety of service annexes including the stables along the north wall and wells. The north and east sides have also been heavily reconstructed.

The building of greatest interest is the **church** (plate 21a) which lies to the west of the palace. The church still impresses today, in spite of the collapse of most of the dome, the southwestern corner and parts of the soaring *triforia* (gallery rooms). The basic shape is a square internal plan, surmounted by a dome but conforming to the three-aisled Syrian format, a difficult combination of shapes that Byzantine architectural practice was still trying to get right. The solution to the problem of squaring the circle – i e supporting the round dome on the square base – was to connect the two elements by devices called pendentives, triangular segments of a sphere which lead down from the base of the dome to the corners of the square. Actually, in this case, the solution is made even more complex by the addition of the *triforia* around three sides of the church and overlooking the central nave. This meant that the dome's weight had to be distributed through the arches supporting the upper storey to the north and south as well as to the substantial piers that carry the main arches across the nave. The total height of the dome was 20 m but the building has a sense of harmony and compactness resulting from the variety and rhythm of the complex internal shapes. (The same effect is sought on a much larger scale in the profusion of shapes supporting the great dome at Hagia Sophia, an earlier project of Justinian.)

The nave itself, excluding the side aisles, measures almost 7 m by 10 m and ends in the customary semi-domed apse. It had entrances to the north, south and west, the latter leading through a wide but shallow lobby or *narthex*. From the *narthex*, a staircase on the northwestern side led to the upper storey which, in the Byzantine tradition, was probably reserved for women. The extensive use of brick (including the only baked brick dome found in Syria) and the use of many different types of stone (including columns and capitals probably recycled from *Apamea, local basalt and imported gypsum, limestone and marble) underlines the exotic nature of the project. Yet though there is much in the structure and the use of materials that recalls metropolitan models, it is likely that the building was largely local in execution. Mango points to the unusual proportions of the building (it is uncommonly tall), the placing of pendentives and the crude style of carving on the capitals, door jambs and lintels as evidence of a Syrian architect imperfectly following Byzantine models.

The third building in the complex was the military **barracks** to the south of the palace (probably AD 558). Of this little remains.

REFS: Butler *EC* 1929: 168–9; Butler *PE* II B I 1907: 26–45 (plans); Klengel *Syrien* 1987: 200; Lassus *Sanctuaires chrétiens* 1947: 146–7; C Mango 1976; Peters 1977–8.

Qatna (al-Mishrife)

المشرفة

VARIANTS: al-Mishrife (Arb) RATING: – MAP: R2

18 kms northeast of Homs. To the north of the modern village of al-Mishrife and left of the road to Selemiye. Road entrance and explanatory panels on western side.

The 100 ha ruins of Qatna, protected by ramparts in earth, were excavated by a French expedition in the 1920s and since 1994 by Syrian and later, Italian and German, teams. Unusually for a Bronze Age city, the site forms a huge quadrilateral whose earth ramparts still reach 15–20 m high. There were four gates, one in the middle of each wall. First occupation levels go back to 2600–2000 BC, a small settlement centred on the citadel hill. The second quarter of the second millennium saw the city's massive expansion with the development of the walls and the royal palace, reflecting the city's importance as a staging post on the newly developed trade routes between the Mediterranean coast and Mesopotamia via the mid-Euphrates.

With over 80 rooms, the palace (1650–1340 BC) is one of the largest found in western Syria. It lies on the northwest slopes of the citadel and has been given a modern mud-brick protective casing. The central throne room and 'ceremonial hall' to the west were immense (40 m by 20 m). A passage (guarded by a pair of basalt statues) led from the throne room to a burial complex under the northern edge of the palace containing inhumations dating back to the early second millennium. The contents of the complex, including a funerary banquet chamber, were found intact by the German team in 2002 and comprise an extraordinary collection of objects serving a royal ancestor cult. Finds are being transferred to the Homs Museum.

The collapse of the roof of the corridor leading to the tombs also brought down tablets from the palace archives above. The 73 cuneiform texts date from the reign of King Idanda, a period (c 1400 BC) in which Qatna was caught in the confrontation between Egypt and its rivals to the north, Mitanni and later the Hittite Kingdom (cf *Tell Nabi Mend). It was probably a Hittite assault that brought the palace's destruction in 1340 BC. Other finds include fragments of frescoes said to be in a Minoan style.

In the lower city between the acropolis and the north gate a second palace may have been used by lesser members of the royal family or a high official.

Qatna continued to be occupied into the Iron Age (palace to the west of the citadel rise) when the city was probably linked to Hama. It was destroyed by Sargon II (721–05 BC), probably at the same time as Hama was incorporated into the Assyrian Empire (720 BC).

REFS: du Mesnil du Buisson 1935; al-Maqdissi & Bonacossi 2005; al-Maqdissi 2003.

Qatura

قاطورة

VARIANTS: Qatoura PERIOD: Rom/Byz ALT: 485 m RATING: – MAP: R3

LOCATION: Just south of *Saint Simeon. Follow the directions for *Mushabbak (25 km) then go on to Dar Tazeh (+5 km). As the road leaves Dar Tazeh and heads north towards Saint Simeon (the peak of Jebel Sheikh Barakat is on the left) it passes over a saddle and begins to descend quite steeply before crossing a small fertile valley. Immediately at the bottom of this descent, a road branches left. Follow this for c1 km. For Jebel Sheikh Barakat, before leaving Dar Tazeh's northern outskirts, instead of turning north to Saint Simeon, turn left then first right and follow sealed road to summit.

The village and its environs contain a number of late Roman and Byzantine remains. If you continue just past the village, you can see on the left, carved into the rocky hillside, roughly cut rock tombs with carvings from the Roman period. The sculptural style is a rather crude version of classical funerary art. There are also touches of Palmyrene, though less stylized and without its oriental embellishments. Tombs in the locality are variously dated between AD 122 and 250. The last tomb on the road that curves around the mountain towards *Zarzita shows a rather decomposed low-relief of a draped figure lying on a banquet couch. The inscription in Greek and Latin refers to one Titus Flavius Julianus, a veteran of the VIII Augusta Legion and his wife Flavia Titia. The tomb probably dates from the late second century.

On the southern edge of the village, a subterranean burial chamber is marked by a two-column funerary monument. This is the tomb, dedicated in AD 195, to Aemilius Reginus. The design is not unlike the nearby bi-columnar monument at *Sitt er-Rum dedicated to Isidotos.

Tchalenko's study of the Limestone Massif brings out the sudden onset of prosperity in the region in the second century, illustrated in the adoption of monumental tombs in settlements as small as this one. On the whole, construction techniques as seen in the extant fragments of ancient housing are not sophisticated, using irregular and polygonal stones. There is no church. Remains of two quadrated stone villas are found in the surrounding fields, one to the north, both probably dating from the fifth or sixth century. The earliest Christian inscription found in the limestone country (dated 336/7) was noted in the northern sector.

On top of **Jebel Sheikh Barakat** (alt 870 m) the second century AD Roman temple site overlooks Qatura from the south (now in a military area). This was a major pilgrimage centre in Roman times (known as Mount Koryphaios), the most important of the 15 or more temples in this area (see also *Baqirha). The temple was dedicated to Jupiter Madbachos (Jupiter of the Altar) and the local god, Selamanes. It was built on a partly artificial terrace 68 m square. The surrounding wall (whose construction was spread over the period late first century AD to 170) was lined with an internal portico pierced by central doors and ramped entrances on three sides. At the centre of the temenos stood a cella oriented east-west with a west-facing portico preceded by four columns. Foundations only remain. It may be no coincidence that the nearby pilgrimage centre honouring St Simeon took over from this pagan site as a major focus of pilgrimage. The summit later housed a Crusader watch-tower and became a Muslim place of pilgrimage: the tomb of the venerated Sheikh Barakat is built against the north wall of the temple compound.

REFS: **Qatura**: Butler AE II 1903: 61, 273–4; Butler PE II B 5 1912: 249–51; Sournia 1966: 112; Tchalenko Villages I 1953: 183–94, II 1953: pl LVII–IX, LXI, LXII, CXXVII. **Jebel Sheikh Barakat**: Callot & Marcillet-Jaubert 1989; de Vogüé 1865–77: pl 94; Tchalenko Villages I 1953: 106–7, II pl XLII, CXXXI; Tchalenko 'Travaux en cours' 1973; Trombley Hellenic Religion II 2001: 144–6.

Qinnesrin

قنسرين

VARIANTS: Chalcis ad Belum (Lat); al-'Iss (Arb)
PERIOD: Rom/Byz RATING: T MAP: R3

LOCATION: 31 km southwest of Aleppo, also known by the modern name of al-'Iss. Take the main Damascus road south from Aleppo Scientific College roundabout (starting point). Turn left after 25 km for the village marked as al-'Iss (+8 km). Ancient remains south of the village; Umayyad town at 4 km east at al-Hadir.

Though Chalcis ad Belum[17] was an important centre on Roman itineraries, more central as a hub than Aleppo, the modern-day visitor should not approach it with any great expectations. The present village of al-'Iss stands near the point where the Quweiq River (east of the site), having struggled to maintain a trickle as it flows through Aleppo, peters out in the marshes of the Madkh before surrendering to the desert. South of the village, the citadel once occupied the 30 m high tell.

The great advantage of the location was its commanding views over countryside which, as in Roman times, is still a flourishing agricultural area as a result of recent efforts to drain the marshes. Qinnesrin, the traditional Arab place name, reflects a pre-Hellenistic (Aramaean) name meaning 'eagle's nest'. From here views could be obtained as far as Jebel Hass to the north, to Jebel Zawiye in the limestone country to the east and to Jebel Isriya to the southeast. It thus surveyed not only the desert margins but the rich undulating country around Aleppo and the hill country east of Antioch. No wonder it was made the junction point of major routes including Antioch-*Palmyra, Aleppo-*Apamea (and south to *Hama, *Homs and Damascus), the east route to Anasartha and Zebed (see *Isriya) and the road southeast to Androna (*Anderin).

17 The 'ad Belum' was added to distinguish this Chalcis from Chalcis ad Libanum in the Beqaa Valley of Lebanon. For Belus, see *Dead Cities – General Note.

The Roman settlement of Chalcis was divided between the acropolis and the lower town to the north (now under the village), the whole being surrounded by a 4 km wall. The site had been founded earlier under the Seleucids by Seleucus I Nicator. By the end of the second century BC, the city may have fallen under Arab control as Seleucid authority weakened. The substantive fortification work, however, was begun by the Romans. Justinian (r 527–65) re-fortified it in 550–1 as part of his extensive works in the desert fringes intended to ward off the Persian threat. It was destroyed in the first shock of the Arab invasion (637), but was revived when the administrative headquarters of the new Umayyad province (*jund*) covering northern Syria was established in the area. It was depopulated by Saif al-Daula (963) during his struggle against the Byzantines. By 1200 the Roman town was abandoned.

A few stones of the Roman-Byzantine walls survive, mainly on the southern and western edges of the citadel. The citadel was once surrounded by two lines of wall, the inner (fortified by square bastions) ran around the edge of the plateau. An outer wall extended as far as the saint's tomb on the crest to the north (hence the modern place name) on the southern slopes of which are quarries and a number of underground tombs.

A long-standing mystery as to why there were no signs of any Islamic occupation at Qinnesrin has now been clarified by the discovery of the Arab settlement 4 km to the east under the modern village of al-Hadir. The square-plan settlement, the initial headquarters of the *jund* of Qinnesrin, was established on a site which had been a gathering point for Arab tribes.

REFS: Monceaux & Brossé 1925; Mouterde & Poidebard I 1945: 7–9; Whitcomb 2000 – Oriental Institute, University of Chicago website.

R

Raqqa (al-Rafiqa)

الرقة

VARIANTS: Nikephorion, Leontopolis (Grk);
Callinicum (Lat); al-Rakka, al-Rafiqa (Arb)
PERIOD:Arb (Abd) RATING:– MAPS: 53, R4

LOCATION: On the left bank of the Mid
Euphrates just before its junction with the
Balikh River (the classical Balissus), 193
km southeast of *Aleppo (134 km northwest of Deir al-Zor).

History

Once a major centre of Arab power,
research in recent decades has highlighted
the fragile remains of Raqqa's past.
Founded, according to Pliny, by Alexander
the Great (but more likely by one of his
generals, Seleucus I Nicator (r 301–281
BC), the first settlement was located
south of Tell Bia, the prominence 2 km
east of the present walled city. The Latin
name Callinicum probably commemorates
Seleucus II Callinicus, the Seleucid king
who expanded the settlement around
244–2 BC. Another foundation legend
ascribes the name to a Greek sophist
Callinicos who was murdered there.
In Byzantine times, it was an important
fortress on the front line between the
Persian and Christian empires. (Remains
of the Byzantine fortifications have been
found south of Tell Bia.) Belisarius,
Justinian's famous general, who did much
of the campaigning against the Persian
threat in Syria, was defeated near the
town in 531.

After falling peacefully to the Muslim
forces (639–40), written records indicate
that the Umayyad Caliph Hisham chose
the flat land to the north of the classical
town as the site for two palaces. Within
the ancient city walls, renamed Raqqa
('the marsh'), an early Umayyad mosque
(recorded in 1907 by Sarre and Herzfeld)
has since been obliterated under the
modern city. Its brick minaret, if it had

survived the 20th century, would have
been a rare example of the square
minarets of the early Islamic world. From
771, the Abbasid caliph al-Mansur (r 754–
75) commissioned the architect, al-Rabah,
to build a 'companion' town to serve as
a second Abbasid capital and control the
province of the Jezira (northeastern Syria)
as well as providing a forward headquarters
against the Byzantines on the Anatolian
plateau to the north. He gave it the
prosaic name al-Rafiqa ('the companion').
Al-Mansur's horseshoe design (1500 m
in diameter) was a modified, but hardly
much less ambitious, version of his earlier
circular plan for Baghdad. The new twin
cities quickly surpassed the old capital,
Damascus, in size and splendour.

The great Abbasid caliph Harun al-Rashid
(r 786–809) favoured the area and
surpassed the old and new towns with a
new metropolis which served as his base
from 796 until 808, gradually acquiring
the old town's identity. The new building
program in Raqqa/Rafiqa was intended not
simply to reinforce the town as a frontier
fort but as a symbol of Abbasid hegemony,
deliberately choosing an area which
had not been central to the Umayyads'
power base. However, after Harun al-
Rashid's death in 809, his widow Zubaida
promptly moved the court to Baghdad.
Raqqa survived as a regional town of note,
a centre of scholarship and a place of
refuge for displaced caliphs but its days as
a centre of empire were gone.

As the Zengids' and Ayyubids' traditional
connections with Mosul (northern Iraq)
emphasised the role of the Jezira, the
symbolic and defence roles of Raqqa were
revived. Saladin (late 12th century) started
the glazed ceramics industry for which
Raqqa became famous. After Raqqa was
ravaged by the Mongols in 1258 at the
time of the catastophic sacking of Baghdad,
it fell into ruin and ceased to play a major
role until the Ottomans partly restored its
citadel in the 19th century and installed a
colony of Circassians.

Visit

Though Raqqa has been intermittently

investigated since 1906, much of what has been unearthed has proved perishable or is of specialised interest. Raqqa preserves only a few scraps of its glory under the Abbasids. Though poorly presented, the remains reveal the extent to which the Islamic world, after the Arab-Hellenistic blending of the Umayyad period, became more heavily influenced by the Persian traditions in art and architecture, particularly through the development of the pointed arch.

There have been recent efforts to reconstruct the semi-circular baked and mud brick **walls** of Abbasid al-Rafiqa

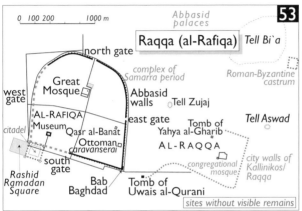

(eighth century), of which two thirds of the length survive (the exception being the south side parallel to the river). The walls were originally of double thickness, strengthened every 35 m by more than 100 semi-circular towers. In the southeastern corner of the walled city lies the **Bab Baghdad** (Baghdad Gate) which may date from the mid 12th century, rather than the original construction phase under the Abbasids. It conveys some idea of the effective use of decorative brickwork (eg the frieze of patterned blind arches above the gateway) which closely followed Mesopotamian styles whose influence in Syria was largely confined to the Jezira.

On the eastern side of the walled city of Rafiqa is the **Qasr al-Banat** ('Palace of the Maidens'), now partly reconstructed.

The building is centred on a courtyard with an *iwan* (high-arched and open hall) on each side, once richly ornamented in brick and sculptured plaster. The purpose and date of the building are unclear but it is almost certainly a secular palace of the Seljuk or Ayyubid periods (11th–12th century) and blends the Iranian four-*iwan* plan with local Syrian treatment. The wide northern *iwan* probably served as a reception hall.

You can also find in the centre of the walled area some remains of the **Great Mosque of al-Rafiqa** whose construction was originally undertaken in 772 under Caliph al-Mansur. The courtyard was rebuilt (1165–6) by Nur al-Din who devoted a good deal of attention to building projects in the Jezira. The remains seen today comprise only two elements: an uncompromisingly plain 25 m round minaret, Mesopotamian in inspiration but probably dating from Nur al-Din's restoration; and part of the courtyard colonnade in mud-brick arches including the inscription recording Nur al-Din's contribution. The mosque was originally almost 100 m² with 11 towers around the periphery. Creswell notes that the square plan and the bastioned walls were Mesopotamian in inspiration while the triple-aisled prayer hall and its parallel gabled roofs are Syrian in origin (cf *Damascus – Umayyad Mosque).

Syrian and German excavators have researched what remains of a huge complex of **Abbasid palaces**, one attributed to Harun al-Rashid, in the zone northeast of the walled city. The palaces were largely built of sun-dried brick with the exterior coated in white plaster and their badly-eroded remains are now covered by modern housing except for one example (the 'East Palace'). Further east again were found remains of earlier settlements including Tell Bia where a MBA palace which resembled the Palace of Zimri-Lim at *Mari was located.

The Raqqa **Museum** contains many interesting finds from local excavations including rare examples of ninth century decorative plaster.

The huge modern shrine to Uwais al-Qurani replaces a modest but historic tomb honouring the early Muslim ascete. Raqqa's importance in the Shiite tradition stems from the burial there of many of the followers of Ali who fell nearby at the Battle of Siffin (*Qalaat Jaabr).

Heraqla

Eight kilometres to the west lie the remarkable ruins of Heraqla, once thought to be a Roman military camp or *castrum*. Later research has unearthed an Arab enclosure which has no parallel in Islam. Clearly not intended for habitation but as a monument, Toueir believes it may have been built by Harun al-Rashid to commemorate his victory over Byzantine forces at Herakleia (modern Ereğli in Turkey) but was never completed. Each side is 103 m long and includes a vaulted hall or *iwan* opening to the outside as well as towers on each corner. The whole stands on a terrace which is in turn enclosed in a circular stone-walled compound 500 m wide. Four gates (each based on a different plan) mark the cardinal points of the outer enclosure.

REFS: Creswell *Early Muslim* II 1940: 139–49; Daiber & Becker *Raqqa V* 2004; Heidemann & Becker *Raqqa II* 2003; Hillenbrand 'Eastern Islamic' 1985; Sarre & Herzfeld 1911: 156–60; Toueir 1983; Toueir 'Raqqa/Rafiqa' *Ebla to Damascus* 1985; Toueir *DaM* 1985.

Ras al-Basit

راس البسيط

VARIANTS: Posideion (Grk), Posidium (Lat)
PERIOD: LBA/Hel RATING:T MAP: R2

LOCATION: 53 km north of Latakia. Take northern route from Latakia towards the hill resort of Qasab (Casambella to the Crusaders), an Armenian village near the Turkish border. At 40 km, turn left and descend +13 km to the coast, weaving through pine forests. The archaeological site, a 25 m tell, lies about 500 m east of the lighthouse that marks the cape (turn left c+1 km when you reach the beach-front road).

French excavations from 1971 to 1984 revealed a small settlement with citadel founded (like *Ras Ibn Hani) as an outpost of Ugarit during the Late Bronze Age, surviving into the Iron Age. It had strong links with Phoenicia and Cyprus and received a Greek colony in the seventh century BC but was destroyed during the Persian period (539–331 BC). Alexander passed this way in 333 BC (the Battle of Issus took place not far to the north, near modern-day Alexandretta) and it became a Seleucid settlement after 313 BC under the name of Posideiôn with a fortress on its small acropolis (southern end of the tell). A new phase of development began with the refortification of the town in the third century AD. A Canadian team has been studying the basilica erected at the foot of the acropolis (north end). The church indicates important links with the liturgical practices of Asia Minor and the Aegean rather than inland Syria. The port was still in use during the Crusades and was a destination for Venetian ships in the 15th to 16th centuries. By the 19th century, it was used only by the local fishing community.

To the north is **Mount Casius** (Jebel al-Aqra). At 1728 m, it is the highest peak on the coast, rising dramatically almost straight out of the sea. It was known in Hittite records as Mount Hazi or Nanni. Being a prominent local high place, the summit was sacred both to the Phoenicians (*Ugarit) and the Greeks (who associated it with Zeus). The Emperors Hadrian and Julian ('the Apostate') climbed to worship on the peak. Hadrian, always keen to associate himself with Zeus, had a particularly momentous visit. He climbed the slope in the hours of darkness, anxious to see the dawn break from the peak. 'A storm was blowing up. As he sacrificed (to Zeus) at the summit the heavens opened and a thunderbolt blasted both sacrificial victim and attendant.'[1] The Crusaders knew it as Mont Parlerius or Parlier.

REFS: Courbin 'Bassit' *CFAS* 1989: 102–6; Beaudry & Perrault *AAAS* 2002–3: 381–91.

Ras Ibn Hani

راس ابن هانئ

VARIANTS: Diospolis (?Grk) PERIOD: LBA/ IrA/Hel RATING: T MAP: R2

LOCATION: 10 km north of *Latakia on the northern side of the promontory extending from the Cham Hotel. Right of the divided road as it passes the hotel entrance (left).

Ras Ibn Hani was dug from 1975 to 1982 by a Franco-Syrian mission. The site complements *Ugarit/Minet al-Beida, continuing the chronological sequence from the end of the Bronze Age until the Byzantine period (13th century BC to sixth century AD).

Founded by a king of Ugarit, probably to survey maritime access to the main port, it also provided a cool summer residence. The settlement is based on a regular grid angled at 45⁰ to the compass. The palace area (east side of the site) is in total larger than the main palace at Ugarit, covering over 8000 m². Excavations uncovered two segments, north and southeast, the latter including an industrial quarter with a supply of copper ingots, probably from Cyprus. A library of tablets in Ugaritic and Akkadian was discovered in the north palace. The original palace was probably destroyed in the Sea Peoples' invasion of 1200 BC after being evacuated by its inhabitants.

Ras Ibn Hani sheds some light on the otherwise obscure period after the Sea Peoples' invasion and indicates a resumption of indigenous Syrian influences, reversing the heavily Mycenaean links of the LBA. The link to Greece revived later (third century BC) with the foundation of a major Hellenistic fortress on the

1 Birley *Hadrian: The Restless Emperor* London 1997: 230.

site, probably by Ptolemy III Euergetes (r 246–21 BC) who campaigned in northern Syria in 246 BC. The town covered most of the neck of the peninsula and was taken by the Seleucids under Antiochus III the Great (r 223–187 BC) after his victory at Panion. The fortress (northeast – square plan, square corner towers) was razed but the site again fell into the hands of the Ptolemies under Antiochus IX Cyzicenus (r 115–95 BC) and a small fortress was erected in the southeastern corner of the ruined compound. This in turn was razed a half-century later. The last significant phase of occupation was during the fourth to sixth centuries AD when the centre's major importance appears to have been industrial.

REFS: Bounni 'Ras Ibn Hani' *CFAS* 1989: 144–6; Lagarce 1987; Leriche 'Urbanisme defensif' 1987; Lagarce (*et al*) *CRAI* 1987: 274–88.

Refade

رفادة

VARIANTS: – PERIOD: Byz   ALT: 509 m RATING: * MAP: R3

LOCATION: On the western slopes overlooking the Plain of *Qatura. Follow directions for *Sitt al-Rum, then continue a few hundred metres further up the hill. The site is also accessible from Qatura from where it can be seen 1.5 km away on the skyline to the north.

Butler describes Refade as 'the most picturesque of all the little deserted cities of the hill country' and Tchalenko saw it as 'an aristocratic village for big landowners'. The striking appearance of the uninhabited village derives from the intact nature of the houses, their elegant decoration and the appearance on the skyline of an isolated tower, evoking a deserted Tuscan hill village.

The buildings are almost entirely domestic but are in a variety of styles, including some built in the early method with polygonal stones. The village contained no church (perhaps the isolated church at Sitt al-Rum below served its needs). The large number of lavish houses, mostly from the sixth century but with some evidence dating back to the first century AD, indicates a sustained high level of prosperity. The agricultural exploitation of this area was begun early compared with the rest of the limestone country and the settlement seems to have been continuously inhabited from the first to the seventh century.

There is no consensus as to the purpose of the tower (sixth century, southwest corner of the village). It is more likely to have been a watch-tower rather than a refuge for a monastic recluse. The tall (9 m) four-storeyed structure (which has been reconstructed since Butler's study) includes a very obvious latrine arrangement protruding from the upper storey. Pena laconically notes that it is 'a rare example in the history of hygiene'.

The double-towered house is clearly a domestic villa (possibly incorporating an earlier independent watch-tower), grouped in a compound with a second, smaller dwelling. The towers were of three storeys with a portico on the façade between. Other dwellings worthy of particular note are a house with a well-preserved double portico (*stoa*) facing south (dated 516) and one with a lighter and more graceful colonnade, plainer in decoration.

REFS: Butler *PE* II B 5 1912: 254–8; de Vogüé II 1865–77: pl 110–1; Hadjar 2000: 163–4; Pena (*et al*) *Reclus* 1980: 259–62; Sournia 1966: 85; Tchalenko *Villages* I 1953: 194–7, II 1953: pl LX, LXIII, CXXVII.

Resafa (Plate 21b)

الرصافة

VARIANTS: Rasapa, Receph (bib); Resapha (Lat/Grk); Sergiopolis (Byz); R'safah; Risafe (Arb)
PERIOD: Byz/Arb RATING: ** MAPS: 54, R4

LOCATION: The nearest main town is *Raqqa. If you head northwest from Raqqa on the road to Aleppo you will reach at 26 km the village of al-Mansura from where a road leads left c+28 km to Resafa. 200 km southeast of Aleppo.

History

Although associated essentially with the Byzantines, the site of Resafa was mentioned in earlier sources, both in Assyrian texts and in the Bible (as Receph – 2 *Kings* XIX, 12; *Isaiah* XXXVII, 12). The Roman emperor, Diocletian (r 284–305) established here a frontier fortress to meet the Sasanian threat. (*Dura Europos had already fallen to the Sasanian Persians in 256.) The Strata Diocletiana, named after the emperor, ran from Sura (on the Euphrates, see below) via Resafa south to *Palmyra and on to Damascus via *Dumeir.

For the Byzantines, the original classical settlement of Resapha took on a new importance with the growth of the cult of St Sergius. A Roman officer in the horse guards serving as a court official, Sergius was martyred here, after refusing instructions (possibly from Maximinus Daia, Caesar in the East in Diocletian's tetrarchy from 305 to 313) to sacrifice to the Roman gods. His cult attracted followers to his place of martyrdom from throughout Syria. To help handle the crowds, as well as to service the garrison which was stationed there, the town's amenities were considerably expanded under the Byzantine emperor, Anastasius I (r 491–518) who officially renamed the city Sergiopolis in honour of its patron saint. A large basilica was constructed and cisterns and ramparts provided.

The sixth century brought a new and more persistent Persian threat. The town became a new focal point of Justinian's great program of military works in Syria (*Halebiye) towards the end of his reign (527–65). Perhaps slightly before the rebuilding of the great fortress of Halebiye, the walls of Resafa were reconstructed on an ambitious scale; stone replaced mudbrick and state-of-the-art military architecture was introduced (for example the galleries to allow movement within from strongpoint to strongpoint). What had begun as a pilgrimage town dedicated to the memory of a soldier-saint took on a more heavily military character, reflecting the frontier nature of the

Christian presence in this area. The policy of forward defence was, however, only partly successful. The Persians penetrated the screen on several occasions in the sixth century (reaching as far as Antioch in 540). Sergiopolis held out against the Persian raids but with great difficulty, notably during the campaigns of Chosroes I. Later it succumbed to the greater Persian campaigns of the early seventh century and was sacked by Chosroes II in his campaign of 616 which did so much fatally to weaken Byzantine control of Syria, softening it up for the Arab invasion two decades later.

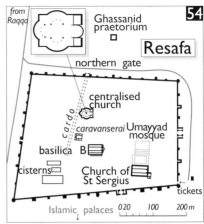

Under the Umayyads Resafa was for a time favoured by the Caliph Hisham (r 724–43) who erected a palace and a great mosque which shared common space with the Sergius cathedral. After the Abbasid conquest in 750, it suffered the vengeance of the new regime's troops who destroyed Hisham's tomb in the city. Further damage was done by a serious earthquake at the end of the eighth century. Though it continued to support a token population, including a sizeable proportion of Christians, into the 13th century, it was depopulated by Baybars (r 1260–77). By the time the Mongols laid waste northern Syria on several expeditions in the 13th and 14th centuries, there wasn't much left at Resafa for a decent sack though they missed a hoard of Christian precious vessels which had been hidden in the courtyard of the Sergius basilica (*Damascus – National Museum) against just such an eventuality.

Visit

You will need a good three hours to see the site properly. As you approach by road, the fortress walls look forbidding across the bare plain. Nothing suggests why such a monumental project was conceived in this bleak spot. After perhaps driving around the road that encircles the site to gain an appreciation of the size of the fortified area, the main entrance is via the ticket office on the east.

Once you enter the enclosure, the size of the city is apparent together with the bareness of the site. Only a fraction of

the surface has been excavated, largely concentrating on the main churches. The rest lies as undisturbed as it was after the last Mongols left, except for the steady encroachment of desert sands protecting what remains underneath. The task of fully excavating the site would be a daunting enterprise.

The city is laid out in a huge rectangle, with the **city walls** extending to the right and left approximately 550 m by 400 m. You can see the intricate nature of the facilities built into the structure including the protected upper gallery and passageways to enable movement from bastion to bastion without coming under fire. The stone used is a local gypsum not dissimilar to the originally sparkling but somewhat friable stone used at Halebiye. Round and square shapes alternate erratically in the layout of the bastions. The walls along the north side are the best preserved and little remains of the gates which once gave entry on the other three sides. The total length of the walls is almost 2 km. Fifty towers or bastions of assorted sizes and shapes strengthen the line of walls.

The first building on your path is the **Church of St Sergius** (plate 21b). This was the focal point of the religious pilgrimage in the last phase of the Byzantine period. The inner walls of this sizeable building have been partly reconstructed in recent years giving you some idea of its scale and grandeur. The basic plan (31 m by 20 m) is a basilica; two side aisles are separated from the central nave by three enormous semi-circular arches resting on cross-shaped piers. The building was constructed in the last quarter of the fifth century when the bold use of broad leaping lateral arches to divide the nave from the side-aisles had been tried elsewhere (*Qalb Lozeh). Additional elements were dedicated in 559.

In Byzantine buildings of the period, the huge weight which had formerly been taken by relatively thin and vulnerable pillars now rested on stout piers. (There is another example in the Church of Bissos at *Ruweiha.) Apparently, however, the engineering principles had not been perfected at the time of construction for at some stage within the next century (probably as a result of an earthquake), each of the broad arches and their superstructure had to be supported from underneath by two smaller arches resting on three columns. The basic insecurity of the sweeping arches was not to be resolved until many centuries later with the full development, in Byzantium and Europe, of the supporting pier and buttress.

Above the arches, the upper or clerestory level provides a row of arched windows to allow light to enter, interspersed with small columns resting on jutting corbels. The apparent lack of transverse arches indicates that the original roof of the main aisle was a wooden structure supported by wide beams. The nave terminates in a semi-circular apse which is relatively well preserved. As is usual in churches of this period, the apse is located between two side chapels of rectangular design. The one on the right, however, is extended out towards the east. The chamber to the left probably housed the martyrium honouring St Sergius.

A large and complex *bema* was located in the nave, occupying most of the space between the central piers. It was provided with a central baldachin, side seating for 28 and a throne surrounded by additional stone seating set in a semi-circle.

A peristyled courtyard, north of the church, probably housed the crowds of pilgrims gathering for the saint's day (6 October). Here German researchers discovered the small treasury of superbly crafted religious vessels, votice offerings for the grave of Sergius buried here just before a Mongol invasion. They are now in the *Damascus Museum. Probably in the eighth century, the atrium was shared with a mosque erected to the north, designed to give access to the saint's martyrium for people of both faiths. The mosque was apparently intended to capitalise on the fame of the Christian pilgrimage centre.

To the west lie the remains of a building called prosaically **basilica B**. This was the site of the first brick-built martyrium of St Sergius, an initiative of Bishop Alexander of Hierapolis (*Menbij), built before 425. This was replaced as the main pilgrimage church by the Church of St Sergius in the late fifth century. A new church on the site was later constructed by Bishop Sergius in 518 though what purpose it served is not clear. It is this church whose outline you now see, though most of the walls are gone. The church was a basic three-aisled Roman-Byzantine basilica plan, extended (probably in Justinian's time) with a fourth aisle on the south side and a broad entrance vestibule or *narthex* on the west. Though smaller than the new Church of St Sergius, it was still one of the largest in Syria (49 by 26m). The main horseshoe shaped eastern apse included a chapel that once contained the remains of a martyr, possibly marking the original burial place of St Sergius. During the Umayyad period, the church was gradually abandoned and used as a quarry for the new mosque (above).

Further to the west, you should note a series of three huge **cisterns** (one with a double row of chambers). Steel barriers now prevent visitors going too close to the apertures of the underground chambers. If you look in carefully, however, the sheer size of the cavernous interiors is astonishing. The largest of the three, the one to the south, is almost 58 m long and 21.5 m wide. The depth of water was 13 m and capacity over 15,000 m^3. The need for such enormous storage capacity is explained by the fact that Resafa has no permanent water supply. It does, however, receive considerable run-off from the Jebel Bishra and Jebel Rujmayn ranges to the south. This collects in pools which could be channeled to the cisterns which held a reserve supply capable of sustaining the city during a prolonged siege or drought. The roofing system is in itself a major achievement. The cisterns are ascribed by the Byzantine historian Procopius to Justinian but there is evidence that they were begun earlier.

Turn right now along the axis that crossed the city roughly north-south. After 100 m you should see on the right the remains of a market. The shape is basically that of a **caravanserai**, later seen throughout Syria. This early example is Byzantine.

Continuing north along the thoroughfare you reach the outline of a curious **centralised church**. The Byzantine love for rather phantasmagoric shapes in church architecture comes out here. There are other Byzantine 'circle within a square' churches in Syria (see box on page 24). All appear to come from the same period, the first half of the sixth century though there is little to indicate any common inspiration. The Resafa example, however, is a tour de force. The basic basilica shape (three naves) is broken up by the clever use of curves to bend outwards the inner and outer rectangles. Three arcaded semi-circles expand the inner area while the rear and side outer walls are gently taken out to accommodate them. The eastern end of the church adopts the familiar Byzantine design of a central apse with semi-circular seating flanked by two square side rooms.

This building has been dated by style to the 520s which would put it slightly after the bold experiments with circular shapes achieved at *Ezraa and *Bosra. Klengel argues that the sarcophagi for the burial of local bishops indicate that it was the metropolitan church as opposed to the two more sizeable pilgrimage churches examined earlier. The building was constructed in a fine gypsum stone in comparatively small blocks.

The **northern gate**, which lies at the end of the main axis, is described by Musil as 'among the most beautiful as well as the best preserved products of Byzantine architecture'. The gate juts out from the line of the wall, a single outer entrance (now gone) sheltering a rectangular court whose inner triple gateway with its rich decoration would not have been seen until the outer gateway had been crossed. The impact of the complex confection of columns and arches would thus have been all the greater, with their typically Syrian embellishment of late Roman ideas. The central passage is flanked by two side doors decorated with friezes, the details of which are now hard to distinguish. As a reminder of the second purpose of the city, defence, towering bastions enclose the entrance gateway on each side.

Outside the north gate is a curious building, a palace or **praetorium** of the **Ghassanid** period. Built around 560, it recalls the alliance in the sixth century between the Byzantine imperial power and the Christianised Arab confederation, the Ghassanids. On behalf of Byzantium, they kept control of the central Syrian desert tribes. The building is of somewhat unusual design based on a central bay surrounded by four barrel-vaulted bays with a semi-domed apse to the east. Some other examples of this cross-in-square shape have been found in the Byzantine world and further east.

On the south side of the city, outside of the walls, were found sparse remains of several palaces, including a so-called '**Palace of Hisham**', an Umayyad building of typical square design based on the Roman *castrum* or military enclosure plan.

Sura

The late Roman town of Sura (northernmost point of the Strata Diocletiana) has not yet been researched in detail. The fortified town's ruins lie 5 kms northeast of al-Mansura, 800 m north of the main road. Little survives above the ground except the contour outlines of the town walls with some evidence of gate structures and the square *castrum* (centre of north side). The river once flowed past the town and 2 km downstream evidence has been found of a Roman bridge.[2] Procopius lists this as one of the towns refortified by Justinian.

REFS: **Resafa:** Butler *EC* 1929: 161–3, 166; Key Fowden 1999; Lassus *Sanctuaires* 1947: 154–6; Procopius *Buildings* II, 9; Sack *Rusafa* V Mainz 1996; Tchalenko & Baccache 1979:-80 pl 499–543; Ulbert *Resafa* II 1986; Ulbert *Rusafa-Sergiopolis* 1985. **Sura:** Procopius *Buildings* II, 9; Ulrich 'Villes' in Dentzer & Orthmann 1989: 287.

Roman Road (Jebel Srir), Dana

الطريق الروماني

PERIOD: Rom RATING:* MAP: R3

LOCATION: 40 km west of Aleppo. Take the main road from Aleppo towards the Bab al-Hawa border crossing. At Urum al-Sughra (23 km) where the road to Idlib branches left, take the right fork and continue +17 km. At this point, Tell Akibrin, the modern road intersects a stretch of Roman road straddling the lower slopes of Jebel Srir.

If you are coming from Aleppo, 5 km before reaching the Roman road lies the village of **Atareb** mentioned (under the same name) in Assyrian archives of the ninth century BC. Atareb was known as Litarba in Byzantine times and became the nearest point to Aleppo fortified and defended by the Crusaders, later destroyed by the Zengids.

Continue on until the road starts to skirt the lower slopes of Jebel Srir. Look out on the right for the start of a 1200 m section of **Roman road** built to take the steep slope. At the top of the rise, the Roman road continues to the left. Syria was once criss-crossed with a network of roads during the Roman period (see box on page 9). Most have vanished, except where aerial photography, traces of installations (water holes and milestones) and written records enable us to reconstruct their path.

2 For a full survey of historic references – Musil *Middle Euphrates* 1927: 323–5.

The road is supported on a base held within containing walls filled with rubble and paved with limestone slabs. This provides a good illustration of Roman road-building techniques, though the road has been partly reconstructed. This section had to be more solidly built to take the slope along the busy route from Antioch (the capital of the province of Syria) to Chalcis ad Belum (*Qinnesrin), Beroea (*Aleppo) and on to Mesopotamia. There is no direct evidence for the date of its construction though a nearby inscription at Qasr al-Banat has Marcus Aurelius (r 161–80) taking the credit. Certainly the later part of the second century saw the peak in Roman construction and road-building activity in Syria.

On **Jebel Srir** (alt 558 m) a few remains of one of the small temples to Zeus contructed in the area in the first to second centuries AD have been found. Built under Hadrian (inscriptions dated AD 116), the shrine became popular when the road was developed for military traffic to support campaigns to the east. (Track to the summit begins on eastern side, from the village of Kfer Kermine.) The temple housed a recluse in Byzantine times. To the west of this peak was the scene of the battle known as **Ager Sanguinis** which resulted in the Crusaders' major defeat at the hands of Zengid forces from Aleppo in 1119. (The actual site was just south of the town of Sarmada on the *Harim road.)

If you are continuing on to Saint Simeon, the turn-off is a little further west (turn right). The road takes you almost immediately through the village of **Dana** (not to be confused with *Dana (South) near Maarat al-Numan). This village contains a remarkable Roman tomb of the second century in the form of a pyramidal canopy supported on four Ionic columns. The tomb is located at the northern end of the town 350m west of the main road. The **Plain of Dana** lies across the two most important access routes through the Limestone Massif. The Antioch-Aleppo road crosses the massif at its narrowest point and here meets the north-south route, the ancient road from *Apamea to *Cyrrhus. It has thus been a strategic crossroads throughout many epochs and is cited as far back as the Egyptian and Assyrian archives. The plain attracted a large number of monastic institutions (80 is Tchalenko's estimate) in the ascetic 'boom' of the late fifth and sixth centuries.

REFS: Hadjar 1979; Saouaf *Saint Simeon* nd: 2–5; Tchalenko *Villages* I 1953: 141. **Dana**: Butler *AE* II 1903: 29, 73; de Vogüé II 1865–77: pl 93; Dussaud 1927: 221, 239, 243; Tchalenko *Villages* I 1953: 117–9.

Roman Road (Wadi Barada)

ودئ بردا

VARIANTS: Abila Lysaniae (Lat); Suq Wadi Barada (Arb) PERIOD: Rom RATING: T MAP: R1

LOCATION: 35 km west of Damascus. 1.5 km east of the point where the new Zabadani road meets the old Barada River road. From Damascus (Umayyad Square), there are two choices.

Follow the highway to Lebanon, taking (at 33 km) the branch to Zabadani then +4 km to the crossing of the Barada River near the old dam. Turn right (east) for c+2 km along the old Barada road until you see the tomb entrances c100 m up the steep sides of the gorge on the left. Alternatively, follow the slower old road from Damascus (via Dummar) until 1.5 kms beyond Suq Wadi Barada (c34 km – the ancient Abila Lysaniae).

Along the steep northern side of the Barada gorge, remains can be seen of several Roman burial places as well as traces (over some 200 m) of a cutting for the Roman road from Hierapolis (Baalbek) to Damascus. A quick (seven minute) scramble up the mountainside takes you to the cutting. The Roman road clung to the upper side of the gorge to avoid raging torrents during floods but the cutting, restored in Roman times on at least one occasion, has partly been swept away by later rock-slides.

Several inscriptions (in Latin) record that Julius Verus, legate of the province of Syria, restored the road after a rock-slide 'at the expense of the people of Abila' (Suq Wadi Barada).[3] The inscriptions are dated to the reigns of 'Emperor Caesar M Aur Antoninus Aug Armeniacus and Emperor Caesar L A–rel. Verus Aug Armeniacus' – ie Marcus Aurelius (r 161–80)and his co-emperor Lucius Verus (r 161–9). The restoration must thus have been carried out between 161 and 169.

By following an old aqueduct cut into the rock a little lower down, the courageous can head east to inspect the rock-cut tombs each of which contained multiple burials.

There are legends associating this area with the Old Testament story of Cain and Abel (hence the Roman Abila). The summit immediately south of Suq Wadi Barada (Tell Habil or Nabi Habil) is the legendary place where Cain buried Abel after murdering him (Genesis 4). A Druze holy place marks the reputed spot. (Tarmac road access from Zabadani turn off from highway, c 8 km.) Legend relates that St Helen built a church there, on the site of an earlier (AD 29) Roman temple to Zeus Kronos though a recent French study raises very tentatively the possibility that the building (seen by travellers in recent centuries but now gone) was a temple tomb to the local figure, Lysanias of Abila. The dramatic mountain country to the north was probably studded with Roman temples erected on traditional 'high places' though little research has been done on the remains scattered along an arch through the southern Anti-Lebanon from Deir Nabi Yunan (northeast of Zabadani) to Cherubim on its spectacular perch above *Seidnaya.[4]

---

3 The inscriptions form matching groups, one at each end of the cutting. Each set comprises a dedicatory inscription and a panel saluting the ruling emperors. It is curious that the southern set had initially failed to include the line, later clumsily inserted, 'inpendiis Abilenorum', 'at the expense of the people of Abila'. Gschwind has speculated that the townspeople were rightly outraged that their considerable (forced) contribution had not been noted. Above the southern set is a blank niche.
4 For an interesting recent survey – Gschwind 2004.

The ancient Abila (of which the only traces are a few recycled stones in the houses of modern-day Suq Wadi Barada) was a Hellenistic foundation. It became an Ituraean principality whose ruler, Lysanias (a son of the king of Chalcis), was killed by Antony in 36 BC. It briefly became a substitute capital for what remained of the kingdom of Chalcis which had extended from the Beqaa to the Ledja (see box on 'Hauran' under *Suweida, page 289) after Augustus relieved the tetrarch of his original seat. Abila was later among lands presented by Claudius and Nero to the pro-Roman clients, Herod Agrippa I and II (r AD 37–44, 52–93 respectively). The tetrarchy was absorbed into the Roman administrative system at an unknown date and controlled a district extending across the Qalamoun as far as *Yabrud to the north. Abila's strategic importance for the Romans reflected a combination of factors including its location on the road between Heliopolis (Baalbek, a Roman military settlement) and Damascus.

REFS: Dentzer-Feydy 1999: 539–41; Gschwind 2004; Jones 1931: 265–75; Mouterde 1951–2.

Ruweiha

رويحة

VARIANTS: Ruwayha, Rouweiha PERIOD: Rom/Byz RATING: ** MAPS: 55, R3

LOCATION: Eastern slopes of Jebel Riha / Jebel Zawiye. Coming from the north, go through Riha and head up the hill. Continue c+5 km down the other side into a more desolate landscape.

Ruweiha comprises extensive ruins with two major churches and other vestiges of the late classical period. The setting in sweeping, open countryside on the edge of the plateau adds a dramatic effect. The town was largely a product of the fifth and sixth centuries.

Just north of the road which intersects the southern part of the town, you will notice a church of the fifth century, a columned basilica built in a severe style. The church courtyard includes the remains of a strange structure perched on eight columns. This may have been a tower to house a recluse.

The *agora* (in the centre of the main cluster of ruins) is built on an ample scale for a rural setting and was surrounded by a two-storey portico. In addition to the great number of villas in the style typical of the region, the *agora* also attracted a concentration of high-density construction.

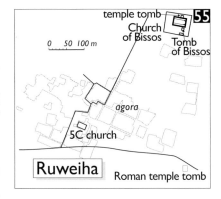

Especially notable on the northern edge of the town is the **Church of Bissos**, named after its sixth century benefactor. The largest church in the Jebel Riha, it is said by Butler to be the second largest in the limestone country of northern Syria. It is clearly a notable architectural milestone with its bold use of two high transverse arches spanning the central nave (not found in Europe until several centuries later) as well as the three more traditional longitudinal arches springing from four massive T-shaped piers. Sadly, though, the transverse arches were not matched by any buttressing in the form of side arches over the outer aisles to transfer the weight to the external walls. The high nave and the structure supporting the clerestory windows above it have thus almost entirely collapsed. At the entrance, the use of horseshoe-shaped arches above the two flanking doorways anticipates later Arab use of this device. The central arch of the *narthex* is more traditional and two towers rise above the outer doorways. The use of ornamentation is restrained, as in most of the churches of this southern part of the Limestone Massif.

The church is flanked by two tombs, the one with a dome honouring Bissos himself. Butler emphasises the unique status of this stone-cut dome, the only extant example in Syria, foreshadowing later Muslim domed saints' tombs (*turba*) which employ this basic design. Above the door on the west façade, the inscription reads: 'Bissos (son) of Pardos. I lived worthily, died worthily and rest worthily. Pray for me.' This is the only tomb of a church founder recorded in the 'dead cities' and it is possible that Bissos was a local priest or bishop. The second tomb (unattributed) in the form of a small but not very graceful Greek-style temple (*distyle in antis*) stands symmetrically on the north side of the church. The church compound is surrounded by a walled enclosure.

Along the tarmac road, 250 m to the east, note another **Roman temple tomb**, dated by inscription over the doorway to 384. The portico comprises two columns with stylized Corinthian capitals *in antae*. (In the necropolis to the southeast, there is another classical tomb, underground with a framed entrance.)

REFS: Butler *AE* II 1903: 84, 99–102, 106, 113–4, 120–3; Butler *EC* 1929: 145–8; Butler *PE* II B 3 1909: 142–8; de Vogüé II 1865–77: pl 68, 69, 91; Pena (*et al*) *Reclus* 1980: 174–9; Mattern 1944: 19–26; Tchalenko *Villages* II 1953: pl CXLI; Tchalenko & Baccache 1979–80: pl 462–80.

S

Safita

صافيتا

VARIANTS: Argyrokastron (Grk); Chastel
Blanc (Cru) PERIOD: Cru   ALT: 380 m
RATING: ** MAP: 56, R2

LOCATION: From *Tartus, 30 km by a
good road.

Safita is one of the most picturesque
towns in Syria, set in beautiful orchard
and olive-growing country dotted with
historic sites. It is equally accessible from
Tartus, the *Krak and Dreikish and the
surrounding valleys contain many picnic

donjon or keep still stands watch, visible
from as far away as the Krak and Tartus.
The area fell early into Crusader hands
and is mentioned in Arab sources as part
of the domains of the Count of Tripoli
from 1112. The building of the first castle
probably dates from that time, part of
the defence in depth for Tartus. In 1167
and 1171, Nur al-Din took advantage of
Crusader   unpreparedness,   occupying
Tartus, destroying Areimeh (*Qalaat
Areimeh) and largely demolishing the first
version of the Safita fortress, partly out of
anger at Crusader piracy against Egyptian
merchant ships.

Either around this time, or later after
Saladin's assault (1188), the Knights
Templar were given responsibility for
securing the Tartus area, having made
their second headquarters in the port

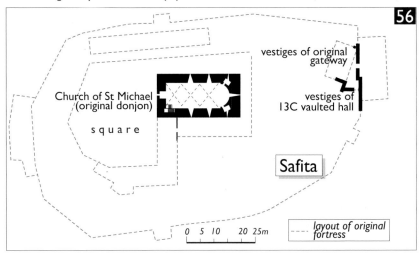

Church of St Michael
(original donjon)

square

vestiges of original
gateway

vestiges of
13C vaulted hall

Safita

0 5 10   20 25m   ---- layout of original
                          fortress

56

spots, idyllic particularly during the spring
when the countryside is covered in
wildflowers. Many of the villages suggest
more the atmosphere of the old Lebanon
or even southern Europe and the bustling
town perches on a hill in an almost Tuscan
scene.

History

At the top of the ridge along which the
town sprawls, the blunt square Frankish

city. They took control of Chastel Blanc
and the major work on the present keep
probably dates from their reconstruction
of the earlier fortress. Damage from an
earthquake in 1202 probably intensified
the need for major improvements and
the present building dates largely from the
13th century.

The castle fell into Muslim hands with
barely a fight in February 1271, taken by
the Mamluk Sultan Baybars en route to

the Krak. The evacuation of the castle was ordered by the Master of the Templars in Tartus, even though the garrison numbered 700 knights at the time. Its fall certainly left Tartus, one of the last Crusader stronghold on the mainland, increasingly exposed, contributing to its abandonment in 1291.

The plan chosen is a typical Frankish design, a stout central tower surrounded by two series of walls. The tower of the donjon or keep is in its own right a work of some note, one of the highpoints of the Crusader style in Syria. It housed the garrison as well as a church. The standard of construction was high with massive walls and stout internal pillars. In spite of earthquakes and the varied purposes to which it has been put, the donjon has survived in an almost perfect state.

Though the town was almost totally Greek Orthodox Christian in the late 19th century, the Christian community had only begun to settle there from the Hauran early in the previous century, gradually displacing the Alawi inhabitants. Today the population is again mixed.

Visit

You access the keep by a lane leading off the main street that circles the ridge. Arriving at the square on the west of the small plateau, it will be immediately obvious that the castle still serves as the main Greek Orthodox church (dedicated to St Michael, Mar Mikhael) for the town.

The exterior of the building (18 m wide by 27 m high) is typically blank, presenting as few weak points as possible to assailants. You enter by the west door (note the faint traces of a cross on the keystone) straight into the church which occupies the lower storey (10 m by 24 m internal dimensions). The vault of the nave is divided into three sections by two arches that rise from pilasters in the side walls. A moulded band passes under the west window and does a circuit of the interior. The apse at the east end is curved and is flanked by two sacristies built into the massive thickness of the walls. There are only five 'windows'

– really firing slits in the 3 m masonry. The height of the nave is almost 18 m, giving the church a surprising feeling of space, in spite of the restricted sources of light. In the southwest corner (hard right as you enter), a narrow staircase built into the walls leads to the next storey.

The staircase brings you out in a large (13 m by 26 m) and surprisingly elegant room used to house the garrison. The walls are slightly less thick than in the church below and the system of arches is different. Three central cruciform pillars divide the room into two parts, each with four bays comprising cross-groined arches. From each bay, a firing point looks over the surrounding countryside. Another staircase leads to the terrace commanding a sweeping view of the hill country as far as the Krak and Tartus, signal fires could be exchanged with other watch points. The parapet consists of alternating loopholes and crenellations. A cistern beneath the chapel was used to store water for times of siege.

Walk round to the back (east) of the church where a path into the town passes one of the gateways of the outer defences and part of a wall which originally belonged to a mid 13th century building. If you skirt around to the south from here you should be able to glimpse between buildings the glacis of the outer protective wall which formed an oval-shape (160 m by 100 m). Originally, an inner wall lay between these defences and the tower but no vestiges remain.

REFS: Deschamps *Châteaux* – III 1973: 249–58; Rey 1871: 85–92.

Saint George Monastery

دير مار جرجس

VARIANTS: Deir Mar Georgis; al-Houmayra (Arb) PERIOD: Arb RATING: – MAP: R2

LOCATION: In the deep valley northwest of the *Krak des Chevaliers. From the Krak, take the road north to Marmarita (5 km) but fork left immediately before the town.

This Greek Orthodox monastery was originally founded in the sixth century AD probably at the time of the Emperor Justinian. It has two chapels of which the older (reached from the lower courtyard) dates from the 13th century with an *iconostasis* in ebony wood (18th century). The lower court also includes remains of the Byzantine monastery. The new chapel (right off first courtyard) was built in 1857.

The monastery is located in the Wadi al-Nasara ('Valley of the Christians') which has been a centre of Greek Orthodox Christianity since the early Christian period. Its feast day (attended by Christians from all over Syria and Lebanon) is 6 May.

REFS: Deschamps III 1973: 249–58; Rey 1871: 85–92

Saint Simeon (Plates 22a, 22b)

قلعة سمعان

VARIANTS: Qala`at Simaan (Arb)
PERIOD: Byz RATING: *** MAP: 57, R3

LOCATION: From Aleppo, take the road direct to Dar Tazeh (30 km). Go through village, take right turn – +6 km to Saint Simeon.

Butler, who led the famous Princeton expedition which surveyed Syrian antiquities at the turn of the century, summed up the importance of Saint Simeon as follows:

> The great cruciform church is unique in the history of architecture and is not only the most beautiful and important existing monument of architecture between the buildings of the Roman period of the second century and the great church of Santa Sophia of Justinian's time, but also ... the most monumental Christian building earlier than the masterpieces of the eleventh and twelfth centuries in Northern Europe. (Early Churches in Syria 1929: 97)

Butler's description sets high claims indeed and few will find the complex of buildings and the magnificent setting a disappointment. The church is notable not only for the boldness of its scale but the classical refinement of its detail.

History

Unlike the later cathedrals of medieval Europe, the great church was conceived and executed more or less as a single project over a short space of time. The cruciform church comprising four separate basilica buildings was probably constructed shortly after the death of the ascete, St Simeon. Born in the area of Antioch around 389–90, Simeon joined the community of monks at Telanissos (*Deir Semaan, at the foot of the present site) around 410–2. He spent the rest of his life in the area, moving only to isolate himself more effectively from the rest of the community. He finally took up residence on a platform atop a column (12 m to 18 m high, 1.5 m to 2 m in diameter) around the remains of which the great building is centred. He died on this spot on 24 July 459, having already become a figure of reverence attracting pilgrims from many parts of the Byzantine world – from neighbouring Antioch but from as far afield as Britain and Persia.

Construction of the complex began a few years after St Simeon's death (probably spanning 476 to 491). This was a time of great ferment in the Antiochene church and the controversy over the Monophysite heresy was at its height. Much of this tension, based on pseudo-theological and contradictory interpretations of the emphasis to be given to Christ's human and divine natures, was partly a revolt by local (Syriac-speaking) Christians against domination from Constantinople. The ascetic and monastic movement too was part of the resistance to the metropolitan church. The cause of St Simeon, however, was tolerated and eventually promoted by the imperial authorities partly as a way of harnessing simple piety to distract attention from the theological-political controversies. Both Constantinople and Antioch vied to honour his memory. Against local (Monophysite) resistance to the removal of his remains, Simeon was buried in Antioch,[1] only to be later

---

1 In 459 Simeon's body was virtually seized

transferred to a new martyrium in Constantinople. Meanwhile, the column and the site of his ascetic deeds was commemorated under imperial patronage (the emperor at the time was Zeno, r 474– 91) thus encouraging the continuation of the cult of St Simeon through pilgrimage.

The colossal scale of the pilgrimage centre reflected the availability of outside resources under imperial patronage with architectural ideas and tradesmen brought in from a wide area. The plan of the building has precedents elsewhere and metropolitan influences and classical styles of decoration are blended with more typically Syrian elements. The ambitious design of the complex thus reflects several architectural styles. The basic concept of the three-aisled basilica already had a long tradition going back to Roman times. The idea of the centralised church focussed on a pivotal point was seen elsewhere in Syria (*Resafa, *Bosra, *Ezraa, *Apamea). The idea of laying out the buildings in the shape of a cross was more novel and was not established as a tradition until the great European religious buildings of the middle ages.

The ridge in its pre-479 state had to be levelled and extended to the west by artificial terracing to accommodate the enormous scale of the four-basilica plan. On this platform, the complex was arranged in several groups of buildings:

- the four basilicas meeting in the central octagonal courtyard
- the monastery complex, adjoining the basilicas to the southeast
- the baptistery, 200 m to the south
- annexes to the baptistery.

In Tchalenko's study of the Limestone Massif, he reconstructs the sequence of building as follows:

by a Byzantine military escort and transported by 600 soldiers to Antioch where he was buried in the city's cathedral. The church of St Simeon is thus not strictly a martyrium but 'a commemorative shrine centred around Simeon's pillar of forty cubits' (Mango 1976: 79).

- 476–92 – the basilica itself and baptistery
- 490+ – monastery; annexes to baptistery
- 500–25 – all other parts of the complex including two hostelries and the monumental arch leading from Deir Semaan.

In 526 and 528, violent earthquakes destroyed Antioch and probably brought down the roof over the central octagon between the four basilicas. The hillside was fortified when the Byzantines retook the area from the Arabs in the tenth century. It was retaken and sacked in 985 by the

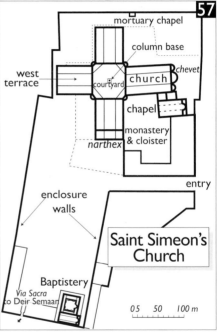

Hamdanids (Said al-Daula's forces) and again in 1017 (by an Egyptian army). It was subsequently abandoned as a monastic-religious centre.

Visit

After passing through the ticket office, you ascend to the ridge on which the church is located, arriving at the point mid-way between the baptistery (to the south, left) and the four-basilica church (right). Before you, the Afrin Valley and the Plain of Amuq stretch westwards to the environs of Antioch with the Kurd Dag line of hills and the Amanus Mountains, lost in the haze to the northwest.

Turn right to the main church, approaching it by the great south *narthex* (plate 22a). You now gain a closer appreciation of the distinctive plan of the church. Four basilica buildings, each big enough to be a major church in its own right, are laid like a cross roughly oriented to the cardinal points. (The overall dimensions of the complex are 100 m east-west, 88 m north-south. The total area enclosed by the cruciform is 3840 m².) The four buildings (each 24 m wide) meet in a central court at whose focal point stands the stub of the column on which St Simeon's platform was poised (plate 22b). (The remains of the column have been chipped away by pilgrims over the centuries.) This court is rounded off by *exedra*-shaped devices to form an octagon. Though no direct evidence remains of the original roof of the court, it is believed to have been erected in wood, perhaps with a dome or a central conical lantern. The design, however, was too ambitious and, after tumbling in the earthquake of 528, was not restored, the court being left uncovered. Though now striking for the simplicity of its honey-coloured limestone, the building was once ornately decorated with polychrome pavements, plastered and painted walls and encrusted decoration.

The eastern basilica, slightly larger than the other three (43 m long, nine bays; as against 30 m, seven bays), was naturally the most important and would have accommodated the major ceremonies in honour of the saint. In practical terms, the other three buildings had little perspective into the main basilica and were probably used for assembly and organisation of the pilgrims rather than for religious ceremonies. The observant visitor will notice that the east building is slightly off axis, being bent fractionally towards the north in order to orient the apse towards the true east.

The detail of the church is worth close examination. The sculptured decoration is superbly executed, extraordinary in its richness and variety. Indeed almost all the concepts exploited later in the churches of the Antioch hinterland are already found, usually in a more classical form, at Saint Simeon. Some features are of necessity experimental and having been tried out on a building of such huge scale are not always fully successful. Note, for example, the way in which the four basilicas are joined by the device of the corner *exedrae*. The square is transformed into an octagon at the points of which stand eight complex piers in line with the columns of the naves. From these piers spring the four arches leading into the basilicas as well as the arches framing the *exedrae*. These framing arches enclosing the trapezoidal *exedrae* are somewhat heavy, more like the local rural churches of the era in their preference for massive monumentality.

Though the architectural ideas are post-Roman, the treatment of the decoration is almost classical. Pillars are used to round off the piers and help support the arches. The capitals are variations on classical orders, with the occasional Byzantine flourish.

While you will want to wander around by yourself to take in the scale and detail of the building, three points are worthy of particular note.

- The first is the *narthex* by which you entered, a beautiful Byzantine adaptation of Roman concepts. The classical detail, including the grooved pilasters facing the piers and the swept acanthus motif of the capitals, is particularly noteworthy. The latter device, first employed in this building, is later widely taken up in the Byzantine world.
- Second, the great west **terrace** which looks down over the rich plain. The *loggia* is built upon an enormous artificial platform constructed over the steep slope of the ridge (cf the similar arrangement at *Burqush near Damascus.) This was necessary in order to balance the length of

the eastern and western basilicas, the central position of the column determining the focal point on the narrow ridge.

• The third point of particular interest is the outer wall of the **chevet** of the eastern basilica. To inspect it, you will have to walk around the outside of the cathedral to the east, through the remains of the attached monastery. The *chevet* echoes some of the ideas employed a few years beforehand in the church at *Qalb Lozeh, notably in allowing the curve of the apse to project beyond the rear line of the building and in decorating the drum wall with two tiers of colonnettes. Note too that the windows' decorated mouldings are passed continuously from frame to frame without interruption.

North of the cruciform cathedral, the upper remains of the enclosure give commanding views of the complex and the surrounding countryside. The tenth century wall was hastily constructed in a slapdash technique during the Byzantine re-occupation of the area. Within the wall are the remains of a mortuary chapel, the lower level carved out of the rock, probably for the storage of skeletal remains.

The segment between the south and east basilica is occupied by the ruins of a **monastery**, apparently intended for resident and visiting clergy. (The general public were accommodated at the foot of the hill in Deir Semaan.) The remains include a small chapel, the whole group forming a great courtyard around the southeastern walls of the cathedral itself.

To visit the rest of the complex, exit the main cathedral by the south *narthex* and continue south along the ridge. This was the great central processional way for pilgrims. The baptistery stands 200 m south. Here converts were sacramentally initiated into Christianity. The main processional path skirted this building to the west, having ascended the ridge at an angle to its slope.

The **baptistery** dates slightly after the main cathedral but is an essential part of the pilgrimage complex. Described as 'one of the finest remnants of Christian architecture in the whole of Syria',[2] it was built in two phases – the baptistery itself first; the associated small basilica later. The octagonal drum which externally tops the square base of the building was once crowned by a wooden roof shaped either like a cone (cf the cathedral courtyard roof) or a dome. The inner octagon (15 m) was enclosed in the square outer building. The two shapes are resolved by arches cutting across the corners of the square, linked to the outer walls by pilasters. At the eastern end of the chamber is a semi-circular *absidiola* which includes a curious channel with steps leading down to it. This was clearly the walk-through 'font' to process the mass baptism of converts. The remains of the associated basilica to the south are minimal.

Southwest of the baptistery, you can trace the remains of ancillary buildings which provided accommodation and facilities to pilgrims. The **processional route** (*via sacra*) entered the complex from this direction, passing through the great monumental arch lower down the slope (described in *Deir Semaan).

REFS: Bavant *CFAS* 1989: 194–8; Beyer 1925: 60–2; Butler *AE* II 1903: 97–109, 156, 184–90; Butler *EC* 1929: 97–105; Butler *PE* II B 6 1920: 281–4; Delehaye 1923: LIX–LXXV; de Vogüé I 1865–77: 141, II pl 139–50; Saouaf *Saint Simeon* nd; Sodini 1982: 277–8; Sodini (*et al*) 2002–3: 353–5; Tchalenko *Villages* I 1953: 223–76; II pl LXI–III, LXXV–IX, LXXXI–IV, LXXXVII; Mattern 1944: 118–34.

Salkhad

صلخد

VARIANTS: Salchah (bib)[3] PERIOD: Arb
RATING: – MAP: R1

LOCATION: From *Suweida (128 km from Damascus) continue +38 km south-east.

One of the most ancient centres of southern Syria, Salkhad has so far yielded

2 *Blue Guide* 1966: 400.
3 Job XII, 5; XIII 11; Deut III 10.

few of its secrets and the only reminders of its past are the citadel and a minaret in the lower town. Salkhad is mentioned in the Old Testament as a frontier settlement, a walled city of the Kingdom of Bashan. A fort was built here by the Fatimid caliph, al-Mustansir, in 1073/4. The most notable visible remains are those of the Ayyubid citadel built (in conjunction with the fortification of the theatre at *Bosra) in 1214–47 to serve as the southern defence of Damascus against the Crusader presence in Jerusalem. The citadel was renewed by the Mamluk sultan, Baybars (r 1264–77).

The fortress was built into the crater of a volcano but the walls which slope steeply down the outer face are now badly crumbled. There is little to see on the crest and Ottoman and later use of the site as a military position have left little intact.

The minaret (erected 1232) is found in the town's main square. The lower 20 m of the tower dates from the Ayyubid period. Hexagonal in shape (a plan unique in Islamic architecture but probably borrowing from Roman models), it is largely made from the local basalt (black, with a dark red section at the top), interrupted by two bands of white with finely inscribed Koranic passages and niches on each face. The original mosque has disappeared but apparently resembled in style the Mosque of Umar in nearby Bosra.

REFS: Abu Assaf 1998; Butler PE II A 2 1915: 117–9; Korn II 2004: 181–4; Meinecke 'Salkhad' in Dentzer & Dentzer-Feydy (edd) Le Djebel al-'Arab 1991; Meinecke AAAS 1997; Miller 1984: 104–5.

Sanamein

الصنمين

VARIANTS: Aere
PERIOD: Rom RATING: * MAP: R1

LOCATION: 51 km south of Damascus, just off the Deraa road.

This temple of the late second century AD survives mainly in the rear wall of the cella and its side walls though the ground plan is clear from the foundation remains. The standard of decoration, however, is exceptionally beautiful. The rear (south) wall of the cella carries a central shell niche of bold design, flanked by niches with particularly effective carved lintels. The building is dated by inscription to the 13th year of the reign of Commodus (AD 191–2). It was erected about the same time as the temple (now disappeared) at nearby Mismiye which had a similar arrangement of a tri-panel adyton. Both projects were perhaps built in association with major intensification of the Roman presence in the area with the building of the Via Ledja but echo typical local temple styles dating back to the first century BC. The use of the shell-form in the apse continued into the third century, eg *Qanawat. The square temple form survived through to Byzantine times until overtaken by the greater popularity of the fifth–sixth century basilica-plan churches.

REFS: Butler PE II A 5 1915: 315–22; Freyberger DaM 1989: 87–108; Sartre-Fauriat 2004: 239–46.

Seidnaya

صيدنايا

VARIANTS: Sardeneye (Cru)
PERIOD: Byz/Arb ALT: 1415 m   RATING: – MAP: R1

LOCATION: On the edge of the Anti-Lebanon Range, 27 km north of Damascus. Take the road to al-Tal (turn-off at 11.5 kms) and continue north +15 km.

Seidnaya is more notable as a place of religious pilgrimage than for any outstanding remains. In fact, few reminders of its origins can be distilled from centuries of legends.

The **Convent of Our Lady of Seidnaya** is perched on an outcrop of rock, looking rather like a castle from some angles. Legend relates that it was founded by Justinian (r 527–65). The miracles associated with the image of the Virgin brought the chapel wide fame particularly during and after the middle ages. It became the most famous centre for pilgrimage in the east, after Jerusalem – 'the Lourdes of the medieval East' (Pena). The Crusaders were fascinated by the legends of 'Notre Dame de Sardeneye' associated with a painting of the Virgin said to have been executed by Luke the Evangelist. Even in times of open hostility between the Franks in Jerusalem and the Muslims of Damascus, Christian pilgrims reached Seidnaya.

After entering through the confined doorway, the interior leading up to the chapel of the Virgin is a maze of indeterminate origins. The shrine itself (right at top of the stairs) contains many mementoes of recent pilgrim traffic. The concealed image of the Virgin is said to be an early copy of the one reputedly painted by Luke (cf *Tartus) and there are other icons said to date from the fifth and seventh centuries. The shrine is usually crowded; perhaps most remarkable is the number of non-Christians, particularly on a Friday, reflecting the long tradition of Muslim interest in the shrine and its attendant legends. The convent is in the care of the Greek Orthodox Church. The main day of pilgrimage is 8 September (Birthday of the Virgin).

The **Chapel of St Peter** is a converted Roman tomb lying west of the roundabout on the approach road to the convent. The design is superbly austere – only a doorway and a deep cornice relieve the basic cube shape (9.5 m by 9.5 m by 7.9 m). The interior is cruciform. A staircase in one corner gives access to the roof.

There are other sites of historical interest in the area, some associated with the monastic tradition of the early Church. To the north and south, caves of holy men and remains of monasteries can be visited. The **Cherubim Monastery** was founded in the Byzantine period and lies on a commanding peak (1910 m) one kilometre to the north in a straight line. (A 5.5 km circuitous tarmac route winds up from the north of the town). Three re-used columns mark the porch, recycled from a Roman temple on this site, as were components of the church walls and part of the new monastery complex. The steep (5 km) road to the peak passes (left) the vastly expanded **Monastery of St Thomas**, also incorporating remains of a Roman temple.

Deir Mar Elias or **Chapel of the Prophet Elijah**, 3 km south of Maarat Seidnaya, lies on the escarpment overlooking the great Syrian steppe. The cave is associated with a local legend that it sheltered the Old Testament prophet, Elijah, in his sojourn in the 'Desert of Damascus' (I Kings 19, 15). Only a few fragments of the frescoes, recently restored with assistance from the Netherlands, survive. They are dated on stylistic grounds to the 11th–12th centuries (*Qara, *Deir Mar Mousa). You may need to ask for keys and a guide from the Greek Orthodox church in Seidnaya.

REFS: anon *Recueil historique*; Keriaky *Saidnaya – History and Ruins* Damascus nd; Gschwind 2004; Lassus '*Deux églises*' 1931: Appendice II; Nasrullah *BEO* 1943–44: 5–38; Pena *Lieux* 2000: 111–2; Pringle *Churches* II 1998: 219–20; Schmidt, & Westphalen 2005: 155–82.

Selemiye and Qalaat al-Shmemis
(Plate 19b)

سلمية قلخة شممامیس

VARIANTS: Salamias, Salamya   PERIOD: Fatimid/Ayy/Ott RATING: – MAP: R2

LOCATION: 30 km east-southeast of Hama.

The remains of the Ayyubid fort today known as **Qalaat al-Shmemis** (plate 19b) lie 5 km northwest of Selemiye. The castle looks more striking from a distance than it does up close but can be approached by a side road that reaches a point half-way up the slope on the east. The walls rise abruptly from an artificial ditch with the entrance on the southeast side, once flanked by two rectangular towers. The fort dates from 1231 and was built on the flattened top of an extinct volcanic cone by the Ayyubid Prince of Homs, al-Mujahid Assad al-Din Shirkuh II (r 1186–1240). The castle was destroyed by the Mongols in 1260 but restored by Baybars, having been incorporated in the province of Damascus. What remains inside the outer shell comprises little but rubble and the slippery slope of the ditch's inner side makes the ascent through a hole in the eastern face somewhat hazardous.

Selemiye is the ancient Salamias, later the seat of a Byzantine bishop. Remains of a church were incorporated in the town's central shrine-mosque. Selemiye was prominent under the Abbasids when a cousin of the first two Abbasid caliphs, Abdallah Ibn al-Abbas, settled there. Its association with the Ismaelis goes back before Fatimid times. The first of the hidden imams of the Fatimids, Abdallah, grandson of al-Sadiq, lived here in the early ninth century and it became the centre from which Ismaeli doctrine was spread to North Africa. The domed tomb constructed on the imam's grave c1009 and rebuilt by the Fatimid amir of Homs in 1088 is still venerated (ask for Makam al-Imam). This singular reminder of the Fatimid period in Syria lies 150m southeast of the Ayyubid-Ottoman citadel, also using ancient spolia, in the centre of town. Selemiye was a staging post on the route to Iraq in the Arab middle ages but neglected under the Ottomans until the amir of Qadmus was allowed to resettle in Selemiye in 1849 with his Ismaeli followers from the coastal mountains. The city then flourished and Circassians were also settled by the Ottoman authorities. The Selemiye Ismaelis transferred their allegiance in 1887 to the Aga Khan and the town became the most important Ismaeli centre in the Middle East.

REFS: **Qalaat Shmemis** – Bylinski in Faucherre (et al edd.) 2004 152–5; Korn II 2004: 200–1; van Berchem & Fatio 1914: 171–3; **Selemiye** – Halm 1986; Korn II 2004: 199–200; Kramers, Daftary 'Salamiyya' EI2; van Berchem & Fatio 1914: 167–70.

Serjilla (Plate 23a)

سير خيلة

VARIANTS: Serdjilla, Sergilla
PERIOD: Rom/Byz RATING: ** MAPS: 58, R3, R3a

LOCATION: Turn east immediately south of *Bara. 4 km to Bauda then +3 km to Serjilla.

One of the most interesting and visited of the 'dead cities', Serjilla, located in a natural basin opening out to the south, comprises extensive remains of houses, a church, baths, tombs and sarcophagi – a complete Byzantine settlement in a superb and isolated setting.

Near the road, on the left, you will notice a necropolis area with **sarcophagi**. Beyond this and a little to the southeast (downhill) lie the substantial remains of the **baths** (plate 23a) and meeting house. A floor of the baths is dated to 473 and their existence in this remote locality indicates the degree of prosperity in the community at the time. The baths are one of the most intact examples found in Syria and are particularly interesting given their origins in the Christian period, as opposed to earlier Roman examples. The main hall of the baths (the largest room, along the north side of the building) measured 8 m by 15 m. The American expedition at the turn of the last century found a large mosaic in this room (since destroyed[4]) dedicated by one Julianos and his wife Domna. In appearance, the building is rather severe, the only decoration being the moulded cornice on top of the walls and gables.

Immediately to the southeast lies an outbuilding, an *andron* or men's meeting place. The building's south front is marked by a double portico, three columns on each level. It is described by Butler as 'one of the most perfectly preserved structures in all the ruined and deserted towns in Syria'.

East of the *andron* and half way up the rise, you will find a small triple-naved **church**. The chamber (*prothesis*) on the north side of the apse is unusual in being enlarged beyond the line of the north wall of the church. On the south side, there is an additional room off the right nave. This communicates with a longer room to the south which gave on to a cloistered court of irregular shape. Beyond this room is a chamber which contained

---

4 In fact, most of the mosaic disappeared in the six years between the first and second American expeditions (1899–1905).

three sarcophagi. Such a mortuary chapel is unusual, possibly intended for ecclesiastical dignatories or town notables rather than venerated saints. Butler judges the church on stylistic grounds to be one of the oldest in the region, perhaps begun earlier than the inscribed date of 372. The building was remodelled and enlarged in the fifth or sixth century.

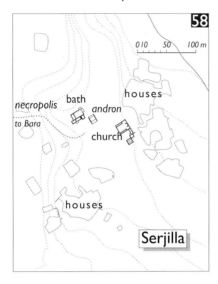

Up the rise to the east are extensive remains of **housing**, mostly of the detached villa variety. Most are ranged along an arc extending from the south to the east, with colonnaded fronts facing a court. Some were large in size, allowing for up to four families. The most extensive is 50–60 m north of the church, a double-fronted villa of the fourth or fifth century with a colonnaded façade (modified Corinthian capitals) giving on to a courtyard. Two ancillary houses were grouped around this triangular space. The house immediately behind the church to the east is also of interest. Its façade, now blank, once bore a double colonnade in addition to the then-fashionable decorative mouldings around windows and doors. The building, somewhat analogous to the *andron* described above, is probably from the late fifth or early sixth century.

Other houses are found on the other side of the valley (southwest of the baths). This group terminates with an isolated tomb. A small square chamber is partly cut out of the rock with a front of cut stone.

Other sites in the vicinity include **B`uda** (1 km west) and a Crusader stronghold, **Rubea** (2 km south). The latter has a pyramidal tomb described by Butler as 'one of the most perfectly preserved of its class in the Jebel Riha'.

REFS: Butler *AE* II 1903: 124; Butler *PE* II B 3 1909: 113–33; de Vogüé I 1865–77: 80; Krautheimer 1981: 147–8; Mattern 1944: 35–40; Tchalenko *Villages* II 1953: pl CXL.

Shahba (Plate 23b)

شهبا

VARIANTS: Philippopolis (anc), Shehba, Shuhba
PERIOD: Rom   ALT: 1100 m   RATING: *
MAPS: 59, R1

LOCATION: 87 km south of Damascus on the *Suweida road. Take the Damascus airport highway; turn right at the Ebla Cham Hotel and head south.

A curious town located between the volcanic region of the Ledja to the west and Jebel al-Arab to the southeast. It is nearly 100 percent Druze, apparent from the dress of the inhabitants. It is dominated by the cone of an extinct volcano (Tell Shihan) 3 km to the north. From an archaeological point of view, it is the only town in the Roman Hauran (ancient Auranitis) – apart from the capital, *Bosra – built to a grid pattern and the walls are broadly oriented towards the cardinal points of the compass. (The terrain of other towns such as *Qanawat was probably too broken to accommodate easily a geometric layout.)

Shahba's square shape and the remains of its Roman walls give it a more 'imperial' feel than other towns in the area. It was founded, possibly on the site of his native village, by the local boy made good, Philip 'the Arab', who was emperor from 244 to 249.[5] This project was timed to be inaugurated on the 1000th anniversary of the founding of Rome. The Italian origins of many of the concepts and techniques is revealed in the lavish scale of the baths, the project was abandoned when the town failed to generate economic self-sufficiency. Less than half of the walled area was built upon and only a small community continued to inhabit the town

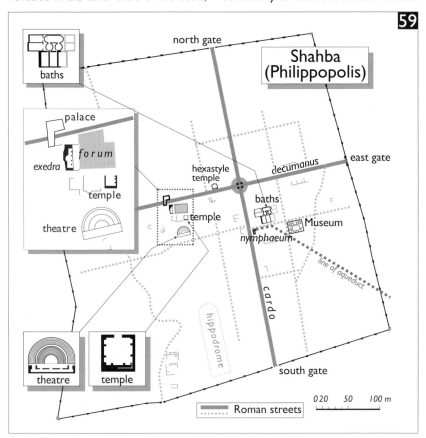

Shahba (Philippopolis)

59

north gate

baths

palace

forum

exedra

hexastyle temple

decumanus

east gate

temple

baths

theatre

temple

Museum

nymphaeum

line of aqueduct

cardo

hippodrome

south gate

theatre

temple

Roman streets

0 20   50   100 m

the use of barrel vaulting and concrete domes and the extensive application of marble cladding on interior walls. It is possible that the 'new town' was intended to house a colony of settlers as well as to honour Philip's family. The new town was not completed on Philip's death and

in the late Empire. It was only in the 19th century that the town was repopulated with the influx of Druze from Lebanon.

The town **walls** include monumental gateways at the cardinal points. The plan is a rough square, described by Hatoum as taking its shape from a Roman *castrum*. The actual dimensions of the walls are – north 800 m, east 800 m, south 900 m, west 1000 m. The two main axes which join the gates were originally c15 m wide excluding the colonnaded pavements (c2.5

5 The assumption that Philip came from the village underlying Philippopolis is supported in the recent study by Darrous & Rohmer (2004). Philip was proclaimed emperor on the death of Gordian III, killed in battle near modern Baghdad.

m on each side). The *insulae* depart from the Greek pattern, being more square (c102 m by 144 m) than the proportions usually adopted in the Hippodamian grid. The north and south town gates, comprising a large central arch flanked by two smaller passages in a severely plain style, have been reconstructed. The main colonnaded streets crossed at the centre of town in a large circular space once marked by remains of a tetrapylon.

The main cluster of ruins is 100 m along the cross street to the west of the central intersection (right as you come from Damascus). There are stray remains here and there: note, for example, the five Corinthian columns, beautiful fragments of a portico that once provided the entrance to a **hexastyle temple** or shrine, 50 m on the right as you ascend towards the palace-theatre area.

The ruins centre on the rather awkward square which is dominated by the **monumental exedra**. This eye-catching façade comprises an elaborate arrangement of niches 30 m wide and 20 m deep meant to display statuary. Some (including the 19th century visitor, the Marquis de Vogüé) saw this curious building as a *nymphaeum* (water fountain). There is, however, no evidence of a water source or associated channelling. Butler concluded that it was a *kalybe* (open-sided shrine) or 'great open-air state apartment ... where, perhaps, the Arab Emperor sat upon his throne'. More recently, researchers prefer to see the arrangement as an elaborate frame for statuary depicting the divinity of Philip's ancestry:

> The great exedra dominating the town from its esplanade took the place of a capitol in other Roman colonies. Thus on the eve of the celebration of the thousand years since Rome's foundation (247), the Emperor's native land was endowed with a unique form of sanctuary, a striking proclamation of the glory of the local boy risen to be master of the eternal city.

(Amer and Gawlikowski *DaM* 1985)

To the right but not directly connected with the monumental *exedra* are the remains of the **palace** with the main *decumanus* penetrating its façade.

The simple but impressive building between the square and the theatre to the south was once assumed to have been a '**Philippeion**' or temple erected in honour of Philip's father, Julius Marinus. It consists of an almost square chamber interrupted only by a broad and lofty entrance doorway on the north side. The exterior is austere, relieved by shallow corner pilasters with Ionic capitals. The doorway, 5.5 m high and 3 m wide, is impressive for its moulding in bold relief. The two flanking brackets were intended for statues, one of Philip's father. Inside, groups of blind arches are set into the walls facing and flanking the entrance, each set comprising a broad central recess with narrower arches to the side. The holes found in many parts of the walls and niches indicate the original use of marble revetments to decorate the interior. The rear (south) wall is considerably thicker in order to accomodate a staircase ascending to the roof. A recent study (Darrous & Rohmer 2004) has raised the possibility that the building was intended as a 'bouletereion' to house the town council rather than a 'Philippeion' as assumed by Butler. This would explain the horse-shaped seating that fills the floor area.

The **theatre** (immediately south of the temple, plate 23b) is small, rather stolid and without decoration but is one of the best preserved in Syria. (With a diameter of 42 m it is not in the same league as the superb example at Bosra to the south). The vaulted passages underneath (based on an unusual and complex arrangement of semi-circular and radial vaults) and access to the seating are well preserved, along with the lower rows of seats and the stage front. This is the last of the Roman theatres constructed in the east.

The **baths** (turn left at 80 m as you go south from the intersection of the two main Roman axes) are on a remarkable scale for a town of this size (covering 5000 m²) and the only identifiable remains in this style in the Hauran. Butler observed that the standard of construction is much higher than, for example, the Baths of

Caracalla in Rome. The domes used a light concrete, mixing small stones and high quality cement. The interior walls were clad with marble and alabaster and the domes faced inside with painted plaster. The plan was complex: to the south, a series of three rectangular rooms (two *apodytaria* flanking a *caldarium* – that on the right was never completed); two round *caldaria* in the centre; and a long room with semi-circular ends to the north, the *tepidarium*. In the street to the south, remains of an aqueduct that fed the baths and nearby *nymphaeum*.

In the same street is a **museum of mosaics** which contains some of the best examples of the art of the late Roman period in Syria. They are believed to date from the 'Constantinian renaissance' of the second quarter of the fourth century, indicating that prosperous urban life continued well beyond the city's foundation. (Other, usually earlier, mosaics from Shahba are found in the Damascus and Suweida museums.) The four intact panels describe (anti-clockwise from entrance):

- **Tethys** (goddess of the sea) – 2.66 m by 2.65 m. The goddess bears in her thick tresses, various manifestations of sea life. A favourite theme of artists from Antioch, the goddess is often depicted as the consort of Oceanos. Not a major deity, she was used as a vehicle for depicting the rich variety of fish life of the region. A recent survey of Roman mosaics describes this as a work of 'astonishing' boldness and vitality.[6]

- **The Wedding of Ariane and Bacchus** – Bacchus and Ariane are seated on a rock (both provided with halos) in a scene typical of the 'love conversation' tradition. Behind stands Hymen carrying a flaming torch symbolising desire. At their feet lies a rather enebriated Heracles. On the left, an aged Satyr-like figure labelled Maron seems to be lunging towards Ariadne's cup.

6 Dunbabin *Mosaics of the Greek and Roman World* Cambridge 1999: 166.

- **Orpheus** – Orpheus, dressed in a Phrygian cap and oriental attire, is sitting on a rock, playing the lyre. He is surrounded by animals entranced by his music. The importance of the mosaic is described by Janine Balty: 'this mosaic, at the level of art history, impresses as one of the most powerful and sensitive in the whole history of late Roman mosaic work'.

- **Aphrodite and Ares** – The scene is from *The Odyssey* VIII, 266–70. Aphrodite and Ares in their love tryst before Hephaistos takes his revenge, ridiculing them before the gods of Olympus. Aphrodite, barely covered but richly bejewelled, stands opposite Ares attended by a rather severe-looking woman, labelled as Charis. Cupids divest Ares of his arms and armour and dispute possession.

These four mosaics were found in a house on this site. The remaining two panels were brought from other sites in the city, notably **Three Graces** and **the Seasons**. The final panel comprises segments from works now incomplete.

REFS: Abu Assaf 1998: 59–63 Amer & Gawlikowski 1985: 1–15; Balty, Janine *Mosaiques* 1997: 141–8; Butler *PE* II A 5 1915: 359–60; Freyburger 1992; Darrous & Rohmer 2004; Hatoum 1996; Hatoum *BEO* 2000: 135–41.

Shaizar

شيزر

VARIANTS: Sinzaru (BrA); Larissa (Grk); Cesara (Lat); Le Grand Césaire (Cru); Seijar, Qalaat Shaizar (Arb) PERIOD: Cru/Arb   RATING: *
MAP: R2

LOCATION: 28 km northeast of *Hama on the road to Qalaat Mudiq (*Apamea) and *Jisr al-Shugur. 27 km southeast of Apamea.

History

Shaizar is located at a vital crossing point on the Orontes. Here the river, after rushing around a bend through a confined gorge to the east, returns to the more leisurely pace of the plains. The settlement has classical origins, local legends recorded by Diodorus Siculus (first century BC) claiming its foundation by a regiment of Thessalonian cavalry from Alexander's forces.

In the early Arab period, a Fatimid castle stood on the site but was seized in 999 by the Byzantines in their effort to reassert their influence in Syria. As the Byzantine hold weakened, a local clan (the Banu Munqidh) seized Shaizar in 1081. By the time the Crusaders had installed themselves briefly in Qalaat Mudiq to the north, the clansmen used Shaizar as a base to harass their presence. It formed a strongpoint of the Arab frontline against the Crusaders. (An interesting Arab perspective on this confrontation is given in the memoirs of a member of the Banu Munqidh family, Usamah (see Bibliography).

Shaizar grew in importance as a centre of Arab resistance, so much so that the Crusaders set up positions in the mountains on the opposite side of the plain to observe and contain Shaizar (*Qalaat Abu Qobeis, *Qalaat al-Mehelbeh). Tancred unsuccessfully sought to take it in 1108 but after another feint in 1110 was forced to settle for a treaty with the amir of Shaizar agreeing to live-and-let-live within existing spheres of influence. The Byzantines attempted in 1134 and 1138 to take the castle but failed. Much of it was destroyed in 1157 by the severe earthquake which affected the greater part of Syria. The Crusaders tried to profit from the decimation of the clan owners in the destruction by moving on Shaizar, occupying the lower citadel. But by then Nur al-Din was active in northern Syria. He expelled them, repaired the damage and installed his own governor.

In 1170 another earthquake did further damage. Saladin's incorporation of northern Syria after 1174 brought it under his control. A new keep was constructed under the Ayyubids (1233). The first Mongol invasion of Syria in 1260 brought renewed destruction but Baybars (1260–77), who did much to revive Syria after the Mongol wave had passed, garrisoned

it. He and his successor, Qalawun, were probably responsible for the substantive rebuilding of a good deal of the castle as seen today (especially the northern defences and the reconstruction of the keep). The castle subsequently fell into disuse as a military post but came to shelter the village inhabitants whose building activities helped erode its fabric until they were moved out in recent decades.

Visit

The elongated (300 m) crag on which it sits provides a natural setting for a fortress. As you pass the village, take a close look on the right at the south end of the crag where a great ditch has been dug out of the living rock to isolate the defences from the connecting hill and give the main castle keep greater elevation. (Similar arrangements were employed at *Qalaat Saladin and *Bakas-Shugur.)

A visit to the castle requires only an hour or so and is a convenient stop on the way from Hama to Apamea. The castle is entered from the north, near the old Turkish bridge and *norias*. The entry bridge leads into a salient of the castle built in 1290 (according to the Arabic inscription above the rear arch of the vestibule) which juts out from the northern walls at an angle and was originally skirted by a glacis. The salient's construction is solid with large bossaged blocks anchored through the use of classical columns. The upper tower is partly missing but one storey and several windows survive.

A vaulted passage takes you through to a relatively open space, the jumbled remains of various epoques left after the villagers were evacuated. There is not much that is identifiable but the views west over the plain or east over the Orontes gorge 50 m below are worth taking in. Head straight for the south end of the ridge, towards the prominent remains of the keep or donjon already noted, towering above the artificial ditch. Poised at the weakest point of the castle's defences, this was originally built in 1233 by the Ayyubids using large bossaged blocks and strengthening columns. (Remains of a Roman arched structure incorporated into the fortifications – base of northern front – were recently identified by Italian researchers.) The quality of work is superior to the entrance gateway. There is an entrance on the north but access is difficult. Inside, the tower comprises a cellar area with vaulted rooms, two large floors and a roof platform. The architecture and siting of the keep has much in common with Crusader techniques though the proportions are not always as regular, especially in the pillars holding up the vaulting.

REFS: Bevan I 1902: 205; Boase 1967: 72–4; Dussaud 1927: 145; van Berchem & Fatio 1914: 177–87; Tonghini (et al) 2003: 179–212.

Shaqqa

شقّا

VARIANTS: Saccaia, Maximianopolis (Grk); Shakka. PERIOD: Rom/Byz RATING: – MAP: R1

LOCATION: From Damascus, take the road to *Shahba (87 km). Immediately before Shahba, a large volcanic cone (Tell Shihan) on the right is being mined for bitumen. A little south, turn left and follow this road for +8 km.

The scale of its buildings indicates the degree of importance Shaqqa once enjoyed, its decline symptomatic of the general neglect of the area once its wider markets were cut off and insecurity prevailed. It had the status of a colony in Roman times and was the seat of a bishop in the Christian era.

Four hundred and fifty metres northeast of the main intersection (head east, take third street to the left) lie the remains of an impressive Roman palace (dubbed in early sources the **Kaiseriye**). Note the finely carved door and surviving niche on the south of the eastern façade. A forecourt led right into a broad hall spanned by five closely spaced wide arches supporting a flat ceiling, a common roofing system in the Hauran reflecting the difficulty of cutting the local basalt into roofing slabs longer

than 2 or 3 m. Northwest of the forecourt is a long hall, its roof once supported on ten transverse arches. South of the same square is part of the façade of a Roman **basilica** building later used as a church.

350 m to the east are the remains of a **monastery** tower (fifth–sixth century) incorporated into a farmyard. The complex once included a three-naved church of which few traces remain (south of courtyard).

Further up the hill to the west (guide needed) you will find a chamber now used as a Druze meeting hall that clearly has classical or early Christian origins, a centralised structure with four internal columns.

The main road continues north to the interesting villages of Hit and Haiyat that also preserve significant remains.

REFS: Abu Assaf 1998: 63–7; Butler AE II 1903: 370–5, 396–7; Butler PE II A 5 1915: 360; Butler EC 1929: 22, 84–5.

Sheikh Suleiman (Plate 24a)

الشيخ سليمان

PERIOD : Byz RATING : MAP : R3

See directions for Mushabbak but 3 kms before, turn right. Village + 3 km along a new sealed road.

Now accessible by sealed road, this site is worth the short diversion en route to *Saint Simeon. The ruins nestle among a lush patch of green in the otherwise rock-strewn environment of the Jebel Semaan.

There are remains of three churches. The northern-most lies amid the modern houses and few remains survive. The small church left of the road just south of the village is dated 602 (lintel of south door), thus one of the latest dated churches in the region – basilica plan with piers separating nave from side aisles. The apse is perfectly intact but much of the rest of the structure lies around in tumbled blocks. (Much has fallen since Butler's visit a century ago, perhaps explained by the fragile nature of the piers, most of which comprised two large superimposed blocks.)

The Church of the Virgin lies further to the south and is earlier (late fifth century), rightly described by Butler as 'one of the most beautiful (churches) in northern Syria' with its intact and superbly decorated apse, colonnaded porch or *narthex* (plate 24a), atrium and what was probably the priest's house on the west. The porch of the church is particularly notable: 'There is nowhere in all Syria a church portico which in any way can be compared to this for beauty and richness of detail' (Butler). North of the village, a recluse's tower.

REFS: Butler *PE* II B 6 1920: 335–41; Hadjar 2000: 118–24; Tchalenko II 1953: pl CXXX.

Sia

سيع

VARIANTS: Seia (anc); Si', Siah, Si`a PERIOD: Rom RATING: – MAPS: 60, R1

LOCATION: 3 km southeast of *Qanawat in the Jebel al-Arab. From the square in front of the Qanawat *seraya*, head down the road which goes past the precariously-poised fragment of a tower east of the main ruins. Continue about 3 km until the road turns sharp left, running below a ridge. It then heads right and ascends steeply to the village of Sia. Stop before the village and ascend to the jumbled remains along the ridge to the right.

Even in terms of the many survival stories of the Jebel al-Arab, Sia is a remarkable site, providing some insight into the pre-Roman Semitic architecture of Syria and its adaptation under Roman influence. It is, however, a site for the true enthusiast and the severely fragmented remains require constant resort to the accompanying plan (next page).

In the first decade of the last century, the Ottoman Turkish forces dismantled entirely the tomb of Hamrath at *Suweida to provide stone for their new barracks. Thus was lost an important (and, until then, largely intact) example of the pre-Roman

and Nabataean architectural tradition. The same barracks project also inspired the mining of a considerable part of the temple complex at Sia, though enough remains of its lower courses to give some idea of this second major example of Nabataean temple architecture and its adaptation under later Roman influence. Fortunately both the Suweida and Sia monuments had been recorded in some detail by the French marquis, Melchior de Vogüé, who visited the site in the mid 19th century. The remains he described were considerably more substantial than those seen today, though he had to employ the villagers to dig out much of the temple façade.

History

The temple complex had its axis along the crest of the east-west ridge, the earliest phase the Baal-Shamin complex at the western end. The increasing popularity of the cult, accessible to followers from the Hauran and from the desert to the east, determined the later phases of expansion with vast new courtyards and additional temples to the east. The layout eventually comprised an outer gateway, two inner courts divided by secondary gates, culminating in the original *cella* preceded by a peristyle court.

Sia began as a Semitic 'high place' attracting worshippers from the surrounding agricultural region. The area came under the influence of the Nabataean Arabs (from present-day Jordan and Saudi Arabia) who promoted the local cult in the form of a temple to Baal-Shamin (for Bel/Baal-Shamin, see box on page 210). There is evidence of three construction periods:

- 50 BC to AD 50 – At this time, Sia marked the northern limit of Nabataean rule as Roman control of Damascus after 64 BC had pushed the Nabataean zone back to the Hauran. The Nabataeans came under constant pressure from the Romans to hand the area over to Herod the Great's kingdom. The original Baal-Shaamin Temple is from the end of first century

BC (in a hybrid Persian-Greek style).

• AD 50 to 106 – Additions were made to the Nabataean cult centre (second courtyard, temple of third courtyard), perhaps reflecting a tussle between Nabataean influence and Herodian control in the area.

• AD 106 to 200 – The creation of the Roman province of Arabia brought more direct Roman influence.

Sia did not become a site for settlement until a village sprang up to service the burgeoning pilgrim traffic encouraged by peaceful conditions in Roman times.

Visit

You enter the complex through remains of the eastern gate (probably Severan). On the left are ruins of a Roman *nymphaeum* which faced the first court (50 m by 19 m) on the south. On the elevated south terrace (left) stood a small temple,

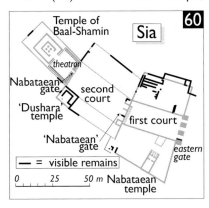

classical in design but with Nabataean ornamentation, probably dated to the period of the last Nabataean king, Rabbel II (AD 71–106). To the west of the first courtyard once stood a monumental triple-arched gateway dubbed by Butler as 'Nabataean' but actually carrying an inscription naming Agrippa II (AD 50–93). The gateway leads into a second courtyard flanked by terraces, the upper a metre above the level of the avenue, the lower

6 m below. On the far end of the upper terrace (left) stood another small temple, ascribed by Butler to the Semitic god, Dushara. This too was constructed in the period of Agrippa II. At the end of the second court was another gateway, also fragmentary. This Nabataean construction dated probably from the first century AD. (Butler found considerably more evidence of the structure than exists today and a reconstruction of the gateway is found in both Berlin and Princeton.)

The processional way entered the forecourt of the **Temple of Baal-Shamin** which took the form of a colonnaded *theatron*, almost square in plan (21 m by 25 m) with raised seating on three sides. Butler found in 1909 that much of the temple itself had been carried away in the ten years before his arrival and nothing remained of its splendid decorations in a florid Nabataean style not found on any other remains of this period. His reconstructions, however, based on earlier findings of de Vogüé and on fragments found at the site indicate a *cella* (built between 32 and 1 BC) preceded by a shallow portico with two columns, flanked on each side by pilastered towers of two storeys. The columns supported a triangular pediment with a sculptured tympanum. A statue of Herod, according to Butler, stood in front of the *cella*. The main door was decorated with vines and the lintel carried a bust of Baal-Shamin (now in the Louvre). Within was an inner chamber, square in plan enclosing a group of four pillars set in another square (perhaps supporting an open space in the roof). This central space enclosed an outcrop of rock rising 1.5 m above the floor, the focal point of the cult centre.

REFS: Abu Assaf 1998: 64–6; Butler *AE* II 1903: 334–40, 421; Butler *PE* II A 6 1916: 366–402; Dentzer 1985: 65–83; Dentzer-Feydy 'Le site et le sanctuaire de 'Si' in Dentzer (ed.) *Le djebel el-'Arab* 1991: 45–7; de Vogüé 1865–77: 30–8, pl 2–4.

Sinhar

See **Batuta and Sinhar**

Sitt al-Rum

ست الروم

VARIANTS: PERIOD: Rom/Byz   ALT: 482
RATING: – MAP: R3, R3a

LOCATION: From the road 1 km south of
*Saint Simeon (2 km north of Dar Tazeh),
walk hard left towards the lower group
of ruins in the distance, c 600 m. The site
can also be approached via the road to
*Qatura.

The ruins of Sitt al-Rum ('Our Lady of
the Greeks') consist of an isolated church
and a Roman tomb. The **tomb** is c200 m
southeast of the church, left of the road as
it crosses a small valley before ascending
to the northern side. It is marked by two
monolith pillars, square in shape, which
once carried a classical entablature.
Near the top of each column is a framed
sunken panel which originally bore bronze
plaques or low-reliefs. Butler notes that
'it is interesting to find so chaste and
well-studied a design in Classic style at so
early a period and at such a distance from
the great artistic centres' and assumes
it is an example of contemporary work
in Antioch. The tomb (entrance 6 m to
the north) is rock-cut and dates from
AD 152. It was a family burial place as 15
sarcophagi were found in the chamber but
the inscription gives a particular dedication
to one Isidotos with explicit directions as
to where his body was to be found ('the
third in the first *arcosolium* on the right as
you enter').

Continue on to the **church** or monastery
chapel, dated to the fourth century and
virtually devoid of decoration. In plan it
is a simple rectangle with one nave but
the walls are tall in proportion to the
width and the windows are placed high.
The sanctuary is set in a rectangle which
protrudes beyond the east wall. The
chancel arch is low and stolid with three
windows above to augment light. The
chapel was surrounded by a monastery
complex of which the double arcading of
one building survives precariously but the
rest is barely recognisable.

It is hard to see the common thread in
these remains. Possibly this is the site of
an early (first century) estate of a Roman
landholder, later overtaken by the nearby
developments at Qatura and *Refade and
used to house a monastic community.

REFS: Butler EC 1929: 149; Butler PE II B 5 1912:
258–61; Tchalenko Villages II 1953: 198–200.

Slim

سليم

VARIANTS: Selaema (Lat); Selim (Arb)
PERIOD: Rom RATING: – MAP: R1

LOCATION: 6 kms north of *Suweida on
the Damascus road. The ruins lie on the
northwest side of the village in the form
of the corner pilaster of a temple façade,
visible above the houses.

Selaema was originally a Nabataean
settlement later incorporated into
Provincia Syria but transferred to
Provincia Arabia in the late second
century. The rather scanty remains of a
small Roman temple consist of the corner
of the badly decomposed façade poking
up incongruously. It is hard to reconstruct
in the imagination the few stones left on
the site but illustrated reconstructions
of the temple reveal a building of some
considerable size and interest with a
number of features in common with the
Syro-Phoenician tradition. Amy's study of
step temples indicates that the building
originally included towers on either side
of an entrance portico comprising two
pairs of pillars set in a 5 m wide staircase.
The small *cella* behind included a semi-
circular chamber set between two flanking
rooms, a plan later employed in the Baal-
Shamin temple in Palmyra and in many
church buildings, particularly in northern
Syria. Above the corners of the façade
the stonework continued upwards, rising
above the level of the entablature (richly
decorated with almost every device in
the pattern books) to support a giant
Corinthian capital. This supported in turn
a further entablature enclosing a flat open
platform-roof, an effect described by a
recent researcher as a 'totally unorthodox

way to achieve an eclectic effect'. Much of the carved decoration is of a high standard. According to Freyberger, the temple dates from the reign of the Roman emperor Augustus (d AD 14) and may have been dedicated to Baal-Shamin.

REFS: Amy 1950; Butler *PE* II A 5 1912: 356–9; Freyburger 'Der Tempel in Slim: Ein Bericht' DaM 1991: 9–38.

Surkunya

See **Burjke, Fafertin, Surkunya and Banastur**

Suweida

السويدا

VARIANTS: Dionysias (Grk); Soada (Lat)
PERIOD: Rom RATING: * MAP: R1

LOCATION: 128 km southeast of Damascus. For exit, see directions for *Bosra or *Shahba.

A Nabataean town dating back probably to the fourth century BC, Suweida would have been ruled by an independent prince until the area was handed by the Romans to Herod the Great in 23 BC. In AD 92, it was annexed to the Roman province of Syria and in 106 incorporated in the new province of Arabia. Under the Romans it was an important market town. It was given the name Dionysias (Dionysus or Bacchus) under Commodus (r 180–5) in honour of the Greco-Roman god of the grape, one of the main products of the region.

Nowadays, Suweida is again a major centre which serves as the capital of the increasingly prosperous province of the Hauran. Unfortunately, most of its ancient remains were mined by Turkish troops for building material for their new barracks in the first decade of the last century (*Sia page 285). A new Museum (1 km on right on road to Qanawat) includes an exceptional collection of sculptures and Roman mosaics of the region, notably from *Shahba (Philippopolis). The rich collection of sculpture dates from the Nabataean to

Islamic periods, demonstrating that even the heavy basalt of the Hauran could not defeat the creative capacities of the sculptors of Roman-Nabataean Syria. The range of themes is wide with a great variety of reliefs decorating architectural details such as lintels and niches.

The mosaics (central hall of the Museum) reveal an extraordinary degree of expressiveness. Those worthy of particular note are:

• **Artemis Taking Her Bath** – first on right from door – mid third century – 4.3 m by 4.3 m – Artemis crouches near a spring, leaning on her left leg. The naked goddess is bejewelled and crowned with a diadem of pearls. She is surrounded by four nymphs. The head of Acteon emerges from the shrubbery. The scene is bordered by a superb frieze of garlands of fruit and foliage.

• **Venus at her Toilet** – second on right of door of central hall – mid third century – 3.24 m by 3.23 m – Venus, framed within a shell, holds in her right hand a tress of her hair and in her left a mirror to adjust her coiffure. Two cupids attend her and she is flanked by two marine divinities. The figure is naked but richly adorned with jewels.

• **Banquet Scene** – right on opposing wall, first quarter of fourth century, 6.5 m by 6.62 m – circular banquet scene enclosed within a square frame.

In the same room, particularly striking are the victory (*nike*) figures aligned with the eastern pillars and a giant female head in Nabataean style (hard left on entry)

There are few remains in the older part of town of the Roman or later periods. Near the central square south of the Governor's office are seven columns (only three visible), all that has survived of a peripteral temple dedicated to Dushara (Dionysus), probably end of first century BC. One kilometre south of the town, remains of a five-aisled basilica (fifth century), a pilgrimage complex constructed on an enormous scale, were partly exposed by the widening of the Bosra road in the 1980s. The only part of the complex visible (now the centrepiece of a traffic circle) is the 'triumphal' arch, restored with the assistance of the German Archaeological Institute. This arch once framed the choir of a second basilica lying to the north. Remains of the Roman odeon have been exposed south of the basilica complex but most of the nearby theatre still lies under the road and the neighbouring houses.

REFS: Abu Assaf 1998: 66–8; Balty, Janine 1977; Brünnow & Domaszewski 1905: 88–102; Dentzer *Le djebel al-'Arab* 1991; Donceel-Voûte 1987; Dunand *Le musée de Soueïda* Paris 1934.

Hauran

This basalt plain, the result of relatively recent volcanic activity, forms an area (100 km north-south, 75 km east-west) of fertile land south of Damascus between Mount Hermon and the desert with the Jordanian border as its southern limit. The plain is protected from the encroaching desert to the east by Jebel al-Arab (alt c1500 m), the Mount Bashan of the Psalms (Asalmanos in Greek-Roman times) noted for its oak.

The Hauran was colonised by the Greeks but with the collapse of Seleucid rule by the first century BC, was raided by rival Jewish and Nabataean groups. The semi-hellenized local kings were overthrown and in the confusion the area largely fell under the control of Arab shepherds and bandits. Herod the Great, as ruler of Judaea (r 37–4 BC), was given most of the area in 23–20 BC as a reward for his last-minute switch to Augustus' cause after Actium (31 BC). It remained in the hands of Herod's son, Philip, until his death in AD 34. Still subject to Nabataean and Bedouin designs, it was annexed to Provincia Syria in 34 but handed by Caligula to Herod Agrippa II. By AD 70 Bosra had become the capital of the Nabataean Kingdom but controlled only the southern part of the Hauran, the rest (including Suweida and Canatha) being included in Syria. The whole area, however, was transferred to Arabia in the late second century. Stable Roman control brought new life to the economy of the Hauran and cultivation of corn was pursued by pushing back the desert limits (*Bosra).

The ancient Hauran in its wider sense was divided into several sub-regions (modern names in brackets):

- Gaulanitis (Jaulan) – the area between the Damascus-Deraa road and Syrian Golan
- Batanaea (Nuqra) – capital Deraa (ancient Adraa)
- Trachonitis (Ledja or Leja – the refuge) – the lava-strewn semi-wilderness area northwest of Jebel al-Arab
- Auranitis (Hauran proper, mainly Jebel al-Arab plus the plain as far as Bosra) – capital *Bosra

To these is sometimes added the area north of Gaulanitis, namely:
- Ituraea west and south of Damascus which was for a time associated with Chalcis (modern Anjar, central Beqaa Valley in Lebanon).

T

Takleh

تِكلة

VARIANTS: Taqle PERIOD: Byz ALT: 520 m
RATING:* MAP:R3a

LOCATION: 300 m before the road diverges to ascend the slope of Saint Simeon
(coming from Dar Tazeh), a sealed road
leads 1.2 kms up the slope in a southeast
direction to the ruins.

This village seems to have comprised a
group of reasonably prosperous farmers
who exploited the fertile Plain of Qatura
below to the west. Tchalenko notes that
the houses all belong to the same period
(mid fifth century) – modest in scale and
of middling execution.

The settlement was grouped around the
church of the same date. The plan of the
church is typical of the columned basilicas
of the mid fifth century with the apse
flanked by two side rooms – a *diaconicon*
or sacristy (north) and martyrium or burial
chamber for a saint (south). Most striking is
the west façade which preserves its three
tiers of windows. On the south side of
the church an arcade leads to a baptistery
in the annexe. Note also the two olive
presses, one attached to the church, the
other accessible to all inhabitants.

REFS: Butler *PE* II B 6 1920: 284; Tchalenko
Villages I 1953: 200–4; II 1953: pl IX, LVII, LXIV–VI,
CXXVII.

Tartus (Plate 24b)

طرطوس

VARIANTS: Antaradus, Constantia (Lat);
Antartus,Tortosa (Cru) PERIOD:Cru RATING:
** MAPS:61,R2

LOCATION: On the coast 220 km northwest of Damascus.

Tartus has been rapidly developed in recent
decades as Syria's second port and more
recently by a range of new leisure facilities.

It has been connected to the national rail
and road grid and the expansion of the
city has robbed it of much of its sleepy
charm as a small Mediterranean fishing
port with its roots firmly planted in the
past. Nevertheless, the old city retains
some of its character and the former
Cathedral of Our Lady of Tortosa is one of
the most remarkable surviving remains of
the religious architecture of the Crusades
outside Jerusalem.

History

Tartus was originally founded by the
Phoenicians to complement the more
secure but less accessible settlement
on the island of *Arwad. Tartus for a
long time thus played a secondary role
to Arwad, a major centre in Seleucid
and Roman times. The classical name,
Antaradus (*anti-Aradus* – 'the town
facing Aradus' or Arwad) reflected this
secondary role. Constantine (r 306–37)
made it a separate city and his successor,
Constantius, renamed it Constantia in 346
as he favoured its Christian inhabitants
over the pagans of Arwad. The town was
already famed for its devotion to the cult
of the Virgin, one of the earliest chapels
in her honour having been built there
before the fourth century. (Legend had
it that St Peter himself had consecrated
the first church in honour of the Virgin.)
The altar of the chapel is believed to have
miraculously escaped destruction by an
earthquake in 487. An icon, said to have
been painted by the evangelist St Luke,
was also venerated there (cf *Seidnaya).

After passing into Muslim hands with the
Arab conquest in the 630s, Tartus was
one of the towns the Byzantine Emperor
Nicephorus II Phocas retook in his effort
to reassert Byzantine sovereignty in Syria
in 968. The Cairo-based Fatimids sought
to take it in 997 during Caliph Aziz's push
into Syria. By the time the Crusaders
arrived in 1099, it was subject to the amir
of Tripoli. The governor was tricked into
surrender by the Crusaders for whom
the acquisition of the port and its easy
communications to Cyprus and Antioch
greatly helped them establish their
foothold in the area.

Tartus quickly reverted to Muslim hands but in 1101, Raymond de Saint Gilles, Count of Toulouse, began his concerted campaign to take Tripoli and the areas connecting the coast and the Orontes near *Homs. He turned Tartus into a fortress city owing allegiance to Tripoli. The Franks strongly promoted the Marian pilgrimage and after 1123 began construction of the Cathedral of Our Lady of Tortosa, presumably in order to house the venerated altar.

Taking note of the lesson, the Templars thereafter took the defence of the region more seriously. By consolidating a chain of outer defences – *Safita, Chastel Rouge (*Qalaat Yahmur), Arima (*Qalaat Areimeh), Akkar (in northern Lebanon) not to mention the other substantial fortresses at Tripoli, Marqab and the Krak – Tartus was no longer a soft target.[1]

The decision of Baldwin IV, King of Jerusalem, to hand Tortosa over to the Templars followed the temporary occupation of the city by Nur al-Din (1152). The Templars undertook what was to become the order's principal fortress after the headquarters at Acre in Palestine. Nur al-Din's incursion profited from the confusion sown by the murder at the hands of the Assassins of Raymond II of Tripoli at the gates of

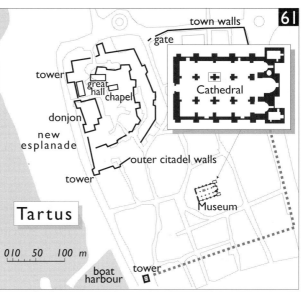

that city. In 1188, Nur al-Din's successor, Saladin, followed up his major victory over the Crusaders at Hattin in Palestine by raiding much of the countryside north of Tripoli. In most cases, he did not press engagements if serious resistance were offered but at Tartus in 1188, he occupied most of the city from 3 to 8 July. He failed, however, to take the donjon in which the Templar garrison had taken refuge (an episode which did little credit to the Templars' reputation as fearless defenders of the Christian realm). Saladin, before departing northwards, took the opportunity to destroy a good deal of the occupied town, for the first time offering a serious challenge to the Crusader presence in the area.

Despite attacks by the Mamluk Sultan Baybars in 1267 and 1270, Tartus remained in Templar hands until the last days of the Crusader presence on the mainland. A 1282 truce between Sultan Qalawun and the Knights Templar prolonged the fortress' survival until after the fall of the great fortress of Acre in May 1291. It finally succumbed on 3 August 1291, by which stage its forward defence posts in the area had all fallen and even the great castles of the Krak and Marqab were in Mamluk

1 Another factor assisting its defence in depth may have been the presence of a considerable number of Christian villages in the mountains behind Tartus. This presence has survived to this day, especially in the so-called 'Valley of the Christians' around the Krak. The town of Tartus, however, has for long been substantially Muslim.

hands. Except for Athlit (the last remnant of the Jerusalem Kingdom evacuated 14 August), Tortosa was the last point on the mainland held by the Crusaders.

The knights slipped away to the nearby island of Arwad without resistance, taking with them the revered icon of the Virgin. From Arwad, they conducted a last-ditch harassment campaign for another decade but by 1303, the last Crusaders had withdrawn to Cyprus from where their descendants carried on the cause through the Lusignan dynasty. For centuries, the cathedral fell into neglect. In 1851 it was use as a mosque and, after 1914, as a Turkish barracks but was restored under the French and used as a museum in the independence period.

Visit

It may be simplest to begin your visit with the **Cathedral of Our Lady of Tortosa** (plate 24b), currently the city's Museum. You enter it from the west, the exterior wall providing a blank but powerful expression of simple Crusader-period style. This dates entirely from the 13th century improvements to the original Crusader redevelopment. It has lost most of its two corner towers which gave the building more the character of a fortress than a church. The eye is now drawn in to the entrance doorway surmounted by twin windows framed with elegant colonnettes and topped by a third matching window. Two small windows to the side mark the axes of the side naves.

Inside, the effect of the simple Crusader style is most impressive – 'the most beautiful interior from the Crusader period in Syria' (Odenthal). The plan is a straightforward three-aisled basilica. Each aisle has four bays and ends in an apse, the central one preceded by a short choir. In the eastern corners, two more towers are located, reached through passageways off the apses.

It is worth paying particular attention to the north aisle. Note the pillar between the central and north aisles which rests on a cube of masonry, pierced by a transverse passageway. This is assumed to represent an attempt during the first Crusader (12th century) rebuilding to preserve some elements of the earlier Byzantine chapel. (The passageway would originally have given entry to the chapel below.) Note also the carved figure of a bird (head missing) at the top of the north apse – presumed to represent the Third Person of the Trinity, the Holy Ghost.

Though the work on the cathedral church was begun in the 12th century (1123 on), it was interrupted in the middle of the century. After Saladin's attack (1188), much damage had to be reconstructed. When major work resumed in the 13th century, under the Templars' guidance, the church took on a more defensive character lying, as it does, outside the main walls of the fortress. The exterior was reinforced, the nearly blank western wall was built and the towers were probably added. (You can still see in the eastern towers the reinforced firing positions.) It was probably at this time that the traces of the Byzantine chapel were built over, bringing the level of the north aisle up to that of the rest of the church. The transition from Romanesque to Gothic in contemporary Europe is also reflected in the new style, particularly in the mix of treatment of the capitals.

The **Museum** has been greatly improved in recent years with many new displays and enhanced presentation. It now provides an important survey of the Tartus region including particularly classical material from Tartus, Amrit and *Qalaat Yahmur. Along the left aisle, Phoenician-style sarcophagi; votive statues and figurines found in the excavations of the Amrit temple; some *kouroi* figures from fifth century Greek colonisation; in the apse, a purely classical sarcophagus (second-third century from Latakia) showing Dionysius, Eros and Medusa; other classical statuary including two striking marble portrait heads of local notables found in a cave near Amrit (case on right of central aisle between first and second pillars); three mosaics on classical themes (apse of right aisle).

Taking your bearing from the church, you

should now head for the remains of the **fortress** itself. Tracing the inner walls of the Crusader city amid the tangle of later buildings can be a challenge. The first defence wall of the castle lay c100 m northwest of the church. Behind it, traces of the Crusader inner walls survive between the houses.

At this point, some appreciation of the layout of Tortosa's defences is needed. The fortress city formed a large, irregular rectangle, its length (350 m) parallel to the sea. The outer (town) wall can be seen along the street which leads from the northwestern tower inland towards the modern main street. Three hundred metres inland it ran south c300 m before taking in the land east of the cathedral. The point where it reached the sea and turned back northwards along the coast is marked by the remains of a tower seen along the seafront about 300 m south of the citadel. The walls were 2.5 m thick in parts and were surrounded by a rock-cut ditch filled with sea water.

In the northwestern segment of this outer compound were two inner defence walls roughly semi-circular in shape and behind them the inner citadel. At the heart lay the donjon where the Templars held out against Saladin. The concentric defences thus consisted of:

- outer ditch and town wall
- inner ditch and concentric defence walls around citadel
- main citadel wall (almost half-circular in plan) with square bastions
- central donjon.

The point you have now reached is between the second and third of these.

If you keep heading in the same direction inside the walled area, you will come to a relatively open space, the modern town square. This is more or less in the centre of the fortress area and from here you could explore what traces remain of the original fortress. On the north side of the square lies the 13th century **great hall**, 44 m long. The south wall is incorporated into later housing; the north wall forms

part of the fortification walls. The hall was on the upper floor; the ground floor being divided by a central row of five pillars into two naves vaulted in six sections. The **chapel** is a little more easily identified to the northeast, behind a reconstructed doorway up a short flight of stairs. The single-naved structure is windowless on the east side which is up against the inner fortified wall. The remains of the original **donjon** (only the ground floor survives) adjoin the square on the west side. This great bastion in fact comprised two thicknesses of concentric square fortifications. The original kernel (pre-Templar) was later duplicated by a second equally stout-walled outer layer with a greater number of firing points except on the western side where it faced the sea. (The structure is at present being cleared and researched for later presentation.)

From this point, if you head a little north you will come to a recognisable gateway on the northern edge of the semi-circular walls. (You may also want to look out for a mosque, a little to the east, which is installed in a former tower of the Crusader castle.) From here, it is a few metres west to the new esplanade fronting the sea. The fortified half-circle is closed by the line of **walls** along the drive that marks the landward side of the esplanade. The esplanade has recently been massively extended to provide new fishing and tourist facilities, extending the shoreline well away from the Crusader walls, once lapped by the sea. If you now head south, the mixture of old stonework, later patching and modern dwellings along the line of wall is impressive. The western face of the donjon survives, indented between two stout bastions. The three doors on the lower face of the donjon allowed direct access to ships. This is where the last Crusaders in 1291 escaped the Muslim besiegers, quietly abandoning one of the last vestiges of their 200 year adventure on the Levant coast.

After continuing south to the other end of this stretch of wall (passing the southern-most tower of the citadel), head eastwards again into the town and you will reach the small square in front of the

Museum from where you started out. (A diversion 200 m to the south will take you to the southwest tower of the outer walls mentioned earlier.)

REFS: Boase 1967: 93–6; Braune 1985: 45–54; Deschamps *Châteaux* III 1973: 287–92; Enlart II 1927–8: 395–429; Odenthal 1998: 221–4.

Tell Brak

تل براك

VARIANTS: ?Nagar PERIOD: EBA/MBA
RATING:T MAP: R5

LOCATION: 40 km northeast of Haseke (Northeast Province). Take the <u>old</u> Qamishli road (fork right c5 km north of Haseke). After c 27 kms, right (southeast) towards the village of Tell Brak, on the banks of the Jaghjagh River (the ancient Mygdonios – a tributary of the Khabur). The ancient mound lies on the right +2 km after the turn-off.

Tell Brak is the site of Mallowan's excavations (1937–9) which were an important landmark in reconstructing the history of this area in the Early Bronze Age.[2] The Khabur region was at the time (as it is becoming again) an important centre for dry-land farming, especially the production of grain given the reliability of the annual rainfall and the benefits of the run-off from the Taurus Mountains in Turkey to the north. Tell Brak sits at the point on the Khabur basin system where the natural communication route from the Jebel Sinjar region of Mesopotamia to the east joins the river before continuing south to the Euphrates.

The tell is one of the largest (43 ha, 40 m high) in northeast Syria. Excavations began again in 1976 by a British team led by David and Joan Oates, concentrating on remains of the **Akkadian fortress** (24th or 23rd century BC) in the southeastern corner of the site. The fortress of the Akkadian ruler Naram-Sin (24th century

BC) which assumed the role of the northern Mesopotamian centres such as Mari, was rebuilt in the third Ur dynasty (22nd century BC) but abandoned at the end of the third millennium. The ruins included those of a substantial palace (façade 90 m long, four internal courts), probably the seat of a regional governor of the Akkadian Empire.

The most celebrated discovery of Mallowan's dig was the 3100–2900 BC Eye Temple found under part of the Akkadian palace complex ('Palace of Naram-Sin') 200 m to the east. The temple was named on account of the hundreds of flat idols discovered there, all bearing an outsized representation of an eye. (They were presumably ex voto offerings for the temple which follows a plan typical of Sumerian religious buildings of the period – long central nave, deliberate use of proportion (18 m by 6 m), double entrance, podium at the far end, service rooms to the left, subsidiary sanctuary to the right.)

The British excavations have also uncovered remains of a third period, a 16th–15th century BC **Mitannian palace** 250 m north of the Eye Temple (50 m northeast of the trig point) on the northern edge of the tell. The palace was destroyed by the Middle Assyrian kings and totally abandoned by 1200 BC.

A Roman legionary camp (5 km to the east, now covered by the modern village of Saibakh just across the Jaghjagh River) was part of a cluster of fortifications defending this access route from the Tigris. Though it is not possible to pick it up from an earthbound perspective, French aerial surveying in the 1920s also revealed a Byzantine fort 91 m[2] with external pentagonal towers 1 km to the northeast. The exact dating of the fort is uncertain (fourth–sixth century). After the loss of Nisibis to the Persians (AD 363), the late Roman-Byzantine line of defence in this area largely receded west of the Jaghjagh. The new line running from Thannouris (10 km southeast of Haseke) was eventually buttressed by the great fortress at Dara (507–8, in modern

2 Mallowan married Agathie Christie who wrote an amusing account of several seasons spent together in the northeast of Syria, including at Tell Brak – *Tell Me How You Live*, London, 1946.

Turkey, 25 km northwest of Qamishli).

REFS: Kennedy & Riley 1990: 187–9, 215; Mallowan 1936; Oates 1990a; Oates 1990b; Oates & McDonald 2001; Poidebard *Trace* I 1934: 143–6; Weiss 'Tell Brak' in Weiss (ed) 1985.

Tell Halaf (Ras al-Ain)

تل حلف

VARIANTS: Guzana (anc), Gozan (bib), Resaina, Fons Chaborae (Lat), Theodosiopolis (Byz); Ras al-'Ain (Arb). PERIOD: IrA/Rom RATING: –
MAP: R5

LOCATION: Tell Halaf (Ras al-Ain) lies on the Turkish frontier at the source of the Khabur River (classical Chaboras). It can be reached from the capital of the Northeast Province, Haseke, on a good sealed road (74 km northwest). The tell itself is 4 km southwest of Ras al-Ain town almost on the Turkish border. The Roman military camp is on a flat tell (Tell Fakhariye) on the southern outskirts of the town.

Tell Halaf has been an important site in the development of Middle Eastern archaeology. The story of the excavation and its aftermath is in itself a remarkable saga. In 1899, the tell attracted the attention of Baron Max von Oppenheim, a Prussian engineer involved in surveying the route of the Berlin/Baghdad railway.[3] Von Oppenheim resigned from his appointment and returned to the area to take on the excavation of the site from 1911. Work was interrupted by the First World War but resumed from 1927 to 1929. Since 2006, the site is again being researched by a coalition of German and Syrian teams.

The site goes back to neolithic times and has given its name to a type of fourth millennium BC pottery found on the tell. The site was then abandoned until the first millennium BC when the revived centre was identified with Guzana mentioned in the Assyrian archives. It was the capital of Bit Bahiani, the eastern-most of the Aramaean states that had spread over

Syria at the beginning of the millennium but its independence was curtailed and an Assyrian governor was installed from 808.

The ninth or eighth century palace of the Kapara dynasty was unearthed with many huge sculptured figures in a somewhat grotesque style found in a less fantastic and prolific form in other sites of the period including Carcemish and *Ain Dara. The greater part of the finds were divided between Syria (now in the *Aleppo Museum) and Berlin where some were set up in a special Tell Halaf Museum. During the Second World War, the building received a direct hit from an Allied bomb and much of the Berlin collection was lost or seriously damaged. The remains were sent to the Pergamon Museum in Berlin and there are plans to rehouse the surviving and restored pieces in a new pavilion to be built within the courtyard.[4]

The palace covered an area 52 m by 30 m on a spur of the citadel mound near the river bank, surrounded by a three-sided fortification with the river forming the fourth (north) side. On the west side of the citadel mound the temple complex included receptions halls for ceremonial purposes. The façade was lined along the lower course of the 61 m wall with sculptured orthostats, black and red in colour. Other monstrous sculptures stood along the ceremonial entrance passage in black volcanic stone – *caryatids*, griffins, lions, a bull and sphinxes. The effect is seen in the replicas at the entrance to the Aleppo Museum which recreates the Tell Halaf temple façade.

The **sulphur springs** to the south (Hammam al-Sheikh Bashir) probably account for the intensity of settlement in this area which in ancient times supported a considerably more active agriculture than today. (The cutting of the forests in the Turkish foothills to the north have probably diminished the region's rainfall.) The springs are worth visiting for the sight of the huge volume of foul-smelling hot water bursting out of the flat ground.

---

3 The railway survives in the Aleppo-Mosul link but is now disused. The line forms the Turkish-Syrian border at this point.

4 Four orthostats are also on display in the Metropolitan Museum in New York.

The site of the Roman military post at **Resaina** (the modern Tell Fakhariye) contains little of obvious visual interest. It is hard to think of this remote spot playing any role in Rome's outer defences but the fortress may date as early as the second century AD. By the late third century, the Roman-Byzantine *limes* were maintained on a line well to the east of here (from Nisibis on the Turkish border to Thannouris, southeast of Haseke). Resaina was for a time an important garrison town (there is evidence that it was the base for the III Parthica Legion under the Severan Emperors) and part of the rear line of defence along the Khabur River that provided defence in depth to the *limes*, controlling a reasonably prosperous district which bore the classical name, Gauzanitis. Resaina was renamed Theodosiopolis when city rights were conferred under Theodosius I (r 379–95) by which stage the frontier had moved west to this line. The city walls probably dated from this period but were rebuilt in the mid sixth century under Justinian.

REFS: **Tell Halaf:** Canby 1985: 332–8; Cholidis & Martin 2002; Honigmann 'Ras al-`Ain' *EI*1; Dussaud 1927: 490–5; Poidebard *Mission* 1930; http://www.tell-halaf-projekt.de/. **Tell Fakhariye:** McEwan (*et al*) 1958.

Ugarit (Ras Shamra)

راس شمرة

VARIANTS: Ras Shamra (Arb)
PERIOD: LBA RATING: ** MAP: 62, R2

LOCATION: Leave *Latakia by the high-way heading north to the resort hotels. At c10 km, at the roundabout in front of the Cote d'Azur Hotel, turn right c+4 km. The site (known as Ras Shamra, 'Headland of Fennel' in Arabic) is clearly marked.

Ugarit is one of the few Bronze Age sites in the Middle East which offers identifiable remains to the casual visitor and not simply to the specialist scholar or those who have the time to familiarise themselves with the wealth of published information. Unlike other centres of the period, the palace and religious buildings were constructed in stone. Whereas the mud brick of cities such as *Mari or *Ebla can quickly erode with rain and wind on exposure to the archaeologist's spade, Ugarit survives with at least its foundation courses and a good deal of its walls clearly delineated in stone.

Ugarit has been described as 'probably the first great international port in history'.[1] Through its ancillary harbour at Minet al-Beida, in ancient times, Ugarit actively engaged in trade around the eastern Mediterranean. From here much of the later Phoenician commercial and cultural expansion took its inspiration, not least through the development of the alphabet. Admittedly the riches of the palaces are now elsewhere (*Damascus – National Museum; the Louvre in Paris) but it is still possible to get an appreciation of the period by wandering between the walls and passageways or scrambling up to the acropolis. Choose a cool day, though, or start early in the morning. If you visit in spring when the wildflowers give the scene a patina of colour, watch out for the vipers that take on the hues of the mottled stone.

Excavated almost continuously over the course of 50 years, Ugarit has served as one of the anchor-points of modern archaeological research and biblical studies illustrating in particular the Canaanite milieu in which the Biblical world later emerged. The chance discovery of the site in 1928 quickly confirmed the identity of the remains with Ugarit, mentioned in the archives of *Mari and of Tell al-Amarna in Egypt. Exploration began in 1929 under French auspices and (apart from a break between 1939 to 1948) continued until 1970 under Claude Schaeffer. They have continued since 1974 under a series of French directors (currently Marguerite Yon), thus continuing the virtual sub-industry of scholarship generated by this extraordinarily rich site.

History

Though it rose to prominence towards the end of the Bronze Age (late second millennium BC), the earliest settlements at Ras Shamra go back much earlier. Neolithic remains were found at the base of the tell, dating from the eighth millennium. The earliest links were probably with the Upper Euphrates area. By the fourth and early third millennium, contacts extended as far as the lower Euphrates or Mesopotamia. The city, lying close to Cyprus, a rich source of copper, shared in the general rise in sophistication of technology and political organisation in the Early Bronze Age (third millennium BC) and through trade was drawn into the orbit of the Mesopotamian world. For the Mesopotamians, it offered access for their goods, a source of permanent building materials (wood and stone) and a point of contact with the wider Mediterranean world.

A dark age descended around 2200 BC. The city at this time seems to have been burnt and its population probably diminished. A new wave of migrations in the region, however, brought fresh infusions of population with the coming of the Amorites around 2000 BC. The

1 Culican in Piggott (et al) The Dawn of Civilization London 1961: 153.

Canaanites (called sometimes proto-Phoenicians), a Semitic-language group from the south, formed the predominant population during the new millennium.

Ugarit's commercial potential as the key point on the Mediterranean-Mesopotamian route was fully exploited during the second millennium. Moreover, a new economic role was added when the Egyptians, in a period of increasing prosperity and stability, turned to Ugarit (along with Byblos in northern Lebanon) as a source of timber and other imports. This golden age saw the establishment of a local Ugaritic dynasty whose authority was underpinned by the balance struck between Egyptian power under the XI and XII Dynasties (c2000–1800 BC) and Hammurabi's dominance in Mesopotamia.

The diverse influences on this city-state are clear from the remains seen today. The walled palaces, almost totally blank viewed from the outside, show Mesopotamian inspiration but the sheer luxury of their appointments (prolific use of courtyards, pools, internal gardens and light-wells) demonstrates a way of life which has its echoes only in Minoan civilisation on Crete.[2] It was at this time that the working of bronze became a specialty of the city and such value-added exports supplemented its role as an entrepôt for local agricultural output.

Even at its peak, the Kingdom of Ugarit did not control extensive territory. The king's writ probably ran no further than the land between the Mount Casius to the north (see below) and *Jeble, 25 km south of modern Latakia, and inland as far as the coastal mountain range. But the land is exceptionally fertile and the city's prosperity was based on the agricultural riches of its hinterland and its trading role rather than extensive political control.

After a period of renewed uncertainty coinciding with the Hyksos invasion of Egypt (which ushered in the break between the Middle and New Kingdoms),

2 A point made by Caubet in *Beaux Arts* (Hors Serie on Syria), 1993: 15.

Ugarit flourished once again in the Late Bronze Age (after 1600) in collaboration with the XVIII Dynasty in Egypt. The transition locally may have been marked by the arrival of a Hurrian élite linked to the new power in the northern Syrian region, the Kingdom of Mitanni. The population, however, remained basically Canaanite. Not the least of the new dynasty's skills was its ability largely to stay out of the great power games of the period, poised as it was between Mitanni and the Egyptians.

Ugarit's resilience and economic strength were shown in its recovery from a severe earthquake and tidal wave which struck in the middle of the 14th century BC (1365?) as a result of which most of the city had to be rebuilt. The subsequent golden age (late 14th–13th centuries BC) accounts for much of the building achievements now visible when the city benefited most directly from the Egyptian-Mitannian peace. The warehouses were overflowing and one of the earliest alphabets greatly simplified record-taking and accounting; 30 cuneiform symbols based on the principle of 'one sound, one sign' were a much simpler method of recording language than the unwieldy pictogram-based cuneiform. The results of this greater facility can be seen in the range of correspondence and archives from this period: political dealings, tax and commercial accounts and religious texts, the latter throwing much light on the Semitic world in which the Israelite colonisation of Palestine was to unfold three centuries later. As well, there was an extensive archive of diplomatic correspondence in Babylonian syllabic cuneiform (the 'diplomatic language' of the time), some scholarly texts in Hurrian and a few in Cypriot-Minoan script.

Once the more remote power of the Hittites (based in Anatolia, central Turkey) came directly into play in the late 14th century BC, the balance was less easily maintained and the correspondence unearthed at Tell al-Amarna in Egypt (the capital of the heretic pharaoh, Akhenaten) reveals much of the nervous state of mind in Ugarit with the king urging the pharaoh to appease the Hittites with gifts.

Maintaining sound relations with the Hittites (the Ugaritic navy was put at the Hittites' disposal), Ugarit avoided taking the Egyptian side in the century-long struggle which culminated in the great battle at *Qadesh, just south of modern Homs in southern Syria (Tell Nabi Mend).

The 13th century brought other changes, in particular links with the Aegean. But more ominous developments were about to end Ugarit's days of creative prosperity. The secondary effects of the population movements (c1200 BC) touched off by the invasion of the Sea Peoples, probably accounts for the destruction of the city's prosperity though there may also have been internal reasons resulting from the excessive demands of the palace-based economy.

Though there are later traces of casual or light occupation, the local economy probably reverted to a more traditional village-based system. There are some signs of a prosperous class re-emerging during the Persian period, but the tell was never again to accommodate the sizeable and prosperous urban community that had brought it to prominence for much of the second millennium. The beginning of the Iron Age which the Sea Peoples ushered in demanded new skills and technology and these were found elsewhere.

Visit

You enter the site on the western side. The following brief description does not necessarily follow the arrows installed among the ruins as some were apparently missing when last visited and they provide no apparent sequence to guide the visitor.

If you turn hard right from the ticket office, you will see the remains of the **fortress, walls and postern gate** which once protected the palace complex on this side of the city. Descend the stairs on the right for a closer inspection. This defensive work was begun in the 15th century BC,

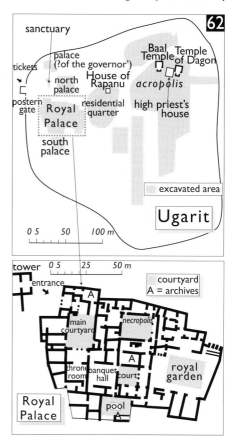

not long after the city's recovery at the beginning of the Late Bronze Age, but was later considerably rebuilt. The city walls were formed by smoothing off at 45° the slope of the mound created by preceding occupation layers and covering this with a stone glacis (a seamless surface intended to give attackers no purchase). At this point (the only surviving section), the glacis was supplemented by a tower protecting the official entry. The walls of the tower are up to 5 m thick. Defenders could, at a later date, exit to harass besieging forces through a postern gate to the right. A passage to the gate was formed by tunnelling down through the mound and covering it with a corbelled vault.

Return to the courtyard before the **Royal Palace**. In front of you (west) is a small open area which dates from the second half of the Late Bronze Age phase of the city's occupation (late 14th–13th century BC). A portico with two pillar bases marks the main entrance to the palace. The central passage between the pillars (originally wood on the present stone bases) leads into a small reception area for guests from which the palace proper opens to the south (right after you cross the entrance threshold). The rooms on the left (A) of this vestibule were used to store one of the important archives unearthed in the French excavations.

Right from the vestibule is the main courtyard of the palace, the paving of which still bears evidence of the channels used to feed water throughout the building. A well in the southwest corner was the main water source for the palace. The throne room lay to the south, preceded by a portico marked by two columns.

Before you get further immersed in the maze of 90 rooms (6500 m^2) comprising the main palace, pause here to note the fine quality of the stonework, showing the increasing sophistication of building methods of the time. What you see is only the first storey layout of a complex of buildings that often rose at least another storey (where the bulk of the living quarters were probably located). This is a royal residence of a dynasty which had established itself comfortably in a society based on commercial acumen and high craftsmanship. The proliferation of rooms during the 200 year life of the building reflected the growing administrative burden of its affairs, the accumulation of extensive archives as well as the need to accommodate an expanding court.

From the first courtyard, take time to wander through the rest of the maze. East (left) of the throne room is a space now considered as a banquet hall. To the east again lay a second courtyard. To its north a complex of rooms included archival spaces and, further north again, a series of five large underground chambers which served as the palace necropolis.

The corbelled vaulting technique seen in the postern gate is again evident in these remarkable spaces.

Return to the banquet hall. To the south lies a space, trapezoidal in shape, which contained a large ornamental pool fed by an elaborate water supply arrangement. Archives of political records were contained in the rooms to the south and west. To the east of the main palace was the 'royal garden' with verandahs and pavilions once equipped with ivory-encrusted furniture.

Immediately to the north and south of the Royal Palace complex, **subsidiary palaces** are found. To the north of the same entrance courtyard that leads to the Royal Palace lies a complex of buildings including a shrine (far left), a so-called 'Queen-Mother's residence' and to the right a 16th–15th century palace, possibly never rebuilt after the mid 14th century earthquake. The palace south of the principal complex covers 1000 m^2 and 33 rooms. East of the Royal Palace was a **residential quarter** for the well-connected.

The main temple area or 'acropolis' is on the hill about 200 m to the northeast, the highest point of the site. In scrambling through the intervening ruins, you may come across the **House of Rapanu** (75m from the northwest corner of the main palace) under which lies a burial vault, a domed rectangular underground chamber approached by a descending corridor (*dromos*).

There are two main temples on the acropolis, to Dagon and to Baal. Baal was the patron deity of the city (as distinct from the supreme deity in the Ugaritic pantheon who was known as El). The worship of Baal (originally a lesser god representing strength, fertility and control of the weather) or various local manifestations under this name, became closely associated with Canaanite religion later recorded in the Bible.[3] Baal

3 The worship of Baal in this area is associated with the classical Mount Casius which rises from the coast to a height of 1728

worship and its attendant fertility rites survived among the Semites of Syria. The cult of the Semitic Baal/Bel ('lord' – see box page 210) in various manifestations continued into Roman times when Baal was syncretised into the local version of the Roman pantheon. Here at Ugarit, the Syro-Phoenician temple tradition (see box on page 20) begins on a modest scale.

The **Baal Temple** lies on the northwestern side of the acropolis. Its plan consists of an open courtyard (south) with a central altar. Beyond this on the north, the sanctuary is preceded by a vestibule. The walls of the latter were extraordinarily thick in order to conceal internal staircases on three sides leading upwards to form a tower rising above the *cella*. From this artificial 'high place' sacrifices could be performed, commanding a superb view of the great natural high place on which Baal was believed to dwell, Mount Casius to the north. Between the Baal and Dagon temples, in the remains of the priests' quarters, an archive of religious texts was discovered including chants.

The **Temple of Dagon** (god of fertility in the Ugaritic pantheon) is 40 m to the southeast. Its outline can only be seen in the foundation remains but it follows much the same basic plan as the Baal Temple though the walls are even thicker (4–5 m).

Excavation trenches have been dug to extend knowledge of Ugaritic life into areas occupied by the classes dependant on the court. An area has been unearthed north of the acropolis and two long extensions of the excavations on the citadel exposed private houses (some with burial vaults). These have provided evidence of the variety of artisanal activity in the city including ceramics, cosmetics, weaving and (in the port area) shipbuilding and the smelting and working of bronze, thus supplementing the wealth generated by the mass exportation of local produce such as wine, grain, dyed fabric (requiring the preparation of dye from the murex shell), wood and salt.

Minet al-Beida

The port (**Minet al-Beida** – 1 km northwest) is currently a military area to which access is restricted. Excavations of the mound (1928–32) unearthed buildings of a more mundane nature. This was the Leucos Limen ('white harbour') of Greek sources, reflecting the fact that this port regained a degree of importance up to Seleucid times (330 BC on).

REFS: Sa'adé *Ougarit* 1979; Yon *La cité d'Ougarit* 1997.

---

m to the north of *Ras al-Basit.

Y

Yabrud

يبرود

VARIANTS: labruda (Lat)
PERIOD: Rom RATING:– MAP: R1

LOCATION: Left turn off Damascus-Homs highway 81 km north of Damascus (9 km before Nabk). 5.5 km west to the centre of town. Turn left at major T-intersection. At 330 m, turn right. Cathedral is almost immediately on the right.

Yabrud lies in a fertile pocket of the Qalamoun, bordering the forbidding terrain of the Anti-Lebanon, and has evidence of settlement going back tens of thousands of years. It formed part of the domains of Agrippa II, perhaps ceded to him as part of the Tetrarchy of Lysanias by Claudius in AD 53 (*Roman Road – Wadi Barada). The Greek Catholic Cathedral of Constantine and Helen was built using elements of the former Temple of Jupiter. The worship of Jupiter in his local form (Jupiter Yabrudis) seems to have achieved wider fame and an altar to Malekiabrudis has been unearthed in Rome. labruda was the seat of a bishop in the early Christian period. The church contains a good collection of icons (sacristy to right of altar). The bases of three Roman columns (part of a peripteral colonnade) can be seen to the south. Some of the Islamic buildings southwest of the cathedral are on the sites of other Byzantine churches.

At Ras al-Ain, 4 km along the road leading southwest via the mountains to *Maaloula, there are several Roman tombs, cut into the limestone rock – one (third century) with two lions in relief beside the door (not easy to distinguish) and 11 carved relief panels.

REFS: Jalabert, Mouterde *IGLS* V 1959: 308–13; Nasrallah 1956: 63–86.

Z

Zalebiye

زلبية

VARIANTS: Annoucas (?Grk); Regia Dianae Fanum (Lat) PERIOD: Byz RATING: – MAP: R4

LOCATION: 2 km downstream along the mid Euphrates from *Halebiye. From Halebiye, cross via the pontoon bridge north of the site. Road continues to the railway station from where a dirt track leads +2 km to the ruins.

The history of Zalebiye marches closely with that of the complementary fortress on the right bank of the Euphrates, Halebiye (with which it shared control of river traffic). Being in a worse state of preservation, smaller in extent and until recently less accessible, Zalebiye has been infrequently visited.

The fortress, like Halebiye, was established in the period when the Palmyrenes were unwisely attempting to assert their control in the area to test Roman dominance (*Palmyra – for Zenobia's rebellion). The fortress was improved as part of the defensive works of the Byzantine Emperor Justinian. The use of less solid construction techniques and the effects of earthquakes and river flooding (not to mention the recent use of its stone as ballast for the railway) have done considerably more damage to the fabric than is the case at Halebiye. The basic plan is an elongated rectangle narrowing to a point at the northern end, strengthened by square towers. Only the eastern half of the rectangle survives, the wall on the west having been swept into the river. The east wall (which carries eight towers) gives on to the plateau and is marked by an imposing entrance gateway. To the north and east lay suburbs greater in extent than at Halebiye.

One kilometre upstream from Zalebiye a dam was built across the Euphrates and, on the eastern bank, an off-take canal.

These works probably date back at least to the first century AD and possibly to the Late Bronze Age. The canal was still in use in the Arab middle ages when it was named after Samiramis, the Arab queen.

REFS: Bell *Amurath* 1911: 67–8; Calvet & Geyer 1992: 19–26; Lauffray *Halabiyya* 1983, 1991; Poidebard *Trace* 1934: pl LXXXIII–IV.

Zarzita

زرزتا

PERIOD: Byz ALT: 550 m RATING: – MAP: R3

LOCATION: On the western slopes of Jebel Sheikh Barakat in the Jebel Halaqa region of the Limestone Massif. Branch left 1.5 km south of Saint Simeon for *Qatura then continue c+3.5 km west.

Rather bleak stone ruins, a few arches but, on the whole, nothing memorable except the splendid view over the Plain of Amuq, the rich plain to the east of Antioch.

This appears to have been an ancient village with a monastic establishment including a recluse's tower to the south. Little remains of the sixth century church (track south at eastern entry to the village) with a single nave but 30 m south of the church lies a tower, the two once connected by a *stoa* or colonnade. Built of large stone blocks, the tower measures 4 m by 4 m with the two floors separated by a prominent cornice. The lower floor housed the altar of a small chapel. The second storey was presumably a recluse's living quarters. There is an inscription on the cornice which reads: 'Simon, priest, built this in the month of June 500. Eusebius, architect, John Mar [...]. Lord, help us.' A small (detached) porch 4 m to the east is dated earlier (423) and was once attached to a building now disappeared.

The village seems to be basically of the fifth and sixth centuries when the local agricultural industry was flourishing and there was surplus to support a large number of monastic communities.

REFS: Butler *PE* II B 5 1912: 246–8; Hadjar 2000: 161–2; Pena (*et al*) *Reclus* 1980: 165–9.

4

ITINERARIES, REGIONAL AND THEMATIC MAPS

ITINERARIES

306

I. Damascus (maps 17–27)

The ten walking itineraries described in the Gazetteer are largely self-explanatory. Six describe areas of the old city of Damascus and mostly take as their starting point the western end of the Suq al-Hamidiye. Two describe areas in the Ottoman extension of the city (Tekkiye Mosque, National Museum) and the remaining two (Salihiye, Midan) cover older extensions of the city beyond the walls. For the latter, you may need to use a taxi to reach the starting points.

2. Hauran (map R1)

All of the Hauran can be visited in day trips from Damascus. The Hauran is divided between two programs, though it would be possible to see all of the main sites (Ezraa (**), Bosra (***), Shahba (*), Qanawat (**)) in one itinerary by combining the two.

2a Eastern Hauran – 320 km round trip – one day. Exit Damascus via Deraa highway – 51 kms, road west to Sanamein (*) – 80 km south turn off left to **Ezraa** (**) – return to highway for remainder of distance (25 km) to **Deraa** – take road 42 km east to **Bosra** (***) – [either; take up Itin 2b at Suweida (*) – 7 km east then 40 km north – or return to Damascus either via Deraa road or via Suweida].

2b Jebel al-Arab – 285 km round trip. Exit Damascus ring road via Sitt Zeinab road – 87 km south to **Shahba** (*) – then follow location notes and Jebel al-Arab map for tour around Jebel al-Arab beginning with side trips to **Slim, Atil, Qanawat** (**) and **Sia** and then anti-clockwise circuit **Suweida**(*) – **Salkhad** – **Mushennef** (*) – **Shaqqa**.

3. Around Damascus (map R1)

There is limited scope for combining these sites given their location on separate roads radiating from Damascus, but loop itineraries combining small groups of sites might be organised as follows.

3a Dumeir – Haran al-Awamid – c90 km – half-day circuit. Exit Damascus via Palmyra road – follow site directions for **Dumeir** (**) (43 km) then **Haran al-Awamid** (27 km) – return via direct road to Damascus.

3b Seidnaya – Maalula – Yabrud – 180+ km – half-full-day circuit (full day with lunch stop). Exit Damascus via road north to al-Tal (turn-off at 11.5 km) – +15 km N, **Seidnaya** – +26 km north to **Maalula** (*) – **Yabrud** c12 km north – continue 8 km to Nabk (Damascus-Homs highway) – possible visits to **Deir Mar Mousa** (*) (14 km northeast of Nabk) or **Qara** (15 kms north of Nabk) – return to Damascus via highway (81 km).

3c Burqush – Barada gorge (Roman Road – Wadi Barada) – Zabadani – c125 km – half-day circuit. Follow directions for **Burqush** (*) – return to Beirut highway, continue west 9 km to turn-off to Zabadani – follow directions for **Roman Road – Wadi Barada** – after visiting Roman road cutting, return west 2 km to Zabadani road – turn right at intersection (small dam) 13 km to Zabadani-Bludan (restaurants, mountain resort) – return to Damascus via Beirut highway.

4. Orontes Towns (map R2)

Several of these sites can be covered by prolonging the half-day trip from Damascus to Aleppo as few require an extensive diversion from the main north-south highway. Certainly **Homs, Hama** (*), **Apamea** (***), **Shaizar** (*) and Tell Nabi Mend could be covered in this way. **Deir Soleib** (*) is more accessible from Masyaf (*) and could be visited in conjunction with a trip to or from the coastal mountains. However, there are many advantages in a more leisurely circuit of the Orontes area from Hama which could also provide a base for expeditions into the steppe area to the east.

Orontes Towns – 150+ km – full day. From **Hama** (*) – take northwest road (to Mhardeh) 28 km to **Shaizar** (*) – after

Shaizar, take road west 20 km to Suq al-
Biye, then +7 km north to Qalaat Mudiq
(for **Apamea** (***)) – from Tell Salhab
(+17 km south of Tell Mudiq) road south
leads 38 km to **Masyaf** (*) [*but you may
wish to divert into foothills from Tell Salhab
to take in* **Qalaat Abu Qobeis** *which, along
with Masyaf, is on itinerary 5c*] – as you meet
Hama-Masyaf main road, turn left (east) c3
km before taking road right (south) for
Deir Soleib. Return to Hama 30 km.

Further options from Hama include **Qasr
Ibn Wardan – Anderin** (*) – Itin 11b
– and **Isriya** (*) (see location notes and
map R4).

5. South Coast (map R2)

5a **Tartus and Inland** – 162 km – full day.
Follow directions for **Qalaat Areimeh** –
take road back to Tartus as far as the Safita
turn-off – follow directions to **Qalaat
Yahmur** – return to Safita road and
follow directions to **Safita** (**) (164 km)
– continue north by following directions
for **Husn Suleiman** (**) (27 km) return
to Tartus via Dreikish.

5b **Krak des Chevaliers** – half day (full
day if combined with parts of 5a). The
Krak (***) can be visited as a one-day
trip from Damascus (and is so described
in the Gazetteer location notes). It could
more conveniently be visited from Tartus,
either as a half-day trip or combined with
elements of 5a. Leave Tartus by the Homs
highway – after Tell Kalakh turn left, picking
up the location guidelines – visit Krak
– visit nearby **St George Monastery**
– either return to Tartus [*or take direct
road west to* **Safita** (**) (*continuing on to*
Qalaat Yahmur *and Tartus) or return to
Tartus highway*].

5c **Tartus – Ismaeli Castles – Qalaat
Marqab – Baniyas** – *a long itinerary (190
km if done as a round trip) which you may
want to trim to a more comfortable one-day
program. Exit Tartus via highway to Latakia
– follow notes for* **Qalaat al-Kawabi** (T)
*(22 km) – visit castle and return as far as
Sheikh Badr road – continue to Sheikh Badr
(10 km) – pick up location notes for* **Qalaat**

al-Kahf (**) *(13 km) – visit al-Kahf and
return to Sheikh Badr – take direct road east
to* **Masyaf** (*) *(c24 km – see also itinerary
4) – [note: possible option to include Qalaat
Abu Qobeis – see itinerary 4] return to
coast highway (54 km), by retracing Masyaf
direction notes to Baniyas – short side trip (12
km round trip) to* **Qalaat Marqab** (***)
*– return to Tartus via highway (40 km) or
continue north to Latakia (c45 km).*

6. Central Coast (map R2)

6 **Qalaat Maniqa–Qalaat Ben Qahtan-
Jeble – Qalaat al-Mehelbeh** – 200+ km
– full day, depending on starting/finishing
points. Start either from Tartus or from
Latakia (from Latakia, order of visits could
be reversed) – reach Baniyas and follow
location notes for **Qalaat Maniqa** (*)
(21 km) – return to coastal highway and
continue c+20 km north to just before
Jeble turn-off – follow notes for **Qalaat
Ben Qahtan** (round trip 48 km) – return
to coastal road – visit **Jeble** (*) – continue
north on coastal road to Snobar – turn
inland following location notes for **Qalaat
al-Mehelbeh** (c45 km round trip) –
return to coastal road – return to Latakia-
Tartus.

7. North Coast (map R2)

7a **Qalaat Saladin** – use location notes
for half-day (70 km) round trip from
Latakia. [*Could be combined with* **Qalaat
al-Mehelbeh** (*) *from itinerary 6 or* **Qalaat
Burzey** (**) *from itinerary 7b.*]

7b **Jisr al-Shugur – Bakas – Qalaat
Burzey** – c175 km – full day. From Latakia,
follow notes for **Qalaat Burzey** (**) (c55
km) – continue 15 km along road
that follows west side of Orontes Plain –
visit **Jisr al-Shugur** – take main road to
Latakia, following direction for turn-off to
Bakas (T) (9 km round trip) – return to
main road and continue along Latakia road
(80 km).

7c **Ugarit – Ras al-Basit** – 110+ km –
half to full day (picnic at Ras al-Basit). From
Latakia, follow location notes for **Ugarit**

(**) (14 km) – from there, rejoin main Latakia-Qasab road (to Turkish border) and pick up notes for **Ras al-Basit** (T) – return to Latakia.

8. Aleppo (maps 2–8)

Except for the tour of the Mashhad al-Hussein, all the ten walks described are in the old walled area of the city or the adjoining Jdeide area immediately to the northwest.

9. Dead Cities (Limestone Massif, maps R3, R3a)

There are literally hundreds of so-called 'dead cities' in the limestone country west of Aleppo, as explained in *Dead Cities – General Note. The three itineraries described here take in most of the sites selected for this survey, grouping them as much as possible to rationalise a program of visits.

9a **Jebel Semaan area** (map 68, below) – c100 km round trip without diversions. From Aleppo, start with location notes for **Sheikh Suleiman, Mushabbak** (*) – then pick up directions for **Qatura, Zarzita, Refade** (*) and **Takleh** (*) – visit from there **Saint Simeon** (map: 29) (***) – take Afrin road north 14 km to **Barad** turnoff – 10 km to Barad – return to Afrin road [*possible diversion 3 km further north to Ain Dara (*) which could also be done with itinerary 10a*] – return to Saint Simeon to pick up directions for **Basofan, Burjke, Burj Haidar** (*), **Fafertin** and **Kharrab Shams** (*) – return to Aleppo by continuing east to Afrin road and heading south for Aleppo. For a two-day itinerary with Barad included, a natural break would come after Saint Simeon.

9b **Jebel al-Ala** (map R3a) – 150+ km without diversions – one/two day(s) (one day if you confine your tour to sites with one or more * – ie the Harim road plus **Qalb Lozeh**). A complex itinerary given the bewildering range of roads in the area. To reach the starting point of the tour, exit Aleppo via the Damascus highway,

turning right along the road that is sign-posted as leading to the main Turkish border crossing at Bab al-Hawa (40 km) (via Urum al-Sughra, Atareb) – before the border post, turn left at the road junction that also leads south towards Idlib – avoid, however, the Idlib road and take the turn-off immediately to the right that goes initially through the village of Sarmada and leads eventually to **Harim** (*).

Using this Bab al-Hawa junction as 'point zero', the following sequence of sites is recommended – **Braij**, diversion to **Baqirha** (*) (+7 km), **Bamuqqa** (*), **Harim** (*) (21 km), **Kirkbizeh, Qalb Lozeh** (**) – [*if you wish to undertake the longer itinerary continue south from Qalb Lozeh for Behyo, Beshindlaye, return to Kirkbizeh for Kokanaya, Dayhis and/or Meez*].

9c **Jebel Zawiya – Bara – Maarat al-Numan – Jebel Riha** – A relatively long (c200 km if done as out-and-back one-day trip from Aleppo) which can, however, be abridged and made a half-day diversion while travelling Aleppo-Latakia or Aleppo-Damascus. Leave Aleppo via Damascus road – at Saraqeb junction (c38 km from Aleppo), take highway to Latakia – pass Riha (+19 km) and after +6km, at Urum al-Joz, pick up directions for **Bara** (**) – visit Bara – immediately south, pick up road east towards **Serjilla** (**) – return to Bara road and continue south for 5 km – at Basqala, turn left (east) for **Maarat al-Numan** (*) (10 km) – visit Maarat, then take Aleppo highway north and after 4 km, take left turn for **Dana (South)** (*) – proceed north along Riha road to **Jerade** (*) and **Ruweiha** (**) – return to Aleppo or resume journey to Latakia or Damascus.

10. North of Aleppo (maps R3, R3a)

10a **Cyrrhus – Ain Dara** – 200+ km round trip – half/full day. Exit Aleppo by north road to Afrin – follow location notes for **Cyrrhus** (*) (76 km from Aleppo) – return to Azaz and main road (+32 km), continuing on west to Afrin (+10 km) – take road south +10 km and turn right (west) for **Ain Dara** (*) – visit Ain Dara and return to Aleppo via Afrin or take road south through Saint Simeon (+17 km – see Ain Dara location notes) and take Dar Tazeh-Aleppo road (+36 km).

10b **Menbij – Qalaat Najm** – 200 km round trip – full day. Exit Aleppo via east (airport) road – at c12k (airport on right) turn left (north) on Menbij-Jezira road – follow direction notes for **Menbij** – visit Menbij – return to Jezira road, turn right after +17 km for **Qalaat Najm** (*) (+3 km) – return to Aleppo via same route.

11. South of Aleppo (map R4)

11a **Qinnesrin – Ebla** – 157 km round trip – half-day. Exit Aleppo on main road to Damascus – follow location notes for **Qinnesrin** (T) (31 km) – return to main Aleppo-Damascus highway – south to Saraqeb junction (50 km from Aleppo) – pick up notes for **Ebla** (*) +9 km – return to Aleppo via main highway or continue with itinerary 11b.

11b **Qasr Ibn Wardan – Anderin** – probably best done as part of a wider itinerary (eg Aleppo-Damascus), this itinerary involves a detour of 162 km from the main Aleppo-Damascus highway at Hama – allow a half day. From Hama bypass, follow notes for **Qasr Ibn Wardan** (**) – continue northeast following notes for **Anderin** (T) +25 km – return via same route [*though four-wheel drive vehicles would have option of picking up the* Khanazir *route covered in itinerary 11c*].

11c **Khanazir [- Isriya]** – 130+ km round trip to Khanazir – full day+. Exit Aleppo by east road (airport/Raqqa) – just as new Jezira road diverges northeast, take the road heading south towards al-Sfire (14 km from turn-off) – continue heading southeast +40 km along track to Khanasir [*+56 km to* **Isriya** (*) *from where options for continuing west (track only) to connect with* **Anderin** *(itinerary 11b) or southwest on sealed road to Isriya-Selemiye*].

12. Mid Euphrates (maps R4, R5)

12a **Qalaat Jaabr – Resafa** – 345 km without diversions – full day. Best covered as one-way itinerary Aleppo-Deir al-Zor (or vice versa). Exit Aleppo on airport/ Raqqa road – 146 km southeast to turn-off for Tabqa/al-Thawra (new town for Euphrates dam) – take turn-off (left) and cross dam wall (permission may be needed), picking up location notes for **Qalaat Jaabr** (*) – return to main road – continue southeast +21 km to al-Mansura – turn-off to right (south) for **Resafa** (**) +28 km, see location notes – visit Resafa, return to main road – continue +26 km E to Raqqa turn-off – turn left (north) and cross Euphrates to **Raqqa** – return to main road and resume southeast road +85 km (12 km before Tibne) – turn-off left 8 km to **Halebiye** (**) – visit Halebiye and return to main road – resume journey southeast via Tibne to Deir al-Zor (58 km from Halebiye turn-off).

12b **South of Deir al-Zor (Qalaat Rahba – Dura Europos – Mari-Baghuz)** 270 km plus diversions – full day round trip. Exit Deir al-Zor by Abu Kemal road (right bank of Euphrates heading southeast) – 45 km pick up directions for **Qalaat Rahba** (*) – resume southeast journey +48 km – pick up directions for **Dura Europos** (**) – return to main road and resume road southeast +24 km – turn left, for **Mari** (*) (see location notes) – return to main road, continue southeast towards Abu Kemal and pick up location notes for visit to **Baghuz** on left bank of Euphrates – return same road to Deir al-Zor.

13. Northeast Syria (map R5)

13a **Circesium** – 52 km round trip from Deir al-Zor. See Circesium (T) location notes.

13b **Tell Brak – Tell Halaf – Ain Divar** – three destinations difficult to combine into a single itinerary but which could separately be visited from either Qamishli or Haseke using the location notes. Except for **Tell Brak** (T) (42 km northeast of

Haseke), each requires a good half-day though the roads are relatively fast in this part of Syria.

14. Central Desert (map R4)

Qasr al-Heir East-Palmyra – Qasr al-Heir West – Harbaqa Dam – 470 km plus diversion – at least two full days needed to include both Umayyad castles and Palmyra (including *Qalaat Shirkuh (*)). For many visitors, however, Palmyra will be an out-and-back itinerary from Damascus (and it is so described in the location notes). This itinerary includes it as a final prize in the clockwise tour of Syria but the order could as easily be reversed.

Exit Deir al-Zor by Palmyra-Damascus road across the central desert – at c100 km point, pick up directions for **Qasr al-Heir East** (*) – return to main road and continue 110 km to **Palmyra** (***) – after Palmyra (at least one day required for a full survey) continue along road to Damascus, picking up directions for **Harbaqa Dam** (*) and **Qasr al-Heir West** from the second turn-off to Homs – return to Damascus road and continue via **Dumeir** (**, see itinerary 2a).

KEY TO REGIONAL MAPS

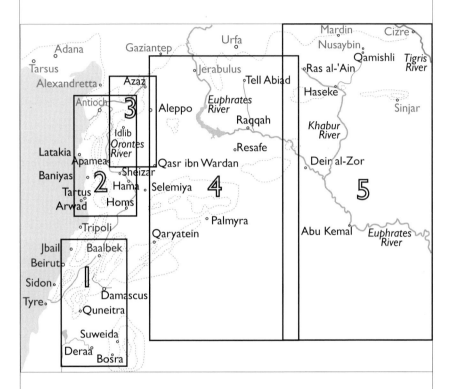

Mardin
Cizre
Urfa
Nusaybin
Adana
Gaziantep
Qamishli   Tigris
River
Tarsus
Jerabulus
Ras al-'Ain
Alexandretta
Azaz
Tell Abiad
Haseke
Antioch
3
Aleppo
Euphrates
River
Sinjar
Idlib
Raqqah
Khabur
River
Latakia
Orontes
River
Resafe
Apamea
Qasr ibn Wardan
Dein al-Zor
Sheizar
Baniyas
2
Hama
Selemiya
4
Tartus
Arwad
Homs
5
Tripoli
Palmyra
Qaryatein
Abu Kemal
Euphrates
River
Jbail
Baalbek
Beirut
Sidon
I
Damascus
Tyre
Quneitra
Suweida
Deraa
Bosra

road	————————
track	··························
motorway	▬▬▬▬▬▬▬
railway	- - - - - - - - - -
river	〰〰〰
lake, sea	▨
wall, fortification	
geographic feature	*Jebel Ansariye*
place not described	Gaziantep
fortification	□
town, village	○
peak or tell	△
detailed or neighbouring map or plan	6

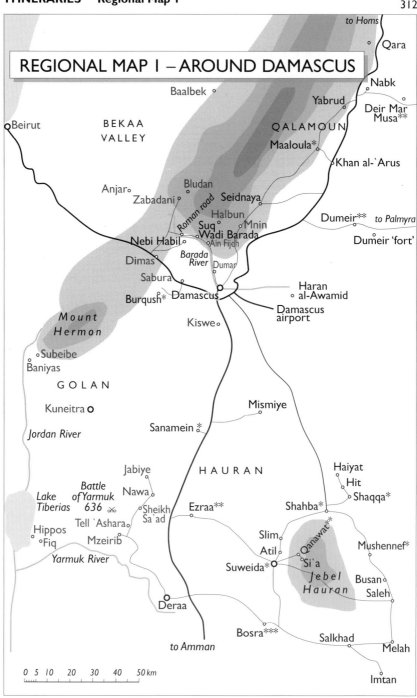

REGIONAL MAP I – AROUND DAMASCUS

to Homs

Qara

Nabk

Baalbek

Yabrud

Deir Mar Musa**

BEKAA VALLEY

QALAMOUN

Beirut

Maaloula*

Khan al-ʿArus

Anjar

Bludan

Zabadani

Seidnaya

Halbun

Dumeir**   to Palmyra

Roman road

Suq

Mnin

Wadi Barada

Ain Fijeh

Dumeir 'fort'

Nebi Habil

Barada River

Dimas

Dumar

Sabura

Damascus

Haran al-Awamid

Burqush*

Damascus airport

Kiswe

Mount Hermon

Subeibe

Baniyas

GOLAN

Kuneitra

Jordan River

Mismiye

Sanamein*

Jabiye

HAURAN

Haiyat

Hit

Nawa

Lake Tiberias

Battle of Yarmuk 636

Shaqqa*

Ezraa**

Shahba*

Sheikh Saʿad

Hippos

Tell ʿAshara

Fiq

Slim

Mzeirib

Qanawat**

Mushennef*

Yarmuk River

Atil

Siʿa

Suweida*

Jebel Hauran

Busan

Saleh

Deraa

Bosra***

Salkhad

Melah

to Amman

Imtan

0 5 10   20   30   40   50 km

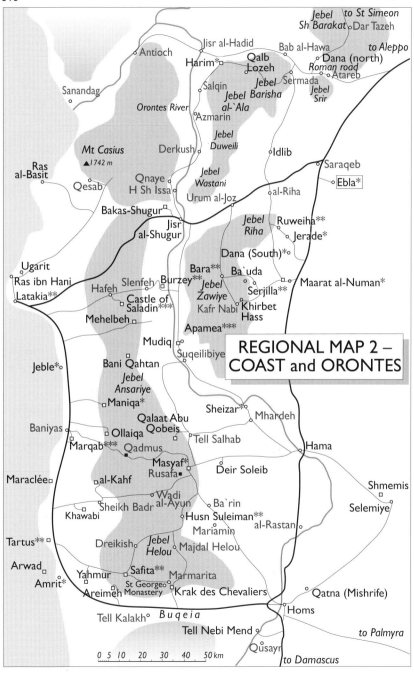

REGIONAL MAP 2 –
COAST and ORONTES

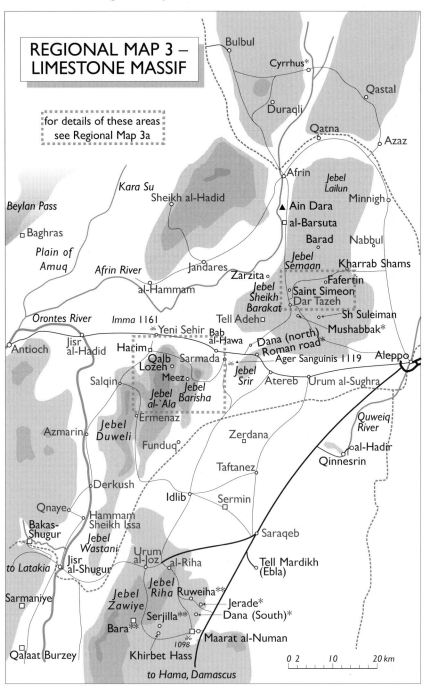

REGIONAL MAP 3 – LIMESTONE MASSIF

for details of these areas
see Regional Map 3a

Bulbul

Cyrrhus*

Qastal

Duraqli

Qatna

Azaz

Kara Su

Afrin

Jebel Lailun

Minnigh

Beylan Pass

Sheikh al-Hadid

▲ Ain Dara

al-Barsuta

Baghras

Barad

Nabbul

Plain of Amuq

Afrin River

Jandares

Zarzita

Jebel Semaan

Kharrab Shams

al-Hammam

Fafertin

Jebel Sheikh Barakat

Saint Simeon

Dar Tazeh

Orontes River

Imma 1161

Tell Adeh

Sh Suleiman

Yeni Sehir

Bab al-Hawa

Dana (north)

Mushabbak*

Antioch

Jisr al-Hadid

Harim

Roman road*

Qalb Lozeh

Sarmada

Ager Sanguinis 1119

Aleppo

Salqin

Meez

Jebel Srir

Atereb

Urum al-Sughra

Jebel al-'Ala

Jebel Barisha

Ermenaz

Quweiq River

Azmarin

Jebel Duweli

Funduq

Zerdana

al-Hadir

Qinnesrin

Taftanez

Derkush

Idlib

Sermin

Qnaye

Hammam Sheikh Issa

Bakas-Shugur

Jebel Wastani

Saraqeb

Jisr al-Shugur

Urum al-Joz

al-Riha

Tell Mardikh (Ebla)

to Latakia

Sarmaniye

Jebel Riha

Ruweiha**

Jerade*

Jebel Zawiye

Serjilla**

Dana (South)*

Bara**

1098

Maarat al-Numan

Qalaat Burzey

Khirbet Hass

0 2   10   20 km

to Hama, Damascus

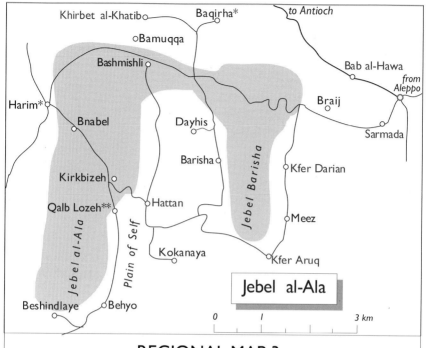

Khirbet al-Khatib○   Baqirha*   to Antioch

○Bamuqqa

Bashmishli○   Bab al-Hawa

                                          from
                                          Aleppo
Harim*○   Braij

    Bnabel   Dayhis   Sarmada

                 Barisha○   *Jebel Barisha*   Kfer Darian

Kirkbizeh○

Qalb Lozeh**○   ○Hattan   *Jebel al-Ala*   Meez

    Plain of Self

          Kokanaya○   Kfer Aruq

                             Jebel al-Ala

                    0   1   3 km

Beshindlaye○   ○Behyo

REGIONAL MAP 3a -
Limestone Massif Itineraries
('dead cities') - Jebel al-Ala and Jebel Semaan

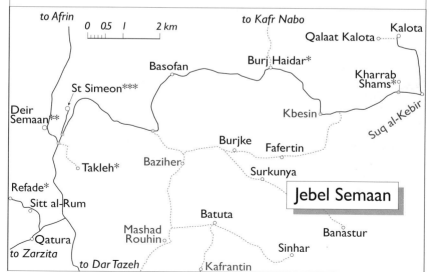

to Afrin   0   0.5 1   2 km   to Kafr Nabo   Kalota

                                   Qalaat Kalota○

                         Burj Haidar*
              Basofan○   Kharrab
                                              Shams*○
    St Simeon***

Deir   *Suq al-Kebir*
Semaan**   Kbesin○

    ○Takleh*   Baziher○   Burjke○   Fafertin

Refade*   Surkunya

Sitt al-Rum   **Jebel Semaan**

○Qatura   Mashad   Batuta○   Banastur
to Zarzita   Rouhin○   Sinhar
    to Dar Tazeh   ○Kafrantin

REGIONAL MAP 4 – EAST, SOUTH OF ALEPPO

Jerabulus

Ras al-Ain
Tell Halaf
Tell Abiad
Khabur River

Azaz
Menbij
Qalaat Najm*
al-Bab
Jebel Khalid
Balikh River
Aleppo***
Abu Qalqal
Lake Assad
Qalaat Jaabr*
Heraclea
Raqqa
Euphrates River
al-Thawra
Djazla
Nheyle
Halebiye**
Zalebiye
Resafa**
Anderin
Qasr Ibn Wardan *
Isriya *
Jebel al-Bishra
Deir al-Zor
Selemiye
al-Taybe
Qasr al-Heir East*
Sikne
Qalaat Shirkuh*
Palmyra***
Khan al-Hallabat*
Bkhara
Qasr al-Heir West
Qaryatein
Harbaqa Dam*
al-Bisiri
+ Deir Mar Musa**
Khan al-Manqura
Kh Butmiyat
to Baghdad

0 5 10 20   50 km

Jebel Seis

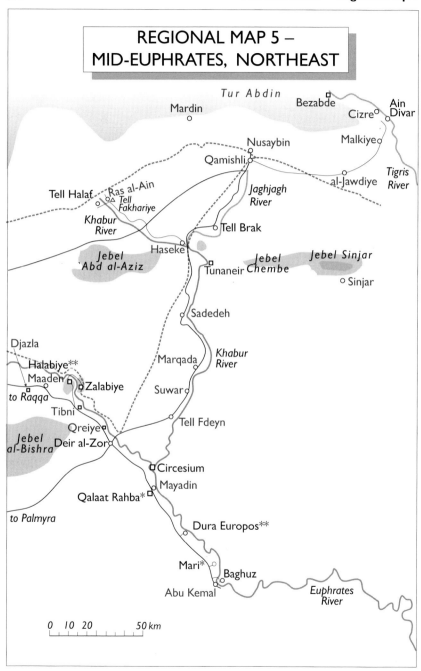

REGIONAL MAP 5 –
MID-EUPHRATES, NORTHEAST

Tur Abdin

Mardin

Bezabde

Cizre   Ain Divar

Malkiye

Nusaybin

Qamishli

Tigris River

al-Jawdiye

Tell Halaf   Ras al-Ain   Tell Fakhariye

Jaghjagh River

Khabur River

Haseke   Tell Brak

Jebel 'Abd al-Aziz

Tunaneir   *Jebel Chembe*   *Jebel Sinjar*

Sinjar

Sadedeh

Djazla

Halabiye**

Marqada   *Khabur River*

Maaden   Zalabiye   Suwar

to Raqqa

Tibni

Oreiye   Tell Fdeyn

Jebel al-Bishra   Deir al-Zor

Circesium

Mayadin

Qalaat Rahba*

to Palmyra

Dura Europos**

Mari*

Baghuz

Abu Kemal

Euphrates River

0   10   20   50 km

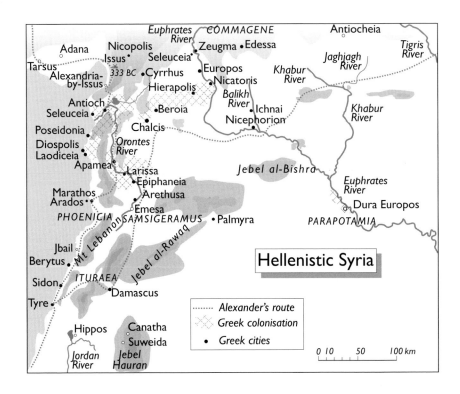

Hellenistic Syria

.... Alexander's route

⬚⬚⬚ Greek colonisation

• Greek cities

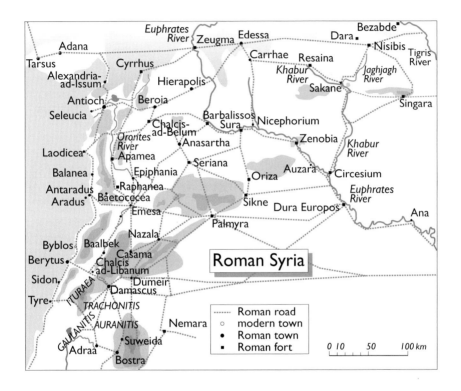

Roman Syria

Euphrates River · Zeugma · Edessa · Dara · Bezabde
Adana · Carrhae · Resaina · Nisibis · Tigris River
Tarsus · Cyrrhus · Khabur River · Jaghjagh River
Alexandria-ad-Issum · Hierapolis · Sakane
Antioch · Beroia · Singara
Seleucia · Barbalissos · Nicephorium
Chalcis-ad-Belum · Sura
Orontes River · Anasartha · Zenobia · Khabur River
Laodicea · Apamea · Seriana
Balanea · Epiphania · Oriza · Auzara · Circesium
Antaradus · Raphanea · Euphrates River
Aradus · Baetocecea · Sikne · Dura Europos · Ana
Emesa · Palmyra
Nazala
Byblos · Baalbek · Casama
Berytus · Chalcis-ad-Libanum
Sidon · Dumeir
Tyre · ITURAEA · Damascus
TRACHONITIS · Nemara
GAULANITIS · AURANITIS
Adraa · Suweida
Bostra

------ Roman road
○ modern town
● Roman town
■ Roman fort

0 10   50   100 km

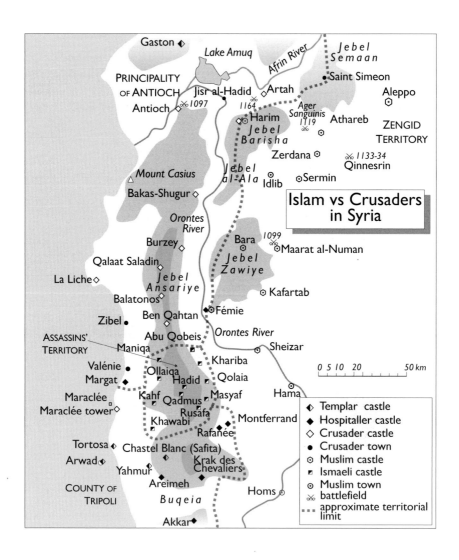

Gaston ◈
Lake Amuq
Afrin River
Jebel Semaan

PRINCIPALITY
OF ANTIOCH   Jisr al-Hadid ◇Artah   •Saint Simeon
                                                          Aleppo
Antioch ◇✕1097   1164   Ager   ⊙
                          •Harim Sanguinis Athareb
                          Jebel   1719 ✕ ⊙   ZENGID
                          Barisha   TERRITORY
                              Zerdana ⊙   ✕1133-34
                                                 Qinnesrin
              Mount Casius *Jebel*
                △   *al-Ala* Idlib ⊙Sermin
           Bakas-Shugur ◇
                                          Islam vs Crusaders
              Orontes   **in Syria**
              River
           Burzey◇   Bara 1099
                                  ✕
   Qalaat Saladin◇   ◉Maarat al-Numan
                          Jebel
La Liche◇   *Jebel*   *Zawiye*
              Ansariye
   Balatonos◇   ⊙ Kafartab
      Zibel • Ben Qahtan ◈Fémie
                        ◇
ASSASSINS'   Abu Qobeis • *Orontes River*
TERRITORY   Maniqa   •Sheizar
                          ◙ Khariba
   Valénie • ◙Ollaiqa ◙ ⊙Qolaia   0 5 10 20   50 km
   Margat ◆ ◙Hadid ◙
Maraclée • Kahf ◙ ◙Masyaf   Hama
Maraclée tower◇ ◙Qadmus   ◙   ⊙
           Rusafa   Montferrand ◈ Templar castle
      Khawabi ◙   ◆ Hospitaller castle
           Rafanée ◆   ◇ Crusader castle
Tortosa ◈ Chastel Blanc (Safita) • Crusader town
Arwad◈   Krak des   ⊙ Muslim castle
   Yahmur◆ Chevaliers ◆   ◙ Ismaeli castle
COUNTY OF Areimeh ◆   ⊙ Muslim town
TRIPOLI   *Buqeia*   Homs ◉   ✕ battlefield
                                - - - approximate territorial
           Akkar◆   limit

Glossary of Architectural and Other Terms

ain   spring, well (Arb)

ablaq   alternating courses of contrasting stone, especially in Mamluk or Ottoman periods (Arb)

absidiola   large niche, usually semi-circular, often built into a corner (Lat)

acropolis   elevated (usually fortified) administrative or religious centre of a Greek city (Grk)

acroteria   ornaments placed above the outer angles of a pediment (Grk)

adyton   inner sanctuary within the *cella* of a temple, usually in the form of a broad niche (Grk)

aedicule   niche or shrine housing a cult image (Lat)

agora   open meeting place or market (Grk)

aisle   in a basilica, the elements of the building lying either side of the central passage or nave

ambulatory   colonnade with roof encircling a small temple

amir (emir)   military leader

ambo   pulpit in a Christian basilica (Grk)

andron   men's meeting room (Grk, Lat)

anta   squared pilaster continuing the line of a side wall, eg of a *cella* (pl *antae*, Lat)

apse   structure (often semi-circular in shape and vaulted by a semi-dome) terminating the east end of the nave of a church

apodyterium   changing room of a Roman bath (Lat)

arcosolium   burial niche, carved into rock with roof in the form of an arch (Lat)

architrave   lowest division of an entablature; or the moulded frame around a window or door

ashlar   square-shaped stones laid in regular courses

atabeq   regent (Tur)

atrium   courtyard (in a Roman house) or forecourt (in front of a Byzantine church)

bab   door, gateway (Arb)

baldachin   or baldaquin – free-standing canopy above an altar, tomb, reliquary or throne (fr Itn 'baldacchino')

baptistery   part of a church (or separate building) intended for the baptism of converts

barrel vault   vault in the form of a half-cylinder

barbican   gateway usually defended by twin flanking towers

basilica   building of Roman origins in the form of a central nave flanked by two aisles. The nave is higher than the aisles and is lit by a clerestory supported on double colonnades

bastion   strongpoint in a fortification, usually a fortified tower

bayt or *beit*   house, living quarters (Arb)

bema   raised platform with seating arranged in a horseshoe, found in the main nave of a Byzantine church (Grk)

bimaristan   see *maristan*

bossage   practice of leaving the outer surface of a block of stone rough and projecting, thus providing a rusticated appearance

brattice   see machicolation

burj   tower (Arb)

caldarium   the hot room of a Roman bath (Lat)

cardo maximus   main (usually north-south) thoroughfare of a Roman city comprising a wide central carriageway flanked by colonnaded pavements on each side and lined with stalls, shops and public buildings (Lat)

caryatid   figure of a woman or man serving as a column or pier to support an architectural element (roof or portico) (fr Grk)

castrum	Roman fortress, rectangular in shape with corner towers (Lat)		often flanking an open colonnade (*porticus*) (Grk/Lat)
cavea	semi-circular seating forming the auditorium of a Roman theatre (Lat)	*cupola*	dome (Itn fr Lat)
		curtain wall	long run of straight wall between towers or bastions
cella	central sacred chamber in a *Syro-Phoenician temple enclosure (Lat)	*deir*	monastery (Arb)
chancel	section (usually raised by a few steps) surrounding the altar of a church	*decumanus*	major cross street (east-west) of a grid-planned Roman city intersecting with the *cardo maximus* (Lat)
chemin de ronde			
	walkway around the battlements of a medieval castle (Fr)	*diaconicon*	small chamber, used as a sacristy, to the left of the chancel of a church (Grk)
chevet	wall terminating the east end of a church – often semi-circular or rounded in shape (Fr)	*dikkah*	platform in a mosque for the recitation of prayers (Arb)
ciborium	canopy construction, usually raised over the high altar (Lat)	*diwan*	see *iwan*
		donjon	central fortified refuge or keep of a Crusader castle
citadel	stronghold commanding a city	Doric	classical order based on a simple undecorated capital
clerestory	the upper structure supported on columns or piers set between the side aisles and the nave. Usually broken by windows to provide light to the interior of a basilica	*distyle*	two columns at the front of a temple (Lat)
		distyle in antis	two columns set between protruding pilasters (*antae*) at the front of a temple (Lat)
colonnade	columns set in rows supporting a roof structure or entablature	entablature	horizontal elements connecting a series of columns (comprises cornice, frieze and architrave in the classical order)
colonia	colony (usually of Roman veterans) (Lat)		
conch	semi-dome in form of a conch (shell), usually surmounting a niche	*exedra*	a semi-circular indentation in a wall or line of columns; room opening across its full width into a larger space, often furnished with seats (Lat)
corbel	projecting stone supporting a decorative element or statue on the face of a wall	*fleuron*	sculptured ornament in the form of a flower (Fr)
Corinthian	type of capital (Grk in origin) decorated with acanthus leaves	fluting	vertical grooves or ridges set in the surface of a column
cornice	top section of the classical entablature, usually a projecting moulding	fosse	ditch surrounding a Crusader or Arab fortification (fr Fr)
crypt	chamber (often underground) set beneath the floor of a church	frieze	middle segment of a classical entablature
cryptoporticus	a dark passage, usually semi-underground,	glacis	smooth sloping surface of stone intended to deter scaling of a medieval

fortification and to expose attackers to fire (fr Fr)

groin vault vault formed over a square bay by the intersection of two barrel vaults

hammam public bath (Arb)

haremlek private quarters of an Ottoman house (Tur)

Hippodamian grid
urban plan developed by Hippodamus of Miletus based on a grid with segments (*insulae*) c110 m by 55 m

hypogeum underground tomb chamber (Lat fr Grk)

iconostasis screen bearing icons separating nave from chancel in a Byzantine or Orthodox rite church (Grk)

in antis façade comprising a number of columns set between *antae* (see *anta*, Lat)

insula grid segments of a Greek-Roman city plan (see Hippodamian grid), rectangular in the proportion of 2:1 (Lat, 'islands' pl *insulae*)

Ionic style of column capital deriving from one of the three classical Greek orders; the shape is based on a scroll

iwan (or *liwan*) large open reception area off a courtyard with high arch opening (Arb)

jami`a large congregational mosque (Arb)

jebel mountain (Arb)

joggled voussoirs
voussoirs (elements of an arch – see below) the edges of which are not straight but cut to fit together in a pattern

kalybe open-fronted shrine with niches for the display of statuary ('hut' or 'cabin' – Grk)

keep innermost structure of a castle, strengthened to serve as a last refuge

khan combined warehouse and hostel for merchants (Arb)

khanqah Sufi monastery (Arb)

khatun princess, especially a woman with élite connections during the time of Nur al-Din and the Ayyubids (Kurdish)

khirbet ruin (Arb)

kouros (-oi) statue(s) depicting a naked youth, usually of the Greek Archaic period

Kufic type of script employed especially in the early Arab period, highly stylized and with pointed terminals (Arb)

limes limits of Roman administration or control; military line of control (Lat)

lintel horizontal member above a doorway or window to support surmounting masonry

liwan synonymous with *iwan*

loculus niche inserted lengthwise into wall of a burial chamber or tower to contain a body (Lat)

loggia a colonnaded arcade providing a sheltered extension of a hall or other entertainment space (Itn)

machicolation a projection from a masonry wall intended to allow liquids or missiles to be rained upon attacking forces. It usually takes the form of an opening with corbels on each side supporting a surmounting shelf, to which the term brattice is also applied

madrasa school for the teaching of Islamic law, often endowed by a prominent citizen

maqsura enclosed section of a mosque reserved for the ruler (Arb)

maristan (*bimaristan*) institution for medical care and training (Arb fr Persian)

martyrium small chamber or

chapel for the burial or preservation of relics of a saint or martyr (Lat)

masjid local mosque (Arb)

mashhad building (literally 'place of witness') constructed over the tomb of a religious notable (Arb)

medina city, central city area (Arb)

merlon architectural embellishment rising above a parapet; a Mesopotamian device (often introduced into buildings of the Roman period) in the form of a step-sided triangle

mihrab niche, usually ornately decorated, intended to show the direction (*qibla*) of Mecca (Arb)

minaret tower of a mosque (fr Arb)

minbar pulpit in a mosque (used particularly for the preaching of the Friday sermon) situated to the right of the *mihrab* (Arb)

mithraeum temple devoted to the cult of the Persian god, Mithras (Lat)

muezzin man who recites the call to prayer from a minaret (Arb)

muqarnas decorative treatment of an arch or dome support by clusters of triangular segments of a sphere, giving a 'stalactite' effect (Arb)

naos sanctuary (Grk)

narthex entrance vestibule located at the western end of a Byzantine church, usually running the full width of the building (Grk)

nave central part of a basilica between the colonnades dividing off the side aisles

necropolis burial ground (Grk)

noria large wooden water wheel to elevate water from a river, usually to supply an aqueduct (Arb)

nymphaeum structure enclosing a public fountain (dedicated to the nymphs), usually with niches for statues (Lat)

odeon small theatre for the performance of music (fr Grk)

orchestra paved space (semi-circular) between stage and auditorium of a Roman theatre

oratory small chapel devoted to prayer (from *oratorium* Lat)

orthostat large slab of stone (usually basalt) set to line the lower part of a wall

pandocheion large building to house pilgrims (Grk: 'inn' – origin of the Arabic *funduk*)

palaestra courtyard or open exercise area often attached to Roman baths (Lat)

pasha Ottoman honorific usually bestowed on the governor (*wali*) of an Ottoman province (*vilayat*) (Tur)

pediment triangular, low-pitched gabled end to a classical building, framed by a cornice

pendentive triangular segment of a sphere, used to carry the transition between a square base and a round surmounting dome

peribolos outer area of a sacred enclosure, surrounding an inner enclosure or *temenos* (Grk)

peripteral temple with *cella* surrounded by a colonnade or peristyle

peristyle colonnaded and roofed corridor running around the edges of an internal courtyard; or the outer colonnade of a peripteral temple

pilaster engaged pier, usually a shallow rectangle in section

portal doorway, usually treated in a monumental style

portico porch or structure

	sheltering the outer part of a doorway, usually supported on columns
portcullis	heavy wooden grill gateway designed to drop from within a tower, preventing access by invaders
praesidium	camp or military headquarters (Lat)
praetorium	residence of a Roman senior official (Lat)
principia	headquarters area in a Roman camp (Lat)
pronaos	porch at the entrance to the cella of a temple (Grk)
propylaeum	monumental pillared entrance to a temenos or sacred precinct (pl propylaea – Lat fr Grk)
prothesis	small chamber on the right of the chancel of a church (cf diaconicon on the left) used in the preparation of the liturgical offerings (Grk)
pseudo-peripteros	use of pilasters on the outer wall (eg of a cella) to resemble a peristyle
qa`a	reception room (Arb)
qadi	Muslim judge (Arb)
qaisariye	lockable shops for sale of precious goods
qalaat (qalaa)	castle, fortress; also refers to ancient remains assumed to have served that purpose (Arb)
qasr	palace, lodge (Arb)
qibla	place towards which prayer is directed in Islam – ie the wall of a mosque which faces in the direction of Mecca (Arb)
qubba or qubbet	dome (Arb)
redoubt	central place of refuge in the event of a Crusader castle being overrun (cf keep) (Fr)
riwaq	arcaded spaces enclosing a courtyard (Arb)
scaenae frons	elaborate stone façade behind the stage area of a Roman theatre, usually

	richly decorated with columns and niches (Lat)
selamlek	public entertainment quarters of an Ottoman house (Tur)
sentry walk	see chemin de ronde
serail, seraya	palace; headquarters of a governor or senior administrator (Tur)
soffit	exposed lower surface of a lintel or ceiling beam
squinch	a small arch or niche placed across a corner in order to carry the transition to an octagonal or domed upper structure
stela	upright narrow slab of stone, usually inscribed
stoa	porticoed structure supported at the front by columns, at the rear by a wall (Grk)
suq	market (Arb)
synthronon	raised platform or semi-circular bench, often intended to frame a bishop's throne in the apse of a Byzantine or Orthodox church (Grk)
Syrian arch	broad semi-circular arch, usually framed within the pediment of a building or arch, with an ornately decorated architrave
tabula ansata	rectangular panel for inscriptions of an official character (Lat)
talus	synonymous with glacis
tekkiye or tekke	Dervish monastery (Tur)
temenos	sacred enclosure providing space (mostly outdoors) for worshippers to gather. See also peribolos (Grk)
tell	mound or artificial hill formed by the debris of centuries of occupation (Arb)
tessera	small pieces of stone used in mosaics (Lat fr Grk)
tepidarium	the warm room of a Roman bath (Lat)
tetraconque or tetraconch	structure formed from four conches (semi-

	circular niches with surmounting semi-domes) (Grk 'four shells')
tetrakionion	four-way arch structure (Grk)
tetrapylon	arrangement of columns (often in four groups of four) used to mark a major intersection of a Roman city (Grk)
tetrastyle	four columns at the front of a temple (Grk)
theatron	small area reserved for religious rituals or gatherings, usually stepped around three sides of a square; common feature of Nabataean cult centres (Grk)
transept	a transverse section inserted in a basilica plan, usually between the main nave and the apse, thus transforming the rectangular plan into a cross shape
triclinos	Grk equivalent of triclinium
triclinium	dining room of a Roman house (originally with three divans) (Lat)

triforium	gallery above the arches flanking a nave (Lat)
turba	tomb or mausoleum (Arb, Tur)
tycheion	shrine or temple in honour of a city's protecting goddess (Tyche) (Grk)
vilayat	see wali
vomitorium	corridors and stairway system enabling a large number of spectators to enter or exit a theatre (Lat)
voussoir	wedge-shaped stone used to form the components of an arch (fr Fr)
wadi	valley or watercourse, dry except during rain (Arb)
wali	governor of a Turkish province (vilayat) (Tur)
waqf	endowment intended for the upkeep of a mosque or madrasa, usually the proceeds of rent from shops or land (Arb)
zawiya	place associated with an Islamic holy man (Arb)

Chronology of Main Events

The list does not attempt to give comprehensive details of rulers, confining itself to those who are mentioned in the text or who made a substantial impact in their Syrian domains.

Entries in italics are references to major building programs or external historical events affecting Syria.

Bold is used for references to significant battles, and to major headings, places or personalities.

BC

c3100–2150   Early Bronze Age

c2900	founding of Mari, Ebla
post-2500	development of Mari
2340–2150	*Akkadian Empire – Sargon of Akkad (r 2340–2284)*
2400–2250	*apogée of Ebla*
c2250	Mari and Ebla razed by Akkadians

c2150–1600   Middle Bronze Age

c2100	arrival of Amorites
2050–1786	*Middle Kingdom in Egypt*
c2000	Ebla rebuilt
1900–1759	Mari's second golden age – Amorite dynasty (Zimri-Lim (r 1775–60)
18C	Amorite kingdoms of northern Syria
c1792–50	reign of Hammurabi of Babylon
1759	Hammurabi of Babylon razes Mari – **Amorite Kingdoms** of north Syria escape direct Babylonian rule
1674–1567	*Hyksos period in Egypt*
c1600	*Ebla destroyed – by Hittites*

c1600–1200   Late Bronze Age

1595	***Babylon falls to Hittites***
1567–1085	*New Kingdom in Egypt*
1550	Hittites arrive in Syria
post-1500	Egypt, **Hittites** and Mitanni compete for control of Syria
c1450–1360	Kingdom of Mitanni flowers
1425–17	*Thutmose IV pharaoh*

	of Egypt
1417–1379	*Amenhotep III pharaoh of Egypt*
1400–c1365	Ugarit's golden age – development of the alphabet
14th century	Egyptian campaigns in Syria
1350	Hittites dislodge Mitanni in Syria
1304–1237	*Ramses II Pharaoh of Egypt*
1286	**Battle of Qadesh** – Ramses II vs Hittites
1284?	Egypt-Hittite peace treaty settles spheres of influence in Syria
13th century	Ugarit in contact with Mycenaean Greece

1200–539   Iron Age

c1200	**Sea Peoples invade Syrian coast**
12th century	*period of prophets in Israel*
1200–1150	Aramaean people arrive in Syria
970–31	*Solomon King of Israel*
9th century	Aramaeans establish 'Neo-Hittite' city states in the North
890–42	Kingdom of Aram-Damascus resists expansion of Israel's influence northwards
856–612	Assyrian dominance
853	**Battle of Qarqar** – Assyrians defeat Aramaean states' combined forces
732	**Assyrians take Damascus** – end city-state of Aram-Damascus
605–539	**Neo-Babylonians** (Chaldeans) control Syria
604–562	*Nebuchadnezzar neo-Babylonian (Chaldean) ruler*

539–333	**Persian Period**		41–54	*Claudius emperor*
			54–68	*Nero emperor*
539	Cyrus takes Babylon and		66	*Jewish revolt against*
	acquires Neo-Babylonian			*Roman rule*
	realms in Syria		69–79	*Vespasian emperor*
521–486	*Darius I ruler of Persia*			*(Flavian line begins)*
490	*Greeks defeat Persians*		70	*Romans (under command*
	at Battle of Marathon			*of Titus) take and*
486–63	*Zerxes ruler of Persia*			*destroy Jerusalem*
			81–96	*Domitian emperor*
333–64	**Hellenistic (after 301,**		98–117	*Trajan emperor*
	Seleucid) Period		105	Trajan annexes
				Nabataean Kingdom
333	**Battle of Issus –**			– creates Provincia
	Alexander of Macedonia			Arabia based on Bosra
	defeats Persians		113	Trajan annexes
	under Darius III			Dura Europos
323	death of Alexander		114–6	Trajan's aggressive
311–281	Seleucus I Nicator			policy in East against
301	army of Seleucus Nicator			Parthians results in
	occupies northern Syria			annexation (temporary) of
223–187	Antiochus III Megas			Mesopotamia and Armenia
	(the Great)		117–38	Hadrian emperor – less
198	Antiochus the Great			aggressive policy in
	seizes southern Syria			East, moves frontier
	from Ptolemies			back to Euphrates
175–64	Antiochus IV Epiphanes		117	Damascus raised to
	– raids Egypt			*metropolis* by Hadrian
164–38	**civil wars** bring		119	Hadrian visits Palmyra
	breakdown of			– renames city
	Seleucid control			Palmyra Hadriana
			138–61	*Antoninus Pius emperor*
64 BC – AD 395 – Roman Period				*(Antonine line begins)*
			161–80	*Marcus Aurelius emperor*
64	**Pompey annexes**		late second century	
	Syria – creation of			major Roman road-
	Provincia Syria			building projects in Syria
51–30	Cleopatra VII Philopater,		162–6	major campaign against
	Ptolemaic ruler			Parthians – Dura
43–36	Mark Antony			Europos retaken
	governor of Syria		180–92	*Commodus emperor*
37–4	*Herod the Great's*		187	Septimius Severus marries
	rule in Judaea			Julia Domna (daughter of
31	**Battle of Actium**			High Priest of Emesa)
	(Octavian defeats Antony)		193–211	Septimius Severus
27–14 (AD)	*Octavian (Augustus) emperor*			emperor (Syrian
20	Roman-Parthian			line begins)
	treaty establishes		193	Governor of Syria,
	agreed boundary			Pescennius Niger, revolts
				against new Emperor
AD			194	Syria reorganised into
				four provinces
14–37	*Tiberius emperor*		211	Dura Europos de-
24–37	*Pontius Pilate Procurator*			clared Roman *colonia*
	of Judaea		212	Palmyra declared

	Roman *colonia*
211–17	*Caracalla emperor*
212	*constitutio antoniniana declares all free inhabitants of Empire Roman citizens*
218–22	*Marcus Antoninus (Elagabalus) emperor*
222–35	*Alexander Severus emperor*
224	Sasanian dynasty under Ardashir (r 224–41) takes power in Parthia
241–72	*Shapur I ruler of Sasanians*
244–9	*Philip 'the Arab' emperor*
244	founding of Shahba to commemorate Philip's family
253–60	*Valerian emperor*
256	**Dura Europos falls to Sasanians**
260	amid anarchy in Syria (Shapur I conquers as far as Antioch), Valerian captured (and later killed) by Sasanians at Edessa
260–8	*Gallienus emperor*
260	Gallienus seeks help of Odenathus (Palmyrene leader) in pushing Sasanians back to Euphrates
267/8–72	**Zenobia** takes control on Odenathus' death
270–5	*Aurelian emperor*
272	**Aurelian takes Palmyra** – Zenobia captured
273	Aurelian puts down second revolt in Palmyra
284–305	*Diocletian emperor*
305–11	*Constantius emperor (west), Galerius (east)*
306–37	*Constantine I emperor*
313	*Edict of Milan recognises Christians' right to practice their faith*
325	*First Ecumenical Council, Nicaea*
326	pilgrimage by Helena (Constantine's mother, later St Helen) to Jerusalem
330	*Constantine dedicates **new capital, Constantinople***
337–61	*Constantius II emperor*
361–3	*Julian 'the Apostate' emperor*
375	*Arian schism in church*

379–95	*Theodosius I emperor*
381	*Second Ecumenical Council – Constantinople*
395– 636	**Byzantine Period**
395	*Roman Empire formally split between east and west*
395–408	*Arcadius emperor (east)*
389–459	*life of St Simeon 'the stylite"*
422	'One Hundred Year Peace' with Sasanians
post-423	*rise of Nestorianism*
431	*Third Ecumenical Council, Ephesus – condemns Nestorians*
451	*Fourth Ecumenical Council, Chalcedon – condemns Monophysites*
474–91	*Zeno emperor*
post-475	*pilgrimage centre honouring St Simeon built*
518–27	*Justin I Emperor*
527–65	*Justinian emperor*
532	Justinian's 'eternal peace' with Sasanians
532–7	*building of Hagia Sophia, Constantinople*
553	*Fifth Ecumenical Council – Constantinople – fails to deflect Monophysite split by reviving condemnation of Nestorianism*
565–78	*Justin II emperor*
573	Chosroes I (Persian ruler) raids Syria as far as Apamea, Antioch
582–602	*Maurice emperor*
590–627	*Chosroes II Persian ruler – gains throne with help from Maurice*
602	Maurice murdered by usurper Phocas – Chosroes II subsequently breaks treaty and invades Syria in retaliation
610–41	*Heraclius emperor*
611–4	*Chosroes II takes Syria, including Damascus*
622	Muhammad leaves Mecca for Medina – **Hijra**
622–8	Heraclius' counter-offensive against Persians – reaches Ctesiphon

632	***death of Muhammad***		disaffection encourages
632–4	*Abu Bakr caliph*		spread of Shiism
634–48	*Umar caliph*	*868–905*	*Tulunids in Egypt*
635	Muslim army takes	*935–969*	*Ikhshidids in Egypt*
	Damascus for first time	*944–1003*	Hamdanid dynasty
636	**Battle of Yarmuk**		controls Aleppo
	results in Arab defeat	*944–67*	Saif al-Daula's
	of Byzantine forces –		rule, Aleppo
	opens Syria to Islamic		
	rule – Damascus taken	**969–1055**	**Fatimid Period**
637	Aleppo falls to Muslims		
637	**Battle of Qadissiye** –	*969*	*Fatimids set up rival*
	Arabs defeat Persians		*Caliphate – establish new*
638	last Syrian towns		*capital al-Qahira (Cairo)*
	fall to Arabs	*978–1076*	*Fatimids in southern Syria*
640–61	*Muawiya governor of Syria*	*969–997*	*Byzantine push to*
644–56	*Othman caliph*		*regain Syria – ends*
656–61	*Ali caliph*		*in treaty recognising*
656	*Muawiya refuses loyalty to*		*Fatimid supremacy*
	Ali – first Arab civil war	*996–1021*	*al-Hakim second Fatimid*
661	*Ali murdered*		*caliph – Druze later*
			revere him as last Imam
661–750	**Umayyad Period**	*1037*	*Seljuk Turks in effective*
			control in Baghdad
661–81	**Muawiya Caliph –**		
	makes Damascus	**1055–1128**	**Seljuk Period**
	his capital		
668–85	*Constantine IV emperor*	1055	Seljuks take northern Syria
672	*Umayyad forces reaches Sea*		on behalf of Abbasids
	of Marmora – subsequently	*1070–72*	*Alp Arslan, Seljuk sutlan*
	besiege Constantinople	1071	**Battle of Manzikert** –
679	Umayyad-Byzantine truce		Seljuks defeat Byzantine
	– Umayyads abandon		army, control all Syria
	attempt to control Aegean	*1072–92*	*Malik Shah I Seljuk sultan*
680–3	*Yazid caliph*	*post-1078*	*Seljuks begin fortification*
685–705	*Abd al-Malik caliph*		*of Damascus Citadel*
705–15	*Abu al-Abbas al-*	*1095*	*Pope Urban II preaches*
	Walid caliph		***First Crusade** at Council*
706–14	*building of Umayyad*		*of Clermont-Ferrand*
	Mosque, Damascus	1098, March	Edessa taken by Crusaders
post-715	*construction of Great*	1098, June	Crusaders take Antioch
	Mosque, Aleppo		after nine month siege
724–43	*Hisham caliph*	1098, December	
744–50	*Marwan II last*		Crusaders massacre
	Umayyad caliph		population of Maarat
			al-Numan
750–968	**Abbasid Period**	*1099, July*	***First Crusade takes***
			Jerusalem
754–75	*al-Mansur caliph*	*post-1100*	*first Ismaeli presence,*
762	*foundation of Baghdad*		*beginning in Aleppo*
772	*construction of Raqqa*	1108	Latakia taken by Crusaders
786–809	*Harun al-Rashid caliph*	1109	Crusaders take Tripoli
813	Damascus revolts	*1116–54*	Tughtagin dynasty in
	against Abbasids		Damascus – nominally
842	further revolts in Syria –		on behalf of Fatimids

1118	al-Ghazi invited by Aleppo to garrison city against Crusader threat		truce with Saladin – Christians allowed access to Jerusalem
1119	'Ager Sanguinis' battle near Sermada – Crusader forces defeated by Seljuks from Aleppo	1193–1215	al-Zaher Ghazi Ayyubid governor of Aleppo
1124/5	Crusader attack on Aleppo fails	post-1193	on Saladin's death, succession disputed, empire fragments

1128–1174   Zengid Period

		post-1200	*major Ayyubid-endowed building programs in Damascus – especially for promotion of Islamic learning and for fortification of city*
1128–46	Zengi atabeq (regent) of Aleppo		
1128–9	first Crusader attack on Damascus	1202–4	*Fourth Crusade – occupies Constantinople*
post-1128	*Zengid push to restore Sunni orthodoxy*	1217–21	Fifth Crusade – fails to take Egypt
post-1130	*Ismaelis (Assassins) move into coastal mountains*	1227	Cairo Ayyubid, al-Kamil, hands back Jerusalem to Christians
1144	Zengi regains Edessa	1244	Turkish invaders
1146–74	Nur al-Din's rule		restore Muslim control of Jerusalem
1147–9	**Second Crusade –** unsuccessful attack on Damascus	1248–50	St Louis' Crusade in Egypt fails – retires to Acre
post-1162	active career of Ismaeli leader, Rashid al-Din Sinan ('Old Man of the Mountain')	1258	Mongols sack Baghdad – caliph murdered
1171	*Saladin restores nominal Abbasid authority in Cairo – ends Fatimid Caliphate*	1260	**first Mongol invasion** – under Hulaga

1176–1260   Ayyubid Period

1260–1516   Mamluk Period

		1260	**Battle of Ain Jalud –** Mamluks defeat Mongols
1176–93	*Saladin's rule – invited to take succession to Nur al-Din*	1260–1382	*Bahri Mamluks*
1186	Saladin takes full control of Aleppo – unites central Muslim lands from Baghdad to Cairo	1260–77	al-Zaher Baybars Mamluk sultan
		1261	Baybars installs al-Mustansir in Cairo as caliph
1186–1216	al-Zaher Ghazi Ayyubid governor of Aleppo	1268	Antioch falls to Mamluks
1187	**Battle of Hattin** – Saladin defeats Crusader army – goes on to take Jerusalem	1271	Krak des Chevaliers falls to Baybars
		1280–90	Qalawun Mamluk sultan
1187–92	**Third Crusade –** recovers coastal ports	1281	Qalawun defeats Mongol invasion
1188	Saladin's campaign along Syrian coast against Crusader positions – Qalaat Saladin (Saône), Burzey fall	1285	Marqab falls to Qalawun
		1287	Latakia falls
		1289	Tripoli falls
		1291	Tartus falls
		1300–3	**fourth Mongol invasion** – Damascus occupied
1192	Richard Coeur de Lion's	1302	Arwad, last Crusader position in Syria, falls to Muslims

1312–40	Tengiz Mamluk governor of Damascus	1832–40	Ibrahim Pasha administers Syria on behalf of Muhammad Ali
1382–1516	*Burji Mamluks*	1840	Ottomans restore their authority in Syria, Egypt
1400–1	**last Mongol invasion** – under **Timur** – Damascus besieged for 40 days	*1840*	*Druze-Christian tensions in Lebanon break out*
1453	*Constantinople falls to Ottoman Turks*	1860	massacre of Christians in Damascus
1468–96	Qaitbey Mamluk sultan	1863	paved road Beirut-Damascus completed
1500–16	Qansawh al-Ghawri Mamluk sultan	1893	major fire in prayer hall of Umayyad Mosque, Damascus

1516–1918	**Ottoman Period**

1516	**Ottoman Turks** take Syria	**post-1918**	**Modern Period**
1520–66	*Suleiman ('the Magnificent') Ottoman sultan*	1918	**Allied forces enter Damascus**
1548f	*first Ottoman 'capitulation' treaties with European powers – subsequently led to European consulates being established in Aleppo*	1918–9	Feisal king of Syria
		1920–45	French Mandate
		1925	revolt begins in Hauran against French rule
1555	Suleiman undertakes building of Tekkiye Mosque, Damascus	1936	France cedes Antioch and Alexandretta to Turkey
1590–1635	*Fakhr al-Din's rule in Lebanon, Muhammad Ali, pasha in Cairo*	1945	Syria admitted to the United Nations
		1946	last French troops leave

Bibliography

The following list of books and journal articles consulted for this survey is in two parts. Books and articles cited in REFS at the end of each gazetteer entry are listed in the first section, considerably updated since Monuments of Syria initially went to press (1991). The second section lists works of wider background interest.

Those titles on both lists which are of most interest to the general reader are marked with a □ before the title though this is not intended to imply that the works are in print.

Abbreviations

Three important journals are devoted to the publication of reports on research in Syria - the *Annales archéologiques arabes syriennes* (**AAAS**) published in Damascus by the Directorate-General of Antiquities and Museums, the annual **Syria** published by the Institut français du Proche-Orient (IFPO) in Beirut and *Damaszener Mitteilungen* (**DaM**) by the German archaeological institute in Damascus. In addition, a vast amount of relevant information is contained in the two editions of the *Encyclopedia of Islam* published by E J Brill in Leiden, now also available in electronic form (see **EI** below).

Other abbreviations:

AE   Butler, Howard Crosby (et al) Publications of the **American** Archaeological **Expedition** to Syria, 1899–1900 New York 1903, including:
          Part II – Architecture and Other Arts
BEO   Bulletin d'Etudes Orientales
BG   **Blue Guide** (Hachette World Guide) The Middle East Lebanon, Syria, Jordan Iraq, Iran (Boulanger, Robert ed.) Paris 1966
CFAS Contribution française à l'archéologie syrienne 1969–1989 Damascus 1989
CRAI Comptes rendus des séances de l'Academie des Inscriptions et Belles-Lettres
EC   Butler, Howard Crosby **Early Churches** in Syria, 4ᵗʰ to 7ᵗʰ Centuries (re-print) Amsterdam 1969
EI   **Encyclopaedia of Islam** – published in two editions, EI1 Leiden 1913–1938; EI2 Leiden 1971–1999 (electronic edition 2003)
IGLS Inscriptions grecques et latines de la Syrie Institut français du Proche-Orient (IFPO), Paris-Beirut since the 1930s
MUSJ Mélanges de l'Université Saint Joseph
PE   Butler, Howard Crosby (et al) Publications of the **Princeton** University Archaeological **Expedition** to Syria (1904–5, 9) Leiden 1907–20 including:
                    Division II, Ancient Architecture, Section A – Southern Syria
                    Division II, Ancient Architecture, Section B – Northern Syria
REI   Revue des études islamiques
WW – Damaskus antike
          Watzinger, C & Wulzinger, K Damaskus, die antike Stadt Berlin 1921
WW – Damaskus islamische
          Wulzinger, K & Watzinger, C Damaskus, die islamische Stadt Berlin 1924
var   various

Works cited in REFS and Footnotes

Abu Assaf, Ali 'Ain Dara' *Ebla to Damascus* (Weiss, Harvey ed) Washington 1985

Abu Assaf, Ali *Der Tempel von 'Ain Dara* Mainz am Rhein 1990

Abu Assaf, Ali □ *The Archaeology of Jebel Hauran* Damascus 1998

Allen, T Ayyubid Architecture Occidental (Calif) 1999 (http://sonic.net/~tallen/ palmtree/ayyarch/

Amer, Gh (*et al*) 'L'ensemble basilical de Qanawat (Syrie du sud)' *Syria* 1982

Amer, Gh & Gawlikowski, M 'Le sanctuaire impérial de Philippopolis' *DaM* 2 1985

Amiet, P 'La Syrie ... l'époque des royaumes Amorites XXe-XVIe siècle av. J.-C. *Au Pays de Baal et d'Astarté* Paris 1983

Amy, R 'Temples à escaliers' *Syria* XXVII 1950

anon *Recueil historique – Couvent Patriarcal Orthodoxe de Notre-Dame de Saydnaya* Damascus n.d.

anon *Places in Time – 25 Years of Archaeological Research in Syria 1980–2005* Damascus 2005

Arnaud, D 'Histoire et civilisation écrite 2200–1600 av. J.-C.' *Au Pays de Baal et d'Astarté* Paris 1983

Arush, Abu-l-Faraj al- *Musée National de Damas – Département des Antiquités Arabes et Islamiques – (catalogue)* Damascus 1976

Arush, Abu-l-Faraj al- (*et al*) *A Concise Guide to the National Museum of Damascus* Damascus 1982

Al-As'ad & Yon, J-B *Inscriptions de Palmyre* Beirut 2001

Asakir, Ibn al- *Description de Damas* (trans Elisséeff, Nikita) Damascus 1959

Atassi, Sarab (*et al*) *Damascus Extra-Muros – Midan Sultani* Damascus 1994

Bahnassi, Afif *Damascus* Tunis 1982

Bahnassi, Afif 'Visite archéologique de la vieille cité d'Alep' *BEO* 1986

Bahnassi, A *The Great Omayyad Mosque of Damascus* Damascus 1989

Ball, W *Rome in the East* London 2000

Balty, Janine □ *Mosaïques de Syrie* Brussels 1977

Balty, Janine (ed) 'Apamée de Syrie – Bilan des recherches archéologiques 1973–1979 – Aspects de l'architecture domestique d'Apamée' *Actes du colloque tenu à Bruxelles ... 1980* Brussels 1984

Balty, Janine & J C 'Apamée de Syrie, archéologie et histoire. I. Des origines à la Tétrarchie' *Aufstieg und Niedergang der römischen Welt* II.8 Berlin 1979

Balty, J C 'Le groupe épiscopal à Apamée, dit "Cathédrale de l'est" – premières recherches' *Actes du colloques Apamée de Syrie* Brussels 1972

Balty, J C □ *Guide d'Apamée* Brussels 1981

Barbir, K K *Ottoman Rule in Damascus, 1708–1758* Princeton 1980

Bauzou, T *A finibus Syriae* Paris Ph D thesis, Univ Paris I 1989

Bavant, B (*et al*) 'La mission de Syrie du nord' *Contribution française à l'archéologie syrienne 1969–1989* Damascus 1989

Bell, Gertrude *Amurath to Amurath* London 1911

Bell, Gertrude □ *The Desert and the Sown* London 1985

Berchem, Max von & Fatio, Edmond *Voyage en Syrie* Cairo 1914

Bermant, Chaim & Weitzman, Michael *Ebla – An Archaeological Enigma* London 1979

Bevan, Edwyn Robert *The House of Seleucous* London 1902 (2 vols)

Beyer, H W *Der syrische kirchenbau* Berlin 1925

Bianca, S *Syria – Medieval Citadels Between East and West* Turin 2007

Biller, Thomas & Burger, Daniel
'Qalat Yahmur, castrum
    rubrum: Ein Beitrag
    zum Burgenbau der
    Kreuzfahrerstaaten' *DaM*
    14 2004
Biller, Thomas (*et al*)
    □*Der Crac des Chevaliers*
    Regensburg 2006
Biscop, Jean-Luc & Sodini, Jean-Pierre
'Qal`at Sem`an et les
    chevets à colonnes de
    Syrie du nord' *Syria* 1984
Bloom, Jonathan
    Minaret – Symbol of Islam
    London 1989
Boase, T S R   □*Castles and Churches
    of the Crusading Kingdom*
    London 1967
Bonatz, D (*et al*)
    *Rivers and Steppes,
    Catalogue to the Museum
    of Deir ez-Zor* Damascus
    1998
Bounni, Adnan'Le sanctuaire du Nabu ...
    Palmyre' *CFAS* Damascus
    1989
Bounni, Adnan'Ras Ibn Hani' *Au Pays de
    Baal et d'Astarté* Paris 1983
Bounni, Adnan & Alas`ad, Khaled
    *Palmyre – Histoire,
    Monuments et Musée*
    Damascus 1982
Braune, M   'Die mittelalterlichen
    Befestigungen der Stadt
    Tortosa' *DaM* 2 1985
Braune, M   'Untersuchungen
    zur milteralterlichen
    Befestigung in
    Nordwest-Syrien: Die
    Assassinenberg Masyaf'
    DaM 1993
Bredel, B & Lange, B
    A House in Damascus
    Copenhagen 2003
Brisch, K   'Das omayyadische Schloß
    in Usais' *Mitteilungen des
    deutschen archäologischen
    Instituts Abteilung Kairo*
    1963, 1965
Browning, Iain □*Palmyra* London 1979
Brümmer, Elfriede
    'Der Römische Tempel
    von Dmeir. Vorbericht'
    DaM 2 1985
Burman, Edward
    *The Assassins – Holy Killers
    of Islam* London 1987
Burns, Ross   □*Damascus – A History*
    London 2005
Butler, Howard Crosby

AE – Publications of the
    American Archaeological
    Expedition to Syria, 1899–
    1900 New York 1903,
    including:
    *Part II – Architecture and
    Other Arts*
Butler, Howard Crosby
    PE – Publications of the
    Princeton University
    Archaeological Expedition
    to Syria (1904–5, 9) Leiden
    1907–20 including:
    *Division II Section A –
    Southern Syria
    Division II, Section B –
    Northern Syria*
Butler, Howard Crosby
    EC – Early Churches in
    Syria, 4ᵗʰ to 7ᵗʰ Centuries*
    Princeton 1929
Bylinski, Janusz
    'Survey of the Arab
    Castle in Palmyra'
    *Polish Archaeology in the
    Mediterranean* 1993
Bylinski, Janusz
    'Qal`at Shirkuh at Palmyra:
    A medieval fortress
    reinterpreted' *BEO* LI 1999
Callot, O & Marcillat-Jaubert, J
    'Les Temples romains du
    massif calcaire de Syrie
    du nord' *CFAS* Damascus
    1989
Calvet, Y & Geyer, B
    Barrages antiques de Syrie
    Lyon 1992
Canby, Jeanny Vorys
    'Guzana (Tell Halaf)' *Ebla
    to Damascus* (Weiss,
    Harvey ed) Washington
    1985
Canivet, Marie-Thérése & Pierre
    'L'ensemble ecclésial de
    Huarte d'Apamée (Syrie)'
    Syria LVI 1979
Canivet, Pierre'Huarte – l'ensemble
    ecclésial' *CFAS* Damascus
    1989
Cathcart King, D J
    'The Taking of Le Krak
    des Chevaliers in 1271'
    Antiquity XXIII 1949
Cathcart King, D J
    *Defences of the Citadel of
    Damascus* 1951
Chad, C   *Les dynastes d'Emèse* Beirut
    1972
Chapot, V   *La frontière de l'Euphrate*
    Paris 1907

Chéhab, Kamel
'Le musée de Ma`arat al-
Numan' *Syria* LXIV 1987
Chéhab, Maurice
*Fouilles de Tyr – la
Nécropole – I l'Arch de
Triomphe* special issue
of *Bulletin du Musée de
Beyrouth* 1983
Cholidis, Nadja & Martin, Ludz
*Der Tell Halaf und sein
Ausgräber Max Freiherr von
Oppenheim* Berlin 2002
Clarke, G. W.
*Jebel Khalid on the
Euphrates. Report on
Excavations 1986–96 I*
Sydney 2001
Clarke, G W & Jackson, H
'Jebel Khalid on the
Euphrates: An Overview'
AAAS XLV–XLVI 2002–3
Clauss, P
'Les tours funéraires du
Djebel Baghouz dans
l'histoire de la tour
funéraire syrienne' *Syria*
79, 2002
Cluzan, S (*et al, edd.*)
☐ *Syrie – Mémoire et
Civilisation* Paris 1993
Cohen, Getzel *The Hellenistic Settlements
in Syria, the Red Sea Basin
and North Africa* Berkeley
2006
Colledge, Malcolm
☐ *The Art of Palmyra*
London 1976
Courbin, P 'Bassit' *CFAS* Damascus
1989
Creswell, K A C
☐ *Early Muslim Architecture*
vol I, parts 1 and 2,
Oxford, 1969, vol II
Oxford 1940
Creswell, K A C
'The Great Mosque
of Hama' *Aus der Welt
der islamischen Kunst –
Festschrift Kühnel* Berlin
1959
Crowfoot, J W
*Churches at Bosra and
Samaria-Sebaste* London
1937
Crowfoot, J W
Early Churches in Palestine
London 1941
Dabrowa, E *Roman and Byzantine Army
in the East* Krakow 1995
DAI (Deutsches Archäologisches Institut,
Damascus Branch)

☐ *Places in Time – 25 Years
of Archaeological Research
in Syria 1980–2005*
Damascus 2005
Daiber, V. & Becker, A.
*Raqqa V – Baudenkmäler
und Paläste* 2004
Dangles, Philippe
*Saône – Rapport
préliminaire de la mission
effectué du 15 au 20
mai 2002* website:
castellorient.com 2004
(accessed Jan 2006)
Darrous, N & Rohmer, J
'Chahba-Philippolis
(Hauran) : Essai de
synthèse archéologique et
historique' *Syria* 81 2004
David, Jean-Claude & Degeorge, Gérard
Alep Paris 2002
Delehaye, H *Les Saints Stylites* Paris
1923
De Lorey, E & Wiet, G
'Cénotaphes de deux
dames musulmanes à
Damas' *Syria* II 1921
de Lorey, E 'Mosaics of the Great
Mosque of Umayyads in
Damascus' in Creswell
Early Muslim Architecture,
New York 1979
Dentzer, J-M 'Six campagnes de fouilles
à Si" *DaM* 1985
Dentzer, J-M (ed.)
☐ *Hauran I – Recherches
archéologiques sur la
Syrie du sud à l'époque
hellénistique et romaine*
Paris 1986
Dentzer, J-M 'Bosra' *CFAS* Damascus
1989
Dentzer, J-M 'Fouilles et prospections
à Si` (Qanawat)' *CFAS*
Damascus 1989
Dentzer, J-M & Orthmann, W (edd.)
*Archéologie et histoire de la
Syrie* Saarbrucken 1989
Dentzer, J-M *Le Djebel al-`Arab* Paris
1991
Dentzer, J-M, Blanc, P-M, Fournet, T
'Le développement urbain
de Bosra de l'époque
nabatéenne à l'époque
byzantine : bilan des
recherches françaises
1981–2002' *Syria* 79 2002
Dentzer-Feydy, J
'Les Temples de l'Hermon,
de la Bekaa et de la Vallée
du Barada' *Topoi* 1999

Dentzer-Feydy, J (et al)
> Bosra, aux portes de l'Arabie
> Beirut 2007

Deschamps, Paul
> Les châteaux des croisées en
> Terre Sainte – I Le Crac des
> Chavaliers – étude historique
> et archéologique Paris 1934
> (2 vols)

Deschamps, Paul
> Les châteaux des croisées en
> Terre Sainte – III La défense
> du Comté de Tripoli et de la
> Principauté d'Antioche Paris
> 1973 (2 vols)

de Vogüé, Melchior
> Syrie Centrale – architecture
> civile et religieuse du Ier au
> VIe siècles Paris 1865–77
> (2 vols)

Dignas, Beatriz
> The Economy of the Sacred
> in Hellenistic and Roman
> Asia Minor Oxford 2003

Dodd, Erica Cruikshank
> 'The Monastery of
> Mar Musa al-Habashi
> near Nebek, Syria' Arte
> mediaevale I 1992

Dodd, Erica Cruikshank
> □ The Frescoes of Mar
> Musa Al-Habashi : A Study
> in Medieval Painting in Syria
> Rome 2001

Donceel, R   'L'exploration de Qanouat
> (Qanawat)' AAAS XXXIII
> 1983

Donceel-Voûte, P
> 'A propos de la grande
> basilique de Soueida-
> Dionysias et de ses
> évêques' Le Muséon 1987

Downey, Susan
> 'The Citadel Palace at
> Dura Europos' Syria 1986

Downey, Susan
> Mesopotamian Religious
> Architecture Princeton 1988

du Mesnil du Buisson, Robert
> 'La basilique chrétienne du
> quartier Karm al-Arabis à
> Homs' MUSJ XV 1930

du Mesnil du Buisson, Robert
> Le site archéologique de
> Mishrifé-Qatna Paris 1935

Dunand, Maurice
> Le musée de Soueida Paris
> 1934

Dunand, Maurice & Saliby, Nessib
> Le temple d'Amrith dans la
> pérée d'Aradus Paris 1985

Dussaud, Réné
> Topographie historique de la
> Syrie antique et mediévale
> Paris 1927

Dussaud, Réné
> 'Le Temple de Jupiter
> Damascène' Syria III 1922

EC   see Butler, H C

Ecochard, Michel
> 'Consolidation et
> restauration du portail du
> temple de Bel à Palmyre'
> Syria XVIII 1937

Ecochard, Michel
> 'Note sur un édifice
> chrétien d'Alep' Syria 1950

Ecochard, Michel & le Coeur, Claude
> Les bains de Damas Beirut
> 1942

Edwell, Peter   Between Rome and Persia
> London 2008

Eidem, Jesper 'Across the Euphrates
> – The Region of Qal`at
> Najm and Reflections on
> Some Trans-Euphrates
> Routes' AAAS XLIII 1999

Elisséeff, N   'Les monuments de Nür
> al-Din' BEO 1949–51

Elisséeff, N   La déscription de Damas
> d'Ibn 'Asakir Damascus
> 1959

Elisséeff, N & Paillet, J L
> 'Deuxième mission au
> château de Rahba' AAAS
> 1986

Enlart, Camille Les Monuments des
> Croisées dans le Royaume
> de Jérusalem – Architecture
> religieuse et civile Paris
> 1927–8

Ettinghausen, Richard & Grabar, Oleg
> □ The Art and Architecture
> of Islam 650–1250
> Harmondsworth 1987

Eydoux, Henri-Paul
> Les châteaux de soleil Paris
> 1982

Faucherre (et al, edd.)
> La fortification au temps des
> Croisades Rennes 2004

Fedden, Robin
> Crusader Castles – A
> Brief Study in the Military
> Architecture of the Crusades
> London 1950

Finsen, Helge (ed)
> 'Le levée du théâtre
> romain à Bosra, Syrie'
> Analecta Romana Instituti
> Danici VI Supplementum
> 1972

Flood, Finbarr Barry
'Umayyad survivals
and Mamluk Revivals:
Qalawunid Architecture
and the Great Mosque of
Damascus' *Muqarnas* 14
1997

Frankfort, Henri
☐ *The Art and Architecture
of the Ancient Orient*
Harmondsworth 1970

Freyburger, Klaus S
'Untersuchungen zur
Baugeschichte des Jupiter-
Heiligtums in Damaskus'
DaM 2 1985

Freyburger, Klaus S
'Einige Beobachtungen
zur stätdtbaulichen
Entwicklung des römischen
Bostra' *DaM* 4 1989

Freyburger, Klaus S
'Die Bauten und Bildwerke
von Phillippolis' *DaM* 1992

Freyberger, Klaus S
'Der ‚Peripteraltempel'
in Qanawat: Ein
Arbeitsbericht' *DaM* 7
1993

Freyberger, Klaus S
*Die frühkaiserzeitlichen
Heiligtürmer der
Karawanenstationen im
hellenisierten Osten* Mainz
am Rhein 1998

Freyberger, Klaus S
'The Roman Kanatha: The
Results of the Campaigns
in 1997/1998' *BEO* 2000

Freyberger, Klaus S
'Das Heiligtum in Hössn
Soleiman (Baitokaike)'
DaM 14 2004

Frézouls, Edmond
'Cyrrhus et la
Cyrrhestique jusqu'à
la fin du Haut-Empire'
*Aufstieg und Niedergang der
römischen Welt* II, 8 Berlin
1979

Frézouls, Edmond
'Mission archéologique de
Cyrrhus' *CFAS* Damascus
1989

Gabrieli, Francesco
*Arab Historians of the
Crusades* London 1984

Gatier, P-L 'Palmyre et Émèse, ou
Émèse sans Palmyre' *AAAS*
1996

Gatier, P-L 'La principauté d'Abila de
Lysanias dans l'Antiliban'
Dossiers d'archéologie 279
2002

Gawlikowski, M
'Palmyra as a Trading
Centre' *Iraq* 56 1994

Gawlikowski, M
'Un nouveau mithraeum'
CRAI 2000

GB Guide Bleu – Syrie, Palestine,
Iraq, Transjordanie Paris
1932

Genequand, Denis
'Al-Bakhra (Avatha)'
Levant 36 2004

Genequand, Denis
'From "desert castle" to
mediaeval town: Qasr
al-Hayr al-Sharqi (Syria)'
Antiquity 79 2005

Genequand, Denis
'Some Thoughts on Qasr
al-Hayr al-Gharbi' *Levant*
38 2006

Geyer, B & Monchambert, J-Y
*La basse vallée de l'Euphrate
syrien* Beirut 2003

Gibb, Hamilton A R
'Arab-Byzantine Relations
under the Umayyad
Caliphate' *Dumbarton Oaks
Papers* 12 1958

Gogräfe, R 'Die Datierung des
Tempels von Isriye' *DaM* 7
1993

Gogräfe, R 'The Temple of Seriane-
Esriye' *AAAS* 1996

Goodwin, Godfrey
'The Tekke of Suleyman I,
Damascus *PEFQ* 1978–79

Goodwin, Godfrey
☐*A History of Ottoman
Architecture*, London, 1987

Goosens, G *Hiérapolis de Syrie* Louvain
1943

Grabar, Oleg 'La Grande Mosquée de
Damas et les origines
architecturales de la
mosquée' *Synthronon* Paris
1968

Grabar, Oleg (*et al*)
*City in the Desert – Qasr
al-Hayr East* 2 vols Harvard
University Press 1978

Grainger, J D *The Cities of Seleukid Syria*
Oxford 1990

Gray, John *The Canaanites* London
1964

Gschwind, Markus
'Zum Stadtgebiet von Abila
Lysaniae' *DaM* 2004

Hadjar, Abdallah
'Die römischen Straßen in
Syrien' Das Altertum 1979
Hadjar, Abdallah
Church of St Simeon Aleppo
nd
Hadjar, Abdallah
☐Historical Monuments of
Aleppo Aleppo 2000
Hakim & Jawish
Ma`lula und Saydnaya
Damascus 2000
Hallam, Elizabeth (ed.)
Chronicles of the Crusades
London 1989
Halm, Heinz 'Les Fatimides à Salamya'
REI 1986
Hatoum, Hassan
Philippopolis Damascus
1996
Hatoum, Hassan
'L'antique Chahba-
Philippopolis' BEO 2000
Heidemann, Stefan & Becker, Andrea
Raqqa II – die islamische
Stadt Mainz am Rhein 2003
Herzfeld, Ernst
'Damascus, Studies in
Architecture' I–IV Ars
Islamica 9 1942, 10 1943,
11/12 1946, 13/14 1948
Herzfeld, Ernst
Inscriptions et Monuments
d'Alep (vol 1) Cairo 1955
Hillenbrand, R 'La Dolce Vita in Early
Islamic Syria: The Evidence
of the Later Umayyad
Palaces' Art History 5/1
March 1982
Hillenbrand, R 'Eastern Islamic Influences
in Syria: Raqqa and Qal`at
Ja`bar in the Later 12th
Century' The Art of Syria
and the Jazira 1100–1250
Oxford 1985
Hitti, Philip K ☐History of Syria –
Including Lebanon and
Palestine London 1951
Holod-Tretiak, Renata
'Qasr al-Hayr al-Sharqi
– A Mediaeval Town in
Syria' Archaeology 23/3
June 1970
Hopkins, Clark☐The Discovery of Dura-
Europos New Haven 1979
Hourani, Albert
☐The Islamic City – A
Colloquium Oxford 1970
Huygens, R B C
'La campagne de Saladin en
Syrie du nord (1188)' Actes

du colloque Apamée de Syrie
Brussels 1972
IGLS   Inscriptions grecques et
latines de la Syrie Paris/
Beirut, various dates
Immerzeel, M 'The Wall Paintings in
the Church of Mar Elian,
Homs' Eastern Christian Art
2 2005
Issa, Abed   A Guide to the National
Museum of Damascus
Damascus 2007
Jones, A H M 'The Urbanization of
the Ituraean Principality'
Journal of Roman Studies 21
1931
Kader, Ingeborg
Propylon und Bogentur
Mainz 1996
al-Kayem, Ali Bimaristan Nur al-Din
Damascus (n.d.)
Keenan, Brigid Damascus – Hidden
Treasures of the Old City
London 2000
Kennedy, David and Riley, Derrick
☐Rome's Desert Frontiers
from the Air London 1990
Kennedy, Hugh
☐Crusader Castles
Cambridge 1994
Keriaky   Maaloula History and Ruins
Damascus 1996
Key Fowden, E
The Barbarian Plain 1999
Khayyata, Wahid
Guide to the Museum of
Aleppo – Ancient Oriental
Department Aleppo 1977
King, G R D 'Archaeological Fieldwork
at the Citadel of Homs,
Syria: 1995–1999' Levant
34 2002
Kissel, Theodor
'Die Brücke bei Nimreh'
Antike Welt 2/2000
Klengel, Horst
Syria antiqua – Vorislamische
Denkmaler der Syrischen
Arabischen Republik Leipzig
1971
Klengel, Horst
'Hosn es-Suleiman – ein
Heiligtum in Syriens
Küstenbergen' Das
Altertum 22 1976
Klengel, Horst
Syrien zwischen Alexander
und Muhammad –
Denkmale aus Antike und
frühem Christentum Vienna
1987

Klinkott, Manfred
'Ergebnisse der
Bauaufnahme am "Tempel"
von Dmeir' *DaM* 4 1989

Kohlmeyer, Kay
'Ugarit (Ras Shamra)'
Ebla to Damascus (Weiss,
Harvey ed) Washington
1985

Korn, Lorenz *Ayyubidische Architektur
in Agypten und Syrien*
Heidelberg 2004 (2 vols)

Krautheimer, Richard
☐*Early Christian and
Byzantine Architecture*
Harmondsworth 1981

Kreikenbom, D (*et al*)
*Urbanistik und stätische
Kultur in Westasien und
Nordafrika unter den Severn*
Worms 2005

Krencker, D & Zschietzschmann, W
Römische Tempeln in Syrien
Berlin 1938

Lagarce, J & E *Ras Ibn Hani – archéologie
et histoire* Damascus 1987

Lagarce, J (*et al*)
'Les dixième et onzième
campagnes de fouilles
(1984 et 1986) à Ras Ibn
Hani' *CRAI* Apr-Jun 1987

Lapidus, Ira M ☐*Muslim Cities in the Later
Middle Age* Cambridge
1947

Lapidus, Ira M *A History of Islamic Societies*
Cambridge 1988

Lassus, Jean *Sanctuaires chrétiens de
Syrie* Paris 1947

Lassus, Jean 'Deux églises cruciformes
du Hauran' *Bulletin d'études
orientales de l'Institut
français de Damas* I 1931

Lauffray, Jean *Halabiyya-Zenobia – place
forte du limes oriental et la
Haute-Mésopotamie au VIè
siècle* Paris 1983, 1991 (2
vols)

Lauffray, Jean 'Halebiye-Zenobia' *CFAS*
Damascus 1989

Lawrence, T E *Crusader Castles* London
1986

Lenoir, M 'Dumayr, Faux Camp
Romain, Vraie Résidence
Palatiale' *Syria* 1999

Leriche, P & al-Mahmoud, A
'Doura Europos' *CFAS*
Damascus 1989

Leriche, P 'Urbanisme defensif ' in
*Sociétés urbaines, sociétés
rurales dans l'Asie Mineure
et la Syrie hellénistiques et
romaines* (Frézouls, E ed.)
Strasbourg 1987

Leriche, P & al-Mahmoud, A
Doura-Europos Etudes Beirut
1988

Leriche, P & Gelin, M
Doura-Europos Etudes IV
Beirut 1997

Leroy, Jules 'Decouvertes de peintures
chrétiennes en Syrie' *AAAS*
XXIV 1974

Lightfoot, J L *Lucian: On the Syrian
Goddess* Oxford 2003

Loosley, E *The Architecture and Liturgy
of the Bema in Fourth–
to Sixth–Century Syrian
Churches* Kaslik 2003

Maalouf, Amin ☐*The Crusades Through
Arab Eyes* London 1977

Mallowan, M 'The Excavations at Tell
Chagar Bazar and an
Archaeological Survey of
the Habur Region, 1934–
35' *Iraq* III 1936

Mango, Cyril *Byzantine Architecture* New
York 1976

Mango, Marlia 'Excavations and Survey
at Androna, Syria: The
Oxford Team 1999' *DOP*
2002

Mango, Marlia 'Excavations and Survey
at Androna, Syria: The
Oxford Team 2000' *DOP*
2004

al-Maqdissi, M 'Note sur les sondages
réalisés par Robert du
Mesnil du Buisson dans la
cour du sanctuaire de Bel
à Palmyre' *Syria* 2000

al-Maqdissi, M 'Recherches
archéologiques syriennes à
Mishirfeh-Qatna au Nord-
est de Homs (Émèse'0'
CRAI 2003 : 1587–1515

al-Maqdissi, M & Bonacossi, D M
Metropolis-of-the-Orontes
Damascus 2005

Marcus, A *The Middle East on the Eve
of Modernity: Aleppo in the
Eighteenth Century* New
York 1989

Margueron, J-Cl
'Emar et Faq`ous' *CFAS*
Damascus 1989

Margueron, J-Cl
'Mari – Le Palais du
second millénaire' *Au Pays
de Baal et d'Astarté* Paris
1983

Margueron, J-Cl (*et al*)
'Ugarit au IIe millénaire'

Au Pays de Baal et d'Astarté Paris 1983

Margueron, J-Cl
'Mari ou les debuts de la civilisation urbain en Syrie' *AAAS* XLV–XLVI, 2002–3

Margueron, J-Cl
Mari – Métropole de l'Euphrate au IIIe et au début du IIe millénaire av. J.-C. Paris 2004

Marino, Brigitte
Le faubourg du Midan à l'époque ottomane, Damascus 1997

Matheson, Susan
'Dura-Europos on the Euphrates' *Ebla to Damascus* (Weiss, Harvey ed) Washington 1985

Mattern, J *Villes Mortes de Haute Syrie* Beirut 1944

Mattern, J, Mouterde, R & Beaulieu, A
'Dair Solaib – Les deux églises' *Mélanges de l'Université Saint Joseph* XXII 1939

Matthiae, Paolo
☐*Ebla – An Empire Rediscovered* London 1977

Matthiae, Paolo
'Tell Mardikh, 1977–1996' *Akkadica* 101 1997

Matthiae, Paolo
'Fouilles à Tell Mardikh – Ebla, 1998–2001' *AAAS* 2002–3

McEwan, Calvin W *(et al)*
Soundings at Tell Fakhariyah Chicago 1958

Meinecke, Michael
Der Survey des Damaszener Altstadtviertels as-Salihiya' *DaM* I 1983

Meinecke, Michael
'Raqqa on the Euphrates' *The Near East in Antiquity* vol II Amman 1990

Meinecke, Michael
☐*Mamlukische Architektur in Ägypten und Syrien* Glückstadt 1992

Meinecke, Michael
Patterns of Stylistic Change in Islamic Architecture New York 1996

Meinecke, Michael *(et al)*
☐*Islamic Bosra – A Brief Guide* Damascus 1990

Meinecke, Michael & Aalund, Flemming
Bosra – Islamische

Architektur und Archäologie Rahden 2005

Meyer, M (ed.)*Oxford Encyclopaedia of Archaeology in the Middle East* 1997

Michalowski, Kazimierz
Palmyra New York 1970

Michaudel, Benjamin
'Le Crac des Chevaliers, quintessence de l'architecture militaire mamelouke' *Annales islamologiques* 38/1, 2004

Milburn, R *Early Christian Art and Architecture* Aldershot 1988

Millar, Fergus 'Paul of Samosata, Zenobia and Aurelian: The Church, Local Culture and Political Allegiance in Third Century Syria' *Journal of Roman Studies* 61 1971

Miller, Doris S
The Lava Lands of Syria: Regional Development in the Roman Empire New York 1984

Moaz, Abd al-Razzaq
'Suwayqat Saruja' *Fondation Max van Berchem Bulletin* 1994

Moaz, Khaled & Ory, Solange
Inscriptions arabes de Damas – Les stèles funéraires – I Cimetiére d'al-Bab al-Sagir Damascus 1977

Monceaux, P & Brossé, L
'Chalcis ad Belum' *Syria* VI 1925

Mortensen, Inge *(et al)*
New Museum at Hama Damascus 2000

Mougdad, Sulaiman
☐*Bosra* Damascus 1974

Moussli, M. 'Griechische Inschriften aus Emesa und Laodicea ad Libanum.' *Philologus* 1983

Mouterde, R & Poidebard, A
'Le `Limes' de Chalcis et la route d'Antioche à Palmyre' *Melanges de l'Université Saint Joseph* XXII 1939

Mouterde, R & Poidebard, A
Le limes de Chalcis – Organisation de la steppe en Haute Syrie romaine Paris 1945 (2 vols)

Mouterde, R 'Antiquités de l'Hermon, de la Beqa' *MUSJ* 1951–2

Moussli , M 'Griechische Inschriften aus Emesa und Laodicea ad Libanum' *Philologus* 1983

Mukdad, Khalil
Bosra – le théâtre antique Damascus 2001

Musil, Alois *The Middle Euphrates – A Topographical Itinerary* New York 1927

Musil, Alois *Palmyrena – A Topographical Itinerary* New York 1928

Nasrallah, Elias Antoun *Ma`loula* Damascus 2003

Nasrullah, Joseph 'Voyageurs et Pèlerins au Qalamoun' *BEO* X

Nasrallah, Joseph 'Le Qalamoun à l'époque Romano-Byzantine' *AAAS* 1952, 1956, 1958

Nour, Antoine Abde *Introduction à l'histoire urbaine de la Syrie ottomane (XVIe-XVIIIe siècle)* Beirut 1982

Oates, David & Joan 'Tell Brak – l'empire akkadien' *Les Dossiers d'archéologie* 155 Dec 1990a

Oates, David & Joan 'Aspects of Hellenistic and Roman Settlement in the Khabur Basin' *Resurrecting the Past* (Matthaie *(et al)* edd.) Istanbul 1990b

Oates, David, Joan & McDonald, Helen *Excavations at Tell Brak 2* Oxford 2001

Odenthal, J *Syrien (DuMont Reiseführer)* Cologne 1998

Omran & Dabboura *The Citadel of Damascus* Damascus 1997

Ory, Solange 'L'inscription de fondation de la mosquée al-`Umari à Busra' *DaM* 11 1999

Parr, Peter 'The Tell Nebi Mend Project' *AAAS* 1983

Parr, Peter 'The Tell Nebi Mend Project' *Journal of the Ancient Chronology Forum* 4 1990/91

Parrot, Andre *Mari – capitale fabuleuse* Paris 1974

PE see Butler, H C

Pena, I with Castellana, P & Fernandez, R *Les Stylites syriens* Milan 1975

Pena, I with Castellana, P & Fernandez, R *Les Reclus syriens* Milan 1980

Pena, I with Castellana, P & Fernandez, R *Les Cénobites syriens* Milan 1983

Pena, I *Inventaire du Jebel Baricha* Milan 1987

Pena, I (*et al*) *Inventaire du Djebel el-A'la* 1990

Pena, I *Lieux de pelèrinage en Syrie* Milan 2000

Pensabene, P 'Marmi d'importazione' *Archeologia classica* 1997

Perkins, Ann ☐ *The Art of Dura Europos* Oxford 1973

Perkins, Ann (*et al*, edd.) *The Excavations at Dura Europos – Final Reports 8* vols New Haven various dates

Peters, Frank E 'Byzantium and the Arabs of Syria' *AAAS* 1977–78

Peters, Frank E 'City Planning in Greco-Roman Syria: Some New Considerations', *DaM* 1 1983

Pettinato, Giovanni *The Archives of Ebla – An Empire Inscribed in Clay* New York 1979

Pézard, Maurice *Qadesh* Paris 1931

Pinnock, Frances 'The Urban Landscape of Old Syrian Ebla', *Journal of Cuneiform Studies*, 53, 2001

Piraud-Fournet *Le 'Palais de Trajan' à Bosra. Présentation et hypothèses d'identification*, *Syria*, 80, 2003

Poidebard, A 'Mission archéologique en Haute Djéziré (1928)' *Syria* XI 1930

Poidebard, A ☐ *La trace de Rome dans le désert de Syrie – le limes de Trajan à la conquête arabe – recherches aériennes* Paris 1934 (2 vols)

Pouzet, Louis *Damas au XIIIe siècle – vie et structures religieuses d'une métropole islamique* Beirut 1991

Pringle, Denys *The Churches of the Crusader Kingdom of Jerusalem – A Corpus II (L–Z)* Cambridge 1998

Pritchard, James (ed) ☐ *The Times Concise Atlas*

of the Bible London 1991

Raymond, Andre
□Great Arab Cities of the Sixteenth to Eighteenth Centuries New York 1984

Rey-Coquais, J-P
Arados et sa pérée aux époques grecque, romaine et byzantine Paris 1974

Richmond, I A
'Palmyra Under the Aegis of Rome' Journal of Roman Studies LIII 1963

Rihaoui, Abdulkader
The Krak of the Knights Damascus 1982

Rihawi, Abdulqader
□Damascus – Its History, Development and Artistic Heritage Damascus 1977

Riis, P J
Temple, Church & Mosque Copenhagen 1965

Rostovtzeff, M
Caravan Cities Oxford 1932

Rostovtzeff, M
Dura-Europos and Its Art Oxford 1938

Rostovtzeff, M
Social and Economic History of the Roman Empire Oxford 1957 (2 vols)

Roujon, Y. & Vilan, L.
Le Midan Damascus 1997

Runciman, Steven
□A History of the Crusades Harmondsworth 1965 (3 vols)

Ruprechtsberger, Erwin (ed)
Palmyra – Geschichte, Kunst und Kultur der syrischen Oasenstadt Linz 1987

Sa`adé, Gabriel
'Le château de Bourzey, forteresse oublié' AAS 1956

Sa`adé, Gabriel
'Saint Elian de Homs' Beirut 1974

Sa`adé, Gabriel
'L'exploration archéologique de Lattaquie' AAAS 26 1976

Sa`adé, Gabriel
Ougarit – Métropole Cananéenne Beirut 1979

Sa`adé, Gabriel
'Histoire du Château de Saladin' Studi Mediaevali 9 1968

Sachau, Eduard
Am Euphrat und Tigris

Leipzig 1900

Sack, Dorothée
'Damaskus, die Stadt intra muros. Ein Beitrag zu den Arbeiten der Internationalen Kommission zum Schutz der Altstadt von Damaskus' DaM 2 1985

Sack, Dorothée
□Damaskus – Entwicklung und Struktur einer orientalisch-islamischen Stadt Mainz am Rhein 1989

Sack, Dorothée
Rusafa V Mainz 1996

Sadan, Joseph
'Le tombeau de Moïse à Jéricho et à Damas' REI XLIX 1981

Sader, Hélène S
Les états araméens de Syrie Wiesbaden 1987

Saliby, N
'Amrith' CFAS Damascus 1989

Saouaf, Soubhi Alep – son histoire, sa citadelle, ses monuments antiques et son musée – Guide des visiteurs Aleppo 1975

Saouaf, Soubhi Saint Simeon Aleppo (n.d.)

Sarre, F & Herzfeld, E
Archäologische Reise im Euphrat- und Tigris-Gebiet Berlin 1911, 1920

Sartre, Maurice
'Le territoire de Canatha' Syria LVIII 1981

Sartre, Maurice
Bostra des origines à l'Islam Paris 1985

Sartre-Fauriat, A
Les voyages dans le Hawran (Syrie du Sud) de William John Bankes (1816 et 1818) Beirut 2004

Sauvaget, Jean 'Deux sanctuaires chiites d'Alep' Syria IX 1928

Sauvaget, Jean 'Inventaire des monuments musulmans de la ville d'Alep' Revue des etudes islamiques V 1931

Sauvaget, Jean Les monuments historiques de Damas Beirut 1932

Sauvaget, Jean 'Le plan de Laodicée-sur-mer' Bulletin d'études orientales 4 1935

Sauvaget, Jean 'Esquisse d'une histoire de la ville de Damas' Revue des études islamiques 1934 VIII

Sauvaget, Jean 'Les Caravanserails syriens du Hadjdj de Constinantinople' *Ars Islamica* 1937

Sauvaget, Jean 'Les ruines omeyyades du Jebel Seis' *Syria* XX 1939

Sauvaget, Jean □*Alep – Essai sur le développement d'une grande ville syrienne des origines au milieu du XIXème siècle* Paris 1941 (2 vols)

Sauvaget, Jean 'Le plan antique de Damas' *Syria* 1949

Sauvaget, Jean 'Châteaux umayyades de Syrie' *Revue des études islamiques* (1967) Paris 1968

Sauvaget, Jean 'Halab' *EI2* Leiden 1971

Sauvaget, Jean & Ecochard, M *Les monuments ayyoubides de Damas* Damascus 1938–50

Scharabi, Muhammad 'Der Suq von Damaskus und zwei traditionelle Handelsanlagen: Han Gaqmaq und Han Sulaiman Pasa' *DaM* I 1983

Schatkowski Schilcher, Linda *Families in Politics – Damascene Factions and Estates of the 18th and 19th Centuries* Stuttgart 1985

Schlumberger, Daniel 'Les fouilles de Qasr el-Heir el-Gharbi (1936–1938) – Rapport préliminaire' *Syria*, 1939

Schlumberger, Daniel *Qasr el-Heir el-Gharbi* Paris 1986

Schmidt, A. & Westphalen, S. *Christliche Wandmalereien in Syrien – Qara und das Kloster Mar Yakub* Wiesbaden 2005

Segal, Arthur *Town Planning and Architecture in Provincia Arabia* Oxford 988

Segal, Arthur *From Function to Monument* Oxford 1997

Seyrig, Henri 'Palmyra and the East' *Journal of Roman Studies* XL 1950

Seyrig, Henri 'Aradus et Baetocaece' *Syria* XXVIII 1951

Seyrig, Henri 'Antiquités de la nécropole d'Emese' *Syria* XXIX 1952

Seyrig, Henri 'Caractères de l'histoire d'Emesse' *Syria* XXXVI 1959

Seyrig, Henri 'La culte du soleil en Syrie à l'époque romaine' *Syria* 1971

Shéhabé, K *The Mosaics of the Ma'arra Museum* Kaslik 1997

Smail, R C □*Crusading Warfare (1097–1193)* Cambridge 1985

Sodini, Jean-Pierre 'Déhès (Syrie du Nord)' *Syria* 1980

Sodini, Jean-Pierre 'Qal'at Sem'an et les chevets à colonnes de Syrie du nord' *Syria*, 1982

Sodini, Jean-Pierre 'Les églises du massif de Belus' *Au Pays de Baal et d'Astarté* Paris 1983

Sodini, Jean-Pierre & Tate, Georges 'Maisons d'époque romaine et byzantine (Ile-Vle siècles) du massif calcaire de Syrie du nord – étude typologique' Balty, Janine (ed.) *Apamée* 1984

Sodini, Jean-Pierre (*et al*) 'Déhès (Syrie du Nord) Campagnes I–III (1976–1978) – Recherches sur l'Habitat Rural' *Syria* 1980

Sodini, Jean-Pierre (*et al*) 'Qal'at Sem'an et son environnement : Essai de synthèse' *AAAS* XLV–XLVI 2002–3

Sournia, Jean-Charles & Marianne *L'orient des premiers chrétiens* Paris 1966

Starcky, Jean 'Palmyre – guide archéologique' *Mélanges de l'université Saint Joseph* Beirut 1941

Starcky, Jean *Palmyre (L'ancien orient illustré)* Paris 1952

Starcky, Jean & Gawlikowsky, Michael *Palmyre* Paris 1985

Strube, Christine 'Androna / al Andarin – Vorbericht über die ungskampagnen in den Jahren 1997–2001' *Archäologischer Anzeiger* 2003/1

al-Tabbaa, Yasser Ahmad *The Architectural Patronage of Nur al-Din (1146–1174)* Ph D dissertation, New York University 1982

al-Tabbaa, Yasser Ahmad *Constructions of Power and*

Piety in Medieval Aleppo, 1178–1260 Pennsylvania 1997

Talass, As`ad *Les mosques de Damas d'après Yousouf Ibn `Abd el-Hadi* Beirut 1943 (Arabic)

Tate, Georges 'Les villages du massif calcaire' *Au Pays de Baal et d'Astarté* Paris 1983

Tate, Georges *Les Campagnes de la Syrie du Nord du IIe au VIIe Siècle* Paris 1992

Tchalenko, Georges *Villages antiques de la Syrie du nord; le massif de Belus à l'époque romaine* Paris 1953–8 (3 vols)

Tchalenko, Georges 'Travaux en cours dans la Syrie du nord' *Syria* L 1973

Tchalenko, Georges 'La basilique de Qalb-loze' *Annales archéologiques arabes syriennes* 24 1974

Tchalenko, Georges & Baccache, E *Eglises de villages de la Syrie du nord* Paris 1979–80 (2 vols)

Teixidor, Javier 'Un port romain du désert – Palmyre et son commerce d'Auguste à Caracalla' special issue of *Semitica* XXXIV Paris 1984

Toll, N P *Excavations at Dura-Europos – Ninth Season 1935–36 – Part II The Necropolis* New Haven 1946

Tonghini, C *(et al)* 'The Evolution of Masonry Technique in Islamic Military Architecture: the Evidence from Shayzar' *Levant* 35 2003

Toueir, Kassem 'Heraqlah: A Unique Victory Monument of Harun al-Rashid' *World Archaeology* 14/3 Feb 1983

Toueir, Kassem 'Der Qasr al-Banat in ar-Raqqa' *DaM* 2 1985

Toueir, Kassem 'Raqqa/Rafiqa' *Ebla to Damascus* (Weiss, Harvey ed) Washington 1985

Trombley, Frank R *Hellenic Religion and Christianization* Boston/ Leiden 2001

Ulbert, Thilo 'Rusafa-Sergiopolis: Pilgrimage Shrine and Capital' *Ebla to Damascus* (Weiss, Harvey ed) Washington 1985

Ulbert, Thilo *Resafa II, Die Basilika des Heiligen Kreuzes in Resafa-Sergiopolis* Mainz 1986

Ulbert, Thilo 'Villes et fortifications de l'Euphrate' *Archéologie et histoire de la Syrie* tome 2 Saarbrücken 1989

van Berchem, Max & Fatio, Edmond *Voyage en Syrie* Cairo 1914

Viviers, D 'Travaux de la Mission archéologique belge à Apamée de Syrie XLe campagne' *Revue belge de Philologie et d'Histoire* 2007

Weber, Stefan 'The Transformation of the Arab-Ottoman Institution – The Suq (Bazar) of Damascus from the 16th to the 20th Century' *Seven Centuries of Ottoman Architecture* Istanbul 2000

Weber, Stefan *Zeugnisse kulturellen Wandels: Architektur und Gessellschaft des osmanischen Damaskus im 19. und frühen 20. Jahrhundert* Utrecht 2006

Weber, Thomas 'Haran al-Awamid' *Antike Welt* 28 1997

Weber, Thomas *Sculptures from Roman Syria in the Syrian National Museum at Damascus* Damascus 2005

Weiss, Harvey (ed.) *Ebla to Damascus* Washington 1985

Wiet, Gaston 'Une inscription de Malik Zahir al-Gazi à Latakieh' *BIFAO* 30 1931

Will, Ernest 'La tour funéraire de la Syrie et les monuments apparentées' *Syria* XXVI 1949

Will, Ernest 'Développement urbain de Palmyre' *Syria* 1983

Willey, Peter *Eagle's Nest – Ismaili Castles in Iran and Syria* London 2005

Wulzinger, K and Watzinger, C **WW – Damaskus –**

antike
Damaskus, die antike Stadt
Berlin 1921–4
Wulzinger, K and Watzinger, C
**WW – Damaskus –
islamische**
*Damaskus, die islamische
Stadt* Berlin 1924
Yon, Marguerite
*La cité d'Ougarit sur le Tell
de Ras Shamra* Paris 1997
Ziadeh, Nicola A
☐*Damascus under
the Mamluks* Norman
(Oklahoma) 1964

**Books and Articles for Further
Reading**

anon   *Au Pays de Baal et d' Astarté*
             Paris 1983
anon   *Contribution française
             à l'archéologie syrienne*
             Damascus 1989
anon   *Syrian-European Archaeology
             Exhibition – Catalogue*
             Damascus 1996
Aharoni, Yohanan
             *The Land of the Bible – A
             Historical Geography*
             London 1974
Baduel, P R (ed)
             *Villes au Levant – Hommage
             … André Raymond* Aix-en-
             Provence 1991
Ball, Warwick *Syria* London 2007
Ball, Warwick ☐*Rome and the East: The
             Transformation of an Empire*
             London 2000
Bourchier, E S *Syria as a Roman Province*
             Oxford 1916
Bowersock, G W
             Roman Arabia Cambridge
             Massachussets 1983
Bowersock, G W
             Hellenism in Late Antiquity
             Cambridge 1990
Butcher, Kevin
             *Roman Syria and the Near
             East* London 2003
Cahen, Claude
             ☐*La Syrie du nord à
             l'époque des Croisades
             et la principauté franque
             d'Antioche* Paris 1940
Caubet, Annie 'Des premiers villages
             aux cités-états' *Beaux Arts*
             (Hors Serie) Paris 1993
Colledge, Malcolm

'Greek and Non-Greek
Interaction in the Art
and Architecture of the
Hellenistic East' *Hellenism
in the East* (Kurht, Emilie
(*et al*, edd.) London 1987
Dalrymple, Willam
             From the Holy Mountain
             London 1997
Davis, Ralph *Aleppo and Devonshire
             Square – English Traders in
             the Levant in the Eighteenth
             Century* London 1967
Davis, Norman & Kraay, Colin M
             *The Hellenistic Kingdoms –
             Portrait Coins and History*
             London 1980
Degeorge, Gérard
             ☐*Palmyre – Métropole du
             désert* Paris 1987
Degeorge, Gérard
             ☐ *Syrie – Art, histoire,
             architecture* Paris 1983
Degeorge, Gérard
             ☐*Damas des origines au
             Mamluks* Paris 1997
Degeorge, Gérard
             ☐*Damas des Ottomans à
             nos jours* Paris 1994
Dentzer, J-M & Dentzer-Feydy, J
             *Le Djebel al-'Arab – Histoire
             et patrimoine au Musée de
             Suweida* Paris 1991
Donner, Fred McGraw
             The Early Islamic conquests
             Princeton 1981
Downey, Michael
             *A History of Antioch in Syria
             – from Seleucus to the Arab
             Conquest* Princeton 1974
Fedden, Robin *Syria – An Historical
             Appreciation* London 1946
Fowden, Garth
             *From Empire to
             Commonwealth* Princeton
             1993
Freyburger, Klaus S
             'Der Tempel von Slim: Ein
             Bericht' *DaM* 5 1991
Freyburger, Klaus S
             'Die Bauten und Bildwerke
             von Phillippolis' *DaM* 6
             1992

Frézouls, Edmond
             'Recherches sur les
             théâtres de l'orient syrien'
             Syria 1959,1961
Frézouls, Edmond
             'Cyrrhus et la
             Cyrrhestique jusqu'à

la fin du Haut Empire'
Aufstieg und Niedergang der Römischen Welt II/8 Berlin 1977

Fugelstad-Aumeunier, V
Alep et la Syrie du Nord Aix-en-Provence 1992

Gaube, H & Wirth, E
Aleppo – Historische und geographische Beitrage (Beihefte zum Tübinger Atlas des Vorderen Orients) Wiesbaden 1984

Gawlikowski, Michael
'Palmyre et l'Euphrate' *Syria* LX 1983

Grabar, Oleg 'Islamic Art and Byzantium' *Dumbarton Oaks Papers* 18, 1964

Grabar, Oleg □ *The Formation of Islamic Art* New Haven 1987

Green, Peter □ *Alexander to Actium – The Hellenistic Age* London 1990

Hillenbrand, Robert
□ Islamic Architecture – Form, Function and Meaning Edinburgh 1994

Houghton, L C
'Survey of the Salihiye Quarter of Damascus' *Art and Archaeology Research Papers* 14 1978

Hourani, Albert
□ *A History of the Arab Peoples* London 1991

Isaac. Benjamin
The Limits of Empire Oxford 1990

Jones, A H M *The Cities of the Eastern Roman Provinces* Oxford 1937

Kennedy, David (ed.)
The Roman Army in the East Ann Arbor 1996

Key Fowden, Elizabeth
The Barbarian Plain: St Sergius Between Rome and Iran Berkeley 1999

Klengel, Horst
The Art of Ancient Syria New York 1972

Kohlmeyer, Kay & Strommenger, Eva (edd)
Land des Baal – Syrien – Forum der Volker und Kulturen Mainz am Rhein 1982

Konzelmann, Gerhard
Damaskus – Oase zwischen Haß und Hoffnung,

Frankfurt/M 1996

Kuhrt, Amélie
□ *The Ancient Near East c 2000–330 BC* London 1995 (2 vols)

Lapidus, Ira M □ *A History of Islamic Societies* Cambridge 1988

Lassus, Jean *Inventaire archéologique de la région Nord-Est de Hama* Damascus 1935 (2 vols)

Lewis, Bernard
The Assassins – A Radical Sect in Islam London 1985

Lifschitz, B 'Etudes sur l'histoire de la province romaine de Syrie' *Aufstieg und Niedergang der römischen Welt* II/8 Berlin 1977

Lovell, Mary S *A Rage to Live: A Biography of Richard and Isabel Burton* London 1998

Lovell, Mary S *A Scandalous Life: The Biography of Jane Digby* London 1995

Lyttelton, Margaret
Baroque Architecture in Classical Antiquity London 1974

Marcus, Abraham
The Middle East on the Eve of Modernity – Aleppo in the Eighteenth Century New York 1989

Margueron, J-Cl & Pfirsch, Luc
Le Proche-Orient et l'Egypte antiques Paris 1996

Mesqui, Jean Châteaux d'Orient, Paris 2001

Michell, George (ed.)
□ *Architecture of the Islamic World – Its History and Social Meaning* London 1978

Milburn, R *Early Christian Art and Architecture* Aldershot 1988

Millar, Fergus □ *The Roman Near East 31 BC – AD 337* Cambridge Mass. 1993

Miller, D S *Lava Lands of Syria* PhD thesis, New York Univ 1984

Moosa, Matti *Extremist Shiites – The Ghulat Sects* Syracuse 1988

Mougdad, Sulaiman A
Bosra – Guide historique et archéologique Damascus 1974

Müller-Wiener, W
□ *Castles of the Crusaders* London 1966

Pirovano, Carlo
    *Da Ebla a Damasco –
    Diecimila Anni di Archeologia
    in Siria* Milan 1985
Raymond, André
    'La conquête ottomane
    et le développement des
    grandes villes arabes' *Revue
    de l'Occident Musulman et
    de la Méditerranée* 27 1979
Rey, Guillaume
    *Etude sur les monuments de
    l'architecture militaire des
    Croisés en Syrie et dans l'isle
    de Chypre* Paris 1871
Rey-Coquais, J-P
    'Syrie romaine, de Pompée
    à Dioclétian' *Journal of
    Roman Studies* 1978
Rey-Coquais, J-P
    'Laodicée-sur-Mer et
    l'armée romaine' *The
    Roman Army in the East* (ed.
    E Dabrowa) Krakow 1995
Riley-Smith, Jonathan (ed)
    ☐ *The Atlas of the Crusades*
    London 1991
Riley-Smith, Jonathan (ed.)
    ☐ *The Oxford Illustrated
    History of the Crusades*
    Oxford 1995
Rostovtzeff, M
    'Syrie romaine' *Revue
    Historique* CLXXV 1935
Salibi, Kamal *Syria Under Islam – Empire
    on Trial 634–1097* New
    York 1977
Sartre, Maurice
    *L'Orient romain – provinces
    et societé provincials en
    Mediterrannée orientale
    d'Auguste aux Sévères* Paris
    1991
Sartre, Maurice
    ☐ *The Middle East Under
    Rome* Cambridge Mass.
    2005
Sauvaget, Jean
    'L'architecture Musulmane
    en Syrie' *Revue des Beaux
    Arts Asiatiques* VIII/1 1934
Seyrig, Henri 'Seleucus 1er et la
    fondation de la monarchie
    syrienne' *Syria* 1949
Smail, R C   'Crusaders' Castles of
    the Twelfth Century'
    Cambridge Historical Journal
    X, 2 1951
Smail, R C   *The Crusaders in Syria and
    the Holy Land* London 1973

Stark, Freya   *Letters from Syria* London
    1946
Stark, Freya   ☐ *Rome on the Euphrates*
    London 1966
Stilwell, Richard (ed.)
    *The Princeton Encyclopedia
    of Classical Sites* Princeton
    1976
Stoneman, Richard
    *Palmyra and Its Empire –
    Palmyra's Revolt Against
    Rome* Ann Arbor 1992
Tchalenko, Georges
    Eglises syriennes à béma
    Paris 1990
Usamah Ibn Munqidh (trans Philip K Hitti)
    ☐ *An Arab-Syrian Gentleman
    and Warrior in the Period
    of the Crusades – Memoirs
    of Usamah Ibn-Munqidh*
    London 1987
var   *Highlights of the National
    Museum of Damascus*
    Damascus 2006
Watenpaugh, Heghnar
    *The Image of an Ottoman
    City – Aleppo in the
    Sixteenth and Seventeenth
    Centuries* Ph D thesis,
    UCLA 1999
Weiss, Harvey (ed.)
    ☐ *Ebla to Damascus – Art
    and Archeology of Ancient
    Syria* Washington 1985
Whitcomb, Donald
    'Hadir Qinnesrin'
    Archéologie islamique 10
    2000
Will, Ernest 'Damas antique' *Syria* LXXI
    1994
Wood, Robert
    *The Ruins of Palmyra,
    otherwise Tedmor in the
    Desert* (re-print of 1753
    edition) Westmead, Hants
    1971

Index to Places and People

Quick Index of Sites

(sites in **bold** are included on the UNESCO World Heritage List 2007)

Site	Period	Map or Plan	Rating
Ain Dara	Ira/Grk	R3	*
Aleppo	BA/Ott	2, 68, 71–2	***
Amrit	Phn/Grk	9, R2	*
Anderin	Rom/Byz	R4	T
Apamea	Hel/../Arb	10, R2	***
Arwad	Phn/../Arb	R2	T
Atil	Rom	R1	*
Baghuz	Rom	R5	-
Bakas (Shugur Qadim)	Cru	11, R2	T
Bamuqqa	Rom/Byz	R2, R3a	-
Baqirha	Rom/Byz	R3, R3a	*
Bara	Byz	12, R3	**
Barad	Rom/Byz	13, R3	-
Basofan	Byz	R2, R3a	-
Behyo	Byz	R3, R3a	-
Beshindlaye	Rom/Byz	R3, R3a	-
Bosra	Rom/Byz/Umd	14, 15	***
Braij	Byz	R3a	-
Burj Haidar	Byz	R3, R3a	*
Burjke	Byz	R3	-
Burqush	Rom/Byz	R1	*
Circesium	Rom	R5	T
Cyrrhus	Hel/Rom/Byz	16, R3	*
Damascus	All	17–27, R1	***
Dana (South)	Rom/Byz	R3	*
Dayhis	Rom/Byz	R3, R3a	-
Deir Mar Mousa	Byz	R1, R4	**
Deir Semaan	Byz	28, R3, R3a	*
Deir Soleib	Byz	R2	-
Deir al-Zor	-	R5	-
Deraa	Rom/Arb	R1	-
Dumeir	Rom	R1	**
Dura Europos	Grk/Rom	R5, 29	**
Ebla	EBA/MBA	30, R3	*
Ezraa	Byz	R1	**
Fafertin	Byz	R3, R3a	-
Halebiye	Rom/Byz	31, R5	**
Hama	Arb	32, R2	*
Haran al-Awamid	Rom	R1	-
Harbaqa Dam	Rom	R4	*
Harim	Arb	33, R3	*
Homs	var	34, R2	-
Husn Suleiman	Rom	35, R2	**
Isriya	Rom	R4	*
Jebel Khalid	Hel/Rom	R4	-
Jebel Seis	Umd	R4	*
Jeble	Rom	R2	*

Jerade	Byz	R3	*
Jisr al-Shugur	Rom/Arb	R2	-
Khan al-Hallabat, Bkhara	Rom/Umd	R5	*
Kharrab Shams	Byz	R3a	*
Khirbet Hass	Byz	R3	-
Kirkbizeh	Byz	R2	-
Kokanaya	Byz	R3a	-
Krak des Chevaliers	Cru/Arb	36, R2	***
Latakia	Grk/Rom/Arb	37, R2	*
Maalula	Byz	R1	*
Maarat al-Numan	Arb	R3	*
Maraclée	Cru	R2	T
Mari	EBA/MBA	38, 39, R5	*
Masyaf	Cru/Ism	R2	*
Meez	Rom/Byz	R3a	-
Menbij	Grk/Rom/Arb	R4	-
Meskene	M/LBA/Byz/Arb	R4	*
Mushabbak	Byz	R3	*
Mushennef	Rom	R1	*
Palmyra	Rom/Arb	41, 42, R4	***
Qadesh (Tell Nebi Mend)	LBA	R2	T
Qalaat Abu Qobeis	Ism/Cru	R2	-
Qalaat Areimeh	Cru	44, R2	-
Qalaat Bani Qahtan	Cru	R2	-
Qalaat Burzey	Cru/Arb	45, R2	**
Qalaat Jaabr	Arb	R4	*
Qalaat al-Kahf	Ism	R2	T
Qalaat al-Khawabi	Ism	R2	T
Qalaat Maniqa	Cru/Ism	R2	*
Qalaat Marqab	Byz/Cru/Arb	46, R2	***
Qalaat al-Mehelbeh	Cru	47, R2	-
Qalaat Mudiq (Apamea)	Ayy	10, R2	-
Qalaat Najim	Arb	R4	*
Qalaat Ollaiqa	Ism	R2	-
Qalaat Rahba	Arb	R5	*
Qalaat Saladin	Byz/../Arb	48, R2	***
Qalaat Shirkuh (Palmyra)	Ayy/Mam/Ott	R4	*
Qalaat Yahmur	Cru	49, R2	-
Qalb Lozeh	Byz	50, R3, R3a	**
Qanawat	Rom/Byz	51, 52, R1	**
Qara	Byz/Arb	R1	-
Qasr al-Heir East	Byz/Umd	R4	*
Qasr al-Heir West	Byz/Umd	R4	-
Qasr Ibn Wardan	Byz	R4	*
Qatna (Mishrife)	E/M/LBA/IrA	R2	-
Qatura	Rom/Byz	R3a	-
Qinnesrin	Rom/Byz	R4	T
Raqqa	Arb (Abd)	53, R4	-
Ras al-Basit	LBA/Grk	R2	T
Ras Ibn Hani	LBA/../Byz	R2	T
Refade	Byz	R3a	*
Resafa	Byz/Umd	54, R4	**
Roman Road (Jebel Srir)	Rom	R3	*

Roman Road (Wadi Barada)	Rom	R1	T
Ruweiha	Rom/Byz	35, R3	**
Safita	Cru	56, R2	**
Sanamein	Rom	R1	*
St George Monastery	Arb	R2	-
Saint Simeon	Byz	57, R3, R3a	***
Salkhad	Arb	R1	-
Seidnaya	Byz/Arb	R1	-
Selemiye	Fat/Ayy/Ott	R4	
Serjilla	Rom/Byz	58, R3	**
Shahba	Rom	59, R1	*
Sheizar	Cru/Arb	R2	*
Shaqqa	Rom/Byz	R1	-
Sheikh Suleiman	Byz	R3	-
Sia	Rom	60, R1	-
Sitt al-Rum	Rom/Byz	R3a	-
Slim	Rom	R1	-
Suweida	Rom	R1	*
Takleh	Byz	R3a	*
Tartus	Cru	61, R2	**
Tell Brak	EBA/MBA	R5	T
Tell Halaf	IrA/Rom	R5	-
Ugarit	LBA	62, R2	**
Yabrud	Rom	R1	-
Zalebiye	Byz	R4	-
Zarzita	Byz	R3	-